Discover Beauty in Your Own Backyard with a FREE YEAR of *Birds & Blooms*!

As a *Birds & Blooms* subscriber, you'll look forward to:

- **100+ Full-Color Photos**…action pictures of your favorite birds, not to mention amazing flowers

- **Bird-Feeding Tips**…all new "secrets" to bring feathered friends flocking to your yard

- **Helpful Gardening Hints**…to make your yard a lush haven for the birds who "visit"

- **Instant Access to Our Exclusive Website**… a neighborly place to get proven tips for attracting more birds and growing bigger blooms at www.BirdsandBlooms.com!

Send for your FREE YEAR today!

BIRDS & BLOOMS

SUBSCRIPTION FULFILLMENT CENTER
PO BOX 5502
HARLAN IA 51593-1002

BEST OF
BIRDS&BLOOMS

BIRDS & BLOOMS

A BIRDS & BLOOMS/READER'S DIGEST BOOK

Editors: Heather Lamb, Stacy Tornio
Art Directors: Scott Schiller, Kim Sumrall
Contributing Art Director: Nicole Trapp
Art Director, *Birds & Blooms*: Sue Myers
Copy Editor: Susan Uphill
Contributing Editors: Melinda Myers, George Harrison, Tom Allen
Photo Coordinator: Trudi Bellin
Assistant Photo Coordinator: Mary Ann Koebernik
Editorial Assistant: Kirsten Sweet

Senior Editor, Retail Books: Jennifer Olski
Creative Director: Ardyth Cope
Vice President, Executive Editor/Books: Heidi Reuter Lloyd
Editor in Chief, Home & Garden: Jeff Nowak
President, Home & Garden and Health & Wellness: Alyce C. Alston
President, North American Consumer Marketing: Dawn M. Zier
President and Chief Executive Officer: Mary G. Berner

Photos on front cover: Blue jay, Marie Read; lilies, Nancy Rotenberg;
blue metalmark, Larry Ditto/KAC Productions
Photos on back cover (from left): Irene Jeruss; Marie Read; Orean family;
Ray Herrick/Racinphoto.com; Alan and Linda Detrick

International Standard Book Number (10): 0-89821-685-0
International Standard Book Number (13): 978-0-89821-685-1
Library of Congress Control Number: 2007938813

For other *Birds & Blooms* books and products, visit *www.birdsandblooms.com*.
For more Reader's Digest products and information,
visit *www.rd.com* (in the United States)
www.rd.ca (in Canada)

Printed in China
1 3 5 7 9 10 8 6 4 2

WELCOME

How does a book earn the title *Best of Birds & Blooms*? Simple—when it contains the most useful, interesting and lively backyard features from 2 YEARS' worth of magazines! (To learn more about *Birds & Blooms*, see page 4.)

You'll find…

• Complete profiles of 79 beautiful plants, including all the information you need to add them to your yard.

• Features about 25 different backyard birds and 22 unique butterflies, plus tips on how to attract them.

• Detailed stories on 31 bursting-with-color gardens. These friendly "green thumbs" show you how to easily achieve the same results in your yard.

• Page after page of tried-and-true backyard ideas, simple solutions and handy hints from seasoned readers.

• Over 100 useful Q&As from nationally recognized bird, plant and butterfly experts.

• Charts to help you track birds in your area, know the best flowers to plant, and build a proper birdhouse.

• Step-by-step illustrated plans for 17 useful backyard projects.

• A special bonus section that addresses everything from winning the war on weeds to no-fail tips for attracting more hummingbirds.

All of these stories are accompanied by brilliant, full-color photos and detailed in a complete index to help you find just the information you're looking for.

It truly is the best *Birds & Blooms* book yet!

Photos, counterclockwise from left: Maslowski Productions; Donna and Tom Krischan; Doug Locke/Dembinsky Photo Assoc.; Faith Bemiss; Dick Dietrich; Maslowski Productions

What is *Birds & Blooms*?

Birds & Blooms is all about celebrating the "beauty in your own backyard." Started in 1995, this reader-written magazine invites people like you to share their gardening and birding stories, ask questions of staff experts and swap the secrets to their success. And, with over 1.6 million subscribers, *Birds & Blooms* is the largest bird and garden magazine in America, so you can bet there's always plenty of unique and useful information to share.

Each issue features profiles of birds, flowers and butterflies, along with tips to use in your own yard. There are simple ideas for attracting birds, an expert Q&A section, "how they did it" information from green thumbs, and readers' favorite bird and garden tales. Packed with vivid, full-color photos from front to back, *Birds & Blooms* captures the simple beauty in a bird's feathers or the delicate texture of a flower petal.

If you'd like to learn more, see the *Birds & Blooms* Web site at *www.birdsandblooms.com*, or mail in the subscription card you find in this book.

CONTENTS

60   198   228

FLYING FLOWERS 168

BLOOMING BEAUTY 218

ALL ABOUT HUMMINGBIRDS 290

PLAN A GREAT GARDEN 328

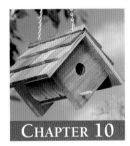

34

60

47

24

TOP BILLING

18

13

Photos: song sparrow (left), Richard Day/Daybreak Imagery; cedar waxwings (above), Ray Packard; opposite page (clockwise from top left): grosbeak and indigo buntings, Bill Leaman/The Image Finders; killdeer, Marie Read; loons, John Rockwood

AMERICAN ROBIN

This early bird will sing its way into your heart.

By George Harrison, Contributing Editor

ALIVE WITH ACTIVITY.
Robins are often bustling about the backyard. And contrary to common belief, they will stick around in winter in areas with an abundant food supply.

Come springtime, my wife, Kit, often gets a predawn wake-up call.

"How did you sleep?" I'll ask her.

"Fine. Until 4:30, when the robin started to sing," she'll answer.

Spring in our southeastern Wisconsin yard means the morning chorus of birds is at full volume, led by a male American robin that sings just outside our bedroom window.

Kit loves the robin's song, but it does awaken her early, almost every spring morning. I sleep through the serenade, since I wear hearing aids that spend the night on a side table.

American robins have been part of my love of nature nearly all my life. I was 6 years old when I had my first close-up experience with the bird. Neighbors in my boyhood town in Pennsylvania invited me across the street to see their nesting robin. When I gazed through their kitchen window at the female sitting on her nest on the sill, 3 inches from my nose, I was truly amazed.

Though I was only a little boy, my fascination with that robin was one of the building blocks of my career as a nature journalist. It was a classic example of experiencing the wonders of nature through the eyes of a child.

"Robins have been part of my love of nature nearly all my life…"

A BIT OF SUNSHINE. It's hard not to smile when a robin hops across your lawn. But did you know that it cocks its head (left) to look for earthworms, not listen for them? The juveniles (above) have spotted breasts.

Clearing Up Myths

Though it is true that the American robin is the best known of all song birds in North America, this familiarity has led to some widespread myths about the backyard favorite.

For example, the American robin is not a true "robin" at all. It is a thrush, misnamed by our founding fathers. Its red breast reminded them of the European robin, a smaller dainty bird with a red breast that is not found in North America. Like all other thrush babies, young robins have spotted breasts, which they lose when they get their adult plumage.

Another legend about the robin is how it finds earthworms as it hops across our lawns. The bird doesn't listen for earthworms as it cocks its head. It sees them. Because a robin's eyes are located on the sides of its head, it has to turn toward the ground to see its prey.

Then there is the mystery about why robins (and northern cardinals, too) fly themselves into windows. This strange behavior is caused when a robin sees its own reflection in the glass and tries to chase the "other" robin away from its territory.

Snow Birds?

Finally, it used to be said that seeing the first robin in February or March in northern states meant spring had arrived. Although that was once generally true, warmer winters and abundant food mean the robin—and that other sentinel of spring, the bluebird—now spends winter almost anywhere on the continent, even the North.

Yet, competition to see the "first robin" of the year continues. Every spring, Rhonda Norris of Elkton, Maryland and her aunt compete for the first sighting. It was her aunt who got Rhonda excited about nature when she was a little girl.

"Now I relish and anticipate each year's competition more and more," Rhonda writes. "It doesn't matter if I win or lose. Every time I see a robin in my yard, I'm reminded of my aunt's spirit, strength and unselfishness for passing on her love and knowledge of nature."

One Nest, Then Another

The home life of the American robin starts with the selection of a nesting site, but this usually isn't a snap decision. Female robins often are indecisive.

I found this to be true when I watched a female robin build

a nest on the ledge of a backyard shed in Pennsylvania. Then she built another nest and another, until she built 13 nests side by side before selecting where to lay her eggs.

Another female robin, and her generations of offspring, has nested on a coach lamp at the side of my house almost every year for 3 decades. She usually builds a second nest on a similar coach lamp at my neighbor's house before deciding which to use.

Sometimes a robin's confusion over her nests becomes unbelievable. Near Cincinnati, Ohio, photographer Steve Maslowski took pictures of an American robin nest shared with a northern cardinal.

"Three young cardinals and four robins were all reared together," Maslowski says. "The four adults shared parental duties, though each species was apparently more inclined to take care of its own brood."

Lost and Found

The female builds a nest by first gathering mud in her bill and carrying it to the nesting site. Then she adds grasses and other items, such as string—or whatever else she can find.

A robin building a nest in Mt. Vernon, Illinois collected strings from the price tags at a lawn ornament shop owned by Marvin and Joyce Eller. Joyce assumed the wind had blown the tags away, until Marvin noticed a robin's nest above the shop's window with small white tags dangling from it. Mystery solved!

In autumn, when all the babies have grown, American robins gather into large flocks that may or may not move south. They sustain themselves by searching out berries and other fruits during winter.

If you want to give them a helping hand, offer fruit or mealworms on a tray feeder. You may discover that a midwinter robin is the perfect reminder of your favorite springtime sights—and sounds.

Backyard Birding Bio

Common Name: American robin.
Scientific Name: *Turdus migratorius*.
Length: 10 inches.
Wingspan: 17 inches.
Distinctive Markings: Adult has a slate-gray back, brick-red breast and belly, and a white line above and below the eye. Juvenile is speckled gray above and spotted orange below. Males and females look alike, although the female is duller overall.

Distinctive Behavior: Hops around lawns in search of earthworms, often cocking its head to one side to look for them.
Habitat: Grassy yards with plentiful shrubs and trees, farmland and open woods.
Song: Male performs a caroling, liquid and thrushlike song that is delivered in two or three phases, often repeated. Alarm call is a low mellow "putt" or a sharp cluck.

Roland Jordahl

Nesting: Female builds a nest of mud in a shrub or tree fork, along a horizontal branch or on a ledge. It contains grasses, strips of cloth and string worked into the soft mud; the contours of the female's body mold the nest into a deep cup. The female incubates three or four blue eggs for 12 to 14 days; young fledge 14 to 16 days after hatching. Pairs often raise two broods a year.

Summer
Year-Round
Winter

Diet: Mostly earthworms, but also cutworms, caterpillars, spiders, grasshoppers, fruit, berries and occasionally cracked sunflower seeds.
Backyard Favorite: Both adults and youngsters often use birdbaths. May use a nesting shelter with two sides, a roof and a floor (6 inches square and 8 inches tall), placed on the side of a building or fence.

Richard Day/Daybreak Imagery

ALIVE WITH ACTIVITY. Robins are often bustling about their nests, whether it's tending young (above left) or watching a cozy clutch of "robin's-egg blue" eggs (left).

CEDAR WAXWING

Discover the mystery behind this masked flier.

By George Harrison, Contributing Editor

Nowhere in the bird world is there a species with plumage as smooth, sleek and silky as the cedar waxwing's. The deerlike appearance of its feathers is punctuated with red wing tips, holding true to its name because they look like drops of red wax. The finishing touches to these beauties—males and females look alike—are a black mask and a bright-yellow tip on the tail.

Ruth Ratliff lives in Sylvan Springs, Alabama, and she'll never forget the time she saw her first flock of cedar waxwings.

"I told my husband, Jerry, to get out the bird book be-

cause I had just spotted a gorgeous group of birds," she says. "The fliers were grayish-brown and had tails that looked like they had been dipped in yellow paint. And they looked like they had sunglasses on, too."

It didn't take long for Ruth and Jerry to figure out that the birds were cedar waxwings. As they read more, they learned that it's common to see the fliers in a flock. In fact, if you see one of these birds, you almost always see more. The gregarious fliers often nest close together in a loose colony, and they remain in groups year-round.

Barbara Spence of Charleston, South Carolina can

Backyard Birding Bio

Roland Jordahl

Common Name: Cedar waxwing.

Scientific Name: *Bombycilla cedrorum.*

Length: 7-1/4 inches.

Wingspan: 12 inches.

Distinctive Markings: Sleek, silky brown and tan bird with a black mask, yellow belly, yellow tip on the tail and wing tips that resemble dabs of red sealing wax, for which it was named. Sexes look alike.

Habitat: Open groves, orchards, urban and suburban backyards, and wild areas where native berries grow.

Voice: Their wheezing call is high-pitched and often difficult to hear.

Nest: Late nesters that build their loosely woven nests of grass, twigs and sometimes yarn on horizontal branches 4 to 50 feet above the ground. Female incubates the four to five pale-gray eggs blotched with dark brown for 12 to 13 days. Young leave the nest 2 to 2-1/2 weeks after hatching.

Diet: Fruit, sap from maple trees and insects in summer.

Backyard Favorite: Birdbaths will attract cedar waxwings to backyards, as will a variety of berry-producing shrubs and trees.

■ Year-Round
■ Summer
■ Winter

vouch for this. It was a cold and rainy day when she looked outside to find a wonderful surprise.

"I saw as many as 300 cedar waxwings in a tree across the street from my house," she says. "They gathered in the top of that tree, and then flew across into my backyard, where I had a holly tree loaded with berries."

On the Assembly Line

Cedar waxwings do love their berries. They feed on a wide variety, including those from mountain ash, crabapple, holly and cranberry.

If you do have berries in your yard, you might even get to see waxwings put on a show. The birds often perform a ritual of passing a berry up and down a line of perched birds. They may repeat the passing several times before it finally stops, and one of the birds eats the berry. Now how they decide which bird gets to eat the berry is a mystery to me. But it's fascinating to watch.

Like American goldfinches, cedar waxwings are late nesters. One reason for this goes back to their love of berries. In addition to insects and other items, waxwings

BIRD-WATCHER'S SECRET

Don't get cedar waxwings confused with bohemian waxwings. Both are masked fliers, but the cedar waxwing is smaller and has a distinctive yellow belly.

Maslowski Productions

Richard Day/Daybreak Imagery

feed their nestlings fruit. So they coordinate nesting season to when the berries will be ripe.

It isn't easy to find a waxwing nest. At least that's the case for many people. Most people suffer some high-pitched hearing loss by middle age. Since these birds have a high-pitched call, people with younger ears are more likely to hear it. You can find a nest if you know where to look, though.

It usually consists of loosely woven grasses, from 4 to 50 feet above the ground on a horizontal tree branch. The female incubates the four to five eggs. The male remains on guard, ready to feed the youngsters when the eggs hatch 12 to 13 days later.

Fledgling cedar waxwings are light gray overall with gray stripes on their breasts. They do have the black masks and yellow-tipped tails of their parents, but lack the namesake red "wax" on their wings.

Come and Go

Though cedar waxwings generally nest in the North, like their close relatives, the Bohemian waxwings, they are nomads throughout the year. If cedar waxwings are in your area one year, that's no guarantee they'll return.

So if you do see these stunning birds in your backyard, enjoy it while it lasts. It probably won't be long before they move on, impressing others with their sleek feathers and mysterious masks.

Ray Packard

HAVE A BITE. Berries are a favorite among cedar waxwings, as the two fledglings (above) show. The stripes on the breasts of these two young fliers will be replaced with smooth, silky plumage as adults. Top, a pair of waxwings feed several hungry mouths.

Bill Marchel

NEITHER SLEET NOR SNOW STOPS THE
COMMON REDPOLL

By Rachael Liska, Associate Editor

Don't feel sorry for the common redpoll. If you spot a group of these tiny brown-streaked birds burrowed in a snowdrift, they're far from cold and miserable. More likely, they're just fine.

Weighing only half an ounce each, these diminutive finches are some of the toughest songbirds around. That stint in the snowdrift? Burrowing in wet snow is one way common redpolls bathe themselves in the winter.

A familiar sight in Alaska and the upper regions of the Canadian territories, common redpolls are right at home in scrub forests, tundra, brushy pastures, and open thickets of willow and birch.

Food Followers

During the winter months, when food is scarce in the North, foraging flocks numbering a few million may leave their breeding grounds and travel south, even as far as California, Oklahoma and the Carolinas, in search of a meal.

These sporadic invasions are greeted with enthusiasm by bird-watchers, who sometimes see dozens of these gregarious visitors squabbling for a turn at their winter feeders.

At the backyard feeder, nyjer, millet and sunflower seeds are satisfying substitutes for the common redpoll's natural winter diet of birch, willow, grass, weed and alder seeds. It's not uncommon to spy these hungry vagabonds feverishly tearing apart dried flower stalks and then rushing to the ground to pick up the seeds that have fallen.

These high-calorie food sources are essential to provide the oils common redpolls need to keep their bodies warm when temperatures plummet.

Just before darkness, redpolls fill a special storage pouch in their esophagus, called a crop, with food. As the birds roost overnight, the seeds are digested and converted into energy, warming their bodies.

What's in a Name?

Look up "poll" in the dictionary, and you'll find it means "head." So, it's not surprising that the common redpoll gets its name from the bright-red or orange spot that marks its forehead.

Backyard Birding Bio

Common Name: Common redpoll.

Scientific Name: *Carduelis flammea*.

Length: 5-1/4 inches.

Wingspan: 9 inches.

Distinctive Markings: Brown-streaked finches with red foreheads and black throats. Adult males have rosy feathers on their upper breast.

Distinctive Behavior: Large flocks often wander south in search of food. They can survive extremely cold temperatures and are almost fearless around people.

Habitat: Scrub forests, tundra, brushy pastures, as well as open willow and birch thickets.

Song: A series of short, repeated notes; mainly call notes and short trills.

Nesting: Raises one to two broods a year; females choose a nesting site 3 to 6 feet off the ground. Low shrubs, rocky outcroppings and the crotch of alders or willows are common choices. Nests are constructed first with twigs, then loosely lined with grass, moss, feathers, rootlets and animal fur. Females lay four to five greenish eggs marked with spots.

Diet: Seeds of birch, alder, willow, pine, elm and basswood; seeds of grasses and weeds; insects in summer.

Backyard Favorites: Nyjer, millet and sunflower seeds.

Summer
Year-Round
Winter

Marie Read

HUNGRY VISITORS. The rosy breast of the male common redpoll brightens up the bleak winter landscape (far left). Always on the lookout for food, it's not unusual to see dozens of these friendly birds at the feeder (above), especially tube feeders.

Both males and females sport this conspicuous cap, as well as a tiny yellow bill, white wing bars, a black throat, a blackish-brown notched tail and dark gray-brown streaks on their backs and sides.

It's the males, however, that really stand out in the snow-covered landscape. By their second year, their white upper breast becomes a brilliant rose hue.

But you don't have to see a common redpoll to know one is in your backyard. Just listen for their bubbly song. It's a series of short trills and repeated notes that sound like "chit chit chit twirrrrrr toweeoweeowee chrr chit chit chit tiree tiree."

Back Home They Go

Mid-March marks the start of the breeding season and the common redpoll's journey home. Once back in the northern wilderness, they begin courting. The female crouches with drooped wings and twitters, while the male stands rigidly in front of her and bows. If the courtship dance is successful, the pair may raise one to two broods that year.

Believed to be monogamous and nonterritorial, common redpoll pairs often nest close to one another. Between April and August, females choose a site for their nest, generally hiding them in dense low shrubs. The birds line their twig nests with grass, moss, feathers, rootlets and animal fur, creating cozy shelters for the eggs in their often unforgiving northern surroundings.

The female lays four to five pale green to blue-green eggs with purple to reddish-brown spots. She incubates them for 10 to 11 days until they're ready to hatch. The male usually pitches in by feeding his partner during this time.

After hatching, the new brood is well-cared for, as both parents gather insects for their young ones to eat. Twelve days later, the fledglings leave the nest, and another generation of these remarkable and resilient birds takes to the sky.

So why not set out some of their favorite seed this winter? Perhaps this will be the year the common redpolls wander into your backyard.

READER TIP

Common redpolls will visit backyard feeders to eat nyjer, millet and sunflower seeds. They'll also tear apart dried flower stalks, then eat the fallen seeds from the ground.

SONG
SPARROW

This talented vocalist puts on a show in backyards across North America.

By George Harrison, Contributing Editor

Already the most widespread of all North American birds, song sparrows are becoming more universal in winter as well.

I used to look forward to the first song sparrow of spring in my Wisconsin backyard. It would herald the season with its clarion "sweet, sweet, sweet" song, followed by shorter notes and a trill. But during the last couple of years, there has been a song sparrow at our bird feeders all winter long.

Not Your Ordinary Sparrow

Though on first glimpse it looks like any other sparrow, I know it is a song sparrow by its unique behavior. It seems busier—a little nervous—as it darts in and out of cover, almost always on the ground and ever alert to the other activity in the yard.

It has a slightly longer tail than the other sparrows, which it pumps while in flight. But its definitive field mark is a large central breast spot. And, it is usually alone or with a mate, not in small flocks like most sparrows. The sparrow that looks most similar is the fox sparrow, but that bird is more reddish and a little larger, and never stays around very long.

Song sparrows frequently live near people in brushy fields and hedgerows. That's why you'll find them in most backyards across North America—in deserts, mountains, wetlands and prairies. Yet, there are 30 or so forms of song sparrows that vary somewhat by region.

For example, the song sparrows in Alaska's Aleutian Islands look and sing differently than those in California. And the song sparrows in Arizona vary from those in my Wisconsin backyard or those on the East Coast.

Yet, they all share that lovely, spirited song for which they were named. Its first three notes have been compared to the first three notes of Beethoven's Fifth Symphony—and the avian version is a masterpiece that will make any bird-watcher stop and listen.

Bursting with Song

As early as February, a male song sparrow will perch in my yard, and with tail lowered and head thrown back at a 45-degree angle, he'll unleash his liquid melody. Over and over he'll sing his three notes, followed by a trill.

After the males have established their territories—areas typically less than 1 acre—they pair up with females. The female bird then builds a nest, often hidden on the ground under a tuft of grass or brush pile. Later in the season, she may build it in a low shrub or tree. The pairs normally raise two broods each year.

My father, Hal Harrison, recalled a memorable song sparrow experience from an April day one year in Pennsylvania. He was walking along a country road bordered by shrubby meadows and a meandering creek—perfect song sparrow habitat.

BIRD-WATCHER'S SECRET

Song sparrows are common backyard visitors in winter. To attract them, offer birdseed near shrubs or other natural protection.

Backyard Birding Bio

Bill Marchel; opposite page, Richard Day/Daybreak Imagery

Common Name: Song sparrow.

Scientific Name: *Melospiza melodia.*

Length: 6-1/4 inches.

Wingspan: 8-1/4 inches.

Distinctive Markings: Coarsely streaked brown bird—dark on the back and light underneath—with streaks on its sides that join to form a central breast spot. Its crown is brown with a narrow stripe, and a broader grayish stripe over each eye. The male and female look alike.

Habitat: Any low, open, weedy or brushy areas around farms, cities or suburbs.

Voice: The male's song begins with three clear notes of "sweet, sweet, sweet" followed by shorter notes and a trill. Its distinctive call note is "chimp."

Nesting: A well-hidden ground or low nest of grasses, weed stems, leaves and bark fibers lined with finer materials. The three to five eggs are greenish white and heavily splotched with reddish brown and purple.

Diet: In fall and winter, small weed and grass seeds. In summer, insects make up half of their diet. Winter residents frequent bird feeders.

Backyard Favorites: A ground-level tray feeder with seeds or a birdbath, each surrounded by thickets or brush.

Summer
Year-Round
Winter

"Song sparrows were in their territories, and the population was so dense that year that about 50 feet along the road represented the average frontage for a single territory," he wrote.

"Suddenly, one songster flew up to a small bush and started to sing. Like so many jumping jacks, song sparrows appeared for as far as I could see, each mounting to a singing perch and declaring its territory, too. A dozen or more birds were singing at once.

"Then, just as suddenly, all was silent. The birds returned to their feeding. But let one bird again take the initiative, and a dozen more popped up from the ground to join the chorus. Seemingly, they needed only one bird's urging to start them all singing."

Indeed, there are few bird species that bring happiness to so many birders over such a large part of the continent as the lowly song sparrow.

Long may he sing.

BLUEBIRDS

They give cheerful meaning to having the "blues."

By George Harrison, Contributing Editor

Chapter 1

W hen I was a boy, I remember that the appearance of the first bluebird meant spring was close behind. Numerous poets and songwriters latched on to this connection over the years, and penned verse that further intertwined bluebirds with springtime.

But that notion is no longer true.

Fifty years ago, bluebirds, especially eastern bluebirds, were true signs of warmer weather when they returned to northern states in March. But with mild winters during the past couple of decades, many bluebirds now spend winters in their nesting areas all across the North.

Spring Song

Still, for me, the soft notes of the first bluebird warble "tru-al-ly, tru-al-ly," are among the most welcome sounds of spring.

There sits the male eastern bluebird on a fence post along the country road where I live in Wisconsin, and I watch with thankful eyes. He appears to wear the velvet-blue sky on his back and shoulders, and his breast reflects the reddish-brown earth.

The activity will pick up a week or two later, when the female appears. Then, to the accompaniment of his own warbling, the male will pursue his chosen mate from one perch to another, often showing her areas available for nesting.

That's a signal for me to set up a tray feeder and fill it with the live mealworms I buy at a local pet store. In my experience, placing the feeder in the vicinity of the birdhouses encourages bluebirds to nest there.

Making a Comeback

There was a time, in the early to mid-1900s, when bluebirds were in trouble. Due to loss of habitat and competition for nesting sites, people thought the birds would disappear.

But through the great efforts of many people who love bluebirds, trails of birdhouses made just for them have popped up throughout North America, especially in the East.

The millions of bluebird houses nailed to fence posts along rural roads and highways, 100 yards or so apart, produced a recruitment of bluebirds beyond anyone's dreams.

Today, all three species of bluebirds—eastern, mountain and western—are at healthy population levels, and the future looks bright.

That doesn't mean that bluebirds are without challenges.

Bill Leaman/The Image Finders; opposite page, Maslowski Productions

Hal Harrison

Indeed, competition for nesting sites from house sparrows, house wrens, European starlings and tree swallows is a major problem that both bluebirds and their fans face every spring.

Just about the time a pair of bluebirds settles into a birdhouse and begins to nest, one of the four enemy birds takes over the house and keeps the bluebirds from claiming it for themselves.

House wrens will even poke holes in the bluebirds' eggs. The frustrating part of this aggressive behavior is that once they win the battle, these other bird species often vacate the house.

Invite Bluebirds to Nest

Nesting starts early among bluebirds, so they can raise at least two broods each year. Tree cavities are natural nesting places, but they readily accept man-made nest boxes.

There is a great variety of bluebird houses, but most are as good as any other. The house should be made of untreated wood, 4 by 4 inches to 5 by 5 inches square and 7 inches high, with a 1-1/2-inch entrance hole about 6 inches above the floor.

A removable overhanging lid makes for easy observation and cleaning, and it should be ventilated at the top with drainage holes in the floor. Paint or stain it a natural color, then place it on a post 5 to 10 feet above the ground at the edge of an open grassy field, facing away from the wind and sun.

The North American Bluebird Society (NABS) is one of the organizations that formed to help save the bluebird. This group recommends that bluebird houses be spaced at intervals of 100 to 150 yards (300 yards for mountain bluebirds). If house wrens

> *He appears to wear the velvet-blue sky on his back and shoulders.*

BLUEPRINT FOR SUCCESS. Want to attract bluebirds? Place a house for them in an open area, and these spirited songsters might start a nest, like this eastern bluebird pair (left). The female bluebirds of all three species—eastern, western and mountain (at top)—lay four to six pale-blue eggs (inset).

Western bluebird

Mountain bluebird

are in the area, be sure the box is mounted at least 200 feet away from a wooded or brushy area.

If tree swallows or violet-green swallows are likely to use the box, try setting out two boxes about 10 feet apart. That way, bluebirds can use one and swallows the other.

Most bluebird box landlords have found this practice allows both species to nest side by side in relative peace, according to NABS.

To keep house sparrows away from bluebird houses, NABS emphasizes the importance of box location.

Avoid placing boxes near farmsteads, feedlots, barns or old outbuildings. Boxes placed in or around towns and cities will likely be claimed by house sparrows. If sparrows do take up residence, one option is to relocate the box to a site farther away from people.

Watching in Awe

If the bluebirds are successful, and you're able to watch the whole process, from nest building to the young birds fledging, it is one of the most rewarding experiences in nature.

I remember the pair of bluebirds that set up housekeeping in a nesting box attached to an apple tree in our backyard a few years ago. I set out a feeder tray with mealworms about 10 feet away. I watched the pair carry grasses into the house for a few days, and then the female laid one egg a day for 5 days.

The female began incubating on the fifth day, and she sat on them for 14 days, while the male brought her food—often a mealworm from the tray feeder. During one of the rare times when she left the house, I peeked inside to admire the pale-blue, almost white, eggs she had been incubating.

> **READER TIP**
>
> In my experience, placing a mealworm feeder in the vicinity of my bluebird houses encourages bluebirds to nest there. **—George Harrison, Contributing Editor**

OPEN WIDE. Even after the juvenile bluebirds take flight from the nest box, the adults continue to feed them, like the male eastern bluebird offering mealworms to a fledgling (above right). Residents of the West have two bluebirds that could frequent yards—the mountain (above) and the western (above left).

When the young hatched on the 15th day, both parents began feeding them. The morsels of insects they delivered were tiny at first, but as the days passed, the offerings increased in both size and frequency.

Nothing is cuter than a pudgy bluebird fledgling awaiting a meal.

By the time they were 18 days old, the youngsters were ready to leave the house. One at a time, they sat at the entrance and then popped out of the house and proceeded to fly erratically to the safety of a nearby tree or bush.

Bluebird fledglings (like the one above right) have spotted breasts, similar to other members of the thrush family, including the American robin. Nothing is cuter than a pudgy bluebird fledgling waiting for a meal, as it hunkers down on a tree branch.

New Beginnings

Far from slowing down, the bird activity once the young left the box was feverish. While the male was running a "meals on wings" service to the young, the female was preparing for the second brood.

She built another nest on top of the first, in the same house, rather than selecting another house nearby.

Before I knew it, the first youngsters were on their own, and the male was attending to his mate, who had started laying eggs.

Later, after the eggs hatched, I saw the young of the first brood helping their parents feed the second brood. This practice, called "cooperative breeding," is common among bluebirds.

Bluebirds are one of the most beautiful avian species around. The sight of them often elicits gasps of amazement, and I feel lucky to have witnessed their complete nesting routine many times.

As the song goes, they truly are the "bluebird of happiness," bringing excitement, color and adventure to any yard.

Chapter 1

Eastern bluebird

Richard Day/Daybreak Imagery

Backyard Birding Bio

Common Name: Eastern bluebird.
Scientific Name: *Sialia sialis*.
Length: 7 inches.
Wingspan: 13 inches.
Distinctive Markings: Males have a blue back, wings and head, with a white belly (above). Orange on breast extends onto throat. Females have the same markings, but duller.
Habitat: Open backyards and farmland.
Song: Soft warble, "tru-al-ly, tru-al-ly."
Nesting: Built mostly by the female, the nest is made of dried grasses and lined with finer grasses, hair and feathers. She lays four to six pale-blue, sometimes white, eggs between March and July, then incubates them for 12 to 14 days until they hatch. Both parents feed the nestlings.
Diet: Insects and berries.
Backyard Favorite: Live mealworms.

Common Name: Western bluebird.
Scientific Name: *Sialia mexicana*.
Length: 7 inches.
Wingspan: 13-1/2 inches.
Distinctive Markings: Males have a blue back, wings, head and throat, plus a bluish tinge on belly (see photo above far left). Orange on breast extends onto back. Females have the same markings, but are much duller and have a grayish cast.
Habitat: Open woodlands with scattered old trees, plus farmland and orchards.
Song: A subdued "f-few, f-few, f-few."
Nesting: Pair builds a nest of grasses, then lines it with finer grasses. The female lays four to six pale-blue eggs in April and May, then incubates them for 13 to 14 days until they hatch. Both parents feed the nestlings.
Diet: Insects and berries.
Backyard Favorite: Live mealworms.

Common Name: Mountain bluebird.
Scientific Name: *Sialia currucoides*.
Length: 7-1/4 inches.
Wingspan: 14 inches.
Distinctive Markings: Males are brilliant blue all over (see photo above near left). Females are gray overall with pale-blue feathers on their tail and wings.
Habitat: Meadows, clearings and open forests up to elevations of 10,000 to 12,000 feet.
Song: Similar to the eastern bluebird's song, but slightly higher pitched.
Nesting: Pair builds a grass nest often lined with finer material. The female lays four to six pale-blue eggs between April and July, then incubates them for 13 to 14 days until they hatch. Both parents feed the nestlings.
Diet: Insects and berries.
Backyard Favorite: Live mealworms.

Summer
Year-Round
Migration
Winter

COMMON LOON

This alluring bird is anything but common.

By Stacy Tornio, Associate Editor

I'll admit it. In the beginning, I was completely clueless. I moved from Oklahoma to Wisconsin 5 years ago and had never even heard of the common loon before.

That didn't last long, however. I was soon introduced to this mystical bird early one summer day in June.

It was a gorgeous morning, and my husband, Steve, and I were at his parents' cottage in the northwoods of Wisconsin. We were out on the deck, looking across the calm, clear waters of the lake, when I heard a loud, captivating wail. My mother-in-law, Vicki, hurried to the edge of the deck and looked out over the water. Her face immediately lit up.

"They're back," she said.

I tried to find what she was talking about, but I could not see anything. "Right there," she said, pointing.

This time I saw it. A sleek, black-headed bird was swimming in the water. Then, before I could admire it any longer, it dove swiftly into the lake.

"Where did it go?" I asked, almost in a panic. "Is it okay?"

I breathed a sigh of relief when the bird resurfaced. "What was that?" I asked.

Everyone smiled, as if they knew some sort of secret. "That was a loon," my husband said.

Wild About Loons

I later learned just how special that sighting was. While common loons migrate across the United States, you can only find them regularly in specific locations. Loons summer throughout Canada and in northern parts of the United States, and they winter along the coasts. And even then, they spend nearly all of their time on the water, where they eat, sleep and even nest on floating bogs.

Maybe this is why so many people seem to be smitten with these unique birds. Just mention the word "loon" here in Wisconsin, and everyone seems to have a story to tell.

Contributing editor George Harrison knows exactly when he'll see common loons fly in on the lake near his house in southeastern Wisconsin.

"As soon as the ice breaks, loons will show up within 48 hours," George says.

The birds have been visiting the lake regularly for the past 30 years. They make a brief stop there as they migrate farther north for the summer.

"The whole neighborhood looks forward to seeing the loons," George says. "I always get eight or nine calls the first day they fly in."

The striking summer plumage of the common loon is not the type of thing you forget. The bird has a jet-black head that has a greenish sheen and a black bill. It also has a striped white "necklace" around its throat, piercing ruby-brown eyes and a black-and-white checkered back.

Water Birds

There's a reason you only see these swift swimmers in the water. Common loons have large feet that are set far back on their bodies, so it's nearly impossible for them to walk. They do go on land during nesting season, but are careful to keep their nest as close to shore as possible so they don't have to travel far.

Loons raise one brood each year. Both parents incubate the eggs for 29 days, and after the babies hatch, they immediately take them to water. There, the young will feed on tiny fish at just 1 day old.

Early on, chicks often ride on their parents' backs. During this time, one chick usually becomes dominant and chases the other away.

Like their parents, a young loon quickly becomes a skilled swimmer and diver. The bird's primary food source

---

ROOM TO FLY. When common loons prepare for flight, they run on the water's surface to generate enough speed (below). The birds need at least 20 yards to become airborne.

Backyard Birding Bio

Common Name: Common loon.

Scientific Name: *Gavia immer.*

Length: 32 inches.

Wingspan: 46 inches.

Distinctive Markings: All-black head and bill with distinct ruby-brown eyes and a white striped "necklace" around its throat. A black-and-white checkered back with white underparts. The male and female look alike. In winter, head, neck and back fade to a dark brown or gray.

Habitat: Spends nearly all of its time on water; prefers remote locations with plenty of small islands available for nesting.

Voice: Four calls, including the hoot, the yodel, the wail and the tremolo, also known as the bird's laughter.

Nesting: Prefers islands or sheltered areas along the shore for its nest built of matted grasses and twigs. Birds mate for life and often use the same nest site every year. Usually lays two olive-green to dark-brown eggs with brown scattered spots between mid-May and mid-June. Both parents incubate the eggs for 29 days, starting with the first egg, and then feed and raise chicks.

Summer
Migration
Year-Round
Winter

Diet: Dives from water's surface up to 200 feet to catch fish in its bill; also eats crayfish, shrimp, crab, snails and frogs.

is fish, and a loon will dive up to 200 feet underwater to catch one with its strong bill.

The loon has four different calls and each has its own meaning. Many people recognize the loon for its tremolo call, also known as the bird's laughter. But that's just the beginning.

The haunting wail call of the loon is most often heard in the evening. The birds use the wail to keep in touch with other loons, sometimes miles away. Males make a yodel call to defend nesting territory. And finally, there's the hoot call, which loons use to keep in touch with one another.

Pat Blue Moon of Sunriver, Oregon remembers hearing the loon while camping around the lakes in northeastern Washington.

"I have always been an early riser, and I have fond memories of hearing the loon call at early light," Pat says. "Those who have heard the call will probably never forget it."

I have to agree with Pat. When I first heard the mystical sound of the loon, I was hooked.

I finally understand why this extraordinary bird mesmerizes so many people. Now I'm in on the secret—and I'm completely smitten.

BIRD-WATCHER'S SECRET

These birds nest as close to water as they can get. So if you can hear this bird but can't find it, try looking near shore.

CHANGING COLORS. In summer, loons have vibrant black-and-white checkered backs and an iridescent green sheen to their signature jet-black heads and bills (bottom). For winter, the bird's plumage begins to molt to a dark brown or grayish color (below).

John Rockwood

John Rockwood

Chapter 1

YELLOW WARBLER

This bright songster is a summertime delight.

By George Harrison, Contributing Editor

Photo: Marie Read

27

Even in this family of brightly colored birds, the yellow warbler stands out. Not only do the males display overall golden feathers, but they're also less timid than the 55 other North American birds in the wood warbler family. In fact, it's the only wood warbler that regularly visits backyards.

The first time I witnessed yellow warblers up close was at the Pymatuning State Park headquarters in northwestern Pennsylvania. They were in a multiflora rose hedge that had grown out of control.

Perfect Habitat

Multiflora rose is one of those shrubs that farmers hate because it takes over land for grazing and crops. It is even outlawed in some states. Yellow warblers, on the other hand, love it because it is dense and prickly. This makes it a good hiding spot that also provides protection for their nests, and its blossoms attract insects they can eat and feed to their young.

This particular rose was so perfect that a whole colony of yellow warblers nested in it. It was an amazing sight, though

Their ongoing musical display of "sweet sweet sweet" is one reason its "warbler" name is quite fitting.

rare, since warblers generally do not nest in groups.

More recently, my observation of yellow warblers is at the tiered recirculating birdbath on my southeastern Wisconsin patio. There, a pair of yellow warblers frequently bathes and drinks from May through July.

I love to watch one particular male stand on the spillway, face upstream and dip his head into the flow. Even when his bright-yellow feathers are soaking wet, I can plainly see the distinctive reddish-brown streaks on his breast.

Yellow warblers are interesting birds for many reasons. Not only are they one of the most widespread of any native songbird (they breed from Mexico all the way to the Arctic Circle), but they spend less time in their breeding grounds than other songbirds—arriving in May and leaving just a few short months later, by August.

The yellow warbler is also one of the most frequent targets for the brown-headed cowbird, a species which lays its eggs in the nests of other birds, then abandons them.

When this happens, yellow warblers will often build a new

LOVELY LADY. You can recognize the female yellow warbler (like the one at left) by the slightly duller—but still eye-catching—feathers. While females incubate eggs, males continue to sing frequently and bring food to her. At right, yellow warblers prefer birdbaths with recirculating water.

Al Cornell

floor in its nest to cover the cowbird's egg. This defense keeps the eggs from hatching.

Life at the Nest

Though yellow warblers build neat and compact cup-shaped nests of plant fibers and down, they are known to steal some of that material from neighbors' nests, or from a nest they've previously built and deserted.

It takes the female about 4 days to complete construction, while the male sings and supervises. Then he feeds her as she incubates four to five eggs for 11 to 12 days. Once the eggs hatch, the male pitches in to help feed the young, mostly with small caterpillars.

Though he is busy gathering food and feeding young, the male yellow warbler continues to carol his lovely "sweet sweet sweet" song at a rate of about once every minute. The ongoing musical display is one reason its "warbler" name is quite fitting.

Southward Bound

In another 9 to 12 days, the young are ready to leave the nest, though they require feeding and protection for another couple of weeks. As soon as the young are able to take care of themselves, the adults leave the breeding territory and head south. They seem to disappear overnight, which may be exactly what happens, because they migrate after dark.

Though yellow warblers are frequent visitors to backyards, they also inhabit swamps, marshes and bottomlands. I spotted one in a marsh in Cuba, and was surprised to discover it was the very same species that I see bathing in my Wisconsin backyard.

Because it is so widespread, the yellow warbler appears in several different geographic forms. Those in the North and West have slightly drabber yellow plumage; in the Southwest, they're paler. In the Florida Keys, yellow warblers reside year-round and exhibit rich golden feathers.

But no matter where you are, the sight of this bright-yellow bird of summer is an event to cherish.

Backyard Birding Bio

Common Name: Yellow warbler.
Scientific Name: *Dendroica petechia*.
Family: Wood warbler.
Length: 5 inches.
Wingspan: 8 inches.
Distinctive Markings: Adult male is bright yellow with reddish-brown streaks on its breast; adult female is duller yellow; first-year juveniles may be gray overall.
Distinctive Behavior: Hunts for food in shrubbery and thickets; male hunts higher in vegetation than females.
Habitat: Backyard gardens, along waterways, swamp edges, marshes, brushy bottomlands, orchards, hedgerows and roadside thickets.
Song: "Sweet sweet sweet sweet sweeter sweeter," or "sweet-sweet-sweet-chit-tit-tit-teweet."
Nest: Strong compact cup of firmly interwoven milkweed fibers, hemp, grasses and plant down that's lined with felted plant down, hair and fine grasses. Female places the nest in an upright fork or crotch of a shrub, tree or briars, 3 to 8 feet above the ground. She then incubates the four to five eggs for 11 to 12 days while the male brings food to her.
Diet: Insects, mostly caterpillars, but also the mayflies, moths, treehoppers and other insects, plus spiders.
Backyard Favorite: Birdbaths, especially those with moving water.

Summer
Migration
Winter
Year-Round

TEACHING BIRDS TO FLY

Conservation groups take to the sky to keep whooping cranes from becoming extinct.

By Stacy Tornio, Associate Editor

Photos courtesy of the Whooping Crane Eastern Partnership and Operation Migration

"Eventually, we won't need to use ultralights."

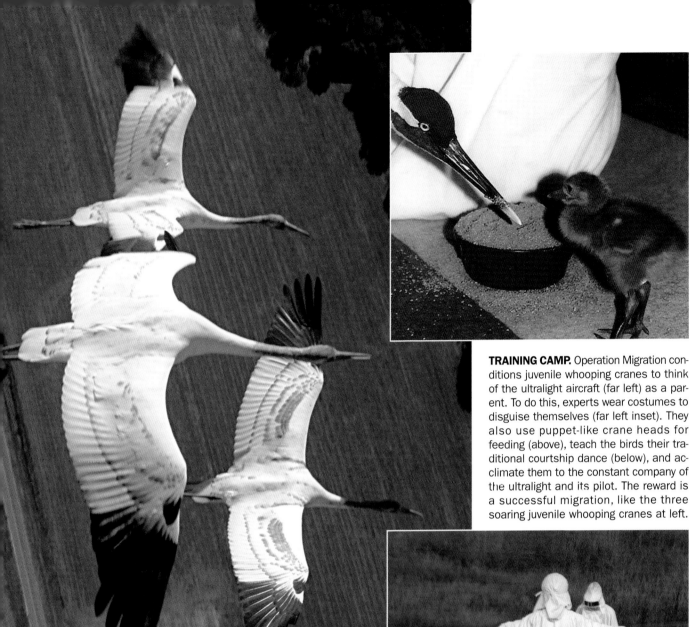

TRAINING CAMP. Operation Migration conditions juvenile whooping cranes to think of the ultralight aircraft (far left) as a parent. To do this, experts wear costumes to disguise themselves (far left inset). They also use puppet-like crane heads for feeding (above), teach the birds their traditional courtship dance (below), and acclimate them to the constant company of the ultralight and its pilot. The reward is a successful migration, like the three soaring juvenile whooping cranes at left.

"Daddy is flying with the birds." According to 5-year-old Alex, this is where her father, Joe Duff, goes each fall. And that description isn't just the result of a child's creative imagination, either.

Every October, Joe climbs into a tiny ultralight aircraft to lead a flock of graceful whooping cranes from Wisconsin to their winter home in Florida. He is the cofounder of Operation Migration, a group chosen by Canadian and U.S. wildlife officials to help keep the whooping crane population from becoming extinct.

To do this, the organization does exactly what Alex says—they fly with the birds.

A Fading Treasure

By the early 1940s, the population of whooping cranes—the largest bird in North America—had fallen as low as 15 birds. The U.S. government took action and created a winter

refuge for this migrating Canadian whooping crane flock at the Aransas National Wildlife Refuge along the Gulf of Mexico in Texas. The location is still used by the wild population today, which has grown to include nearly 200 birds.

But experts knew they couldn't rely on this single flock to avoid extinction, so in the early 1990s, they established a group of nonmigratory whooping cranes at Kissimmee Prairie in Florida.

Meanwhile, the rest of the birding world was starting to hear news of an innovative concept. Humans were teaching birds how to fly…or more specifically, how to migrate.

In 1993, Joe joined pilot Bill Lishman on the first human-led bird migration of a flock of Canada geese. That experience led Joe to help with the 1995 movie about the subject, *Fly Away Home*. He didn't lose sight of his goal, however. He continued studying the concept of using ultralight planes to lead migrating birds.

The more he and his colleagues learned about the process,

the more excited they became. Test trials with Canada geese and sandhill cranes continued to be successful. It didn't take them long to convince officials that a similar plan could work to establish a new migratory flock of whooping cranes. They would simply teach the youngest chicks to follow the aircraft.

Plan Takes Off

It was December 3, 2001, when six whooping cranes made the first airplane-led flight from Necedah, Wisconsin to the Chassahowitzka National Wildlife Refuge in Florida. The 1,250-mile trip had taken nearly 2 months, three ultralights and a 14-member team.

"During that flight, I didn't relax for a minute," remembers Joe, who was the lead pilot. "When we arrived with the first flock, it was a huge relief."

The following years continued to be demanding. Weather conditions have to be perfect for flying, which means the team and cranes often spend hours, or even days, grounded.

"Last year, the migration took 64 days, and we only flew on 23 of those," Joe says. "We do a lot of sitting in a trailer, waiting on the weather so we can take off."

With the amount of time and effort it takes to help the birds migrate, it's no surprise that the project carries a hefty price tag. Joan Garland is the outreach coordinator for the International Crane Foundation, one of the organizations that help support the effort. She said it takes an estimated $1.8 million to complete the migration each year.

Migration Milestone

The fall of 2005 was an important time for Joe and his team. Twenty-one juvenile cranes—the fifth and largest flock—made the trip. Upon their successful arrival, the Wisconsin/Florida migratory group will have more than 60 birds.

Another new development is a change in the training. Unlike previous years, when all newly hatched chicks train with the ultralight aircrafts, in 2005, five chicks did not receive the same preparation.

Joan says they are hoping these five birds will have the natural instinct to follow the other migrating birds.

"Eventually, we won't need to use ultralights," she says. "Once enough birds are making the migration on their own, hopefully those older birds will be able to show the new chicks the proper migration route."

Cranes from previous years already are migrating to and from Florida on their own. The ultralight training will continue until there are enough mature birds to teach the younger ones every year.

Whooping crane supporters want the birds to be able to live like they once did, as wild migratory birds. This is why the handlers at the Necedah National Wildlife Refuge in Wisconsin—

SOUTH FOR THE WINTER. It's hard to imagine that such majestic birds were once on the brink of extinction. The juveniles are just as beautiful as the adults, but display tan markings on their wings and neck (above left). Soon, that coloring will begin to fade until the bird displays the snow-white feathers and red crown of an adult (at right). At left, a whooping crane surveys its surroundings at the Necedah National Wildlife Refuge in Wisconsin. Once the birds are taught the migration route, they can then make the trip on their own.

where the chicks hatch and train—take careful precautions to disguise themselves when working with the birds.

"We have to eliminate everything that is human," says Joe, who is one of the few people who work one-on-one with the birds. "We wear a big costume, we don't talk anywhere near the birds and we carry a recorder that plays crane sounds."

It's important for the birds to avoid any human contact, so they can learn to survive on their own. Imprinting starts when the chicks are only 7 days old. The handlers use puppet-like crane heads to feed the chicks and train them to think of the ultralight aircraft as a parent. That way, when it comes time to migrate, they will follow it.

One unique aspect of the whooping crane effort is the amount of support it receives from people and organizations throughout North America. Chester McConnell lives in Tennessee and is a retired wildlife biologist. He says he's a preservationist at heart, which is why he belongs to the group, Whooping Crane Conservation Association.

"This is my life," he says. "I love it, and I just can't turn it loose."

Chester says it's encouraging to know groups like his are making a difference, as seen in the rising numbers of whooping cranes.

"This is the symbol of conservation in this country," Chester says. "So many people have come together for the same joint effort."

Currently, there are roughly 450 whooping cranes throughout North America. As the number continues to grow, supporters have their eyes on a common goal—improving the cranes' status so they can be removed from the endangered species list. They know it's something that won't happen overnight, but are confident it's attainable.

"So many endangered species programs just focus on why there is a decline, but with this, we get to give back," Joe says. "We get to save the species."

ROAD TRIP. This map shows the migration route of the whooping cranes. Beginning each October, they travel from Wisconsin to their winter home in Florida. The Whooping Crane Eastern Partnership and Operation Migration provide an up-to-date route tracker and information about the cranes. Visit *www.operation migration.org* or *www.bringback thecranes.org*.

Did You Know?

■ As the tallest bird in North America, the whooping crane can reach up to 5-1/2 feet with a wingspan of 7 feet.

■ These cranes got their name from their distinctive whooping call. Sometimes referred to as a duet, this loud mating ritual can be heard from more than a mile away.

■ Whooping cranes select a mate for life between the ages of 2 and 3. The ritual includes a courtship dance known as the unison call.

■ They can live up to 25 years, but whoopers face a lot of dangers along the way, including predators and disease.

■ The birds feed on insects, crabs, crayfish, rodents, roots, seeds and marsh plants.

■ Whooping cranes lay two eggs, which hatch after about 34 days.

INDIGO BUNTING

These birds are far from "blue," with ever-present songs and vibrant hues.

By George Harrison
Contributing Editor

Every morning from early May until late August, I listen for the familiar sound of a male indigo bunting. He rarely disappoints, singing his high-pitched, boisterous warble from the top of a poplar tree along the lake road where I walk each day.

For 3 decades, I've walked that 1-1/2 mile trail of blacktop for exercise…and bird-watching. In summer, especially on hot days, I always hear an indigo bunting, cutting through the chorus of birds. In fact, in recent years, there have been three males singing along the road, spaced about a 1/4 mile apart.

The only time I see a female is at my birdbath, where she drinks and bathes. I often see a male there, too, but they do not visit the bath together.

Nesting Time

Indigo buntings are found primarily in the eastern half of the United States and southern Canada. Reader Maria Tremblay of Sault Ste. Marie, Ontario was happy to witness a pair nesting in her parents' raspberry patch one spring.

"After my mother noticed the nest while picking raspberries, we started watching to see what kind of bird was nesting there," Maria writes. "Then I caught sight of the dark-blue male indigo bunting.

"I actually heard the pair peeping near the nest. The male was in a tree and the female was flying around the vegetable garden, trying to ward us off to protect the nest.

"I took pictures of the eggs and chicks until mid-August, when the nest was empty one day. We assumed the chicks had safely flown away."

Despite his beauty and delightful song, the male indigo bunting is not very helpful when it comes to nesting and raising young. I found this out the hard way, while trying to photograph a pair of indigo buntings at their nest in southern Ohio a few years ago.

It was a lovely, well-built grass nest in the crotch of a small shrub. From a blind some 30 feet away, I was able to take photo after photo of the female feeding her four nestlings.

Though she is a lovely bird in plain, light-brown feathers with some subtle blue on her wings and tail, she is not a bright beauty like her all-blue mate. For that reason, I was determined to wait him out. I wanted that photo! Surely he would stop by to feed sometime over the couple of days I had allotted to this project.

Finally, totally confused and discouraged about failing to get a single photo of the male at the nest, I used my cell phone to call my father from the blind. He had photographed indigo buntings at their nests many times.

"Dad, why doesn't this male indigo bunting feed his young?" I asked.

"Because male indigos don't feed at the nest," he responded.

"Never?" I asked.

"Not in my experience," he said.

With all due respect to my father, I have since seen at least one photo of a male indigo bunting feeding at the nest, but apparently it is very unusual. So, I folded my tent and gave up my dream of photographing this gorgeous blue bird at its nest.

More Than Meets the Eye

I did get some good close-ups of Mr. Blue at the birdbath, but the wetter he got, the less blue he appeared.

A little research into this curious color condition was very revealing. I learned that the male indigo bunting isn't really blue at all. It's brown.

According to ornithologist John Terres, some of the colors we see in birds, such as blue, aren't the result of actual pigments, but rather are from light reflecting off the special structures in their feathers. This is true of other "blue" birds, too, including blue jays and bluebirds. The moisture can interfere with this reflection.

It reminded me of the very first indigo bunting that I ever saw as a boy in Pennsylvania. I spotted the spectacularly colored all-blue bird perched on the top branch of a

> *"I learned that the male indigo bunting isn't really blue at all. It's brown."*

SITTING SIDE BY SIDE. It's not difficult to see the differences between sexes when together, but when apart, look for hints of blue on the wings and tail to identify a female.

Photos: opposite page and above, Bill Leaman/The Image Finders

TRUE COLORS. Indigo buntings aren't truly blue, as their name suggests. They just appear that way because of the way light reflects off of their feathers. In fact, when these birds get wet, they will start to show their true color, which is brown.

roadside apple tree, singing in a high-pitched voice.

On a rainy afternoon a few days later, I heard the bird again near the same apple tree. I knew the bird was back. I looked in vain for its vibrant, blue feathers, but on that dark, rainy day, the bird was brown, almost black. So Terres must be right.

The Last to Go

As the summers along my lake road wear on, I hear fewer and fewer birds as I go along on my morning walks. By late summer, the indigo bunting's song is all that is left of the dawn chorus that once greeted me. It rings through the air loud and clear.

I have often been thankful for that solitary song on an August morning, because it seems to be the last remnant of spring. When the indigo buntings finally go quiet, I know the end of summer has arrived.

By then, the brilliant blue buntings have become mottled with brown and are headed for their winter homes in southern Mexico, Central and South America and the West Indies.

My walks become quieter again, until next spring.

BIRD-WATCHER'S SECRET

At first glance, female indigo buntings look more like sparrows, not at all like their stunning male counterparts. Look closely, though. Females do have a few blue feathers on their wings and tail.

Backyard Birding Bio

Common Name: Indigo bunting.

Scientific Name: *Passerina cyanea*.

Length: 5-1/2 inches.

Wingspan: 8 inches.

Description: The male's brilliant blue body is the distinguishing namesake feature. The female could pass for a sparrow, with her overall cinnamon-colored body, but she does have a few blue feathers hidden in her wings and tail.

Voice: The male's song is a high, sharp and loud warble that is repeated, "ti ti sweet sweet serre serre sip sip."

Nesting: A carefully woven nest of grasses, bark strips and weeds in the crotch of a shrub or small tree, 2 to 10 feet above the ground. The female alone incubates the three or four pale, bluish-white eggs for 12 to 13 days. She also raises the young without help from the male, who is usually nearby singing from a high branch throughout nesting season.

Diet: Insects, berries and seeds.

Backyard Favorites: Nyjer or cracked sunflower seeds from a tube feeder. Will visit birdbaths to drink and bathe.

Summer Migration

NORTHERN MOCKINGBIRD

Lively songs and antics are this bird's calling card.

By George Harrison, Contributing Editor

Few birds are as well named as the northern mockingbird. This species does exactly what its name implies: It "mocks" the songs of other birds. It also deftly imitates many other sounds—creaky gates, bells, telephones, factory whistles…the list goes on and on.

More than 200 years ago, colonial naturalist Mark Catesby reported that American Indians called it *Cencontlatolly*, or "400 tongues." Fittingly, scientists named it *Mimus polyglottos*, or "many-tongued mimic."

Play It Again…and Again

Northern mockingbirds are tireless songsters, sometimes beyond reason. I'll never forget one hot summer night in Richmond, Virginia when a lovesick male mockingbird kept me awake most of the night.

At 3 a.m., I'd had enough. I picked up a shoe, headed for the back porch, and threw it as hard as I could at the black silhouette at the top of a magnolia tree. I missed, of course, but at least I had the satisfaction of stopping—for a few seconds—that irritating torrent of clatter. The famous book *To Kill a Mockingbird*, which isn't about mockingbirds at all, came to mind.

Samuel Grimes, an old friend in Jacksonville, Florida, was probably one of the world's leading authorities on the mockingbird's song. He recorded the bird around his home and farther afield, and accumulated 45 hours of songs from more than 500 mockingbirds.

One bird he recorded in Harlem, Georgia changed his tune 310 times in 15 minutes, and interspersed 114 notes and phrases from 29 others bird species among 196 phrases of its own. From this research, Sam estimated the songs of the northern mockingbird are two-thirds its own and one-third mimicry.

Some of the sounds a mocker can make are incredible. Sam told me about one in Louisiana that imitated a dinner bell so well that the farmhands left the field to come to lunch. Another mockingbird in Miami imitated an alarm clock to perfection, regularly awakening a man living nearby ahead of schedule.

Another observer tells how a mockingbird in Nashville, Tennessee did a first-rate takeoff of a squeaky washing machine.

I'm no longer angry when I hear a mockingbird sing. After moving to Wisconsin, I actually missed hearing them.

Although "northern" is part of this species' official name, it's not commonly found in upper Midwestern or western states or in Canada. Instead, the moniker helps differentiate it from other mockingbirds, like the Bahama, which lives in the tropics.

BIRD-WATCHER'S SECRET

If you have a northern mockingbird that frequents your backyard, try having a little fun. See if you can get it to mock certain sounds or phrases. You just might be surprised by its talents!

Chapter 1

On business trips to Washington, D.C., I'd hear mockingbirds singing from the utility poles as I walked to lunch with colleagues. No one else seemed to notice the bubbly, enthusiastic songs amid the traffic noise, but it was an exciting and refreshing sound to my northern ears.

Protective Parents

The songster is a feisty defender of its nesting territory. I remember a mocker that hounded the cat that lived next door to my suburban Richmond backyard.

The cat ruled the yard until the mockingbirds moved in and began threatening the poor feline every time it appeared. It got to be such a sport that the birds would spot the cat coming out of the house and attack even before it reached the porch steps. After a few weeks of that treatment, the cat became afraid to leave the house.

The feathered fighters are dedicated parents. They build a bulky nest that is well hidden in a hedge or shrubby thicket at about our eye level. The male selects the location and places nesting material on the spot. If the female approves, both birds build the nest.

Northern mockingbird youngsters, like all songbird babies, are vulnerable to predators, and most do not reach 1 year.

However, those mockingbirds that do survive have extended their historic breeding range from the Deep South north to New England, and to the West Coast. It still remains most common in the South, where it is the state bird of Arkansas, Florida, Mississippi, Tennessee and Texas.

When Texas legislators adopted the mockingbird as their state bird in 1927, they made note of the bird's perseverance. According to Gary Clark, a professor at North Harris College in Houston, "they wrote a resolution describing the bird as 'a fighter for the protection of his home, falling, if need be, in its defense, like any true Texan…' "

In autumn, mockingbird pairs split and establish their own winter feeding territories. They defend these with a zeal similar to their summer behavior.

And yes, they keep right on singing.

Backyard Birding Bio

Common Name: Northern mockingbird.

Scientific Name: *Mimus polyglottos*.

Length: 10 inches.

Wingspan: 14 inches.

Description: A medium-sized, slender, dull-gray songbird with long legs, white wing patches and white outer tail feathers. Males and females look alike.

Voice: A creative and extensive repertoire of songs and noises—from natural sounds to man-made ones. Its own alarm note is "tchack."

Habitat: Hedges and thickets in backyards, farmlands and brushy woodlands.

Nesting: Builds a bulky nest hidden 3 to 10 feet above the ground in a thicket (above). Four light blue-green eggs, heavily blotched with brown, are incubated by the female for 12 or 13 days. Youngsters leave the nest 10 to 12 days after hatching.

Diet: More than half its diet is animal matter, mostly insects, that it often flushes out of the grass by raising and lowering its wings while on the ground. Also eats berries and other fruit.

Summer
■ Year-Round

Backyard Favorites: Raisins (left) as well as bird cakes made with suet and cornmeal. Berry-producing shrubs (far left) provide food and nesting sites.

Tom Uhlman/The Image Finders

WHIP-POOR-WILL

Harrison Productions

Listen up, or you may not spot this hidden songster.

By George Harrison, Contributing Editor

The whip-poor-will has been a special bird for me ever since I was a little boy. One of these talented vocalists would sing me to sleep every night at my family's cottage, which was along the Allegheny River in western Pennsylvania.

I remember its haunting call, "whip-poor-will, whip-poor-will, whip-poor-will," continuing on and on until I fell asleep. It often called from the top of a 50-gallon oil drum outside my bedroom window, a fact I confirmed one night by using my dad's big flashlight to find the bird's reflective red-orb eyes in the dark. Those eyes made the bird seem even more mysterious to me.

I have heard its nighttime call on many occasions since then and in various locales. One time while visiting friends in the Blue Ridge Mountains of Virginia, I lay in bed wondering how many times the bird would call without stopping. So, I started to count them like sheep. I got well into the hundreds before sleep overtook me. John Burroughs, one of the nation's greatest ornithologists, once recorded 1,088 repetitions without a pause.

Like most people, I used to think that whip-poor-wills sounded their name exactly. But one night, when I was very close to a singing bird, I could hear an additional "chuck" sound between the "whip-poor-will" calls.

Hearing this member of the nightjar family is far easier than spotting the highly camouflaged bird. Its brown mottled feathers and squat shape don't make it the most attractive bird around, but they're the perfect characteristics for hiding among leaves on the ground or along tree branches.

Maslowski Productions

Todd Fink/Daybreak Imagery

MASTER OF DISGUISE. The whip-poor-will's mottled feathers and squat shape are excellent camouflage. This allows the females to blend in while incubating eggs among dried leaves (like the bird at left), and helps the birds keep a low profile on daytime roosts (far left). The dappled markings on the young birds (below) and eggs mimic the sunlight and shadow pattern of the bird's leafy forest habitat.

Perfect Camouflage

One day, I accidentally scared a female whip-poor-will off her eggs. I was surprised that she made no noise when she flew. She fluttered about 20 yards away, as silent as a moth, and began feigning a broken wing to draw me away from the eggs.

A few days later, I returned with a camera to photograph the bird and could not find her, even though I had memorized the nest's location. After 15 minutes of looking, I finally saw her in the exact spot I had been staring the whole time. It was as if I'd put on 3-D glasses that brought the forest floor to life. She blended in almost perfectly.

In late April or early May, whip-poor-wills arrive in their northern nesting grounds in mature hardwood forests. The boisterous males immediately make their presence known, using their distinctive call in hopes of attracting a mate and to defend their territory. They'll continue to sing until the nesting season ends in late July or early August.

Once coupled, the female lays two gray-spotted eggs on the dry and dead leaves of the forest floor. Although there is no nest, as the female incubates the eggs, the depression in the leaves becomes deeper. She keeps the eggs warm until they hatch 19 days later. The pair may raise a second brood in warmer regions.

In-Flight Meals

The way a whip-poor-will gathers food is unique—even among some birds in the same family. Unlike close relative the common nighthawk, which darts around the sky to gather insects, the whip-poor-will flies close to the ground in smooth silent motions.

With its mouth agape, it funnels mosquitoes, moths and other nocturnal flying insects into its wide mouth. The hair-like feathers around its bill help direct the insects into its mouth.

Unfortunately, whip-poor-will numbers have declined in recent decades due to several factors, including the loss of habitat in both summer and winter ranges; pesticides that reduce the number of insects for food; and losses to nocturnal predators, such as great horned owls.

Though these birds have never been a common backyard species, any bird enthusiast who can hear a whip-poor-will through the bedroom window is in for a nightly treat.

Backyard Birding Bio

Common Name: Whip-poor-will.
Scientific Name: *Caprimulgus vociferus*.
Length: 9 inches.
Wingspan: 19 inches.
Distinctive Markings: Heavily mottled with gray, black and brown above and paler gray and black mottling below. The male has white patch borders below its black throat and the tips of its outer tail feathers. Females are buff-colored in those areas.
Distinctive Behavior: Nests, almost unseen, among dried leaves on the ground.
Habitat: Open deciduous woodlands, where dead leaves carpet the forest floor.

Summer
Migration
Year-Round

Summer
Year Round
Migration

Song: Distinctive nighttime call that resembles its name, "whip-poor-will," repeated over and over again.
Nest: None. The female lays two oval light-brown eggs with gray spots and blotches in dead leaves on ground, typically where light and shadows filter through the trees to help the incubating bird blend in with its surroundings.
Diet: Small flying insects caught in flight.

WESTERN TANAGER

This colorful flier loves a sweet treat.

By George Harrison,
Contributing Editor

It was like a fine art masterpiece. A male western tanager was perched on a fir tree limb, surrounded by dark-green boughs. Its brilliant-yellow body, red face and head and black wings glowed in the dark wooded background. Here, I decided, was surely one of the most beautiful birds on the continent.

This event happened a few years ago while I was serving sugar water to birds at a campground in the Madera Canyon in Arizona. I was expecting to attract hummingbirds, but my first visitor was a male western tanager instead.

He wasn't alone, either. A few minutes later, there were six males lined up, waiting to have their turn at the sugar water. I couldn't believe my luck. All of these gorgeous birds were right in front of me.

Setting out orange halves is another way to lure these birds to Western backyards and campgrounds. Doug Sparks of Clackamas, Oregon knows this firsthand.

Sweet Surprise

One summer while sitting in his backyard, Doug looked up and saw a rather different bird perched on the hanger of his bird feeder. "I immediately grabbed my field guide and identified it as a male western tanager," Doug says.

The guide said the birds would come to feeders for orange halves. So Doug sliced an orange and used a piece of coat hanger to wire it so it was facing up near the hanger feeder. Then he sat back to watch.

Unfortunately, the tanager didn't return that day. Doug was disappointed. He figured the bird was migrating, so he thought it might have been his only sighting—until the next morning.

Doug woke up, opened his blinds and was greeted by

a dozen male tanagers, sitting in the sun and patiently waiting their turn at the orange halves.

"They really go crazy for them," Doug says. "I had to put new oranges out almost every day because they would scrape them down to the peel."

To Doug's delight, the tanagers stayed for nearly a

> *The western tanager does not develop the red coloration on its head naturally. Instead, it must be acquired from the bird's diet.*

---

month, eating from his backyard feeder before continuing on to their nesting territories.

As members of a tropical family, most species of tanagers never reach North America. The western is one of only four tanagers that breed here. The males of these four—the scarlet, summer, hepatic and western—all display bright red during breeding season, while females are a dull yellow green.

A Balanced Diet

According to the Cornell Laboratory of Ornithology, the red color in the face of the western tanager is rhodoxanthin, a pigment that is rare in birds. Unlike other red tanagers, the bird does not develop the color naturally. Instead, it must be acquired from the bird's diet.

In fall, western tanagers migrate to the tropics to spend the winter in Mexico and Central America. In April and May, they head north into the coniferous forests of North America, from the high desert mountains of the Southwest and north to Canada and southwestern Alaska. The males arrive on the breeding grounds first, establish a territory and sing to attract females, who arrive a week or two later.

While the male sings his song, which resembles that of an American robin with a sore throat, the female gets busy building a nest. Then she lays three to five eggs. Because the summers are short in the western tanager's mountain habitat, the pair will raise only one brood of three to five youngsters a year.

Despite their short breeding season, western tanagers don't seem to be in a hurry to migrate south and may loiter in western gardens that offer fruit, jelly and sugar water.

If you're one of the lucky ones to see these amazing birds, I think you'll agree with my assessment. Western tanagers really are one of the most beautiful birds on this continent.

BIRD-WATCHER'S SECRET

Western tanagers love sweets. Attract them to your yard with an oriole feeder filled with sugar water or sliced oranges.

Backyard Birding Bio

Francis and Janice Bergquist

Common Name: Western tanager.

Scientific Name: *Piranga ludoviciana*.

Length: 7-1/4 inches.

Wingspan: 11-1/2 inches.

Distinctive Markings: Male has a bright-yellow body, black wings and tail, and a vibrant crimson head. The female (above) is greenish on top and yellowish underneath. It is also the only North American tanager with distinct white wing bars. In fall and winter, the male's face and head change to yellow green, and it looks much like the female.

Habitat: Mature, coniferous forests; mountainous regions.

Voice: The male's song is similar to an American robin, but it is a hoarser repetition of short "pit-ic" or "pit-i-tic" phrases with rising and falling inflections. The call note is "chee-tik."

Nesting: Builds a shallow nest, 15 to 65 feet above the ground, in a fork of a pine, spruce or fir tree. The female incubates the three to five spotted bluish-green eggs for 13 days before hatching. Both parents feed the single brood.

Diet: A diverse diet of wasps, ants, caterpillars, cicadas, grasshoppers and many other insects; also berries and other fruit.

Backyard Favorites: Fresh fruit including citrus and fruit jelly. Try offering sugar water in an oriole feeder or dried fruit in a tray feeder.

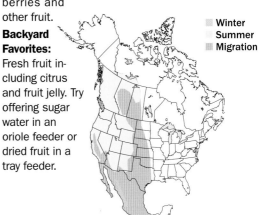

- ▨ Winter
- ▨ Summer
- ▥ Migration

BLUE JAY

These boldly colored birds are nature's noisemakers.

By George Harrison, Contributing Editor

Photo: Marie Read

A blue jay's call may warn other birds of danger.

They certainly aren't a secretive species. If you have blue jays in your yard, they're almost impossible to miss. When I'm outside watering the garden, taking out the trash or walking along the road, I can often hear one or more blue jays screaming at me, "jay, jay, jay."

One of the most noticeable characteristics of this bright member of the crow family is the noise it makes. And blue jays have quite a repertoire of calls.

In addition to the alarm call (the "jay, jay, jay" that many of us recognize), there is its charming bell-like "tull-ull" call that it uses to communicate with its mate and other members of its family. There also is the so-called "whisper call" that parent birds use around their nests during a period when they are otherwise very quiet.

Blue-Feathered Bandits

Blue jays also imitate the sounds of winged predators to chase other birds and squirrels from feeders.

Typically, a flock of blue jays will arrive at feeders screaming like hawks to scare away the other birds. Then four or five of these cocky impersonators, showing off their flashy blue and white feathers, sail into the empty feeders and begin to eat whatever and wherever they want.

Sometimes, they are like wolves in blue suits that will raid the nests of other birds, eating eggs and nestlings. This flashy and arrogant behavior is why some people consider blue jays "bully birds" that are unwelcome at their feeders.

Yet, other birds sometimes benefit from the blue jay's boisterous personality. Their calls may warn of danger, like the scene Pattie Glaze witnessed in her Claremore, Oklahoma backyard.

"Early one fall day, my husband, Richard, and I were sitting on our back patio enjoying the small birds at our feeders," Pattie writes. "I looked up and saw a rather large brown bird sitting at the top of our neighbor's tree.

"As I wondered what species it was, a blue jay perched in another tree began making a loud steady noise. The smaller birds quickly disappeared.

"Just then, the larger bird swooped toward us. As it flew

TURN UP THE VOLUME. Blue jays often make quite a racket in the backyard. They may imitate hawks to scare other birds away from a feeder (top photo). However, when they're nesting, they become very quiet. Both the male and female build the nest (above photos) and incubate the eggs until they hatch.

over our heads, we realized it was a Cooper's hawk! The blue jay's screams apparently had warned the smaller birds that danger was near."

In addition to warning of nearby predators, blue jays will often attack hawks and owls by "mobbing" these larger and more dangerous birds of prey. This usually causes such a ruckus that other songbirds heed the warning about the raptors' presence.

Hide and Seek

When I was a boy helping my dad photograph birds, we often had blue jays living in our home. Keeping native wild birds as pets was legal then, and I'm glad I had the experience of having jays inside. I recall that it was not safe to leave anything shiny lying around the house when the birds were loose. Invariably, they would pick up those objects and carry them around or hide them.

I also learned a great deal about their eating habits. I watched a blue jay swallow one whole sunflower seed after another, not eating them, but stashing the seeds in its throat pouch to transport to a more secluded site. The jay later coughed up the seeds and either cracked them open and ate or hid them.

Researchers have found that blue jays do, in fact, remember where they cache some of their food, but much of it is either pirated by other wildlife or forgotten.

Creating a Family

Courtship for blue jays begins in early May, when a troop of seven or eight jays gathers in the top of a large tree to play follow the leader, stopping now and then to bob their heads up and down. Presumably, the leader is a female, and the followers are hopeful male suitors. When the leader flies away, the

FLOCKING FOR FOOD. In the winter, blue jays often travel in groups, searching woodland areas for fruit, grains and nuts. They will often visit backyard feeders to eat sunflower seeds and suet.

group of other jays is always right behind it.

After the female selects a mate, the new couple gathers twigs and carries them around until they locate a suitable nesting site.

Those sticks eventually wind up in a well-hidden bulky nest, usually in the crotch or outer branches of a tree, 10 to 25 feet above the ground. Four or five greenish eggs hatch 17 to 18 days after being incubated by both blue jay parents.

Three weeks later, the blind and naked chicks have transformed into fully feathered miniatures of their parents, and are ready to leave the nest. It's common for pairs in the North to raise one brood a year, while southern parents usually raise two broods.

Watching these young birds interact with the world around them is a thrilling experience, as Lynda Saye discovered while witnessing a fledgling blue jay as it learned to fly in Panama City, Florida.

"I noticed that the bird was not hopping very fast and realized that it was a baby blue jay," Lynda writes. "The parent birds soared back and forth over its head, while the baby flapped its wings as fast as it could, but only seemed to clear a couple of inches above the ground before crash landing.

I was reminded of my grandchildren learning to walk. It was an amazing sight."

By late August or early September, both youngsters and adults join other blue jays in groups of several families. These flocks stay together through the winter, cruising woodland areas in search of food, and pestering owls and hawks at every opportunity.

Some jays migrate farther south, while others remain near their nesting range. Wherever they end up, however, you're sure to hear them.

READER TIP

Attract blue jays by offering sunflower seeds at a tray feeder or supplying suet cakes. They'll also bathe and drink from birdbaths and pools.

Backyard Birding Bio

Winter
Year-Round

Common Name: Blue jay.
Scientific Name: *Cyanocitta cristata*.
Length: 11 inches.
Wingspan: 16 inches.
Distinctive Markings: Males and females are alike. Pale blue above with paler underparts, a blue head crest and a black necklace. Its wings and tail are barred with white.
Distinctive Behavior: Will noisily chase other birds from feeders.
Habitat: Open woods, parks, wooded farmlands and backyards.
Voice: A noisy jay, jay, jay or jeer, jeer, jeer is the blue jay's most familiar call, but

a bell-like double note "tull-ull" is also characteristic. The male's courtship song is a whispering chatter.
Nesting: In a bulky nest 10 to 25 feet above the ground, the female lays four to five spotted olive to buff-colored eggs. Both parents help incubate the eggs for 17 to 18 days until they match.
Diet: Although jays are omnivorous, about 75 percent of a blue jay's diet is fruit, grain and nuts. The remainder consists of insects as well as small animals.
Backyard Favorite: Sunflower seeds and suet cakes. They will also bathe and drink from a birdbath or pool.

ROSE-BREASTED GROSBEAK

These charming birds are a striking springtime sight.

By George Harrison, Contributing Editor

One of my greatest delights each spring is the sudden appearance of several male rose-breasted grosbeaks at my feeders. Without any fanfare, they peacefully perch on the edge of a wooden tray, cracking one seed at a time.

Though spring brings many other spectacular arrivals to my yard, such as Baltimore orioles, indigo buntings and ruby-throated hummingbirds, there is something special about the rose-breasted grosbeak, and I believe the reason dates back nearly 100 years.

If it were not for one particular male rose-breasted grosbeak in the early 1900s, I may not have become a nature journalist. My father, Hal Harrison, a pioneering bird photographer and writer, once confessed that as a grade-schooler, he shot a male rose-breast.

He'd planned to use it as a taxidermy mount, but within an hour, all the glamour of taxidermy disappeared. From that day on, my dad vowed to shoot birds only with a camera, which he did for the next 80 years.

This family anecdote may be why I so eagerly anticipate the first male rose-breasted grosbeak each spring. It must be in my genes.

All Dressed Up

But I'm not alone. With a black-and-white "tuxedo" and a bright blush of red on their chests, the male birds are a stunning sight.

Below, Mark Werner/The Image Finders; previous page, Bill Leaman/The Image Finders

Once I get over my admiration for their striking beauty, I wonder how far have they flown to get here. Most rose-breasted grosbeaks spend winter in southern Mexico, central and northern South America, Puerto Rico and the West Indies.

Regardless, they always look fresh, well rested and quite content to be eating sunflower seeds in my backyard.

The males appear to migrate together, ahead of the females, because I do not see any females for 1 to 2 weeks after the first males arrive. Even then, males and females remain peaceful as they munch on seeds, sometimes in groups of a half dozen or more.

Then, as suddenly as the males arrived, all but one disappears. The remaining male will pair with a female, claiming my backyard as their territory.

I soon hear the male singing his melodious warble, a long, broken carol that's similar to the song of the American robin, but sweeter and more varied. The female rose-breast sings, too, but her song is softer and shorter.

The pair has an affectionate courtship, which lasts for weeks. They often touch bills or exchange food.

An Unlikely Pair

Two birds of the same species could not look more different than male and female rose-breasted grosbeaks. By comparison, the female is drab, much like an overgrown sparrow, with thick, brown stripes punctuated by a white stripe above each eye. Her dull colors must serve as protective camouflage to avoid predators while she sits on the nest.

Curiously, the brightly colored male also helps incubate the eggs. Perhaps he sits on the nest mostly at night when his location is not as noticeable.

When the young leave the nest 9 to 12 days after hatching, their presence becomes a bit unnerving. They sit in the nearby basswood tree and call and call in mournful, off-key notes.

The sound is an effective method to get their parents to feed them, but after days of listening to their endless bleating, I begin to wonder why I looked forward to their parents' arrival.

Yet all is forgiven when the fledglings become juveniles, quiet down and settle into an enter-

SHOWING ITS COLORS. While the male rose-breasted grosbeak displays a distinctive red shield on its chest, the coloring of the female and juvenile (like those at right) is subdued, more closely resembling a sparrow. At left, brown streaks begin to develop on the male's feathers at the end of summer.

taining routine of feeding and taking baths.

At that stage of life, the young resemble their sparrow-like mothers, with one exception. Juvenile males have rose-colored underwing patches, like their fathers, while the juvenile females have the yellow underwing patches of their mothers. It's always satisfying to be able to identify the sex of a juvenile when it raises its wings. It's a small indicator, but it tells you exactly what you want to know.

At the same time, the adult males begin to look shabby as they start to change into their winter plumage, with spots of dull brown marring their once-perfect feathers. I know it is near time for them to disappear, leaving the youngsters to fatten up for a few more weeks before they, too, head to the tropics.

It's a sad day when I realize that I haven't seen a rose-breasted grosbeak at the feeders or birdbath for a few days. I know at that moment that it will be a long and cold winter before these birds delight me with their presence once again.

BIRD-WATCHER'S SECRET

When male rose-breasted grosbeaks first arrive in spring, the females are nowhere to be found. Keep looking, though. Roughly 1 to 2 weeks later, the females will follow. Then let the courtship begin!

Marie Read

Backyard Birding Bio

Anthony Mercieca/Dembinsky Photo Assoc.

Common Name: Rose-breasted grosbeak.

Scientific Name: *Pheucticus ludovicianus.*

Length: 8 inches.

Wingspan: 12-1/2 inches.

Distinctive Markings: Males are mostly black with a white chest accented by a brilliant-red shield. Females have heavy, brown streaks and a white stripe above each eye.

Distinctive Behavior: Small flocks of males visit feeders in spring.

Habitat: Deciduous woods, swamp borders, old orchards and wooded suburban lots.

Voice: Song is a long, broken warble that's similar to the song of an American robin. The call note is an unmistakable metallic kink.

Nesting: Flimsy nest of twigs and dried weeds is lined with finer materials; generally 10 to 15 feet above the ground. The eggs often may be seen through the lining from below. The four eggs are greenish blue and speckled with brown. The pair shares the 14-day incubation period.

Summer
Migration

Diet: Insects, seeds and flower buds.

Backyard Favorites: A tray feeder filled with sunflower or safflower seeds.

BREAKFAST
WITH THE
EAGLES

*In winter, majestic birds savor
"Eagle Lady's" morning buffet.*

By Cary Anderson, Anchorage, Alaska

FLY-IN RESTAURANT. For almost 30 years, Jean Keene, the "Eagle Lady" (above), has fed fish to hungry bald eagles each winter near her Alaska home.

A long finger of land, known as the Homer Spit, juts out into Alaska's Kachemak Bay. From here, you can marvel at a jagged horizon of snow-capped mountains, inhale an ocean breeze and watch waves lap the beach.

You may witness a passing whale or a flock of seabirds. And if you're lucky, you may glimpse the "Eagle Lady."

Eighty-one-year-old Jean Keene is the Eagle Lady. Better known by her nickname than her real name, Jean and her eagles are legendary. But unlike many legends, the Eagle Lady's story is unembellished.

A Modest Start

Jean lives in a small mobile home at the Homer Spit Campground, surrounded by a driftwood-ornamented fence. Fishing floats, whale bones and snowshoes decorate her small yard.

The seeds of Jean's notoriety were planted on a gusty winter day nearly 30 years ago, when she spotted a pair of bald eagles standing on the gravel beach near her home. Jean had long maintained a feeder stocked with sunflower seeds for finches and other small birds, but eagles seldom came near.

Perhaps, Jean thought, the eagles might like something to eat. Jean worked at the nearby fish processing facility, where salmon and cod scraps were plentiful, so she had a steady supply of eagle food. She took home some leftover fish heads and tossed them over the short fence to the eagles. They eagerly devoured them.

"It all started with a few fish heads in a bucket and two eagles," Jean recalls. "It grew from there."

The following day, she offered them more. Jean continued to feed the birds daily. Tossing fish to the pair of eagles soon evolved into a morning ritual during that winter in the late 1970s. By the end of winter, four or five eagles were showing up at Jean's place for breakfast.

When spring arrived, the handful of eagles disappeared as their breeding season began. But once winter returned, and the birds had finished nesting, the eagles came back. Jean began feeding again. In a matter of weeks, more than a dozen eagles were showing up. Jean fed them throughout winter. As before, the eagles left in spring.

Growing Clientele

The pattern continued. Eagles arrived in winter and departed in spring. Each year, the number of eagles increased. Within 7 years, more than 100 eagles were homing in on the Eagle Lady's generosity.

Like squadrons of warplanes, eagles flew in from the distant shores of Kachemak Bay. They came from miles around. Other fish-eating birds, including ravens and gulls, also gathered for the feast.

After 10 years, more than 200 eagles were stopping by for fish handouts. The morning arrival of so many eagles at the Homer Spit Campground became an astounding phenomenon that must be seen to be believed.

To keep pace with the rising demand for eagle food, Jean brought home more and more surplus fish from the seafood plant.

"I hate to see anything go to waste," Jean says. "Not when

WINGED RESIDENTS. In winter, it's common to see eagles soaring over nearby resorts or perched on buildings.

someone can make good use of it."

Jean's morning routine steadily evolved from a minor chore into a strenuous job. Few people realize the depth of her dedication or how much work is involved. By the mid-1980s, Jean was no longer doling out mere buckets of fish. She was serving up scraps of salmon, herring, cod and halibut by the barrel.

On average, Jean distributes more than 50,000 pounds (that's 25 tons) of fish to the eagles from late December through mid-April. That works out to an average of 500 pounds per day.

Some people have criticized Jean over the years for feeding the eagles, even though it is not against the law in Alaska. And wildlife authorities concede that offering fish to eagles is not much different than dispensing seed to songbirds at a backyard feeder.

None question her dedication.

Always There with a Meal

From January through mid-April, day after day, Jean persists. Eagle attendance at Jean's place has fluctuated, but typically 200 to 300 eagles fly in for her fish breakfast.

Through wind-driven rain, blizzards and sub-zero weather, Jean dutifully feeds them. When frostbite injured one of her toes during a sub-zero cold snap, she carried on with little complaint. There'd be time to rest later.

"I'm a tough old bird," she once told CBS TV news correspondent Jerry Bowen.

In his coverage of the Eagle Lady, the journalist agreed. He concluded his story by saying that Jean was, perhaps, "the toughest bird of them all."

Editor's Note: Read more about Jean in Cary Anderson's new book, *The Eagle Lady.* It contains nearly 100 fascinating photos and is available on-line at *www.eaglelady.com.*

> ## *Jean and her eagles are legendary.*

MOURNING DOVE

These tame birds are flocking to backyards across the country.

By George Harrison
Contributing Editor

Shy is not a word I would use to describe the mourning dove. My friend Joe Staudacher lives in Milwaukee, Wisconsin and had a pair of mourning doves nest on a ball of twine outside his back door one summer.

I was visiting Joe and his wife, Rose, when he pointed out the female sitting peacefully on her two eggs.

"That dove is so tame she will let me stroke her back," he said.

As I peered into the bird's beady brown eyes, I realized for the first time how much these fliers have adapted to our urban environment.

By the time I visited the Staudachers again, the hatchlings were 5 days old. Inside the house, I set up my camera at the open kitchen window and waited. Within a few minutes, the larger and more colorful male mourning dove landed on the edge of the nest. The female rose off the chicks and made room for her mate to feed them.

Harrison Productions

The activity around the yard didn't bother these loyal birds. Instead, they went about their business, oblivious to the rest of the world. Yes, these birds are not shy.

It's All Relative

As a close relative to the passenger pigeon, mourning doves share many characteristics. In the autumn of 1813, John James Audubon observed a flight of passenger pigeons along the Ohio River in Kentucky that was so dense it eclipsed the light of the noonday sun.

Passenger pigeons are now extinct, but mourning doves have similar autumn flights as they fly over cultivated fields and into roosts of dense cover. There aren't as many doves as there were passenger pigeons, but there still are around 400 million of them in the lower 48 states.

Why is it, then, that mourning doves are so prolific, while billions of passenger pigeons now cease to exist? The quick answer is that mourning doves are a protected migratory bird. They are game birds in many states, but only hunted during specific times of the year. The more vulnerable passenger pigeons predated game laws.

Also, mourning doves are more adaptable than passenger pigeons were. Historically, mourning doves have been a farmland species, but in recent years, there has been a shift to urban habitats, possibly due to backyard feeding. During the last decade, surveys by the Cornell Laboratory of Ornithology in Ithaca, New York have shown that the mourning dove is one of the most reported birds at backyard feeders across North America.

Another reason for the mourning dove's success is its potentially high reproductive rate. Every year, a pair of mourning doves is capable of producing five broods of two chicks each. That's a lot of new mourning doves.

Changing of the Doves

In most of the country, the mourning dove's nesting cycle begins in March or April with the male's melancholy "coo-ah, cooo, cooo, coo" call. The bird was named after this mournful hoot, but it could have easily been called the "morning" dove instead. The U.S. Fish and Wildlife Service reports mourning doves are most active calling from 30 minutes before sunrise to 30 minutes after.

Courtship for the birds begins when the slightly larger male puffs up all his feathers, flashes his iridescent neck and towers over the female while following her around their territory. My dad, Hal Harrison, was an ornithologist and nest expert. He taught me that mourning doves select a nesting site, often on a branch of an evergreen, 10 to 25 feet high. Then the female lays two pure-white eggs on a flimsy platform of sticks, where both parents incubate them for 13 to 14 days.

Trica Bonenberger lives in Pottstown, Pennsylvania and has fond memories of watching a pair of mourning doves during nesting season one year. She first noticed the birds outside her kitchen window while washing dishes.

"I remember one rainy day, seeing a mama or papa bird

NOW THAT'S DEDICATION. Joe Staudacher had a mourning dove in his backyard that was so tame and unflappable that she would even let him stroke her back while incubating her eggs (above). Below, a parent mourning dove sits with one of its young.

Bill Carter; opposite page, Maslowski Productions

sitting on the nest, with beads of water running down their back," Trica said. "They were forever diligent, sitting on the nest and protecting their eggs."

Trica said the birds actually made her look forward to washing dishes. One afternoon, she even got to witness what she calls the "changing of the doves," when the pair took turns incubating the eggs.

"In my romantic eye, it looked like they hugged as they put their necks around each other and exchanged places in the nest," she said.

Hatchling mourning doves may be one of the least attractive of all baby birds, but with constant care and feeding from the parents, the squabs quickly grow into handsome fledglings. All members of the dove and pigeon family feed their offspring "pigeon milk." Adults deposit this milk-like granular fluid of partially digested seeds directly into the throats of the chicks.

After about 10 days, the youngsters leave the nest and are on their own within a week. Meanwhile, the parents are already preparing a new nest for the next brood.

Despite declines in some regions of the country, mourning dove populations are very healthy throughout their breeding range. In fact, there are so many mourning doves at feeders that people often ask me what they can do to keep the doves from hogging the food and chasing other birds away.

I don't have a perfect answer for this, but one thing is for sure: These bold birds can take care of themselves!

BIRD-WATCHER'S SECRET

These backyard visitors are not shy. It often takes little more than an ongoing supply of cracked corn to have an up-close experience with this feathered friend.

Backyard Birding Bio

Common Name: Mourning dove.

Scientific Name: *Zenaida macroura*.

Length: 12 inches.

Wingspan: 18 inches.

Distinctive Markings: A brown, pigeon-like bird that is larger than an American robin, but smaller and slimmer than a pigeon. It has a long, pointed tail with white edges conspicuous in flight. Sexes look alike.

Habitat: Open woods, evergreen plantings, orchards, farmlands, roadside trees, and suburban backyards and gardens.

Voice: A coo that consists of five to seven notes: "coo-ah, cooo, cooo, coo."

Nesting: Commonly found in an evergreen, 10 to 25 feet above the ground on a horizontal branch. Builds a loose, bulky platform of sticks (above) in which it lays two pure-white eggs. Pairs raise two to five broods each year.

Diet: About 98 percent seeds and plant materials.

Backyard Favorites: Tray feeder filled with wild bird seed mix or cracked corn (left). They will visit birdbaths to drink and bathe.

Summer
Year-Round

PILEATED WOODPECKER

This red-crested wonder is the head of its class.

By George Harrison, Contributing Editor

Anyone who has spotted a spectacular pileated wood-pecker will tell you the sight of this large dramatic bird is second to none.

Although bird enthusiasts around the world are focusing on the rediscovery of another member of the woodpecker family—the larger and once believed extinct ivory-billed—the pileated is remarkable in its own right.

Not only is it a breathtaking creature to watch, but unlike the ivory-billed, both males and females sport red crests, making them a handsome couple.

A Sight to See

A pileated woodpecker in flight is something you won't soon forget. About the size of crow, the pileated soars powerfully

with rowing-like wing beats, often through lush dark forests. Its black wings flash white patches underneath, and its red crest and long neck and tail make for an eye-catching sight.

When Mark Catesby first discovered the pileated woodpecker in 1731, he gave it the name "log-cock." Ornithologists later renamed it "pileated," from the Latin word *pileatus*, which means capped.

It is a reclusive woodland bird, but is more common than it might appear. This red-crested wonder breeds on both coasts, southern Canada and the eastern half of the U.S.

Defending the Nest

The bird's prominent markings make it hard to miss when it's flying through the air or hammering on a tree, but the nests can be difficult to detect.

Despite a lifetime of bird-watching, I've seen only one pileated woodpecker nesting cavity. It was in mature woodland at Cook's Forest State Park in Pennsylvania, 35 feet above the ground in a dead white oak.

It was early May as I approached the nesting cavity, and the female inside was either incubating eggs or brooding young. She left the nesting hole and noisily flew to a tree trunk about 100 hundred yards away, then began expressing her discontent. The beating of her great wings was surprisingly loud, and a little intimidating. The bird made a terrific clucking racket, causing the woods to ring with her cries. Instantly, a male appeared, but remained silent.

Confronted with this protective display, I retreated some distance away and watched as the female flew back to the nesting hole and disappeared inside.

Pileateds create a new cavity for each brood they raise, and add no nesting material to the 2-foot-deep tunnel they chisel out with their bills.

The entrance to a nesting cavity is usually round. If you spot a pileated near an oblong or triangular hole—their trademark—these are used for roosting or created as the woodpecker searches for food in the wood. At the bottom of the cavity, the female lays three to five pure-white eggs, which both parents incubate for 18 days until they hatch.

Youngsters' Fare

A few weeks later, when I returned to that nesting tree I had found in Pennsylvania, two young pileated woodpeckers were hanging out of the cavity, stretching their necks and calling for food in rasping voices.

Staying out of sight, I watched the parent birds feed the youngsters several times, depositing partially digested food into their mouths.

Though I can only guess what the parents were feeding their young, I do know that the pileated's preferred food is carpenter ants, which they gather by ripping the bark off dead trees with their hammerlike bills. I've also seen a female gather food by pushing her bill into the soft wood of a stump and stretching out her long sticky tongue to collect ants.

HOLE IN ONE. Pileated woodpeckers are known for the holes they create. They chisel out round ones for nesting, but use triangular or oblong entrances (left) to roost or search for food.

FEEDING TIME. You can distinguish the males from the females by looking for the red "mustache" of the male. These birds might eat suet (below) or forage for insects (at right).

Pileateds in the Backyard

In winter, pileated woodpeckers remain in the general area where they nested, and will use the round nesting cavity or drill a new oblong cavity for roosting. The pair bonds are quite strong among pileateds, and they will remain together throughout the year.

I have never been lucky enough to attract pileated woodpeckers to my own backyard feeders, but I know several people who have. Among them are friends in Rhinelander, Wisconsin and in rural Pittsburgh, Pennsylvania. They reported that the big red-crested birds regularly came to eat suet in the feeders hanging from mature trees in their forested backyards.

Both friends were ecstatic about attracting pileated woodpeckers, as they should be. These birds are very wary and often elude would-be observers with their great alertness.

Though they may be vocal during their breeding season, drumming on trees and other surfaces, or loudly protecting their nest, pileateds are silent for much of the year. That makes the challenge of finding one—and the reward of a sighting—even greater. ◄

READER TIP

If you spot a pileated near an oblong or triangular hole—their trademark—these are for roosting or created as the woodpecker searches for food in the wood. The entrance to a nesting cavity is usually round.

Backyard Birding Bio

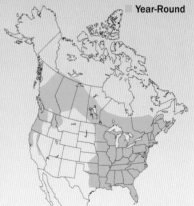

Common Name: Pileated woodpecker.
Scientific Name: *Dryocopus pileatus*.
Length: 16-1/2 inches.
Wingspan: 29 inches.
Distinctive Markings: Prominent red crest, black wings and tail, and a white stripe on its long neck. Males and females look alike, except the male has full red crest that extends to the top of his bill, and a red "mustache" (like the one at left). The female has a red crest on the back of her head and a black mustache (see photo above).
Distinctive Behavior: Searches for carpenter ants by ripping large oblong or triangular holes in the trunks of standing or fallen timber.
Habitat: Mature conifer and deciduous forests and large tracts of mixed woodlands.

Year-Round

Voice: Contact call is a deep and loud "wek" or "kuk." Its territorial call is a higher-pitched cackle that sounds like "flick-a, flick-a, flick-a."
Nest: Pairs excavate a new nesting cavity each year in generally the same area. It's located in a tree 15 to 70 feet high, typically faces south and has a round entrance hole. The pair spends about a month creating the cavity, which is up to 24 inches deep.

Using no nesting material, the female lays 3 to 5 white eggs, which both parents incubate for 18 days. They raise one brood per year.
Diet: Mostly carpenter ants, as well as beetles, insect larvae, wild berries and acorns.
Backyard Favorite: Suet in feeders, located at least 10 feet above the ground on the trunk of a mature tree in wooded habitat.

NORTHERN SAW-WHET OWL

By George Harrison, Contributing Editor

A trusting little northern saw-whet owl perched and stared at me through round golden eyes, dotted with big black pupils. It was the first saw-whet I'd ever seen. I knew that it was the smallest owl in the East, but I was not prepared for this dainty beautifully marked bird that appeared to have no fear of me.

I was on Mt. Desert Island, Maine, helping my dad search for a nest of these diminutive owls to photograph for his *Peterson Field Guide to Eastern Birds' Nests*. We had put up a half dozen nesting boxes in the hope of attracting these cavity nesters, but the birds had not used them, even though we heard them calling in the area at night.

Northern saw-whet owls have a number of utterances. The one I heard in Maine reminded me of the beep of a truck backing up. It also has a call that early ornithologists thought sounded like a lumberjack sharpening his saw. Thus, the name "saw-whet."

Finally, a friend and resident of Mt. Desert Island, Ralph

Chapter 1

Long Jr., found a nest for Dad in an old woodpecker cavity. He noticed a swarm of mosquitoes at the entrance, indicating that a warm-blooded animal was inside.

The little guy I spotted was perched in a hemlock tree, about 10 feet above the ground. Though females are slightly larger, the sexes look alike, so I did not know which I was looking at, even at close range.

Getting to Know "Hoo"

Because saw-whets are totally nocturnal, people rarely see them. But reader Emily Grey of Onancock, Virginia has seen many of them. That's because she assists with the banding of the birds at the tip of the Delmarva Peninsula near her home. The banding effort is part of a much larger program known as Project Owl Net, with banding stations in many eastern states.

Emily says that the average saw-whet she handles weighs about 3 ounces and is covered in down and feathers, even on its legs, almost to the ends of its needle-sharp talons. Except at the banding sites, Emily had never encountered a saw-whet owl in the wild. That is, until one cold March evening, when she spotted a tiny bird no larger than an American robin drinking from a puddle at her mother's house.

"I watched in fascination as the buff-colored adult owl lowered its head, raised up and slightly tilted its crown back, swallowing the cool refreshment," she relates.

Moving South

Despite the fact that the northern saw-whet has been banded more often than any other North American owl (more than 60,000 individuals), relatively little is known about its behavior and movements.

It was once believed to be a strictly northern dweller of coniferous and mountainous forests. But recent banding records have shown that it is more widespread than anyone knew, especially in winter.

A northern saw-whet was found as far south as northern

> ## *It is more widespread than anyone knew.*

Florida. Like northern finches, some populations of this owl seem to "irrupt" periodically—moving south en masse to search for the small mammals like mice, moles and shrews that comprise most of their diet.

Although most northern saw-whet owls nest in abandoned woodpecker tree cavities, they can be enticed into man-made nesting boxes. If you live in or near northern or mountainous coniferous forests, you might want to build a couple of nesting boxes for your backyard. Visit the Shaw Creek Web site for building plans for a saw-whet owl box *www.shawcreekbird-supply.com/plans_saw_whet_owl.htm*).

Perhaps one night, you'll find yourself peering into the captivating yellow eyes of a northern saw-whet owl.

NEED A HAND? A northern saw-whet owl (above) perches for a moment on volunteer Kristina Baker after it was banded at the Big Oaks National Wildlife Refuge in Madison, Indiana.

READER TIP

You can find a hidden saw-whet owl nest by looking for signs like a swarm of mosquitoes at the entrance of an old woodpecker hole. That indicates there is a warm-blooded animal inside.

—George Harrison, Contributing Editor

Backyard Birding Bio

☐ Summer
☐ Winter
☐ Year-Round

Common Name: Northern saw-whet owl.
Scientific Name: *Aegolius acadicus*.
Length: 8 inches.
Wingspan: 17 inches.
Distinctive Markings: Adult is reddish-brown above, white below with reddish streaks. Facial disks are reddish, without dark borders, and its beak is dark. Juveniles are strongly reddish above, tawny-rust below. Males and females look alike.
Distinctive Behavior: Hunts almost entirely at night, using sound and sight to find its prey.
Habitat: Coniferous forests, sometimes oak woodland or streamside groves in arid country.
Call: Repeated low whistled toots. Also has a wheezy, rising, catlike screech or soft nasal barks, or a soft and whining whistle.

Nest: In a cavity, usually an abandoned woodpecker hole, that's 14 to 60 feet above the ground. Will use a birdhouse. Uses no nesting material, only breast feathers. Lays five to six pure-white eggs, laid at intervals of 1 to 3 days. The female incubates for 21 to 28 days, beginning with the laying of the first egg. The male helps feed the young.
Diet: Mostly small mammals, but occasionally insects and frogs.
Backyard Favorite: Nesting box, 16 inches tall and 12 inches wide with a 3-inch entrance hole.

KILLDEER

Don't be fooled by this bird's theatrics.

By George Harrison, Contributing Editor

I bet there's not a farm kid around who does not know the unique quirks of the legendary killdeer. I knew the birds as a kid on my grandfather's farm in southwest Pennsylvania. I remember them in the spring, flying low and calling behind my grandfather's tractor as he plowed new furrows. Killdeer were snapping up the insects exposed in the fresh soil.

As I got older, I was not surprised to learn that the killdeer is the most well-known and widely distributed shorebird in North America. Yet, this member of the plover family usually stays away from the water's edge. Instead, it prefers lawns, golf courses, cultivated fields and gravel driveways.

Between its preference to live near people and the loud, distinctive call of its own name, it is easy to see why this bird is so admired. Farmers love the killdeer because 98 percent of its diet consists of insects removed from their fields. Others enjoy the killdeer because it's fairly tame, especially near its nest, where it will perform the famous "broken-wing" act to lead predators away.

Photos: above and opposite page, Marie Read

Now You See It, Now You Don't

You would think a bird with a white ring around its neck and two black bands across its breast would be fairly easy to see at close range. But it's not.

This pattern, called eruptive markings, is a kind of camouflage that helps the bird blend into its surroundings. When it stands perfectly still, even at close range, it's nearly impossible to see. You have to know exactly what you're looking for.

The same is true of the killdeer's nest and eggs. Actually, there is no traditional nest. The birds simply lay four heavily marked eggs on bare gravel (above). The camouflaged eggs usually point toward the center of the nest like pieces of a pie, and look like the stones that surround them.

On several occasions, I have found a killdeer's nest by accidentally scaring the parent bird off of it. After marking it with a stick, I would go to get my camera. Yet, every time I returned to the area, I would spend a long time trying to relocate the nest. Sometimes, I was staring straight at it without knowing it.

Once a parent is off the nest, it performs its broken-wing act to lure predators away. My neighbor's English setter was one of those duped predators a few years ago.

I watched the dog run from the driveway, and then suddenly stop and point at a killdeer feigning a broken wing. The bird made a pathetic call as it slowly led "Berkley" away from

Richard Shiell

its nest in the gravel driveway. When they were both safely away, the killdeer flew across the road, loudly calling, "kill-dee, kill-dee, kill-dee." On the ground, killdeer are silent and nearly invisible, but in the air, they are among the noisiest birds I've ever heard. I guess their scientific name, *Charadrius vociferus*, rings true, since vociferous means to make a loud outcry.

Born to Run

Killdeer also use their camouflage pattern while searching for food. Their diet of insects requires skilled, stealthy hunting. When killdeer stop, they freeze in a position that blends into their surroundings. This fools both the insects they are after and predators that are after them.

During nesting season, both parent birds incubate the eggs for the 24 to 26 days required for hatching. In turn, this long incubation period produces chicks that are in an advanced stage of development. They are ready to leave the nest as soon as they dry, within an hour or so after hatching.

Like ducks, geese and cranes, the killdeer parents never feed the babies. They show them the food, and the youngsters eat on their own.

The chicks are a sight to behold. They look like little balls of cotton on two toothpick legs with a single black band across their breast. Even though they are developmentally advanced, they still have a lot of growing to do. A young killdeer's flight feathers are slow to develop, so the chicks are almost fully grown before they can fly (about 25 days after hatching).

During this growing period, baby killdeer depend on their

IT'S ALL AN ACT. If a predator gets too close to a killdeer's eggs, the parent pretends to be injured (left) until it lures them safely away. Adult killdeer have two black bands across their breast, while the young start with just one (above right).

protective coloring to hide themselves from predators. When danger approaches, they lie flat on the ground to blend into the background.

Though migratory, killdeer remain as far north as Alaska well into the fall, and return to the North early in the spring. They winter in warmer areas from the southern U.S. to Peru.

Populations of killdeer are healthy, but the long-term outlook may not be favorable. Because they nest in disrupted landscape, such as housing developments and sand traps of golf courses, many nests are destroyed.

Yet, killdeer have proven they are adaptable to incursion on the land, which gives hope they will be around for many years to come.

BIRD-WATCHER'S SECRET

Don't be alarmed if you see a killdeer pretending that it's injured. The bird is trying to lure you away from its nest. Let it do its job, and then try to avoid that area until after nesting season.

Francis and Janice Bergquist

Backyard Birding Bio

Mark Werner/Unicorn Stock Photos

Common Name: Killdeer.

Scientific Name: *Charadrius vociferus*.

Length: 10-1/2 inches.

Wingspan: 24 inches.

Distinctive Markings: A large, lanky plover with a brown back, white neck ring, two black bands across a white breast and a long tail with an orange rump that shows only in flight or display.

Habitat: Lawns, cemeteries, parking lots, golf courses and cultivated fields, usually away from water.

Voice: Noisy call of "kill-dee" and repeats "dee-dee-dee."

Nesting: No nest. Its four eggs, heavily marked with brown spots, scrawls and blotches, blend in with the surroundings. The pair incubates the eggs for 24 to 26 days until they hatch.

Diet: Nearly all of its diet consists of insects gleaned from the fields and lawns where it lives. It also consumes earthworms, crayfish and weed seeds.

Backyard Favorite: A gravel driveway where it can lay its eggs, even though it may be at risk at that location.

- Summer
- Year-Round
- Winter

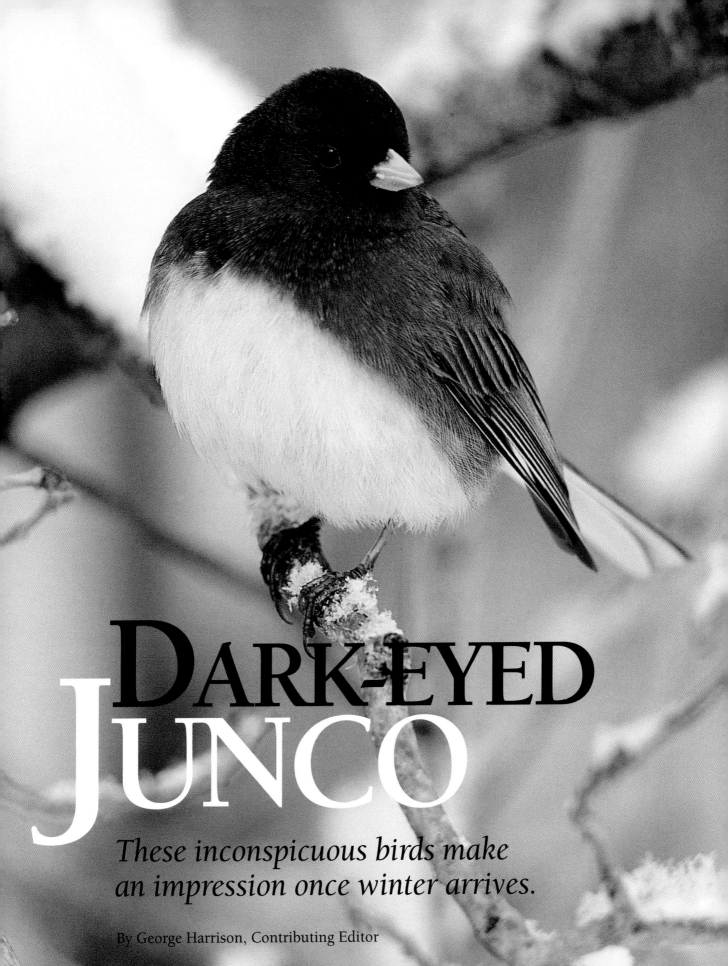

DARK-EYED JUNCO

*These inconspicuous birds make
an impression once winter arrives.*

By George Harrison, Contributing Editor

Gray-headed

Oregon

Pink-sided

Just call them stealth birds. It seems that dark-eyed juncos are rarely on anyone's radar screen. Despite the fact that these little ground sparrows are the most widespread feeder birds in North America, they frequently go unnoticed.

Granted, they don't have the charisma of a northern cardinal, American goldfinch or cedar waxwing, but these little gray and brown birds that flash white tail feathers are the most friendly and sociable, yet quietest, of all backyard birds. Many people call them "snowbirds," because juncos seem to show up in northern backyards about the time of the first snowflake, and then quietly disappear at the end of winter.

They are never alone. Quite gregarious in winter, dark-eyed juncos are always in small flocks of a half dozen or more birds, usually on the ground, and often in search of birdseed dropped from hanging feeders.

Dancing for Food

I love to watch their two-step dance as they search for food. It's a double shuffle with spread feet and a quick jump backward to throw snow or leaves behind them and uncover any seeds beneath.

One such junco that I watched for two winters was "Long John Silver," a one-legged male that performed a perfect two-step dance with just one leg. He was undeterred by his handicap, and quickly became a favorite.

Like other northern songbirds in winter, dark-eyed juncos have an amazing capability to stay warm in severely cold weather. They depend on a thick layer of fat that both insulates and generates energy. During cold nights, juncos burn 12 to 15 percent of their body weight just to keep warm. That means that they must replace that weight the next day or die of starvation. That's why juncos and other feeder birds eat most actively at sunrise and just before dark.

With the arrival of spring, the snowbirds seem to just disappear. They have moved north, paired off and are seeking nesting territories in coniferous woodlands.

POWER IN NUMBERS. There are six separate populations of dark-eyed juncos. These inconspicuous birds are all considered to be in the same species. The separate names refer to the different color variations or regions for individual populations.

WHAT'S IN A NAME?

Years ago, the dark-eyed juncos we know today were separated into six different species in North America. But then the ornithologists responsible for naming North American birds decided to group them under one name—the dark-eyed junco. They believed all were simply different populations of the same species.

These populations still exist as variations of the dark-eyed junco:

- **Oregon junco:** Resides in the West; has a black head and brown body.
- **Pink-sided:** Found in the Rocky Mountains; displays a gray head, brown back and pinkish sides.
- **Slate-colored:** A gray and white bird that's common throughout North America (see page 33).
- **White-winged:** A smaller population in the Rockies that's slate colored with white on its wings.
- **Gray-headed:** Gray bird found in the Southwest with a reddish spot on its back.
- **Red-backed:** Southwestern resident nearly identical to the gray-headed.

There is still one other species, the rare yellow-eyed junco in the extreme Southwest, which has remained separate from the dark-eyed.

Backyard Birding Bio

Hidden Homes

Many times I have visited the junco's northern nesting range, where I once again hear their familiar trills on their breeding grounds.

One thing I've learned during these excursions is that finding a junco's nest is no easy task. They typically are concealed under the overhanging grasses and mosses of a creek bank or woodland road. The trick is to locate a singing male, and then watch for the female that will unwittingly lead you to her nest.

At times, the parent birds have helped me find their nest by calling a "tsip" chip alarm note as I neared it. By searching under embankments in the immediate area, I was usually able to locate the hidden nest.

The female incubates the four or five pale, bluish-white eggs with dark spots for 12 to 13 days until they hatch. The young birds remain in the nest for another 2 weeks. If the first nest is successful, the parents will move on to a second nesting before the young of the first brood are fully on their own.

I found one such fledgling on the forest floor in Maine. It was hiding like an ostrich, with its head under a leaf, but its stubby little tail was sticking out in plain sight.

The next time you see a little gray bird, take a closer look. I believe you'll find a new feathered friend.

BIRD-WATCHER'S SECRET

When winter arrives, so do these birds. Attract dark-eyed juncos to your backyard with wild birdseed mix, cracked corn or millet.

Common Name: Dark-eyed junco.

Scientific Name: *Junco hyemalis.*

Length: 6-1/4 inches.

Wingspan: 9-1/4 inches.

Distinctive Markings: Small, slender, sparrow-like birds with striking white outer tail feathers. Some are all gray and white; others are black on the head, with brown on the back and/or sides.

Distinctive Behavior: Ground-inhabiting birds that shuffle both feet backward to uncover food.

Habitat: In summer, juncos breed in coniferous woodlands. In winter, they inhabit open woodlands, brushy clearings and backyards.

Voice: Song is a high-pitched trill. Alarm call is a high-pitched tinkling chip.

Nesting: Usually concealed on the ground under overhanging grasses. Compact nest is made of grasses, rootlets and mosses. The female incubates four or five pale, bluish-white eggs with dark spots for 12 to 13 days.

Diet: Mostly weed seeds and feeder food in winter. In summer, they will consume many kinds of insects.

Backyard Favorite: A tray feeder on or near the ground, filled with wild birdseed mix, or a combination of cracked corn and millet, which will attract flocks of juncos.

Winter
Summer
Year-Round

Marie Read

BLACK-CAPPED CHICKADEE

*These little charmers
are true feathered friends.*

By George Harrison, Contributing Editor

Of all the common backyard birds, the black-capped chickadee takes the prize as the most entertaining.

The little birds are so delightful that my wife, Kit, often says she'd like to come back as one in another life, if there were such a thing as reincarnation.

Why? "Because chickadees seem to enjoy life," she says.

It's true. These vivacious and carefree birds do exhibit a friendly energy. When two or more of them are together, they are full of conversation, exchanging cheerful remarks.

A Bird in Hand

Another of the black-capped chickadee's many remarkable traits is its tameness. It is so approachable around bird feeders that it may even eat seeds from an outstreched hand.

Hugh Wiberg, the author of several books, including *Hand-Feeding Backyard Birds*, still remembers the first time a black-capped chickadee snapped a seed from his open palm 25 years ago.

"Of the many species that have eaten from my hand since

Chickadees are named after the sound of their alarm call.

---

then, those fearless black-and-white bundles of energy are without question the easiest birds to charm to your hands," he says.

I, too, was thrilled the first time a black-capped chickadee fed from my hand. I was just a little boy helping my dad maintain a bird-feeding station behind our house in western Pennsylvania.

"If you stand very still with sunflower seeds in your hand, a chickadee may stop for a snack," my dad said.

So I did as he instructed and sure enough, in a few minutes, a tiny chickadee landed on my hand. In a flash, the bird seized a seed in its bill and was gone. The chickadee was so lightweight that I really couldn't feel it, until it pushed off. The most memorable part was seeing all the detail in the bird's feathers, beady black eyes and sharp tiny bill. I was ecstatic.

But don't let a chickadee's petite appearance fool you.

"Chickadees are not the suburban wimps that some people think they are," says wildlife ecologist Margaret Clack Brittingham, who studied the birds at the University of Wisconsin in Madison.

For three winters, she kept track of 576 black-capped chickadees. As the small birds struggled against starvation and stinging cold, they earned her respect, too.

"They are tough survivors that live close to the edge of life," she says.

One notable finding was that chickadees don't depend on bird feeders, even when they're readily available. During normal winter weather, chickadees that had access to feeders survived at the same rate as those chickadees without feeders.

In fact, despite the feeders, the birds still gathered a majority of their food from the wild. This should ease the concerns of people who cannot replenish their bird feeders on winter days when they are away from home.

George Harrison

BACKYARD ATTRACTIONS. Black-capped chickadees are common—and welcome—backyard visitors. They'll stop by for a bite of sunflower seeds (far left) or raise their young in a birdhouse (above), preferably one with a 1-1/4-inch entrance.

"The thing that really impressed me about chickadees is their metabolism," she says. "We weighed birds early in the morning and found that they had virtually no body fat. Yet, the same birds examined in the afternoon of the same day were bulging with fat."

These fat stores are what allow these tiny imps to make it through a long sub-zero night.

They Will Survive

Chickadees have other winter survival strategies as well.

Marie Read

Donna and Tom Krischan

ALWAYS ON THE GO. The endless energy of black-capped chickadees makes them a delight. So it's no surprise that many bird-watchers list this bird as their favorite species. It's common to spot them plucking sunflower seeds or other treats from a feeder (left). But this sight of a chickadee hovering in mid-air as it sips water from a melting icicle (above) is simply amazing.

During winter nights, they can reduce their metabolism by slowing their heartbeats, breathing and energy consumption.

They also are adept at finding fluids in winter—sometimes from unexpected sources, like the scene Elizabeth Williams witnessed in her West Bloomfield, Michigan yard.

"As I peered out from my sunroom, I noticed the icicles on my pussy willow were beginning to thaw," she says. "The melting ice must have caught the eye of a black-capped chickadee, too, because it flew to a branch directly below one of the dripping icicles. As the drops fell, the chickadee opened its bill and caught each one. What a sight!"

Music with Meaning

Chickadees also are very vocal birds. Named for their alarm notes, "chick-a-dee, dee, dee," they communicate a great deal more with that call than we might realize. New research at the University of Montana has shown that their "dee" calls are filled with information.

Researcher Christopher Templeton discovered that the spacing of the "dees" describes the level of danger from a nearby predator. Large birds of prey, like great horned owls, which don't pose much threat to tiny chickadees, elicited fewer "dees" than did smaller, more maneuverable raptors, like pygmy owls. More "dees" drew a greater group defense of fellow chickadees against the predator.

Larry Mishkar/Dembinsky Photo Assoc.

HAND IT TO THEM. One of the black-capped chickadee's most remarkable traits is its tameness. These birds are among the easiest species to feed from your hand (left). Summer is a busy time for chickadee parents as they tirelessly work to keep their six to eight hungry young ones fed (above).

A totally different black-capped chickadee vocalization is the male's courtship song, a sweet and lazy "phee-be" that's used to maintain pair bonds and nesting territories. When I hear the first black-capped chickadee's courtship song in the late winter, I know spring is not far behind.

Pairs of chickadees begin checking out nest sites as early as March, and gather nesting material in April. Barbara Humes of Orcas, Washington inadvertently began providing chickadees with a unique nest material several years ago. It all started when she left an old cotton mop on her porch. Later that day, she noticed a black-capped chickadee inspecting it.

"Glancing around occasionally, the bird removed strings one by one until its bill was full of them," Barbara says. "A few minutes later, it returned to take more fibers. Obviously, the bird was building a nest.

"We've left that old mop on our porch for 3 years now. Each spring, we watch more birds discover the advantages of its soft fibers. And to think that I almost threw it away!"

If you miss the nest-making process, there's another way to determine if black-capped chickadees are raising young nearby. In my southeastern Wisconsin yard, I look for this clue: bedraggled parents.

Keeping six to eight hungry balls of fluff fed is a full-time job, and it takes a toll on the adults. A fresh-looking chickadee at the feeders in summer tells me that it is a juvenile, though otherwise it looks like its parents.

The black-capped is the most common and widespread of the seven species of chickadees in North America. But all are fairly similar in appearance and display many of the same entertaining behaviors.

But don't just take my word for it. Set out a tube feeder of sunflower seeds to attract these little charmers, and you can see for yourself.

Backyard Birding Bio

Common Name: Black-capped chickadee.
Scientific Name: *Poecile atricapilla*.
Length: 5–1/4 inches.
Wingspan: 8 inches.
Distinctive Markings: Gray and buff feathers, bright-black bib and skullcap and white cheeks. Males and females look alike.
Distinctive Behavior: Acrobatic, friendly, curious and will often hang upside down. May become tame at bird feeders, and fly to an outstretched hand for seed.
Habitat: Woodlands, thickets, parks and wooded backyards.
Voice: Contact call is "chick-a-dee, dee, dee." In spring and early summer, the male's courtship song is "phee-be."
Nest: Both male and female dig a natural nesting cavity in dead tree trunks or branches. The nest may be lined with wool, fur, hair, moss or feathers. The six to eight white eggs with reddish-brown spots hatch in 12 to 13 days. They also will nest in old woodpecker holes or birdhouses with a 1-1/4-inch entrance. Both parents then work to feed the nestlings. Pairs raise only one brood per year.
Diet: Primarily insects, but up to 50 percent of their diet may be plant matter, especially pine seeds.
Backyard Favorite: A tube-style bird feeder containing sunflower seeds, either cracked or in the shell.

■ Year-Round

100

84

108

75

97

GREEN THUMB

FORGET THE MOWING

Minnesota gardener sidelines her lawn mower, opting for lush gardens, ponds and blooming pathways.

By Vivette Botner
Field Editor, Duluth, Minnesota

Amazing! That's what I said the first time I saw Kathy Bomey's garden.

I was taking photos of another backyard nearby when the owner pointed out Kathy's home. Beautiful blooms, abundant shrubs and a picturesque pond covered the entire front yard. That was just the appetizer.

When I walked out back, I was awestruck again. What would have been a carpet of grass at just about any other house in this Duluth neighborhood was another spread of annuals, perennials, ground covers and shrubs.

DIFFERENT APPROACH. Kathy Bomey (inset) chose ponds (left) and flowers instead of a lawn.

COME SEE WHAT'S BLOOMING. Three snails adorn a colorful welcome sign in Kathy's garden (left)—just don't let these slug relatives eat the nearby hostas! Garden accents like these are a common feature in Kathy's yard. Above, trilliums and lady's slippers are wildflowers that thrive in the shade.

den," Kathy says. "Soon, whenever family or friends took vacations, they'd bring home more rocks. Once I had enough to create a flower bed, I'd get to work."

Although Kathy hired landscapers to install a 700-gallon water garden in the front yard, she learned from watching and built a smaller pond in back herself, even adding a waterfall.

"I'm not sure how I did it all, but I'm glad I did," she says with a laugh. "It's so peaceful. I can't imagine not having it."

The water garden in the front yard was nearly destroyed after a harsh winter, but Kathy decided to expand it rather than repair it. She nearly tripled its size to 2,000 gallons and added a 3-foot-high waterfall, a gurgling stream, fish, water lilies and other aquatic plants.

Countless Varieties

When visitors ask Kathy if there's a plant she doesn't have in her yard, she's hard-pressed to answer.

"I have so many," she says. "I planted quite a few varieties of shrubs, from weigelias to barberries, spirea and more. I think the weeping larch in front is one of my favorites. It's so dramatic, with its drooping branches."

To add color after many of the shrubs are finished flowering, Kathy tucks annuals in and around them.

"I particularly like Wave petunias because they'll wind around and up into the bushes, making it look like they're blooming again," Kathy says.

She also relies on lots of pansies, impatiens, marigolds, plus perennials and new favorites—ornamental grasses.

"Perennials, such as daylilies, purple coneflowers and hostas, are part of the mix. And you'll find between eight and 12 different kinds of ornamental grasses. They look interesting all year.

"I also have several container gardens of trilliums and lady's slippers stationed at the south end of the backyard where it's very shady. Those I change each year."

Containers aren't the only items that vary from one summer to the next. Kathy regularly "remodels" sections of her

"I hate to mow," Kathy explains. "I started eliminating the lawn when I bought the house nearly 20 years ago."

The process was slow at first, she admits. But her project really got growing when she removed a dilapidated garage from the property.

"There was no way I was going to cover that space with more turf," she says. "I started buying plants that looked interesting and went on garden tours for new ideas."

> *"I'm not sure how I did it all, but I'm glad I did..."*

Today, only a tidbit of lawn is left, a mere 9- by 16-foot strip. The rest of her 75- by 150-foot lot is a complex web of gardens intertwined with paths and ponds.

One Stone at a Time

Rocks help define the rambling beds that blanket the property. Kathy hauled the majority of the stones herself, with some help from her sister-in-law and grandson.

"Every time I went on a trip, I'd bring back rocks for my gar-

FLORAL TAPESTRY. Flowers weave a colorful pattern in Kathy's yard (above). Several flower-lined walks (like the one at right) invite visitors to slow down and enjoy the garden, while also allowing easy access for flower bed maintenance.

backyard, moving rocks, plants and garden accents to new locations.

"Once every inch of property was used up, I began looking at the gardens and thinking about what I'd like to do differently. For example, I decided to move some ground cover plants in order to make room for roses, which I haven't grown before."

Ways to Save

To save money, Kathy starts most of her annuals from seed. She also works for a friend who owns a nursery.

"Instead of cash, I get paid in plants," she shares. "Honestly, though, I can't possibly put in enough hours to earn all of the ones I want."

Even though her gardens fade as the weather cools, Kathy still finds ways to keep her green thumb busy.

"I never consider autumn as a time for closing down my gardens for winter," she says. "I prefer to think of it as the season when I start planning for spring."

READER TIP

Landscapers installed the water garden in my front yard. But I learned the process by watching them and then built a smaller pond myself.

—Kathy Bomey, Duluth, Minnesota

BEAUTY ON THE FARM

This rural Ontario gardener created a beautiful backyard oasis amid the fields.

An avid gardener and lifelong farmer, Joyce Walters was not afraid to get her hands dirty when she and her husband, Elmer, decided to landscape their St. Mary's, Ontario home some 12 years ago.

"Putting in the fish pond was our first project together," Joyce says. "Elmer and I had just gotten married and built our house on a 73-acre farm. The only things on the lot were several evergreens standing in front of the fence. The space really called out for something dramatic."

Eager to get started, Joyce volunteered to dig the pond, with visions of a lily-covered lake dancing in her head.

"I've done my share of shoveling, so I knew what I was

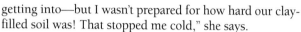

getting into—but I wasn't prepared for how hard our clay-filled soil was! That stopped me cold," she says.

Renting a small backhoe was the answer. And quick as a wink, the pond started to take shape.

Because they wanted to hear the soothing splash of moving water, they included a waterfall on one side, then lined the pond with rocks and created flower beds around it.

Today, the pond is home to frogs, fish and water lilies galore. Plants like black-eyed Susans, allium, iris and ornamental grasses surround it on all sides.

"It turned out to be the spectacular centerpiece our yard needed," Joyce says.

Garden Keeps Growing

Of course, the couple didn't stop there. Each year since, they've added a new flower bed, path or some other garden feature.

"My son, who lives a 1/2 mile away with his family, does the farming," Joyce says. "Elmer and I are retired and we have time to do a lot more gardening than we ever could before."

One summer, they constructed a brick sitting area to the side of the pond and surrounded it with rosebushes, so they could enjoy a cup of coffee and the outdoors at the same

time. Then Joyce and Elmer put in a patio on the other side of the pond, complete with a table and a small bench that serves as a planter. And more flower beds followed after that.

"I decided to put a new bed in the front yard after paging through a bulb catalog," Joyce says. "I was just amazed at the huge variety of tulips you can buy these days."

In addition to a huge array of spring bulbs, the area holds perennials and annuals, as well as a flagpole and a birdbath.

Another plot that makes Joyce especially proud is her butterfly and hummingbird garden for attracting these gorgeous fliers.

"I tried to coordinate colors by choosing varieties with pink or purple blooms," Joyce says.

"Other beds have come about just because I'm fascinated by flowers. Some of my favorites are roses, tulips and lilacs—their scent is heavenly," Joyce adds. "But honestly, I love any kind of flower."

Although Joyce has plenty of green-thumb experience and an obvious appreciation for blossoms and greenery, she's the first to admit that she and Elmer made some mistakes as they expanded their gardens.

"On several occasions, I'd make a flower bed and put in these little plants and shrubs, only to find a few years later that I should have made the bed bigger when everything outgrew the surroundings," she explains.

"I've also planted bushes too close to the house, because I didn't account for how large they'd be when mature," Joyce continues. "But every time we make a mistake, we learn something new, so nothing is ever wasted."

Even a heron taught Joyce and Elmer a lesson after they spotted one flying around the pond.

"We heard that a fake heron would stop the real ones from landing, so we added one to the shore," Joyce says. "It worked for a few minutes, until a live heron landed right next to it and tried to make friends!"

Room with a View

Bringing the outdoors in became easier when Joyce and Elmer added a four-season sunroom on to their home about 3 years ago. Windows line the room and patio doors open onto the deck and attached gazebo, where containers filled with annuals sit. It even has a fireplace in it for use during chilly weather.

"The room is just amazing. It overlooks the pond and just about the whole backyard. Being able to see our flowers in bloom with acres of green behind them is awesome," Joyce says. "My daughter-in-law named it my 'room with a view.'"

Apparently, the birds like it, too.

"One day, two hummingbirds flew in—and it was quite a chore to coax them back outside," she recalls. "I guess they wanted to see things from my perspective."

Joyce's three children and six grandchildren like to explore the yard as well.

"They all look forward to coming to our house and walking through the garden, searching for new flowers or garden accents we've tucked in different spots," Joyce says.

"And the grandkids can't wait to sit by the pond and watch me pet the frogs. I'm glad the little ones have developed an admiration for nature, and I hope they become gardeners someday, too.

"I think there's a pretty good chance," Joyce adds. "After all, I'm living proof that once you start gardening, you just can't stop."

GREEN THUMB TIP

Choose flowers with sweet scents. When they bloom, you'll have something nice for the eyes...and the nose!
—*Joyce Walters, St. Mary's, Ontario*

PERFECT PATHWAYS

Everyday objects transform this yard into a delightful realm of unique walkways.

You won't find formal gardens or precise hedges in Brenda Sensenig's yard. Instead, her Ephrata, Pennsylvania property is a colorful collage of uniquely shaped shrubs, inventive paths, refreshing water features and some of the most creative flower containers around.

It wasn't always like this, Brenda admits.

"My husband, Ed, and I have lived in this house for 35 years, but I've really only spent the last 12 of them creating gardens," she says. "When our four children were small, I dabbled in organic vegetable gardening, then swapped that for a part-time job after the kids moved out."

However, when her daughter was expecting twins, Brenda decided to quit her job to help out, and started landscaping to fill up her spare time.

Putting in a pond was the first project.

"I just started digging with the rototiller. I didn't have a plan, nor did I really know anything about ponds," she recalls. "I managed to dig so deep I couldn't get the rototiller out."

Daring to Dream

At that point, Brenda thought she ought to do some research, and was lucky enough to meet up with a neighbor who had a stash of water gardening books. The end result was a pond with a small stream that has provided her family years of enjoyment. Brenda later called in a professional to add a waterfall.

"That's how I do things," Brenda says. "I dive right in because drawing up plans just doesn't work for me. I can see what I want to do in my mind's eye, but I can't put it on paper."

There is a method to Brenda's madness. She keeps her

imagination open and always looks for a way to put a different spin on things. For instance, the winding path that leads to a fountain in front of her house came about after Brenda picked up an old arbor (below) for $5 at a yard sale.

"I thought it would be fun to turn the arbor into a doorway to the fountain, but rather than remove part of the lawn to create a normal stone walkway, I put in flower beds on either side of a strip of grass and let the sod serve as the path," she says.

Lining the path are elegantly shaped arborvitae interspersed with planters of annuals.

"I've been pruning arborvitae, yews, blue spruce and other evergreens into cones, spirals and other forms for a while now. I love the way they look, and they're easy to do," Brenda says.

"Plus, I'm big on annuals. You just can't beat the show they put on all summer long. Marigolds, geraniums, fuchsia, zinnias—you name it, I've probably grown it at one time or another. Right now, dragon-wing begonias are my favorites."

Bargain Hunting

Planters are another necessary element in Brenda's yard—and almost anything is fair game. Brenda gets most of her soon-to-be containers at yard sales.

"I've made a container for flowers from a pedestal sink as well as an old-fashioned washing machine, a rinsing tub and a wicker hamper," she says.

"My daughter and I go to yard sales and basically buy the stuff nobody else wants, then I find a way to use it in the yard, Brenda explains. "A rocking chair, an old pair of blue jeans, a birdcage, even an old stove—if I can fill it with soil, I can turn it into a planter."

One of her favorite finds is a canopy bed.

"I brought home the old frame with the idea of turning

DIVE IN. When Brenda Sensenig (left inset with husband Ed) started planning her garden, she says she dove right in instead of making up formal plans. The results include this pathway (left) lined with pots that feature vibrant pink dragon-wing begonias. These are just a few of the many bold planters that Brenda likes to use in the rest of her garden.

SOMETHING DIFFERENT. If you're looking for unique landscaping ideas, then Brenda's garden is the perfect place to visit. Whether it's colorful flower beds (above), distinctive planters (at left), or the fun garden railway (below), she seems to have something to offer just about everyone.

it into one of those classic 'flower beds,' but it needed something more," she says. "So I asked Ed if he could come up with a different way to use it. He's a sheet metal worker, so he was able to make the metal canopy that I now fill with trailing petunias each summer." (See inset photo above.)

Ed also helped Brenda rig up the bathtub-and-shower fountain behind the house.

"He handles all the plumbing and wiring for my projects," Brenda says. "He installed lights so we can enjoy the garden at night and the miniature train that runs along the tracks in my garden railroad near the porch."

Right on Track

The railroad (above right) is a highlight for everyone who visits, including the Sensenigs' 11 grandchildren. Brenda got the idea after a guest observed that their garden had everything but a railroad.

"He was a garden railway enthusiast and was kind enough to help me get started," Brenda says. "I opted to keep the tracks and the train simple because I was more interested in adding succulents, mini shrubs and pots of impatiens around it."

Gardening now occupies most of Brenda's waking hours during the growing season.

"I save housecleaning for winter because once the weather warms up, I'm outside most of the time," she says. "Adding new plants, mulching and moving older flowers to new spots is all-consuming."

Of course, Brenda can always find a few spare moments to come up with new ideas.

"This summer, I think I'll turn our old porch swing into a planter and get Ed to hang it in one of our trees," she says. "And who knows what I'll find when I shop at yard sales? That's what keeps me going!"

GREEN THUMB TIP

You don't have to spend a lot of money to have unique planters. Go to yard sales to look for bargains. From a laundry hamper to an old sink, ordinary objects can be extraordinary with blooms.
—Brenda Sensenig
Ephrata, Pennsylvania

SNIP, PLANT, GROW

Add to your garden without spending a cent.

By Melinda Myers, Contributing Editor

Taking cuttings is a great way to expand—or share—the beauty of any garden. Perhaps you'd like to preserve a flower with family history, increase your collection of favorite blooms or reproduce that hard-to-find plant.

Most gardeners have had success rooting leafy plants like coleus or philodendron. A short stem with leaves will quickly form roots in water, potting mix or vermiculite—and then you are well on your way to a full-sized plant.

The same does not hold true for trees and shrubs, however. With these plants, you'll need to pay more attention to timing and the type of cutting you take. And these factors will vary depending on the type of plant.

But with a little know-how, you'll soon be able to grow cuttings of plants like roses, lilacs, forsythias and spireas. The extra effort will be worth it.

Pay Attention to Patents

Before you take a cutting of that fancy new rose (like the one at right) or lilac, it's important to understand some of the laws of the plant world.

Many new varieties are patented. This means you cannot take a cutting from an existing plant to start a new one without the permission of the patent owner. This right is reserved for the company that spent time and money developing the new or unusual variety. If this is the case, a close look at the tag or growing information will reveal a patent number or note that the patent is pending.

Patents are good for about 20 years. After that, you are free to take cuttings and start your own plants. Although it may seem like an inconvenience, remember that respecting the patents helps support those who work to introduce new plants for us to enjoy.

When checking the tag, you also may see ® or ™ symbols. You can take cuttings and plant these varieties in your garden, as long as they are not patented.

If all this sounds too confusing, don't be intimidated. There are plenty of old family favorites and traditional garden beauties that aren't protected—and these make great candidates to grow from cuttings.

Getting Started

There are several types of cuttings you can use to propogate new trees and shrubs.

Hardwood cuttings are the key to starting plants like roses, forsythia, privet, olive, wisteria, spirea, hemlock and many other deciduous and needled trees and shrubs.

During the dormant season, which is late fall or winter, remove a 4- to 8-inch stem piece of the previous season's growth that contains two nodes—the place where leaves attach (see top right photo). Pack the cuttings in peat moss or sawdust and store them in a cool dark place until spring. As the weather warms, stick the cuttings—with the end that was closest to the roots down—in a flat of moist vermiculite, perlite or sand (see lower right photo). To increase the success for these types of cuttings, or any others, dip the end in rooting hormone first.

Summer is the time to take semihardwood cuttings—the new growth that's starting to harden up and mature. This works for varieties like holly, azaleas, pittosporum, euonymus, citrus, olive and other broadleaf evergreens and deciduous trees and shrubs.

Take 3- to 6-inch cuttings in the morning when the stems are firm and full of moisture. Remove the lower leaves and cut the remaining leaves in half to reduce moisture loss.

Then root semihardwood cuttings in moist vermiculite, perlite or sand in a shaded and humid location. Loosely cover the container with plastic to increase the humidity and monitor the temperature to prevent overheating.

Softwood cuttings from tender new growth are another way to propogate plants like lilacs, roses, forsythias, magnolias, weigela, spireas and fruit trees.

Take 3- to 5-inch cuttings early in the day and plant them right away for the best results. Root in a warm and moist rooting medium in a humid location that's out of direct sun (like in a cold frame).

No matter what kind of cuttings you're using, once they've rooted, you can treat them like bare-root plants and add them to your garden. Or, move them to a large container filled with well-draining potting mix. This allows the plants to develop stronger root systems before transplanting.

As you begin trying to grow trees and shrubs from cuttings, I do have some last words of wisdom: Professionals often spend years perfecting this process, so don't be disappointed if your cuttings don't root right away. Just keep trying!

GROWING IN CIRCLES

Gardener rounds up a lush new look for her once-barren backyard.

By Ina Johns, Harrogate, Tennessee

BLOOMS AROUND EVERY BEND. Ina Johns (above inset) created bright, curving flower beds that wind through her yard (top).

A small flower bed for irises and a few other perennials…that's what I had in mind when I decided to give gardening a try back in 1996. Little did I know that some 9 years later, I'd have a bounty of blooming beds all over our 1-acre backyard!

I've always loved flowers, but my only green-thumb activity after moving into our home in 1978 was planting a few marigolds, impatiens and geraniums next to the house. Still, I knew our expanse of half-dead grass lined with trees needed something.

My answer was to create a simple circular patch of irises

flanked by daisies, veronica, yarrow, phlox and purple coneflowers. The experience, from start to finish, was so gratifying that I couldn't wait to do it again.

You could say I've been gardening in circles ever since. A glance at our yard reveals that none of my beds have straight edges. All of the new gardens I've created are either round or oval.

The reason for this consistency is simple: To plan a new flower bed, I don't pull out paper and pencil or stakes and twine, I place a garden hose on the lawn in a pleasing shape. That way, I wind up with a gently curving outline. Then I etch out the edges with a shovel before my husband, Bill, uses the tractor to dig up the grass and add compost.

MANY HAPPY RETURNS. Pretty perennials and birdhouses dominate Ina's garden. Above: Purple coneflowers, ornamental grasses and sunflowers surround a birdhouse. Others like daylilies, lambs' ears and coreopsis (below) spread each year.

Learn from Mistakes

Nowadays, I generally have an idea what kind of flowers I want to plant in a new flower bed. But when I started, I'd go to the garden center and pick out whatever caught my eye.

After a few failures, I began to pay more attention to the conditions each plant preferred. I also started primarily focusing on perennials, both for their beauty and the fact that they come back year after year. I love that many varieties are self-sowing and will spread throughout the garden with little effort from me.

I don't completely ignore annuals, however. I like to add them here and there for extra color, especially sunflowers, lantanas and petunias. I've learned to save the seeds and use them to start plants for the following growing season.

For the past several years, cultivating daylilies has become a passion. I love these easy-care flowers that provide pretty blooms from summer to fall. To date, I have planted over 125 daylilies, with plans to add even more.

Ornamental grasses have also caught my fancy. They add a sense of peacefulness to my gardens and seem to almost sing in the wind.

Another hobby of mine, thanks to my 19-year-old daughter, Ashley, is raising flowers and plants that attract butterflies and provide spots for these "flying flowers" to lay their eggs.

When Ashley was young, she used to collect caterpillars and care for them until they turned into butterflies. She got me interested back then, and today we have a patch of milkweed, which monarchs lay eggs on, as well as dill to attract black swallowtails. We wait in anticipation each year for caterpillars to emerge and watch them transform.

Character Building

My 27-year-old son, Shawn, contributes to my gardening efforts as well. He likes to build birdhouses out of old barn wood and perch them on posts in the midst of the flowers. He has also crafted wooden tepees for growing vines and rustic wheelbarrows that add so much character to our yard.

I like to make things for the garden, too, like wind chimes using old silverware. I've even fashioned one from dog tags and car gears and another by tying kitchen utensils to a tin teapot.

Probably the most interesting decoration that graces our yard is the old outhouse from my mother's place. I use it to store tools and display antiques. It's a real conversation piece.

One of the things I enjoy about our yard is that it constantly inspires new ideas. I know I started with a small plan, but now I just can't contain myself.

Every morning, I wake up knowing something different is waiting to be discovered. I guess you could say gardening is a never-ending joy that feeds my soul.

READER TIP

To plan a new flower bed, I don't pull out paper and pencil or stakes and twine, I place a garden hose on the lawn in a pleasing shape. That way, I wind up with a gently curving outline.

—Ina Johns, Harrogate, Tennessee

ROCK THE GARDEN

*This couple carved out
a flowering haven
with natural materials.*

By Pat Becker, Mishicot, Wisconsin

I have flower fever. It's true. I caught it from my mother, an avid gardener who grew the most beautiful flowers when I was growing up.

While I've "suffered" for years, my husband, John, did not catch the fever until he married me, but once he did, there was no stopping him. Our infectious love of flowers has led us on quite an odyssey over the years!

We started out small by landscaping around the urban home we owned for 18 years while we raised our eight children. During that time, we purchased 27 forested acres in the country. Then, with help from my sister and her husband, we cleared a space in the woods and built a cozy cabin that we visited often.

We all loved the cabin so much that we decided to add on to it and turn it into our permanent home when our oldest daughter graduated from high school. After we settled into the house, our flower-growing efforts really took off.

Rocky Inspiration

In order to put in flower beds, we had to clear some more land. In the process, we wound up uncovering a treasure trove of interesting rocks. Jackpot!

Instead of plain flower gardens, we used our new find to create rock gardens. It was both inexpensive and fun. Then to further keep costs down, I filled the beds with flowers from my mom and other family members and friends.

After that, we put in a few small lily ponds and kept expanding our gardens. By this time, John and I were full-fledged empty nesters. We had a big house and an even bigger yard to care for, so we decided to downsize. We built a smaller home at the other end of our land, and sold our cabin to our youngest son and his wife.

Our gardening efforts at the new house were modest at first. But then John and I retired, and we knew exactly what to do with our free time.

Just like at our old place, we started accessorizing our new abode with rock gardens. Multiple loads of rocks and 5 years later, we wound up with our own personal paradise. Not surprisingly, we ended up with more flower beds than we had at the big house!

Over the years, I've learned some very practical things about gardening. For instance, I know now to avoid flowers that multiply, not by reseeding, but by sending out roots underground, particularly lilies of the valley. One time I had to dig up an entire bed because the roots spread too aggressively and made a real mess.

Water Wisdom

Adding our pond taught us the importance of weighing down the plastic sheet that serves as a liner. When we first developed our pond, we had everything ready. It was set up, we added water and all looked good—until a heavy rainfall brought about a big surprise. The plastic worked away from the bottom and floated up to the top.

We had to drain the pond, reposition the liner and top the entire thing with 1/2 inch of limestone. We haven't had a problem since.

Both John and I have found that gardening has a lot to offer people beyond creating a pretty vista. We truly believe that cultivating flowers helps you cope with tough times. We lost a daughter at age 18, a tragedy that took a lot out of us. Our gardening efforts helped us work through our grief.

Budget-wise Beauty

Raising a large family teaches you how to make the most of a dollar, and I still look for ways to save as we add yard decorations and work on our gardens. The rock gardens we build are probably one of our most easy and inexpensive projects. With permission, we gathered many stones from farmers' fields. Now they look great stacked around pots of flowers and along our small pond and flower beds.

We also put dead stumps to use by turning them into unique planters. It's cheap and easy to hollow them out and fill with flowers. They add a nice woodsy touch to the landscape. Straight branches and bark gathered from fallen trees in our woods provided the materials to create paths in our shade garden.

An old stepladder now works as a plant stand in the middle of one flower bed. Even leaky watering cans can be handy planters.

All of these accents, plus a collection of statues, birdhouses, benches and feeders, enhance the many perennials we've planted. We've also included a variety of trees and shrubs in and among the flower beds.

For example, you'll find maples, weeping cherries, weeping crabapples, tamaracks, blue spruces and weeping willows, as well as three kinds of weigela, burning bushes, holly, lilac, mock orange, spirea and more.

You know, a gardener's work is never really done. John and I can always find a new project to tackle or new blooms to add. Our flower-filled haven in the middle of the woods is a work in progress—and we wouldn't have it any other way.

GREEN THUMB TIP

Stones can be an attractive and inexpensive addition to your garden. It might take a little effort to collect them, but the end result is worth it and will last for years.
—Pat Becker
Mishicot, Wisconsin

HER GARDEN
GROWS IN PERFECT HARMONY

By Judy Hominick, Dallas, Texas

Carolyn Bush is in perfect tune with her garden. You could say she's conducting a blooming symphony out her back door in Dallas, Texas, thanks to musical roots that have fed a growing love for gardening.

It all started when her interest in collecting stringed instruments from flea markets took a new twist. She spied an old tuba and had to add it to the mix.

"There was something about the shape of a tuba that made me think of flowers," says Carolyn, who planted the huge instrument in her garden out of necessity. "There was no room for it inside the house, so I put it outside. It kind of grew from there."

Soon a trombone found its way into another flower bed, standing tall among a group

---

Gardening is a lot like music because nothing is ever static.

---

of bush honeysuckle. When a small pond was added, a second tuba appeared, plus a bugle rising from the water next to a lizard's tail plant and Texas star hibiscus.

Working in Concert

Now, 15 musical instruments have taken root among nearly 200 different plants and trees in her yard. It's even certified as a Texas Wildscape Backyard Wildlife Habitat and as a Butterfly Habitat.

Music has always been a part of Carolyn's life…long before she thought of taking up gardening. Her father, a musician, planted that seed early on. And her mother, an organist, fertilized Carolyn's continued musical interests.

"I grew up with music", says Carolyn, who earned her certification as a Master Gardener in 2000. "Gardening is a lot like music because nothing is ever static. The seasons change, we try new plants that may or may not make it and continue to learn new things. It's another wonderful outlet for being creative."

For many years, Carolyn raised vegetables in her backyard until a cedar elm grew so large it began to cast some serious shade. Not that it mattered to this sentimental gardener…the lovely tree grew enough to be designated cochampion in the Texas Big Tree Registry.

But the additional shade forced Carolyn to make the transi-

BRASS AND BLOOMS. Carolyn Bush (inset, left) has assembled a band of instruments as unique additions in her Texas garden. Clockwise from left: Virginia creeper and impatiens surround a trio of clarinets…a solo tuba accents containers of impatiens…ferns and a saxophone work together in harmony.

tion from sunny to woodland backyard. She decided it was time for her yard to take on a more natural look.

Shrubs like the blue-berried mahonia, oakleaf hydrangea and strawberry bush helped anchor the garden. Turk's cap lily, obedient plant, St. John's wort and other shade-loving perennials started filling in the woodland setting. It wasn't long before birds, squirrels, butterflies, raccoons and possums were drawn to this peaceful retreat punctuated by retired instruments.

Carolyn designed the large garden with wandering in mind. Visitors are pleasantly surprised when they come upon a stand of clarinets forming a tepee beside purple coneflower. Accompanying a French horn are fall-blooming oxblood lilies, while wood fern plays a duet with a saxophone.

Carolyn's garden soon became a magnet for a young friend, Christin Colden, who, as a child was so drawn to the magical yard, that she adopted it as her secret garden.

Christin, now 16, fondly recalls those carefree days spent acting out *Swan Lake* and the *Nutcracker*, with the enchanted instruments each playing a part.

"I used to spend hours there," says Christin. "I got involved with band partly because I loved the instruments in Carolyn's yard. Being there is like an old friend giving you a hug."

Like the roots of her many perennials, Carolyn's love of gardening and the arts has also spread to Christin's yard.

"A few years ago, Christin dug her own pond and surrounded it with gardens," reports Carolyn. "I like to think that perhaps my garden helped inspire her."

Carolyn continues to fine-tune her native and perennial plantings. They constantly change with the seasons, offering subtle shades of green in spring, occasional blooms in summer and stunning fall color. Together, they're a perfect melody.

And, with a bit of imagination, you can almost hear the strains of long-ago concerts blowing in the breeze.

Chapter 2

BRING IT TO THE TABLE

This small-space, no-bend gardening method is just what the doctor ordered.

By Reilly Maginn, Daphne, Alabama

BEDSIDE MANNER. Reilly Maginn (left), a retired doctor, now cares for plants. His tabletop garden yields colorful and tasty results without bending or kneeling.

No doubt about it—downsizing to an apartment or condominium can seem like the end of gardening. After all, how can you raise bumper crops of veggies or armfuls of flowers without a sizable plot of soil?

Before you table all of your garden efforts, however, consider this—you can create a flourishing patch on top of a table just outside your back door. I like to call this method tabletop gardening, and it's truly amazing how much a 3-foot-square garden can yield!

What's more, this type of gardening is great for those of us who are white of hair and less than limber. Why? Because you no longer need to bend, kneel or squat. You can do all your green-thumb work in a comfortable and strain-free seated position (that's the retired doctor in me talking).

Don't Contain Yourself

So let's get started! First, you'll need a sturdy table that can hold about 50 pounds. Stay away from card tables—they may collapse under such weight.

You'll also need to gather containers to fit on top of your table. I often use old wooden ammunition boxes I find at an Army surplus store. They're a good size and already have open cracks in the bottom for drainage. Any kind of wooden box—or other container—will do, of course. Just check for drainage holes. If the container doesn't have any, drill your own.

Potting soil, a trowel, a watering can or bucket and a few dollar's worth of seeds are the only other tools necessary. There's no call for shovels, rakes, hoes or wheelbarrows. And you won't have to spend hours in the hot sun weeding, hoeing or thinning plants. Only minimal upkeep is needed, and garden pests are the exception rather than the rule.

That means no dirty knees, aching back or sweaty blistered palms. It might sound too easy, but it's true—and tabletop gardening is fun!

Time to Sow

I like to place my table in a sunny spot that I walk past regularly, so it's easy to check the garden boxes. I fill my boxes with potting mix, dampen the mix and make shallow depressions about every 4 inches. Then I place a single seed in each depression and cover with a bit more mix.

For me, a square foot section yields about 16 plants—such as radishes, lettuce, beets or carrots—in a few short weeks. This is plenty of produce for a twosome to enjoy.

I train climbers like cucumbers and beans to grow up small wooden trellises nailed to the back of a box (see photo above center). Broccoli, tomatoes and other larger veggies still fit into the boxes as well. Devote a square foot of space to each plant.

If you'd rather raise flowers, these boxes will work, too. I've had a lot of success with zinnias and other small annuals, as well as herbs of all kinds.

The key to success is keeping it small. Believe me, tabletop gardening is easy, stress-free and affordable. Give it a try—I know you'll like it! ◀

TAKING THE PLUNGE

They made a splash by turning their inground pool into a garden and patio.

By Pam Dirnberger, Benton, Missouri

When my husband and I became empty nesters 5 years ago, we decided to make some changes around our house. Rather than remodel the interior, Henry and I headed outdoors to see what we could do with the backyard.

This wasn't the first time we'd tackled a big project. When we bought our 35 wooded acres in 1970, the road back to the property had washed out, and the brush and undergrowth were so thick we couldn't even tell if there was a good spot for building a house.

With lots of help from Henry's dad, we cleared the land and rebuilt the road. We lived in a mobile home for 5 years before we were ready to start building a house.

After our third child was born, we installed an inground pool. We got many years of use out of it, and we all enjoyed it tremendously.

But once our children left home, the pool lost its appeal. Henry and I spent more time maintaining it than swimming in it—and pool chemicals aren't cheap.

Pulling the Plug

At this stage in our lives, turning the area into a garden-lined patio made more sense to us. Henry drained the pool and pushed in its concrete sides with a bulldozer.

It took 8 dump truck loads of sand poured on top of the concrete to fill the hole. We flooded the area to make sure the sand settled and filled any cavities.

Once the area was stable, Henry and his uncle got busy building the brick patio, a task that took most of the summer. We had no plan to follow—we just knew we wanted the patio to include a fish pond, a waterfall and some flower beds.

Henry and Uncle Leonard brainstormed as they went, and the design just seemed to fall into place. Some 10,000 bricks later, we had the patio of our dreams.

Since then, we've been busy planting and adding new features. Now we can't seem to stop!

The summer after we completed the patio, we put in a covered pavilion with a wooden bar and stools so our guests would have a pleasant place to relax. Then we installed a fountain surrounded by an interesting semicircular hedge.

Henry also made a water wheel and water-filled wishing well for the flower beds, giving us a total of four water features, including the original pond and waterfall.

Our three flower beds—one is crafted in the shape of the state of Missouri—overflow with an assortment of blooms. I planted hostas and daylilies as soon as the beds were completed, and they come back beautifully each year. For extra color, I add annuals like impatiens, petunias, begonias and geraniums.

We tucked an old section of wrought-iron fence in one

HITTING THE BRICKS. Pam and Henry Dirnberger (far left) are too busy enjoying their patio to miss the inground pool it replaced. Henry and his uncle used 10,000 bricks to build the patio, which includes a fountain overlooking a natural 1-acre pond. The koi pond (above) is visible from an inviting open-air bar. At left, a frog peers out from the lily pads in the pond.

of the beds to provide architectural appeal and support the clematis I planted around the bottom. The fence looks lovely covered in blooming vines.

Handy Accents

My husband has made lots of items for our yard from the *Birds & Blooms Backyard Projects* book, like the wishing well and a wheelbarrow planter. He also created a flower cart with iron wheels salvaged from old farm implements. His handmade houses and feeders entice birds to our yard year-round.

Henry loves decorative woodworking, too, so we have

pink flamingos in our fishpond. Hand-cut swans, ducks, geese and chickens populate the flower beds.

We recently added a set of winding stairs to connect the patio with our natural 1-acre pond and the spacious screened-in building next to the dock. We added a small koi pond in this area, too, along with more flowers and foliage plants.

This is a great spot to watch the abundant wildlife drawn to the pond. We often see Canada geese, wood ducks, wild turkeys and deer. We've counted as many as 42 deer around the pond at one time!

In the summertime, we like to entertain a lot, and our patio seems to be a favorite gathering place with our friends. Whether we invite a large group or a small one, there's always plenty of food and laughter out there.

After a barbecue, we love to sit and watch the deer walk through the yard in the early evening. It's so peaceful and beautiful, plus the view is amazing.

Best of all, no one misses the pool! Our new patio, brimming with gardens and appealing water features, satisfies everyone all summer long.

GREEN THUMB TIP

An old wrought-iron fence can make a great trellis in your flower bed. Plant climbing vines like clematis around it, and you'll have a beautiful addition to your garden.
—*Pam Dirnberger, Benton, Missouri*

FINISHING TOUCHES. Henry made several decorative items for the patio in his backyard. His flour mill (top) has a working water wheel. His mobile flower card (middle) uses an iron wheel salvaged from an old farm. Above, his hand-cut wooden birds pop up throughout, adding a whimsical touch.

Chapter 2

THE HEALING GARDEN

This couple's restful retreat grows strong hearts and spirits.

By Hilde Lange, Field Editor, Axtell, Nebraska

Sometimes, the answer to a prayer is just outside your back door. That's what Harriett and Doug McFeely (above inset) discovered years after they purchased 2-1/2 acres of cow pasture in Hastings, Nebraska.

They didn't know then that their unassuming plot of land would one day bring inspiration to others.

Now a beautiful garden called Country Meadows, the property is open to hundreds of visitors year-round. Many find the lush oasis the perfect backdrop for special occasions, while others come seeking solace.

It's also a godsend to Harriett, who had hoped for a way to stay home and take care of her aging mother. It was only after a few strangers came knocking on her door, asking to use the garden for a reunion and a wedding, that she realized her prayers had been answered...and a home business was born.

Blessed Bounty

Although Harriett humbly admits she's not a professional gardener, it's obvious she has one mighty green thumb. Years of hard work have transformed this once plain pasture into a garden thriving with yuccas, hostas, barberries, evergreens and many others.

There's also plenty of water. A 100-foot stream, two waterfalls and two ponds teeming with koi are inviting additions to the tranquil surroundings.

But it's the Three Trees Miracle Garden that's possibly the most captivating spot in the yard. It was inspired by garden visitors

who have shared stories of how miracles have touched their lives.

A welcoming path leads guests to a grove of trees, where an arbor, pond and benches beckon. Harriett also records the stories, and sets out a plant and commemorative stone for each one.

A small chapel rests in the center of the garden. Bought at auction for $100, the old building was in dire need of repair. Formerly a farm summer kitchen, Harriett, with the help of a few friends and a volunteer carpenter, transformed it into the ideal place for reflection.

Personal Details

Everywhere you look, Harriett's garden is dedicated to friends and causes in her life.

A small rock garden, marked with a sign reading "Cody County," is a memorial to her famous cousin, U.S. scout Buffalo Bill Cody. The rocks are from Lookout Mountain in Colorado, where Bill and his wife are buried.

There's the Mothers Against Drunk Driving Memorial Garden, and a special Kids' Garden that's cared for by children with developmental disabilities.

Finally, a large broken fountain—a gift from a local group home—decorates the landscape. Although visitors often ask about it, Harriett has no plans to repair the fountain.

Instead, she says it's a reminder that we all may be "broken" in some way, but nature has the power to bring us peace, especially in places like Harriett's healing garden.

A WARM WELCOME

Pennsylvania couple happily shares their garden with visitors.

By Patrick Brezler, Waynesboro, Pennsylvania

M erle and Beulah Cordell don't want your money. This former farm couple graciously opens their garden to the public without asking for anything in return.

On average, more than 2,000 visitors stop by every year. Even tour buses have been known to make the drive down Grindstone Hill Road to their home just outside of Greencastle, Pennsylvania to see the spectacular flowers.

"We've had people come from England, Canada, California and almost every part of the eastern states," Beulah says. "There have also been visitors from Poland and Puerto Rico."

Merle loves checking the guest book that visitors sign and admits his favorite part of having the garden is the people it brings.

Their country road, which once saw the daily arrival of a milk

COME ON IN. Merle and Beulah Cordell (left inset) believe in sharing. With a simple welcome sign (at right), they invite people in to tour their immense garden.

truck, now greets visitors with a wall of beautiful colors. Massive hollyhocks, rose of Sharon shrubs and bee balm create a bold entryway and serve as a daily feast for bees and butterflies.

As you approach their farmstead, you'll see far more flowers than you would have imagined. The real showstoppers are red canna lilies (next page). These tall plants can reach 6 feet or more. The Cordells plant 18 varieties of the statuesque flowers—which they chose for their eye-catching nature.

"They're the showiest and they bloom from July to frost," Beulah says.

But there is a catch. Cannas are a tropical and subtropical species that don't survive winters in the North. That means the Cordells must dig up the rhizomes every year and carefully

store them over winter—a task that isn't easy on the back. Merle estimates they dig up and preserve 1,000 cannas every autumn to replant in spring.

Years in the Making

Adding cannas isn't the only change the couple has made since they purchased the farm in 1964. When they moved in, the only thing in the front yard was a tree stump with three hosta plants growing around it. Over time, they've created more than 50 flower beds that are are now scattered across the acre of land surrounding their house.

Beulah started gardening in the early years of their marriage. She raised four children, and Merle worked as a farmer, minister and geography teacher. But she still wanted an activity for her spare time. Gardening was the perfect fit.

"My husband was on the road a lot as a minister, so it gave me something to do," Beulah says.

She is quick to tell you that her favorites are the daylilies— a carefree bloomer. She gave up on roses early on because they required too much care.

Annual Display

A sea of annuals surrounds the sidewalk leading up to the Cordells' home. Beulah plants dozens of flats every year to form a colorful collage of marigolds, scarlet sage, impa-

tiens and petunias, to name a few.

But that's only the preview to the main show on their expansive porch. It holds pot after pot of massive geraniums, a collection Beulah started when they first married.

"After years of trading plants with friends, I have just about every color," she says.

A local farmer gives Beulah the pots for her geraniums, and they never go unfilled. She jokes that she needs a bigger porch, but admits she would use the space to pack in more plants.

Times have changed for Merle and Beulah, but they are still young at heart. After 30 years of traveling around the country on a motorcycle, their daughter convinced them to trade it in for a safer mode of transportation. When the couple isn't in their garden, you might find them zipping around in a two-seater sports car.

As lifelong farmers, Merle and Beulah are accustomed to hard work. Even though they have sold the cows, it's obvious the two aren't ready to accept a rocking-chair way of life…you need only look at their garden for proof.

Chapter 2

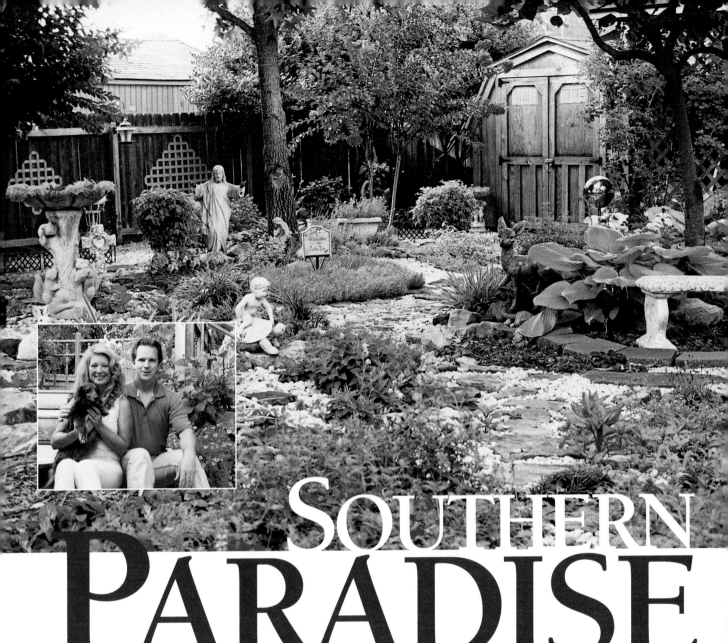

SOUTHERN PARADISE

Novice gardeners turned their plain backyard into a lush place to escape.

By Sheila Jasper, Memphis, Tennessee

Why not turn an otherwise ordinary yard into something really special? That's what came to mind as I sat on my patio one day, surveying our property. There wasn't anything wrong with it—but at the same time, it just didn't make much of an impression.

Closing my eyes, I could clearly envision a colorful re-treat with a pool, pond and a flower-lined walkway, instead of our simple fenced-in lawn. When I told my husband, Carl, he jumped at the idea, and together we developed our plan.

It quickly became apparent that this transformation would involve a lot of work. Even though we were both novice gardeners, we decided to tackle the entire project ourselves. Little did we know how much time and elbow grease it would require!

Making Waves

The first major job on our "to-do" list was the pool. We agreed on an aboveground model and chose a spot for it that was close to the patio. Then we rented a small backhoe to excavate a hole for the pool and level the site. Then the two of us got to work installing the actual pool.

Once the pool was in place, Carl turned his attention to the pond. The plan was to position it between the pool and the house and stock it with goldfish so we could watch

FIRST THINGS FIRST. Sheila and Carl Jasper began creating their backyard oasis by installing a pool and pond near their patio (top). Next, they filled the garden with color by planting a vivid selection of perennials, annuals and shrubs along the stone walkway that runs throughout their yard (above). Sheila gave the area more personality by adding yard decor.

the aquatic creatures from our kitchen window. To give it a bit more dimension, Carl decided to add a waterfall at one end, too.

While Carl got busy digging, putting in the pond's liner and tinkering with pumps, I focused on fashioning the flower gardens and a winding fieldstone path. Because I wanted to fill the whole area with color, the flower beds and the walkway kept expanding, until both eventually encompassed a good portion of the yard.

Additional size meant additional effort, of course. All told, it took 6 months of hard work, several pallets of fieldstone, and 200 bags of small white rocks used to fill in and anchor the stones. Finally, Carl and I had the structure of our backyard haven in place.

Exercising Green Thumbs

With all that heavy labor behind us, we could hardly wait to get planting, a process I thought would move along quickly. However, the gardens were so extensive that there wasn't enough time or money to fill them in one growing season. It actually took two summers to install all our flowers, shrubs and trees.

The first plants to go in were an assortment of perennials, including verbena, balloon flowers, phlox, dianthus, ferns, lavender, clematis, coneflowers and hostas.

I made sure to leave plenty of space for shrubs and trees, too. My choices for these substantial garden anchors run the gamut from fairly common to rather exotic, but they all have one thing in common—they add plenty of color and interest to the gardens.

Take a walk through our yard today, and you'll see everything from rich junipers to stately boxwood, pom-pom evergreens, a sycamore, redbuds, a Japanese maple, barberry bushes, hydrangea, pink dogwood, holly, spirea and several fruit trees. I also added crepe myrtles that produce blooms in a range of hues.

Annuals will always have a place in my flower beds, thanks to the vivid tones they provide each summer. My top picks each year are geraniums, petunias, vinca and impatiens.

The pond is surrounded by rocks peppered with moneywort, while yellow and pink water lilies grace the pond's surface and provide cover for the goldfish. We recently added a lotus that produces brilliant red blooms—it's quite a sight come summer.

Hooked on Yard Art

After most of the planting was complete, I decided it would be fun to add a few decorations…and once I got started, it was hard to stop! Our yard now contains angels and other religious mementos, signs, fairies, birdbaths, urns and an inviting bench.

I've also hung plaques and lamps on the fence, along with sections of lattice that I use as accents. A duck stands next to the pond beside a pair of plaster children sitting on a bench. We even made sure our wood tool sheds were attractive by surrounding them with unique outdoor art, too.

We're by no means finished with the yard. In fact, I've come to view it as an evolving part of our home. It isn't unusual for me to dig up a mature perennial that's gotten a bit too tall and reposition it so it doesn't block more diminutive blooms. I also love to bring home new varieties to try.

Carl hasn't put his tools away, either. Over the past several years, he's designed and built a tiered deck around a portion of the pool, and a cover for the patio.

When we're not busy planting or completing new projects, we enjoy relaxing outside and watching the many visitors we now have in our backyard. Butterflies, dragonflies and birds make regular stops in the garden, and we often see playful rabbits, chipmunks and squirrels.

My favorite is the dove that often drinks from the pond in the morning while I sip coffee on the patio. But the best treat of all, as far as Carl and I are concerned, is the vibrant view that we created from scratch.

No. 1 Green Thumb

GREEN THUMB TIP

Don't forget to leave room for shrubs in your garden. They add great texture and color, and the birds love them.
—*Sheila Jasper, Memphis, Tennessee*

EVERYTHING OLD IS NEW AGAIN

The Old West kicks up its heels in this couple's Michigan yard.

100

Chapter 2

Debbie and Nick Altman don't live in the Old West. It just looks that way—at least in their backyard.

The Altmans' home in Montrose, Michigan sits on 2-1/2 acres, and Debbie admits that landscaping it was a constant challenge.

"When we first moved in 21 years ago, the only things on the property were the house and some pine trees," she says. "One year, our two children and I had 53 pine tree stumps professionally removed as a Father's Day gift for Nick. That should give you some idea where we began!"

The mature trees that remained gave the yard a peaceful, old-fashioned feel. Debbie capitalized on that atmosphere by creating garden areas that looked natural and unplanned. Then she took the idea a step further, adding Old-West accents to the rest of the area.

"I've made lots of Western-themed decorations for the gardens, including barbed-wire wreaths trimmed with bandannas, horseshoes and stirrups," Debbie says. "One wreath includes a cowboy boot planted with hens and chicks, and I recycled another cowboy boot into a birdhouse."

Weathered wood lawn furniture and vine-draped fences enhance the yard's vintage look. The Altmans even have their own "general store," a cozy retreat built with wood that was salvaged from an old barn.

"We originally built the store to house all my planting utensils, flowerpots and potting soils," Debbie says. "But it turned out so cute that I don't want to put anything dirty in it now, although there are a few well-washed flowerpots in there."

Alongside the store's front porch, Debbie created flower beds filled with shade-loving plants like hostas, ferns and bergenias. The store's front porch posts are wrapped with chicken wire for vining plants to climb.

Antique barrels, boxes and other vintage pieces serve as planters for annuals. An antique buckboard sits in a clearing near the general store. Debbie planted ferns and ornamental grasses around it to complement the frontier feeling.

"For Nick, the buckboard is the heart and soul of our backyard," Debbie says. "We found it while rummaging around at an antique sale, and it was love at first sight. The buckboard seat is just big enough for two. Our dog 'Jazz' jumps onto the buckboard whenever I do. She thinks the second seat is hers!"

The most extensively landscaped area of the Altmans' yard started with a simple purpose—hiding the propane tank behind the house. "It was a real eyesore," Debbie says.

They started with a rustic fence to hide the tank, then began adding flowers around it. But one thing led to another, and by the time she and Nick were finished, they'd created a koi pond with a waterfall and footbridge. Now it's one of the main attractions in their yard.

They surrounded the area with a footpath and multiple garden beds. One of those sunny beds is the home of Debbie's beloved bonnet girl (above inset), that stays hard at work in the garden.

"She's a small evergreen that I trim out to resemble a young girl pushing a wheelbarrow," Debbie explains. "Each year I buy her a new bonnet to wear. With her to keep me company, I'm never alone in the garden."

Debbie says visitors are always enchanted by their property's natural beauty.

"No one has ever walked into our yard without raving about it," she says. "It's a rather different twist to gardening, and it took a lot of love and hard work. We're very proud of what we've achieved here." ◢

NEW FRONTIERS. Even "city slickers" enjoy the Old-West atmosphere created by Nick and Debbie Altman. From a koi pond to a boot birdhouse, it all adds to the yard's frontier feel.

GREEN THUMB TIP

Try planning a theme in your garden. Whether you duplicate the Old West, like this garden, or something else, annuals can make anything shine!
—*Debbie and Nick Altman*
Montrose, Michigan

THE FLOWER FARM

"Retired" farmers use their talents to produce a colorful crop of blooms.

By Ray Timmons, Holden, Missouri

My wife, Charlotte, and I used to coax crops from the earth on our small farm. When we retired, we could not get growing out of our systems, so we turned our energies to producing floral "crops" instead.

Over the last 15 years, we've created almost every kind of flower bed we could imagine, transforming our 4-acre farmstead into something truly fantastic.

An Annual Event

The first of May is when the real fun begins. That's when we start planting our colorful array of about 5,000 homegrown annuals.

We prefer annuals because they offer more color and a longer bloom period than most perennials. Plus, there are so many different varieties. This makes it easy to change the look of our flower beds from one year to the next.

To save money, we start most of our annuals from seed. We converted an old hog house into a small greenhouse, which creates the perfect conditions for our plants to thrive.

Some of our favorite flowers include marigolds, zinnias, rudbeckia, geraniums, begonias and petunias. We like these varieties for their abundant long-lasting flowers that look tidy with little deadheading.

To keep our flower beds full and vibrant all season, we al-

A BOUNTY OF BEAUTY. Every spring, Ray and Charlotte Timmons (left) plant 5,000 homegrown annuals on their 4-acre farmstead. They also have some unique flower beds, including (from top right) island plantings...an arch...and terraces.

low the volunteer plants that sprout up later in summer to grow. Also, we sow additional seeds a month or so after setting out the original bedding plants.

Bulbs and More

In addition to annuals, many of our beds boast a vibrant collection of spring-flowering bulbs. These harbingers of warmer weather may be more work to plant, but they provide a welcome abundance of showstopping color in an otherwise lifeless post-winter landscape.

One piece of equipment we've found to be a huge back-saver is a drill with a 24-inch bulb auger attachment. These are available at most home and garden stores. By using the auger to dig holes in our hard clay soil, we can easily plant up to 1,000 annuals or bulbs in a single day.

Despite our preference for annuals, we've found a spot for some pretty perennials in our flower beds, too. Purple coneflowers, butterfly weed, balloon flowers, roses, iris, poppy and daylilies all add a dazzling punch of color that we can count on season after season.

We especially like blue perennial salvia, which is hardy and coordinates well with the other colors in the garden. They also reseed themselves and are easy to transplant if it's necessary.

Flower Bed Frenzy

Every year, we add more flower beds to our yard. We've created beds that thrive on islands in the lake we dug ourselves (top right), others bordered with rocks or timbers, and still oth-

ers on large stair-step terraces (above).

By far, the most unique garden feature is our "hill bed" (see photo above center). A rainbow-shaped flower bed arcs over a small pool with a waterfall and stream, and we planted mandevilla to grow along the graceful curve. We built the 7-foot-wide pool from an old fertilizer tank, which we lined with cedar, and then fashioned the edging and wood arch from treated plywood.

With all the beauty that blooms in our backyard, we enjoy sharing it. Friends and relatives often stop by to fish or paddleboat in the lake while admiring our blooming bounty, and the local garden club has included our yard on their tours.

We guess it proves that our *annuals* have a *perennially* positive effect on people.

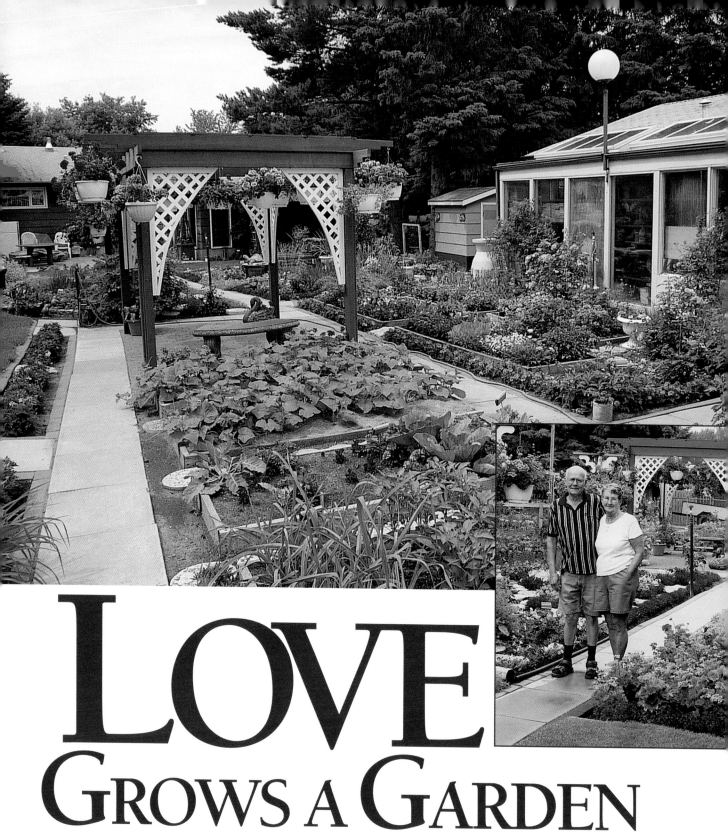

LOVE
GROWS A GARDEN

*The union of hard work and devotion
help this couple create a blooming paradise.*

By Edna Manning, Saskatoon, Saskatchewan

NEAT PATHWAYS and colorful flower beds are the signature in Steve and Helen Fosty's yard. Above, stepping-stones accent a bed of lilies. At left, raised beds flank the pergola Steve built. They use their backyard greenhouse to start many of their annuals.

The neatly planted rows of flowers and orderly walkways in Steve and Helen Fosty's Saskatoon, Saskatchewan backyard seem to contradict the couple's relaxed attitude toward gardening.

"We don't spend all winter thinking about what we're going to plant and where," Helen says. "God didn't take time to color-coordinate, He just planted."

"We do the same, and it seems to work out," Steve adds.

The spectacular results—and numerous landscaping awards—speak volumes for their laid-back approach. It's obvious the two enjoy every moment they spend working side by side in the yard.

Helen explains their simple secret as "love and tender care."

A Blank Slate

Neither Steve nor Helen grew up with a gardening background, but when they purchased their property in 1981, their green thumbs grew and blossomed along with their yard.

"The property is large, and we had to do something with it," Steve says.

They removed some trees to open up space, leaving rows of pine and spruce running along two sides and surrounding their greenhouses.

"That first year we started with over 5,000 bedding plants in a single greenhouse," Helen says. "Now we're down to 2,800."

The Fostys prefer annuals because of the large selection, the season-long color, and how simple it is to alter the garden's look from year to year.

One of the striking things about the Fostys' gardening style is the absence of untidy or neglected areas.

For example, in the shady nook under a stand of pines and spruces, Steve constructed two semicircular beds where hostas, ferns and elephant's ears thrive. Begonias and large pots of cannas add color. The bed is a beautiful use of an area that might otherwise be ignored.

Picture-Perfect Pergola

The focal point to the Fostys' yard is a large pergola and patio (photos opposite page) that Steve constructed. About 35 baskets and containers overflow with an assortment of petunias, geraniums and ivy. It is a favorite spot for the Fostys to relax and enjoy the entire yard.

A series of beds around the area feature low-growing annuals such as ageratum, salvia, petunias, gaillardia and pansies, planted among benches, birdbaths, gazing globes and the stepping-stones Steve makes.

Despite their preference for annuals, the couple has recently converted a few beds to perennials.

"We had a landscape designer come in and give us some ideas," Steve says. "We wanted some low-growing shrubs to provide continuous color, yet not block our view of the rest of the garden."

They chose dwarf European cranberrybush viburnum, variegated dogwood (which they plan to keep trimmed), golden spirea, miniature bleeding heart, mugo pine, gold potentilla and Little Princess spirea.

Other areas of their yard now feature a variety of perennials like silver mound, Veronica, juniper, Morden Fireglow

Their green thumbs grew and blossomed along with their yard.

COLOR EVERYWHERE. Containers play a large role in the Fostys' yard. Above, they add instant height to an area. At top, pots brighten the shade without disturbing a tree's roots.

roses, coral bells, lady's mantle and wintergreen.

Near the back of their yard are the greenhouses for growing annuals, and six raised beds, largely for vegetables.

"We started with the raised beds and found they work well for a number of reasons, not the least of which is the ease of upkeep," Steve says.

The soil in raised beds warms up quicker in the spring, giving some plants a head start, he says. They provide better drainage and aeration, and offer more control over the soil conditions. Plus, working in raised beds is easier on the back during planting, weeding and harvesting.

More to See

A description of the Fostys' yard could go on and on. You'll find a small water feature next to the raised rock garden…lush ferns, hostas and colorful containers lining the front walkway…a thriving rose garden…prolific kiwi trees…and an arbor covered with mandevilla and passion flower vines.

It's enough to make passersby want to follow the wooden "Welcome" sign and enter this overflowing backyard retreat that the Fostys have so lovingly created.

"It's good to do these things together," Helen says. "It builds a bond."

Sounds like the "love and tender care" that nurtures their garden, nurtures their marriage as well.

GOING BANANAS

With determination, this gardener created a tropical escape in the Northeast.

By Nancy Moffett
Coopersburg, Pennsylvania

GROWING UP. It was the unlikely centerpiece of Jeff Hauck's tropical dream, but the banana (with Jeff, at top) thrived. A variety of vines (above) and other plants complete their paradise.

The Energizer Bunny has nothing on my husband, Jeff Hauck. He has always been interested in gardening, and constantly is adding trees, shrubs and flower beds to our yard. But I had my doubts the year he declared his plans to design a tropical garden near our backyard pool.

This may not sound difficult, except for the fact that we live in the Northeast and have a limited growing season. Nevertheless, Jeff dug into the project with dreams of creating a lush tropical-looking haven.

Planning Paradise

It was a cold day in January when Jeff came home with the first plant for our garden—a Japanese fiber banana (*Musa basjoo*). He bought it because it's supposed to be the hardiest of all bananas and survive in -20° weather when properly mulched. As I looked at the meager plant, however, I was skeptical it would ever make it outside. Shortly after, two of the leaves on the plant died and three more turned brown.

Jeff kept working toward his paradise, though. He searched stacks of seed catalogs and made notes, trying to decide what other plants would add heat to our Pennsylvania version of the tropics. Meanwhile, the banana plant was perking up and slowly growing in the light of one of our windows.

In the spring, Jeff sowed a variety of summer poinsettia (*Amaranthus tricolor*) and vine seeds in a temporary area by our kitchen window. He then built several 6-foot cedar trellises and two raised beds around our pool.

The banana plant, now 20 inches tall, was the first thing to go into the soil. Surrounding it were a mixture of hibiscus, cannas and calla lilies, as well as a sprinkling of annuals like pink and white cleomes and a border of vincas.

In the second bed, Jeff planted Persian shield, verbena and morning glories. By then, the newly sprouted seeds were ready to go. He added the summer poinsettias between the two beds and found spots for the vines—cardinal climber, hyacinth bean, moonflower, love-in-a-puff and Spanish flag—along the homemade trellises.

Backyard Getaway

By midsummer, our tropical fantasy had become a reality. The true highlight was the banana plant. It grew 12 feet tall, and towered above the pool to create the perfect tropical setting.

We spent many hours relaxing in the water, soaking up our spectacular view of paradise.

As soon as summer was over, Jeff was already making plans to improve our poolside retreat. He has his eye on an Arizona yucca, which resembles a small palm tree. He thinks it will be the perfect addition to the banana plant.

That's just how Jeff is…he keeps going and going!

BEST GARDEN IDEAS

Readers share ways to make yards special.

Garden Dishes Out Smiles

WE HAVE LOTS of flower and vegetable beds scattered about our 1-acre yard. Most are outlined with stones or railroad ties—but there is one bed with an unusual border that catches everyone's eye.

To surround the blossoms I planted there, including butterfly bush and Texas sage, I turned to china plates and saucers (see photos above). Some of the dinnerware belonged to my grandmother and mother, and the entire design has become a real conversation piece!

That's not the only spot I've dressed up with unlikely supplies. I transformed an old iron bed frame into a zinnia patch, and my husband and I built a bench using stones from his grandparents' fireplace.

But I have to say the focus is on whatever's growing—and since I plant everything from azaleas to zucchini, there's always something to feast your eyes on.

—*Karen Nettles, Groesbeck, Texas*

SERVING UP BLOOMS. Karen Nettles has many varied flower beds in her yard, but one is especially unique—it has a border of old china plates and saucers (above left). Purple brachyscome blooms (above right) accent the pretty platters.

A GROWING GAME. Blooming daffodils form a unique tic-tac-toe board (above left) and the word "Ohio" (above) in this reader's yard.

Daffodils Spell Out Fun

RATHER THAN PLANT daffodils in typical flower beds, I like to play around with the bulbs—literally!

About 4 years ago, I used the bulbs to create a large tic-tac-toe board, complete with the X's and O's. Above the board, I added the date in Roman numerals, which I change each fall so it's current for the following spring (top left photo).

Then, a couple years ago, I added more bulbs in order to spell out "Ohio" in our yard (above right).

My "designer flowers" catch everyone's attention when they stop in for a visit.   —*Richard Balmer, Ironton, Ohio*

Everlasting Geraniums

THANKS TO my husband's green thumb, we haven't had to buy geraniums in a long, long time. The ones in this picture (below right) are at least 9 years old!

Each fall, Jim pulls up the plants, shakes off the dirt, then lays them in a large, covered cardboard box, which he tucks into a corner of the basement.

Throughout the winter, he sprays water on the plants once a month. In spring, he replants them and they come back bigger than ever, with even more red blooms.

If you want to try this yourself, it helps to be patient. The plants look dry and dead when they're replanted, but if you keep them in their pots and water them as you normally would, they eventually bounce back.

To help keep plants shorter and more compact, try cutting them back to 4 to 6 inches above the soil line. It will take several weeks to see the new growth, so don't give up!   —*Kathie Speas*
Marshalltown, Iowa

Geraniums That Last

I HAD TO SHARE my husband's own money-saving method for overwintering his bright geraniums to plant again the following year.

Every fall, he cuts the stems off our geraniums and places them in canning jars with water so they'll root. Then he puts the plants in our sunroom, where there's plenty of natural light. The geraniums bloom all winter long. When spring

comes, the plants go back outside and into the soil to add color to our window boxes, planters and garden.

This method has really saved us money. My husband has been growing the same geraniums for years. And we no longer have to buy them each spring from the garden center.   —*Marilyn Redden, Columbus, Ohio*

Scent of the Times

LAVENDER often is associated with old-fashioned sachets, but this fragrant flower isn't just for grandmas.

It's true that as far back as Victorian times, lavender was used to scent sachets, linens, furniture polish and cosmetics. People even dried their bedding on top of lavender plants so the cloth could soak up the soothing aroma.

Dried blossoms were brewed as a tea to treat insomnia, added to face creams to clear blemishes and speed healing, and used as edible garnish for pastries. Who knew this little garden herb was so useful?

Lavender isn't as common in modern gardens, but I love bringing this plant's lovely scent from my yard into my home. I fill muslin bags with dried blossoms and toss them into the dryer and clothes hamper. I use them to make herbal pillows for the couch and my bed, and add them to candles for a relaxing aroma.

Adding just one lavender plant to your garden can provide a lifetime of sweetly scented pleasures. So maybe Grandma was on to something with those old-fashioned sachets! —*Jennifer Ziegler, Sullivan, Missouri*

Garden Strikes a Graceful Note

I'M A MUSIC teacher, so a garden with a musical theme is right in tune with my style.

My husband, sons and I poured this concrete pond (above) and painted on the keys after measuring my piano to get the correct proportions. The keys need a touch-up of paint each summer, but it's not too tough.

At the corner of the pond, we included an old French horn. My husband ran tubing to it from the fountain to create a miniature waterfall.

The wind chimes on the treble clef sign behind the pond were a gift from a gardening friend who sang in my church choir. She's since passed away, so they're very special to me.

Off to one side, although not visible in the photo, are wooden chimes my nephew brought from Chile, and a garden bench a friend made from old piano parts.

This summer, I plan to add a brick path through the nearby flower bed and paint the bricks to look like piano keys. And when my niece is married in our yard in July, we'll all have something to sing about! —*Teresa Rotert, Sutherland, Nebraska*

A New Twist for Faded Bulbs

WHAT CAN YOU do with those unsightly leftover leaves after your spring bulbs have bloomed?

You can't cut them off until they turn yellow or brown, or the bulbs won't get the food they need to flower the following year.

But not everyone can live with 6 weeks worth of straggly leaves. To hide the not-so-green greenery, some gardeners fold the leaves over and tie them. And then there's the approach Lois Smith takes.

This Duncansville, Pennsylvania gardener braids bulb leaves and tucks them under once the blooms are spent (see the photo at left). Her method works with most bulbs except for tulips, whose leaves are too sparse and broad.

The braided leaves add extra dimension to a garden —and have even prompted people to ask her what kind of new plant she's put in the beds because the twists look so unusual.

This spring, don't be afraid to give your bulbs a brave new "do." Then wait to see if your neighbors take notice! —*Barbara Dunn, Field Editor*
Hollidaysburg, Pennsylvania

Bumper Crop of Cukes

MY METHOD for growing cucumbers produces a prolific crop in record time. Last year, I planted six hills on May 15. I picked my first cucumber a little more than a month later, on June 24.

And the bounty continued throughout summer. I stopped counting the harvest when I got to 700!

My secret for quick maturation and extended productivity is feeding and watering through a tube. I put a 12-inch section of 4-inch pipe in the center of each cucumber hill and plant five seedlings around it.

To water, I fill the pipe to overflowing every other day. Once a week, I mix in a dose of vegetable or flowering plant fertilizer and fill the pipe again.

This slow-watering method encourages the plants' roots to grow deep. I've raised cucumbers this way for 10 years and have never harvested fewer than 450 cucumbers in a season.

I've found the technique works on other vine plants as well. Give it a try with pumpkins, zucchini, squash and melons.
—*Ken Sohl*
Richmond Heights, Ohio

A Wall with a View

HERE'S a suggestion for readers who have a large outdoor wall that they'd like to decorate: Hang an old window on it!

Larry and Sue Lapp of Ozark, Alabama found some old window frames and put mirrors where the glass would normally be. Then they placed the frames in a prominent spot to reflect their flower beds.

"We hung these frames on the back of the garage to reflect the beautiful view of our backyard," write Larry and Sue. "They blend in perfectly because they're from the original windows of our 100-year-old house.

"It's a nice effect, and the 'view' is different each time we look at it."

Believe it or not, the garden in the photo above is the *reflection* of their flowers!

Get the Message?

HAVE YOU ever had the feeling your plants were trying to tell you something? Faith McDowell certainly did when she spotted this interesting scene.

"These Oriental poppies looked like they were illustrating the saying, 'See no evil, hear no evil, speak no evil,' " says Faith, who snapped this series of photos in her Mt. Sidney, Virginia yard.

It just proves that you never know what garden surprises await…if you take the time to look.

Love Those Bedding Plants!

This floral display in our yard (above) gives new meaning to the term "flower bed"! I love watching people's reactions when they see it. Cameras always come out!

We create this display every year, from June to late September. The flowers on the bed are in metal containers. We use various shades of impatiens, with alyssum in the corners.

The pedestal sink holds red impatiens and white alyssum, and the nightstand has purple lobelia spilling out of the drawer. —*Barbara Thompson*
Caribou, Maine

A Garden of Ideas

Do you need some new ideas for beautifying your backyard? Here's an easy one. Visit your local botanic garden. The plants growing outdoors there are guaranteed to be suited to your area's climate, and they're generally identified with plant markers, so it's easy to take notes on the varieties you like.

You might be surprised at what you find growing in your area. It's a great way to break out of your usual gardening routine to try something new.

If you have questions while you're visiting, seek out garden staffers or volunteers—they'll have a wealth of helpful information.

Ask if the garden hosts plant sales, too. You could get some great deals while supporting a good cause.

Little Sprouts Grow with Elementary Garden Club

HERE AT Strafford Elementary School, where I teach, three other teachers and I started a garden club for students in grades one through five. The only requirement for membership is simple—an interest in "playing in the dirt"!

At our first meeting, we gathered seeds, talked about the plants we had at home and discussed ideas for sprucing up our school's existing garden. We moved dirt and rocks, turned over the soil in the garden beds to see what was there and got rid of the weeds that were trying to take over.

The students' energy and enthusiasm has rubbed off on others, too. We wrote letters to seed companies, and they sent the children seed packets for next season. Our principal's husband recruited two friends to put in a new sidewalk near the garden. A local business even donated a truckload of topsoil.

Since then, we've received a grant from the Missouri Conservation Department and have added a water garden, 16 benches and lots of native wildflowers. —*Linda Maune, Strafford, Missouri*

She's Proud to Share
Her Gardening Legacy

My grandson Connor loves to pick produce. Granddaughter Bailey delights in snapdragons, creating characters out of the flower heads. I sit in the garden with them, pleased that I can pass on my passion for gardening to a new generation. It's one of the best gifts we can give a child.

Children love working in the soil. Pumpkins, gourds and sunflowers fascinate them, and fast-growing vegetables like leaf lettuce, onion sets and radishes hold their interest. Big seeds like beans, squash and sunflowers fit well in small hands. Let children plant bulbs, and they'll be hooked for life!

A big plot can overwhelm young gardeners, so I measure each child's height and make a garden of equal size. When I told one granddaughter I'd made a "Brooke-sized garden" just for her, she beamed with pride.

An old Chinese proverb states, "He who plants a garden plants happiness." I have to agree with that.

— *Carol Hammond, Louisburg, Kansas*

Luck of the Irish

My garden is a welcoming haven for blue jays, northern cardinals, various finches, squirrels, chipmunks, and even a pair of ducks. But in March, the love of my homeland inspired me to create this shamrock garden (above) to roll out the welcome mat for leprechauns, too!　　—*Frank Mullin*
Toronto, Ontario

The Tables Have Turned

This topsy-turvy idea from Dorie Hughes of Stanfield, Oregon proved a winner in more ways than one.

"Dorie came up with this idea after purchasing a new patio set," explains her mom, Leona Beckstead, of nearby Hermiston. "Instead of throwing away the old table, she tipped it next to the fence, stabilized it with wood blocks and wire, and turned it into a shelf and plant hanger (above)."

This savvy recycling gave Dorie lots more room for container plants. And her new display improves her backyard view, too.

"Now, instead of looking through the fence and seeing Dorie's dog run and winter woodpile, passersby see something unique and beautiful," Leona says.

High-Flying Colors

While most people fly Old Glory on the Fourth of July, these clever garden displays show the owners' patriotic colors all summer long.

The blooming flag display at Jeraldine Roberts' home didn't cost a dime. Jeraldine (right, with family), from Biglerville, Pennsylvania, built the planter from skids salvaged from the greenhouse where she works.

"I think of myself as frugal, so I also used flowers that I was able to get for free," she says.

Jeraldine chose red impatiens and red and white begonias for the stripes, and blue and white lobelias for the field of stars. When the lobelias didn't make it, her husband saved the day.

"Pete is a jack-of-all-trades, so he painted me these 50 perfect stars," Jeraldine says proudly.

Jeanne Longworth's clever planter (bottom left) conserves resources, too. Her son made it for her as a surprise, using an old ladder, wood scraps and leftover paint.

"The planting boxes looked like drawers, but they seemed to be missing something," Jeanne writes from Oak Harbor, Washington. "I found some old knobs to attach to the front. Then, since July 4 was coming, I planted lobelias and red and white geraniums."

Linda Kay Tanner credits *Birds & Blooms* with giving her an idea for showcasing a patriotic antique water pump (right).

"We had it stored for a long time and loaned it out as a prop to our community theater and a fund-raiser at our daughter's school," Linda writes from Carlsbad, New Mexico. "I never thought of using it as a yard decoration until I saw the idea in a past issue of the magazine. One of our daughters suggested painting the pump red, white and blue."

They paired a heart-shaped rock and an old meter cover to create the "love water" message at the base of the pump.

"In our desert climate, this is a constant reminder that water is a precious resource," Linda explains.

That's the patriotic spirit. Happy Fourth of July!

Garden Characters

Some gardens have character...and others have characters.

Sandra Daigle's storybook garden in Colchester, Connecticut has separate beds to illustrate fairy tales and children's stories.

"The central character is a permanent, life-sized 'pot man' built out of various clay pots," she says. "He plays a different role every year." He served as the Tin Man for a *Wizard of Oz* display, and as the Queen of Hearts for *Alice in Wonderland*.

Last year, he was Old MacDonald (below), complete with straw hat and blue fescue "hair," and a tractor made from old tires and a steering wheel.

"I want guests to have fun in my garden and be surprised by what they find," Sandra says.

Mary Griffin found a similar surprise at the Antique Rose Emporium in Independence, Texas (lower right). The "pot man" there rides an old tricycle in the Children's Garden.

"This really caught my eye," Mary writes from Houston. "Wouldn't you love to have this whimsical character in your garden? I know I would."

Mike Canter of Johnson City, Tennessee spotted his favorite "garden character" (right) in John and Nancy Scott's yard, which abuts a pedestrian-friendly green belt in nearby Kingsport.

"If you walk past their gardens, you'll marvel over the beauty and variety of their flowers, greenery and landscaping," Mike says. "But beware if you're a plant snatcher. Your fate awaits you at the compost pile!"

No. 1 Green Thumb

She Grows Profits In Her Garden

Looking for a way to earn some pocket money? Fern Mc-Cormack of Red Wing, Minnesota turns to her garden's flowers into funds.

Each spring as she thins out her old favorites, she places the extras in 4-inch pots, four plants per container. Then she sells the flowers at her annual garage sale.

"I have repeat buyers every year, so I'm always trying to add new plants and combinations," she writes.

"I'm 81 years old and have limited garden space, so this keeps my beds the same size and provides a little extra income. I don't charge much, but I often make a good profit—even though I give some of the flowers away to friends."

Sunny Pumpkin

If you don't have time—or the skills—to carve a pumpkin to dress up your entryway this autumn, take a cue from Field Editor Margie Casey of Norwich, New York. With artificial sunflowers and a few sprigs of faux greenery, Margie created a lighthearted seasonal decoration in a snap.

"I just decorated my pumpkin with sunflowers and set it on my front steps," she says. "I got so many compliments on this simple decoration!"

This Bloom's Quite a Dish!

We took an eyesore—an old satellite dish—and turned it into a beauty. Now this sunflower "blooms" in my backyard all year long.

My husband, Steve, did the metalwork. The leaves are made of tin and sway in the wind. My friend Susan Pickett and I did the rest with spray paint. It took us about a weekend to finish, and it is gorgeous!
—Pam Takacs, Midway, Georgia

GREEN THUMB TIP

Plant marigolds alongside your tomatoes and peppers to control root nematodes without chemicals. It works—just ask the pros. Some commercial vegetable growers rotate marigolds with food crops to kill nematodes in the soil.

Pulling the Plug

I had lots of trouble cleaning my large yard fountain when I first got it. The only method that seemed to work was taking the whole thing apart. Then I came up with an easier way.

I drilled a 3/4-inch hole in each tier of the fountain and plugged the openings with wooden stoppers. Whenever the fountain needs to be cleaned, I just "pull the plugs" and spray the tiers with a garden hose. Then I replace the plugs and refill the fountain with water. It's a simple solution that saves me a lot of time and energy.

This works well for winter, too. I remove the plugs before cold weather hits, and replace them in spring. By doing this, I've eliminated the need to cover the fountain or take it apart for the winter months.
— James Conlee
Elizabeth, Indiana

From Office To Garden

I've tried many methods for marking my seedling containers, but none worked as well as I would have liked. Then I discovered plastic-coated paper clips.

Not only do they come in different colors, shapes and sizes, they're also durable—standing up to moist soil conditions.

When I'm ready to plant my seeds indoors, I simply assign each plant a different clip and attach it to the container. The clips are a snap to move when I transplant the seedlings to larger pots, and they easily attach to marking stakes in the garden.

This method has been such a time saver!
— Flavio Gallegos, Fort Lyon, Colorado

Perfect Frame Up

A windowframe from an old barn really lightened up the backyard potting table my husband and father built for me (left).

I also discovered that old barn windows and panes look great paired with lots of landscape structures, from flower boxes to retaining walls. They're a nice accent for your plants during the growing season, and they're easy to decorate at Christmas or other holidays.

I hung a second barn window on our shed (below), and used old barn boards to make a vintage window box underneath it. Barn boards work well for making decorative garden benches, too. There's no end to the creative ways you can use them!
—Suzanne Livingood
Owatonna, Minnesota

Put Your Soil to the Test

Here's how to get the "dirt" on your dirt.

By Melinda Myers, Contributing Editor

Even on my little city lot, the soil isn't consistent. Some areas are clay, some are loam and others are gritty and well-draining. Then there's that "mystery spot." I suspect it was once used to dispose of ashes, bottles and other debris.

All this variability in just one tiny lot. How can a home owner be sure they're doing the right thing when adding fertilizer and other amendments to their backyard soil?

The answer is simple—take a test. A soil test, that is. I promise, you won't even have to study.

The results from this simple lab analysis will take the guesswork out of what nutrients should be added to your backyard gardens and lawn.

"Soil tests may take a little time and cost a little money, but it's not a large expense compared to the amount of fertilizer you put on that may not be needed," says Sherry Combs, director of the Soil and Plant Analysis Lab at the University of Wisconsin in Madison.

Costs for soil tests vary depending on where you're located in the country, but you should basically get the information you

Faith Bemiss

need for around $15 for each test.

For your time and expense, you'll receive printed information that takes the mystery out of fertilizing. The recommendations save you time and money because you'll only add the nutrients your plants need.

Start from the Beginning

Your first task is to find a soil lab that's "state certified." That way, you know you'll receive accurate results.

Many states provide a public lab through their county Extension Service. If this isn't available in your area, check under "soil testing" in the yellow pages.

Soil tests can be taken any time, except when the ground is frozen. Sherry recommends jotting a note on the calendar to test in fall.

"That's when the soil is somewhat drier, which gives a longer window to take the samples," she says. "Spring samples usually are pretty wet, making turnaround time even longer because the soil has to dry out first before it can be tested.

"Plus, that's when the labs are busiest…gardeners are anxious to get results and into the garden."

Another time to soil test is when you're planning a new garden or landscape. Also, if your current gardens are looking sickly or just aren't as vibrant as they used to be, a soil test helps pinpoint any nutrient deficiencies.

"It's best to conduct several soil tests in a yard," Sherry says. "Because the front, backyard and gardens are used differently, separate tests should be conducted in each area."

It's especially important to conduct separate tests for problem areas in a yard.

Only as Good as Your Sample

The most critical step in soil analysis is in the sampling process.

"It's the most important part," Sherry says. "We recommend you take at least five samples from each area of the yard you're having tested." (See illustration above right.)

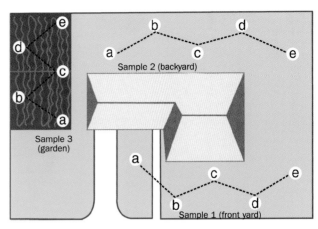

A THOROUGH SOIL TEST includes samples from different parts of a yard. Five samples (labeled a-e) are mixed from each area. This gives an "average" soil sample for each location.

A simple hand trowel works fine. Simply brush away any mulch or debris and take a slice of soil, starting at the surface, down to about 6 inches below ground level.

Collect several samples from the area being tested. Mix them in a clean bucket and let the soil dry for several days. Besides reducing the time it takes to analyze the soil, drying the soil first lightens the mailing load and costs.

Once in the mail (be sure to follow instructions carefully), enjoy your window of relaxation because when the test results are returned, you'll most likely want to immediately "dig in" and put them to use.

The results tell you everything you need to know about your soil, from its texture and pH levels to the nutrients it contains, plus the recommendations to improve it.

While soil testing is scientific, it really isn't daunting when you have the experts on your side. They'll give you the results and you'll reap the benefits of less work, less money spent and gardens that are noticeably more lush and productive.

The Answers to a Soil Test

WHAT CAN YOU EXPECT when you send soil in for laboratory testing? The results include a whole lot of information on what your soil already contains and recommendations for improving it. Here are some typical factors that soil tests measure:

■ **Organic matter**—Organic matter, such as fallen leaves and decaying plant roots, influences water retention, provides some nutrients and feeds worms, insects and microorganisms that help improve the soil structure. Ideal soils contain about 5% organic matter.

It takes time to alter the level of organic matter in your soil because 100 pounds of organic material breaks down to 10 pounds the first year and only 1 pound the second year.

■ **Soil pH**—This tells you if your soil is acid, neutral or alkaline. It's also difficult to change. Though the difference in numbers may be small, it takes huge amounts of energy and materials to change them. Lime raises the pH in acid soils and sulfur lowers pH in alkaline soils. Don't add either without a soil test.

■ **Nitrogen**—Plants use nitrogen for growth.

Nitrogen dissipates through the soil quickly and is usually added regularly. Too much, however, isn't a good thing. It leads to thick green growth, fewer flowers and may damage your plants.

■ **Phosphorous and potassium**—Plants use these nutrients in smaller amounts. Unlike nitrogen, these move slowly through the soil. The test will tell how much to add, if any.

■ **Soluble salts**—This measurement reflects the amount of soluble chemicals, such as sodium, in the soil. A high level indicates over-fertilization, exposure to deicing salts or soils that are naturally rich in these chemicals.

■ **Calcium, magnesium and sulfur**—Many soils have adequate levels of all three, and some labs will test for them only if a deficiency is suspected.

140

146

132

122

CHAPTER 3

BACKYARD BIRD HAVEN

166

144

Photos: above, Bill Leaman/Positive Images; left, Larry Dech; opposite page: top left, Dave Ryan; pond, Dave Dornberg

BACKYARD HABITAT

*The National Wildlife Federation
wants to make your yard animal friendly.*

By Stacy Tornio, Associate Editor

Dave Dornberg

Animal Planet

David Mizejewski is on a mission.

"We have more than 70,000 backyards certified, but we're not finished yet," he says.

David is the head of the Backyard Wildlife Habitat program for the National Wildlife Federation, and 2006 marked the federation's 70th anniversary. To honor it, the habitat program wanted to certify 70,000 backyards by the end of the year—a goal that they easily achieved.

The Wildlife Federation started the Backyard Wildlife Habitat program in 1973 as a way to encourage people to create more natural environments for wildlife. The program has been growing steadily for more than 30 years, but it recently got a big boost, thanks to the power of television.

The federation is working with Animal Planet to produce the TV series, *Backyard Habitat*. The show works to create wildlife habitats in backyards across the country, honoring participants with certification at the end of each show.

"Millions of people are now hearing about the concept of our program," David says. "This is my personal passion and has been ever since I was a little kid."

David says creating a backyard habitat doesn't have to be a big project. "It can be as simple as adding a few shrubs or putting out a birdbath and planting flowers," he says.

For a yard to be eligible for certification, it must have five basic elements outlined by the Wildlife Federation. These include everything animals need for survival—food, water, cover, places to raise young, and sustainable plantings that conserve natural resources.

Once your yard has these elements, you fill out an application and send it to the federation, along with a $15 processing fee. Then you can join the ranks of certified backyards across the country.

Backyard Habitat No. 33,213

When Leisa Royse moved to her home in Lexington, Kentucky, the backyard was completely bare with little cover for birds. The lawn was neatly manicured, but there wasn't a sign of wildlife in sight. Then she decided to hang up a bird feeder.

"Birds started coming, and before I knew it, I bought a small ID book," Leisa says. "After that, I began to learn what specific birds liked to eat, so I put out more food and feeders. The more I read, the more I learned. It just snowballed."

Leisa never thought her backyard would become a destination for area wildlife. After all, she was living in a subdivision, not out in the country. But that didn't matter. Soon, Leisa was attracting butterflies, dragonflies and birds that she had only seen in pictures before.

"My backyard was kind of like my secret garden," she says. "I was so proud of all the different things I could attract to it."

Among her favorites are cedar waxwings and hummingbirds. One year, a rufous hummingbird spent the winter in her backyard. She said the resilient little flier encouraged

WARM WELCOME. David Mizejewski and Molly Pesce (left) host Animal Planet's television show, *Backyard Habitat*. They help create yards that are wildlife friendly, similar to Dave and Cheryl Dornberg's backyard (at left), filled with shrub roses.

Photos on both pages: Leisa Royse

her to do even more to welcome wildlife the next year.

Having a backyard habitat can be easy, Leisa says. For people just getting started, she recommends planting purple coneflowers, black-eyed Susans and shrubs.

Now, Leisa can't imagine her home without birds, insects and other critters in the yard.

"Every day I go out to explore my garden, and I see something new each day," she says. "I could sit in my yard for hours."

Backyard Habitat No. 27,815

Janet Allen has been gardening all her life, but it wasn't until she had her backyard certified that she changed her perspective on it.

"I became a steward for wildlife," Janet says. "A garden isn't just filled with plants. It also has birds, butterflies and even bees."

Janet lives in a suburb of Syracuse, New York and teaches a 5-week community class about habitat gardening. One thing she emphasizes is the importance of planting native species, though they're not always the most ornamental.

For instance, in her area, many people think of milkweed and goldenrod as weeds. But Janet says a wide variety of these plants are available, and they're excellent food sources for butterflies and birds.

"Many people believe a garden should look a certain way, but it's whatever you want it to be," she says. "You can really connect with the natural world through your garden."

BIRD-WATCHER'S SECRET

Insects are friends, not foes. Don't try to eliminate all the insects in your yard. The good ones will often take care of the bad ones.

—Janet Allen, Syracuse, New York

For her own yard, Janet is proud to garden pesticide-free and to plant native shrubs and flowers. If Janet has one piece of advice for others, it is this—invite insects into your yard. The good ones take care of the bad ones.

"I've learned how important insects are to the garden, and they are fascinating to watch," Janet says. "I don't use chemicals, but I have virtually no damage to my plants."

Last year, there were frogs in Janet's yard for the first time, and she enjoyed listening to their songs during mating season. She looks forward to many more years of gardening for wildlife, and can't wait to see what her backyard brings next.

Backyard Habitat No. 38,121

Cheryl Dornberg credits her husband, Dave, for introducing her to birding.

"We've been married for 13 years, and Dave was always the big bird-watcher," she says. "But now I look for birds, too, and I see our backyard in a new light."

WILDLIFE SANCTUARY. Leisa Royse loves the animals that visit her backyard. From opposite left: A chipmunk surveys the area...purple and white coneflowers and garden phlox attract all sorts of fliers...a Baltimore oriole perches on a red hot poker plant...a red-bellied woodpecker finds a place to drill... a bright monarch sips nectar from a butterfly bush.

Dave and Cheryl live in Munster, Indiana and had their backyard certified in 2002. Now they do what they can to teach others about the National Wildlife Federation program.

"It's a lot less work than many people think," Cheryl says. "Many people already have what they need to be certified."

With their own backyard, Cheryl and Dave credit their pond area for attracting most of the wildlife. "Once we put that pond in, our wildlife probably tripled," Cheryl says. "We see so many different things now."

Dave remembers watching a great horned owl in a tree in their backyard one day. He started hooting at it, and the

bird hooted right back.

"It kept staring at me, trying to figure out what the strange creature was," Dave says. "After about 15 minutes, it finally got tired of the game and flew away, but I'll always remember that day."

On another morning, Cheryl was looking out the window when she thought she saw a strange-looking dog near their fence. She called for Dave, and he came to look. Staring back at them was a red fox, investigating some leftover sunflowers seeds from the bird feeder.

One tip the Dornbergs offer is to keep lots of trees in your yard, no matter what condition they're in. For instance, when a tree dies in their yard, they don't remove it. They leave it for the birds.

Cheryl says it's those little things that really make a difference in the amount of wildlife they see. "Look closely in your own backyard," she says. "You might be surprised at what you find."

WATER WORKS. When Dave and Cheryl Dornberg added a pond to their backyard, they say their wildlife tripled. Above: A rufous hummingbird, a golden garden spider and a bullfrog are all considered equals in this garden area.

Did You Know?

Contributing Editor George Harrison had a hand in the creation of the Backyard Wildlife Habitat program. In the early 1970s, George was the managing editor for the National Wildlife Federation's magazine, *National Wildlife*. A feature he produced in the April 1972 issue told how researchers at the University of Massachusetts recommended using food, cover and water to create a wildlife haven in suburban backyards. The following year, the habitat program was born. Later, George was happy to become No. 604 in certified backyards.

IT'S FOR THE BIRDS

This tree-filled yard tempts all types of feathered friends.

A REAL TREE PARTY. It all started with a few trees—and turned into a backyard worthy of a celebration. Opposite page: Danny and Lisa's private "park" invites you to take a stroll. This page, clockwise from above: A cedar waxwing finds a backyard perch...Lisa spots a tiger swallowtail on a butterfly bush... a homemade fountain provides a place for birds to bathe.

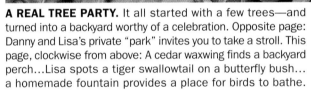

Four-hundred pounds of birdseed is a lot to go through in one winter—even for nature lovers like Danny and Lisa Reed.

The couple always stocks six feeders to satisfy the hundreds of birds that flock to their tree- and flower-packed backyard in Hays, North Carolina.

But even Danny was amazed last winter when he realized just how much the birds had eaten.

"I counted the empty bags and I checked the receipts, and I just thought, *Wow*," he says.

"Wow" is exactly the word most people would use to describe the Reeds' 2-acre yard.

In the past 9 years, the industrious pair has planted hundreds of trees and flowers, converted their garage into a sunroom, and created their own backyard park (above left), complete with classic wood benches, a rock fountain and a jasmine-covered trellis.

Danny and Lisa love their private paradise—and so do the local finches, bluebirds, robins, hummingbirds, doves and wrens, many of which raise two broods or more in each of the couple's 20 birdhouses and surrounding trees.

"My wife and I are both from mountain areas, so we've

always had a soft spot for wild critters," Danny says. "We wanted our yard to be livable for us and for the animals and birds.

"It turned out great."

Trees for Two

When the Reeds first moved into their white ranch home, their yard had only three trees: a weeping willow, a poplar and a maple.

They kicked off their outdoor makeover by planting lines of Leland cypresses on both sides of their house, then enclosing the area by joining the two rows with a backyard slatwood fence.

Since then, they have filled their lot with crape myrtles, weeping cherries, maples, apple and mimosa trees, English ivy and more.

From their plant-packed sunroom, the couple can look to their front yard—where the main attraction is a Yoshina cherry tree circled with mums, evening primrose and other blooms—or head out back for a stroll through their self-made park sectioned off by a split-rail fence.

Their yard also boasts an arbor with a swing, a miniature

READER TIP

Don't overlook trees if you're trying to find plants to attract hummingbirds. These tiny fliers love the sweet blooms of the mimosa trees in our backyard.
—**Danny and Lisa Reed, Hays, North Carolina**

windmill, several wooden wells, a banana plant that's taller than Danny…even a small vegetable garden, which they pack with tomatoes, potatoes and gourds (above).

"I told Lisa each thing I added to the yard would mean less grass I had to cut," Danny jokes.

But all joking aside, this pair truly works with Mother Nature in mind.

Danny compliments Lisa on her gentle touch with the flowers and genuine love for all living creatures. Lisa says she and Danny work together in the garden—and relax together in its beauty.

"A lot of evenings we'll just take a walk around the yard to look at what's blooming," she says.

Winter, Spring, Summer or Fall…

Danny and Lisa also love watching the wildlife that gathers in their yard. Hummingbirds feed on their mimosas and fight for spots on the feeders, and a couple of doves "practically live here," Danny adds.

"This year we're lucky enough to have a family of cedar waxwings, the type that look like they're wearing a mask," he says. "The tips of their tails are so yellow, just like they've been dipped in a can of paint."

Besides birds, the Reeds' plant display attracts butterflies and some four-legged creatures as well. Lisa says she loves to be outside with the wildlife, especially in spring.

She also loves summer, when she can bask in the heat of the North Carolina sun. Danny says he prefers fall.

It may not make their list of favorite seasons, but when winter approaches, at least one thing is certain: This couple better start stocking up on birdseed.

BATTLING BULLY BIRDS

By George Harrison, Contributing Editor

Photos: Harrison Productions

For those of us who feed birds, there's nothing more frustrating than a flock of so-called bully birds descending on our backyard feeders.

Not only do they eat the feeders clean in minutes, but their aggressive behavior also can discourage some of our favorite songbirds.

That's why controlling these species is one of the most common concerns among many *Birds & Blooms* readers.

For example, reader Georgia Wacker of Canton, Ohio wrote to ask for a solution to keep blackbirds and grackles from pillaging her bird feeders. And in Steger, Illinois, Mrs. Joseph Kraus says an invading swarm of house sparrows is eating her out of house and home.

European starlings are ruffling Wayne Taylor's feathers. These non-native birds are frightening away more desirable species from his Bethlehem, Pennsylvania yard.

Bully birds include blackbirds, grackles (above left), pigeons, European starlings (above center with red-bellied woodpecker) and house sparrows. The last three are non-native species and are not protected by law.

These hungry avian invaders are often attracted to a yard by the cheap wild birdseed mix or suet that's made available on the ground or in easy-access feeders.

If you're one of the people frustrated by the behavior of bully birds in your backyard, don't give up the fight. Here are some solutions that will help you keep these pest birds at bay, so you can continue feeding the birds you love.

■ **Lock Them Out.** Because virtually all bully birds are larger than more desirable birds, you can adapt your feeders to accommodate only smaller species.

Try enclosing the feeders with large-mesh hardware cloth or chicken wire with openings big enough to allow smaller birds to pass through (a 2-inch opening should do). This will exclude the large bully birds. You can also purchase caged-in tube or tray feeders at your local bird, hardware or garden store (like the feeder above with an American goldfinch). Just be sure to get one with the feeder portion located several inches inside the cage, so bullies can't reach the seed from the outside with their long bills.

■ **Outwit Starlings.** European starlings have a fondness for suet and often take over the feeders. Next time they're at your feeder, foil them by hanging the suet up and under a domed squirrel baffle.

Starlings are reluctant to go underneath any kind of cover and usually will avoid the hard-to-reach meal. A special starling-proof feeder, in which the suet can be eaten only from underneath, is also available in bird stores.

■ **Keep It Clean.** Some backyard birders have the greatest problems with bully birds that eat the cast-off seeds below hanging and post feeders. Pigeons are notorious for gathering in flocks underneath feeders for their meals.

The solution for this problem is to collect the fallen seeds in a deep container, such as a plastic garbage can or pail, that the pest birds cannot or will not get into. You can make a hole in the center of the container and place it right on your feeder pole.

■ **Feed Favorites.** Selective feeding is another way to control the kinds of birds that pillage feeders. Generally, bully birds prefer bread, corn, millet, wheat and sunflower seeds. To get rid of them, supply food they won't eat.

To feed finches, fill hanging tube feeders with only nyjer seed (thistle). For cardinals, chickadees and nuthatches, provide safflower seed in hopper or tray feeders.

If you do this, grackles, crows and blackbirds generally will look elsewhere for the foods they like. ◀

SETTING THE TABLE

Tips to transform your yard into a bird haven.

Well-Rounded Feast

You can feed your feathered friends and be festive, too. That's what I've been doing for the past 2 years around the holidays. First I buy an evergreen wreath, and then I place a birdseed wreath in the middle. I add a few touches like holly berries, and then sit back and wait for the birds to arrive.

They must like the edible decoration. I always have plenty of visitors, like this male northern cardinal and female downy woodpecker (above). It's a quick feeder solution that always puts me in the holiday spirit.   —*Darlene Lause, Fort Jennings, Ohio*

Heightened Advantage

Around my home, black bears are everywhere and destroy bird feeders in no time. But I came up with an easy solution to keep the furry critters away: suspend the feeders out of the bears' reach.

I hung a chain 15 feet high between two trees in my backyard. I tried it at 12 feet the first time, but some of the bigger bears could still reach the feeders.

Using a pulley system, I attached the chain to a rope that hangs down from one of the trees. I suspend about four feeders across the chain, and when I want to refill the feeders, I just use the pulley.

Now the bears can't reach the feeders, and I still have feathered friends in my backyard.   —*Carol Haines*
Shohola, Pennsylvania

Child's Play

I protect my bird feeder from the squirrels by using a traditional child's toy. I hang a Slinky (right) from the top of the feeder pole, and let it dangle all the way to the bottom.

When the squirrels try to climb up the pole, the Slinky moves and they can't get a firm grip. It's actually a little funny to see them try.

The best thing is that it's an easy fix and inexpensive. For a child's toy, it sure does a good job in my backyard.   —*Betty Stawick Amherst, Ohio*

Water Works Wonders

We have a great tip that always attracts birds to our backyard during winter. All you need is a little warm water!

On extra cold days, flocks of 15 to 20 eastern bluebirds descend on our heated birdbath (above). We know it sounds too simple, but it really is that easy! This has worked wonders for us, and the colorful birds really brighten our yard.

—*Lowell and Marlene Wenger*
Mount Sidney, Virginia

Living in Harmony

A single corncob can go a long way. To keep squirrels fed and away from my bird feeders, I set out whole pieces of corn. When the squirrels are finished eating the cob, I spread it with peanut butter and roll it in birdseed.

Then I twist wire around the end and hang it from a nail on my deck. The birds love it!

—*Lorrene Pierson*
Marionville, Missouri

Stockings for the Birds

Goldfinches actually fight over the food at these feeders that I made out of old knee-highs (above). They are easy to make. Just fill them with nyjer (thistle seed) and watch the birds gather.

Using stockings like these works great because they are inexpensive, washable and reusable. I use the kind with the reinforced toe because they hold seed better and last even longer. —*Tessa Murr*
Kingsport, Tennessee

Flowerpot to Birdbath

My daughter Stephanie made me this mosaic birdbath (below) for Mother's Day. It's a creative design that anyone can make!

First, she took a large clay flowerpot and whitewashed it. Then she covered the rim of the pot and the inside of its saucer with pieces of old, mismatched antique plates. She turned the pot upside down, placed the saucer on top and then filled it with water. Everyone compliments me on the unique design, and best of all, the birds love it!
—*Pamela Maly, Tiverton, Rhode Island*

Perfect Perch

Since many feeder birds perch in trees, it seemed only natural to attach tree branches to my feeders.

Branches provide cover and protection for birds, hiding them from predators and blocking strong wind or precipitation. They are also an attractive addition to an unnatural looking feeder, and they offer additional places to perch.

It's easy to do. Simply prop branches against your feeder or attach them using twine or clamps. You should see more birds in no time, like this rose-breasted grosbeak (below) I spotted in my yard. —*Matthew Studebaker*
Hudson, Ohio

Hang It Up

My mother lives on a mountain ranch in Colorado and has fed hummingbirds for years. It's not unusual for her to count as many as 15 birds at her feeder at one time.

She has several sugar-water feeders that hang up high around her home. It got to be quite a chore for her, getting up and down on a ladder to refill them. Then my son came up with a simple solution.

He took an old broom handle and screwed the top of a coat hanger into the end to make a useful hook (above). Hanging feeders is now a snap—no more ladders!

—*Harriet Holloway, Colby, Kansas*

Get a Grip

Since I started putting out suet cages in my backyard, I've noticed that many larger birds have a hard time clinging to the cage. So I came up with an idea.

I attached a small wooden dowel through the bottom of the feeder. Now bigger birds, like this northern mockingbird (above), don't have to struggle to get the suet inside. It's an easy fix that doesn't cost a lot of money. And it's fun to see the birds perched nearby! —*Keith Johnson*
Balch Springs, Texas

Eggshell Suet

I adapted this suet cake recipe from an old issue of *Birds & Blooms*. The eastern bluebirds in my area love it. The eggshells are especially good to use during nesting season because they provide birds extra calcium.

   1 cup lard
   1 cup chunky peanut butter
   2 cups rolled oats
   2 cups yellow cornmeal
   1 cup flour
 1/3 cup sugar
 2/3 cup chicken scratch
 1/3 cup washed, dried and crushed eggshells

Melt lard over low heat. Add peanut butter. Stir until melted. Add other ingredients and mix well. Line a baking pan with wax paper. Spread into pan and then cut mixture into squares. Freeze, remove cakes and store in freezer.

There's no need to thaw before serving. Just put them out and enjoy watching your feathered friends!

—*Carol Nagy, Calico Rock, Arkansas*

In Good Taste

My decorative handmade feeders aren't just pretty—they're also quite popular with the birds that live in our area.

I've crafted a number of the feeders and put them up in my yard or given them to friends, and the feeders always draw a crowd. Blue jays, northern cardinals, sparrows, American robins and orioles are all frequent visitors.

To make one, I first paint the design—bees, ladybugs, sunflowers or whatever catches my fancy—on a clean 1-gallon metal coffee can. Then I punch holes all around the bottom edge with a can opener before attaching the can to a metal pie tin with a 1/2-inch screw.

Finally, I fill the can with seed, which spills out of the holes and fills the pie tin. Before I hang the feeder in the yard, I pop the plastic lid back on top.

—*Susan Johnson, Lyons, Kansas*

Brow-Raising Idea

I discovered that brow brushes, typically used for shaping eyebrows, are great for cleaning out the water ports on hummingbird feeders. The one I found is 6 inches long, and has a little flat brush on one end that is great for cleaning around the crevices in the reservoir. There also is a tubular brush on the other end, which is the perfect size for cleaning out the ports on feeders. —*Steve Lake*
St. Joseph, Michigan

Back to Nature

We have a weekend retreat in the Rocky Mountains. Between our neighbors and us, we do a good job of keeping the birds well fed.

Some of our feathered friends' most popular dining spots are near natural feeders. My neighbor Diana has a couple of different log feeders that she regularly uses. One is like a stump that she fills with peanuts. The jays love it, like this Steller's jay (above, top).

A second, smaller log, has holes drilled in the sides that she fills with peanut butter. Birds like hairy woodpeckers frequent it (above). —Sarah Brickett
Calgary, Alberta

Dinner on a Sour Note

I always leave leftover biscuits for the feathered friends in our backyard, and they never last long. Then one day, I decided to crumble some homemade sourdough bread to see if they would eat it.

The usual birds enjoyed the bread, but the real surprise was the new visitors it attracted. Several eastern bluebirds couldn't get enough.

I leave mealworms for my bluebirds every morning, but now I'm also making sourdough bread for them. They come several times a day to feed. —*Janet Henry*
Alexander City, Alabama

Don't Freeze Up

Offering fresh water for birds in winter isn't as difficult as it might sound. You can keep water from freezing with these easy tips from three different readers.

"We put our birdbath over the exhaust of our heating system," says Edna Bissette of Pikeville, North Carolina. "Now the birds have water to drink even when it's below freezing."

"Our idea is really simple," write Randy and Linda Reiffer of Barryton, Michigan. "Just use a heated dog water bowl. The water dish has a built-in thermostat, so there's always fresh water. We use it year-round and just unplug it for the summer."

Sherry Schoberg from Elkridge, Maryland says the obvious solutions are sometimes best.

"I don't have a heated birdbath, but I still provide water for my feathered friends during the cold season. In the morning when the water is frozen, I simply pour hot water over the ice. It quickly loosens it, and I pop the ice right out of the birdbath. Then I refill it with warm water. When it's really cold, I'll do this a few times a day."

Squirrel Buster

For years, squirrels raided my feeders—until I came up with this solution. I drilled a hole in the bottom of two soda bottles and slipped them over my feeder pole (above). To dress it up, I put plastic flowers inside.

The squirrels can't figure out how to climb up the bottles, and I have created an interesting conversation piece for my backyard. —*Ron Jones*
Hermitage, Pennsylvania

Easy Log Feeder

THIS PINE log peanut feeder (at right) is a favorite with our red-bellied, downy and hairy woodpeckers. Even better, it's a cinch to make!

Cut an 8-inch length of a small pine log (mine was 3-1/2 inches in diameter). Using a 1-inch spade bit, drill a series of 1-inch-deep holes around the log at roughly a 45-degree angle. Then fill each hole with peanuts, suet or your favorite combination of ingredients.

A few inches from the top of the log, drill a 1/4-inch hole through the log and thread it with a piece of 16-gauge galvanized wire, twisting it together at the ends to form a hanger.

—*Stefan Delloff, Pequannock, New Jersey*

Strike Up the Band

WITH A LITTLE IMAGINATION, it seems almost anything can be transformed into a bird feeder.

When a friend was going to throw out a set of cymbals, my husband asked if he could have them. Placing one a few inches above the other (see photo above), he threaded the cymbals onto a steel rod. A nut above and below each one helped stabilize the feeder.

Now that we've filled it with sunflower seed, it's "drummed" up a lot of attention. —*Audrey Kalivoda-Sanders Fairview, Tennessee*

Snowman Serves Seed

WHEN MY TOWN was socked with 11 inches of snow, I came up with a fun way to feed the birds. I built a snowman with the usual details—scarf, earmuffs, derby and a carrot nose. Then I made arms from the stems of dried coneflowers and filled the top of its hat with birdseed.

A few days later, I was delighted to spy a chickadee pulling at seeds in the coneflower arms, while another nabbed food from the snowman's cap. —*Lori Qualls Midland, Michigan*

A Grape Idea

WE LEARNED a while back that oranges could attract whole flocks of orioles, but our newest find is grape jelly!

We've observed the orioles eating this for several weeks, so we know they love it. In fact, most of them now go directly to the jelly and completely ignore the sugar-water mixture we provide. —*Joe and Sharon Heynoski Erie, Pennsylvania*

Birds of a Feather

DURING nesting season, I buy several packages of feathers from a craft store and scatter bright and drab colors alike under my maple tree. Within minutes, the sparrows arrive, pick them up and fly off to add the feathers to their nests.

The birds return time and again until all the feathers are gone—which only takes about 30 minutes. I've seen as many as 10 birds at a time bickering over the feathers.

I also put out bits of string, yarn, dog hair and slender strips of packing paper. They always use it all.

—*Carolann Lucente, Beavercreek, Ohio*

Sprouting a Birdbath

RHUBARB PLANTS provide the template for these colorful birdbaths (below). To make one, I curved a rhubarb leaf over a mound of sand (to give it a nice shape), then covered the leaf with Quikrete Vinyl Concrete Patcher and allowed it to dry.

Then I turned the leaf over and carefully submerged it in water, soaking until the leaf tissues softened. Using a soft brush, I removed the remaining leaf membrane, digging it out in a few spots with a small pointed tool.

Once the leaf was completely dry, I was ready to paint. I used brightly colored craft paints and then added a coat of clear varnish, but you could seal it with polyurethane instead. If you use outdoor paint, and you can skip the sealing

step entirely.

These rhubarb-leaf birdbaths are so much fun to make, and you can decorate them however you wish. I made 10 to give to friends as gifts. —*Yarda Ervin, Lansing, Michigan*

Fruitful Solution

WHEN WE MOVED to our home in the country, we decided to try to attract Baltimore orioles—something we'd never been able to do when we lived in the city.

My husband, John, built a "fruit table" to hold the sweet treats we knew would attract orioles and stationed it at the perfect vantage point in our yard.

As you can see from our photos (right), we were richly rewarded for our persistence. Not only did a flock of orioles fly in to enjoy the feast, but a male scarlet tanager (center) and a male rose-breasted grosbeak (bottom) also stopped by for a bite. The birds munched on our offerings of grape jelly, oranges, grapes and watermelon.

Thankfully, our brother-in-law, who loves to take pictures, happened to be visiting and captured these colorful sights on film. —*Linda Wysocki, Coal City, Illinois*

Hummingbird Beacon

YOU COULD SAY I roll out the red carpet for hummingbirds. I set a red plastic tablecloth in the yard to catch the attention of migrating hummers, so they know they should investigate. I anchor it with flowerpots at each corner, then drive in a tall metal garden stake to hold a hummingbird feeder.

You can find a red plastic tablecloth at a party store, but an old red oilcloth or a dyed bedsheet would work, too. Just find a spot that's clearly visible to birds flying above the treetops.

This trick brings many hummingbirds our way. In fall, we've had as many as 40 of them swarming our feeders as they make pit stops during their migration to warmer climates. —*Anne Speers, Conroe, Texas*

Ice Idea

WE'VE BEEN MAKING our own suet for years. The only difficulty was finding the right containers so we could freeze it in a size that fit our various suet holders.

That all changed when I worked on a craft project using ice cube trays. It dawned on me that the trays would make great containers for freezing suet.

The suet cubes pop right out, and it's easy to remove only the number you need. Plus, the cubes fit any size feeder, and the trays stack neatly without taking up a lot of space.

To make suet, I simply melt 2 cups of shortening and 2 cups of crunchy peanut butter in a saucepan over medium heat. While that's cooking, I mix together 4 cups of yellow cornmeal, 1 cup of sugar and 2 cups each of flour, nyjer (thistle) and instant oats in a large bowl.

I stir in the melted mixture, then spoon it into the trays and pop them in the freezer. That's all it takes to make six to seven trays of suet. —*Jerry and Kathy Hitzemann Everett, Washington*

Sugar-Water Shortcut

IN SUMMER, I have to fill my five large hummingbird feeders daily in order to keep up with the big appetites of these petite birds. And that means boiling up a lot of sugar water for the broad-tailed, rufous and occasional black-chinned hummers that visit us.

In order to cut down on the work and leave room in the refrigerator for our food, I now make a syrup with a one-to-one ratio of water and sugar. When I fill the feeders, I simply mix a cup of the syrup with 3 cups of water (to get the four-to-one ratio of water to sugar). It works great. —*Carole Miller, Meeker, Colorado*

Bluebird Buffet

WE REMODELED a gazebo-style feeder in our yard to create an enclosed buffet that caters exclusively to our eastern bluebirds.

We covered the five openings with 1/8-inch-thick Plexiglas and drilled 1-1/2-inch holes on two of the sides to give the birds access. We also adjusted the top of the gazebo so we could easily remove it for filling.

Then we placed it on a fence post about 12 feet away from our bluebird house, filled it with a cup of mealworms and waited to see what would happen.

We were soon rewarded with the sight of a female bluebird entering the gazebo, grabbing a mouthful of worms and exiting (above right).

We never saw the male go inside the feeder, but we know the feeder worked well since we had to replenish the mealworms two to three times each day. —*Carmelite Moreau Diamondhead, Mississippi*

Sentimental Showpiece

THE OLD CONCRETE birdbath that once belonged to my grandfather had a large crack in the basin, making it both unusable and unattractive. I just couldn't throw it away, so my husband repaired the crack, then I dressed it up (right).

I lined the bowl with colorful pieces of tile and glass, along with some marbles, and glued them in place. Next, I used bathroom tile grout to fill in the spaces between the decorative pieces and finished the whole thing with concrete sealer.

Now we proudly display the birdbath in our yard. Grandpa would have loved the transformation. —Judy TePastte
Grand Rapids, Michigan

Nice and Easy

I GROUPED our finch feeders together in this special holder (left) that makes them easier to maintain and provides extra feeding spots, too.

I cut holes in five cedar boards, just a hair bigger than the diameter of the tube feeders. Then I assembled the boards in a hexagon shape, slid the tubes through the holders and screwed the caps on to keep the feeders in place. My design holds five feeders, but this idea would adapt easily to accommodate as many—or as few—as you'd like.

Filling the feeders is a snap because they're all in one place. And it's really something to see all the finches that come to visit. I've counted more than 35 birds feeding together at one time! —Greg Tuggle, Hillsboro, Illinois

Shooing Away Sparrows

FOR SEVERAL YEARS, I watched in frustration as sparrows chased the wrens away from my backyard. Then I came up with a simple solution, and it has worked well for the past several years.

In spring, I take down the feeder that holds mixed birdseed and put it away. I still offer the birds suet, nyjer and sunflower seeds, and I keep my hummingbird and oriole feeders out, too. For whatever reason, the sparrows soon leave my yard—and I still get to see all my favorite birds, including my beloved wrens.

Come fall, I put the mixed seed feeder back up and feed the sparrows and other species all winter long.

—Mossie Peterson, Lowell, Indiana

Creating a Sanctuary

WHILE WE typically see all kinds of birds at our backyard feeders, one spring they were overtaken by starlings, pigeons, squirrels and mallard ducks. At times, there were as many as 50 "bully birds" frequenting our yard! They would not leave until they consumed all the seed, and they scared away the smaller birds.

We finally took down the feeders and cleaned up the dropped seeds in an effort to discourage the varmints. The trouble was, the smaller birds were gone as well.

After a week of silence, I decided to create two "feeding sanctuaries" (see photo below) to hold our bird feeders and provide protection for the smaller birds.

For the top and bottom of each holder, I used 18- by 24-inch pieces of galvanized steel. The frames are pieces of lumber attached to the metal with screws.

I wrapped three sides with chicken wire, then cut four small holes on each side to create entrances that are perfect for little

birds, but keep out squirrels and larger birds. One side also features a hinged door, so we can easily refill and clean the feeders I placed inside.

The squirrels gave up after a few attempts to get at the feeders. And because the steel floor catches dropped seeds, we no longer have problems with ground feeders like pigeons, starlings or ducks.

What we have seen is the happy return of the smaller birds we enjoy so much. —Dave and Barb Getz
Greenwood, Indiana

Ribbons Do the Trick

AFTER SEEING a tip from a reader in a previous issue of *Birds & Blooms* about tying red ribbons onto hummingbird feeders to attract birds, I thought I'd give it a try.

We have several feeders, and I topped each one with a generous length of red ribbon. That did the trick. The photo (right) shows one feeder hanging near our front porch—see how busy it is!

Overall, I'd estimate we now have three or four times more

hummingbirds at the feeders in summer than we did before. One feeder regularly attracts 20 to 25 birds at a time.

—Ruth Lee, Frisco City, Alabama

No-Weed Feed

TO PREVENT fallen birdseed from sprouting, I contacted experts to find out what to do. I learned a useful tip and wanted to pass it on to other readers.

Birdseed can be heated in a microwave oven to prevent the sprouting of weeds. For each pound of seed, microwave for 2 minutes at high power. The seeds can also be baked in a conventional oven by spreading a thin layer on a cookie sheet and baking at 250° for 30 minutes.

One more way to prevent sprouting is by using seeds out of the shell like hulled sunflower, cracked corn or peanut hearts.
—*Tom Kovach, Park Rapids, Minnesota*

Act of Diversion

IF YOU CAN'T BEAT them, feed them. At least that's what works for me when dealing with squirrels. To keep these critters away from my bird feeders, I divert them to a dining spot of their very own.

I put a screw eye into the end of a dried corncob, and then hang it on a shepherd's hook in my yard (left). I've learned to make sure the screw isn't too loose around the hook, though. These crafty creatures will figure out how to remove the hanging cob and be off with it in no time.
—*Mark Bozicevich*
Cordova, Texas

Sticky Situation

SINCE WOODEN peanut butter feeders are hard to clean and usually collect mildew, my son John and I decided to take action. We make our own feeders from PVC pipe (right). The body is constructed from 1-1/2-inch pipe, and the cups for peanut butter are 1-inch pieces attached to the body with PVC cement.

The feeders are quick to make and easy to clean, too. I coat the cut edges of the cups with clear lacquer or epoxy, which helps prevent mildew. And when it's time for a thorough scrubbing, the feeder fits in the upper section of the dishwasher.
—*Howard Williams, Athens, Georgia*

A Real Hit

I GET SO MANY suet-loving birds in my backyard that small suet feeders aren't practical. Instead, I bought a CD holder and added a board to the back and the bottom (left). Now I use large pieces of bulk suet, and the birds love it. —*Kenneth Sabel*
Friendship, Wisconsin

War of the World

I HAVE WON most of my battles with the squirrels that try to eat from my bird feeders. My secret? I block squirrels from the feeders with various baffles—from plastic pumpkins to globes. Here are the results (above photos) from my latest victory.

In the first picture, the squirrel appears to be pondering its plan of attack. Next, it descends on its target, only to be left "spinning." The third picture shows the critter scurrying away in defeat.

I guess you could say the world got the best of this squirrel!
—*S.M. Kent, West Caldwell, New Jersey*

Window Feeder

WHEN MY husband and I moved into our first home, I was relatively new to feeding birds and certainly new to home ownership.

One of the first modifications we made to the house was removing an old window-unit air conditioner. We didn't get around to taking down its platform right away, and for that, I'm glad. As I was looking at it one day, I realized it would be a perfect place to feed birds.

I set out seed on this windowsill feeder, and we have close encounters with birds all the time. Children of all ages love to come to our home to see the birds up close. In this case, I guess procrastination was a good thing. —*Susan Moussette*
Huntington, Massachusetts

Leave the Lights on

THIS YEAR, I wanted to try something different for our purple martin houses, so I went to a salvage yard for inspiration. There, I found a brass chandelier for $5.

After cleaning it up, we attached our gourd birdhouses to it and installed it on a retractable pole (below). The purple martins loved it!

They even ignored our other gourd birdhouses, and would only use the one on this hanger.

My bargain bin find turned out to be an attractive and functional addition to our backyard.

—*Judy Wolfe*
Dunnellon, Florida

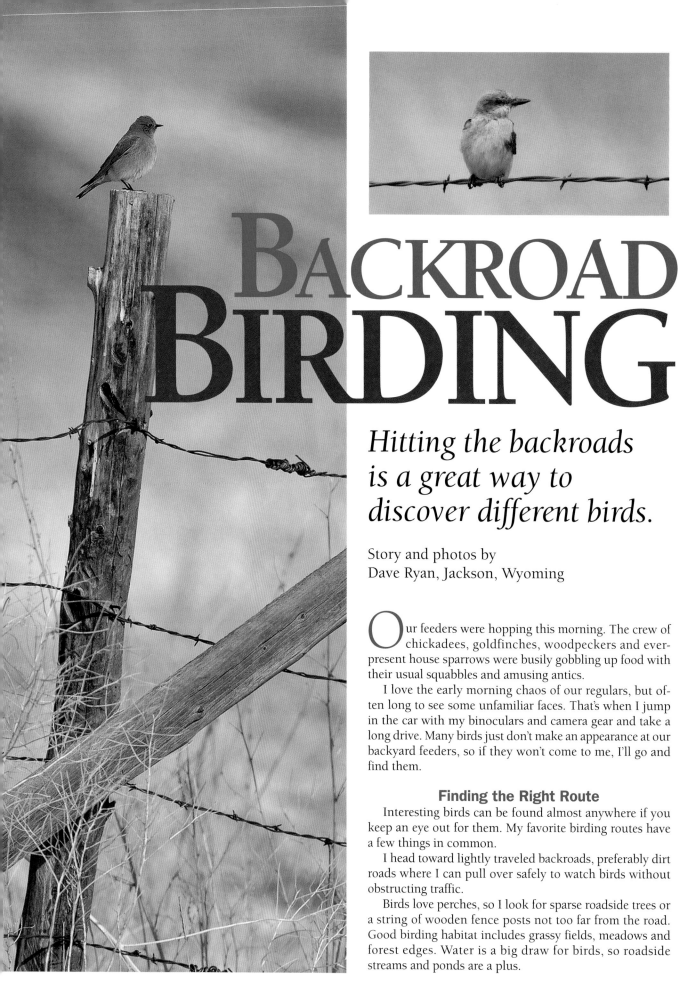

BACKROAD BIRDING

Hitting the backroads is a great way to discover different birds.

Story and photos by
Dave Ryan, Jackson, Wyoming

Our feeders were hopping this morning. The crew of chickadees, goldfinches, woodpeckers and ever-present house sparrows were busily gobbling up food with their usual squabbles and amusing antics.

I love the early morning chaos of our regulars, but often long to see some unfamiliar faces. That's when I jump in the car with my binoculars and camera gear and take a long drive. Many birds just don't make an appearance at our backyard feeders, so if they won't come to me, I'll go and find them.

Finding the Right Route

Interesting birds can be found almost anywhere if you keep an eye out for them. My favorite birding routes have a few things in common.

I head toward lightly traveled backroads, preferably dirt roads where I can pull over safely to watch birds without obstructing traffic.

Birds love perches, so I look for sparse roadside trees or a string of wooden fence posts not too far from the road. Good birding habitat includes grassy fields, meadows and forest edges. Water is a big draw for birds, so roadside streams and ponds are a plus.

I discovered my favorite roads by looking for the tiniest lines on maps, and then driving them to scout for that combination of habitat and nice perches.

Keep It Quiet

Choosing good driving tours is a start, but a few tricks can make the difference between a frustrating or a great birding drive.

Most birds will startle at the sound of a car abruptly stopping. It's amazing how birds will sit still for passing cars but take off when a car stops near them. You can increase your chances by driving slowly while scanning ahead for any interesting birds.

When you see one, coast slowly to a stop and stay inside your car, which makes a great observation blind. The good news is that many birds that flee at first will return if you sit still for a few minutes.

I've learned that western meadowlarks often disappear for only a moment before picking a nearby perch to resume singing. And groups of immature mountain bluebirds are very tolerant, usually returning moments after being startled. Try driving with your windows rolled down—you'll often hear birds before you see them.

I was driving along, scanning some high trees for raptors, when I heard the beautiful song of a white-crowned sparrow (above). It took me a minute to locate the beautiful soloist, but I finally saw it, singing from a shrub next to the road. The bird was so engaged in its song that it allowed me to drive right up to it.

Take in the Scenery

It's easy to develop tunnel vision while slowly scanning a fence line, but don't forget that lots of birds prefer perching on wires or nearby shrubbery.

If your driving tour takes you past any old bridges, take a peek underneath for nesting swallows or phoebes. In the spring, it's not unusual to find hundreds of cliff swal-

BIRD-WATCHER'S SECRET

When bird-watching, don't give up if a bird flees before you get a good look at it. If you're patient and still for a few minutes, it will often return.

—*Dave Ryan, Jackson, Wyoming*

ACROSS THE FENCE. Country roads are great for bird-watching. Clockwise from top left: A white-crowned sparrow belts out a song...a marsh wren gathers nesting material...cliff swallows busily build nests. Opposite page, a mountain bluebird and a western kingbird check out the view from up high.

lows (above), their faces covered in mud, busily dabbling away at their homemade adobe nests. Old rusty bridge pilings are a favorite nesting location for these birds.

Sometimes a driving tour turns up some surprising birds. Once, on the way to a local marsh, I did a double take to find a willet perched on top of a fence post. It didn't seem concerned with me at all as I drove a bit farther, did a careful U-turn and coasted up for a photo session. This long-legged wader is more often seen pecking for food along muddy shorelines, so it was a real treat.

If you'd like to visit with birds that don't frequent your feeders, take a drive and do some backroad birding.

They happily share their yard with birds and critters.

WHOSE HABITAT IS IT, ANYWAY?

By Marie Fletcher, Leoti, Kansas

Years ago, my husband, Ralph, and I moved to a new place on the south edge of a small western Kansas town. We planted a lot of shrubs, flowers and trees...not realizing how attractive we were making our 5 acres to the wildlife around us.

From our patio, we look over a miniature forest of staghorn sumac (top photo) that forms a natural canopy to cool the area in summer—and turns brilliant gold and red in fall.

A small redwood bridge arches over a homemade stream, making an entrance into the backyard. Beyond are a variety of trees, including Russian olive, black walnut, sunburst locust, golden-rain tree, Scotch pine, ponderosa pine and red cedar.

Between the backyard and the small field to the west grow a variety of plums, plus choke cherries, elderberries, currants and mulberries.

To break the searing summer wind, we planted a 200-foot

LIVING IN HARMONY. Marie and Ralph Leoti (above inset) created a lush backyard wildlife habitat that includes plantings like larkspur (top) that grow near their "miniature forest" of staghorn sumac. Other plants that produce berries attract various birds.

ALL ARE WELCOME HERE. The Leotis enjoy watching the variety of wildlife that pass through their yard looking for food or shelter. From top near right: A young eastern cottontail peers through grasses...a pair of mule deer stop for a visit...an eastern black swallowtail feeds on coneflower... two juvenile western kingbirds find a protected perch.

hedge of lilacs on our southern boundary.

Those many plantings really enhanced *our* habitat. But as we sat on our patio enjoying the results of our work, we began to notice that we were not alone.

The Wild Kingdom

Eastern cottontail rabbits filtered into the yard from the grassy areas around our property. More and more birds started coming in to build their nests. To accommodate them, I put out birdbaths and pans filled with water.

American robins could not get enough of our elderberries and juniper berries, so I planted more.

Deer slipped in during the night or early morning hours to browse on the buffalo grass in the backyard. Pheasants began patrolling our lilac hedge, digging in the dead leaves and taking dirt baths. We could hear northern bobwhites doing their "bob white" call in the field. I put out scratch grain for them.

Realizing we catered to a variety of animals and birds, we decided to plant flowers that would attract butterflies as well. Soon, painted ladies, viceroys, red admirals and others were visiting. I saved milkweed wherever I saw it, because it's a favorite of monarch butterflies.

At first we referred to the animals, birds and butterflies as visitors, but now we've come to think of them more like extended family. They eat, drink and relax in *our* habitat...because it has become *their* habitat as well.

Natural Rewards

Of course, these animals do provide compensation for our hospitality—we get to enjoy the wonderful sights and sounds of our natural world.

There's the pleasure of seeing a beautiful male ring-necked pheasant strut his stuff alongside his more subtle mate...and hearing the songs of brown thrashers and northern mockingbirds.

There are flashes of color from American goldfinches, American robins and eastern towhees...and the soft coo of mourning doves and Eurasian collared-doves, plus the twitter of western kingbirds and a variety of others.

Of course, the backyard habitat is also occupied by a few less-desirable critters. A sleepy skunk occasionally follows the hedge back to its bed after a long night of hunting. We don't bother it, and the skunk ignores us.

Snakes are another matter. We added a small garden pond that provides water for birds and other animals, but it also attracted garter snakes. I frequently pluck these harmless snakes out of the pond with a pair of old kitchen tongs and carry them out into the field. Ralph teases that they simply slither back, and I suppose he's right.

In the end, it really doesn't matter what kind of wildlife comes passing through our backyard. We're just glad to be sharing it!

BETTER BIRDHOUSES

Attract more nesting birds with these 5 basic tips.

By George Harrison, Contributing Editor

There are few bird-watching experiences more reward-ing than setting up a birdhouse and having a pair of birds select it as their home to raise young.

Not all backyard birds use houses, including many popular species like cardinals, orioles and goldfinches. But enough common birds *do* nest in birdhouses to make it worthwhile to set up a few to see what happens.

About 30 bird species in each region of the country are so-called cavity nesters, which means that most of them will also use a birdhouse. Bluebirds, purple martins, house wrens, chickadees, tree swallows and house sparrows are the most common occupants. You might also be able to en-tice nesters like wood ducks, screech-owls, woodpeckers, titmice and nuthatches.

But setting up a successful birdhouse isn't as simple as

"build it and they will come." There are several key fac-tors to consider that will give you the best chance to at-tract nesting birds.

1. Select a Suitable Location. Each bird species has dif-ferent habitat requirements, and this includes the envi-ronment they'll choose for nesting.

For example, the best location for a bluebird house is an area facing or surrounded by open fields, where the in-sects they eat and feed to their young are plentiful. Chick-adees (like the Carolina species above) are just the opposite. They prefer houses in a thicket or a stand of small trees and shrubs. House wrens like their house to hang from a small tree in a more open yard.

Purple martins select apartment houses placed on a tall

pole in the middle of a lawn or open field. And tree swallows want to be close to water where they can find insects to eat and feed to their young.

2. Pick the Proper House Design. In addition to specific habitats, different bird species also require varied types of birdhouses. Purple martins like to live in communities of many birds of their species. Therefore, an apartment-style house or multiple nesting gourds work best (bottom right).

House wrens live in single, small houses, and prefer not to have other wrens close by. Bluebirds require single-room dwellings, typically 50 to 75 yards apart.

3. Use a Birdhouse That Fits. Generally, small birds need small houses; large birds require large houses. House wrens are happy with an 8-inch-tall house with a 4- by 6-inch base, while a chickadee might select an 8-inch-tall house with a 5- by 5-inch base.

Bluebirds need more room, so a box that's 5-1/2 by 5-1/2 inches and 10 inches tall is perfect. Wood ducks and screech-owls need big houses, 10 by 10 inches and 24 inches high.

4. Focus on the Front Door. A very important aspect of selecting the right house for the birds you want to attract is the size of the entrance hole.

House wrens require the smallest entrance, only 1-1/8 inches. This will also keep out competing nesters, since almost no other birds can fit through such a small opening.

Wood ducks and screech-owls like an elliptical doorway that is 4 by 3 inches and about 20 inches above the floor of the house. The oval-shaped entrance helps prevent predators like raccoons from entering.

Chickadees, tufted titmice and nuthatches are comfortable with a 1-1/4-inch hole, while bluebirds need about 1-1/2 inches to get inside.

5. Get the Height Right. The final factor to consider is that birds prefer their houses at different heights.

Purple martin houses need to be about 15 to 20 feet above the ground. Wood ducks and screech-owls also need lofty homes, 12 to 40 feet high.

For bluebirds and tree swallows, place houses about 5 to 8 feet high on a post. House wrens prefer them 6 to 10 feet above the ground and hanging from a tree. Chickadees are most likely to nest in houses that are 4 to 8 feet above the floor of a thicket.

No matter what type of birdhouse you use, wood is the best material. The houses also should have ventilation around the top and drainage holes in the floor, and be painted or stained an earth tone. The exception is martin houses, which often are made of aluminum (or dried gourds) and painted white to reflect heat.

Even if you follow these five requirements, not every birdhouse will attract birds. The best way to increase your odds is to offer multiple houses of several types. Then, chances are good you'll have some winged tenants to admire come nesting season.

Photos: above, Bill Leaman/Positive Images; opposite page, Maslowski Productions

Potential Tenants

There are over 30 bird species that will regularly nest in birdhouses. Some of the birds you might see in your yard include:

American kestrel
Bewick's wren
Bluebirds
Carolina wren
Chickadees
Downy woodpecker
Flickers

Great-crested flycatcher
Hairy woodpecker
House finch
House wren
Nuthatches
Prothonotary warbler
Purple martin
Saw-whet owl
Screech-owls
Tree swallow
Tufted titmouse
Violet-green swallow
Wood duck

Maslowski Productions

HOME TWEET HOME

Readers share their most creative birdhouses.

Norwegian Chapel for the Birds

"My husband, Norman (above), constructed this birdhouse for our son and his wife," writes Bridget Walton of Newark, California. It's a scaled-down version of the Chapel in the Hills, the traditional Norwegian wooden church in South Dakota where they were married in 2003.

"Norman used cedar fence boards to make the church, including the more than 6,000 shingles that cover the multiple roofs. It took several months and was by the far his most challenging birdhouse project so far."

All-Time Favorite

"This is my favorite birdhouse of all time," raves Denise Deodato of Mineola, New York. "I saw the plan in a magazine and showed it to my husband. A few weeks later, he surprised me with this gorgeous work of art."

Denise painted and decorated the house, and "landscaped" it by gluing colorful wooden flowers to the heads of bent nails.

Right on Track

"My father made this birdhouse for my two children, Joshua and Anna," writes Laura Kurth of Greenfield, Wisconsin. "Now Joshua walks around the backyard saying, 'All Abird!' and Anna says, 'Choo-choo!'"

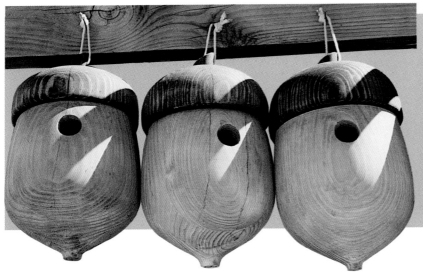

In a Nutshell

"My husband, Mike, and son David have been busy as squirrels making acorn-shaped birdhouses to hang in our numerous oak trees," writes Debbie Chamberlain of Willard, Missouri. "Each wooden house is ventilated, and, with the turn of a few screws, the top comes off for easy cleaning. When we have company, our guests request houses for their yards!"

Stylish Slate

"Since my husband retired, he's been busy building birdhouses. So, when a friend brought him some slate pieces left over from a flooring project, he used them to construct this multicolored dwelling," explains Joyce Whipple of Garden Grove, California. "Those colorful, flat stones made quite a distinctive look. It's the perfect home for our feathered friends, and it's durable."

Hitting a High Note

"Because I love birds and dabble in sculpture, I decided to combine my two interests by creating sculpted birdhouses," says Ray Garrett of St. Simons Island, Georgia. "I used laminated cedar or birch to form stylized, three-dimensional musical notes, then painted them with oil or acrylic paints. I've found that the bright colors appeal to many varieties of birds, and they amuse friends and visitors."

Storybook Ending

"This birdhouse looks like it came straight from a charming storybook," writes Peggy Shull of Seattle, Washington. "My mom, Marjorie Floyd, lives in Mesa, Arizona and crafted it out of clay. She has always loved birds, and began sculpting after she retired. I guess you can say she gave her birds a storybook ending."

Hard Hat Zone

"To make the top of this birdhouse, I used the hard hat that I wore for 31 years when I worked at a steel mill," explains Donald Bourgeois of Greenville, Illinois. "I built the rest from wood, then painted on a face."

All in the Family

"I constructed these little birdhouses from durable cedar and painted each one differently," says Pearl Ditch of Imperial, Missouri. "My husband, Paul, then helped me secure them to sturdy posts, which I'd decorated by painting flowers up the sides.

"I also added house numbers on each post—one is our address and the other three are for our married children—before securing them onto a cement slab in our yard. They sure do help brighten things up!"

148

We've Got the Birds Covered

"This covered-wagon birdhouse makes for an interesting conversation piece in my backyard," says Donald Isom of Klamath Falls, Oregon. "The wheels rotate freely on the axle and also turn right and left, so it's a home on the go!"

Hit the Slopes

"I have been making birdhouses out of recycled material since I retired in 1992," says Len McCaughan of Kent, Washington. "I use anything I can get my hands on—barn boards, cedar fencing, carpenter scraps and even siding. Then I hit the jackpot with these old skis. They are perfect for the snowbirds in my backyard!"

Attention to Detail

"When my boyfriend, Sean, starts a hobby, he puts his whole heart into it," writes Laura Bergeron of Waterford, Michigan. "One year he decided to start building birdhouses, and he spent all of his spare time in the garage, perfecting every last detail. Then he gave them away as gifts. I hope others find them as beautiful as I did."

South-of-the-Border Abode

"THERE'S ENOUGH ROOM in this hacienda (above) for two bird families," writes Gerry Vincent of Bailey, Colorado. "There's an entrance hole in each front window—I painted them black so they'd blend in. The house unscrews from the base for cleaning. I originally built it for an auction, but couldn't part with it. Now I have this and more than a dozen other birdhouses in my backyard."

Fit for a King

"I LIVE for my birds," says Vic Robbins of Fleetwood, Pennsylvania. "I've been a commercial artist all my life and enjoy making gourd art and birdhouses. I'll try anything I feel is 'birdable.' My lion has rope for a mane and seedpods for eyes."

De-light-ful Gift

"ONE OF my hobbies is making birdhouses from old and weathered wood," says David Snyder from Port Orchard, Washington. "So when my wife's birthday approached one year, I thought a replica of the Coquille Lighthouse in Bandon, Oregon would make a great gift. Her mother used to play in the historic building as a child, so it's very special to my wife."

Back to School

"USING a simple band saw and basic hand tools, this redwood birdhouse took me 6 months to construct," writes Richard Gorthy of San Ramon, California. "It's a model of the one-room Tassajara schoolhouse in our area. I furnished the inside of the birdhouse with old-fashioned desks, bookshelves, a blackboard and a potbellied stove, leaving space in the 'attic' for birds to nest.

"Forty miniature daffodils adorn the outside, representing the hundreds that bloom on the school's grounds each spring."

Two Was the Bear Minimum

"MOM LOVES Bluebirds, Dad loves chain saws. It's a rather strange pair of interests, you might say," writes daughter Kelsey Needham of Lawrence, Kansas. Her parents, Keith and Margaret, live in Mound City.

"Dad carved a 2-foot-tall bear birdhouse from a catalpa log and addressed every detail, including a clean-out door in back and a predator guard for the pole.

"Then he decided one bear wasn't enough, so he carved another—this one with overalls. On Christmas morning, Mom was surprised with the most unique birdhouses around."

Double Vision

"THIS CHARMING birdhouse (above) is a replica of our home," says Linda Pratico of Rutland, Vermont. "My husband, Randy, fashioned it using leftover building materials from our house. Every bit is handmade, including the miniature shutters that accent each window."

Drilling It Home

"MY SON Kenneth had great fun making this one-of-a-kind oil rig birdhouse," says Maxine Bednar of Kouts, Indiana. "But it's the birds who have really struck pay dirt. Within an hour of setting up the house in my front yard, a pair of birds moved in."

Do Birds Prefer Chevys?

"OVER THE YEARS, I've built close to 500 nest boxes for bluebirds," says Len Vest of Chester, Virginia. "To challenge myself, I decided to build a house in the shape of a 1953 Chevy truck. I constructed all the parts from cedar and used a Dremel tool to make the curves. I worked on it for 5 months, and spent 800 hours in the shop."

This Barn Has Birds and Blooms

"MY HUSBAND, Randy, and I designed and built this multipurpose birdhouse and planter (below) based on the barn on his family's farm," writes Paula Simpson of Churchill, Ontario.

"There's a wren house on top, and two silos in back that are made from tube feeders. On the bottom is a flower box and a storage area for my small gardening tools. It sure brightens up the old satellite pole in our backyard."

Bedtime Reading

"MY BROTHER Bert Burmeister has become quite a birdhouse builder since he retired," explains Bonnie Chastain from Omaha, Nebraska.

"He built a workshop behind their home in Orlando, Florida, and he spends many hours there making creative birdhouses, like this stack of books. We think he's very talented!"

Taking a Break

"I RECENTLY started making mosaics from broken dishes, tiles, sea glass...whatever I can find," writes Janice Austin of Salinas, California. "I've loved bird-watching since a dear friend introduced me to it a number of years ago. So naturally, my favorite mosaic projects are birdhouses and feeders."

Up to the Challenge

"AFTER spotting an elaborate birdhouse while visiting our son in Bavaria, my wife asked if I could build one for her—only better," writes Gary Pomeroy of Springfield, Vermont.

"I took up the challenge, and after more than 30 hours at the work bench, I finished this birdhouse. There are two nesting compartments, one in front and another in back, and two balconies that hold seed. I used five different kinds of wood and added copper flashing to the roof peak and edges."

A Capitol Idea

TO CREATE this birdhouse, which I modeled after the U.S. Capitol in Washington, D.C., I started with a 5-gallon bucket and a plastic flowerpot," writes LaRoyce Shiver from Mobile, Alabama. "Then I added columns and the rest of the architectural features using wood and other materials.

"It has become quite popular with our backyard friends. Once the purple martins leave each year, squirrels move in and raise their families."

Hats Off!

"I WAS searching for unique gifts for the college friends I see only once a year, when I came up with the idea of red hat birdhouses," says Pam Fraser of Tallahassee, Florida. "We were all planning to wear red hats for our upcoming get-together, so I thought matching birdhouses would be fun.

"My dad, Ken Bope (above), who lives in Maggie Valley, North Carolina, loves to work with wood and happily agreed to design and make the houses. He crafted them so they'd open underneath for cleaning. The birdhouses were challenging, but he did a fantastic job!"

Full Steam Ahead

"MY FATHER, Patrick Holliday, has constructed several unique and beautiful birdhouses over the years, but I think this old-fashioned paddle-wheel boat is his best effort yet," writes Debbie Green from Palmyra, Missouri. "The birdhouse is stationed outside my cousin's restaurant, which overlooks the Illinois River in Hardin, Illinois."

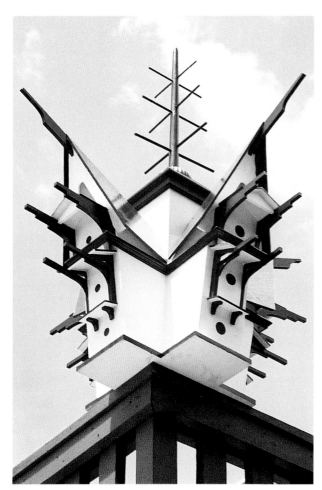

Victorian Villa

"IT TOOK 3 months, but I finally completed this Victorian-inspired birdhouse complex," says Ken Konvicka of Garland, Texas. "I based the design on a photo I took at Butchart Gardens in British Columbia. I was impressed with the structure, so I wanted to try making one myself.

"It seems like I took about 100 trips to the hardware store while building this project, but now it's ready for my backyard birds to enjoy."

A Birdhouse, to Boot

"MY OLD ski boots remind me of the good times I've had on the ski slopes," writes Richard Adamus from Penfield, New York. "So instead of throwing them away, I converted one into a birdhouse.

"I made the entrance hole with a large drill bit and capped the top of the boot with a block of wood."

Fanciful Fortress

"AFTER COMPLETING several other woodworking projects, I had a pile of scrap lumber on my hands, so I decided to build a birdhouse," explains Ken Hawkins of Decatur, Indiana.

"What I ended up with was more like a huge bird playhouse (below)! The building is 32 inches tall, 60 inches long and weighs about 50 pounds. It took me about 6 months to make it in my spare time."

Garden Musician

"I LOVE growing my own gourds and using them to create birdhouses," says Jo Ann Sutherland from Santaquin, Utah. "I was looking through all my gourds, hoping for inspiration for a project to add to my copper garden, when I located the perfect one. The shape of this gourd was just right for a kokopelli, which is the Native American musical figure that's popular in Southwestern art."

HOMEGROWN HOMES

Gourds are a natural choice for feeders and birdhouses.

By Bill Moore, Wentworth, New Hampshire

If you're like me, there's no such thing as too many bird-houses. That's why I enjoy growing gourds. Once dry, gourds can easily be transformed into the perfect nesting spots.

Gourds are simple to grow, and so prolific that one crop is enough to create a housing glut. But that's no problem—I turn the surplus into unique bird feeders. After all, birds use houses only a couple of months a year, while feeders stay busy year-round.

For "homegrown" houses and feeders, look for seeds of any type of lagenaria gourd. The rounded, bottle-shaped varieties are often known as birdhouse or bottle gourds. Not surprisingly, they're the most popular choice for birdhouses and are becoming easy to find at garden centers (or see the list of sources on page 81). Some other types that will work well for this are swan, dolphin and dipper gourds.

From experience, I've learned a few hints that will help you cultivate a successful gourd crop.

154   *Chapter 3*

HUNG OUT TO DRY. Growing gourds (left inset) is a great way to combine your interests of gardening and birding. After harvesting the gourds, allow them to dry by hanging them in a ventilated area (left). Then they're ready to be cleaned and converted into birdhouses, or even feeders (like the ones below).

Start with Seed

First of all, most of these gourds take about 120 days to ripen. Give them a head start by planting them indoors, 4 to 6 weeks before the last frost date in your area. I plant mine in peat pots so I can transplant them into the garden without disturbing the roots.

Put five seeds in each pot, a 1/2 inch deep, and place the pots under grow lights or on a sunny sill. When it's time to thin the seedlings to one per pot, use scissors. Pulling them out can damage the roots of the remaining plants.

When temperatures begin to warm, start hardening off the seedlings outdoors. During the day, place the pots in a shady spot. They can stay outside overnight as long as there's no threat of frost.

Then it's time to find a sunny planting site—and make it a big one. Space the plants 3 to 6 feet apart. That sounds like a lot, but trust me, these plants ramble!

For each seedling, dig a hole 18 inches wide and a foot deep, and amend the soil with organic matter. Once planted, surround the gourds with mulch to inhibit weeds and protect the shallow roots.

If your garden space for gourds is limited, just go vertical. This has advantages—it makes the gourds more uniform and less susceptible to slugs and fungal problems. However, gourds grown on trellises generally have straight necks. If you'd like the necks to curve, gently bend them after the gourds first emerge.

READER TIP

Give your gourds a head start by planting them indoors, 4 to 6 weeks before the last frost date in your area. Also, plant them in peat pots, so you can transplant them to the garden without disturbing the roots.

—Bill Moore, Wentworth, New Hampshire

The gourds are ready to harvest when the stems dry and turn brown. Cut the stem with pruning shears or a sharp knife, leaving about 6 inches attached to the gourd. Cutting the stem too close encourages rot.

All Dried Up

Gently wash and dry the gourds, then place them in a well-ventilated area to cure. An attic is ideal, but anyplace indoors works. Keep gourds in a single layer, not touching each other. Don't worry if the gourds get a little moldy—that's normal. However, discard any that become soft or wrinkled.

You'll know the gourds are dry when their color changes from green to tan, they become noticeably lighter weight and the seeds rattle. If you can use them as maracas, they're ready to go! Wash off the gourds and buff away any mold with a little sandpaper or steel wool.

Move-in Condition

To create a birdhouse or feeder, make an entryway with a hole saw. Then remove the seeds and dried pulp.

Drill a few small holes on top for ventilation, and in the bottom for drainage. If you'd like, insert a small stick or dowel under the entry hole for a perch, and affix it with waterproof glue.

To hang the gourd, hook the stem or neck over a branch, or anchor sturdy cord or twine through the top hole. Sometimes I get creative and add a second gourd as decoration (see photos above left).

The birds will love them, and you'll love the natural look and budget price.

Ready, Set...Gourd!

Gourd seeds are almost as easy to find as they are to grow. They're available from nurseries, garden centers and numerous catalog and on-line retailers. But if you can't find them in your local stores, here are a few sources to get you started:

Baker Creek Heirloom Seeds
2278 Baker Creed Rd.
Mansfield MO 65704
1-417/924-8917
www.rareseeds.com

Nichols Garden Nursery
1198 N. Pacific Hwy.
Albany OR 97321
1-800/422-3985
www.gardennursery.com

Pinetree Garden Seeds
P.O. Box 300
New Gloucester ME 04260
1-207/926-3400
www.superseeds.com

Onalee's Home-Grown Seeds
226 Benes Rd.
Brooksville FL 34604
1-352/544-2999
http://onaleeseeds.scifstore.com

Gourd organizations offer a wealth of information for both novice and experienced growers, including growing tips, craft ideas, information on gourd artisans and news about area gourd art shows and competitions.

To learn more, contact the American Gourd Society, P.O. Box 2186, Kokomo IN 46904 (www.americangourdsociety.org). Canadian residents should check with the Canadian Gourd Society, 44 Edgevalley Rd., Unit 48, London ON Canada N5Y 5P7 (www.canadiangourdsociety1.homestead.com).

MARTIN METROPOLIS

When it comes to attracting martins, no one does it better than these savvy Southerners.

By Laura Cartwright, Booneville, Mississippi

ROOMS FOR RENT. Over 600 purple martins (like the ones above inset) zip among a towering complex of gourd houses and apartments in this rural Mississippi yard (top). It's perhaps the largest and oldest martin colony in the United States.

Purple martins in the East largely depend on man-made housing. Near Booneville, Mississippi, *over 600* martins look to Luther and Joan Moorman for homes.

The martin colony on the Moormans' 107-acre farm may be the largest—and oldest—in the U.S.

"My father began putting up martin houses here in the '40s," Luther says. "I just kept adding them over the years. Now we have more than 300."

Growing Homes

It truly is a homegrown operation, since most of those houses are made from the gourds Luther raises each year.

He plants them in April, then lets the gourds grow as big as possible before harvesting. After frost kills the vines in late October, Luther lets the gourds dry.

"It takes a long time," he says. "At first they get moldy and look like they're rotten, but they finally dry out."

To prepare the gourds for martin homes, Luther and Joan

WORTH THE EFFORT. Luther and Joan Moorman put a lot of care into their purple martin hobby. They grow gourds in their garden to make houses (above), then diligently check the homes (at right) to keep out nest raiders like European starlings.

use an electric buffer to clean them to a beautiful shine. Then they cut a 2-3/4-inch entry hole in the short-necked gourds or cut the tip off the long-necked ones for a natural entryway.

After they remove the seeds and membranes, they apply a coat of waterproof sealant to the gourds. Luther also adds a small "awning" over each entry hole to help keep rain out.

Once they complete the gourd houses, they hang them among a large stand of poles that hold 16 houses each.

All of the poles have cables so Luther and Joan can raise and lower the racks to check the nests and clean the houses as needed. This allows them to keep European starlings in check. Otherwise, these non-native birds will push martins out of the homes.

And that's not the only martin challenger the Moormans have to fight. At the bottom of every pole is a disk-shaped guard that prevents snakes from climbing to the houses.

Helpful Hobby

All this may sound like a lot of work for a hobby, but Luther and Joan have always put plenty of effort into their outdoor activities. Until Luther was sidelined by back problems, he and Joan ran a lawn service business.

Their own yard still is a showplace of manicured grass and well-tended flower beds, surrounded by trees and shrubs. It's often filled with visitors during spring and summer, when birders come to marvel at the Moormans' purple martin majesty.

Luther and Joan are happy to share information about the birds with their guests.

He explains that martins have a very strong migratory instinct and arrive at the farm each year on February 11 or 12. After settling into the cozy gourd houses, female martins lay

several eggs—three to eight per nest.

"As the eggs hatch, I've seen the males hanging upside down on the gourds," Luther says. "I figure they're making sure everything is okay.

"Purple martins eat only insects, so we don't have to buy any seed for them," Luther says. "When the babies grow a bit, the adult birds will bring dragonflies to feed them."

In July, when the young martins first come out of the gourds, it's something to see—there are hundreds of them!

"The adult birds try to keep the babies from coming back to the nest, but they don't always succeed," Luther says with a grin.

Time to Move on

The martins leave during the second week of August, as soon as the baby birds can fly, and migrate to Brazil and northern Argentina. Then the Moormans take down all of the houses—the gourds plus the larger "apartments"—for cleaning and storage. In January, the process starts over.

"I can't help but get excited when I put the houses up," Luther says. "Because I know that I'll soon be seeing my purple martins again."

READER TIP

We add small "awnings" over each gourd house entry hole to keep the rain out.
—Luther and Joan Moorman, Booneville, Mississippi

FANTASTIC FEEDERS

These feeders offer birds fine dining year-round.

Dinner Music

"Bird-watching and building harps are two of my favorite hobbies, so it was only natural for me to combine the two," says George Phillips of Oswego, New York. "Using scraps of harp wood, I constructed a harp-shaped bird feeder for our yard. The top comes off so I can fill the feeder with several days' worth of seed. This harp doesn't make music though—I leave that up to the birds!"

Cleanup's a Breeze

"The shallow terracotta trays I attached to this feeder are so simple to remove, they make cleaning and refilling the feeder easy," says Jim Kral of Arroyo Grande, California. "My wife and I retired to the Central Coast area about 6 years ago, and our property has a creek running through it that attracts plenty of birds. I enjoy watching them eat at the many feeders I've crafted over the years."

Space Needle Dining

"Our local Eagles club will auction off this bird feeder in spring," writes Mel Minion of Longview, Washington. "I crafted the design after the Seattle Space Needle. The base is from a poplar tree, which I soaked in water to make it bend. The rest is from scrap wood that I had around the house. It was fun to create, and it's easy to fill from the roof."

Big Rig Diner

"Our neighbor drives a semitruck, so we made this feeder in honor of him," writes C.O. Knap of Tucson, Arizona. "The birds appreciate the 'big load' of seed that it carries."

Come and Get It

"After I attended a nearby covered bridge festival, the unique designs inspired me to create one for my feathered friends," writes Jimmy Curlow of Carmel, Indiana. "This feeder (above) now has a permanent home in our backyard. My wife and I enjoy sitting on the porch, reading the morning paper and watching the birds feed."

Given the Green Light

"My stoplight bird feeder gives my feathered friends great protection," writes Curtis Hall from McDowell, Kentucky. "It was inexpensive to build, using mostly basic lumber and coffee cans. I refill the seed from the top. And, as you can see, the birds love it."

Open Concept

"My husband offered to build me a cabin-style bird feeder to replace the one in my garden that had seen better days," writes Trish Wyss, Christmas Valley, Oregon. "Using scrap wood, he created a log cabin design with open walls. The feeders started out little, but eventually grew into large lodges. I just toss in some seed and watch as different birds arrive to feast."

Ready to Ride

"THIS FEEDER (left) was a cooperative effort," writes Mrs. Ed Carpenter of Capac, Michigan. "Our son built the flatbed for the corncobs, and some family friends added the detailed tractor, which is a replica of the one my husband drives. We placed the feeder in our backyard, where both squirrels and birds hop aboard to dine."

Winter Fuel

I'VE BEEN building feeders and houses for birds ever since I retired," says Dave Bott from Lacombe, Alberta. "This one is a replica of an old kerosene lantern. It's made entirely of wood, except for the glass globe. There are six feeding ports, which provide enough room for numerous birds, such as common redpolls."

Work of Art

"MY HUSBAND, Larry, spent more than 100 hours creating this beautiful feeder that's similar to the gazebo on our pond," writes Doris Tyler from Hartford City, Indiana. "It's built from western red cedar and features a double-curved copper roof."

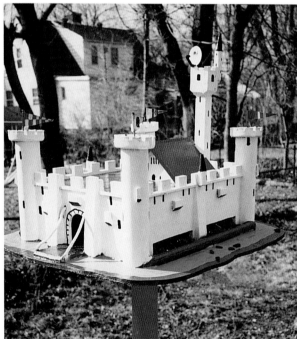

Great Gift

"WE ARE avid bird-watchers and feed many birds in our yard," write Roy (left) and Vonnie Nelson of Murdock, Minnesota. "So you can imagine our delight when we received this elaborate bird feeder as a gift from a friend, John Hugo of Mason City, Iowa. We get quite a selection of birds visiting it for a meal."

Eat Like a King

"MY GRANDSON and I built this castle bird feeder," writes Bob Dewitz from Williamsville, New York. "We added details like a satellite dish and a drawbridge, which we left open so birds could investigate under the seed tray."

Father Knows Best

"MY FATHER, Gene Lowe, enjoys taking care of the birds that visit his backyard. That's why he built them this lovely nine-port feeder," says Genia Turbyfield of Simpsonville, South Carolina.

"When my husband and I started to take up bird feeding ourselves, my dad went back to the wood shop and surprised us with our own handcrafted feeder. And guess what? Our birds love it, too!"

Backyard Cabin

"DURING OUR long winters, my husband, George, stays busy building feeders like this intricate cabin," says Carol Goodson from Worley, Idaho. "He doesn't use plans—just his imagination. On this one, the seed spills out the front door and down the steps.

"He builds birdhouses, too, and has filled our 2-1/2-acre property with a variety of houses, feeders and baths—all for the birds."

Whimsical Windmill

"THIS UNIQUE bird feeder is a replica of the DeZwaan, a 240-year-old working Dutch windmill that was sent to our town from the Netherlands," says Ken Dozeman from Holland, Michigan. "I copied its likeness by projecting the windmill's image onto a sheet of paper using slides I had made. Then I traced the image onto wood and cut it out. The large walkway that circles the landmark is the perfect place for seed."

Feeding Frenzy

"GOLDFINCHES flock to this unique feeder my husband, Harold, built," writes Trudy Barnes of Centralia, Missouri. "It has a copper roof and a pan to catch any seeds that fall. There are small holes in the pieces of Plexiglas to allow access to the seed.

"The birds can dine from 10 feeding ports, including four where the finches feed upside down. The roof and the feeding portion both lift off, so it's easy to refill."

Victorian Charmer

"WHEN WE revamped our backyard with a Victorian cottage garden theme, my father, Larry Himenes (below, with my daughter Alexandra), made this wonderful birdhouse and feeder to go with it," says Laurie Swindell of San Lorenzo, California. "I sprinkle birdseed on the platform that encircles the house, and the birds seem to love it. I love it, too, because it was made with tender loving care by my father."

A Sterling Effort

"I BUILT this rustic feeder for a neighbor whom my wife, Helen, and I often see on our daily walks," says Vernon Fellows of Peshastin, Washington. "I constructed it with scrap wood and aluminum roofing."

Ready for a Spin

"WHEN I get up every morning, the birds and squirrels are waiting for me to fill this Ferris wheel feeder," says Lenard Smith from Orange, Texas. "Each box-type 'seat' holds a cup of birdseed and has a drainage hole in the bottom.

I have two feeders like this. I keep one on the front porch, and the other in the yard near the swing where I like to relax. The squirrels have a ball on them."

Rocky Feeder

"MY BROTHER-IN-LAW Chris Jasan built this feeder (above) for my sister," says Kimberly Smith of Vacaville, California. "When I saw it, I knew that it was wonderfully unique with its river rock chimney and base. He even made a one-of-a-kind post for it using a tree trunk."

All Aboard the Feeder Train

"WE CAN'T FILL this dual bird and squirrel feeder fast enough," says Edward Shinkle of Ocala, Florida. "It's popular with all our backyard visitors.

"I got some of the feeder ideas from *Birds & Blooms*, and some are original creations. It has plenty of character with old license plates as roofs and two hanging feeders. But the real eye-catcher is the train, especially when there's a squirrel in the engineer's seat."

"Mort" Is a Different Sort

"I'D LIKE you to meet 'Mort,' the bird feeder I created from nearly all recycled materials (below)," writes Leonard Kuster of Green Bay, Wisconsin. "His body parts, shoes and hat were created from a fallen poplar tree. The pipe in his mouth is an ear of corn (picked clean by squirrels). The seed tray is a pie crust pan, and his teeth were made from a tomato sauce can."

Cactus Creation

"OUR FRIEND Tom Krieg constructed this uniquely shaped feeder for his home in Prescott Valley, Arizona," say Michael and Gloria Danek of Laingsburg, Michigan.

"As a retired engineer, he took special care with the design he crafted for his feathered friends. He formed it from long-lasting PVC pipe and drilled slightly angled holes to prevent the seed from spilling out. Tom has since passed away, but his wife, Ruby, continues to enjoy the variety of birds this saguaro cactus brings to their desert backyard."

WANT MORE BIRDS?

Here's the Menu:
Sunflower
Nyjer
Safflower
Suet Cake
Sugar Water

By George Harrison, Contributing Editor

Richard Day/Daybreak Imagery

Autumn is the time of the year when many backyarders think about feeding the beautiful songbirds in their neighborhoods. I'm not sure why this revelation happens this time of year—feeding birds year-round has many rewards.

Yet autumn is when birdseed sales are held and feeders are widely promoted to consumers…and I'm not talking about the feathered variety.

You could say once the autumn winds hit, bird-feeding season is in high gear —people are buying birdseed by 50-pound bagfuls. But what kinds of foods attract the birds you most want in your backyard?

Black-oil sunflower seeds and out-of-shell sunflower meats are both excellent offerings for lots of birds.

Sunflower Seed—Top of the List

If you want to rely on just one type of seed that is most attractive to the greatest number of backyard birds, hands down sunflower seed is the right pick in any form—in the shell (black-oil or white-striped) or medium cracked out-of-the-shell meats. All forms of sunflower seeds are relished by finches, chickadees, nuthatches, grosbeaks, cardinals, jays and even some species of woodpeckers.

There's only one problem with sunflower seed—bully birds, such as blackbirds, European starlings and grackles, also love it, especially if it's served in a tray feeder.

There's a simple solution. Serve sunflower seeds from a feeder that allows only the smaller birds to enter the feeding chamber. These feeders are often called "exclusion feeders," with smaller perches, weight mechanisms or fencing to keep the larger birds out.

Nyjer Seed (Thistle)

If finches are your fancy, like the brilliant-yellow American goldfinches (left) that frequent my area, then you'll want to serve up this tiny, black seed some people call thistle. It's best served in a special tube feeder that has tiny ports to keep the small seeds from pouring out.

Chickadees love nyjer seed, too, and their acrobatic behavior allows them to extract the seeds from the tiny food ports. It's also a good choice if you're overrun by larger bully birds. They have a problem feeding from the tiny ports.

Safflower Seed

Though it may take some birds a little time to get acquainted with safflower seeds, northern cardinals, grosbeaks, mourning doves and house finches will frequent feeders that serve it. Because northern cardinals prefer a flat surface to stand on when eating, a tray feeder or hopper feeder with a wide rim makes it easier for them to eat safflower seed. Even chickadees will remove a single safflower seed and fly to a nearby branch to crack it open.

Perhaps best of all, squirrels don't like safflower seed! Consider switching to it if these rascals often pester your feeders.

Squirrels don't eat safflower!

Sugar Water

During spring and summer, sugar water mixed in the kitchen (one part sugar to four parts water, boil and cool before serving) is dynamite for feeding hummingbirds and orioles. Because most hummingbird feeders are made of red plastic, and oriole feeders of orange plastic, the sugar water doesn't even need to be colored to attract the birds' attention. Once these desirable birds find the feeder, it will be a challenge keeping it filled.

Chapter 3

"Mystery mixes" will not always attract your favorite feathered friends.

Suet Cakes

One of my pet peeves is the commercial suet cake selection in bird stores. Most suet cakes contain a smorgasbord of foods other than suet, such as berries, oranges and even insects. The most common extra ingredient in suet cakes is birdseed. Birds that eat suet, including woodpeckers, nuthatches, chickadees and titmice, eat it to get the energy that the suet offers, so all the extras are virtually useless. If they require seeds, berries or insects, they'll find those food items elsewhere. For my backyard, I purchase only pure suet cakes.

Wild Birdseed Mixes

This is often the "mystery mix" you'll find at grocery stores or on sale at the local discount store. It's usually a mix of lots of millet, cracked corn and very few sunflower seeds. The basic problem with these feed-all mixes is that they're not discriminating and may attract mostly undesirable birds and night critters, such as rats and raccoons. I recommend avoiding these

do-all mixes, and stick with the specialty foods listed.

Feeding the most desired birds is probably much easier than you thought. Order off the right menu, and you're likely to see the birds you want feasting right outside your favorite picture window.

Feeders Hold More Than Food

There's more to filling feeders with the right seed to attract the birds you want. A feeder's shape, placement in the yard and distance above the ground will determine what kinds of birds actually use it. And yes, proper cover and habitat play an equally important role.

Here's a quick rundown of the most effective bird feeders:

Tray feeders, on a post or hanging, are open pantry shelves that attract most seed-eating birds. Problem is they also attract rain, snow and ice, so you have to maintain them more than other feeders.

Certain birds, such as cardinals, grosbeaks, bluebirds, woodpeckers and robins, will basically feed from only these types of feeders. Try to get one with screening or holes in the bottom for drainage to keep seed from spoiling.

Tube feeders are hanging cylinders with portholes and perches that are favored by small finches. Chickadees and nuthatches will use them, too.

If the bully birds figure out how to eat from a tube feeder, you may want to shorten the perches slightly, or enclose the feeder in a wire mesh that will allow only the little birds to get to the food. Commercially made exclusion feeders are available.

Hopper feeders, either on a post or hanging, are targeted to most kinds of seed-eating birds. They usually have an enclosed reservoir for seeds that slides food down to the open feeding tray below. The advantage is that the hopper keeps the seeds dry and always available to birds.

Suet feeders are usually small, square laminated cages that hold blocks of suet. They can hang on a tree trunk or be suspended from a branch. They're great for attracting woodpeckers, as well as titmice, chickadees and nuthatches.

Sugar-water feeders are for hummingbirds and orioles. Tanagers, finches and other birds may also use them. Simply keep them topped off with fresh, homemade sugar water…and stand back.

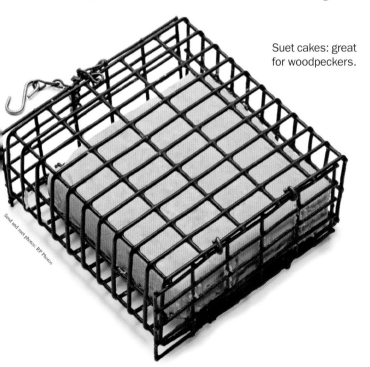

Suet cakes: great for woodpeckers.

Seed and suet photos, RP Photos

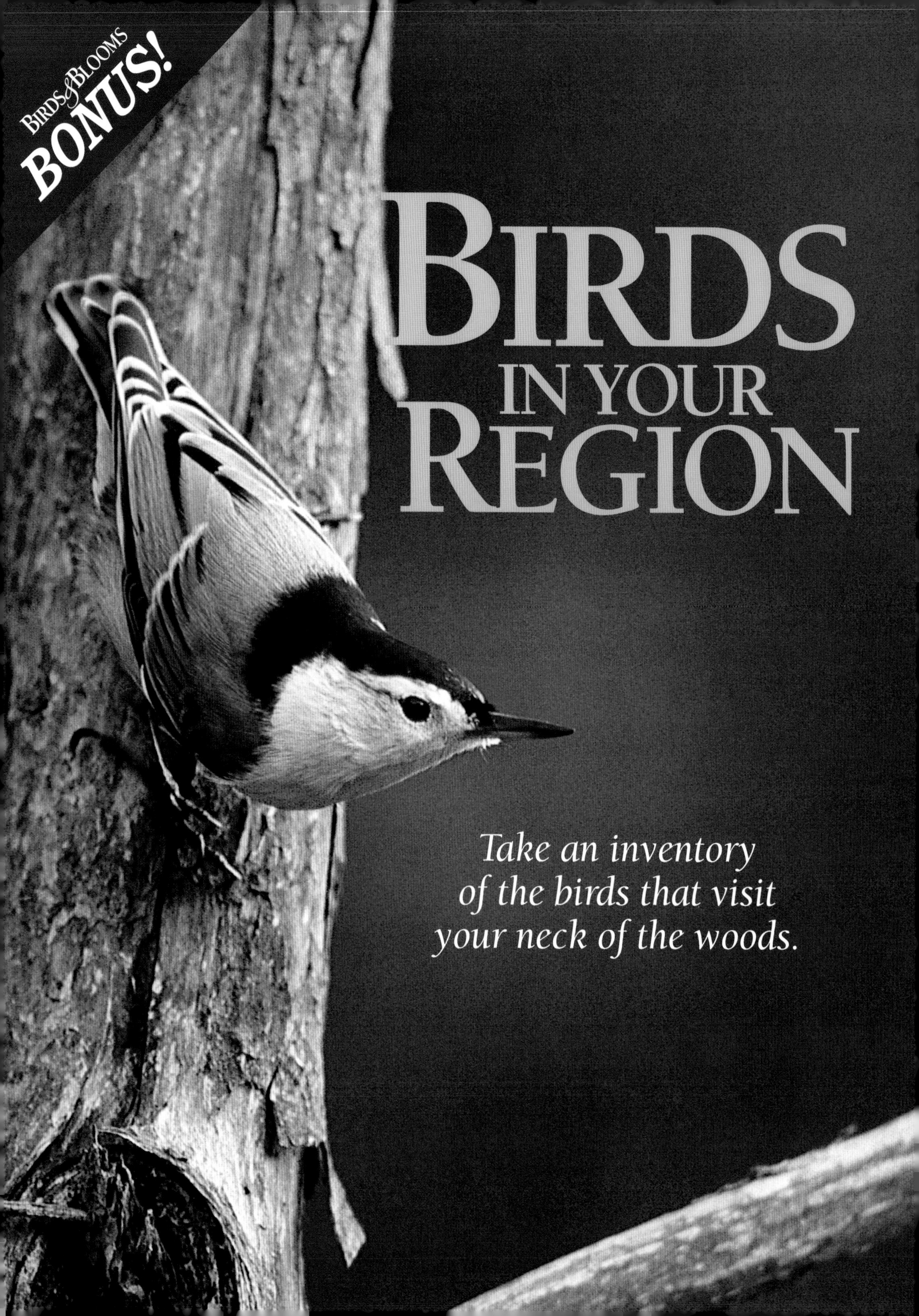

BIRDS & BLOOMS BONUS!

BIRDS IN YOUR REGION

Take an inventory of the birds that visit your neck of the woods.

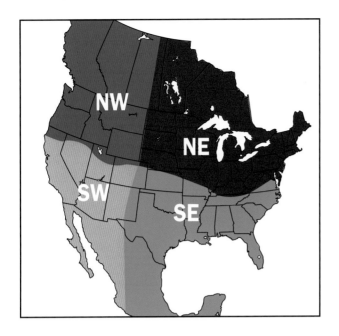

Map regions: NW, NE, SW, SE

BLACKBIRDS	SUMMER				WINTER			
	NE	NW	SE	SW	NE	NW	SE	SW
Brewer's blackbird		●				●	●	●
Red-winged blackbird	●	●	●	●	●	●	●	●
BLUEBIRDS								
Eastern bluebird	●		●		●		●	
Mountain bluebird		●		●				●
Western bluebird		●		●		●		●
BUNTINGS								
Indigo bunting	●		●					
Painted bunting			●				●	
CARDINAL								
Northern cardinal	●		●	●	●		●	●
CHICKADEES								
Black-capped	●	●			●	●		
Carolina			●				●	
Mountain		●		●		●		●
FINCHES								
American goldfinch	●	●	●	●	●	●	●	●
House finch	●	●	●	●	●	●	●	●
Pine siskin		●		●	●	●	●	●
Purple finch	●	●			●	●	●	●
GROSBEAKS								
Evening	●	●		●	●	●		●
Rose-breasted	●	●	●					
HUMMINGBIRDS								
Anna's		●		●		●		●
Broad-tailed				●				
Ruby-throated	●		●					
Rufous		●						
JAYS								
Blue jay	●		●		●		●	
Western scrub-jay		●		●		●		●
Steller's jay		●		●		●		●
JUNCO								
Dark-eyed junco	●	●		●	●	●	●	●

MIMIC THRUSHES	SUMMER				WINTER			
	NE	NW	SE	SW	NE	NW	SE	SW
Brown thrasher	●		●				●	
Gray catbird	●	●	●				●	
Northern mockingbird	●		●	●	●		●	●
NUTHATCHES								
Red-breasted	●	●		●	●	●	●	●
White-breasted	●	●		●	●	●	●	●
ORIOLES								
Baltimore oriole	●		●				●	
Bullock's oriole		●		●				●
PIGEONS								
Mourning dove	●	●	●	●	●	●	●	●
SPARROWS								
House sparrow	●	●	●	●	●	●	●	●
Song sparrow	●	●	●	●			●	●
SWALLOWS								
Purple martin	●	●	●	●				
Tree swallow	●	●	●	●				
Barn swallow	●	●	●	●				
TANAGERS								
Scarlet tanager	●							
Summer tanager			●	●				
Western tanager		●		●				
THRUSHES								
American robin	●	●	●	●			●	●
Hermit thrush	●	●		●				
TITMOUSE								
Tufted titmouse	●		●		●		●	
TOWHEES								
Eastern towhee	●		●				●	
Brown towhee				●				●
WARBLERS								
Common yellowthroat	●	●	●	●				
Yellow warbler	●	●	●	●				
Yellow-rumped warbler	●	●				●	●	●
WAXWINGS								
Bohemian waxwing						●		
Cedar waxwing	●	●					●	●
WOODPECKERS								
Downy	●	●	●	●	●	●	●	●
Hairy	●	●	●	●	●	●	●	●
Red-bellied	●		●		●		●	
Red-headed	●		●		●		●	
Northern flicker	●	●	●	●	●	●	●	●
WRENS								
Cactus wren				●				●
Carolina wren	●		●		●		●	
House wren	●	●	●	●			●	●

Photo opposite page: Larry Dech

Backyard Bird Haven

204

216

198

FLYING FLOWERS

186

Photos: mourning cloak at left, Francis and Janice Bergquist; opposite page from top left: comma, Martin Withers/Dembinsky Photo Assoc.; giant swallowtail, Richard Day/Daybreak Imagery, cecropia; Rob Curtis/The Image Finders

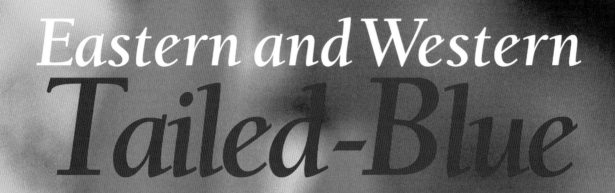

Eastern and Western
Tailed-Blue

*Diminutive beauties
charm onlookers
from coast to coast.*

There's nothing small about the impression these chipper little fliers make. The tailed-blue, measuring a mere 1 inch across, adds noticeable flashes of azure wherever it goes.

People all across North America can spot these butterflies because two related species—the eastern and the western—populate much of the U.S. and Canada.

Not-Quite Identical Twins

The eastern butterfly frequents the eastern U.S. from the Atlantic coast to the Rocky Mountains and south to Texas and Georgia. It can even be found as far as southern Ontario and Quebec.

The western tailed-blue is common in the West, from the Rockies to the Pacific Ocean and north to Alaska. It is also the species seen in most of Canada, from the Yukon and British Columbia east to Ontario.

The differences between the two species are very subtle. Males have bright-blue topwings outlined in black with white fringed edges.

Orange and black spots, which are more pronounced on eastern males, rim the hind wings and draw attention to the butterflies' threadlike tails. Females tend to be a darker hue, ranging from gray to brown with black and blue shading.

The best way to tell these cousins apart is by looking at their gray underwings. Eastern tailed-blues bear more distinct orange and black markings. But getting a good look is tough because the butterflies tend to twitch their wings when perched on flowers to feed.

This is actually a defense mechanism. It is designed to draw attention to their tails, which in turn, distracts predators from attacking.

The tailed-blue is one of the most abundant butterflies in North America and can be found in almost any sunny, open area. Both the eastern and western species have adapted well to the presence of people and can often be seen flitting through gardens containing flowers like butterfly bush, yarrow, lavender, zinnia and even dandelion.

Playing Host

When it comes to host plants, these butterflies rely on legumes, but their tastes differ somewhat. Eastern tailed-blues prefer peas, beans and clovers, while their western relatives flock to locoweed and vetch. Both species lay their eggs inside the flower buds or on stems. Then the last brood of the season will seek shelter inside seedpods where they will stay over the winter.

The resulting caterpillars typically are a shade of green, ranging from dark to light (westerns may also have yellow bodies), with subtle stripes.

The caterpillars produce a sweet, protein-rich liquid called honeydew that attracts ants. The ants feed on the honeydew and, in return, attend to the caterpillars by guarding them from predators and parasites. They may also seek protection by feeding inside seedpods. These defense mechanisms help assure plenty of tailed-blue butterflies in seasons to come.

So the next time you're in the garden and see a glint of sapphire, take a closer look—a tailed-blue might just be finding a meal on your flowers!

Flying Flower Facts

John and Gloria Tveten/KAC Productions; opposite page, Richard Day/Daybreak Imagery

Common Names: Eastern tailed-blue and western tailed-blue.

Scientific Names: *Everes comyntas* (eastern) and *Everes amyntula* (western).

Family: Blue.

Wingspan: 1 to 1-1/8 inches.

Distinctive Markings: Iridescent blue topwings with striking white fringed wing edges and threadlike tails.

Distinctive Behavior: The butterflies twitch their hind wings as they drink; they also fly low and close to the ground.

Habitat: Open, sunny areas like fields and roadsides, as well as yards and gardens.

Caterpillar: The eastern tailed-blue caterpillar typically is dark-green with subtle brown stripes. The western tailed-blue caterpillar varies in hue from deep-green to yellow-green with pink or maroon stripes.

Host Plants: Eastern tailed-blues lay their eggs on peas, beans, clover and even other legumes, while western tailed-blues will seek out vetch and locoweed.

■ Range

BUTTERFLY BIT

Try planting nectar-rich flowers like butterfly bush, yarrow, lavender and zinnias to attract these gorgeous butterflies to your backyard.

CLOUDED SULPHUR

Have you ever seen a pair of small yellow butterflies spiraling upward in the air? Then you've witnessed one of the spectacular behaviors of the common sulphur, also known as the clouded sulphur.

While this behavior might *look* romantic, the truth is the female sulphur is rejecting the male. The male will pursue the female a bit longer, but eventually he'll head off in search of a more receptive mate.

Common sulphurs often bask in the sun with their wings closed. The undersides of the wings (at right) feature two silvery spots encircled in red, which helps distinguish them from other sulphurs.

The tops of the wings are yellow for all males and most females, particularly those that live in southern regions. You may spot white females in cold climates.

Regardless of color, females' wings have light-black borders with yellow dots, while males' wings have solid, ink-black borders (like the one above). Their wingspan typically is 1-3/8 to 2 inches.

Male common sulphurs are often confused with orange sulphurs (also known as alfalfa sulphurs) because they look almost identical. The butterflies, however, have no trouble telling each other apart—whether it's due to ultraviolet colors we can't see or the production of certain chemicals, called pheromones.

These butterflies are common in western Canada and across most of the United States. They prefer open areas, such as meadows, parks and large backyards. They like clover, dandelions and wildflowers for nectar, and the females usually select clover or alfalfa as host plants for their chartreuse eggs.

The common sulphur caterpillar is small and green with light side stripes and darker back stripes (inset at right). Each one forms a bright-green chrysalis in fall that protects it over the winter months.

Common sulphurs are active from March to November. They often congregate around puddles to collect salts and other nutrients. In fact, creating an area of damp sand or soil in your yard is a great way to coax these sunny flying flowers to pay you a visit. 🗡

READER TIP

These butterflies are common in western Canada and across most of the United States. Look for them in open areas, such as meadows, parks and large backyards.

Cabbage White

This fair beauty is found across the country.

No matter where you live, chances are you've seen this gossamer creature floating above a field of flowers or fluttering through the rows of a vegetable garden. Named for both its coloring and its offspring's appetite for cabbage and other crops, the cabbage white is one of the most widespread species in North America.

It may come as a surprise, however, to discover that this dainty butterfly isn't native to our continent. Instead, it hails from Eurasia.

The cabbage white was virtually unknown here until the 1860s, when it was accidentally introduced in Quebec. It quickly made itself at home just about everywhere in North America except South Florida, extreme southern portions of Louisiana and eastern Texas. Some 140 years later, it's common in both rural and urban environments, ranging from pastures, roadsides and gardens to mountain meadows and desert washes.

The cabbage white's striking, 2-inch-wide wings have distinctive charcoal tips and pale yellow-green or gray-gray undersides, so it's easy to spot. The wings also feature inky dots that help identify the gender. Males (like the one above) have only one mark on each forewing, while the females possess two.

This ephemeral flier sips nectar from yarrow, dahlias,

TAKE A CLOSE LOOK. With cabbage white butterflies, it's easy to recognize the differences between the genders. Female butterflies have two distinct marks on each forewing (like the one above on fleabane), while males have only one (opposite page).

Mark Werner/The Image Finders

lavender, sedum, marigolds, verbena, zinnias and other garden favorites. Cabbage whites like to congregate with other members of the white and sulphur butterfly family at mud puddles, or rest on rocks in the sun.

Friendly Pursuit

It's not unusual to see a male cabbage white hovering near a veggie patch, waiting for a willing damsel to woo. Once he spots a likely candidate, he engages in a friendly pursuit to evaluate the female's interest.

If the male has the bad luck to pick a female who isn't interested, the pursuit can make his head spin. The female will lead him on a dizzying upward chase, called a spiral dance, which ends when she suddenly tucks in her wings and rapidly descends, leaving the bewildered male aloft.

Once the male finds a receptive partner, he spends most of his time with her. The pair will flit about the garden until it's time for the female to lay individual yellow, vase-shaped eggs on the undersides of host plants, including cabbage, mustard, nasturtiums, broccoli, collard greens and radishes.

Hungry Caterpillars

The larvae have a reputation as garden pests, as they can damage entire crops of their host plants with their voracious appetite. An individual caterpillar can be hard to spot in the garden, though. Its fuzzy, bright-green body has subtle yellow lines and dashes, so it blends in quite nicely amid the veggies.

Thanks to their big appetites, cabbage white caterpillars grow rapidly, molting up to five times. When they reach about 3/4 inch in length, they build speckled green or

Flying Flower Facts

Alan and Linda Detrick

Common Name: Cabbage white.

Scientific Name: *Pieris rapae.*

Family: Whites and sulphurs.

Wingspan: 1-1/2 to 2 inches.

Distinctive Markings: The forewings have dark tips; males also bear a single black spot on each forewing, and females have two dark spots. Undersides are yellow green or gray green.

Distinctive Behavior: When a male cabbage white chases a disinterested female, she will start a spiral dance to get rid of him. The two circle each other as they fly up, then the female plummets down, leaving the male alone in the sky.

Habitat: Gardens, farm fields, pastures and meadows, cities, suburban and rural areas, foothills, roadsides and areas near streams.

Caterpillar: Bright green with a thin yellow line down its back and yellow dashes on the body. Larvae are covered in short soft hairs that look fuzzy.

Host Plants: Eats cabbage, broccoli, collards, radishes, nasturtiums, pepper grass and mustard plants.

■ Range

brown chrysalides.

Caterpillars living in the South transform into butterflies in just a few weeks because the weather is warm enough for both the adults and the larvae to be active all year long.

In the North, caterpillars remain in the chrysalis and hibernate during the colder winter months. A few months later, they emerge as adults in early spring, ready to fly and continue their amazing cycle of life.

Majestic beauty reigns the garden.

MONARCH

Ask almost anyone to name a butterfly they know, and chances are, "monarch" will be the response you hear most often. It's no wonder—these distinctive fliers are found almost everywhere!

Ranging from southern Canada to the mountains of central Mexico, from California to the East Coast, and all points in between, the monarch is as abundant as is it widespread. And the flier's large size and striking orange-and-black wings make it easy to spot.

The monarch is a year-round resident in southern California, southern Florida and Hawaii, but it isn't a permanent fixture in colder climates, thanks to its preference for temperatures above 60°. Monarchs living in northern areas head to the far South, Southwest or Mexico as soon as chilly weather begins to set in.

In fact, monarchs are the only butterflies that regularly migrate from north to south as birds do. You might see thousands of them roosting in trees during fall as they make their way to warmer locales for the winter.

Pacific Grove, California plays host to countless numbers of the species, earning it the nickname "Butterfly Town, USA." Florida, Texas and Mexico are also destinations for these kings of the road. (For more on monarch migration, see pages 178-179.)

Flight of Fancy

Watching a monarch fly is a real treat—whether it's hurriedly zipping by or leisurely gliding along, occasionally stopping to sip nectar from aster, verbena, ironweed, sedum, zinnia and butterfly bush flowers. The butterfly is quite approachable, so it's easy to get close and observe its behavior.

Monarchs are commonly found in city and suburban gardens, as well as open prairies, weedy fields, pastures, roadsides, rugged foothills and marshes. If you want to attract some to your yard, install a butterfly feeder filled with sugar water or plant the flowers they prefer—and be sure to add several milkweed plants also.

Why milkweed? Because this regal butterfly is a member of the milkweed butterfly family, a clan that lays eggs on milkweed plants.

READER TIP

To attract this beauty to your yard, install a butterfly feeder with sugar water or plant nectar-filled flowers. And don't forget the milkweed!

Richard Shiell/Dembinsky Photo Assoc.

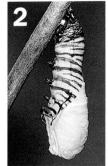

Metamorphosis photos: Richard Day/Daybreak Imagery

AN AMAZING PROCESS. The metamorphosis of a monarch from caterpillar to adult butterfly is a remarkable process to witness. First, the caterpillar hangs upside down in the shape of a 'J' (1) until it slowly sheds its skin (2) to enter the chrysalis stage. Within an hour, the soft casing hardens to form a protective shell (3). Nine to 14 days later, the chrysalis becomes clear and splits open so the adult can emerge (4). After allowing its wings to dry (5), the monarch is ready to take flight.

The plants serve as the major food for monarch caterpillars, with an important added benefit—the poison found in milkweeds provides a lifetime of protection from predators. As the caterpillars munch on milkweeds, they store the plants' toxins in their bodies, transferring the noxious chemicals into the butterflies they become.

Visual Clues

The adult monarchs' vivid wing markings serve as a warning to birds and other predators. Inexperienced hunters that decide to eat one quickly learn that these beauties don't make a tasty meal!

The message a monarch's wings send is so effective that the viceroy species of butterfly mimics its markings as a defense mechanism.

Monarch caterpillars are as stunning as their parents, with bold yellow and black stripes covering their plump white bodies and two antennae-like filaments crowning each end. They grow to about 2 inches long.

When it's time to begin the transformation, each caterpillar forms a delicate-looking jade green chrysalis that becomes increasingly transparent. (See photo series above right.) After 2 weeks, a butterfly emerges...and the cycle of life continues.

Flying Flower Facts

Common Name: Monarch.
Scientific Name: *Danaus plexippus*.
Family: Milkweed.
Wingspan: 3-1/2 to 4 inches.
Distinctive Markings: Bright orange with multiple black veins. Wings are edged in black with white speckles.
Distinctive Behavior: Caterpillars dine on milkweed plants. Adult butterflies migrate north and south.
Habitat: Widespread during migration, from cities to suburban gardens to rural fields and mountain pastures. When breeding (before the southward migration), they prefer open areas with plenty of milkweed plants.

Summer
Year-Round

Caterpillar: White with yellow and black stripes, measuring up to 2 inches long.
Host Plant: Milkweed.

MYSTERIOUS MONARCHS

This butterfly's migration is nothing short of amazing.

By Tom Allen, Contributing Editor

Many butterflies from around the world migrate each year, but no butterfly can match the incredible journey of the monarch.

In autumn, these regal butterflies travel up to 2,000 miles over 2 months. Those from east of the Rocky Mountains head to a 30-by-50-mile patch of forest in the mountains of south-central Mexico, and those west of the Rockies winter in southern California. The only exception is a nonmigratory population in southern Florida. There, monarchs continue to breed and produce caterpillars year-round.

Butterflies in "Training"

But monarchs just don't flap their wings and head south. With a cruising speed of 12 mph, they would be exhausted after a short journey if they didn't adequately prepare. In fact, many monarchs arrive in Mexico five times fatter than when they started in their summer range.

So how do they do it? First of all, it's important to know there are three to six generations of monarchs each year, and only one of those generations makes the preparations to migrate. The monarchs that emerge in spring and summer live only 4 to 5 weeks and simply produce the next generation.

Then, as autumn approaches, the butterflies sense the temperature change and shortening daylight. This signals the caterpillars that develop in fall to delay maturing into adults, al-

Robert E. Barber/Unicorn Stock Photos

THE AIR IS ALIVE. Monarchs gather by the hundreds of thousands in their mountain wintering sites (far left). To conserve energy, they cling to branches (left) and remain semi-dormant.

the next generation completes the journey back to their original summer range.

No Map, No Guide

One of the great mysteries of this journey is that no monarch making the trip has ever traveled the route before. How they know where to go and how to get there continues to baffle the scientific world.

Although they may not have understood it, this migratory phenomenon was well known to the regions' ancient cultures. Monarchs and other butterflies appear on pre-Columbian Meso-American Indian art and embroidery. Yet, the monarchs' wintering grounds were not discovered by modern scientists until the mid-1970s.

Mysterious as it may be, there are several theories about how and why the monarchs migrate.

One theory is that the monarch originally was a tropical species that followed its main food source, milkweed, as the plant became more common in the North after the last ice age. Unable to withstand cold winters, the butterfly would head south each winter and return north in spring.

There's a possible explanation for the location of their concentrated wintering sites as well.

While the butterflies can't withstand freezing temperatures, neither can they remain in warm climates where they would be active and deplete their stored fat reserves. This might also cause them to use up milkweed in an area, since the warm weather could trigger continued mating and egg laying.

That's why the temperate climate in their mountain roosting sites high in the Sierra Nevada range is perfect for them. The butterflies can remain semidormant for winter, living off their fat stores. Although the monarchs do not feed during hibernation, they do require moisture, which they get in the high-elevation coniferous forests.

A Delicate Balance

Due to the concentrated roosting sites, when local people began harvesting forest trees for timber, it placed the wintering monarchs in grave danger. Even removing a few trees changes the forest's critical temperature—making the nights frostier and the days warmer, which altered the environment the butterflies needed to hibernate.

A cry for help came from conservationists around the world and forced the Mexican government to take action. News quickly spread of the monarch's plight. Unfortunately, this attracted droves of visitors to the area, and thousands of butterflies that fell from the trees were trampled.

In recent years however, the Mexican government has taken steps to protect the monarch's wintering grounds. In 1986, the country established a preserve to protect the area. And slowly but surely, tourism and guided walks are replacing the need to harvest timber as a means of supporting the local economy.

With ongoing preservation and concern, the monarch will have a bright future...and continue to intrigue butterfly enthusiasts for a long time to come. ◄

lowing extra time to begin storing large fat reserves for the journey south.

When the newly hatched adult butterflies take flight in fall, they head for warmer areas as quickly as possible, feeding and storing fat as they go. They fly south by riding on wind and thermal currents, even if it is not a direct route.

As they get farther south, they become more selective and ride higher on the thermals to conserve energy. Once they reach Texas and the Gulf of Mexico, they begin a more direct route and fly closer to the ground, unless the winds are blowing in the right direction. While traveling across the Gulf, they rest on any structures they can find, such as oil rigs and ships.

When they arrive at their mountainous roosting sites in Mexico and California, the butterflies congregate in huge groups, numbering in the hundreds of thousands. The orange-and-black striped beauties often cover entire groves of trees—dangling from every branch and limb (see photo above). There, at elevations of 10,000 feet, they remain semidormant for the winter.

As winter ends, the butterflies increase their activity and fly farther and farther from the colony until they begin to return north. They then mate and lay their eggs along the route, and

QUEEN

It may look like a monarch, but this regal beauty is actually a cousin of that well-known flier. The queen butterfly bears monarch-like markings, including black veins and white spots along the edges of its wings and on its body. But this species is slightly smaller, with a wingspan of about 3-3/8 inches (compared to a monarch's 4-inch span), and noticeably different in color—it's more mahogany brown than orange.

The queen is no fan of cold temperatures and typically keeps to the southern United States from Nevada east to Missouri, southern Georgia and the Carolinas and south through Florida. It is a common sight in the Sonoran Desert in Arizona, California and Mexico, and can be found in South America, too.

The queen may also visit northern states like Massachusetts, Illinois or Idaho if the weather is unusually warm.

When in flight, queen butterflies take several strong wing flaps, followed by a leisurely glide. Look for them in open areas like brush-filled fields, grassy roadsides, prairies, meadows, deserts and open waterways.

Queens are only active when it's warm and sunny. On cool mornings, you might spot one basking in the sun to raise its body temperature and gain enough heat to fly.

Like monarchs, queens are milkweed butterflies, named for their preference for this plant. Females lay eggs *only* on milkweed, typically producing several broods from April to November.

The caterpillars that hatch sport bright bands of white, black and yellow, with three pairs of black "tentacles" (see bottom photo at right). They munch entirely on milkweed leaves, which provide both nutrition and protection in the form of a toxin that doesn't bother the caterpillars, but makes them taste terrible, even after they've become butterflies. Most birds and other predators simply leave queens and other milkweed butterflies alone.

Each caterpillar completes its metamorphosis inside a 1-inch-long, bright-green chrysalis suspended from a nearby leaf, stem or twig. The delicate, winged creature that emerges dines on the nectar of many plants, including milkweed, goldenrod, aster, daisy and thistle.

A HEALTHY DIET. Like its monarch cousin, the queen butterfly gets protection from toxins in the milkweed it eats. These butterflies are found in the southern United States.

Alan and Linda Detrick; insets from top: Richard Day/Daybreak Imagery; Tom Allen

Flying Flowers

American Snout

Distinctive butterfly will definitely catch your eye!

Michael Shedlock

Catch one glimpse of this butterfly as it perches on a plant, and you'll know how it got its name. The American snout's beaklike mouthparts, called "palpi," stick out a good 1/4 inch or so from its head and look like a long nose.

The palpi don't serve a specialized function for feeding or mating, but they create a visage that certainly sets this species apart from other butterflies!

A member of the large brush-footed clan, the American snout is also unusual because its direct family is the smallest in the butterfly world. There are only about 10 snout species in the world.

You might think the tiny size of the family indicates snouts are the new kids on the block, but that isn't the case. Fossil evidence suggests snouts have been around for quite a while—as long as 30 million years.

A Common Sight

Its family size notwithstanding, the American snout is widespread on our continent. It's found throughout much of the United States and Mexico, ranging from the desert Southwest to the temperate East Coast. It also makes appearances as far north as southern Ontario and as far south as Argentina.

In addition to prominent palpi, this butterfly also sports distinctively shaped and colored wings. The tips of the forewings are quite square, while the bottom edges are nicely scalloped. The top sides of the wings are a mellow brown, with rich, orange-red patches near the body and splashes of white closer to the wing edges. Wingspans range from 1-3/8 inches to 2 inches.

The wings' undersides are mottled or a smooth purplish gray, which provides clever camouflage. When the snout sits on a branch with its wings folded up and holds its long antennae and palpi downward to resemble a stem, it looks just like an unappetizing dead leaf—a good defense against any potential predators.

On the Move

Adult American snouts overwinter in the southern portions of their range and undergo impressive migrations in places like Texas and Arizona.

These fliers prefer brushy fields, river edges, canyons, mountains, forest clearings and roadsides. However, they'll also show up in gardens, especially those with asters, zinnias, dogwoods, lantanas and butterfly bushes.

The American snout also makes regular appearances at mud puddles and can sometimes be spotted basking in the sun with wings outspread. If you have a hackberry tree or two on your property, you're almost guaranteed to see this species, because the hackberry is the American snout's only host plant.

Males hang around hackberries looking for females. After mating, the females lay small groups of green eggs on the tree's leaves.

The eggs hatch into caterpillars with a bright-yellow stripe racing down either side of their bodies and a swollen thorax near their head, similar to those found on swallowtail caterpillars.

American snout caterpillars feast on hackberry leaves until they are large enough to transform. Then they construct an angular, bright-green chrysalis that hangs from a silk mat attached to a hackberry leaf or branch.

After several days in this form, the adult butterfly emerges, snout and all, and the cycle of life continues. ◀

David Liebman

ABOUT THE SNOUT. This butterfly's beaklike mouth really stands out, either in a profile (opposite), or when the butterfly rests with wings outstretched (right). The caterpillar (inset) sports a yellow stripe on both sides of its body.

Flying Flower Facts

Common Names: American snout, southern snout.
Scientific Name: *Libytheana carinenta.*
Family: Brush-footed.
Wingspan: 1-3/8 to 2 inches.
Distinctive Markings: Brown topwings with tawny orange patches and white spots. Undersides are mottled or solid violet gray. Prominent mouthparts are visible when the butterfly is perched.
Distinctive Behavior: Often seen visiting mud puddles or sitting on garden plants, this butterfly likes to open its wings and soak up the sun. It also migrates in large numbers.
Habitat: Brush-filled fields, thorny scrub, forest edges, wooded swamps, river edges, canyons, and desert mountains and washes.

■ Range

Caterpillar: Dark green with yellow stripes and a pale underside, with a spiny hump near the head.
Host Plant: Hackberry trees.

Ann and Rob Simpson

WHITE PEACOCK

With a name like "peacock," you expect to see something pretty flashy—and the white peacock butterfly definitely delivers!

From its large, silvery-white wings outlined in orange to the intricate pattern of brown and orange scrawls—and small, black eyespots that highlight them—this butterfly is a standout beauty.

A member of the brush-footed family, the white peacock is a close relative of the buckeye butterfly. It is fairly small, with a wingspan of about 2-3/8 inches.

While it prefers the humid climates of southern Florida and Texas, it sometimes shows up in surprising locales. These butterflies have wandered as far north as Missouri and Kansas, North Carolina and even Massachusetts.

However, the white peacock isn't very hardy, so it tends to stick close to the Deep South and other balmy areas. The butterflies can also be found in the tropics of Central and South America.

One behavior that makes this butterfly unique is that it's active year-round, due to the warm climates, rather than finding a protective spot to overwinter as a caterpillar or chrysalis like many other butterfly species do.

Look for this fanciful flier in swampy spots, along shorelines and near water, in weedy fields and in places where the ground has been disturbed. Pay close attention to flowers like bacopa and verbenas, too. The butterflies prefer the nectar these blooms produce.

Don't expect a white peacock to perch on you, though. This beauty is people-shy. It isn't a strong flier and often flies in a low and erratic manner.

Females lay pale-yellow eggs on water hyssop and ruellia leaves. The eggs hatch into spiny black caterpillars with silver spots that avidly feed on their host plants.

Each caterpillar (right inset) forms a smooth, green chrysalis that darkens with age...until the graceful fair-winged beauty emerges. ✒

Mourning Cloak

Age is an asset to this unique butterfly.

Francis and Janice Bergquist

On the surface, the mourning cloak is anything but subtle. Its velvety, reddish-brown wings, measuring about 3 inches across, are banded in soft yellow and highlighted with a row of brilliant-blue dots. But that's just the view from above.

The undersides of the wings bear more modest markings—and for good reason. The ashy-brown striations accented with faint-blue dashes and a dirty-yellow border closely resemble tree bark. In fact, when a mourning cloak is perched on a branch or a trunk with its wings folded up, it becomes almost invisible.

This disguise, called cryptic camouflage or cryptic coloration, allows it to avoid the attention of hungry predators—or the curiosity of inquisitive humans.

The mourning cloak hasn't cornered the market on this defense mechanism, however. In fact, it belongs to a group of butterflies, the tortoiseshells and anglewings. These unique fliers are known for this type of camouflage.

The tortoiseshell family shares other characteristics as well, including jagged-edged wings with colorful tops. However, the mourning cloak is by far the most noticeable member of the group.

Name Game

As for its unusual moniker, the butterfly earned it during the 1800s. Victorian butterfly enthusiasts decided that the mourning cloak's dark wings with light edges resembled a long, black dress—typically worn by a grieving widow—with a light petticoat peeking out beneath the hem of the skirt.

Although imposing that image on a butterfly might be a bit of a stretch by today's standards, the end result is a truly unforgettable name.

The mourning cloak is distinctive for another reason, too. If a bird or other predator startles one while it's at rest, the butterfly emits an audible snapping sound when it bursts into flight. This behavior will surprise the hunter, giving the flier enough time to avoid becoming a meal.

Male mourning cloaks are very territorial and will vigorously defend a large area. They flit from perch to perch as if on patrol and will chase almost any intruder, even if it happens to be a bird.

Quite a Survivor

In a way, you could say that time is on the mourning cloak's side. Unlike other butterflies that live for maybe a month or two, this one can live as long as 10 to 11 months, making it the longest-lived butterfly species around.

Found in open forests, meadows, gardens and parks across most of North America, the mourning cloak is also one of the first butterflies to appear each spring. After hibernating under loose bark, fallen branches or in some other sheltered spot, it emerges on warm days to bask in the sun with outstretched wings. If temperatures drop, it simply finds another hiding spot and waits for the mercury to rise again.

So what does a mourning cloak do for food if it appears before the flowers are even in bloom? Rather than relying on nectar, it eats tree sap. It also dines on the juice of rotting fruit.

Adult females lay clusters of pale eggs in spring on or near elms, willows, hackberries, poplars and other deciduous trees that serve as hosts to the caterpillars. The caterpillars themselves are quite eye-catching with white speckles on their black bodies, rust-colored legs, a row of crimson spots along their back along with several rows of black bristles.

They tend to feed together and can munch a lot of leaves on their host plants, even to the point of stripping entire branches, but they don't do irreparable damage. Then each caterpillar forms a spiny chrysalis that ranges from light tan to blue black as the captivating butterflies prepare to emerge again.

FUN IN THE SUN. Mourning cloaks often sunbathe on warm days. This flier is the longest-lived species around, living up to 11 months. It hibernates over winter, lays its eggs in spring and then the colorful caterpillars will form spiny chrysalides.

Flying Flower Facts

Francis and Janice Bergquist

Common Name: Mourning cloak.

Scientific Name: *Nymphalis antiopa.*

Family: Brush-footed.

Wingspan: 2-7/8 to 3-3/8 inches.

Distinctive Markings: Dark maroonish or purplish brown outlined with creamy-yellow borders and bright-blue dots on top. Undersides are striated, blackish brown with subtle blue marks and a dingy-yellow border.

Distinctive Behavior: Adult males are particularly territorial and will chase away trespassers, including birds. If startled, males and females make a distinctive clicking sound as they take flight.

Habitat: Open woodlands, parks, backyard gardens, forest edges and near waterways.

Caterpillar: About 2 inches long. Body is black with white speckles, a row of red spots along their back and several rows of black bristles. Legs are rust colored.

Host Plants: Deciduous trees including elm, willow, birch, hackberry and poplar.

■ Range

BUTTERFLY BIT

This butterfly hibernates over winter, so during this time, try looking for it under loose bark, fallen branches or another sheltered spots.

Rick Poley

Larry Ditto/KAC Productions

These distinctive fliers show their stripes.

ZEBRA LONGWING

Tom Allen

Kevin Barry

The zebra longwing's bold stripes and black wings make it stand out. On opposite page, a longwing feeds on firebush flower while a trio of zebra longwings gathers on a red penta plant. On this page at far left, a curled chrysalis clings to a stem before an adult butterfly emerges to dry its wings (left).

There's no question how this striking beauty got its name. The pale-yellow, zebra-like stripes on its wings are impossible to miss. The butterfly's long, narrow wings, measuring about 3-1/2 inches across, are distinctive as well.

This year-round resident of southern Texas and Florida frequents forest edges, thickets and flower gardens. If you vacation at Walt Disney World in Orlando, Florida, you might notice longwings gracefully flitting among the flowers there. What's more, these butterflies are easy to observe, since they fly slowly and don't easily startle.

Zebra longwings will venture north during the summer months to places like Georgia, South Carolina, Nebraska and Colorado and, on rare occasions, southern California.

Many butterfly houses at public gardens, museums and zoos also include the attractive zebra longwing in their collections. So no matter where you live, chances are you don't have to travel far to see one.

Time Is on Their Side

In addition to their attractive coloration, these fliers exhibit a number of other noteworthy traits. For instance, they return to the same spot each night to roost in clusters for protection. And unlike many species that survive only a few weeks, adult zebra longwings have life spans as long as 3 months.

There are a few good reasons zebra longwings are so long-lived. First, they rely solely on native passionflowers as host plants for their offspring. Since they are closely tied to their host plant, they usually don't stray far from them.

Also, females lay only a few eggs per passionflower, and may lay far fewer eggs each day than many other butterfly species. Female longwings definitely need to survive longer to deposit the 1,000 or so eggs they produce during their lifetimes.

Why don't females lay more eggs on each host plant? For one thing, zebra longwing caterpillars are very hungry after they hatch and will compete for the few leaves available on the vine. Spreading them out increases their chances of becoming butterflies and reduces predation on the caterpillars and eggs.

The passionflower isn't the most hospitable home either. The plant's nectar attracts ants and parasitic wasps, both of which will eat longwing eggs and caterpillars. To protect her eggs, the female tries to lay them on the growing tips of the passionflower vine, a spot that has little nectar and few predators.

Flying Flower Facts

Common Name: Zebra longwing.
Scientific Name: *Heliconius charitonius*.
Family: Brushfoots.
Wingspan: 2-1/2 to 3-5/8 inches.
Distinctive Markings: Long narrow wings are black with yellow stripes. Undersides have crimson dots at the base of the wings.
Distinctive Behavior: Zebra longwings are one of only a few butterfly species known to eat pollen in addition to nectar. Pollen gives them protein and provides energy.
Habitat: Forest edges, woodlands and flower gardens.
Caterpillar: Bluish to white with a white head and six rows of black branched spines on its body. Grows about 1-5/8 inches long.
Host Plant: Native passionflowers.

Summer
Year-Round

Rick Poley

A BLACK-AND-WHITE BEAUTY. The zebra longwing caterpillar's white body is marked with rows of black branched spines. This one (right) is feeding on a native passionflower.

Eye-Catching Caterpillars

Just like its parents, the zebra longwing caterpillar is distinctive in appearance, with a white body and multiple rows of black spines. It spends its time munching on the leaves of the passionflower vine where it hatched, absorbing the toxin these tropical bloomers contain.

Although this toxin doesn't harm the caterpillars, it does make them unpalatable, even into adulthood. In fact, the butterflies' bright stripes serve as a warning for predators to stay away.

Eventually, each caterpillar forms a spiny mottled chrysalis with metallic spots on the sides, and attaches it to the underside of a passionflower leaf with silken strings. Ten to 14 days later, the chrysalis becomes transparent, splits open and an adult butterfly emerges. Once its wings are dry, the zebra longwing is ready to fly—attracting attention wherever it goes.

Paul Rezendes

Common Buckeye

This multicolored flier is quite an eyeful.

If you glance at a sunny spot on the side of the road and see a pair of eyes staring back at you, don't be startled. It's likely one of North America's most distinctive butterflies, the common buckeye.

Known for the striking eyespots that accent both sides of its orange-banded, brown wings, this creature really makes an impression. The dark circles are edged in yellow and black with shimmery blue or light-purple centers.

These spots aren't just pretty accents, though. They provide the butterfly with clever camouflage. When birds

Richard Day/Daybreak Imagery

David Liebman

and other predators see those eyelike spots, they're often fooled into thinking they're looking at a much bigger animal...maybe one that would like to make a meal out of them.

And if that's not enough to keep the buckeye safe, its rapid, erratic flight patterns do the trick. This strong flier tends to move in a speedy, zigzag fashion, making it hard to see or follow.

Well-Traveled

The butterfly can claim most of the U.S. and parts of southern Ontario as its home turf, with the exception of the Rocky Mountains and the state of Washington. However, this sun lover can't withstand cold temperatures, so they frequent northern areas only on a seasonal basis.

The onset of fall prompts this beauty to fly south in magnificent masses. Coastal areas tend to see the biggest migrations, with numbers rivaling that of the buckeye's well-known cousin, the monarch. Cape May, New Jersey, located on the Atlantic Ocean, is a prime spot to witness swarms of buckeyes on the move each autumn.

In summer, look for this flying flower in bright, open spaces with low-growing vegetation, from sun-drenched gardens to treeless fields, meadows, shorelines, railroad embankments and swamp edges.

And watch your step if you walk along dirt roads. Male buckeyes often stake out such places, perching right on the road to wait for a potential mate to wander by.

If the weather turns cool, you might spot a buckeye basking in the sun to warm its wings. Hot temperatures, on the other hand, cause it to fold its wings.

Plant a Buckeye Buffet

To attract the common buckeye to your garden, cultivate a variety of flowers that will provide a constant source of nectar for the hungry creatures. Some of the buckeye's favorite blooms include zinnias, verbenas, goldenrod, anise hyssop, asters and tickseed sunflowers. A patch of bare earth will also draw in the butterfly.

Snapdragons, stonecrop and plantain—a common lawn weed—are the preferred host plants for the butterfly's offspring. Almost as eye-catching as its parents, the buckeye caterpillar sports a dark-green or off-black body embellished with yellow and orange dashes and rows of intimidating, black bristles edged with bright blue.

The only time a common buckeye isn't a standout is

Flying Flower Facts

Common Name: Common buckeye.

Scientific Name: *Junonia coenia*.

Family: Brush-footed.

Wingspan: 2 to 2-1/2 inches.

Distinctive Markings: Warm, brown wings with bright-orange forewing bars and large, black eyespots rimmed in yellow with iridescent blue or lilac centers.

Distinctive Behavior: Males often perch on patches of bare earth or dirt roads to bask or look for potential mates. Both males and females fly quickly in a zigzag fashion. In fall, buckeyes migrate south in large numbers, particularly along the East Coast.

Habitat: Open, sunny areas including fields, dunes, roadsides, shorelines, meadows, railroad embankments and swamp edges.

Caterpillar: About 1-1/4 inches long. Dark green to off-black with yellow and orange markings and bristly, black spines edged with bright blue.

Host Plants: Stonecrop, plantain, figwort, snapdragon, clover, false foxglove and gerardia.

■ Range

Field Notes: The striking eyespots of a common buckeye aren't mere decorations—they are clever camouflage, tricking predators into thinking it's a larger animal. Even the caterpillars have intimidating black spikes (above left).

when it forms its chrysalis, which is dull tan or brown with white flecks. Of course, what emerges puts on quite a show!

Even though it's a member of the brush-footed family and can count such illustrious fliers as the great spangled fritillary, red admiral and painted lady as relatives, the buckeye's appearance is different from the rest of its clan.

Two other buckeyes make their home in the deep south of Florida and Texas—the mangrove buckeye and the tropical buckeye. Both resemble the common species, with slight differences. The tropical species is a little darker overall with less pronounced eyespots, and the mangrove buckeye has an orange hue to its wings.

BUTTERFLY BIT

It's difficult to admire this interesting flier while in flight. It has a speedy, zigzag flight pattern that is hard to follow. Wait for it to land so you can get a good look.

PAINTED LADY

A s ornate and colorful as the Victorian-style home that shares its name, the painted lady butterfly makes a grand impression everywhere it appears. And this beauty, also known as the "cosmopolite," gets around. It's the most widespread butterfly in the world!

The painted lady can be found on every continent except Antarctica and Australia. A permanent resident of the Sonoran deserts in Mexico and the southwestern U.S., this flier travels northward during March and April, either in scattered numbers or impressive swarms. It permeates the countryside from coast to coast and moves well into Canada until the first hard frost, usually in October.

Unable to survive freezing temperatures, its annual trek is one way. However, the painted lady's prevalence in all parts of the country during warm weather virtually ensures anyone the chance to see this well-traveled creature.

The painted lady isn't too hard to pick out of a crowd. Its recognizable wings are highly patterned and measure 2 to 2-1/2 inches across. On top, they are salmon orange with striking black and white markings (left). The hue is pinker underneath (top inset), where the wings are covered in an elaborately colored web with a row of four to five small bluish eyespots.

It looks very similar to the less common American lady butterfly (sometimes called the American painted lady), which has two large eyespots on its underwings.

At home in any open landscape, this butterfly is as likely to grace an alpine meadow as it is to flit about a coastal garden or an urban park. You might spot it feeding on thistles, asters, sunflowers, zinnias, mallows and various legumes.

When it comes to selecting a host plant for its eggs, the female painted lady most often chooses a thistle or a related plant. The caterpillars (lower inset) that hatch are eye-catching and measure about 1-1/4 inches in length.

These larvae are dark colored with a yellow stripe, and all have short white or gray spines. The lavender-brown chrysalis each caterpillar forms is bumpy and measures just less than 1 inch.

There often are two broods of these butterflies each summer, assuring plenty of painted ladies for all to admire. ◄

SPLIT PERSONALITY. Although the painted lady displays showy colors on both side of its wings, the markings are so different that you may think they belong to two different butterflies.

White Admiral

White is only one of the colors that marks this flier's dramatic "uniform."

This beauty can really command attention. The white admiral's striking wings are hard to miss as it dances about tree-lined clearings or glides through a grove of hardwoods. These butterflies are black and white with flashes of blue and red on top, and with a collage of brick-red and blue marks against a reddish-brown background underneath.

For predators, it's a different story. The pattern that catches the human eye is disruptive to birds and other hunters, making the flier's size and shape unclear, confusing and ultimately difficult to catch.

As eye-catching as it is, however, the design on the butterfly's wings didn't inspire its unusual name. Instead, naturalists on this side of the Atlantic borrowed the moniker from a British butterfly called the "white admirable," which has a similar appearance.

Into the Woods

You might spot this butterfly in deciduous forests, especially stands of aspen and birch, as well as in clearings or along forest edges.

Watch for its distinctive flap-and-glide motion and its territorial behavior. The white admiral will dart out to chase away insects and other creatures that stray into its area.

Ray Herrick/Racinphoto.com

The butterfly also perches on leaves and twigs to rest or sample the honeydew produced by aphids.

Flower nectar is another food source, as are rotten fruit, dead animals, manure and tree sap. The white admiral's offspring also feed on a variety of trees, including the leaves of birch, willow, poplar, aspen or hawthorn.

Just like its parents, the caterpillar's appearance is remarkable. It's covered in mottled milky white, olive and greenish-yellow markings, and bears a pair of bristly horns on the large hump behind its head. In fact, the white admiral caterpillar looks exactly like the red-spotted purple, its close cousin.

These two butterflies actually are part of the same species, separated only by range. Where the two ranges overlap in the northern states, many red-spotted purples will be found with partial white bands on their wings.

The caterpillar will assume a variety of odd, lumpish positions when resting during the day, apparently to fool hungry birds into thinking that it is nothing more than a large bird dropping.

When fall rolls around, the caterpillar nibbles off the end of a leaf and curls the base to form a tube. Then it attaches the rolled-up leaf to a stem with silk before crawling inside and closing the opposite end.

Long Winter's Nap

This handy little bedroll, or hibernaculum, keeps the creature cozy all winter. Come spring, the caterpillar emerges from its leaf "sleeping bag" and begins to devour tender new growth on its host tree to complete its development.

By mid- to late spring, the caterpillar is ready to spin a chrysalis and complete its transformation into one of the most attractive butterflies around.

Flying Flower Facts

Common Name: White admiral.

Scientific Name: *Limentis arthemis*.

Family: Brush-footed.

Wingspan: 2-1/2 to 3-5/8 inches.

Distinctive Markings: Black topwings with distinctive white bands that run across the middle on both sides.

Distinctive Behavior: White admiral caterpillars wrap themselves in leaves and hibernate during the winter months in a half-developed state. White admiral butterflies tend to be territorial and will chase insects or other butterflies that fly into their territories.

Habitat: Areas with deciduous trees or mixed with evergreens, especially near forest edges and clearings.

Caterpillar:
Mottled off-white, olive and greenish-yellow body with a bristled hump behind its head.

Host Plants: A variety of hardwood trees and shrubs including birch, poplar, willow, black cherry and hawthorn.

Range

RED-SPOTTED
PURPLE

Here's a beautiful butterfly that's surely a colorful character. The red-spotted purple's wings are awash in several vibrant shades, making it one of the most attractive flying flowers in North America.

A member of the admiral family, this butterfly's distinctive hues vary depending on your point of view. When viewed from the underside (at left), its scalloped wings are brown with blue and white edges, and distinctive brick-red spots cluster around the border markings.

The view from above (see photo below) is surprisingly different. The topside wings are black with a brilliant-blue to blue-green iridescence most noticeable in bright sunlight. Spanning 3 to 4 inches, these lovely butterflies are hard to miss.

Their coloring isn't only beautiful, it helps them survive. That's because they look a lot like the foul-tasting pipevine swallowtail, which birds will not eat.

The red-spotted purple is most active from early spring to fall and shows up almost anywhere from southern New England to central Florida and west to Colorado, Nebraska and the Dakotas. It's also found in canyons and arroyos dotting the Southwest and northern Mexico.

Their caterpillars are mottled creamy gray with a pair of prominent brush-like bristles behind their head (below right). They'll eat the leaves of a number of host trees, including willows, poplars, aspens, apples, cherries and hawthorns. Adult butterflies are attracted to nectar, fruits and sap.

Red-spotted purples are seen in fields, forests and along shorelines, roads and paths. But keep your eyes open. They also feed in gardens with plenty of nectar-producing plants.

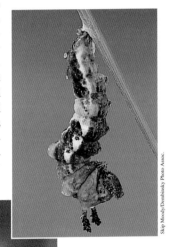

Skip Moody/Dembinsky Photo Assoc.

POINT OF VIEW. The red-spotted purple takes on different looks, depending on how it's perched. Its underside (far left) is brownish with red spots, while the top of its wings (left) are bright blue. Their caterpillars (above) are mottled gray.

Skip Moody/Dembinsky Photo Assoc.

Richard Day/Daybreak Imagery

197

Rob Curtis/The Image Finders

Cecropia

With its enormous wings, this
dramatic moth is hard to miss.

Charles W. Melton

If its sheer size doesn't grab your attention, the cecropia moth's arresting coloration certainly will. Markings on this flier's grayish-brown wings include eyelike spots, red and white bands, and a quartet of creamy crescents outlined in reddish orange. Even the moth's red-and-white striped body is interesting.

This lively combination of colors would stand out on the most diminutive specimen, but the cecropia is far from small. With a wingspan that can reach 6 inches, it's the largest moth in North America.

Still, the sizable cecropia often evades notice because it isn't active during the day. The cecropia is attracted to bright lights, however, and people often witness it at night, perched on surfaces next to a light.

Moth or Butterfly?

If you spot one of these beauties in your backyard, you'll likely notice several characteristics that help distinguish this moth, and others, from butterflies. These include large, feathery antennae—which are more noticeable on males—and a bulky, robust body.

An individual cecropia moth isn't around for long. It emerges from its cocoon when the weather gets warm, usually in late May or early June, and it lives for a brief week or two.

This member of the silk moth family, sometimes referred to as a robin moth, has no mouth and doesn't eat. Instead, it focuses its energy and attention on finding a mate, breeding and laying its eggs.

As soon as the female emerges from its pupa, it emits a powerful scent, called a pheromone. This is designed to attract a mate. Males are equipped with larger antennae that allow them to detect a female's pheromones up to 1 mile away.

Once a pair is established, they stay together for only a few hours. Then the female flies off to lay her eggs. She'll deposit them, as many as 100 at a time, on the foliage of the various host plants. These can include dogwood, box elder, sugar maple, birch, pear, cherry, plum and apple.

Hungry Caterpillars

In a week to 14 days, the eggs hatch and tiny mosquito-sized black caterpillars begin gobbling up everything they can find. These hearty eaters would decimate their host plants if it weren't for their many natural predators that keep their numbers under control.

The caterpillar's enormous appetite fuels its rapid growth, and it sheds its skin, or molts, several times before reaching maturity. Each time it molts, it changes color and eventually becomes a light-green hue dotted with a series of colorful spikes, or tubercles.

By late summer, the hefty green caterpillar (above right), now measuring an impressive 5 inches long, has eaten its

---

Flying Flower Facts

John Fowler/The Image Finders

Common Names: Cecropia moth or robin moth.

Scientific Name: *Hyalophora cecropia*.

Family: Silk moth.

Wingspan: 4-3/4 to 6 or more inches.

Distinctive Markings: Its grayish-brown wings are marked with dark eyespots and four pale crescents. It has a reddish-brown and white striped body, and a white collar behind its head.

Distinctive Behavior: Adults are active mainly at night and only live for 1 to 2 weeks. After females emerge from their cocoons, they emit a powerful pheromone that can attract males up to 1 mile away.

Habitat: Forests, gardens and open areas.

Caterpillar: The larva molts several times, changing colors from black to light green with red, yellow and blue spikes, or tubercles, before it is ready to spin a cocoon. At maturity, it measures up to 5 inches long.

■ Range

Host Plants: Dogwood, alder, birch, sugar maple, box elder, pear, plum, cherry, apple.

---

fill and is ready to settle in for the winter. It spins a large, weather-resistant brown silk cocoon attached to a branch or tree trunk. This cocoon is tough enough to withstand subzero temperatures. Once spring arrives, a striking adult cecropia emerges and flies off to continue the cycle of life.

BUTTERFLY BIT

Welcome the largest moth in North America to your backyard by offering one of its favorite nighttime attractions—bright lights.

LUNA MOTH

These elegant creatures shine in the moonlight.

Nancy Rotenberg

You won't find this beautiful "flying flower" basking in the sun—it's nocturnal by nature. In fact, its name, luna, is Latin for "moon."

This spectacular creature has lovely pale-green wings that can measure more than 4 inches across, making it hard to miss, even in the moonlight. It gets its name from the fact that it's active at night, like most moths, but also because of the silvery, crescent moon-shaped eyespots on its wings.

Those eyespots aren't for decoration, however. They serve as a protective disguise, fooling predators into thinking it's a much larger animal.

If the eyespots don't dupe an animal on the prowl, the luna relies on another trick. Its head is so well covered by its wings that hunters often misjudge their target and go after the long curving tails on the luna's hind wings instead. This gives the moth a chance to escape.

Widespread Beauties

Its large wings make the luna a strong flier, and this species is quite common throughout its range in the eastern United States and southern Canada. It's attracted to bright light, so it isn't unusual to see one resting on the side of house or a tree.

Readers Robin and David Byard of Somerset, Pennsylvania recall the luna that perched on a hanging basket of flowers in their yard.

"I awoke one morning in May to find this beautiful moth clinging to the basket," Robin says. "It remained there for 2 days before flying off."

Nancy Rotenberg

GET A GOOD LOOK. The feathery antennae and stout body of this luna (left) help observers distinguish it from butterflies. Below, lunas perch with their wings open, often near a bright light at night.

Many people who spot a luna erroneously believe it's a butterfly instead of a moth. Although moths tend to have duller wing colors than butterflies, that's certainly not the case with the luna.

The best way to separate moths from butterflies is to examine their antennae. Moths usually have feathery or filament-like antennae with fine tips, while butterfly antennae always end with a club or knob. Moths, especially the larger ones, also generally are more robust than butterflies.

Fly by Night

Like many large moths, the luna will only survive for a few days once it emerges from its cocoon as an adult. It will quickly attract a mate, then the female immediately begins laying eggs on the leaves of trees such as paper birch, sweet gum, hickory, walnut, persimmon and sumac.

The luna caterpillar is lime green with a thin, yellow line on each side and tiny orange spots. It has a hearty appetite and will grow to be about 3 inches long. It needs to store plenty of energy, because once it's a moth, it stops eating entirely. The adult luna doesn't even have a mouth.

The caterpillar eventually turns reddish before spinning a brown, papery cocoon, often among leaves on the ground below a tree.

In the northern parts of its range, luna moths typically emerge between May and July. In the South, there may be as many as three generations of these moths from March into September.

Flying Flower Facts

Common Name: Luna moth.
Scientific Name: *Actias luna*.
Family: Giant silkworm.
Wingspan: 3 to 4-1/2 inches.
Distinctive Markings: Pale-green wings with two sets of silvery eyespots. They have dark-colored margins along the front of their forewings and long tails on their hind wings.
Distinctive Behavior: Strong fliers that are attracted to light.
Habitat: In deciduous woodlands.
Caterpillar: Green with a yellow stripe down each side, tiny orange spots and hairs along back. Grows to be about 3 inches long.
Host Plants: A variety of deciduous trees, including paper birch, persimmon, sweet gum, hickory, walnut and sumac.

■ Year-Round

Sharon Cummings/Dembinsky Photo Assoc.

David Liebman

IN THE BEGINNING. The lime-green luna caterpillar (top) eats voraciously and grows to about 3 inches before spinning a papery cocoon (above) among leaves on the ground.

Nancy Rotenberg

VERY HUNGRY CATERPILLARS

You can't have your plants and butterflies, too... or can you?

By Gilbert S. Grant
Sneads Ferry, North Carolina

SOMEONE has been eating my garden!

Although I enjoy the beauty of a butterfly flitting among my flowers, I was still shocked to discover that a group of black swallowtail caterpillars had been munching away on my precious fennel and dill.

Of course, in order to have those adult jewels flying through the garden, we must welcome a few caterpillars as they dine on their host plants. These plants provide a place for the female butterflies to lay eggs, and then supply food for the growing caterpillars.

So my solution to that hungry group of black swallowtail caterpillars? Plant more fennel!

Now, I have enough plants for me and the caterpillars to enjoy. On occasion, I've noticed as many as 20 caterpillars eating the spread I have offered.

I applied this same lesson to the other common caterpillar plants in my yard.

For instance, in late summer, passionflower vines appear in some of my flower beds, and are soon visited by female gulf fritillaries and variegated fritillaries in search of a place to lay eggs. Since I have a lot of these vines, I don't mind when I see the colorful caterpillars (like the one top right) eating the leaves. Later, the butterflies (top far right) are a delight as they fly among the lantanas in late summer and early fall.

I've also noticed that another prevalent butterfly—the common buckeye—prefers my toadflax and snapdragons, so I added more plantings of those as well.

To be able to enjoy winged jewels like these, we must accept the damage the caterpillars sometimes cause. With extra plantings, we can enjoy both our flowers and the colorful *flying* flowers they attract.

WANT BUTTERFLIES? START AT THE BEGINNING

Attract "flying flowers" by selecting plants to feed caterpillars.

By Tom Allen, Contributing Editor

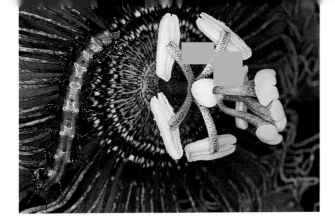

TIME TO DINE. Caterpillars (like the monarch, far left) see your garden as a big buffet. Select the right plants to attract certain species, like passionflower for gulf fritillary caterpillars (above left), which will transform into beautiful adults (above).

One of the best ways to attract butterflies is to fill your garden with plants for caterpillars to eat. You can even combine the plants into a butterfly and caterpillar garden.

You don't need to worry that the caterpillars will destroy all your plants. That's a common misconception.

Most garden butterfly species lay only one or two eggs on each host plant before moving on to look for another plant. As a result, the caterpillars don't appear in large enough numbers to cause great harm to any single plant. In addition, very few butterflies lay their eggs in clusters, as several moths are known to do.

In fact, moth caterpillars often are responsible for the plant damage gardeners find. While some moths can be a welcome backyard addition, such as the attractive hawk moths or Saturn moths, many can be quite destructive. A good example is the eastern tent caterpillar that appears in early spring and consumes cherry tree foliage to the very last leaf.

Be a Good Host

Knowing the proper host plants is the secret to attracting butterflies. A good place to start is with black swallowtails, a species found throughout much of the United States. This butterfly is easy to please and will feed on plants in the carrot family. While they especially like fennel, they will also lay their eggs on dill, carrots and parsley.

Plant a variety of these so the caterpillars spread around your garden, ensuring some survive potential predators to become adult butterflies. Plus, it leaves plants for you, too.

If you live in a warmer climate, try passionflowers to appeal to gulf fritillaries and zebra longwings. Use native plants if possible for these species, since the butterflies will not feed on some of the hybrid passionflowers. Two favored types are maypops and corky-stemmed passionflower, both native to the South.

Plant your passionflowers in sunlit areas to attract gulf fritillaries, or in the shade for zebra longwings. Add several along fences or on a trellis, and there will be enough to go around.

Variegated fritillaries also use passionflowers as a host, but they seek out flax, pansies and violets as well.

A Blooming Favorite

Violets are a popular host plant for many fritillary butterflies. In addition to the variegated species, violets will attract great spangled, Aphrodite and Atlantis fritillaries—all common in the eastern U.S.—as well as most of the western fritillaries (like the callipe, Mormon and zerene).

So no matter where you live, adding violets in shady garden spots (just don't let them invade your lawn) should catch the attention of members of this family. You may see the fritillaries in summer, but the caterpillars won't show up until the following spring.

There are many other common host plants you can add

16 Plants for Caterpillars

To attract butterflies, host plants are a good place to start. These plants provide a spot for butterflies to lay their eggs, and they also offer food for the caterpillars. Butterfly expert Tom Allen recommends the following "sweet 16" to attract some common species.

1. Aster—Pearl crescent
2. Everlasting—American lady (at right)
3. Carrot—Black swallowtail
4. Choke or black cherry—Tiger swallowtail
5. Dill—Black swallowtail
6. False nettle—Red admiral, eastern comma
7. Fennel—Black swallowtail
8. Flax—Variegated fritillary
9. Milkweed—Monarch
10. Pansy—Variegated fritillary
11. Parsley—Black swallowtail (at right)
12. Passionflower—Gulf fritillary, zebra longwing, variegated fritillary
13. Snapdragon—Common buckeye
14. Toadflax—Common buckeye
15. Violet—Most fritillaries
16. Willow—Viceroy, western tiger swallowtail, red-spotted purple, mourning cloak

Eastern *Comma*

Unique scallops punctuate the wings
of this small but strong butterfly.

Flying Flower Facts

Common Name: Eastern comma.

Scientific Name: *Polygonia comma.*

Family: Anglewings.

Wingspan: 1-3/4 to 2-1/2 inches.

Distinctive Markings: Brown-and black-spotted orange wings. Undersides of wings resemble bark or dried leaves. In the center of each wing's underside, there is a small silver or white comma, which gives the butterfly its name.

Distinctive Behavior: If challenged, the butterfly flies away to hide.

Habitat: Forest areas, tree-lined river and marshes.

Caterpillar: Varies in color from black to brown, yellow or cream with formidable white or yellow spines running the length of their bodies (above).

Host Plants: American elm, nettles and hops.

F rom the top, it's hard to miss this beauty with brown-and black-spotted orange wings. If the eastern comma is perched on a tree trunk with its wings folded up, however, you'll probably walk right by—the undersides of its wings resemble bark or dried leaves (above). They provide perfect camouflage for this forest dweller.

The undersides of this butterfly's wings are distinctive for another reason. Positioned in the center of each wing is a small silver or white comma, the marking that gives the butterfly its name. The angular, almost ragged looking edges of the wings also indicate that the eastern comma is a member of the anglewing family.

This butterfly is on the small side with a wingspan that ranges from 1-3/4 to 2-1/2 inches, but it is a strong flier. Like most anglewings, the eastern comma is wary, yet it will aggressively dart at other butterflies, insects, birds and even people that enter its territory.

If challenged, it retreats and alights upside down on a tree trunk to hide. Males also tend to sit on trunks or leaves to watch for females.

You won't see this butterfly flitting about flowers in search of nectar. Instead, it prefers to feast on rotting fruit and tree sap. Look for the eastern comma in moist forest areas, tree-lined rivers and marshes.

Unlike other members of its family that reside all across the country, the eastern comma mostly confines itself to the eastern half of the U.S. and southern portions of Canada. Its range extends from southern New Brunswick to Florida and as far west as eastern Texas, the Dakotas and southern Manitoba.

While eastern commas don't migrate, they do have a way to make it through winter. Those butterflies that develop in September or October seek shelter in logs or wrap themselves up in leaves and hibernate. These are referred to as the fall or winter form.

The fall form commas then emerge in spring and lay eggs until the end of April. The butterflies that come from these eggs are called summer form. They fly from May to September and produce the eggs that develop into fall form commas.

Eastern commas are picky about where they lay their eggs. Females will only choose the leaves and stems of certain host trees and plants, including American elm, nettles and hops.

The caterpillars vary in color from black to brown, yellow or cream with formidable white or yellow spines running the length of their bodies. They tend to feed at night and will form daytime shelters from leaves by fastening the edges together.

The chrysalis each one spins is brown with scattered gold or silver spots and is irregular in shape, giving it the appearance of a twig.

BUTTERFLY BIT

Eastern comma caterpillars are sometimes called "hop merchants" because they often munch on hops, one of their host plants.

BANDED HAIRSTREAK

Unlike other butterflies with striking colors or intricate patterns, the banded hairstreak is a study in subtle beauty.

Viewed from above, its small 1- to 1-1/2-inch-wide wings are a rich, sooty black. But that's a rare sight, since this species rests with its wings closed, displaying the more interesting undersides.

Even so, the patterns underneath are quite simple. They consist mainly of several rows of black dashes outlined in white, a small splash of orange along the bottom outer edge, and a patch of blue positioned above the thin white and black tail on each hind wing.

Another small, almost unnoticeable tail sits a bit above the longer one, usually in line with the smattering of orange.

The only distinction between males and females is the small oval area along the upper inside edge of the male's forewing, which the female lacks. Otherwise, they are almost identical.

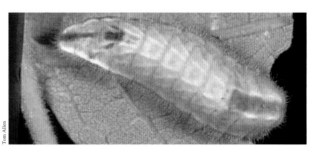

This quiet beauty prefers life among the trees.

Richard Day/Daybreak Imagery

Common Denominator

And speaking of similarities, several cousins so closely resemble the banded hairstreak, it can be challenging to tell them apart. These related butterflies include the striped, king's, hickory and Edward's hairstreaks.

You don't have to rely on wing coloration alone to pick a banded hairstreak out of the crowd, however. Sheer numbers are on its side, since it's the most common of the bunch, thanks to its widespread range and ability to adapt to a variety of habitats.

You'll find this flier from Nova Scotia and Maine to North Dakota and southeastern Saskatchewan, as far south as Texas and Florida, and just about all points in between. Chances are, if you think you've seen a banded hairstreak, you're right.

It also engages in hard-to-miss behavior. This territorial insect responds to every banded hairstreak that enters the area it calls home, and it will charge after the intruder in an effort to drive it away. Sometimes, as many as six may be spotted chasing each other.

Also, look for males perched during daylight hours on shrubs and tree branches located near the ground, where they have the best chance of finding a mate.

EYE OF THE BEHOLDER. Though subtle, this flying flower displays plenty of beauty. Clockwise from far left, the banded hairstreak rests its wings…two hairstreaks feed on butterfly weed …a pupa waits for spring…a caterpillar munches on a leaf.

Tom Allen

Into the Woods

The graceful creature prefers to flit about hickory, walnut or oak forests or hot oak-filled canyons in the westernmost reaches of its range. It will frequent forest edges and clearings, roadsides and city parks, too, as long as hickories, walnuts and oaks grow nearby.

The trees are important because they serve as hosts for banded hairstreak caterpillars. Adult females lay beige or pale-lavendar eggs on twigs during the summer, and the larvae hatch the following spring.

The caterpillars vary in color from brown to green or white, with dark blotches on the head and tail. Some even have yellow stripes along each side. They dine on spring growth, including catkins and leaves, before each forms a hairy, mottled, brownish-pink chrysalis that is tightly fastened to a leaf or twig with a sturdy silken string.

The butterflies emerge in late spring and early summer, and can be found sipping nectar from milkweed, dogbane, daisies, sumac, meadowsweet, white sweet clover and yarrow— when they aren't chasing each other, that is!

So if you live near the woods in southern Canada or the eastern U.S., keep your eyes peeled for this quiet beauty—and get ready to bask in its understated yet breathtaking glory.

Flying Flower Facts

Common Name: Banded hairstreak.
Scientific Name: *Satyrium calanus*.
Family: Gossamer wing.
Wingspan: 1 to 1-1/2 to inches.
Distinctive Markings: Undersides of wings have black dashes outlined in white, an orange patch toward the bottom and a blue area above a thin, black tail.
Distinctive Behavior: Adult butterflies are very territorial and will chase any newcomer. Males can be found during the day perched on low shrubs and tree branches, watching for females. It rests with wings in upright position.
Habitat: Deciduous forests containing oak, hickory or walnut trees, woodland clearings, roadsides and city parks.
Caterpillar: Yellowish-green or brown with dark blotches at either end. May have yellow stripes and dashes.
Host Plants: Oak, walnut and hickory trees.

Year-Round

Donna and Tom Krischan

Common Wood Nymph

This butterfly is a beguiling but elusive beauty.

Blessed with grace and subtle beauty, the common wood nymph certainly makes a lasting impression—if you manage to catch a glimpse of one. Its finely patterned markings and quiet coloration let this butterfly blend in to the open forests, meadows and waterways it calls home.

Even though its wings can span as much as 3 inches, the uneven brown and gray striated patterns on the undersides are easily hidden. The wings mimic tree bark, fallen leaves and brown grass so effectively, that when perched and holding still, the common wood nymph is all but invisible.

Only the dramatic eyespots—two large ones of the forewings and a series of smaller versions on the hind wings—stand out, but not enough to attract undue attention. Those eyespots serve as a defense. When a common wood nymph is spotted by a predator, they can frighten them away.

Variations on a Theme

Moreover, while this species is widely distributed across much of the U.S. and Canada, its coloring and size vary by region, which can be confusing when you're trying to identify one.

For instance, common wood nymphs that live in coastal and southern areas are typically larger, and they often sport splashes of yellow or pale orange toward the outside of their forewings. The smaller inland populations or subspecies tend to show little or no yellow patches.

So how do you know if you've seen a common wood nymph? Look for those large eyespots on the forewings—this species is the only member of the satyr family of butterflies that has two dominant spots in that position.

Its flight pattern is distinctive, too. Although it's not the speediest creature, the common wood nymph darts quickly and skillfully through tree branches and tall

Chapter 4

COLOR CODING. The common wood nymphs in southern areas are flashier, with yellow markings on their topwings (above). Those elsewhere are a more subdued brown (right).

grasses alike, weaving and dodging rather than flying in a straight line.

Just about anything sugary attracts this acrobatic butterfly, which readily sips nectar from garden flowers and indulges in tree sap. Those that live in the western plains prefer wild geranium, thistle and alfalfa nectar, while its eastern cousins prefer rotting fruit.

Picky Eater

Regardless of location, though, the common wood nymph caterpillar is a bit more selective about its supper.

Adult female butterflies lay round yellow or greenish eggs on or near tall grasses like purpletop in late spring or early summer, and the larvae that emerge then munch exclusively on these grasses.

Like the butterfly it will become, this caterpillar blends well with its environment. With a yellow-green hue and faint stripes that resemble grass, its only standout feature is a pair of reddish tails that punctuate the end of its body.

It really needs the added camouflage, too. Unlike other species that mature in a matter of weeks, the common wood nymph caterpillar will eat and grow over the course of several months before burrowing in clumps of grass and weathering through the winter. Those that hatch later in summer sometimes seek shelter immediately and only begin eating when springtime arrives.

The onset of warmer temperatures prompts fully developed caterpillars to form a plump, green chrysalis so they can transform into adults.

So keep your eyes peeled. This butterfly and its caterpillar may be common, but in light of such keen camouflage, glimpsing one takes uncommon dedication! ◄

Flying Flower Facts

Common Names: Common wood nymph, large wood nymph, blue-eyed grayling.
Scientific Name: *Cercyonis pegala.*
Family: Satyr and wood nymphs.
Wingspan: 1-7/8 to 3 inches.
Distinctive Markings: Common wood nymphs typically have light to dark cocoa wings on top with two large eyespots amid a splash of yellow or lighter brown on both the top and bottom sides of forewing. The lower part of each wing also bears one to three eyespots on top, and up to six eyespots underneath.
Distinctive Behavior: Both males and females will perch on tree trunks or boughs, where the busy brown patterns on their folded wings provide perfect camouflage.
Habitat: Open oak, pine and mixed woodlands, meadows, prairies, bogs, along slow rivers and streams with overhanging vegetation, thickets and grassy roadsides.
Caterpillar: Yellow-green and furry with alternating dark and light stripes running the length of its body.
Host Plants: Purpletop and other grasses.

■ Range

BUTTERFLY BIT

If you're looking for a common wood nymph caterpillar, be sure to look in the grass. It feeds exclusively on tall grasses, and almost looks like a piece of grass itself!

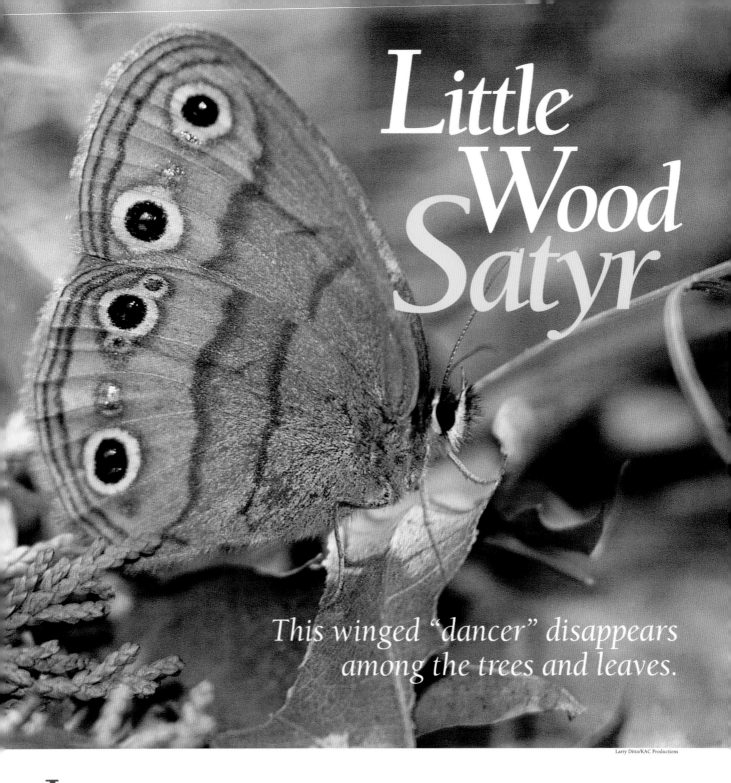

Little Wood Satyr

This winged "dancer" disappears among the trees and leaves.

Look along grassy, shrub-filled forest edges, and you'll likely see this enchanting flier pirouetting effortlessly above the greenery, casting its spell across the countryside.

When the little wood satyr waltzes into the woods, you'll be hard-pressed to find it again, thanks to the butterfly's unassuming complexion. Its drab brown wings act as an important disguise, helping it blend into the woodsy environment it frequents.

Unlike more colorful butterflies that dine on poisonous plants to make them inedible, the little wood satyr's diet of grasses and sedges offers no such protection. Instead, it has to depend on its surroundings and coloration to serve as camouflage.

If that doesn't work, the creature does have one other trick up its sleeve. Edging both sides of its wings are dark eyespots outlined in yellow. These marks aren't designed to frighten predators, though. They're meant to distract them.

Birds and other predators that catch sight of the butterfly try to bite these spots rather than aiming for the butterfly's body. A little wood satyr often survives such attacks, perhaps a little worse for wear, but still flight-worthy.

Aside from forests, this beauty can also be seen leisurely sashaying about meadows and clearings, or meandering

LOOK ONCE, LOOK TWICE. The little wood satyr caterpillar (above) and chrysalis (right) easily blend with their surroundings. Look closely at the the caterpillar to see the tiny projections over its body, making it appear fuzzy.

beside slow-moving streams in search of a mate or nectar.

Though this butterfly is small, as its name suggests, it's actually larger than most other satyrs, with a 1-7/8-inch wingspan. Since it's not a strong flier, the little wood satyr doesn't migrate, although it is common across more than half of the United States.

The grasses that offer this butterfly protection also serve as host plants for the little wood satyr's offspring. While females will lay pale, yellow-green eggs directly on blades of wild grass or sedges, they will also launch their eggs from the air. When the haphazardly scattered eggs hatch, the caterpillars then creep to those plants they can eat.

The brownish caterpillars that emerge resemble the grasses that house and feed them. They bear a single black stripe down their backs and patches of brown on their sides. Tiny white projections also cover them from head to tail, giving the larvae a soft, almost fuzzy, appearance.

About 4 weeks after hatching, each caterpillar forms a simple brown chrysalis. Then after about 2 weeks, the adult emerges.

In the northern portions of its range, the little wood satyr produces a single brood in a year. Those living in warmer southern regions create two, with the second one occurring as late as October.

So keep your eye out. You just might spot this beauty dancing among the trees and grass.

Flying Flower Facts

Common Name: Little wood satyr.

Scientific Name: *Megisto cymela*.

Family: Satyr.

Wingspan: 1-5/8 to 1-7/8 inches.

Distinctive Markings: A series of yellow-rimmed black or dark brown eyespots stand out against the overall drab brown coloring of the wings. Typically, two eyespots mark the tops of the forewing and each hind wing.

Distinctive Behavior: Slow, dance-like flight habits help the little wood satyr coast among tall grasses and dense shrubs, as well as stands of trees.

Habitat: Woods with open glades, thickets and meadows edging forests, clearings, grassy margins, slow-moving sections of streams and saltwater bays.

Caterpillar: Brownish with a dark stripe marking its back and brown patches trimming its sides. Tiny white tubercles, or projections, give the caterpillar a slightly fuzzy appearance.

■ Range

Host Plants: Various sedges and grasses, including orchard grass and species of bluegrass.

BUTTERFLY BIT

There's a reason this butterfly has the word "wood" in its name. Go for a stroll around the forests in your area, and you just might find this flier blending in with its background.

PIPEVINE
SWALLOWTAIL

At first glance, the pipevine swallowtail isn't as flashy as its swallowtail cousins.

But once the sun strikes those inky unmarked wings, watch out! This flier's plain appearance disappears in a burst of brilliant, iridescent blue with a smattering of white spots. The underwings, featuring orange and white spots atop shimmering sapphire markings, are more flamboyant without the help of sunlight.

The pipevine's appearance has little bearing on its name,

however. The moniker stems from the fact that its caterpillar's sole source of food is, naturally, the pipevine. And fittingly, it's the only kind of plant the adult female will use to lay her rust-colored eggs.

Aside from nutrition, these plants also offer something else—protection. Pipevines contain noxious chemicals that the caterpillar tolerates and stores in its body. If an animal eats the caterpillar or adult butterfly, the toxins will make it sick. Experienced predators know that the pipevine's markings

Mark Werner/The Image Finders

Two photos: Richard Day/Daybreak Imagery

A RED FLAG. The pipevine swallowtail's markings serve as a warning to predators that it contains toxins. Even the caterpillar (above) sports fleshy tubercles, which give it a formidable look.

indicate illness, and they stay away.

This defense mechanism is so effective, several other butterfly species mimic the adult pipevine's underwing markings. Female spicebush swallowtails, some female eastern tiger swallowtails, female eastern black swallowtails, female Diana fritillaries and red-spotted purples are among the copycats with similar wing markings.

The pipevine swallowtail caterpillar has another form of security. Its rusty-black body is studded with red or black fleshy tubercles, giving it a formidable appearance.

You'll likely see this graceful butterfly throughout most of the eastern U.S., north into southern Ontario and as far west as Arizona, California and Oregon, thanks to the spread of pipevine plants, which have become popular with gardeners.

Aside from flower beds, the pipevine swallowtail is a common sight in open woodlands, canyons, meadows, orchards and roadsides, and can be found throughout most of the eastern U.S., north into southern Ontario and as far west as Arizona, California and Oregon, thanks to the spread of pipevine plants.

Despite its size—this flying flower's wingspan can reach a huge 5 inches—it's speedy, moving with rapid and shallow wing beats. The pipevine also tends to flutter its wings while feeding, making it difficult to photograph.

READER TIP

This graceful flier prefers to sip nectar from plants like honeysuckle, orchid, butterfly bush, azalea, lilac, thistle and swamp milkweed. Its host plant is pipevine.

Eastern Black Swallowtail

This garden visitor makes a lasting impression.

By Kathleen Zimmer-Anderson
Waukesha, Wisconsin

"Look, Mommy—that butterfly is black!" I glanced up from the dandelion I was trying to destroy and saw my 7-year-old daughter pointing excitedly at the phlox-filled hanging basket on our front porch. Perched delicately amid the flowers was the darkest flier I'd ever seen.

While we watched in awe, the butterfly danced about the pot, barely holding its wings still as it drained nectar from the abundant clusters of blooms.

The few times it paused, I was able to glimpse more color on its wings. It had lines of yellow dots, a halo of bright blue and a pair of orange eyespots on the topside. Underneath, a riot of orange, yellow and blue markings dotted an inky background.

I didn't have much time to look at it, but it only took a second to realize its beauty. After I caught my glimpse, the dog barked, or the wind picked up—I'm not sure which—and the creature sped away.

Common Garden Guest

Our exotic-looking visitor was none other than the eastern black swallowtail, and like other members of its family, it bore distinctive tails on its hindwings.

While we'd never seen one before, I've since discovered that this butterfly is a familiar figure across much of the country—its name not withstanding. The creature's home turf runs from the East Coast as far west as the Rocky Mountains and from southern Canada to Mexico.

With such dramatic coloring and wings that measure as much as 3-1/2 inches across, the eastern black swallow-

tail is hard to miss in the gardens, fields, pastures, meadows and marshes it prefers. Aside from phlox, it enjoys nectar from milkweed, butterfly bush, butterfly weed, ironweed and zinnias.

Host plants for these brilliant butterflies include Queen Anne's lace and rue, as well as garden goodies like parsley, celery, carrots, fennel and dill. This preference for herbs and veggies leads some folks to consider its caterpillar a pest. And for good reason—the larvae frequently nibble away at these plants in the garden.

Eye-Catching Caterpillar

The eastern black swallowtail caterpillar is as hard to miss as its adult counterpart. Its chunky, lime-green body, which measures 2 inches long at maturity, sports striking black bands dotted with yellow or orange spots.

It also has a noticeable habit, although it isn't a very pleasant one. If you poke an eastern black swallowtail caterpillar gently behind its head, orange "horns" called osmeterium emerge and emit an odor that deters would-be predators.

The adult eastern black swallowtail has its own defense mechanism—but this one is easier on the senses, at least for humans. The butterfly mimics the coloration of the pipevine swallowtail, a poisonous cousin. This clever trait is often enough to trick hunters into leaving it alone.

The chrysalis formed by the caterpillar ranges in color from green to brown, depending on the time of year and where it is formed. Some of the offspring of the summer butterflies will overwinter in the chrysalis and wait to emerge the following spring when the weather warms again.

Flying Flower Facts

Common Name: Eastern black swallowtail.

Scientific Name: *Papilio asterius.*

Family: Swallowtail.

Wingspan: 3-1/2 inches.

Distinctive Markings: Jet-black topwings bear two rows of pale dots (females have cream-colored spots, while the male's are brighter yellow), as well as a pair of orange eyespots and blue dashes near the tails. The underwings feature splashes of color that stand out against the inky background. The flier's black abdomen is highlighted with lines of yellow dots.

Distinctive Behavior: Males and females are both strong, agile fliers, preferring to flit from flower to flower in a field or garden until disturbed, which causes them to zip away just a few feet above the ground.

Habitat: Open spaces, including gardens, farm fields, pastures and marshes.

Caterpillar: Measures 2 inches long when mature. Lime-green body with black bands and yellow or orange dots.

Host Plants: Queen Anne's lace, yarrow, parsley, celery, dill, fennel, carrots and rue.

■ **Range**

Olivia and I still talk about our encounter with that eastern black swallowtail, and can't wait to repeat it next summer. We'll be adding zinnias, phlox, dill and carrots to our garden in a few months to entice the fliers to visit more regularly. We may even see some caterpillars and get to witness their magical transformation into adults!

BUTTERFLY BIT

This flier is considered a mimic butterfly. Its only line of defense is to mimic the coloration of a poisonous butterfly, the pipevine swallowtail.

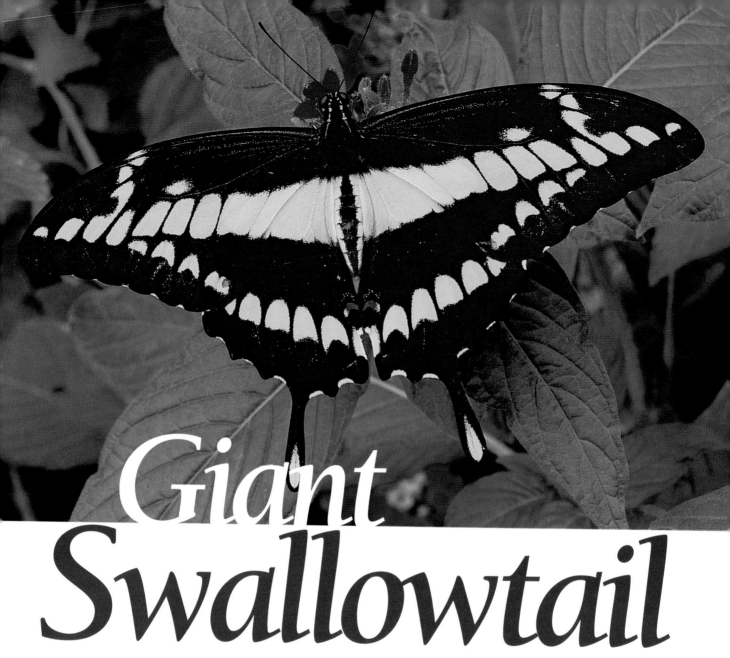

Giant Swallowtail

It's not just size that makes this beautiful butterfly impressive.

With wings that can measure as much as 6-1/4 inches across, this king of the sky certainly lives up to its name. The giant swallowtail is easily the largest butterfly of its kind in North America.

It doesn't hurt that the regal butterfly's wings are visually arresting, too. On top, they're a rich brownish-black, providing the perfect backdrop for a ribbon of brilliant yellow spots that run horizontally across the wings.

More yellow dots outline its wing edges, while a lone orange dot, topped with blue, marks the lower portion of each wing close to the body. Splotches of yellow highlight the tips of the large tails, making them look like spoons.

The undersides of the wings are just as fascinating. Primarily yellow—like the bottom portion of the butterfly's body—they're marked with black veins and a series of blue and orange dashes. Black scallops emphasize their edges.

Coasting Along

The giant swallowtail's flappers don't just look pretty, though. Thanks to their size, they can easily catch a breeze and carry the butterfly a good distance with little effort, resulting in a distinctive, almost leisurely flying style that consists of long glides interrupted by an occasional flutter.

A strong flier, the giant swallowtail is capable of traveling long distances. Although it is often considered a Southern species, it does pop up as far north as the eastern Rockies, the Midwest and southern Canada.

Look for the creature soaring along the edges of forests

and rivers, across sunny, open fields and near citrus groves and roads. The giant swallowtail will also appear in gardens, particularly those with lantana, yarrow, butterfly bush, honeysuckle, rue, milkweed and pentas (like the one perched below).

You might also spot a cluster of males perched near a mud puddle, delicately sipping water and nutrients. Otherwise, male giants are often actively searching for a mate.

Brilliant Disguise

After mating, an adult female will lay greenish eggs that turn yellow then orange as they develop. She lays the eggs on the tips of citrus leaves or the foliage of related host plants, including rue, hopwood and prickly ash. The markings on the larva that emerge from each egg provide a masterful means of disguise.

The giant swallowtail caterpillar's mottled brown body is splashed with cream and buff patches, creating a costume that closely resembles a large, fresh bird dropping. Its appearance is so unappetizing that most hungry creatures steer clear.

But if that doesn't deter a predator, the caterpillar has a backup line of defense. When threatened, it pushes a pair of red horns from its body that release a strong, unpleasant odor.

The critter loves to munch on orange, lemon and lime trees. Since several can do quite a bit of damage, citrus growers justifiably consider the giant swallowtail caterpillar a harmful pest and refer to it as an "orange dog."

Once the caterpillar reaches maturity, it forms a brown chrysalis on its host plant. A few weeks later, it emerges, and another giant makes its mark on the world.

Flying Flower Facts

Common Name: Giant swallowtail.

Scientific Name: *Papilio cresphontes*.

Family: Swallowtail.

Wingspan: 3-3/8 to 6-1/4 inches.

Distinctive Markings: Striking horizontal bands of yellow dashes divide dark wings on top. Additional yellow spots line the edges. The tops also bear an orange spot flanked by blue close to the body on each side. Large tails have yellow centers. Undersides of wings are mostly yellow with black veining and blue and orange spots.

Distinctive Behavior: Flight is slow and almost leisurely because the giant swallowtail prefers to glide for long stretches rather than flap its wings rapidly.

Habitat: Citrus groves, sunny open areas, forest edges, roads, rivers and glades. They will also visit gardens.

Caterpillar: Brown with mottled white patches over the middle and the rear. Markings resemble a fresh bird dropping. Measures almost 2-1/2 inches at maturity. When threatened, the caterpillar will produce a pair of red horns that emit a powerful, unpleasant scent.

■ Range

Host Plants: Citrus trees, prickly ash, hopwood and rue.

272

266

282

220

BLOOMING BEAUTY

255

Photo this page: hibiscus, Richard Shiell; opposite page, clockwise from top left: coreopsis, David Cavagnaro; coneflowers, K.B. Sau/itsaulplants.com; tulips, R. Todd Davis; mums, Alan and Linda Detrick

R. Todd Davis

Tulip

These vivid showstoppers chase away winter's chill.

Nothing heralds the change of seasons quite like tulips.

These graceful flowers are the best indicators that spring is in full swing, turning barren flower beds into lively islands of color and whispering the promise of even warmer weather yet to come.

It's no wonder winter-weary gardeners can't get enough of them!

Available in numerous sizes, bloom times and almost any color except true black and true blue, tulips are one of the most versatile bulbs in the world. That makes it easy to find a variety that suits your style—whether it's cottage-garden casual or strictly formal.

And these blooms have had plenty of practice adapting to different gardens. They've been brightening countrysides across the globe for thousands of years.

Deep Roots, Ageless Beauty

Archeological evidence indicates people cultivated tulips in Central Asia as early as 2200 B.C. European traders discovered them much later, at the end of the Middle Ages in the gardens of Turkish sultans.

Tulips—named after their likeness to the turbans (called tulibands) worn by Turkish men—arrived in Holland by the early 1600s and quickly became popular. By 1634, "Tulipmania" gripped the country, causing prices for unique bulbs to skyrocket.

It didn't take long for the market to crash and send the

country's economy reeling, but Dutch farmers eventually recovered, and Holland is known today as the top tulip grower, producing 90 percent of the tulip bulbs that are sold worldwide.

Dutch colonists introduced the blooms to the New World, where they became favorites from coast to coast. The number of modern tulip festivals in the U.S. and Canada, not to mention commercial tulip farmers, clearly indicates that enthusiasm for the blooms still runs strong.

Selecting the Best

Horticulturists have been hybridizing tulips for hundreds of years, giving gardeners an abundance of choices. But this incredible diversity can seem like too much of a good thing when you're faced with the prospect of making selections for your backyard.

You needn't feel overwhelmed, however. Tulips have been divided into different groups based on flower characteristics like size and shape, making the selection process relatively easy. Categories include:

Single Early tulips bear single, 3-inch-wide and cup-shaped blooms in colors ranging from white to dark purple. Contrasting colors often appear in streaks or flecks or

ONE FOR ALL. Nothing perks up a yard in spring quite like tulips. The array of colors and forms you can find is astounding. Some of the choices include, clockwise from top left: *Tulipa tarda*, a kind of species tulip…lily-flowered blooms…fringed tulips… and Green Wave, a unique multicolored parrot tulip.

line the edges of the petals. The plants grow between 6 and 8 inches tall and bloom from early to mid-spring.

Single Late tulips, as their name suggests, bloom toward the end of the season. Flowers are either cup- or goblet-shaped and range from 18 to 30 inches in height.

Fringed tulips produce single, cup-shaped flowers in white, yellow, pink, red or violet. Petal edges are fringed and often feature a contrasting color. These late-season bloomers grow 14 to 26 inches tall.

Double Early specimens feature double, bowl-shaped flowers that appear in mid-spring. Heights range from 10 to 12 inches and typically are dark red, yellow or white with contrasting margins.

Double Late tulips are known for their peony-like blossoms that measure up to 5 inches across. Some are solid, others feature contrasting flame-like colors.

Darwin Hybrids are great mid- to late-season choices,

Blooming Beauty

growing as tall as 32 inches in a range of bright hues, including pink, yellow, orange and red. The flowers may sport a second color, and the flower base typically contrasts with the rest of the bloom.

Lily-flowered varieties are slender, elegant flowers with petals that curl out when they bloom in late season.

Parrot tulips offer exotic bicolor blooms with fringed or twisted petals in late spring.

Botanical or Species tulips are smaller, wild varieties. They are long-lived and spread easily, making them a good choice for reliable blooms year after year.

With a little bit of planning—and all these choices—you can plant tulips that bloom at different times, ensuring that your garden will be awash in vivid color throughout the season.

Time to Chill Out

In cooler northern areas, gardeners plant tulip bulbs in fall, from the end of September up to the first hard frost. This allows the bulbs to establish themselves before winter's freezing temperatures. And enduring the cold is an important part of the process. Without it, tulips simply won't bloom.

So what do gardeners in warmer climates do? They must use artificial methods to chill the bulbs. Placing them in a refrigerator for 12 to 16 weeks before planting does the trick.

No matter where you live, you'll want to choose planting sites with rich, well-draining soil that will be sunny in springtime. Don't overlook areas under deciduous trees, however. Before the trees leaf out, the ground beneath them typically receives enough sunlight for tulips.

Pick only full, firm bulbs and plant them 6 to 8 inches deep and 6 to 9 inches apart. Make sure you set the bulbs in the holes with the root ends facing down (pointed end up). Otherwise, the sprout has to work harder to reach the surface. To maximize the impact of these beauties, plant large clusters of bulbs in beds and borders.

Once the planting's done, water the soil thoroughly and apply a standard bulb fertilizer. Continue to water whenever the ground feels crumbly. After the blooms have faded, let the leaves and stems turn yellow before you remove them—the foliage provides the bulbs with food that helps sustain the plants when they bloom again.

In the North, bulbs can stay in the ground from year to year. Adding mulch will help retain moisture and keep them cool over the summer. Enriching them with an annual dose of fertilizer is a good idea as well.

Southern summers, on the other hand, are too hot for tulip bulbs, so it's best to treat them as annuals and discard the bulbs after they've flowered, or dig them up and keep them cold in the fridge.

Hybrid tulips can be short-lived, blooming profusely for a few years, then fading away. Dig up those bulbs, divide any that have split and put them back in the ground.

Or start over with new ones, tossing in a few of the varieties that have been bred to thrive longer...then sit back and wait for these spectacular flowers to bring your garden back to life next spring.

Plant Profile

Alan and Linda Detrick

Common Name: Tulip.

Botanical Name: *Tulipa.*

Bloom Time: Early to late spring.

Hardiness: Blooms reliably in Zones 4-6. Gardeners in milder climates can force tulips to bloom by chilling the bulbs in the refrigerator or by buying precooled bulbs. Or, check for varieties suited to your region.

Flower Colors: Almost all colors are available except true black and true blue; includes many striped, streaked, blended and bicolor varieties.

Flower Shape: Most produce cup-shaped flowers, but some have goblet- or star-shaped blooms. Petals are rounded, pointed or fringed.

Height: 4 to 36 inches.

Spread: 6 to 8 inches.

Light Needs: Full sun.

Soil Type: Rich and well-draining.

Planting: Plant firm bulbs 6 inches deep (8 inches deep if your soil is well-draining), making sure the roots face down and the pointed ends face up. Space 6 to 9 inches apart, cover and then water thoroughly.

Special Care: Prevent hungry chipmunks and squirrels from eating bulbs by placing wire mesh or chicken wire on top of newly planted bulbs. After the blooms have faded, allow foliage to turn yellow before removing.

GREEN THUMB TIP

If you like variety, then this is a flower for you. Tulips come in just about every color imaginable. To maximize their impact, plant them in clusters and along borders.

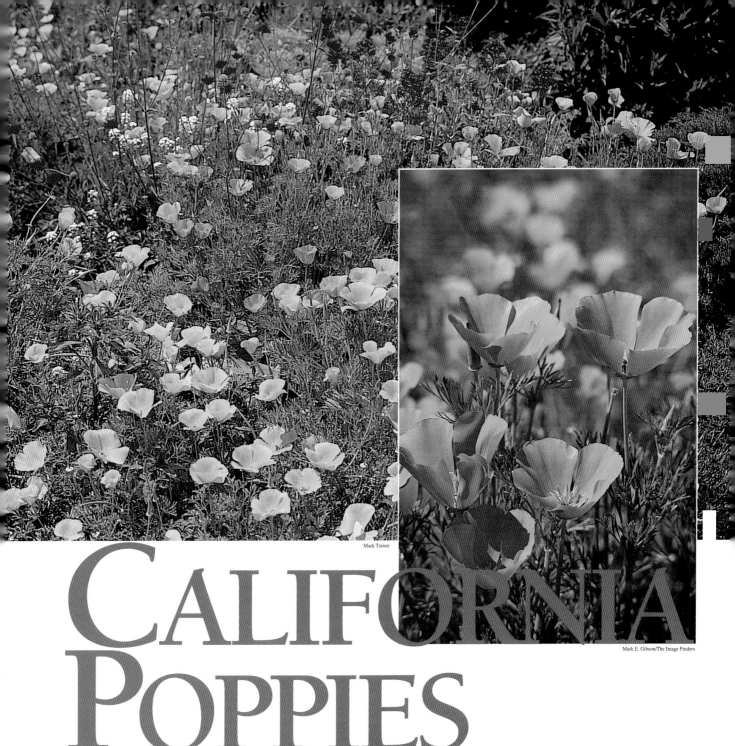

Mark Turner

Mark E. Gibson/The Image Finders

CALIFORNIA POPPIES

Bask in the glow of these golden perennials.

Sweeping across the arid foothills and valleys west of the Sierra Nevada, an endless sea of golden-orange California poppies light up the scenic landscape each spring.

The sight captivates travelers today, just as it did centuries ago, when American Indian tribes living in the area collected the sunny, yet potentially poisonous, blooms as an herbal source. Later, Spanish mariners discovered hillsides ablaze with these brilliant poppies, giving them the most appropriate name—*copa de oro*, or "cup of gold".

Today, they're simply known as California poppies (*Eschscholzia californica*), a fitting name for a plant the state of California adopted as its official flower in 1903.

This fiery beauty is by no means confined to the Golden

State. In fact, they've made their way to far corners of the world in a most unusual way.

After the gold mines in California were "played out" in the late 1800s, miners left the U.S. for Chile, New Zealand and Australia. Inadvertently, they took poppies with them. The ships they sailed needed ballast, so they used local sand, which just happened to be littered with poppy seeds. Now, California poppies are common in these far-flung lands.

In the U.S., California poppies naturally appear in pastures, grassy slopes, vacant lots and along roadways. Rich soil and humid conditions don't suit this tough plant, which is why California poppies are most at home in the West. Specimens crop up in garden beds from southern California to southern Washington and other western states as well.

Lively Offspring

In the wild, California poppies produce 2-inch-wide, satiny, cup-like flowers in shades of pale yellow to deep, golden orange (see the photo at far right). Bloom time generally runs from spring through summer.

Hybrid varieties are available in lots of flower shapes

Faith Bemiss

AWASH WITH COLOR. When California poppies burst into bloom, the vibrant-orange flowers sometimes stretch as far as the eye can see in fields along the West Coast (see photo below). But these flowers are equally colorful in the home landscape. There are a variety of hues available, from hybrid shades of pink (right) to the typical orange (far right).

Bob Coury/Unicorn Stock Photos

Chapter 5

This fiery beauty is by no means confined to the Golden State.

for the color of their flowers, such as Cherry Ripe, Milky White and Purple Violet.

Keep in mind that when these hybrids reseed, you may be disappointed that they lose their unique coloring. The blooms typically revert back to the orange or yellow of their wild ancestors.

And all California poppy blossoms will only open in bright sunlight, closing at night and on cloudy days.

California poppy's blue-green foliage is lacy and small, characteristics that allow it to thrive in arid conditions. The leaves don't have much surface area for water to evaporate. This helps it conserve moisture.

Another trait that guarantees growing success is that California poppies aren't picky when it comes to soil. It doesn't like wet roots, so be sure they're planted in well-draining soil. But if the dirt is dry or poor in terms of organic material, poppies still do very well.

Add a Casual Flair

The tall, nodding blooms are ideal in rock and cottage gardens, rather than formal flower beds. If you do choose to include them in a well-manicured garden, be ready to remove some of the spent flowers regularly to limit reseeding so the plants don't take over.

Poppies don't transplant well, so to grow them, pick a sunny spot and broadcast the tiny seeds across the soil where you want them to root. Sow seeds in fall or mid-spring in areas with mild winters. The plants will act as perennials and self-sow each year. In colder regions, treat California poppies as annuals, planting their seeds each spring.

Be sure to keep the soil moist until the seeds germinate. Then sit back and enjoy the view when these wildflowers bloom in a blaze of glory!

Editor's Note: Tennessee gardeners should check with their local county Extension service before planting California poppies, as they're considered invasive in some areas.

and colors. The Sunset strain has single blooms, while Mission Bells and Ballerina both sport fuller semi-double or double blooms with frilled and fluted petals.

The Thai Silk line is compact at 8 to 10 inches tall and has fluted bronze-tinged flowers ranging from yellow to orange, red, pink, rose, cream and white. Other cultivars are named

READER TIP

These tall, nodding blooms are ideal in rock and cottage gardens, rather than formal flower beds.

Plant Profile

Common Name: California poppy.
Botanical Name: *Eschscholzia californica*.
Bloom Time: Summer.
Hardiness: Perennial in its native habitat, or grow as an annual in all zones.
Flower Colors: Orange, red, rose, purple, yellow, pink, cream and white.
Flower Shape: Four-petal, cup-like blossoms measure 1 to 2 inches across.
Height: 8 to 15 inches.
Spread: 9 to 15 inches.
Light Needs: Full sun.
Soil Type: Well-draining; thrives in poor and dry soil.
Planting: Sow seeds directly on soil in fall or winter in mild climates; sow in spring in cold climates.

R. Todd Davis

Lily-of-the-Valley

Old time beauty shines in the shade.

James A. Hays/Unicorn Stock Photos

This old-fashioned garden belle's diminutive flowers and tender greenery might look delicate...but its appearance is deceiving. Truth is, lily-of-the-valley is tough as nails, able to adapt to conditions that topple even the most robust perennials.

It is one of the few plants that thrive in the deep shade of mature trees and shrubs and in the small spaces between homes in urban settings. In cooler climates, this ground cover queen will even flourish in full sun. It can also handle damp or dry surroundings, slopes and less-than-perfect soil.

Lily-of-the-valley spreads quickly and unfurls slender, 4-inch stalks of white, bell-shaped blooms surrounded by two or three wide, glossy leaves. Many gardeners look forward to the appearance of these wonderfully fragrant flowers each spring.

While the blooms fade after a few weeks, the leaves remain until fall, adding a green blanket in spots other plants avoid.

Mythic Beginnings

Perhaps this flower's strength is due to its legendary origin. According to a medieval European fable, the flower sprang forth after a valiant French saint defeated a terrible

Alan and Linda Detrick

SMALL FLOWERS, BIG IMPACT. Lilies-of-the-valley will brighten shady nooks. The plants spread easily, making them a good ground cover (opposite page). Most have white flowers, but the *rosea* variety (right) is a fresh change with its pink blooms.

dragon in an epic battle.

The springtime staple has religious roots as well. It is mentioned in the Old Testament's Song of Solomon, and it was believed that when Mary cried for Jesus, her tears became lily-of-the-valley flowers.

The plant's supposed healing properties are just as impressive. For some 400 years, it was used to treat everything from gout to migraine headaches.

Today, of course, gardeners know that all parts of the plant are poisonous and should not be consumed.

Although it's no longer a medicinal powerhouse, gardeners still appreciate lily-of-the-valley for its reliability, beauty and fragrance.

Letting in Lily

To introduce this shade lover to your yard, first check at the local garden center for pips. These are the sprouts from the lily's underground stem, called a rhizome, and should be planted in spring. Container-grown plants also are available, and can go into the ground anytime during the growing season.

Although the majority of plants will be low-growing specimens with white flowers, there are a few other options, including the pink-blossomed *rosea* variety and the oversized Fortin's Giant cultivar.

Lilies-of-the-valley will tolerate almost any soil, but plants perform best in areas that are moist and well drained.

Because it spreads so rapidly, the plant can overwhelm flower beds and become a real pest. It's best to select areas surrounded by edging, stones or other barriers that will contain the lily's spread. And, because it has become invasive in some natural forest settings, avoid planting it near wooded areas.

When planting, space container-grown plants 6 to 8 inches apart, or position individual pips every 3 to 4 inches.

Lily-of-the-valley pairs nicely with periwinkle and

Plant Profile

Common Name: Lily-of-the-valley.

Botanical Name: *Convallaria majalis*.

Bloom Time: Spring to early summer.

Hardiness: Zones 2 to 7.

Flower Colors: White or pink.

Flower Shape: Clusters of small, bell-shaped blooms on narrow, arching flower stalks.

Leaves: Large, lance-shaped leaves are glossy green and hug the stem.

Height: 8 to 10 inches.

Spread: Indefinite; can be invasive if not contained.

Light Needs: Partial to full shade, but will tolerate full sun in cooler climates.

Soil Type: Prefers moist, well-drained soil; will tolerate less favorable conditions.

Prize Picks: *Rosea* is the only variety with pink flowers (above right). For cultivars with unique foliage, try Variegata, which has dappled leaves, Albostriata with white stripes or Aureovariegata (above left) with yellow stripes. Fortin's Giant is a bigger version, growing as tall as 12 inches.

Warning: All plant parts are poisonous if ingested.

Alan and Linda Detrick

springtime bulbs like daffodils. It also does well under azaleas, rhododendrons, deciduous trees and evergreens with high, less-dense branches.

Easy TLC

Caring for this beauty is a breeze. If the weather is overly dry, mulch your lilies-of-the-valley and water periodically. For plants under trees and shrubs, a yearly dose of fertilizer in spring will give them a nice boost.

While it's not susceptible to many insects, leaf spot or stem rot can occasionally cause problems, particularly during wet seasons. To control these diseases, remove infected plant parts and destroy them.

In general, it's a good idea to remove old foliage before new growth peeks through in early spring. You will also want to divide plants periodically in order to encourage additional flowering.

Let's face it—gardening doesn't get much easier than this! So pick up some lily-of-the-valley flowers for that dark corner of your yard. By next spring, your garden will be made in the shade.

Scott E. Zinck

Nancy Rotenberg

HAVE A BALL WITH EYE-CATCHING ALLIUM

Add a colorful bounce to your garden with this pretty perennial.

If you want to add a colorful bounce to your garden, there's no better bloomer than allium. This pretty perennial is a winning selection for almost any yard. The allium's flower head is its most striking feature. You've likely admired an allium's globe-shaped cluster of flowers in late spring or early summer. These "ball-headed" flowers (above) range in size from 3/4 inch to 12 inches wide, depending on the variety.

Other types of allium produce loose flower heads, called "tufted" (above far right), with upright or drooping blooms that tend to be smaller but are no less dramatic.

This native of the Northern Hemisphere has more than 700 varieties to its name, providing gardeners with a huge roster of shapes, sizes and colors. You'll find specimens that grow 5 feet tall, petite versions that reach a mere 6 inches, some with interesting foliage or uniquely colored blossoms.

Alliums include edible onions, garlic and chives. Often referred to as ornamental or flowering onions, the name "allium" comes from the Latin word for that pungent vegetable.

Find real proof of the perennial bulb's genetic roots when you crush a leaf. Take a whiff, and you'll encounter an onion-like scent. The blossoms, however, tend to be pleasantly fragrant.

Despite its smelly lineage, it has long been considered a good luck charm. Even today, some believe the yellow-flowered *Allium moly*, also known as lily leek or golden garlic, will bring good fortune to those who cultivate it.

Loyal Fans

Gardeners today find other good reasons to plant this flower. Not only can you find an allium to suit almost any spot in the

Donna and Tom Krischan

garden, the enchanting plant is easy to grow and is readily available as bulbs or container-grown plants.

Most alliums need full sun, although a few varieties will tolerate partial shade. Well-drained soil is the other important requirement—bulbs will rot in standing water. If your soil contains clay, work organic material into it to improve drainage.

Plant these beauties outdoors in fall when temperatures become consistently cool. Place bulbs at a depth about two to three times their vertical diameter, but no deeper than 4 inches. Spacing depends on the variety.

Most alliums look wonderful when combined with other perennials, from purple coneflowers to roses. The only exception is the giant allium. Its large flower head is such a standout it can look out of place with the wrong plants.

Try pairing it up with an equally bold plant like yucca or surrounding it with a finer textured flower like threadleaf coreopsis.

Because many alliums bloom later in the spring, they can serve as a "bridge" between early crocuses and daffodils and summer flowers like daylilies, phlox and yarrow.

Most varieties of allium work well as cut flowers (any onion scent fades once the stems are in water). They last a long time in fresh arrangements and dry well for year-round use.

You don't need to do much maintenance to keep alliums looking their best. If you experience a rainy spring or summer, hold off on watering the plants, or they will become waterlogged and bulb rot can occur. You can also mulch the plants in the fall, after the soil freezes, to provide extra protection from frost heaving or early sprouting.

Divide and Multiply

If your alliums start to look overcrowded, simply divide them in autumn.

You can propagate those that bear seeds by placing the seeds in moist peat moss and refrigerating for 4 weeks. Then remove the seeds from the peat moss and sow in a potting or seed-starting mix. Keep the mix warm and moist. Once sprouted, move seedlings to a sunny window or under artificial growing lights. Just be sure all danger of frost has passed before planting the hardened-off transplants into the garden.

Many varieties drop their own seeds—the easiest way for them to multiply.

Once you have a few alliums in your yard, don't be surprised if these superstar flower clusters attract the attention of a few new fans.

Plant Profile

Common Names: Allium, flowering onion and ornamental onion.
Botanical Name: *Allium* species.
Bloom Time: Late spring to fall.
Hardiness: Zones 2 to 8.
Flower Colors: White, purple, blue, pink and yellow.
Flower Shape: Small star-, bell- or cup-shaped flowers grow in round clusters (ball-headed), or loose upright or drooping clusters (tufted). Flower heads range from 3/4 inch to 12 inches across.
Height: 6 inches to 5 feet.
Spread: 12 to 18 inches or more.
Light Needs: Full sun; some varieties tolerate partial shade.
Soil Type: Well-draining.
Planting: Plant bulbs in fall at a depth two to three times their vertical diameter, but no deeper than 4 inches.
Prize Picks: Giant allium (*Allium giganteum*) grows 3 to 4 feet tall with a striking 6-inch purple flower head. Drumstick chives (below, *Allium spaerocephalon*) produce small tightly packed purple flower heads on 3-foot stems. Ornamental onion (*Allium seneceus* 'Glaucum') features grayish green foliage with 1-inch pink or purple flowers on a plant 6 inches tall.

Michael Shedlock

Faith Bemiss; inset, Alan and Linda Detrick

Wisteria

This stunning vine offers a mass of spring color.

By Stacy Tornio, Associate Editor

Move over American robins and daffodils. Wisteria is a dazzling perennial climber that also deserves recognition as one of the first signs of spring.

With its magnificent hanging branches and signature purple blooms, this woody climber will put on a brilliant show in any backyard. Use it as a vine across a sturdy trellis, fence or wall. Or train it as a small shrub or tree.

Never underestimate its power, though. This command-ing beauty can easily reach up to 30 feet or more in height and spread, and requires a sturdy structure to support its incredible weight. But don't let that intimidate you.

This sweet-scented vine requires very little maintenance. Once you learn to tame this majestic charmer, you'll have a treasure that will last for years.

Scientists originally named wisteria *Glycinia*, after "glykys," the Greek word for sweet. Then, in the 1800s, American naturalist Thomas Nuttall renamed the woody vine to honor Casper Wistar, who was a renowned botanist and professor at the University of Pennsylvania.

Though his name was misspelled, using the letter 'e' instead of 'a', the mistake stuck. Wisteria is the both the common and botanical name for this plant today.

Centennial Masterpiece

There is one community that sticks by Wistar. The Wistaria Festival takes place every year in Sierra Madre, California. It's where the largest wisteria is located—one that has a history 100 years in the making.

This vine is more than 1 acre in size, weighs 250 tons and has 1.5 million blossoms every year. It is one of the seven horticultural wonders of the world, and the *Guinness Book of Records* named it as the largest blossoming plant in the world.

The history of the vine goes back to 1894, when a couple bought a Chinese wisteria for 75¢ at a local nursery and planted it near their home.

Nearly 20 years later, they sold the house to H.T. Fennel, who loved the plant so much that he built extra arbors around it. The added support could only do so much for the expanding vine, however.

As it grew over the house, its weight eventually caused the roof to collapse. Afterward, they built a new house nearby and gave the wisteria more support so it could keep growing.

The public honored the impressive vine in 1918 with the first wisteria festival. Today, about 15,000 people attend the celebration each spring.

Vine-in-Training

With roughly 10 types of wisteria to choose from, the most common backyard varieties include Japanese, Chinese and Kentucky. The blooms can be lavender, pink or white and some emerge before the plant's bright-green leaves.

The vine is part of the legume family, which is evident from the bean-like green seedpods that follow the showy blooms. But don't think of tasting one. All parts of this plant are considered poisonous.

The best time to plant container-grown wisteria is in spring. Select a site with well-draining soil that receives plenty of sun. And keep in mind the experience of H.T. Fennel, whose roof buckled under the weight of the vine. It's best to locate wisteria away from your house, where it can't wreak havoc on rain gutters and downspouts.

Dig a hole the same depth as and at least 2 to 3 times the width of the rootball. You can also take cuttings to start wisteria. Keep them moist and in an area of high humidity until they're ready to move to the garden.

Japanese and Chinese wisteria plants are hardy in Zones 4 and 5, but thrive more successfully in warmer climates. The Kentucky variety is a better choice for regions with colder winters, where the frigid temperatures may damage the buds of other varieties and prevent them from flowering come spring.

And be patient. Wisteria may take up to 7 years to

Plant Profile

Ray Packard

Common Name: Wisteria.

Botanical Name: *Wisteria.*

Height: Can reach 30 feet or more.

Spread: Depends on the size of support; typically 10 to 30 feet or more.

Leaves: 10 to 15-inch-long, bright-green leaflets.

Flowers: Dangling clusters of lavender, white or pink pea-like blooms.

Seeds: Winged, light-brown seeds encased in 4- to 6-inch pods.

Hardiness: Zones 4 to 9.

Light Needs: Full sun to partial shade.

Soil Type: Well-draining; can tolerate drought.

Planting: Plant container-grown wisteria in spring near a sturdy support. Wisteria may take up to 7 years to bloom for the first time.

Prize Picks: Japanese wisteria (*Wisteria floribunda*) is a beautiful choice for southern climates, where its 8- to 20-inch-long, fragrant flowers open just before the leaves emerge. In the North, try the Kentucky variety (*Wisteria macrostachya*). It is slightly less showy because the flowers emerge with the leaves, but it blooms reliably.

flower. To increase the chance of blooming success, you should mulch around the base of the vine, avoid overfertilizing and keep the soil moist, but not wet, during the growing season.

Right after flowering ends, help Oriental wisterias maintain size and shape by pruning. Once established, this is really the only maintenance needed. It's an important requirement, though. If left unattended, this enjoyable vine could take over your growing area and collapse the structure that supports it.

Look at pruning as a benefit. This marvelous spring vine already is beautiful and versatile. Now you have the power to shape it into anything you want.

ELEGANCE COMES EASY WITH CALLA LILIES

By Kathleen Zimmer-Anderson
Waukesha, Wisconsin

From the origin of its name to the graceful flower it produces, the calla lily has "lovely" written all over it! "Calla" comes from the Greek word *kalos*, which translates into "beauty"—and this bloomer certainly is a knockout.

Its lance-shaped, glossy green leaves provide the perfect backdrop as it produces dramatic flowers in spring and summer.

That swirling white petal most think of as the flower is actually a protective leaf known as a spathe, while the golden spike at its center, called a spadix, holds the plant's tiny blossoms.

White is the most common color for the flower-like spathe, but a number of hybrids in shades of yellow, pink or red are also available today. Most produce a wonderful fragrance, too.

SOPHISTICATED SWIRLS. Calla lilies lend a touch of elegance to any backyard garden. Its whirled petal is actually a leaf that protects the tiny blossoms on the center spike. New varieties add to the possibilities with spotted foliage (left) or red flowers (far right).

A symbol of timeless purity, long-lasting calla lilies are often seen in bridal bouquets and other floral arrangements, leading many gardeners to mistakenly assume it's a delicate hothouse plant that can be grown only indoors.

Tough Enough

But that isn't the case. The calla lily is hardy enough to brighten a shady spot in your garden without much fuss.

This native of southern and eastern Africa grows in the wild there along lakes, near streams and in swamps, indicating that it's comfortable in moist conditions.

In North American backyards, the lilies will thrive in shallow pools or ponds and look spectacular when planted in or near water gardens.

That doesn't mean you need to have a water feature in your yard in order to successfully cultivate callas. You can mix them in your flower beds with annuals and perennials in partial or full shade—or even plant them in full sun, as long as you keep the soil moist.

Calla lilies like rich, moist soil that drains well, so if you have clay soil, add organic matter to promote drainage. Do the same for sandy soil to improve water retention.

Northern gardeners may want to get a jump on the season by planting rhizomes indoors in mid-March. Place them in a container filled with well-draining potting mix, then cover with about 3 inches of soil. Water sparingly until you notice green shoots peeking through the surface, then water more generously and add fertilizer. Be sure to keep the soil moist.

Moving Outdoors

You can move them to the yard, gradually acclimating them to outdoor weather, then transplant into the garden once the threat of frost has passed.

Or plant rhizomes directly in the garden once you're sure temperatures will stay well above freezing. Place them about 4 inches deep and about 18 inches apart.

Another option is to purchase potted calla lilies from the garden center and transplant them in your garden. You should plant them at the same level they were growing in the con-

tainer.

Once the plants are in the garden, you don't need to do too much to maintain their graceful appearance. Remove faded flowers for a tidy look and water regularly if the weather turns dry.

R. Todd Davis

Plant Profile

Common Names: Calla lily, arum lily, garden calla and trumpet lily.
Botanical Name: *Zantedeschia* species.
Bloom Time: From late spring to early summer.
Hardiness: Annuals; except common calla lily, which is a tender perennial in Zones 8 and above.
Bloom Colors: White, yellow, pink and red.
Flower Shape: Tiny flowers on a large spike at the center of a flower-like leaf called a spathe.
Height: 12 to 36 inches.
Spread: 8 to 24 inches.
Light Needs: Partial to full shade; will tolerate full sun if soil is kept moist.
Soil Type: Moist and well-draining.
Prize Picks: Hardier and more sun tolerant than other *Zantedeschia aethiopica* varieties, Crowborough produces large 4- to 6-inch-long spathes, while Little Gem is ideal for tight quarters, reaching 12 to 18 inches in height.

Common calla lilies (*Zantedeschia aethiopica*) perform like perennials in warmer areas (Zones 8 or higher) and can remain in the garden all year long. But for locations that experience cold winters, the rhizomes need to be dug up right after the first light frost. Store them in peat moss or perlite in a cool (about 50°) spot.

Two other prevalent types, spotted calla lily (*Zantedeschia albomaculata*) and golden calla lily (*Zantedeschia elliottiana*), are more susceptible to the cold and must be preserved indoors for winter, or replanted each year.

Winter Blooms

Want to enjoy the attractive plant all year long? Consider keeping potted calla lilies in a warm, sunny window during winter and water just enough to prevent the soil from completely drying out.

Increase water as the days become longer and the sunshine grows stronger in the spring and summer. Then set containers outside once warm temperatures return.

You can even place the plants, container and all, directly into your garden. Dig a hole roughly the same depth as the container, and set the pot in the hole. Make sure the lip of the pot is even with the soil's surface.

Then sit back and enjoy the beauty that will abound in your yard as these stylish plants put forth blossom after gorgeous blossom. ◄

HOSTA HAVEN

This reader has eyes for only one kind of plant in his backyard.

By Frederick Ryan, Schenectady, New York

LOVIN' THOSE LEAVES. Ten years of hard work have paid off for Frederick Ryan (below left). He has collected more than 200 varieties of hostas in his backyard, and has added many personal touches along the way that bring attention to his favorite plants. Frederick creates his own planters, like 'V'-shaped ones (above right), and circular and wooden step designs (top left). He also uses unique lighting to make the plants shine.

Ten years ago, I fell in love.

A thunderstorm had just passed through town, and I was out driving around. As I turned the corner, I spotted a bed of radiant hostas glistening in the soft sunlight after the storm.

I had never been a gardener—my hobbies were hot rods and airplanes, not flowers and dirt. But a month later, I still couldn't stop thinking about those hostas, so I broke down and went to a local greenhouse.

Today, I have more than 200 varieties of hostas, and I wouldn't have it any other way.

Wetland to Green Land

Long before I acquired my home, the backyard was like a swamp. A fisherman from my area had lived in the house, and he filled the yard with water so he could practice casting.

I was just a young boy when my parents bought the house from him. I still remember helping my dad fill in the area—it took 27 dump truck loads of soil.

Over the years, my mother put in a few flowers here and there, but the yard didn't see much gardening activity. Even when I inherited the house nearly 20 years ago, I had very little interest in doing any planting. I mowed the grass, and that was it. But once those hostas caught my eye, I was hooked.

I don't have a lot of space to work with, since the yard is only 50 by 75 feet. However, I've made the most of it.

Building a Collection

I have 18 wooden planters, all of which I designed and built myself. My 'V'-shaped creations are probably the most eye-catching. I wanted them to look as if they were barely bal-

ancing on each end (see photo above).

Since I consider myself a romantic, I also built a large heart-shaped planter. It took me a month to finish it. I started by laying out the shape with a rope, and then little by little, it came together. Now, I joke that a piece of my heart will always be in my backyard.

I've never been big on names. I probably couldn't tell you the official names for most of my hostas. I do keep a running planting list, though, which is how my collection has grown.

As a car enthusiast, I often go cruising for a couple of hours at a time. In past trips, if I saw a nursery along the way, I stopped to check out their hostas. When I found one not on my list, I bought it. Then I couldn't wait to bring my new treat home to enjoy.

After years of doing this, my space is filled, but I still find plenty of other projects to keep me busy with the plants. One of these is lighting.

Lights, Hostas, Action

I've always been fascinated by the way lights can emphasize the different features on a car. I decided the same concept could work with my hostas, so I bought some lights at a home improvement store and got to work on my plan.

Now I have dozens of custom-made lights among the plants that help give them an enchanting nighttime glow. My proudest beams are the nine lanterns I made myself. I created them using two lights and red plastic. In the daytime they look clear, but at night the top half shines a beautiful candy-apple red.

People often ask why I'm so infatuated with hostas. I can't explain it, other than I like their reliability. Hostas take care of themselves, and they come back year after year.

You can't ask for much more than that.

Editor's Note: Hostas in raised containers are more susceptible to the damaging effects of winter weather. Some gardeners may need to provide additional insulation for the roots. One common method is to surround the containers with bales of straw for winter.

READER TIP

The backyard isn't just for daytime enjoyment. Use lights throughout the area for an enchanting nighttime glow.

—Frederick Ryan, Schenectady, New York

MORNING GLORY

This climbing annual greets each day with fresh-faced and fuss-free blooms.

By Margene Whitler Hucek, Keswick, Virginia

Photos this page: David Cavagnaro

WINNING STREAKS. Variegated leaves and multicolored flowers are just some of the traits to consider when selecting a morning glory for your yard. Two striking varieties are *Ipomoea nil* 'Mt. Fuji' (above left) and *Ipomoea tricolor* 'Flying Saucers' (above right). There also are several dwarf types that work in smaller planting spaces like hanging baskets or window boxes.

Morning glories conjure up images of lazy summer days, when time is best spent relaxing under an old oak tree, drinking iced tea and enjoying the fruits of my springtime labors. The tomatoes are ripe…there's corn to be picked…and my morning glories are in full bloom, providing an enchanting show well into autumn.

Each spring, I plant a morning glory called Heavenly Blue (like the one at far left) near a pillar in my vegetable garden and along the nearby picket fence. We can see that spot from our dining area and enjoy the incredible blue blooms it produces all season.

Hummingbirds often flit about the azure beauties, feeding on the flowers' sweet nectar. They even rest on the vines from time to time.

Common morning glories climb up and over our mailbox. Their funnel-shaped flowers range from deep purple to bluish purple or red with white throats. Like all morning glories, these blooms last only a day—but because the vine is so prolific, it continuously creates a colorful welcome for friends, family…and our mail carrier!

Family Ties

Morning glories belong to the *Convolvulaceae* family, a large group of vines that includes the sweet potato. In fact, the family name comes from a Latin word that means "to entwine," accurately describing the climbing abilities of most members of this family.

The morning glories commonly grown in gardens go by the botanical names of *Ipomoea purpurea* or *Ipomoea tricolor*, which has many cultivars.

In rural England, the morning glory was once known as "life of man" because its blooming pattern resembles that of a person's life—budding in the morning, full bloom at midday and wilting by evening.

Because these plants devote

no energy to building strong upright stems, they grow quite rapidly. They can reach 10 to 20 feet in a single season. Giving it adequate support, such as a post, trellis, fence or wall, is vital. I use guides—either string or thin bamboo sticks—to direct young plants to the main support.

If your support surface is smooth, provide wire or string "handholds" for the vine to cling to as it grows. Don't worry about the wire or string looking unsightly, though. The fast-growing climber quickly covers up these makeshift handholds.

Morning glories are a good choice if you're looking for a seasonal screen to add privacy to a porch or patio. The speedy climbers will provide attractive temporary cover to a doorway or part of your yard that will eventually be shaded by trees.

They're also ideal for small gardens since their growth is mostly vertical. But even if you have plenty of space, encouraging a few morning glories to climb up a trellis or other upright structure will add extra dimension to your garden.

Although not as common, you can let your morning glories climb up and over stumps or large rocks (a big bonus if there's an area of your yard that needs some work).

Be careful to limit your plantings to areas that can handle the vine's vigorous growth habits—they can easily smother more fragile flowers or greenery.

READER TIP

Morning glory seeds have tough outer coats, so it's best to soak them in warm water overnight before planting. This encourages speedier germination.
—**Margene Whitler Hucek, Keswick, Virginia**

You'll Love These Blooms

However you use the vines, the dramatic, 4- to 6-inch-wide heart-shaped, green leaves make a delightful backdrop for the elegant, funnel-like flowers. Depending on the va-

ALL WRAPPED UP. Morning glories need some sort of support to cling to as they grow. But the plants aren't picky—the vines will wrap around anything, even an old rusty seat (above).

riety you choose, these blooms can measure as much as 5 inches across and are available in a range of colors, although blue and purple are the shades most gardeners associate with morning glories.

Aside from the two I prefer to plant in my garden, there are plenty of other selections, including the red blooms of cardinal climber (*Ipomoea* x *multifida*) and star glory (*Ipomoea quamoclit*), or Spanish flag (*Ipomoea lobata*), a shade-tolerant type with narrow, crimson blooms that mature to yellow and orange.

Another popular variety is moonflower (*Ipomoea alba*), which opens its white blooms during the evening hours. There also are some dwarf varieties that require no support and are especially attractive when used in window boxes or hanging planters.

Sowing Know-How

Morning glories are tropical natives and survive winters only in very warm climates. In North America, they are grown as annuals.

It is best to sow seeds directly in the garden after the soil

warms to about 65°. That's because morning glories don't transplant well. Look for a space in your yard that receives full sun and make sure the soil drains well—these beauties don't tolerate wet conditions.

If you don't have a good spot in your yard to grow morning glories, consider using containers. Just provide support for the vines and remember to water.

Morning glory seeds have tough outer coats, so it's best to soak them in warm water overnight before planting. This encourages speedier germination.

Plant seeds 6 inches apart, covering them with a 1/4 inch of soil. Thin 3-inch-tall plants so they stand about 12 inches apart, then step back and watch them grow! You'll soon have an abundance of blooms.

Morning glories will self-sow, and the resulting blooms usually revert to a purple or reddish flower. (Note: In some areas, this vigor has made them a noxious weed. Check with your county Extension service before adding them to your landscape.) I like to leave some vines in the garden over winter, since finches come looking for seeds in fall.

Pests are few for this vigorous plant, although beetles may cause some problems in late summer. You can control those critters with insecticidal soap.

Ease of care is yet another reason gardeners like morning glories. They do best without fertilizer, which will encourage vine growth at the expense of flower production. And they tolerate dry weather, although a drought may reduce the number of blossoms.

When my husband and I rented homes during the early years of our marriage, I couldn't afford to invest in costly perennials and had to rely on budget-friendly annuals like morning glories for a burst of summer color.

Now that we've settled in our own home, I delight in having beds of phlox, peonies and roses…but I still make room for morning glories. I find there's no better way to start a day than with these colorful blooms twining around my door.

Plant Profile

Common Name: Morning glory.
Botanical Name: *Ipomoea* species.
Bloom Time: Summer until first frost.
Hardiness: Annual.
Flower Colors: Blue, white, purple, pink and red.
Flower Shape: Funnel- or trumpet-shaped blooms.
Height: Vines range from 6 to 20 feet in length.
Light Needs: Full sun.
Soil Type: Moderately fertile and well draining.
Propagating: Plant presoaked seeds directly in the ground after the soil has warmed and the threat of frost has passed. Space the seeds 6 inches apart, then thin 3-inch-tall plants to 12 inches apart.
Prize Picks: The sky-blue flowers of Heavenly Blue are appealing, as are the white blooms of Pearly Gates and the bicolored Flying Saucers. All three are cultivars of *Ipomoea tricolor*. Hummingbirds are attracted to red Scarlett O'Hara and Crimson Rambler. Moonflower (*Ipomoea alba*) is a fragrant night-blooming variety.
Caution: All plant parts are toxic if ingested.

Steve Terrill

Mark Turner

BIRDS&BLOOMS
BONUS!

THE SKY'S THE LIMIT

Things are looking up with this "vine" way to elevate your landscape.

By Jeff Nowak, Executive Editor

Vine-ally, a simple solution to expanding your gardens without having to break large areas of ground—or even a sweat. All you have to do is think *up* rather than *out* and let climbing vines do the rest.

Vines pack a visual punch that will hit you square between the eyes. These plants give your garden new dimension, add vibrant color to your landscape and are a practical problem solver for many unsightly situations.

Looking to hide the trash cans on the side of your house? Let a vine climb a trellis strategically placed in front of them. Want to blend your chain-link fence into the landscape? A nice flowering vine will give it a natural look without sacrificing function. Have a stump that's too expensive to remove and

Blooming Beauty

too big to take out yourself? Plant a vine—it's nature's camouflage. Running out of planting space? Go vertical!

There are plenty of other reasons to select vines for your landscape. Early-blooming sweet peas chase away the chill of winter…Virginia creeper adds beautiful fall color…trumpet vine invites hummingbirds…and grapes are a favorite nesting and feeding site for northern cardinals.

Perfect Planning

But before charging off to the nearest nursery or garden center to pick out the first vine that comes to mind, it's best to plan before you purchase.

There are so many vines to choose from, it would be impossible to list them all (our short list in the box at far right will

GET A GRIP. Each vine has its own method of climbing. Virginia creeper (at left) scales upward using strong hold fasts, which act like natural suction cups. Scarlet runner beans (right) use their main stems to twine around supports.

get you started). However, all vines fall into one of three groups—annuals, perennials or woody vines.

Annuals, such as cypress vine, grow from seed each year. Perennials, like passionflower, die to the ground in winter, but sprout again in spring from the same roots. Woody vines, like wisteria, stand all year.

"One clever gardening trick is to mix annual vines with woody vines," says plant expert and contributing editor Melinda Myers. "Initially, woody vines don't grow very fast. So the annual vines can provide more immediate cover and color.

"It's fun to mix different vines together, such as clematis planted near a climbing rose (below)," she adds. "Together, they really brighten up a yard."

Most landscape vines grow upward, so it's important to understand how they climb and what types of support structures best suit their needs.

Some vines, such as honeysuckle, twine their way up, wrapping around and around as they grow. Others, like passionflower, send out tendrils to grab on. Some, such as climbing

VERSATILE VINES. There are many ways to use vines to add height to your landscape. You can combine two varieties like clematis and rose (below left) for a burst of color, or use them solo to let unique vines like wisteria (right) shine. No matter what types you choose, however, make sure to provide proper support, from strings for morning glory to sturdy structures for wisteria.

hydrangea, have aerial roots, while Virginia creeper and others use hold fasts that serve as natural suction cups.

Selecting Support

A lightweight trellis is perfect for the twisting vines of clematis, but no match for a vigorous climbing rose, which is more suited to a heavier arbor.

If you're a fan of the dangling purple clusters of a blooming wisteria (at right), make sure you have a Herculean structure to support its incredible weight. We're talking major timbers that are located well away from your house, so the vigorous vine doesn't wreak havoc on rain gutters and downspouts.

Any of the clinging vines, like Boston ivy, are perfect plants to green-up brick walls. But be careful if you have a wooden house. Your siding could rot from the trapped moisture, and many of the hold fasts are so strong they can damage the wood.

Use Your Imagination

Elaborate structures are not necessary for planting vines in your backyard. Annuals, like morning glories, are the perfect answer for flimsy fences and lightweight arbors. In fact, they'll even grow on supports as simple as netting or strings.

"My husband, Jim, stretches strong cord diagonally from the ground to the top of our wraparound porch," says Angela Griffin Hatchett from Altoona, Alabama.

"Then he crisscrosses it going the other way. This gives the morning glories plenty of support as they reach toward the sun."

Vines also are great plants to enjoy with children because many grow extremely fast. Make a simple tepee from bamboo poles and let scarlet runner beans cover it for a neat summer hideout.

And if you're not a builder, a simple 4 x 4 post in the middle of a perennial garden is enough to provide a vertical break to your landscape. Just anchor it and stagger a few nails every 6 to 8 inches, so the vine has something to hang onto. ◀

12 Picks to Elevate Your Landscape

Here's a short list of vines that will liven up your landscape. Check with your county Extension service (listed in the government section of your local telephone directory) before planting these vines. Make sure they're not too vigorous in your area. Also ask for recommendations for vines that do well in your climate.

Vine	Planting Zones	Maximum Height	Notes
American bittersweet (*Celastrus scandens*)	3-8	30 feet	Woody and heavy twining vine; fruits provide fall to winter interest.
Clematis (*Clematis* species)	4-9	6-20 feet	Perennial and woody twining climbers with prolific flowers.
Climbing hydrangea (*Hydrangea petiolaris*)	4-9	50 feet	Woody with aerial roots; clusters of white flowers; tolerates shade.
Confederate jasmine (*Trachelospermum jasminoides*)	9-10	20 feet	Woody twining evergreen; fragrant in summer with white flowers; can be wintered indoors.
Mandevilla (*Mandevilla splendens*)	Annual	10-20 feet	Twining vine used as annual with lovely trumpet flowers; can be wintered indoors.
Morning glory (*Ipomoea* species)	Annual	10-12 feet	Fast-growing annual twining vine; flowers open in the morning.
Passionflower (*Passiflora* species)	6-9	6-30 feet	Perennial with tendrils to help climb; host plant to several butterflies.
Scarlet runner bean (*Phaseolus coccineus*)	Annual	5 feet	Annual trailing plant that will climb; red flowers with edible beans.
Sweet pea (*Lathyrus odoratus*)	Annual	6-8 feet	Annual twining vine with fragrant flowers; sow seeds in autumn or early spring.
Trumpet vine (*Campsis radicans*)	5-9	30 feet	Woody vine that clings by aerial roots; flowers attract hummingbirds.
Virginia creeper and Boston ivy (*Parthenocissus* species)	3-9	50-70 feet	Woody climbers with strong hold fasts; vibrant in autumn; can be aggressive.
Wisteria (*Wisteria* species)	6-9	28 feet	Woody twining climber with dangling flowers; needs strong support.

Blooming Beauty

Black-eyed Susan

This easy-care beauty will flower almost anywhere.

The sunny disposition of this simple, old-fashioned flower ensures its spot on any gardener's list of beloved blooms. The black-eyed Susan is well suited for any setting, plus it's a cinch to cultivate. It could very well be the perfect landscape addition to your backyard.

Black-eyed Susans come in a variety of eye-catching, daisy-like blossoms, ranging from yellow to orange, mahogany and rust. The centers are raised and often cone-shaped, featuring hues that usually contrast with the petals, such as black, brown, deep purple and green.

But that's not always the case. Now you can also find these beauties without their signature dark centers, as seen in the Prairie Sun variety (above, inset).

Black-eyed Susans' lance-shaped leaves provide a calm background for the lively flowers that pop up during the summer. Even better, the blooms continue until autumn without deadheading. They make great fresh-cut and dried flowers—and snipping a handful for arrangements will also prolong the bloom time in most cases.

Once the flowers have faded, striking seed heads form

on top of the lanky stems, enhancing the landscape over the winter. This also keeps birds like finches, which love to dine on the seed heads, happy throughout the cold months.

Famed Swedish botanist Carl Linnaeus identified this sturdy North American native during the 18th century. He named it *Rudbeckia*, in honor of his mentor and fellow Swede, Olaf Rudbeck. The popularity of the plant quickly spread throughout Europe, and even prompted English scribe John Gay to feature it in his poem, *Sweet William's Farewell to Black-ey'd Susan*.

Today, the *Rudbeckia* genus includes some 20 related species and numerous varieties of perennials, biennials and annuals. Plants vary in size from 12-inch-tall blooms that are fitting for borders to towering 6-foot specimens that can anchor an island flower bed, serve as a flowering hedge or line a fence or rock wall.

Pretty Pairings

This versatile garden queen looks terrific when planted in lush masses. It's also a good partner with a number of plants, including porcupine grass, red angelica delphinium and butterfly bush.

Adding black-eyed Susan to your yard is a breeze. Although the flower will thrive in most soils, including clay and sand, it prefers a moist, well-draining mix. It also requires full sun for optimum growth, although some shade is fine.

Perhaps the easiest and least expensive way to sow a bunch is to broadcast seeds directly in loosened soil in fall or early spring. Lightly rake dirt over the seeds, press down and water.

For annual and biennial varieties, start seeds indoors, and then move outside after the danger of frost has passed. This will help ensure earlier blooms.

Once established, the perennial flowers don't mind dry spells, especially if you mulch them, but they do appreciate a dose of compost every other year. If they begin to look overgrown or are spreading too aggressively, you can always dig them up in autumn or spring, divide the plants and add them to other parts of your yard or give some to friends.

Staying Healthy

As hardy and fuss-free as they are, black-eyed Susans can fall prey to a few diseases. Powdery mildew will make leaves less attractive, but you can control it by removing leaves, giving blooms full sun and thinning plants to encourage better air circulation.

Though the mildew is unsightly, it won't fatally injure the plants. You can also opt for mildew-resistant varieties.

A couple of leaf spot diseases caused by fungi and bacteria have started to attack some of these plants in recent

Plant Profile

Jodi Bertrand/Positive Images

Common Names: Black-eyed Susan, gloriosa daisy, coneflower.

Botanical Name: *Rudbeckia*.

Bloom Time: Summer through fall.

Hardiness: For perennials, Zones 3 to 9, but it varies by species.

Flower Colors: Yellow, orange and russet petals with black-brown or green centers.

Flower Shape: Daisy-like petals surround a raised, often cone-shaped center.

Height: 1 to 6 feet.

Spread: 18 to 48 inches.

Light Needs: Full sun; will tolerate light shade.

Soil Type: Well-drained.

Planting: Sow seeds of perennials directly in the garden in early spring or fall by scattering them on loosened soil.

Prize Picks: Popular perennials include *Rudbeckia hirta* and *Rudbeckia fulgida*. If you want to make a statement, try *Rudbeckia maxima*, which soars as high as 6 feet when in full bloom. For long-lasting blooms, plant *Rudbeckia triloba*. It produces numerous blossoms well into fall.

Backyard Benefits: The flowers attract butterflies, including the silvery crescentspot, which uses the flowers as host plants. Birds are also attracted to the seed heads that remain on the stems well into winter.

years. These infections are more serious, but you can control them by removing damaged leaves and conducting a thorough fall cleanup.

If the problem persists, treat with a copper-containing fungicide in spring, following label instructions to apply as the plants emerge.

All told, these problems are pretty minor when compared to the immense satisfaction you'll receive when generous bunches of black-eyed Susans grace your landscape next summer.

So what are you waiting for? Go pick out your favorite varieties of black-eyed Susans, and plant them in your garden—you won't regret it!

ROSES

Take your pick—any of these classic beauties will be the crowning glory in your garden.

There's a good reason the rose is often referred to as "the queen of the garden." It has long been prized, not only for its unmatched beauty, but also for its healing properties, delicate flavor and sweet fragrance. And with so many shapes, colors and sizes to choose from, this bloomer stands out in any form.

Roses have been around for ages. Ancient fossils of early roses have turned up in Montana, while active cultivation of the flower started in Greece and Asia more recently—about 3,000 years ago!

Since medieval times, roses have been used as food and medicine. Healers believed roses could cure all kinds of ailments. Their nutritional value was confirmed during World War II when scientists discovered rose hips contain more vitamin C than most fruits or vegetables.

So Many Choices

There are literally *thousands* of roses available to modern gardeners. Luckily, these beauties are divided into distinct categories. Some of the most popular ones include:

Old roses are varieties that were introduced before 1867. These fragrant types include gallica, damask, bourbon and tea roses. They're hardy, disease resistant and easy to grow, but not as showy as newer types.

Hybrid tea roses are the most popular rose. Their flowers are showy and look wonderful in arrangements. They can be more susceptible to disease, however, and need protection from cold winters.

Floribunda roses are a cross between hybrid teas and a low-growing hedge variety called polyantha. These tend to be shrubbier in form and grow 2 to 3 feet tall, producing clusters of blossoms.

Grandiflora types were created by combining long-stemmed hybrid teas and the clustered flowers of floribundas. These roses can grow as tall as 6 feet.

Shrub roses are large full plants that can be hybrids or naturally occurring natives. They're hardy in almost every Plant Hardiness Zone and often fragrant. Some new types are repeat bloomers.

Climbers produce long stems called canes that need to be supported, making them ideal for trellises, arbors and walls.

Which Rose Is for You?

When choosing roses, you need to keep in mind three factors: your soil conditions, the amount of time you have to care for the plant and where you want to use it.

"If you want cut flowers, hybrid tea roses or grandifloras are good choices. Shrub roses, on the other hand, make the garden look great with little care," says Diane Brueckman, rosarian for the Missouri Botanical Gardens in St. Louis. "The best advice is to contact your local rose society and ask what varieties do well in your area."

You can also narrow the field by focusing on the traits you're after, such as scent, stem color or rose hips.

"Damask and alba roses and their hybrids are very fragrant. So are old-fashioned tea roses," offers Stephen Scanniello of Barnegat, New Jersey, who has authored numerous books on roses, including *Roses of America* and *Rose Companions*.

Diane has a few fragrant favorites, too. "I'm a big fan of the

Richard Shiell; opposite page: Alan and Linda Detrick

FALL IN LOVE. Who can resist the timeless elegance of roses, like the red Chrysler Imperial hybrid tea rose (at left)? These bloomers perform best when mixed with other flowers in the garden. Above, a red climbing rose and yellow miniatures make a colorful border with purple irises and evening primrose.

David Austin English roses, especially Pilgrim, a yellow, medium-sized shrub rose," she says. "A floribunda called Apricot Nectar is a good choice, as is Peter Mayle Romantica and Westerland, a climber."

Some roses, such as Mutabalis or Red Meidleind, offer colorful canes or fall foliage.

Abundant rose hips are an added bonus for other types. These rose "fruits" will brighten your garden after the blooms have faded, plus they provide food for the birds. Diane and Stephen both recommend any of the rugosa rose varieties for this purpose.

"Many of the native rose species will produce hips, including prairie, Carolina, Virginia and Arkansas roses," Stephen

READER TIP

If you want cut flowers, hybrid tea roses or grandifloras are good choices. If you're looking for a variety that makes your garden look great with little care, shrub roses are the way to go.

—Diane Brueckman, St. Louis, Missouri

Details: Donna and Tom Krischan

Details: Alan and Linda Detrick

In addition, Diane suggests selecting a spot among your other flowers that receives morning sun, which helps dry the foliage and reduces the risk of disease.

"In areas with hot summers, spots with eastern exposures are best in order to prevent burning and damage from intense afternoon sun," she says. "You'll also have better luck intermingling roses with other plants."

Roses are available as bare-root plants or in containers. It's best to plant bare-root roses in spring while the plant is still dormant—and right after you've soaked the roots overnight. Container plants can go in the garden anytime during the growing season.

Many roses are grafted, a process that attaches a bud from a desired plant onto a hardier root system. The bud graft is easy to spot—it's the swollen knob with branches sprouting from it. To protect the graft in northern regions, plant it 1 to 2 inches below the soil surface. Southern gardeners should keep it even to 2 inches above the surface.

Make the planting hole twice as large as the roots. To avoid disturbing the roots of container plants, cut away the pot rather than pulling out the rose.

Roses are thirsty, and it's important to water them deeply to soak the top 6 to 8 inches of soil. Direct the water at the base of the plant and away from the foliage in order to prevent mildew and black spot. And don't forget the mulch. This will help conserve soil moisture.

Some rose varieties, like hybrid teas, are heavy feeders and require fertilization three to four times during the summer. Shrub, climbing, old rose and floribunda types don't need that much—just give them a dose in spring. Repeat bloomers benefit from an extra application after the first round of blossoms.

If the temperatures in your area drop below 10° in winter, you'll want to protect your hybrid roses after the first week of freezing temperatures. One method is to pile about 10 inches of soil loosely around the base of the plant.

"All in all, roses give you a big bang for your buck," says Diane. "They aren't that expensive, will produce all season long and last for years with a little care."

adds. "Some gardeners don't like the fact that these only bloom once. If that bothers you, try rugosa Scabrosa, which blooms multiple times."

A Little TLC

Ready to get planting? Before you do, Stephen suggests you carefully select your site.

"Make sure it gets 5 to 6 hours of sun, and the ground is a well-mixed combination of compost and soil," he says.

Plant Profile

Common Name: Rose.
Botanical Name: *Rosa.*
Bloom Time: Early summer to autumn.
Hardiness: All zones—check individual varieties for specific hardiness.
Flower Colors: A wide palette, including white, red, pink, cream, yellow, orange, magenta, purple, lavender, tan and brown.

Flower Shape: Single, semi-double or double blooms in many shapes, including flat, cupped, rounded, high-centered, urn-shaped, rosette and pompom.
Height: Varies widely, from 6-inch ground covers to 20-foot climbers.
Spread: 12 to 18 inches or more.
Light Needs: Full sun.
Soil Type: Moist and well draining.
Special Care: Pruning varies with the type of rose and your climate. In general,

shrub roses and climbers need the least pruning. On established shrubs, remove damaged or dead canes before growth begins in spring. Wait until after the first blooms of the season to prune climbing roses.

On hybrid teas, remove any winter-damaged canes in spring. You can also shape and control the size by pruning the remaining stems to anywhere between 12 and 24 inches in height.

Planting a Love of
Roses

*Former teacher encourages
budding gardeners.*

By Jane Miller, Pittsburgh, Pennsylvania

As a high school teacher, Alma Long taught teenagers about chemistry. When she retired, she decided to teach them about roses.

Alma started a project in the Ada, Ohio area to acquaint young people with raising roses. It was part of an American Rose Society initiative to spread an appreciation for roses throughout communities.

With help of local sponsors, she offered a free miniature rosebush to any interested teen in Harden County, Ohio.

They hoped to find about 100 teens to participate. They got that…and more. The response included more than 200 kids in Harden County, and almost 100 more from the next county over. Adults, who joined the rose-planting effort by purchasing bushes at wholesale price, brought the total of new rose gardeners in the area to 760.

Alma, who's known as the "Rose Lady" in her community, has tended roses since she married her husband, Urban, in 1951. As newlyweds, they bought and planted three rosebushes in their yard. One, a McGreddy Scarlet rose, still thrives today. They now have 500 roses planted in long, colorful rows in their farmhouse backyard.

Worth the Effort

Alma grows most of her plants from cuttings of roses given to her by friends. The process takes a bit of time and effort, but the results are worth it. She roots the cuttings in water during summer, plants them in early fall, and covers them with 2-liter soda bottles (with the bottoms cut off) for winter. Then she removes the bottles in spring.

"You can never be sure how many will make it," Alma says "But some of my cuttings have survived better than the original plants."

Sometimes these "friendship cuttings," as she calls them, produce an interesting new flower. The most unusual is a pink and red striped bloom (top left).

"My friends suggested I name it the 'Friend Alma rose,'" she says.

That would be appropriate, since she certainly is a friend to rose gardeners of all ages.

COMING UP ROSES. Alma Long (with husband Urban, center) launched a project to share rose gardening with local teens. She tends roses and other perennials in their rural backyard.

Mark Turner

Phlox

This versatile flower will take your yard from "nice" to "knockout."

With lush clusters of pretty, fragrant flowers and different varieties to suit any yard, there is no question that phlox is a perennial beauty.

Birds & Blooms editor Heather Lamb relies on easy-care creeping phlox to perk up her yard each spring.

"People always stop to ask about my phlox once it starts blooming in May," she says. "The pink and purple flowers spill over the edge of my front flower bed—it's quite a display that takes almost no effort to maintain. That's my kind of plant!"

Creeping phlox (above right) is just one of the many varieties of this versatile flower. It blooms in spring and forms

Photos this page: above, Nancy Rotenberg; top right, Donna and Tom Krischan; bottom right, Skip Moody/Dembinsky Photo Assoc.

PASTEL PALETTE. Bright-pink and soft-pink garden phlox (opposite page) punctuate this summer garden of goldenrod and hollyhocks. In spring, the lavender blooms of creeping phlox (above) pour down slopes to create an eye-catching display. White Miss Jill (right) is a great garden phlox, and wild sweet William (bottom right) is a popular type of wild phlox.

a cascading carpet of bright blossoms. Another common selection is garden or summer phlox, which grows much taller and flowers all summer long (that's it, at left).

Although it is native to North America, phlox wasn't actively cultivated here until European horticulturists introduced it in the 1800s. Then it took off like wildfire—not surprising when you consider that the word phlox is Greek for "flame."

Victorian gardeners were especially fond of the flower and often used it in bouquets and small nosegays called tussie-mussies. According to custom, a gift of phlox was a proposal of love, as well as a wish for sweet dreams.

A Sweet Addition

Mostly, though, people prized the blossoms for their scent. Unlike some old-fashioned flowers that have lost their fragrance due to hybridization, many phlox varieties still retain their delightful aroma.

There are many phlox species, as well as abundant hybrids, to offer a wide selection of colors, sizes and bloom times. With a little bit of planning, almost anyone can find an assortment to brighten their flower beds throughout the growing season. And, as an added bonus, phlox is known to attract butterflies and hummingbirds, too.

Pretty flower clusters atop tall stems make garden or summer phlox (*Phlox paniculata*) a popular selection. One frequently planted cultivar is David, a vigorous beauty that reaches 3 feet in height and blooms from July to September. It produces pearly white flowers that seem to glow both day and night, making your gardens shine.

Other garden phlox choices include Bright Eyes, which bears pink flowers with crimson centers; Laura, with white-centered pink blooms; and Franz Schubert, which produces

elegant lilac and pink clusters.

Creeping or moss phlox (*Phlox subulata*) is another well-known variety that you may want to try. It stays close to the ground, spreads quickly and provides a nice carpet of color and greenery. Creeping phlox also thrives in rock gardens, creating a vibrant carpet of color in lavender, blue, pink, purple or white.

Wild sweet William phlox (*Phlox maculata*, at right) prefers partial to full shade, making it a perfect choice for woodland gardens. Normally light blue, there also are purple and white hybrids of this midsized plant.

There's even an annual version of phlox, *Phlox drummondii*. Its blossoms come in almost any bright or pastel shade except blue or orange, and the plant will thrive in flower beds, containers and hanging baskets.

Planting 101

It's easy to include phlox in your favorite garden setting.

Although most love plenty of sun, there are specimens that do better in partial shade, so be sure to check before you grab the trowel. As far as soil conditions, a rich and well-draining area is the universal preference, although creeping phlox will handle dry situations.

Plant bare-root phlox in the spring when the danger of frost has passed. Container-grown varieties or those you've started from seed and hardened off can be put in the ground any time during the growing season. Space creeping phlox 12 inches apart and taller garden phlox 18 to 24 inches apart.

Water plants regularly, enough to keep the roots moist but not wet. Once they're established, water less frequently and add mulch to conserve moisture and suppress weeds.

As the plants begin to flourish, you'll need to provide just a bit of care to ensure plentiful blooms. Cut back creeping phlox about halfway after flowering. This will keep the plants looking full and may even encourage flowering later in the season. For garden phlox, regularly deadhead spent blooms to promote the formation of more flowers.

Pest Control

The biggest problem phlox faces is powdery mildew. Garden phlox varieties are particularly susceptible. The best way to handle the problem is to select mildew-resistant hybrids like David or the Flame Series.

You can help prevent mildew by improving air circulation around the plants. Avoid planting areas next to fences or walls, and remove about one-third of the stems in spring. If you do notice infected leaves, remove and discard them.

Another threat comes from deer and rabbits. These critters love to munch on phlox, so keep that in mind when deciding where to plant. If they become a problem, repellents and netting can reduce the animals' impact.

Most importantly, don't let these minor irritants discourage you from trying phlox. No matter what type you choose, this easy, breezy garden beauty adds color and texture to almost any kind of garden. You don't want to pass it by!

Alan and Linda Detrick

Jon Gnass/Gnass Photo Images

Plant Profile

Common Name: Phlox.

Botanical Name: *Phlox.*

Bloom Time: Spring or summer to fall. Bloom times vary by variety.

Hardiness: Zones 4 to 8 for most common varieties.

Flower Colors: Blue, white, purple, pink, lavender, red, orange and white.

Flower Shape: Five-petaled blooms with distinct central eyes. Some display clusters of flowers, while others are loose and carpet-like.

Height: 4 to 48 inches.

Spread: 4 to 36 inches.

Light Needs: Most varieties prefer full sun. Wild sweet William thrives in partial to full shade, and creeping phlox works in dappled shade in arid regions.

Soil Type: Moist, well-drained soil. Creeping phlox (above) will tolerate dry conditions.

Prize Picks: David and the Flame Series are garden phlox hybrids that resist powdery mildew. For creeping phlox, try Emerald Blue for light-blue flowers, or the free-flowering McDaniel's Cushion in rock gardens or along a wall. Wild sweet William also resists mildew, even when grown in light shade.

Backyard Benefits: Attracts butterflies; hummingbirds feed on garden phlox.

GREEN THUMB TIP

Phlox comes in just about any shape and size you could want. For a vibrant ground cover, try creeping phlox. Or use tall garden phlox to add summerlong color.

Gay Bumgarner

MYSTERIOUS PLANT CHANGES

Why flowers unexpectedly change color or form.

By Melinda Myers, Contributing Editor

Gardening is full of surprises. One of the most puzzling is when flowers unexpectedly change color or form. I hear from many gardeners who wonder why this happens—a purple patch of flowers that becomes yellow; an oddball red bloom on a white-flowering plant; or flowers that take on the characteristics of the surrounding plants (like the striped tulips above).

Although it may seem like the work of mischievous garden gnomes, there typically are three possible reasons for such plant changes: mutations (also called "sports"), hybridizing, or offspring plants that exhibit different features than the parents. To determine what caused these changes in your yard, start by examining the plant's history.

A Sporting Chance

For instance, reader Dawn Scheppke of Eau Claire, Wisconsin reported that when she planted purple irises in her flower bed of yellow ones, several irises emerged as *purple and yellow* the following spring.

Since the two irises didn't have time to cross-pollinate (that would take longer than a single season), some of the irises probably sported, a spontaneous mutation from the parent plant…though the timing is oddly coincidental.

When flower growers discover a sport, they often propagate them and sell the new plants for their unique size, color or flavor. The golden delicious apple is a tasty example of a plant that first emerged as a sport.

Many variegated plants also are the result of sports. But sometimes, these plants revert back to the parent plants' original color and form.

That's what happened in Phyllis Felton's garden in Castle Creek, New York. She wrote to ask about her variegated hostas that are turning solid green.

Unfortunately, there's nothing a gardener can do to stop this process. Just enjoy the new surprises each season.

Plant changes also occur through hybridizing—when two plants cross-pollinate. This results in a reshuffling of genetic material, with the offspring taking on various characteristics from both parent plants.

Jane Elliott of Manchester, New Jersey experienced a somewhat different dilemma. A division of her blue balloon flowers turned white after she transplanted them.

While this may be a sport, it could also be the result of the offspring not growing true from seed—a common problem with hybrid plants, which typically don't produce seeds that carry the genetic material needed to grow an exact copy of the parent plant.

It's possible the transplanted portion died, but then dormant seeds in the soil sprouted and grew. These seedlings didn't come true from seed, causing the resulting flower color to be white instead of blue.

Other Explanations

Donna Schubert of Republic, Ohio knows that grafted roses—including most hybrid teas—also can change color. For 7 years, her rosebush boasted orange blossoms. Then one year, red roses appeared on the same plant.

This happened because propagators graft a single bud of the desirable rose, orange in this case, onto a hardy root system. If part of the grafted portion dies, often as the result of cold temperatures, the hardy rootstock will take over.

Believe it or not, diseases can also cause changes in plant characteristics. Europe's 17th-century tulip craze, known as Tulipmania, was the result of a virus. The disease infected a plant, causing a yellow streak to develop in a red flower. The resulting bloom caused people to go gaga trying to obtain the unique bulbs.

The bottom line when it comes to plant changes? Remove the new plants if you don't like them or if they compete with your desirable plants. Or leave them be.

You just might end up with a sport or a hybrid that's better than the plant you purchased.

DAZZLING DAHLIAS

These garden darlings provide beautiful bursts of color well into fall.

By Kathleen Zimmer-Anderson
Waukesha, Wisconsin

If variety is the spice of life, then this lush bloomer is one of the zestiest flowers around! With more than 20,000 different cultivars, dahlias come in all shapes, sizes and colors (except for blue), making them a favorite among gardeners across North America.

Dahlias have cast their spell on me. I've been a fan ever since I saw them growing at my younger brother Mike's new home. Once I'd gotten over the fact that he had a hidden green thumb, I caught sight of the full red and yellow blooms gracing his flower bed and couldn't look away.

Mike figured out pretty quickly what had captured my attention and promised he'd help me pick out a few for my garden. I've been growing dahlias ever since.

New-World Native

Appreciation for these members of the daisy family dates back to the Aztecs in Mexico, who used the indigenous plant they called *cocoxochitl* as a cure for epilepsy. Elsewhere in Central and South America, the fleshy, sugar-filled tubers were used for food. Later on, sugar extracted from the tubers served as a treatment for diabetes.

Spanish conquistadors admired the plant's beauty and brought the blooms to Spain in the 18th century. In 1789, the king of Spain bestowed the name "dahlia" on the plant. He chose the moniker in honor of Swedish botanist Anders Dahl, who'd created numerous hybrids.

Hundreds of years later, the flowers are more popular than ever before.

"Dahlias have as broad a range as you'd find in any flower group in terms of size, shape and color," says Alan Fisher of the American Dahlia Society, who raises hundreds of varieties at his home in Rockville, Maryland. "Many gardeners grow

SHAPING UP. There are 11 different dahlia shapes, providing enough variety to satisfy any gardener. They pair well with other flowers, too, like the ball dahlias with cleome above left.

them to enjoy their beauty, while others like to cultivate show-quality blooms and compete in local dahlia shows.

"There's really something for everyone, from tiny specimens to huge tree dahlias that thrive on the West Coast. They can reach as high as 20 feet in a single season and produce flowers as late as November."

Take Your Pick

Because of this huge variety, dahlias are separated into six categories for size and 11 categories for bloom type. The flowers range from dainty 1-inch pompoms to 6- to 8-inch mid-size varieties and giant versions that can measure well over 15 inches wide.

Shape categories include decorative dahlias with full curving, multipetaled blossoms; ball-shaped dahlias with a full pompom of petals (top far left photo); cactus dahlias that sport spiky petals (center left); collarette varieties that have a ring of rounded petals topped by smaller ones; orchid dahlias that feature a pinwheel of inward-curling petals and single dahlias (bottom left) that look like daisies. And that's just the tip of the iceberg!

Most dahlias are on the tall side, standing anywhere from 2 to 5 feet high, with some soaring to 6 feet or more. The loftiest varieties need to be staked in order to prevent the wind from damaging them.

Even the dwarf varieties are sizable, measuring 1 to 2 feet

in height. They are ideal for filling the center of smaller flower beds or in containers.

Aside from catching attention, dahlias will attract hummingbirds and butterflies during summer, and provide a blaze of color until the first frost, much like chrysanthemums.

Friends and Foes

Dahlias pair up nicely with a variety of garden favorites. Try bunching together several short and medium-sized varieties in different spots in a garden that's filled with perennials or annuals.

You can also combine them with threadleaf coreopsis or ornamental grasses—the contrast between the finely textured plants and the bold and leafy dahlias works nicely.

Pests can be a problem on occasion. I've had trouble with slugs that savor my dahlias' meaty foliage, and my brother has battled mites and aphids.

Insecticidal soap will help control insects, and there are a number of commercial sprays and traps for slugs. I've found that sinking containers of yeast and water into the ground near my dahlias to capture slugs works well, too.

Don't forget that dahlias aren't hardy unless you live in an area that doesn't see frost. If your home is in a colder cli-

DIGGIN' DAHLIAS. Although dahlias' tuberous roots (above) have to be stored indoors for winter in cold regions, the vibrant blooms that emerge in summer (below and left) are well worth the effort.

mate like mine, dig up each plant's tuberous roots after the first light frost in fall. Then dry them off and store in a cool, dark place, like a cellar, until planting them in spring.

Not only do these lovelies brighten sunny gardens, they also make outstanding cut flowers, thanks in large part to their sturdy stalks and ability to look fresh for a long time.

Early morning or early evening are the best times to snip the long-stemmed blossoms for a bouquet. Cut the stems at a 45-degree angle, then submerge them—flower and all—in a container of warm water. After a bit, move the flowers to a vase filled with cold water. Trim 1 inch off the stems before creating an arrangement.

A Little TLC

Some gardeners start their dahlias indoors each spring for earlier blooms, but I've never bothered with this. I just pop the tubers, with the "eyes" up, into 4-inch-deep holes once the threat of frost has passed. This method results in later blooming, but I don't mind.

Whether you plant dahlias indoors in early spring or head straight for the garden before summer begins, remember that these beauties like plenty of light. Plant them in a spot that receives 5 or more hours of sun each day.

Dahlias prefer rich, well-draining soil and regular watering. Add mulch to help retain moisture in the soil and apply fertilizer from time to time—these babies have a big appetite! If you don't fertilize regularly or if you water a bit too much, you'll notice because the leaves will turn yellow.

For short, bushy plants with an abundance of smaller blooms, pinch off the growing tips and deadhead spent blooms regularly.

READER TIP

Early mornings or early evenings are the best times to snip these long-stemmed blossoms for a bouquet. Cut at a 45-degree angle, submerge in a container of warm water and then move to a vase filled with cold water.

Dahlias will produce larger, more dramatic flowers if you confine the plant to a single major stem. Remove the side shoots as they grow, as well as any flower buds that develop along the stem, leaving one bud at the very top. The resulting blossom will be worth the effort!

Editor's Note: If you want to find out more about the flowers or meet other gardeners who share your enthusiasm for dahlias, contact the American Dahlia Society. Visit its Web site at *www.dahlia.org* to learn how. Or, send inquires to Richard Peters, 931 W. Wellington Ct., Muskegon MI 49441.

Plant Profile

Common Name: Dahlia.

Botanical Name: *Dahlia* species.

Bloom Time: Summer to first frost.

Hardiness: Zones 7 to 11; tubers must be dug up and stored indoors for winter in other areas.

Flower Colors: All colors except blue; many bicolored varieties are available.

Flower Shapes: There are 11 different basic shapes.

Height: 1 to 6 feet.

Spread: 1 to 3 feet.

Light Needs: Full sun.

Soil Type: Rich and well-draining.

Planting: Once the threat of frost has passed, plant tubers about 4 inches deep with an "eye" pointing up. Add mulch to help retain moisture.

Special Care: Stake taller varieties to protect from wind damage. After the first frost in northern areas, bring the tubers inside. Pack the roots in sand and store in a cool, dry place over winter.

Hibiscus

This beauty's amazing blossoms are a tropical treat.

W hen it comes to making a big impression in the garden, few flowers measure up to the hibiscus. The distinctive blooms are awesome, from 6 to 12 inches wide, with five large petals that look like crepe paper. They add texture, bold color and a splash of "wow" to any backyard.

There's no question that its exotic appearance takes center stage, but hibiscus is also a favorite of gardeners for purely practical reasons. The perennial varieties are tough, adaptable and virtually carefree. In fact, minimal attention will yield a continuous bounty of blooms from summer through fall.

Deep Roots

Hibiscus has been brightening flower beds and natural areas around the world for centuries. The word "hibiscus" comes from the ancient Greek name for "mallow," because it was thought to resemble the mallow flower. In fact, the hibiscus is a prominent member of the mallow family.

It's also been called "flower of an hour" and "good night at noon," because the blooms of many varieties last less than 24 hours and will quickly wilt if picked.

The blossoms, which come in a rainbow of hues, have been used to dye cloth and even make a delightful tea. In some Caribbean countries, it's tradition to include hibiscus in wedding bouquets in order to ward off bad luck.

Hawaii is home to more than 5,000 tropical hybrids and recognizes the hibiscus as its official flower. The Chinese have long put the plant on a pedestal, too, prominently featuring it in artwork, including decorated porcelain plates that date back to the mid-1300s.

Close to Home

There are more than 250 different hibiscus species today, including a number of flowers that are hardy in the U.S. *Hibiscus moscheutos* and *Hibiscus coccineus* are a native to North America. Some of these varieties have been known to grow wild in marshes on the eastern seaboard, and many have long been common components of sprawling Southern gardens.

The popular *Hibiscus moscheutos* perennial, sometimes called swamp mallow or rose mallow, varies in height from 2 to 10 feet and produces brilliant flowers measuring 7 to 12 inches across, as well as attractive green foliage. Some hybrids are even tough enough to withstand subzero winter temperatures, making them suitable for areas as far north as Zone 4.

TAKE A VACATION. You'll feel like you're on an island getaway with a tropical hibiscus like the Ross Estey (previous page) in your garden. Even if you live in a colder region, these blooms can grow in containers. Or try perennial hibiscus varieties, which provide huge flowers in Zones 4 to 10.

Tropical Paradise

Another popular type of hibiscus is the tropical variety— botanically known as *Hibiscus rosa-sinensis* and sometimes called Chinese hibiscus or rose of China.

These graceful showstoppers obviously don't tolerate low temperatures, and they thrive in gardens year-round only in warm, humid coastal climates like those found in Florida, Texas and California—but that's not to say you can't enjoy a tropical hibiscus in your backyard if you live in a cooler region.

The plants flourish in containers on decks, patios and porches during summer and can be brought inside for winter. With a little effort, they'll even flower indoors if placed in a well-lit window.

This showy species has a more diverse array of flowers than its perennial cousins, including both single and dou-

Mark Turner; previous page, Richard Shiell

Chapter 5

ble blooms in a wider range of colors. Its flowers tend to be slightly smaller, but still measure 4 to 8 inches across.

Ready to Plant

Before you plant, remember that both tropical and perennial hibiscus crave sunlight. Both also appreciate occasional applications of fertilizer.

Container-grown tropical specimens are readily available at garden centers and require only minimal attention, including a few extra doses of flowering plant food and regular watering if you keep them as potted plants. They can stay outside until temperatures drop.

Perennial hibiscus, on the other hand, can be easily started from seed. If you live in the South, you can sow the seeds directly outdoors in spring. In the North, it's better to start the seeds indoors first, then move them outside once the threat of frost has passed.

Since perennial hybrids originated in swamps and marshes, they prefer rich, moist soil that retains water. And because of their size, most look best when planted in clusters to form a hedge or lining the back of a flower bed to avoid overshadowing smaller plants. Perennial hibiscus is late to emerge, so be patient.

Prior to planting, improve the soil with a mixture of compost and peat moss. This will promote deep root growth, increasing the plant's chances of winter survival. It's also a good idea to add a few inches of mulch on the soil around your hibiscus to help the plant retain moisture during summer and provide insulation in winter.

Believe it or not, that's about all it takes to include these vibrant starlets in your garden. And the reward is months of color each summer, not to mention the "oohing" and "aahing" of visitors when they see the massive and plentiful blooms.

Plant Profile

Common Name: Hibiscus.

Botanical Name: *Hibiscus* species.

Bloom Time: Early summer to first frost.

Hardiness: *Hibiscus moscheutos* and *Hibiscus coccineus* (perennials): Zones 4 to 10; *Hibiscus rosa-sinensis* (tropical): Zones 10 and 11.

Flower Colors: Red, pink, blue, purple, white, yellow.

Flower Shape: Funnel- or trumpet-shaped blossoms have five petals, a distinct central stamen and are 4 to 12 inches in diameter.

Height: 2 to 15 feet.

Spread: 3 to 10 feet.

Light Needs: Full sun.

Soil Type: Rich, moist and well-drained.

Planting: Start seeds of perennials indoors or in the garden. Nick the seeds with a nail file or knife, then soak them in water for 24 hours before planting to encourage them to grow quickly. Container-grown plants of both perennial and tropical varieties also are available.

Prize Picks: Lord Baltimore, a perennial, grows to 6 feet in height, has rich-red 7- to 10-inch flowers and is hardy in Zones 5 to 9. Disco Bell, another perennial, is more compact, offers red, pink or white 9-inch flowers and works well as an annual in colder northern areas.

Fantasia is a tropical variety that bears smaller, reddish-pink flowers with petals that are slightly fringed; Kinchen's Yellow has golden 5- to 6-inch blooms; and Fiesta produces larger, apricot-colored flowers.

GREEN THUMB TIP

Do you want a touch of the tropics in your garden? Tropical hibiscus, though hardy only in Zones 10 and 11, will thrive in containers just about anywhere.

Richard Shiell

RUSSIAN SAGE

This aromatic and elegant perennial is a real winner.

By Stacy Tornio, Associate Editor

The description of Russian sage may sound lofty, but it won't let you down. This perennial promises to be low-maintenance and grow in a variety of soils...and provide eye-catching beauty besides!

It's no wonder the Perennial Plant Association named Russian sage as the Perennial Plant of the Year in 1995. This charmer earned the honor for its striking stems of lavender-blue flowers, long blooming season and easy care.

Russian sage has gray-green leaves and silvery stems, which add to its lovely elegance, but the real treat arrives in late summer. This is when the plant bursts forth with small, lavender-blue flowers, aligned in gentle spiral clusters along the stems.

Like garden sage, Russian sage is part of the mint family, and its scent lives up to the name. The light, sage-like fragrance of the plant is easy to detect in the garden, and the leaves release a lovely aroma when crushed.

A Russian botanist chose the plant's botanical name,

Perovskia atriplicifolia, in the 1800s to honor B.A. Perovski, the governor of a Russian providence. The plant's origins are in central Asia near Afghanistan and Pakistan.

A Versatile Choice

Though many gardeners use Russian sage as a filler plant, it certainly has the presence to shine alone. At maturity, it reaches 3 to 4 feet tall and spreads another 3 feet wide. This makes it perfect as a mass planting to fill in a large space or for a colorful backdrop to other plants.

Choosing companion flowers for Russian sage is as easy as selecting your favorite color. It's hard to go wrong—Russian sage will complement just about any plant. In addition, the extensive blooming season of Russian sage makes it a popular pairing for both summer and autumn perennials.

Purple coneflowers and black-eyed Susans are a couple of the common choices. Others that work well include daylily, bee balm, garden phlox, coreopsis and aster. Just make sure

R. Todd Davis

Alan and Linda Detrick

Plant Profile

Common Name: Russian sage.
Botanical Name: *Perovskia atriplicifolia.*
Bloom Time: Summer to early fall.
Hardiness: Zones 4 to 9.
Flower Color: Lavender blue.
Flower Shape: Small, tubular flowers on panicles.
Height: 2 to 4 feet.
Spread: 3 to 4 feet.
Light Needs: Full sun.
Soil Type: Well-draining.
Planting: Start bare-root plants in early spring or container plants throughout the growing season.
Prize Picks: Blue Spire has deeper purple blooms; Little Spire works well in small spaces, reaching only 30 inches tall.

PURPLE HAZE. With long stems of lavender-blue flowers, Russian sage can shine alone (above left) or share the spotlight. Above, Russian sage accents Joe Pye weed, porcupine grass, daylilies and rudbeckia. The plant's delicate blooms (above right) last from summer until autumn.

the size of the plant you choose is enough to stand up to Russian sage's big and billowy nature.

Most Russian sage plants are self-supporting, but tend to grow loose and open. To encourage stiff growth, try pruning the plants halfway back in June. Or, enjoy its freedom and accent it with other large companion plants.

Up, Up and Away

To add Russian sage to your garden, start bare-root plants in spring or use container-grown perennials throughout the growing season, spacing the plants 30 to 36 inches apart. They will tolerate most soil conditions, including rocky areas.

As you're growing new plantings, make sure to give them plenty of water, but don't overdo it on the fertilizer. Excess fertilization can often lead to floppy stems and meager flowers.

Once you've established Russian sage, the majority of your work is done. As long as it's in well-drained soil where

READER TIP

Russian sage will complement many types of perennials. Some of the top picks include purple coneflowers, black-eyed Susans, daylilies, bee balm, garden phlox, coreopsis and aster.

it gets plenty of sun, Russian sage often blooms from July through October without any maintenance, and it also withstands drought. You don't have to worry about pests or diseases either, which don't bother this plant.

Although Russian sage is categorized as a perennial, its outstretched demeanor makes it quite shrub-like. By late fall, its stems become woody, but you can continue to enjoy the plant throughout winter. The silver stems create a beautiful seasonal show.

Once spring arrives and the danger of frost has passed, prune the stems 4 to 6 inches above the ground. This will help keep the plant compact and allow for new growth.

Take Your Pick

There are several cultivars of the popular garden variety of Russian sage.

Little Spire is a more compact variety that reaches only 30 inches tall. Filigran also is a smaller cultivar at 2 to 3 feet tall and has narrower fine-textured leaves. Longin has wider less dissected leaves and grows in a straight, upright form.

Finally, for a wider choice of bloom colors, try Blue Haze, which has lighter blue flowers with fewer lacy leaves, or Blue Spire for a deeper purple hue.

No matter what type of this dynamic perennial you select for your garden, it's sure to live up to its promises. After all, the plant already has received top honors.

Blooming Beauty

Moss Rose

This annual flourishes under tough conditions.

By Kathleen Zimmer-Anderson, Waukesha, Wisconsin

Whenever I see a container of colorful moss roses at the garden center, it reminds me of the flower bed that lined the south side of my childhood home. The narrow strip was wedged between the driveway and our lannon stone house, a spot that was both hot and dry during the summer...and it was perfect for those sweet little posies.

Each spring, my mom would ask me to help her plant a bunch of nursery-grown moss roses in that garden, and this was one chore I never resisted. It was fun to dig in the dirt next to Mom and uncover any of the previous year's moss roses that had managed to reseed. But the biggest reward of all was seeing those lush little blooms pop out a month or so later, in cheerful shades of red, orange, yellow, white and purple.

If no one was looking, I'd pick a few flowers and take them up to my room, as though they were trophies of my gardening triumph. And now, as an adult, I don't consider my green-thumb efforts successful until I see moss rose

blooms emerging along the front walkway to our house. They make my garden complete.

Longtime Popularity

This old-fashioned garden favorite is actually a South American native and was first introduced to European gardeners some 300 years ago. While gardeners appreciated the moss rose's lovely appearance, it quickly gained popularity for its medicinal properties, which included relieving teeth grinding and muscle spasms, and soothing gunpowder burns.

The plant has a mild, pleasant flavor and was often eaten cold, cooked or pickled, or used to thicken soups and stews. People also consumed the vitamin-rich leaves to prevent scurvy.

There's even a magical side to the moss rose. Many believed that placing a flower on a child's bed kept evil spirits at bay as the youngster slept.

Today, this semi-succulent annual is best known for its

ability to thrive in the kind of hot, dry conditions that cause less stalwart species to shrivel and die.

The moss rose reaches a mere 4 to 8 inches in height, and its low-growing nature makes it the ideal flower for the very front of the garden. It also tends to creep and spread and will look nice in rock gardens, window boxes and hanging baskets throughout the summer months.

The short, narrow leaves cluster profusely along rosy stems, giving the plant a feathery, moss-like appearance and providing a rich backdrop for the vivid flowers.

The cup-shaped blooms come in either single or double form, with the latter truly resembling a rose. What's most notable about the flowers is the fact that they will open only when the sun is bright in the sky.

New hybrids have flowers that remain open later and when skies are cloudy, like the Sundial series and Afternoon Delight. However, you want to be sure to plant your moss roses where you can see them during the day—they definitely can't be enjoyed at night.

Plant a Rosy Picture

Including these garden gems in your yard is easy, whether you plan to sow seeds or use bedding plants. You can start seeds indoors, about 6 weeks before the last frost, by sprinkling them on top of planting mix and watering well in order to embed the seeds in the mix, a technique known as "watering in."

Or you can scatter seeds on top of the soil outdoors after the threat of frost has passed and water to sow them into the ground. One great idea is to position them near spring bulbs and perennials that fade early in the season. As these flowers die back, the moss roses will spread and add color to the landscape.

Bedding plants need no special handling. Just be sure to space them 6 to 12 inches apart in spots that receive plenty of sunshine. Regularly watering young transplants until they're well established is a good idea, but once they begin to thrive, you'll want to cut back on the water to avoid root and stem rot.

You can apply a little fertilizer if you like, and occasionally removing spent blooms is fine. Otherwise, moss roses are virtually carefree!

Below and opposite page: Alan and Linda Detrick

Plant Profile

Donna and Tom Krischan

Common Names: Moss rose, rose moss, sun plant.

Botanical Name: *Portulaca grandiflora*.

Bloom Time: Summer through fall.

Hardiness: Annual.

Flower Colors: Yellow, orange, red, white, purple and rose.

Flower Shape: Roselike blossoms are cup shaped with four to seven petals and measure 1-1/2 to 2 inches across. Available as single or double blooms.

Leaves: Cylindrical and pointed, measuring about 1 inch long. The fleshy, semi-succulent leaves grow in clusters and range in color from bright to dark green.

Height: 4 to 8 inches.

Spread: 6 inches.

Light Needs: Full sun.

Soil Type: Well-drained. Moss rose prefers hot, dry conditions, making them ideal for rock gardens, hanging baskets, containers or any arid spot in the garden.

Prize Picks: Afternoon Delight, the Sundial series and Sundance Mix stay open later or when the sky is overcast. The most common double-flowering cultivars are in the Calypso series. Margarita Rosita is a beautiful semi-double selection.

GREEN THUMB TIP

Plant moss roses near spring bulbs and perennials that fade early in the season. As summer goes on, the plants will spread and add great color to your garden.

BASK IN THE GLOW OF SUNFLOWERS

These bright blooms are a longtime garden favorite for all ages.

By Kathleen Zimmer-Anderson, Waukesha, Wisconsin

Chapter 5

Alan and Linda Detrick

Alan and Linda Detrick

Gay Bumgarner

TOWERING TREASURE. The warm glow of sunflowers will brighten any garden. This beauty also attracts birds, like the white-breasted nuthatch (far left inset) and adds statuesque prominence to backyards with flowers that soar as high as 15 feet. Numerous varieties are available, including (above, from left) Floristan, Music Box and Teddy Bear.

I've always thought of sunflowers as kings of the garden. When I was a young girl, my dad and I tucked sunflower seeds into the earth and tended them until the plants towered majestically overhead.

Nothing else quite measured up to those sturdy-stalked beauties. And the rewards as summer progressed into fall fed both body and soul—amazing flowers and tasty seeds for my brothers and me to munch on. Sunflowers symbolized goodness.

I still feel that way today, which is why I make a point to plant sunflowers with my daughters each spring. Listening to Olivia and Abigail "ooh" and "aah" as the seedlings nudge their way out of the soil and sprout tall and strong is a treat...and I experience the same childhood thrill.

Without a doubt, sunflowers are particularly well suited for teaching youngsters the joys of gardening, mostly because the large seeds are easy to plant, they require just a little TLC, and the results are speedy and stunning. But that doesn't mean more serious gardeners should ignore these sunny specimens.

Universal Appeal

Today, sunflower hybrids come in a wider range of shapes and sizes than ever before, virtually ensuring that you can find one to fit into almost any style flower bed. The colors of the flowers have expanded well beyond yellow to include red, purple, rust and even white.

Among the annual varieties you can choose from, Mammoth Russian and Russian Giant produce traditional 10-inch-wide golden flowers on top of tough stalks that rise as high as 15 feet. Sunspot is a more diminutive cousin, bearing similar sized blooms on 2-foot-tall stems.

The flowers of the 4- to 5-foot-tall Ring of Fire are 5 inches wide and very colorful, from the rich-brown center to the circle of red petals outlined by another circle of warm, yellow petals. Autumn Fire, another midsized variety, has blossoms that range in color from rich mahogany to lemon, gold and bronze,

while the Italian White variety features unusual dark-centered, creamy blooms.

Teddy Bear is a compact cultivar that grows a mere 2 feet tall with 5-inch-wide double flowers. Music Box, a 2-foot-tall, multibranched type, yields a crop of blooms in a slew of shades, including some bicolor combinations.

You also can find dwarf varieties at garden centers in late summer that are perfect for containers or planting in bare spots in your garden. These mini sunflowers match up nicely with mums, pumpkins and asters to create an attractive fall display.

Want something more permanent? Give a perennial sunflower (*Helianthus multiflorus*) like Flore Pleno a try. This double-flowered variety thrives in Zones 4 to 9 and develops 5- to 6-foot-tall stalks with sizable, dark-green leaves, as well as a profusion of brilliant-yellow, dahlia-like blooms that last well into September.

A host of other perennial varieties are available as well, including Capenoch Star and Lodden Gold, both of which produce lovely, lush flowers year after year that are perfect for cutting and in arrangements.

A native plant in North and South America, people have used the sunflower as both a decoration and a source of food for centuries. The Incas in Peru actually worshipped sunflowers. Other Indian tribes were more practical in their approach to the plant, using it in cooking, as hair accents and to make paint.

Multipurpose Posy

Early pioneers spun and wove fibers from the stalk into fabric, used the petals to make dye and discovered the whole plant provided food for people and animals alike. Many sowed sunflowers right next to their sod houses or cabins in the belief that the plants

Blooming Beauty

Alan and Linda Detrick

SUNNY DISPOSITION. With more than 70 species to choose from, you're sure to find a sunflower to love. Traditional varieties tower over the backyard with their sunny flowers (below). Perennials like Flore Pleno (left) return year after year. The Vanilla Ice hybrid shows its cool colors (bottom).

warded off malaria.

Modern fans of sunflowers often rely on them to lend height to a flower bed or to attract butterflies and hummingbirds. Many also harvest the seeds to fill bird feeders during the winter months.

Keeping hungry critters away from the flower heads can be a challenge. In fact, I vividly remember the year we lost our entire crop to the marauding chipmunks who lived in the stone wall that edged my parents' garden.

But there is an animal-friendly solution to this situation. Simply cover the flowers loosely with cheesecloth or netting, and you'll discourage squirrels, chipmunks and other scavengers.

Start the harvesting process when the backs of the flower heads turn brown. You can cut them, leaving 1 to 2 feet of the stems attached. Hang the heads upside down until they are completely dry and brown. Then the seeds will be ready and can be roasted or saved for the birds.

Green-Thumb Care

Growing these showy yet incredibly resilient flowers is a cinch. They will withstand both heat and drought and require only the most basic upkeep.

Pick a spot that receives full sun and has moderately fertile, well-drained soil. You can plant the seeds directly in the ground about 6 inches apart once all danger of frost has passed—or you can start seeds indoors in moist seed starter mix 4 to 6 weeks earlier. Keep the temperature between 68° and 86°, water regularly and seedlings will appear in 10 to 14 days. Transplant hardened-off seedlings outdoors after the last frost.

When seedlings are about 3 inches tall, thin them to a spacing of 18 to 24 inches between each plant. Then water from time to time when the top few inches of soil become crumbly. If you've chosen a taller variety, you could stake the stem as it grows to prevent the plant from bending or breaking, either under its own weight or in very windy conditions.

You might notice that the leaves turn spotty or white. This is caused by leaf spot or powdery mildew, conditions that are unsightly but not fatal. To cover up the leaves, you can plant slightly shorter flowers in front. Aphids can also cause minor damage but won't really do much harm. Otherwise, sunflowers are fairly pest- and disease-free.

In fact, it's almost impossible to find a friendlier blossom to grow in your garden. So start thinking now about what varieties you'd like to include in the mix next spring. You can even enlist the little ones to help you sow seeds when the time comes, and turn sunflower cultivation into a full family affair.

Plant Profile

Mark Turner

Common Name: Sunflower.
Botanical Name: *Helianthus annuus*.
Bloom Time: Summer to first frost.
Hardiness: Annual; perennial types hardy in Zones 4 to 9, depending on variety.
Flower Colors: Typically yellow with dark centers. Some hybrids bear red, purple or white hues.
Flower Shape: Showy, daisy-like blooms that consist of colorful florets surrounding a dark center. Some double-flowered varieties resemble mums or dahlias.
Height: 15 inches to 15 feet.
Spread: 1 to 2 feet.
Light Needs: Full sun.
Soil Type: Moderately rich and well-draining.
Planting: For annuals, sow seeds 6 inches apart after danger of frost has passed. Thin seedlings when they are 3 inches tall, leaving 18 to 24 inches between plants.
Attracts: A variety of hummingbirds and butterflies will feed from the flowers. Later, squirrels and birds will eat the seeds.

Chapter 5

Maslowski Productions, two sunflower photos: Rick Wetherbee

Living Bird Feeders

Sunflowers provide a natural backyard bird buffet.

By Kris Wetherbee, Oakland, Oregon

One of the great traditions of the American garden is growing sunflowers. These cheery sun worshipers have broad appeal, not only for the beauty they bring, but also for the bounty of birds and butterflies they attract with sweet nectar and high-energy seeds.

Sunflower seeds attract a wider variety of birds than any other type of feeder seed. If these power-packed seeds can make your bird feeding stations a favorite destination spot, just imagine what they can do when growing in your garden!

The sunflower family (*Helianthus*) includes about 70 different summer- and fall-blooming annuals and perennials, though this native American plant is best known for the common or giant sunflower (*Helianthus annuus*). Sunflowers grew as early as 3,000 B.C., and American Indians used this versatile flower in medicine and as a vital food source.

"Set the Table" Your Own Way

Despite its history, Americas' love affair with sunflowers is changing—not in the way we use them, but rather in the kinds of sunflowers we grow.

Giant sunflowers like 'Russian Giant,' with its huge head (far right) may have reigned in the past, but the traditional favorite has opened the door to a new generation of botanical beauties with more variety than ever before.

That means gardeners who want to use the plants to attract birds have an array of options.

Compact varieties grow just 1 to 4 feet tall and work well in container gardens, a children's garden, or as border or edging plants.

Taller, multibranching types grow 4 to 6 feet tall, and produce more flowers per plant for a bird buffet with even more appeal. These multibranched varieties are outstanding when mingled in flower beds and borders, as focal points in the vegetable garden or even arranged in semi-circles as "sunflower forts" for kids.

The More, the Merrier

All these choices expand the design possibilities in the garden—just don't limit yourself to one variety or even one plant. Growing several varieties with different forms, colors and heights amplifies the visual interest in your garden and visual attraction to butterflies and birds.

And since sunflowers rely on cross-pollination for best yields, they will only produce ample seed when two or more plants are in bloom. More plants means more flowers for you and more seeds for the birds. What could be better than that?

10 Tempting Treats for Birds

From pint-sized plants to true giants, here are 10 terrific sunflower varieties that will help you attract birds.

1. AUTUMN BEAUTY
2. BIG SMILE
3. FLORISTAN
4. HOLIDAY
5. THE JOKER
6. RUSSIAN GIANT
7. RED SUN
8. SORAYA
9. VALENTINE
10. VANILLA ICE

Purple Coneflower

This perennial princess adds a royal glow to the garden.

By Kathleen Zimmer-Anderson
Waukesha, Wisconsin

It wasn't a case of love at first sight. When I introduced purple coneflowers to my backyard flower bed, I did it more out of necessity than anything else.

My husband and I were new home owners and novice gardeners, so our raised, weed-ridden bed posed a challenge. We cleared it without much trouble, but filling it was another matter.

My mother, the master gardener, suggested I plant purple coneflowers. "They don't take much work, and they're pretty," she said. "You won't regret it."

I have to admit that I didn't listen at first. But after I watched a fussy, high-maintenance rosebush flounder despite all my efforts, I conceded that Mom might be right. I replaced the rosebush with a rather bedraggled, container-grown coneflower.

Though it was late July when I tucked it into the bed, the perennial valiantly produced a few blooms before the weather turned cold. The following year, my coneflower showed its true colors when it provided a continuous blast of rich purple all summer with no help from me...and I fell head over heels for this hearty beauty.

I'm not the only gardener who feels this way. The purple coneflower has long been prized for its sturdy disposition, long-lasting mass of color and ability to attract a variety of fliers (like this bee, inset).

The daisy-like flowers of this North American native

Donna and Tom Krischan; inset, Sylvester Allred/Unicorn Stock Photos

CROWN JEWELS. Whether you choose newer gold or dark-orange varieties (left), or let the popular purple reign (below), purple coneflowers add regal beauty with minimal upkeep.

stand on sturdy stalks that grow to 5 feet in height, making coneflowers versatile enough to anchor an island flower bed or plant along a wall or fence. Prized in flower arrangements, too, its attractive blossoms will last a week or more after being cut.

All in a Name

Part of the scientific name of the species, *Echinacea*, comes from the Greek word for hedgehog—a reference to the flower's prickly looking center.

This botanical moniker may sound familiar for reasons that have nothing to do with gardening. Many people today take Echinacea supplements to fight viruses.

The purple coneflower's medicinal value isn't a new discovery, however. Years ago, people used it to treat colds, scurvy and even snakebites. They'd often harvest the wildflower, sometimes called Indian or scurvy root, from prairies and open woodlands in the central and eastern parts of the U.S. and Canada.

Today, coneflowers crop up in backyards from coast to coast. In addition to the original purplish-red version, often called rudbeckia, a number of hybrids exist in a range of colors that are equally captivating.

For example, Magnus produces sizable, 7-inch-wide blooms with vibrant, dark-orange centers and deep-purple petals that don't droop as much as other varieties. Bright Star offers smaller, maroon-centered rosy flowers. Meadowbrite, a relative newcomer, bears striking orange-petaled blossoms with rust centers and a subtly fragrant scent.

For those who like white flowers, there are a number of cultivars to choose from, including the 32-inch-tall White Lustre, the slightly shorter White Swan and Finale White, with its unusual greenish-brown center and creamy petals. The rosy blooms and compact 15-3/4-inch form of Kim's Knee High rank high among gardeners, too.

Easy-Growing Nature

No matter which variety you choose, you'll quickly find the purple coneflower exceptionally easy to cultivate. You can give your plants a good head start by choosing a sunny spot for them. Light shade is okay, too, but anything more will result in lackluster growth and an absence of flowers.

Keep in mind that this plant prefers well-draining soil that isn't overly rich. If you are cursed with clay, like I am, it helps to loosen up soil and work in some organic matter to improve drainage.

You can sow purple coneflower seeds directly in the garden after the last frost, scattering them across the area you've prepared. Then rake the soil lightly to cover the seeds, tamp it down and water thoroughly. You won't see blooms right away—in fact, it may take several years for the plants to produce flowers.

For faster results, you can turn to bare-root plants, which can go in the ground in spring, or container-grown coneflowers, which can be transplanted any time during the growing season. Water young plants often enough to keep the soil slightly moist.

One word of caution—these beauties reseed easily and will spread. It might be tempting to bring home a bunch of container plants, but one or two is usually enough.

Routine Maintenance

Established coneflowers don't need too much attention. Resist the urge to fertilize; that will cause the plants to fall over and flower poorly.

Thanks to the coneflower's heat-tolerant nature, you don't have to worry about watering, either, although a quick drink during an extended dry period won't hurt.

Though its spear-shaped leaves aren't remarkable, you'll want to keep an eye on them for signs of leaf spot disease. If the stems wilt or foliage yellows, remove and discard the diseased parts. Even if you have to take out the entire

Plant Profile

Jim Baron/The Image Finders

Common Name: Purple coneflower.

Botanical Name: *Echinacea purpurea.*

Bloom Time: Summer through fall.

Hardiness: Zones 3 to 9.

Flower Colors: Purple, pink, crimson, white and new varieties like yellow and orange.

Flower Shape: Daisy-like drooping petals surround a bristly cone-shaped center.

Height: 2 to 5 feet.

Spread: 2 feet.

Light Needs: Full sun; will tolerate light shade.

Soil Type: Well-drained soil.

Planting: Seeds can be sown directly into the garden in fall. Simply scatter on loosened soil, rake to cover, press the area lightly and water. For immediate results, choose container-grown plants and add them to your flower bed any time during the growing season. Bare-root specimens are also available and can go in the ground in spring.

Prize Picks: Meadowbrite and Mango Pixie are orange versions that produce light fragrances. White Lustre and White Swan both have showy white blooms with copper centers. Magnus produces 7-inch-wide purple flowers.

Backyard Benefits: The flowers attract butterflies and bees, and goldfinches and other birds like to eat the seed heads.

plant, other coneflowers will self-sow and fill in the open space in no time.

But be sure to leave some in the garden—besides their value in self-sowing, the seed heads attract goldfinches and other hungry birds.

See what I mean about easy? Whether you want a plant that's colorful, carefree, attractive to wildlife or all of the above, purple coneflowers can't be beat. I think you'll fall in love with them, just like I did!

Mark Turner

HELIOTROPE

This annual is a scent-sational garden addition.

By Kathleen Zimmer-Anderson, Waukesha, Wisconsin

Some say the fragrance of heliotrope reminds them of cherry pie, while others claim the blooms' scent resembles talcum powder…vanilla…cloves…or even licorice.

Whatever comes to mind when you take a whiff, this colorful bedding plant certainly is one of the most aromatic annuals around. It's no surprise that heliotrope flowers once served as a main ingredient in colognes, perfumes, soaps and powders.

The plant also was a favorite among Victorian-era gardeners, although its popularity faded a bit during the 20th century. Heliotropes have begun to make a comeback, however, and are getting easier to find at many garden centers.

Sun Lover

Heliotrope serves as a woody perennial in its native Peru, but is unable to withstand winters in North America. Here,

HEAVEN SCENT. Heliotropes are best known for their fragrance—which resembles cherry pie, vanilla or licorice, depending on who you talk to. Its purple clusters (left) rise above textured leaves. The upright annual works well with a variety of other plants in borders or containers (lower right).

it works as an annual for backyard gardeners.

The shrubby specimen derives its name from two Greek words—*helios*, which translates into sun, and *trope*, meaning turn. The moniker came about thanks to a legend that describes how the flower heads turn to face the sun. That myth might not be completely true, but there's no doubt the plant thrives in bright locations.

Its nicely textured, dark-green leaves create a perfect backdrop for eye-catching masses of tiny tubular blooms that come in a variety of hues, from light blue to rich violet, lavender or white.

Aside from filling a border area, flower bed or rock garden with loads of color, heliotrope is ideal in window boxes, containers or hanging baskets. It partners well with a variety of other flowers, including verbena, geraniums, dusty miller and petunias.

This pretty plant has another appealing feature—its sweet nectar attracts the attention of "flying flowers" like hummingbirds and butterflies.

Hot Growing Hints

Heliotrope can either be grown from seed or from plants purchased at a garden center. However, because heliotrope is so sensitive to cold, it's best to wait at least 2 to 3 weeks after the last frost date before placing the plants in your garden, so the soil has enough time to warm.

Select a spot that receives full to partial sun with moist well-draining soil. Space the plants about 12 inches apart and water thoroughly.

After the heliotropes become established, you'll want to water them whenever the top 1 to 2 inches of soil just begins to dry. If you've added a heliotrope to a container, check it daily and water when the top few inches start to dry out. Conditions that are too dry or too moist will result in unhappy plants.

Container-grown heliotropes also benefit from a little fertilizer. You can add a slow-release version when you first fill the container with soil, or use a liquid fertilizer for flowering plants throughout the growing season.

Pinch to Grow Inches

Nothing's prettier than bushy heliotropes in a container or a flower bed. To encourage them to fill out, pinch back the growing tips of the young plants. If they start to look scrag-

gly later on, another round of pinching will help shape them again.

Deadheading fading flower clusters is another task that yields lovely results. Not only will you remove unattractive spent flowers, you'll promote better blooming from summer into fall.

If you'd like to preserve your container heliotropes over winter, you can bring them indoors before the weather becomes cold. Place the plants in a cool, sunny spot and water regularly.

While the bloomers are relatively pest-free, white flies, spider mites, aphids or mealy bugs can be a problem on plants wintering indoors. If you notice any of these critters, use an insecticidal soap to banish the pests.

As soon as the risk of frost has passed, your heliotropes can head outdoors again—and you can enjoy another sweet season of fragrant flowers! ✦

Coreopsis

Turn up the heat. This sunny charmer can take it!

With its demure veil of jeweled blooms, coreopsis adds charm to cottage gardens and formal flower beds alike. But that's not the only reason gardeners love it.

Dainty flowers, thin stems and fine foliage disguise the fact that this plant is as tough as nails. Coreopsis handles heat and dry conditions with grace, blooming from late spring until fall. It's great for cutting and attracts butterflies.

Native to the arid grasslands and open woodland meadows of North and Central America, coreopsis is often described as having a sunny disposition because so many varieties produce yellow flowers.

Other colors crop up, too, including orange, maroon, red and pink. But overall, yellow seems to reign supreme. This prominent shade even earned coreopsis the nickname "butter daisy."

One More Moniker

This flower is also referred to as "tickseed" because the seeds, which are black and have a little hook on one end, resemble ticks. The word "coreopsis" is Latin for bedbug, another reference to the seeds.

European gardeners were introduced to a perennial

version of coreopsis in 1699, but it wasn't until *Coreopsis tinctoria*, an annual variety, arrived 100 years later that the flower became fashionable.

Today, gardeners can choose from more than 100 species of annual and perennial coreopsis. This sizable selection includes everything from regal, 3-foot plants that produce 3-inch-wide blooms to adorable 8-inch dwarf varieties.

One species that stands out because of its carefree nature is *Coreopsis verticillata*, or threadleaf coreopsis (left). This perennial has finely textured, threadlike leaves and small yellow blooms and is exceptionally easy to cultivate. There's no need for deadheading—this beauty keeps blooming without your help.

Notable hybrids include the popular Moonbeam, a 20-inch-tall variety with pale yellow blossoms; Golden Shower, which offers golden double blooms; and Zagreb, a 12-inch-tall cultivar with yellow blooms.

Rosy Glow

Similar to the threadleaf species, *Coreopsis rosea* also features wispy, fernlike foliage with pink blossoms. It spreads quickly in arid, sandy spots but suffers in heavy clay soils with poor drainage. The hybrid Nana, a dwarf variety that grows to 10 inches, is especially pretty.

Limerock Ruby, another hybrid, offers striking red flowers. Unlike its perennial cousins, it is best treated as an annual in northern areas. It can only tolerate mild winters.

Coreopsis tinctoria, the species that swept Europe off its feet, provides annual selections like Mahogany Midget, a dwarf hybrid with brownish-red flowers. Tiger Flower offers blooms that range from crimson to gold.

And that's just the tip of the iceberg! No matter what variety you choose, you'll enjoy a bounty of blooms if you offer plants a little TLC.

Bare-root plants and those started from seed and hardened off can go into the ground as soon as the danger of frost passes. Perennials or plants purchased from the garden center can be tucked into beds anytime during the growing season.

Fun in the Sun

Pick a sunny site, keeping in mind that coreopsis combines nicely with salvia, sedum and ornamental grasses. Make sure the soil drains well and is moist. It wouldn't hurt to work in some organic material before planting. Space plants 12 to 18 inches apart.

Keep the soil around newly planted coreopsis moist, but resist the urge to overwater—these plants won't appreciate it. Check the soil first. If the top 3 inches or so are on the dry side, then you can pull out your watering can. Once the plants are established, they'll tolerate drier conditions.

Fertilize lightly, if at all. Too much will make the plants flop and produce fewer flowers. Threadleaf varieties need no deadheading. With other types, remove the first spent blooms to encourage successive waves of flowers and control self-seeding.

You may need to stake or otherwise support tall species. When you spot overgrown or floppy plants in spring, divide them and plant the divisions in other parts of your garden...or share a little sunshine with your friends.

Plant Profile

Alan and Linda Detrick

Common Names: Coreopsis, tickseed and butter daisy.

Botanical Name: *Coreopsis*.

Bloom Time: Late spring through late summer.

Hardiness: Both annual and perennial varieties are available; zones vary by variety.

Flower Colors: Yellow, orange, maroon, red and pink; some bicolored hybrids are also available.

Flower Shape: Daisy-like single, semi-double or double blooms 1/2 to 3 inches wide. Petals are often notched.

Leaves: Foliage ranges from light to dark green. Leaves may be lance-shaped, lobed or finely divided.

Height: 8 to 48 inches.

Spread: 8 to 36 inches.

Light Needs: Full sun.

Soil Type: Moist, well-drained soil is best, but not essential. Established plants tolerate dry conditions. Mulch helps reduce the need to water.

Backyard Benefits: Blooms attract butterflies; seeds attract birds.

Prize Picks: Perennial threadleaf varieties offer distinctive foliage and yellow flowers, but require little maintenance. *Coreopsis rosea*, another popular perennial, bears pink blooms and tolerates dry conditions; it's a good ground cover for arid slopes.

GREEN THUMB TIP

If you want blooms that you don't have to deadhead, then threadleaf coreopsis is your best bet. It has small yellow blooms and is easy to cultivate.

More than 16,000 daylilies provide nonstop flowers in this Texas garden.

By Wendy Rudnicki
Friendswood, Texas

A FLOWER A DAY

For Pearland, Texas residents Paula and Leon Payne, their interest in daylilies started in 1987 with a few yellow blooms.

It almost stopped there.

"I read an article in a magazine about all these different colored daylilies we'd never seen, and we started trying to find them, but we couldn't," Paula says. "I called some of the gardening radio shows and they didn't know, either. So we just sort of gave up."

About 8 months later, however, the National Daylily Convention hit Houston, Texas—and Paula found a list in the newspaper of sources for a multihued variety of daylilies. She and her husband bought about $100 worth.

"We thought we broke the bank!" Leon exclaims. "The very next year, I started hybridizing a little bit, and our garden just kept growing."

Growing Paynes

Today, the Paynes grow about 800 different varieties of daylilies—and more than 16,000 daylily plants in all!

In 1995, Leon and Paula bought the two lots behind their house and started their business: Paynes in the Grass Daylily Farm. They sell both full-grown daylilies and daylily seedlings.

"We had so many flowers, we had to do something," Leon explains.

"It was a hobby that got out of control," Paula adds.

About 9 years ago, Paula and Leon even helped start a daylily club in their area. The Lone Star Daylily Society sponsors plant sales, flower shows and garden tours, and is a recognized club of the American Hemerocallis Society.

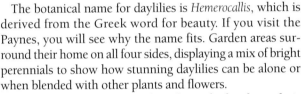

The botanical name for daylilies is *Hemerocallis*, which is derived from the Greek word for beauty. If you visit the Paynes, you will see why the name fits. Garden areas surround their home on all four sides, displaying a mix of bright perennials to show how stunning daylilies can be alone or when blended with other plants and flowers.

In the early '90s, Leon and Paula applied to have their garden added to a list of AHS display gardens. The vice president of their AHS region inspected their place to make sure they had a variety of well-marked daylilies. They did, and today, the Paynes' garden is one of more than 325 display gardens in the United States and Canada.

"We invite people to come even if they don't want to buy anything," Paula says. "We always hope we can get someone else interested in daylilies."

Days in the Making

Leon—who worked as a NASA aerospace engineer for 35 years—attributes his involvement with daylilies to the challenge of trying to develop a better daylily by hybridizing.

"It's easy to get a lot of seedlings, but to get the right one, the one that you're trying to get, that takes a lot of practice," he says.

To hybridize a flower, the Paynes take the pollen from one daylily and dust it onto another. If it works, the result is a seedpod, which they use to collect seeds for planting.

Unfortunately, it doesn't always work.

The Paynes care for about 8,000 seedlings a year, but usually only get about 100 worth trying again.

A BUDDING HOBBY. Leon and Paula Payne (left inset) started growing daylilies (like the one at far left) for their beauty. Now they enjoy creating new hybrids as well. Their collection includes about 800 varieties and 16,000 plants in a huge garden (top left) behind their home (above left). They also add daylilies among perennials like purple coneflowers and mealycup salvia (above) to show how well the different plants complement each other.

Planting, harvesting and other duties keep them busy, though. Some months, they get up at 5 a.m. and work until dark!

Square Dance at Sunset?

The couple registered three new daylilies in 2002: Squaredancer's Curtsy, Sunset Illusion and Rodeo Clown. Since then, they have registered three more: Line Dancer, Lone Star Wagon Wheel and Halloween Masquerade, which is Paula's favorite and won an AHS award in 2003.

"It's an orange daylily with a black edge and eye," Paula explains. "When people see it, they know it. It's great to grow a daylily that you can recognize without a nametag."

But for the Paynes, there are rewards beyond registering a new daylily or seeing the enthusiasm on the faces of their visitors.

"What my husband likes," Paula says, "is to go out in the morning when the seedlings start blooming, and know he's the first person in the world to ever see that flower bloom."

Editor's Note: For information from the American Hemerocallis Society about how to properly plant and care for daylilies, visit its Web site at *www.daylilies.org.*

> ### READER TIP
>
> To hybridize a daylily, take the pollen from one flower and dust it onto another. If it works, the result is a seedpod.
> —**Paula and Leon Payne, Pearland, Texas**

Cleome

These fast-growing flowers stand out in no time flat.

With its crown of feathery blossoms that appear almost immediately, statuesque cleome puts a colorful spin on your garden in no time flat. This fast-growing annual starts flowering when it's a mere 12 inches tall, and doesn't stop blooming or growing all summer long.

By the end of August, when so many other plants look worn or have faded away completely, cleome is at its peak, measuring 4 to 6 feet in height and still blooming like crazy.

The plant's solid yet graceful stems and dark-green leaves are undeniably attractive, but those wispy pink, white and purple blooms are the real draw. The multi-petaled posies are open and delicate, disguising the fact that they can

STANDING TALL. It's easy to see why this beautiful bloom has earned the nickname "spider flower." It has long seedpods (left) that resemble a spider's legs. Above, white cleome stands tall in a backyard flower bed. This plant can grow as high as 4 to 6 feet.

measure as much as 6 inches across.

The blossoms also feature long, pollen-bearing stamens and elongated seedpods that resemble a spider's legs, earning this plant the nickname of "spider flower."

Pros and Cons

Thanks to its stature, cleome serves as a great centerpiece in an island flower bed. It makes a perfect backdrop in a border bed or along a wall or fence, and looks delightful when planted in groups. It even works in a formal setting with the right accessories. If you go this route, try pairing its airy yet sizable appearance with strong vertical plants.

This tropical native is easy to care for and rarely needs to be staked, despite its height. It may slouch a bit toward the end of the season, but you can solve that with a little planning. Simply pair cleome with another tall plant that it can lean on to provide support.

Heat, lack of moisture and less-than-perfect soil conditions don't faze this tough beauty. What's more, cleome often reseeds itself and sprouts again once winter's done.

If you live in a warmer climate, cleome might become a bit aggressive and self-sow to spots where you don't want it. To prevent this, just cut some of the seedpods before they reseed. There will be so many flowers that you can't possibly snip them all, but cutting at least some of them will control the plant's spread.

Aside from providing sumptuous color in the garden, cleome attracts a variety of butterflies, hummingbirds and songbirds. It also makes a great cut flower, adding striking texture to any bouquet.

The stems and leaves emit a distinctive, musky odor that some gardeners describe as skunk-like. It's not strong enough to chase people out of your garden, but you might want to avoid planting cleome right under a window or near a door.

The only other drawback is that the plant can be a bit prickly—literally. Its former botanical name, *Cleome spinosa*, refers to the short spines that line the base of the leaves. Be aware of the spines when transplanting or weeding. It's best to keep cleome away from entrances or next to walkways, so visitors won't get scratched.

Take Your Pick

There are more than 150 different cleome cultivars available today, ensuring that gardeners can find one to suit their needs. If you need a more compact plant, for instance, try the Sparkler series.

These specimens range in size from 3 to 4 feet tall. Sparkler Blush produces 4- to 6-inch-wide blooms in pink with a flush of white. The flowers of Sparkler Rose are a nice, rosy red.

The Queen series offers more color, including large pink, purple, cherry and white blossoms. Color Fountain is a mixture of smaller, narrow-petaled pink, violet-pink, red or white flowers that are nicely scented. Helen Campbell, another popular choice in the Queen series, offers white blooms.

Once you've chosen the perfect cleome for your yard, it's time to plant. You can sow seeds outdoors in the garden in mid- to late spring. In colder climates, wait until the last frost passes.

If you plant seeds, you won't see blooms until midsummer. For a full summer of colorful flowers, plant container-grown specimens after the threat of frost passes.

To start cleomes inside, plant the seeds about 8 weeks before the final spring frost occurs. The seeds need approximately 2 weeks to germinate. Check the seed packet for further directions.

Transplants should be spaced about 2 feet apart in the garden to give them enough room to grow. Be sure to select a sunny spot or an area that sees only light shade. It also helps if the soil drains well.

For optimal results, you must keep this flower's soil evenly moist for the first few weeks after planting. After that, water whenever the top several inches of soil feel dry. You can also add mulch to suppress weeds and conserve moisture.

As soon as it establishes itself, cleome is pretty self-sufficient and requires very little maintenance. This plant enjoys hot weather and doesn't need fertilizer. As summer wanes, lower leaves may die off, giving the plant a leggy look. You can cover that up by surrounding it with lower-growing companion plants like artemisia, mums or red fountain grass.

Cleome will flourish into fall...then look for more to show up in your garden the following spring. It's a perfect addition to any garden. For an annual, this beauty puts on a nonstop show!

Plant Profile

Richard Day/Daybreak Imagery

Common Names: Cleome, spider flower.

Botanical Name: *Cleome hassleriana*.

Bloom Time: Summer to fall.

Hardiness: Annual in all zones, but will self-seed.

Flower Colors: Pink, purple, red and white.

Flower Shape: Airy, spiderlike flowers with long, distinctive stamens and seedpods.

Height: 4 to 6 feet.

Spread: 2 feet.

Light Needs: Full sun to partial shade.

Soil Type: Well-drained soil is preferred, but plants tolerate a variety of soil conditions.

Planting: Start seeds indoors about 8 weeks before the final frost. In the garden, plant container-grown specimens at least 2 feet apart after the threat of frost is past. For seeds, plant 12 inches apart, and then thin later.

Prize Picks: The Sparkler series is fairly new on the scene, with 3- to 4-foot-tall plants that tolerate heat and drought. The taller "Helen Campbell," a variety in the Queen series, has white blossoms. The Queen series also produces rose, pink, purple and cherry-colored flowers.

Backyard Benefits: The flowers attract butterflies, hummingbirds, songbirds and bees. They also make nice cut flowers for bouquets.

GREEN THUMB TIP

Cleome is the perfect flower to start from seed. It's considered an annual, but once established, it often self-seeds the following years.

GO FOR THE GOLDENROD

Strike it rich with this autumn bloom.

It's not easy being gold.

If you point to a patch of goldenrod, the average gardener might tell you it's a weed. Show a friend a sprig of its beautiful yellow blooms, and she'll swear the plant is making her sneeze.

And as far as growing it in your garden…well, you've probably never even considered it.

You're in good company. Although most of goldenrod's 100 varieties are native to North America (you've probably seen them sprouting on the roadsides or near the woods), it

Donna and Tom Krischan; inset; Richard Day/Daybreak Imagery

GOLDEN TOUCH. King Midas or not, anyone can turn a garden to gold by planting a patch of native goldenrod. You'll find that newer hybrids like Golden Baby (right) and Fireworks (left) are worth their weight in gold, especially when paired with other bright autumn blooms like asters or chrysanthemums. These nectar-filled flowers will also attract winged admirers, including monarch butterflies and bumblebees.

took American gardeners until the 1980s to accept this golden treasure as a garden-worthy plant.

Twenty years later, many still shy from its sunny blooms, worried the tall stalks will take over their yards.

Their fears are not completely off base. Some goldenrod varieties are too aggressive, and are best suited for wild gardens. Others, however, are long-lived, trouble-free and will make anyone's backyard sparkle.

Goldenrod has an unusual beauty, captivating admirers with tall leafy stems that erupt into gold-petaled clusters of delicate blooms.

Still worried about hay fever? Ragweed—another tall yellow flower—is the real culprit behind those red eyes and runny noses. Both pollen-packed plants appear in late summer, but goldenrod pollen is too heavy to become airborne.

Tea Time

In fact, 18th-century physicians even believed goldenrod had healing powers. These doctors used its blossoms to mask the flavor of many medicines.

By the time of the American Revolution, dried goldenrod petals were being brewed to make a tasty tea. About 250 years later, the plant had moved on to another type of "tea"— the Model T. Thomas Edison cultivated goldenrod's natural latex to make a set of tires strong enough for the car.

Today, the beauty of this classic bloom is finally beginning to earn the recognition it deserves. In the past 5 years, after conducting in-depth studies of the plant, the Chicago Botanic Garden has put goldenrod on its list of the 19 top plants to grow in the Midwest.

Digging for Gold

Goldenrod, however, thrives as far north as Maine and as far south as Florida. This late-blooming golden perennial will make your garden gleam long after many summer blooms have faded.

Before you break ground for this backyard beauty, there are a few "golden" rules to keep this plant from growing out of control.

Although goldenrod thrives in full sun, it will spread less if you plant it in partial shade.

Goldenrod also grows too vigorously in rich soil. Instead,

READER TIP

If you want to attract butterflies, this is a great bloom for you. Try nectar-filled varieties such as zigzag, prairie or elm-leaf goldenrod.

use it to add color to an area of moderate to poor soil.

And just like real gold, a little bit can go a long way. Keep it from overwhelming your garden by carefully selecting a few sites for this bloom. Large patches are more appropriate for a field or meadow.

With these tips in mind, you can choose from a whole band of varieties of this gorgeous gold.

For a showstopping display, plant a hybrid like Fireworks goldenrod (one of the Chicago Botanic Garden's top picks, pictured at far left), whose flowers seem to shoot out in every direction. Or try Golden Fleece (photo on page 155), a compact plant with arching clusters that will warm up any garden.

To attract butterflies, try nectar-filled varieties such as zigzag, prairie or elm-leaf goldenrod. Silverrod—the only type with cream-colored flowers—also has its charm.

A Winning Selection

Whatever type you select, it's sure to turn heads. Just ask Melody Rose of Benton, Kentucky, who has been growing Canada goldenrod in her backyard flower bed for the past 3 years.

"Pale-pink and pale-blue flowers are really nice, but that's not what you're going to notice in people's yards," she says. "Goldenrod is bright *and* beautiful—and those little blossoms are simply exquisite. It's just a wonderful plant."

Plant Profile

Common Name: Goldenrod.
Botanical Name: *Solidago.*
Bloom Time: Late summer to autumn.
Hardiness: Zones 3 to 9.
Flower Color: Most are gold.
Flower Shape: Clusters of small spiked blooms.
Height: 1 to 5 feet.
Spread: At least 2 feet.
Light Needs: Full sun to partial shade.
Soil Type: Poor soil helps control growth.
Planting: In spring and summer, plant goldenrod about 1 foot apart.
Prize Picks: Golden Fleece is a dwarf variety with arching clusters; Fireworks is known for its unique flowering stems that shoot out in every direction; Golden Baby is compact and blooms early; sweet goldenrod has showy flowers that emit an anise-like scent.

Chrysanthemum

*This garden queen puts on
a vibrant show each fall.*

As summer winds down and most flowers fade away, this feisty late-bloomer warms up its act. The chrysanthemum, a longtime favorite among gardeners and floral designers alike, takes center stage in autumn, when shorter days produce armfuls of bright blossoms.

That doesn't mean mums are invisible during the summer months. Even when the plant isn't splashing dashes of white, pink, purple, bronze, orange, red, mauve and yellow blooms all around the yard, its pretty, deep-green leaves and bushy shape add interest and contrast to border gardens and perennial beds.

Styles of blooms vary as widely as colors for this cousin of the daisy.

"There are 13 different classifications of chrysanthemums based on flower shape," says Carmen Keister, president of the National Chrysanthemum Society.

"The most admired is the decorative type, a lush, double flower head with short petals. People also favor pompon-shaped chrysanthemums, and the daisy-like single and semi-double blossoms," she says. "Spiders, which have long tubular petals that curl at the ends, and anemones generate lots of interest as well."

Time-Honored Beauties

The popularity of the chrysanthemum, which means "golden flower" in Greek, dates back to ancient Asia, when Chinese philosopher Confucius wrote about chrysanthemums in 500 B.C. About the same time, a dedicated Chinese botanist and mum breeder created so many hybrids that his village became known as *Chuh-sien* or

---

MUMS OF MANY COLORS. The vibrant orange (and red and yellow and purple...) hues of chrysanthemums add pop to any fall garden. While many mums have difficulty withstanding cold after they bloom, the Clara Curtis variety (below) is a hardy mum developed to survive winter in northern areas to Zone 4.

Photos: below, Richard Shiell; at right, Faith Bemiss; previous page, Alan and Linda Detrick

"city of chrysanthemums."

Some 400 years later, mums appeared in Japan, where they quickly caught on. At one time, the mum was the national flower of the country, and its image was chosen to decorate the crest of one of Japan's imperial families. The Japanese, who believe mums symbolize happiness and long life, continue to celebrate the legendary flower with a national festival each September.

The flowers eventually made their way to Europe, the U.S. and Canada, although gardeners didn't embrace mums until the mid-1800s. The blooms rapidly gained acceptance and can now be found just about everywhere, from public gardens to private yards. They also regularly crop up in flowers shops.

The growth of chrysanthemum clubs and competitions confirms the flower's favored status today. These competitions feature the efforts of amateur growers who cultivate special varieties called exhibition mums.

Also called disbuds, these exhibition varieties require extra care, including extended periods of darkness to promote blooming at specific times, Carmen says. Commercial growers do the same thing to produce mums for florists year-round.

Everyday Delights

Most folks grow varieties that don't require this extra care and are readily available at garden centers from coast to coast.

Often referred to as hardy mums, these plants are actually considered tender perennials that can be a challenge to overwinter successfully in colder climates.

That's why many northern gardeners treat garden mums as frost-resistant annuals. There are a few types bred to weather the cold. My Favorite Mum is a cultivar developed at the University of Minnesota and is hardy to Zone 3. Clara Curtis, a close relative of the garden mum, produces pretty pink, daisy-like flowers and is hardy to Zone 4.

Garden mums are easy to grow, too, Carmen says. Plant mums 2 to 3 feet apart in a sunny spot with well-draining soil in spring—the sooner the better to encourage successful overwintering in areas where that's a concern. The plant's shallow root system needs time to establish before the onset of cold weather.

Once the mums start sprouting new leaves, pinch back that growth to about 6 inches. Keep pinching until late June in the North and mid-July in the South. This encourages a compact shape.

"If you continue to pinch back after that, the plants won't produce flowers in time," Carmen says.

If you live in a colder climate, once your mums have finished flowering in fall, cover them with mulch and a few evergreen branches after the ground freezes—but don't remove the dead stems and leaves. The erect stalks will grab hold of any snow that falls, ensuring extra insulation against frigid temperatures.

So, do you want to guarantee that your garden ends the growing season with a bang rather than a whimper? Start early by including colorful mums in your planting plans, do a little pinching, and you'll have an eye-catching encore in autumn for sure! ◄

Plant Profile

Richard Shiell

Common Names: Chrysanthemum, mum.

Botanical Name: *Chrysanthemum* x *morifolium* cultivars.

Bloom Time: Late summer through fall.

Hardiness: Varies by species; often grown as an annual.

Flower Colors: Yellow, white, pink, orange, lavender, bronze, purple and red.

Flower Shapes: A wide range of forms is available. Shapes include button, pom-pon, daisy-like, semi-double, single, brush, spider, spoon (above) and decorative.

Height: 1 to 3 feet.

Spread: 2 to 3 feet.

Light Needs: Full sun.

Soil Type: Fertile and well-draining.

Planting: Plant bare-root perennials in spring. Hardened-off and container-grown plants can go into the garden any time during the growing season. Spring planting may help perennials survive winter. To further ensure overwintering success, grow mums in protected areas.

Special Care: To promote compact shape, pinch back new growth until late June or mid-July, keeping the plants about 6 inches tall. Add mulch and cover with evergreen boughs after the ground freezes for cold protection.

Prize Picks: My Favorite Mum is a daisy-like flower that is hardy to Zone 3. Barbara, an early bloomer with showy, 3-inch-wide flowers, does well in containers. The pink, single-flowered Clara Curtis is another great choice, as is the shorter Minnruby with its 2-1/4-inch-wide red blossoms.

GREEN THUMB TIP

If you want chrysanthemums that will survive cold temperatures, try cultivars bred to weather northern winters like My Favorite Mum or Clara Curtis.

Snowdrop

*Plant this white bloom for a
"snow"-stopping floral display.*

By Marissa Conrad, Editorial Intern

Ready to add a drop of life to your sleepy winter garden? If that sounds appealing, then there's a little, white bloom that won't let you down.

Meet the snowdrop: a milky-white perennial that flowers in late winter and often lasts through early spring. Since it grows in almost all climates, this petite plant is the perfect fix for the "nothing's blooming" blahs.

A single snowdrop is something special—its slender stem has only one flower head, with petals that dangle like pearl raindrops ready to plop to the ground. To make a real splash, plant this bloom in larger bunches. It pairs well with cyclamen (another popular cold-weather bloomer). But with or without a costar, snowdrop will steal the show in your garden.

It's "Snow"-time!

Despite its wintry moniker, most snowdrops come up after the snow has melted. Depending on the cultivar and climate, they might bloom as early as January or as late as April.

Snowdrops originally hail from Western Europe, where the plant thrived in alpine areas. It takes its botanical name, *Galanthus*, from the Greek word for "milk flower."

The two types typically planted in gardens are the common snowdrop and the giant snowdrop. The common variety (*Galanthus nivalis*) grows to about 4 inches tall, while the giant (*Galanthus elwesii*) reaches 5 to 9 inches and has a larger flower head. Both display the strappy leaves that are typical of this flower.

Beyond these two types, there are 17 other snowdrop species and hundreds of cultivars, but many sport only minute differences. In fact, despite all the varieties, only one snowdrop color exists—white.

If you're looking for something unique, try the double-flowered cultivar of the common snowdrop, Flore Pleno. Another interesting variety is the Crimean snowdrop, the *Galanthus plicatus*, which has broad, folded-back leaves.

To start your snowdrop garden, head outside in early fall with a few small bulbs. The blooms grow best in rich soil and light shade, so find a good spot and plant each bulb about 3 inches apart. They also look attractive in clumps,

---

CATCH THE DRIFT. To grow snowdrops in your garden, plant the bulbs in fall. Cluster them together to create an attractive floral display that will emerge between January and April, depending on the variety and your climate. Although there are hundreds of cultivars of this plant to choose from, the differences between them are quite small, such as the wider leaves and larger flower heads of giant snowdrops. Any type is a winner.

Chapter 5

Mark Turner

Mark Turner

Common Name: Snowdrop.

Botanical Name: *Galanthus.*

Bloom Time: Late winter to early spring.

Hardiness: Zones 3 to 9.

Flower Color: White.

Flower Shape: A single dangling flower head of three large outer petals and three small inner petals.

Height: 3 to 9 inches.

Light Needs: Partial shade.

Soil Type: Moist and well-draining.

Planting: In fall, plant bulbs 3 to 4 inches deep and 3 to 4 inches apart.

Prize Picks: *Galanthus nivalis* Flore Pleno is double-flowered; Crimean snowdrop boasts broad leaves; giant snowdrop sports larger flower heads.

so feel free to cluster your bulbs together in groups.

Although some gardeners buy new bulbs to expand their snowdrops every year, many simply dig and divide established plantings by transplanting the bulblets that form on the bulbs.

One word of caution, however: The bulbs may irritate your skin and are toxic if eaten, so make sure to wear gloves while working with them.

This toxicity does have its advantages. Squirrels turn up their noses at them, so you don't have to worry about hungry critters devouring your early-spring display before it has a chance to shine.

The Stuff of Legend

Although snowdrops are delicate, understated flowers, this early bloomer doesn't go unnoticed. In fact, people have admired it for centuries.

As a harbinger of spring and returning life, it's a symbol of purity in many European countries. It is even associated with the Virgin Mary and has become the floral symbol for Candlemas Day, which celebrates her purification, on February 2.

GREEN THUMB TIP

Do you have a problem with squirrels eating your bulbs? Try snowdrop. Squirrels don't like them, so you don't have to worry about them disappearing.

In 1819, William Wordsworth wrote a poem praising a patch of snowdrops for weathering a severe storm. In 1863, Hans Christian Andersen published a fairy tale, titled "The Snowdrop," which told the story of a flower brave enough to face the winter frosts.

Other folklore is not so positive. In northern Europe, gardeners have long considered it unlucky to bring even a single snowdrop into the house because it was thought to resemble a shroud.

But even the most superstitious green thumbs will love to see this beautiful bloom appear in their backyards. Let it snow!

Poinsettia

This beautiful plant is a winter delight.

By W.L. Dye, Belle Center, Ohio

Among all the beauty of the winter season, there's one sight that holds a special place in my heart—a bright-red poinsettia.

This ruby-colored plant is a true treasure. And over the years, its rich vibrant color has earned it nicknames like lobster flower, flame leaf and Christmas flower.

Although poinsettias are now closely associated with the Christmas season, that wasn't always the case.

According to legend, one Christmas Eve, a little girl from Mexico wanted to honor Baby Jesus with a special present during the evening church service, but she didn't have any money.

Not knowing what else to do, she picked some flowering weeds as her offering, then placed the makeshift bouquet on the altar. As she set them down, the bouquet burst into a brilliant red poinsettia.

From then on, the plant was known as "Flores de Noche Buena," or "Flowers of the Holy Night."

A Holiday Favorite

The poinsettia is easily the most admired Christmas plant, shining long after outdoor blooms have faded. More than 50 million are sold each holiday season. And it's easy to see why.

The poinsettia is available in more than 100 varieties and in plenty of shades beyond the traditional red—from creamy white, pink or yellow to speckled and variegated forms.

In addition to the container plants commonly seen around the holidays, in its native Mexico, these plants also grow as perennial shrubs that reach up to 10 feet tall.

Don't make the mistake of calling these bright blooms flowers, however. The large colorful "petals" are actually leaves called bracts. The small berry-like clusters in the middle of the bracts are the true flowers.

Joel Roberts Poinsett, the first U.S. ambassador to Mexico, introduced the poinsettia to the United States. He was exploring the countryside one day when he found a beautiful shrub with large red blooms. He took cuttings to his greenhouse in South Carolina.

Chapter 5

HOLIDAY TRADITION. The poinsettia comes in many colors, even speckled varieties (above). At right, the true flowers of this plant are in the middle, surrounded by colorful bracts.

Now sold across North America, the bloom's name honors Poinsett. The U.S. also recognizes the plant and its namesake with National Poinsettia Day on December 12, which marks the date of Poinsett's death.

A Year-Round Treasure

Proper care of this popular Christmas plant should start during transport. When you first purchase a poinsettia, protect it from frigid outdoor temperatures. Have the seller wrap it before you take it outside, and make sure your vehicle is preheated before you place the poinsettia inside.

To continue proper care, set your plant near a sunny window. For ideal conditions, maintain a temperature between 65° and 70° during daylight hours. Then move the plant to a slightly cooler spot at night.

Also be aware that too much or too little watering can harm the plant. Underwatering can cause the bracts to wilt, turn brown or drop entirely. Overwatering, on the other hand, may prevent proper aeration of the soil, causing the leaves to yellow or the roots to die and decay. For watering, use this rule of thumb: If the top inch of the soil feels dry, water it. If it's still wet, don't.

One last tip—avoid placing the poinsettia in drafty areas near doors or heating vents. Both hot and cold drafts can injure the plant.

The end of the holiday season doesn't have to mean the end of your poinsettia. Even after the bracts fade to green, you can still enjoy it for the rest of the year, and even encourage it to display its colors again.

In mid-March, cut the stems back to about 8 inches, rounding its shape. Keep the pot near a sunny window, and by the end of May, you should see the start of some new green growth.

Around June 1, transplant the poinsettia into a larger pot with rich soil, or move it outside. By October 1, it's time to

Plant Profile

Common Name: Poinsettia.

Botanical Name: *Euphorbia pulcherrima*.

Bloom Time: Winter.

Colors: Red, white, pink, yellow and multicolored.

Flower Shape: Small berry-like cluster in the middle of the colorful bracts.

Light Needs: 6 to 8 hours of bright sun during blooming period.

Soil Type: Well-drained potting mix.

Planting: To keep as a houseplant after the holidays, cut it back in early spring and transfer to a larger pot for the summer.

Prize Picks: Lilo White branches freely and has creamy white bracts. Monet (top left) is a white variety with a rose tinge that darkens as the plant matures. For a unique look, try Winter Rose. Its colorful bracts curl downward to resemble a rose.

prepare the poinsettia for its upcoming holiday display. Move it indoors and keep it in complete darkness for 14 continuous hours each night. Then in the daytime, place it in a spot where it will receive 6 to 8 hours of bright sunlight. Stop the dark treatment once the bracts are fully colored.

If you continue this routine for 8 to 10 weeks, your "Christmas flower" should be ready for display, showing off its colorful bracts, proving once again that it's one of winter's true delights. ◀

GREEN THUMB TIP

Shop around to find the perfect poinsettia for your holiday display. These popular winter plants come in white, pink, yellow and even multicolored varieties.

292

313

310

306

CHAPTER 6

ALL ABOUT HUMMINGBIRDS

300

322

Photos this page: Anna's hummingbird, Hugh P. Smith Jr.; daylilies, Daniel Leach; opposite page: top photo of black-chinned hummers, Sid and Shirley Rucker; middle left photo of broad-billed, Rolf Nussbaumer; bottom photo of ruby-throated, Richard Day/Daybreak Imagery

Sid and Shirley Rucker

GAGA FOR HUMMINGBIRDS

Discover why these tiny fliers have everyone talking.

By George Harrison, Contributing Editor

A lmost everything about hummingbirds is amazing. From their dazzling, iridescent colors to their needlelike bills and extraordinary flight, hummingbirds are among the most fascinating birds in the world.

There are as many as 339 species of hummingbirds, all in the Western Hemisphere, and the majority are located near the equator. Of the 19 that enter the U.S., most spend their time in the country's warmer regions. Only one—the ruby-throated—is found in the East.

From the 2-1/4-inch Cuban bee hummingbird to the giant hummingbird of the Andes, the most impressive behavior of these birds is their flight. Not only can they hover in midair while lapping nectar from a flower, but they can also fly backward, shift sideways and move straight up or down. Their unbelievable flying ability is made possible by rotating their shoulder joints, permitting them to turn their wings 360 degrees from both back and front.

Forward flight for hummers has been clocked as fast as 55 to 60 mph. The humming drone this creates during flight is what gave these birds their unique name.

Raising a Family

During mating season, hummingbirds are entertaining to watch. To impress the females watching from tree perches, males perform spectacular, often noisy, courtship flights that take them high into the sky. One male may mate with several females, who, without any help, build the nest, incubate the eggs and raise the young.

Those who have seen a hummingbird nest know how difficult they are to find. The female builds a nest the size of a quarter and camouflages it in a tree. Then she lays two tiny eggs, no bigger than navy beans.

When hummingbirds feed, they use their long, slender bills to probe flowers for nectar with their tubular tongues. When females feed their young, they use their long bills to deposit food directly into their nestlings' throats.

Male hummingbirds often establish feeding territories that overlap with their mates' nesting. They are very protective of their feeding grounds—flower beds or feeders—and chase other males and females away, allowing only their

SMALL TREASURES. There's always something to talk about with hummingbirds. From their quarter-sized nests to the way they hover in the air (right), these tiny fliers are spectacular. Above, a ruby-throated hummingbird looks for nectar at a bee balm bloom. At left, black-chinned hummers crowd a feeder.

mates and offspring to feed.

People often complain that one male hummingbird monopolizes a sugar-water feeder, not allowing other hummingbirds to feed. One way to solve this problem is to hang another feeder around the other side of your house, out of sight of the first feeder. If the male can't see both feeders, he can only protect one.

All Work and No Play

Hummingbirds have the highest metabolism of any animal in the world, with the possible exception of shrews. In order to survive even 1 day, hummingbirds must feed all day long. To conserve energy during cold weather, they put themselves in a dormant state called "torpor," in which their metabolism slows significantly.

Most people never see hummingbirds bathe. That's because their bathing behavior is also unlike other birds'. Sometimes they will bathe in a pool of water caught in a leaf, but it's more common for them to fly through a spray of light water in the backyard.

Whether it's a garden hose or fountain, they fly through the water multiple times to get their feathers wet. Then they preen them dry from a perch in a tree.

All hummingbirds that breed in the U.S. migrate between summer and wintering grounds. The ruby-throated, for example, travels from as far north as Canada, south across the 600-mile stretch of the Gulf of Mexico and into Central and South America for winter.

Even more remarkable is that parent birds leave the breeding grounds first, abandoning their chicks to mature and fatten up for their own long journeys. The youngsters don't have any trouble, though. They are preprogrammed to know when to migrate and where to fly.

From astonishing births to impressive migrations, it's no wonder so many people are captivated by these flying jewels. They are amazing!

All About Hummingbirds

Ruby-Throated Hummingbird

This beauty is one of nature's most intriguing birds.

By George Harrison, Contributing Editor

Maslowski Productions

How does a 3-month-old ruby-throated hummingbird find its way to tropical wintering grounds, making the migration across thousands of miles all by itself?

How can hummingbirds flutter in midair, hovering so perfectly that they appear almost motionless, as if suspended by an unseen support?

How do males summon the tenacity to vigorously defend their territories—taking on intruders of any species and size?

It's true that hummingbirds are among the most fascinating birds in the world—they perform unbelievable feats like these every day. But it is the fall migration of ruby-throated juveniles that's one of the greatest mysteries in all of nature.

This flight to warmer climates in Central or South America includes a 500- to 600-mile nonstop journey across the Gulf of Mexico. And the youngsters go it alone, even though they've never made the trip before!

The parents of the recently hatched hummers leave their northern nesting grounds for the tropics weeks before their offspring do. Until late summer, the youngsters remain near the area where they hatched, busily feeding and preparing their bodies for the long flight ahead.

Then one day, the amount of daylight triggers a migration response, and the ruby-throated youngsters head south. No map…no bird to follow.

How they know when to leave, what direction to fly, how far to go and when they have reached their destinations is the great mystery. And the only plausible answer researchers have offered is genetic programming.

That this programming carries strong influence likely comes as no surprise to people who feed ruby-throated hummingbirds. Because the following spring, another miracle happens:

> *The secret to attracting ruby-throated hummingbirds is red…*

LITTLE GEMS. Ruby-throated hummingbirds shimmer like jewels, especially the mature males (at far left) with their namesake red throats, called gorgets. Clockwise from above, a female tends to young...a birdbath dwarfs this female...a juvenile male starts to show a hint of its developing red throat.

Those same ruby-throats return to the exact locations in the North where they hatched the year before.

They remember precisely where they consumed sugar water the previous summer. Even after decades of admiring these birds, I'm still amazed when the first ruby-throat of spring returns to my Wisconsin backyard and hovers in the same spot where the sugar-water feeder hung last summer, though the feeder isn't there.

That's my signal to mix the first batch of sugar water, fill the hummingbird feeders and get them outside to the hungry ruby-throats, which are the only hummingbird that regularly nests in the East.

Can't Resist Red

The secret to attracting ruby-throated hummingbirds is red. Anything that is red in color will catch their eye. Just ask Alberta Hanson of Cushing, Wisconsin, whose husband was poked by two ruby-throats in his backyard when they probed their bills into the vent holes of his new red cap.

Mairiam Taylor of West Chester, Pennsylvania was shocked while reading a book in her garden when a ruby-throated hummingbird flew right up to her red lips. It obviously was looking for flower nectar, and Mairiam joked that her lips must have looked like red "two-lips."

Then there is the ruby-throated hummingbird's incredible power of flight. Not only long-distance flight, but hovering flight as well.

Hummingbirds can control their positions in midair as no other birds can. Because their shoulder joints are so flexible,

they are able to rotate their wings with each of the 75 times they beat per second. This allows them to fly backward, sideways, up or down, and hover perfectly.

Defending Its Ground

I watch ruby-throated hummingbirds performing aerial acrobatics at the feeders in my yard, where a dominant male maintains his autocratic control over the food and habitat in my garden by chasing away other hummingbirds—all except "his" females.

The same bully male advertises his dominance over the area

FLY-IN DINING. Adding a sugar-water feeder in your favorite backyard spot is sure to be a hit with area hummingbirds. These ruby-throats (above) gather around this feeder for a meal.

with dramatic aerial displays of sweeping pendulum-patterned flights, 40 to 50 feet above the garden. The display impresses the females while warning off other males.

His control is effective, but I have found a way to offer sugar water to other hummingbirds despite the territorial bully. I place some additional feeders on the opposite side of the house—out of the alpha male's sight.

Proof of the male's effective strategy appears every July when green-backed hummingbirds with white bellies appear at the feeders. They are his offspring.

He allows them to feed, but he plays no part in rearing his young. The females do all the work, first by crafting tiny nesting cups of plant down, then attaching them to tree limbs with spider silk.

The nests are so well camouflaged that it took F. Dwain Phillips 20 years to find one in his Stillwater, Oklahoma yard.

"I finally understood why I hadn't been able to find a hummingbird nest before," Phillips explained. "They are only about 1-1/2 inches in diameter, and they blend so well with the tree bark that it looked like nothing more than a bump on the branch," he says.

The female incubates two tiny, pure-white eggs for 14 to 16 days until they hatch. For 3 more weeks, she feeds the youngsters in the nest by regurgitating nectar and tiny insects directly into their throats with her swordlike bill, a somewhat shocking sight to behold.

Another "Cool" Trick

Even short periods of cold weather, such as late-spring frosts, are not a problem for adult hummingbirds. They perform another amazing feat

Backyard Birding Bio

Common Name: Ruby-throated hummingbird.
Scientific Name: *Archilochus colubris*.
Family: Hummingbird.
Length: 3-3/4 inches.
Wingspan: 4-1/2 inches.
Distinctive Markings: Adult male has a brilliant-red throat, white breast and jewel-green back. Adult females are like many other female hummingbirds with jewel-green on their backs and crowns and white breasts; juveniles appear very similar to the females.
Distinctive Behavior: Hovers at flowers and feeders; can fly backward, sideways and up and down, changing direction on a dime. Males court females with swinging pendulum-like flights, humming with each arc. Males often dominate feeders and gardens, allowing only mates and offspring to feed.
Habitat: Backyard gardens near mature mixed woodlands, orchards and shade trees.
Song: The hum of its wings; chases with high-pitched squeaks.
Nest: Tiny nest looks like a mossy knot on the top of a tree limb or twig, 10 to 20 feet above the ground. Over the course of 5 days, the female constructs the nest of plant down, covers the outside with greenish-gray lichens and attaches the nest to a limb with spider silk.

She lays two pure-white eggs, the size of navy beans, and incubates them for 14 to 16 days. The female alone feeds the young in the nest for another 3 weeks before they're ready to fly.
Diet: Flower nectar, sugar water and tiny insects captured in the air, on flowers and from spider webs.
Backyard Favorites: Sugar-water feeders, red flowers (though any color of nectar-rich bloom will do) and misters, which they fly through to bathe their feathers.

■ Summer
■ Migration
■ Winter

by placing themselves into a hibernation-like state called torpidity. This helps them save energy when temperatures are low.

Torpidity slows down their respiratory and metabolic systems, making them appear to be asleep or dead. People who find these "sick" hummingbirds hanging upside down from sugar-water feeders don't realize that the birds are just awaiting warmer weather and improved feeding conditions.

If you want to try feeding ruby-throats in your yard, start by reading the hummingbird feeding basics on pages 164-165. Soon, you will find yourself admiring the fascinating qualities of ruby-throats...and have some amazing stories of your own to share.

READER TIP

I have found a way to offer sugar water to other hummingbirds despite a territorial bully. I place some additional feeders on the opposite side of the house—out of the alpha male's sight.

—George Harrison, Contributing Editor

Bill Stripling

HUMMINGBIRD HEAVEN

Southern hospitality attracts thousands of migrating jewels each year.

By Lola Autry, Hickory Flat, Mississippi

Let the celebration begin!

Each autumn, tiny ruby-throated hummingbirds prepare for their annual vacation to Mexico and beyond. Here in Mississippi, we give these glorious creatures a proper send-off with the annual Hummingbird Migration Celebration in Holly Springs.

The 2005 festival at the Strawberry Plains Audubon Center marked the sixth year of the event, held early each September. Every year, thousands of ruby-throated hummingbirds (like the one above) pass through the center's 2,500 acres of sanctuary. It's a weekend of celebration, education and bird banding.

CATCH AND RELEASE. During the celebration at Strawberry Plains Audubon Center in Mississippi, experts put tiny bands on hummingbirds, including rare finds like the calliope (above right), and then visitors to release them into flight (top right).

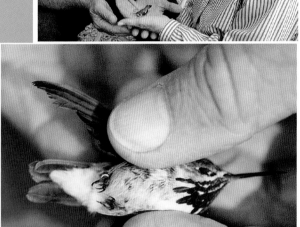

The Chosen Few

A couple of years ago, I was one of the lucky ones who got to release a hummingbird after it was banded. The experience was magical as I held the tiny bird in my hand and then set it free into the crisp, autumn air.

During my visit, I could almost sense the presence of the two sisters who had lived on the plantation years ago. Both nature lovers, they donated Strawberry Plains to the Mississippi Audubon Society. The organization now keeps up the gardens for both the public and the birds to enjoy.

It certainly doesn't go to waste, either. Thousands of people flock to the plantation every year for the festival to see the migrating hummingbirds. One day is even entirely dedicated to kids, who come by busloads for the chance to see a hummer up close and personal.

You can see the excitement in their eyes. Each child hopes to be one of the chosen few who will have the rare opportunity to embrace a hummingbird and then release it into flight.

Observation Deck

The birds flit around the gardens from flower to flower. To avoid disturbing them, onlookers like me watch in awe from a glassed-in solarium at the back of the elegant mansion. These miniature wonders drink up the sweetness from each bloom, storing up energy for their long trip south.

To me, it's no surprise this place has earned the nickname "Hummingbird Heaven." I feel fortunate to live nearby, so I can marvel at the birds every year. This is southern hospitality at its best.

How to Attract Hummingbirds

Use these five easy tips to make your backyard a hot spot.

By George Harrison, Contributing Editor

It's no wonder people are hooked on hummingbirds. With iridescent beauty and lightning-quick speed, there's a lot of spunk packed in their diminutive bodies.

At least 15 species of hummingbirds nest in the U.S. and Canada. Most species—including the broad-tailed, rufous, Anna's and black-chinned (like the one above right)—are found in the West. Only one, the ruby-throated, spends summers in the East (see pages 160-162).

All hummingbirds have a seemingly insatiable appetite for sugar water, which means many backyard bird-watchers attract hummingbirds by setting out a sugar-water feeder (below right) in their gardens.

Unfortunately, it is not always that simple, and I get a lot of questions from readers wondering how to coax hummingbirds to visit their yards.

That's why I've come up with these five basic tips that should help almost anyone successfully attract humming-birds, and deal with some of the problems that can occur along the way.

1. GET THEIR ATTENTION. If you're just starting out, the best way to get hummingbirds to notice your sugar-water feeder is to plant red flowers. Then place the sugar-water feeder among those flowers.

The red blooms will attract the birds, and they will quickly find the feeder. As soon as they are comfortable eating from the feeder, you can move it a few feet a day so it's closer to your viewing window, or wherever you'd like to watch them feed.

As far as the proper placement for your feeder, it's best to keep it out of the sun so the sugar-water mixture does not spoil.

But don't worry about nearby human activity. Reader Evelyn Cook of Springfield, Oregon was concerned that traffic and children playing in the area could discourage hummingbirds from the feeder on her porch. Once hummingbirds find a feeder, they tend to be very tame, and no amount of activity will keep them away.

2. THE RIGHT RECIPE. Mix 4 parts tap water to 1 part sugar. Bring the mixture to a boil, then allow it to cool before plac-

ing it in the feeder. This is the most widely accepted sugar-water recipe. It produces a mixture that is neither too light nor too heavy and resists quick spoiling. Do not use sugar substitutes or honey, which can actually harm the birds.

You can store leftovers in the refrigerator for up to a week. Change the sugar water every 3 to 5 days. It's not necessary to add red coloring because hummingbird feeders usually have red on them. If not, you can try attaching something red—like a gift bow or an artificial flower—to the feeder.

Karin and Walter Mullaney of Arden, North Carolina wondered if they should fortify their sugar-water mixture. There is no need to add other nutrients to the mixture. The birds get any additional nutrients they need from other sources, such as flower nectar and tiny insects.

SWEET TREATS. Hummingbirds aren't the only ones who like sugar water. To keep bees away from your feeders, use bee guards. To keep ants out, hang a water-filled moat (like the one above), which was made from a plastic bottle cap.

3. INSECT-PROOF FEEDERS. Since the sugar-water mixture is so sweet, bees, flies and ants are often attracted to the feeder spouts. This was a problem for Jerry and Lita Fish in Tucson, Arizona, who wrote in looking for a way to stop bees and ants from invading their hummingbird feeders.

Because ants don't fly, you simply need to block their walking pathway to the feeder ports. Deter them with a water-filled moat that hangs between the hook and the feeder. Moats are available at birding supply stores, or you can fashion your own using a deep, plastic bottle cap (see photo above right).

Discourage bees by inserting bee guards, also available at birding supply stores, in the feeder spouts. Some feeders even come with these guards already attached. In addition, you can hang a bee trap near the hummingbird feeder, using the same sugar water as bait. This will eliminate many of the invading insects.

4. OUTWIT BULLY MALES. It's common for a dominant male to chase other hummingbirds away from a feeder. This is one way the male protects his nesting territory. In fact, these males spend most of their time guarding feeders, and will allow only their mates and offspring to feed.

The simple solution is to place other feeders out of sight of the feeder the bully is guarding. He can guard only one feeder at a time, freeing up the others to entertain additional hummingbirds.

5. KEEP FEEDERS CLEAN. When sugar water ferments, it clogs feeder spouts and reservoirs. In hot weather, feeders should be cleaned at least once a week. Sometimes, hummingbirds will let you know when the feeder needs cleaning—they'll stop coming by to eat.

The easiest way to clean the feeders is to wash with a solution of hot water and a little vinegar, and use a pipe cleaner in the tubes. Give the feeder a thorough rinse, and it should look like new.

With these five tips, you're ready to welcome hummingbirds to your backyard this summer!

READER TIP

To get a close-up view of hummingbirds, start your feeders at a distance among red flowers. Then move the feeder a few feet each day until it's at the desired location near your house.

ANNA'S HUMMINGBIRD

*Believe your eyes.
This species may
stick around all winter.*

In the middle of winter, bird-watchers in the Northwest may do a double take before realizing that they have indeed just spotted a hummingbird.

Although it may seem like an extraordinary sighting, it is actually quite common for Anna's hummingbirds to spend winter along the Pacific Coast, reaching all the way north to Alaska.

Though most Anna's still nest in California, their breeding range has recently spread north to Canada and east to Arizona, due to increased availability of the plants they use as food and sugar-water feeders. But when the breeding season ends, many Anna's become vagrants, and may show up almost anywhere in North America during winter.

"Imagine our surprise when we discovered a hummingbird hovering around our red suet bag in November," writes Pat Gould of Kelowna, British Columbia.

"I quickly dug out our hummingbird feeders, and boiled some sugar water to feed to the unexpected visitor. We searched the field guides to discover that our visitor was a female Anna's hummingbird.

"My husband, Frank, had never taken part in my interest in birds, until the Anna's arrived. From that day on, he became the keeper of the feeders, which he brought inside after dark each night to keep them from freezing."

Can't Miss This Redhead

The Anna's hummingbird was named after Anna de Belle Massena, the wife of a French prince who liked to collect hummingbird items.

The males are easy to pick out, since they sport rose-red feathers on their crowns as well as on their throats. Even the females have a small red throat patch. In addition to being simple to spot, the Anna's is also the largest and most common hummingbird in most of its range.

Like most hummingbirds, the male and female Anna's spend time together only long enough to mate. Then each establish and defend separate territories—he for the purpose of feeding; she for nesting.

The female builds a nest of plant fibers early in the season, sometimes amid frost and snow, and attaches it to a tree limb, shrub or power line using spider silk. Though she builds the nest in about 7 days, she often lays the first of two white eggs when the nest is only partially built.

After she lays the second egg, she incubates them for 2 weeks, even while continuing to work on the nest and adding lichens to the outside for camouflage. She raises the young on her own, and the fledglings leave the nest about 3 weeks after hatching.

Within a few days, the young ones establish their own feeding territories, while their mother begins the nesting process again. In fact, she may start building the next nest before she has stopped feeding the fledglings.

Trick Flying

Though the male Anna's does not help rear the young, his role is vital, beginning with one of the most remarkable courtship displays among all birds.

Starting as early as December, a male begins his courtship by hovering in front of a female, then flying in a huge arc to a great height, 100 feet or higher, pausing at the top to sing his squeaky song. Then he speedily dives down to her ladyship, who perches primly on a twig, watching the show. At the last second, the male ends his dive in an explosive squeak, spreads his tail feathers and flashes his brilliant rose-red throat.

In Visalia, California, Cheryl Lockridge observed a similar courtship showing from one of the male hum-

PROMINENT AND DOMINANT. Male Anna's hummingbirds (opposite and below) are easy to spot because of the bright rose-red feathers that cover their crowns and throats. These assertive birds are known to vigorously defend their feeding territories in the far West. They'll keep watch over their treasured space from several prominent perching spots in the area.

Francois Gohier; opposite page, Hugh P. Smith Jr.

Maslowski Productions

Francis Gohier

mingbirds in her backyard.

"'Mad Max' is an Anna's hummingbird that earned the nickname because of his spectacular aerial displays," Cheryl writes. "He would fly high into the sky until he was just a tiny dot, and then swoop down like a little fighter jet."

Aside from his courtship flights, a male Anna's spends much of his time defending feeding territory. He protects nectar-producing plants, such as gooseberry, monkey flower, Indian pink and Indian paintbrushes, and sugar-water feeders.

Anna's hummingbirds will also feed on the sap that oozes from trees that have been drilled by red-breasted sapsuckers. They're after both the sweet sap and the small insects that are attracted to it.

Drawn to the Water

Anna's also will take a keen interest in the water available in Western gardens. Unlike many other hummingbird species, Anna's will perch on the side of a birdbath to drink.

Emerson Stoner of Benicia, California recalls a female Anna's that took a liking to the spray of his garden hose.

"She discovered that she could ride the stream, a solid jet of water about 3/4 of an inch thick," he writes. "Flying up at right angles, she alighted on the jet, as though it were a branch, and permitted it to carry her forward. Over and over she did this, apparently enjoying the stunt. She seemed to be playing rather than bathing."

Perhaps the reason Anna's is one of the most well liked of all hummingbirds is that it is faithful to the backyards of the West. And it is capable of lighting up gardens there anytime of the year.

Common Name: Anna's hummingbird.

Scientific Name: *Calypte anna.*

Length: 4 inches.

Wingspan: 5-1/4 inches.

Distinctive Markings: The crown and throat of the male Anna's are a brilliant rose-red in good light. Females usually have flecks of red on their heavily spotted throats.

Distinctive Behavior: In courtship, the male soars high into the air until almost lost from sight, then dives vertically at great speed toward a perched female.

Habitat: Gardens; after nesting season, it may move to high-altitude coniferous forests.

Voice: A series of squeaky phrases, sung either in flight or from a perch. Both males and females utter a click, especially when feeding.

Nesting: A nest of plant down on a tree limb, shrub or power line. The female incubates two white eggs for at least 14 days until they hatch. Two broods a year are common.

Diet: Eats more insects than many other hummingbirds. Also favors flower nectar, tree sap and sugar water.

Backyard Favorite: A sugar-water feeder surrounded by a garden of red and orange flowers.

■ Year-Round
■ Winter
■ Summer

BIRD-WATCHER'S SECRET

Look for this interesting flier at your birdbath. Unlike many other hummingbird species, Anna's will actually perch there to drink.

SETTING THE TABLE

Transform your yard into a hummingbird haven.

Fine Dining

I made this attractive hummingbird feeder (below) from an old chandelier I found at a yard sale for only $2. After removing all the electrical parts, I painted it with metallic colors—each arm in a different hue.

I purchased the matching jeweled feeders from our local hardware store. To keep them from falling off the arms of the chandelier, I put Styrofoam on the bottoms of the feeders and pressed them onto the arms.

I added the red bow after reading in *Birds & Blooms* that it is a good way to help hummingbirds notice your feeder. It must work. Now they are regular visitors!

—Joan Johnson
Easley,
South Carolina

Feeders on Display

My mom and dad, Delbert and Sibyl Alcorn, came up with this nifty stand to hang their hummingbird feeders in the garden (right). They call it a "hummingbird trapeze."

It's made from pieces of PVC pipe joined in a ladder-like shape and held together with some adhesive. They drilled holes in the top crossbar and added hooks to hang their feeders. Now they can really enjoy the aerial acrobatics of the hummingbirds.

—Jan McPheeters
Kilgore, Texas

No Pests Allowed

I've found two ways to keep pests off my hummingbird feeders. To prevent ants, I stick double-sided tape on the very top of the feeder. Ants won't walk over this.

To deter bees and hornets, I place a birdbath or other container of water within a foot of the feeder. The bees and hornets seem to only want the moisture, so they go to the easiest place to get it. They stay away from my feeder and go to the standing water instead.   —Janet Davis
Liberty Lake, Washington

Getting Antsy?

I know that many people have trouble keeping ants from their hummingbird feeders, so I was excited when my husband and I accidentally discovered a solution.

We started mulching our flower beds with grass clippings to help improve the soil, and also placed the clippings around the pole for our hummingbird feeder. That's when we realized we weren't getting any ants.

I thought it was a fluke, but the same thing happened the next year. As long as nothing else touched the pole, the ants didn't climb it. Once a tree branch touched the feeder and the ants came running, but when I removed the branch, they disappeared once again.

—Marianne Robbins, Grand Ledge, Michigan

Butter Solutions

To keep the bigger birds from spilling or drinking all the hummingbird nectar from my feeder, I came up with this quick and simple solution.

I cut the bottom out of an old plastic margarine tub (right) and fit it over the top of my feeder.

The other birds cannot perch on it, but the hummers can hover and still get to the nectar.   —Norton Egbert
Tucson, Arizona

BLACK-CHINNED HUMMINGBIRD

The black-chinned hummingbird is the western counterpart to the ruby-throated hummingbird. It's the most widespread of all western species, with a breeding range spanning from Mexico to southern Canada.

At one time, these hummingbirds resided strictly near canyons and in the foothill forests of western mountains. However, because of the popularity of sugar-water feeders and hummingbird gardens, these birds are now frequent residents in urban and suburban backyards. And they're very comfortable with their human neighbors.

Like many other hummingbirds, the black-chinned is named for the male's most distinctive feature—its prominent black throat. In the right light, you'll also see a spectacular flash of bright, iridescent violet just above the white bib on its breast. Females are plainer than the male, and have no distinctive markings on their drab gray chins.

Black-chinned hummers almost always pump and wag their tails while in flight. And the males create a dull buzzing sound while in the air.

Besides nectar, these birds also drink tree sap from sapsucker wells and will catch insects by perching on a branch and dashing out to ambush their prey, much like flycatchers do.

READER TIP

Look for black-chinned hummers at sugar-water feeders, hummingbird gardens and on trees as they search for sweetness at sapsucker wells.

BLACK-CHINNED HUMMERS find plenty of room to roam. They are the most widespread of all western hummingbird species. Although most hummingbirds lay two eggs, black-chins can lay one to three.

Photo: Anthony Mercieca/Dembinsky Photo Assoc.

HANGING BASKETS FOR FLYING JEWELS

Use these tips to create an irresistible floating garden of nectar-rich blooms.

By Kris Wetherbee
Oakland, Oregon

Richard Day/Daybreak Imagery; opposite page: Rick Wetherbee

Hanging flower baskets are great ways to brighten the view almost anywhere. But if you plant blooms that also attract hummingbirds, the scene can be even more spectacular.

Imagine several gorgeous hummingbirds hovering around your hanging baskets, each vying for a dining spot. And once they find your flowers, it's likely they'll return again and again all season long.

Luckily, it's not difficult to make that dream a reality. Just start with the simple tips and ideas on these pages.

1. Select the Right Flowers

There are several factors to consider when choosing flowers that will thrive in hanging baskets and attract hummingbirds.

Nectar. First, look for nectar-rich, tubular blooms, such as those on penstemon, salvia and petunia. Hummers are able to access the nectar easily with their long, narrow bills and tongues.

Plant form. Since hummers typically feed while hovering, flowers that stick out from a plant's foliage, by either protruding or dangling, provide ample air space so the birds' beating wings easily clear any leaves.

Color. People often associate hummingbirds with the color red, and for good reason. These inquisitive birds can see red from a great distance, so offering nectar-rich flowers in crimson shades should always get their attention. However, they'll eagerly sip nectar from flowers in almost any color, including orange, pink, purple, white and yellow.

Number of flowers. The amount of blooms a plant produces also plays a big role in attracting these tiny birds. Plants with multiple flowers in open clusters are more appealing than plants like hibiscus that feature a small selection of large blooms.

Think about it from their perspective. How much more enticing is a buffet table laden with multiple food offerings than several tables spaced 10 feet apart, each featuring only a few dishes of food?

Bloom time. Plants with a long flowering season will provide nectar for an extended period of time. Another way to achieve this is to choose flowers with staggered bloom times—whether in one basket or by offering several hanging baskets.

2. Basket Basics

Hummingbirds aren't going to care what type of container you use—whether you select plastic, wood, pottery or a wire basket lined with sphagnum moss. However, the size of the planter will affect its upkeep and placement.

Hanging baskets for hummers should be at least 12 inches in diameter. Lightweight pots or smaller containers are easier to handle, but larger containers hold more plants, make for a more eye-catching display and keep plant roots moist longer.

Just remember that a heavy pot or large container can

easily weigh 50 pounds or more when filled with damp soil and plants. These will need heavy-duty hooks and require strong support.

3. Compose the Display

The sky's the limit when it comes to the variety of flowers and foliage that work well in hanging baskets. You can always count on traditional hummingbird favorites—geraniums, fuchsias, nasturtiums, petunias, lantana and impatiens, for instance—to create a spectacular hanging display.

But even vines and upright perennials, such as garden phlox, veronica or penstemon, can look attractive in larger baskets and appeal to a hummingbird's appetite.

Here are some other design factors to consider:

Color and texture. A combination of both foliage and flowers creates the most alluring effect. For example, the purple foliage of some coral bell cultivars add drama, while the blooms provide nectar.

Combine different leaf shapes or forms for a striking arrangement, and create special tactile interest by using plants with different textures.

Height and form. Bring depth and visual interest to your hanging garden by combining plants with staggered heights and habits.

For example, you could place mounding or upright plants, such as salvia, penstemon or zinnias, toward the center of the pot, then accent with trailing plants—such as verbena, parrot's beak or trailing petunias—positioned along the outer edges to spill over the sides.

Plant requirements. No matter what combinations you select, be sure that plants destined to share the same basket also share similar water and light needs.

4. Put It Together

Now that you know what you'll be planting, it's time to gather the materials needed to make your baskets.

Start with the soil. A good lightweight potting mix is a must, preferably one that includes peat moss and perlite or vermiculite to provide aeration and drainage.

Plan the arrangement. It's a good idea to set out your plants ahead of time to figure out the best arrangement. The spacing needed between each plant will depend on the varieties and the container you've selected, and the nature of the plant's growth habits and characteristics.

Smaller plants can be spaced closer together than larger plants, so the total number will vary. But as a general rule, a 12-inch container will house about five to seven plants. Wire baskets fit more plants since you can also plant in the sides.

Time to plant. Once you've determined the arrangement, fill the pot two-thirds full with potting mix and plant the largest plants and those in the center first, followed by the smaller plants and those around the outer edges of your

---

MAXIMUM CAPACITY. When it comes to attracting hummingbirds to your yard, the more flowers you can plant, the better your chances. That's why hanging baskets are useful because they provide a quick and easy way to increase your floral display. Start with the list on the opposite page for ideas.

Photos on both pages: Rick Wetherbee

Chapter 6

container. Be sure to place the plants at the original depth as they were in their containers. Then secure them in place with additional soil and water well.

Wire baskets are a bit different because in addition to the top, both the sides and even the bottom of the container can be planted, creating a colossal sphere of living color.

Line the basket with a thick layer of damp sphagnum moss or a preformed fiber mat liner. Plant the bottom and sides by poking holes through the moss or liner and gently pushing in the plant's roots from the outside. Add potting mix and secure the roots as you work your way toward the top of the basket. Then plant the surface as you would for a regular basket.

5. Hang It Up

When hanging your basket, you should usually choose a sunny, sheltered location within easy viewing range so you can watch the hummingbirds up close. Or, if your basket contains low-light garden plants, pick an appropriate spot in the shade where you'll have a good view.

And don't limit locations to areas near windows. Think of the other places you spend time outside, and try hanging your baskets around the yard.

Add pizzazz to boring entrance areas by hanging several baskets near the front door, bring a new dimension to walls and doorways, or add colorful charm to a courtyard. Or, why not expand your hanging garden to a balcony, arbor, trellis or gazebo?

Wherever you decide to hang your hummingbird garden, be sure to include a comfortable place nearby where you can sit back, relax and enjoy the view.

Editor's Note: Kris Wetherbee is the author of the book, *Attracting Birds, Butterflies & Other Winged Wonders to Your Backyard.*

Top Hummingbird Flowers for Hanging Baskets

The following list of hummingbird plants for hanging baskets is by no means inclusive, but it offers a variety of colorful choices for a striking display.

Annuals
- Begonia
- Cigar plant (*Cuphea*)
- Cosmos
- Four-o'clock
- Fuchsia
- Geranium (*Pelargonium*)
- Impatiens
- Lantana
- Nasturtium
- Nicotiana
- Parrot's beak (*Lotus berthelotii*)
- Petunia
- Phlox
- Salvia
- Scaevola
- Shrimp plant (*Justicia*)
- Zinnia

Perennials
- Agastache
- Bee balm
- Coral bells
- Dwarf delphinium
- Penstemon
- Phlox
- Salvia
- Verbena
- Veronica

Vines
- Canary creeper
- Cardinal climber
- Clematis
- Morning glory

Fuchsia

Petunia

Clematis

BROAD-BILLED HUMMINGBIRD

This stunning beauty is worth a trip to the Southwest.

By George Harrison
Contributing Editor

Of the 15 or more hummingbird species that breed in the United States, none is as beautiful as the male broad-billed hummingbird. Unfortunately, the broad-billed is a Mexican species that nests in the U.S. only in the deepest Southwest, primarily southeastern Arizona.

In other words, most of us will never get a chance to see this beautiful hummingbird without some traveling.

Though I live in southeastern Wisconsin, I have journeyed to broad-billed hummingbird country in southeastern Arizona to see and photograph this beauty. The best places to see broad-billeds include Madera Canyon, south of Tucson; Ramsey Canyon and adjacent canyons in the Huachuca Mountains near Sierra Vista; and at Chiricahua National Monument, north of Douglas.

Set Up Camp

In all of these parklike locations, campers can easily attract broad-billeds and other birds by setting up temporary feeding stations of sugar-water feeders anywhere around their tents or campers. In a matter of minutes, hungry hummingbirds will appear.

During a 3-day period in late April, when I camped in Madera Canyon, I met Frances and Art Holmes from Bridgeton, New Jersey. They were feeding broad-billed, blue-throated and black-chinned hummingbirds, as well as western tanagers and bridled titmice at sugar-water feeders made of small drinking glasses attached to twigs with masking tape. The birds were coming and going all day long.

It was at that campsite that I began to fully appreciate the beauty of the male broad-billed hummingbird. His carmine-red bill with a dusky tip finished off the striking, sapphire-blue throat. His emerald-green breast, head and back shimmered in the light, and he had a white fleck above and behind each eye.

At sugar-water feeders and blossoms, broad-billeds are not as aggressive as some species are, but they have been observed chasing large swallowtail butterflies that come near. For some strange reason, they fiercely attack these butterflies and run the intruders out of the feeding area. They do not seem concerned by smaller butterfly species, however.

I did not find my first broad-billed hummingbird nest until I visited Sabino Canyon, in the Santa Catalina Mountains, northeast of Tucson.

There, in a dry creek bed, thick with stunted willows and cottonwoods, I spotted a female broad-billed just adding the finishing touches to her tiny nest. She showed virtually no fear as I moved closer for a better look at the nest she was building on a horizontal branch of a willow.

Frankly, the nest was not as neat as any other hummingbird nests I have seen. It was no rounded bump on the branch and there were no lichens on the outside. In fact, there were scraps of materials hanging from beneath, which was very unlike a hummingbird nest.

When she left the nest for more material, I moved in even closer to see what she was using. It was mostly tiny scraps of bark, dry leaves and grass, and was lined with

plant down. While I was still examining the nest, she returned. As if I weren't even there, she made a beeline for the nest, and carried on undisturbed.

As she was forming the nest, I noticed some unusual behavior, which I had never seen before. As she sat in the cup, she beat her wings so fast that they were a blur, just like when she is flying. Yet, she remained in the nest. I assume this was her way of molding her breast into the structure.

When I first spotted this amazing creature, it was early morning, when the desert was still relatively cool. She was not active at midday.

Some ornithologists have reported that broad-billeds lay their eggs 2 days apart, not one a day like most birds. When I returned to the nest several days later, there were two pure-white eggs in the nest and she was incubating them.

What's in a Name?

Broad-billed hummingbirds get their name from the fact that their bills are unusually broad at the base where it's

Maslowski Productions; opposite page, Rolf Nussbaumer

connected to the head. Both males and females have this characteristic.

While observing the female on the nest, I could see her broad bill, which was one of the ways I identified her. Her bill was also orange and she had dark-gray patches on her cheeks. I did not see a male at the nesting site, but found them at the canyon hotspots where they were drinking sugar water.

The males were also performing their courtship flights because it was late April. Like many other hummingbird species, male broad-billeds engage in a pendulum flight, swinging back and forth in front of a female, all the while giving a zinging call that sounded to one observer like the sound of a rifle bullet passing by.

When the young leave the nest after a couple of weeks

Maslowski Productions

Backyard Birding Bio

Bill Carter

Common Name: Broad-billed hummingbird.

Scientific Name: *Cynanthus latirostris*.

Length: 4 inches.

Wingspan: 5-3/4 inches.

Distinctive Markings: Male is dark blue and green with a broad, red bill that has a dusky tip; female is dingy gray below, with dark cheek patches, bronze-green back, dark-bluish tail and a duller orange bill.

Habitat: Thickets in arid country, desert canyons and streamside bushes.

Voice: Song of male is a high, tinkling sound and buzz; call is a dry "tek" or "tekek."

Nesting: A tiny cup, with a 3/4-inch inside diameter, of brown bark, dry leaves, grasses and soft plant down. It's built about 3 to 9 feet above the ground on a branch along a dry streambed. They have been known to nest on a clothesline. The female incubates two white eggs for about 2 weeks before hatching.

Diet: The nectar of bright-red and orange flowers of the arid Southwest, plus many kinds of tiny insects and spiders.

Backyard Favorite: A bright-red or orange feeder filled with sugar water.

☐ Summer
■ Year-Round

of care by their mother, fledgling broad-billeds look like adult females, except with shorter bills and tails.

By the time they arrive at sugar-water feeders, they all resemble females, except that juvenile males may have some small blue patches on the throat. First-year males still do not have the completed sapphire throat, and will not have it filled-in until their second year.

By early October, the broad-billeds that nest in the U.S. depart southward into Mexico. Though in recent years, some have wintered in canyons of the U.S. at lower elevations where sugar-water feeders are abundant. This may be because the habitat in Mexico is vulnerable to grazing, pesticides and even free-roaming domestic cats.

But come March of the following year, the broad-billeds will move back into their breeding territories, which include that chunk of the Southwest, where the most beautiful of all American hummingbirds reigns.

BIRD-WATCHER'S SECRET

Juvenile broad-billed hummingbirds look a lot like adult females, but there are a couple of ways to tell them apart. They have shorter bills and tails.

HUMMER HAPPENINGS

Encounters with these "jewels" are truly magical.

Taking Lunch "To Go"

I spotted this female ruby-throated hummingbird (above) as it was enjoying nectar from a bee balm plant in my mother's garden in Andersen County, Tennessee. When it pulled its bill out of the bloom, the flower came with it! I grabbed my camera and snapped a photo as fast as I could. The bird quickly shook the blossom off.   —Joe Kegley
Charlotte, North Carolina

Picky Eater

My husband and I went out to his workshop one morning and found a hummingbird sitting on the floor.

The bird was barely moving, so we went into the house and mixed up some sugar water. We took it out to the hummingbird, but it wasn't interested in the food.

With some quick thinking, my husband plucked a honeysuckle bloom off a bush near the patio. I held the flower up to the hummer's bill, and it quickly put its head all the way inside for a much-needed drink (above)!

We got a good laugh, and for the next few minutes, we nurtured the hummingbird with the blossoms before it flew off.   —Mary VanBuskirk
Newcastle, Oklahoma

Nest Above the Rest

Our carport contains a system of pulleys with tennis balls suspended from strings. We discovered this hummingbird nest (left) one day, built right on top of one of the balls.

We pulled into the driveway and our daughter Stacia spotted the nest, thinking it probably belonged to wasps.

We carefully climbed a ladder so we could inspect the nest without touching it. Sure enough, it was a hummer nest, but there was no sign of its owner. We kept an eye out, but no bird ever claimed the nest. Hopefully, the hummer made a new home in a more stable spot!
—*Jim and Cherry Bibler, Sequim, Washington*

A Perfect Pose

LAST SUMMER, I was pleased when my zinnias attracted this female ruby-throated hummingbird (left) to my backyard. It visited several times, and one day, I had my camera ready.

I was busy taking a close-up of a monarch butterfly among my zinnias, when the hummingbird zoomed in for some nectar. After flitting from flower to flower, it decided to rest

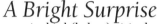

for a few seconds right in front of the camera.

I couldn't believe my luck. It was like she was posing for a photo!

I now plant zinnias every year and would recommend the same to other readers who want to attract hummingbirds.

—*Emily Howald*
Kankakee, Illinois

A Bright Surprise

THIS albino hummingbird (below) visited my sugar-water feeders late last summer. The little white wonder stayed for 2 weeks, stocking up on liquid energy before its journey to the tropics for winter.

I'm sure one reason this pale marvel stayed around so long was the abundant supply of food. My two neighbors and I maintain a total of six feeders in our yards.

I hope our buffet provided the hummer with sufficient nourishment for at least one leg of its long trip.

—*Donna Wolfe, Hebron, Kentucky*

Thirst-Quencher

I WAS watering a blooming hosta in my backyard, when a hummingbird flew within a foot of where I was standing. I figured the bird wanted to get near the bloom, so I slowly began backing away. Much to my surprise, the hummingbird followed!

Turns out, the bird must have been thirsty. I watched in awe as the hummingbird took a drink off a leaf that held a droplet of water. Even more surprising, the hummer returned the next morning and watched while I watered a hydrangea. Perhaps it was hoping for another drink of water! —*Kathy Dolge, Silver Spring, Maryland*

Cold Drink on a Hot Day

IT WAS a steamy 100° afternoon when I decided to change the sugar water in my hummingbird feeder. I added the new nectar, which I store in the refrigerator, then sat back to watch my little friends.

Soon, a male ruby-throated hummingbird arrived. It took a sip of the cold liquid and jumped back, as if startled by the icy drink. It almost fell off the perch. But then it took another sip and sat there for a while, drinking.

Normally, after about 10 to 15 seconds, the hummers fly off, but this one did not. When he did finally leave, he flew quite slowly, almost wobbling. Perhaps he had overindulged a bit on the cool refreshment. —*JoAnn Ennis*
Yardley, Pennsylvania

Granddaughter Knows Best

WHILE visiting our son in Iowa, a hummingbird flew into

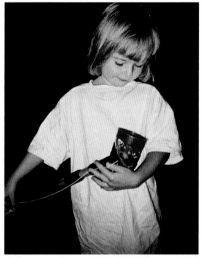

the house and up to the high cathedral windows near the ceiling. The tiny flier would not come down and ended up staying through the entire night.

The next day, our son Eric got an extension pole and tried, unsuccessfully, to guide the bird out the door. Meanwhile, our granddaughter Kali made a "nest" from a plastic cup. She chose a red one because she said hummingbirds like red, and she put dry grass in the bottom.

Kali then asked her dad to attach it to the pole and hold it up for the frightened bird. He did, and within 30 seconds, the bird flew into the cup.

Feeling proud about her role in the rescue, Kali took a moment to say good-bye to her new feathered friend (above), and then released it safely outside.

—*Jerry and Sally Groves, Tucson, Arizona*

On Guard

THE MALE anna's hummingbird who guards the feeders on my patio has earned its nickname, "Bull," short for Bully. As soon as I put this decorative hummingbird stake (right) in my garden, the

hummer immediately took ownership of it. It now serves as its perch for it to keep watch over the nearby feeders.

—LaVerne Otis, Bellflower, California

No Storm Stops 'Em

LAST YEAR, my area in Florida was hit by several hurricanes. But, despite the 40- to 50-mph winds, the hummingbird that frequents my fire bush and salvia made its appointed rounds like clockwork every day. I was totally amazed it could navigate, since it's difficult even to walk in those conditions.

I guess those little hummers have the postal carriers beat, since the hurricanes did stop the mail! *—Karen Lawrence Altoona, Florida*

Wait Your Turn

NOT A single feeder port went unused as these juvenile hummingbirds prepared for their migration (below). And they weren't the only hungry ones. At least 14 others were waiting nearby for their turn at the feeder. It was amazing to see so many hummingbirds in one place! *—Myrtle Stauffacher Englewood, Colorado*

Splish Splash

I WAS helping some vacationing neighbors by filling their bird feeders when I ended up helping out a little hummingbird—big time! One day, I found a hummer spread-eagle on the bottom of a small pan of nectar, stuck and caked with sugar and syrup.

Thinking it was dead, I started to remove it. Suddenly, I heard a feeble chirp. The little guy was alive!

I held it under a faucet to remove all the sugar I could, but it was still covered in the sticky stuff. Not knowing what to do, I put it in a square plastic jar and gingerly drove the 3 miles home. The whole time, I could only think one thing: How do you bathe a hummingbird?

Once home, I put the jar on its side and slowly poured in about a 1/2 inch of water. The hummer started to beat its wings and splashed around, dissolving the crusted sugar on its belly. I picked it up and carried it outside. Eventually, it took off and landed on a limb near my kitchen window.

I spent the next hour watching the bird. I was thrilled when it lifted off, flew directly toward my window and landed on a feeder about 3 feet from my nose. Now that's what I call a day well spent. *—Glen Keith, Junction, Texas*

A Balanced Home

WHEN A bold Anna's hummingbird made a nest on their clothesline, my friends in Wilton, California invited me over to take some pictures. Sure enough, the hummer had built its happy home on a wooden clothespin! I set up my Nikon camera on a tripod, went into the house and watched through the kitchen window. When the bird returned to its

nest, I used a remote to snap this picture (above). *—Boyd Jensen Rancho Cordova, California*

A Top-Notch Meal

A FEW years ago, I read about someone using a small plastic ladle as a temporary feeder for hummingbirds. Intrigued, I tried a version of that experiment, instead using the red plastic top from a mayonnaise jar.

The birds immediately took to it. In fact, they consumed more sugar water from the jar lid than from the regular feeder in my yard, which was completely full.

To fancy up the impromptu porch-rail dining room I had created, I made a tiny roost out of twigs. This little "stool" seemed to suit them perfectly, as you can see in this picture (below) of a female ruby-throated hummingbird.

—Lois Ament, Dillard, Georgia

Better Late Than Never

I'd heard hummingbird feeders should be hung outside in April, so that's when I did it. I even put a red ribbon near them as an added attraction. No hummingbirds.

Week after week, I faithfully changed the sugar water to keep it fresh. I still didn't see any hummingbirds.

The hummers finally showed up in July, when the cannas started to bloom. They had a pattern—first they'd visit the butterfly garden, then the trumpet vine, then the cannas, and then my feeders.

When I had 2 days of vacation, I decided to set my camera on a tripod to try to get some photos. Most of them didn't turn out too well, but I was so proud of this shot of a hummingbird enjoying my cannas (above).

—*Jan Dries, Dover, Pennsylvania*

Hummer...or Hawk?

My husband spotted a hummingbird on the ground under our feeder—something we'd never seen before. As we stared, the hummer shot straight up to attack another hummingbird that was sitting on the perch. He obviously thought desperate measures were required to maintain his turf.

We also watched this same bird buzz another hummer that wouldn't budge from its perch. When that didn't work, he dived down, grabbed the offender with both feet and dragged it off the perch. We couldn't believe what we were seeing—a hummingbird behaving like a hawk!

—*Constance Simmonds, San Benito, Texas*

Caught in The Rain

I mounted a hummingbird feeder outside my kitchen window so I can watch the activity while I'm cooking. One rainy day, I set up my camera just inside of the window and zoomed in on the feeder to try and catch a photo of a hummer up close.

This male Anna's hummingbird stopped by for a quick drink, his little body dripping wet. The flash from the camera makes it possible to see the raindrops on his bill and feathers. —*Desiree Skatvold Livermore, California*

A Bird-Watcher's Diary

One year, a mother hummingbird built her nest on a low branch in our plum tree. It was great for me—I could stand right next to the tree and look down into the nest. I could see it from my kitchen window, too. Here's part of the log I kept:

- **May 8**—Two eggs the size of lima beans.
- **May 19**—Babies getting feathers. Mother left the nest to eat. (She doesn't do this often.)
- **May 28**—Two little bills appear.
- **May 29**—One baby moving.
- **May 30**—Tied limbs down to keep wind from blowing nest out.
- **May 31**—Babies moved from one end of the nest to the other. They had an awful time changing position—they're packed in tight.
- **June 8**—Babies stand on edge of nest, moving their wings and preening.
- **June 9**—Mother feeds one baby in top of the tree.

It was a great experience seeing the birds develop from eggs to fledglings. I really missed them when they left.

—*Elizabeth Dearmin, Rio Rancho, New Mexico*

Wild About Watermelon

One summer morning, my husband, Ron, and I were out on the patio enjoying fresh watermelon from our garden and watching the hummingbirds at the feeder. One juvenile hummingbird hovered around the feeder, but couldn't quite figure out how to get the nectar.

After several attempts to get nourishment, the young hummingbird was chased away by more aggressive birds. The bird flew near the house and hovered there for a few seconds when it noticed the piece of red watermelon in Ron's hand. It headed straight for the melon and had no trouble taking a few sips.

—*Julie Mathews, Tacna, Arizona*

Insect Encounter

At one of my sugar-water feeders, I witnessed an unusual drama unfold between a praying mantis and a hummingbird (left). As the hummer approached the feeder, it was obvious the praying mantis wanted the hummer for lunch.

While the mantis held one bird at bay, another was able to sneak in from behind and grab a drink. It was funny to watch the mantis discover it was outnumbered.

Since the hummingbirds were unable to scare away the praying mantis, I swiftly helped the insect on its way so my feathered friends could eat!

—*Suella Bratton, Ozark, Arkansas*

Ports in a Storm

Three or four hummingbirds regularly visited us last summer. The day before Hurricane Katrina hit, they were feeding heavily. I wanted to make sure they were well fed before the storm, so I decided to wait until dark to take the feeder down. But we were so busy preparing for the hurricane that I forgot.

The next morning, I looked out to check on it. The hummers were feeding as if nothing was happening! Rain lashed the feeder as it swung wildly in 80-mph winds, and still the birds fed. They even seemed to enjoy hanging on and "riding" the feeder as it danced in the wind. Their resilience was amazing.

After the storm passed, we had 30 birds instead of our usual handful, so I bought a second feeder when we were able to get to a store. I think the new visitors were displaced hummers looking for a safe haven. I'm glad I was able to oblige them. —*Regina Hopper, Walker, Louisiana*

Close-Up View

Our family was vacationing at a ranch in Montana when we got to experience hummingbirds up close and personal. The birds there were simply fearless!

It only took us 5 minutes to attract hummingbirds to a hand-held feeder. We all took turns as the birds fed. This is my grandson Nick feeding a female rufous hummingbird (above). Occasionally, a hummer would even fly close enough to look us in the eye! —*Linda Grove, Morris, Illinois*

No Trespassing

The hummingbird feeder hanging on our deck was deserted one morning. Then I noticed a bumblebee circling it, leisurely checking it out.

An approaching hummingbird spotted the bee, braked to a halt, then gathered itself for a swift dash and delivered a poke to the bumblebee's rear.

The startled bee took off, while the feisty little hummer enjoyed its breakfast undisturbed. —*Virginia Kloth, Smyrna, Georgia*

Out in the Cold

It seems like we see hummingbirds earlier every spring, so we put out our sugar-water feeders even when there's still snow on the ground (right).

One year, we were away for a few days, and when we returned, the feeders were as dry as a bone. It was late, and as we unloaded the car, we noticed a hummer sitting at the empty feeder on the porch.

I quickly went inside to get some sugar water. As I took down the feeder to refill it, the bird did not budge. It appeared to be sleeping. (We later learned it was in torpor, a temporary hibernation-like state.)

I poured the mixture in and hung the feeder up again, without disturbing the bird. I went to get my camera, but just as I approached the bird, it flew away.

We hung another feeder nearby, and the hummer immediately flew to it for a midnight snack. I'm glad the bird was able to hang on through the chilly weather and didn't give up on us! —*Vince and Margaret Irwin, Hayfork, California*

Power in Numbers

Hummingbirds mesmerize me. One morning, I looked out my kitchen window at my sugar-water feeder and saw more hummingbirds than I could possibly count.

I was so excited that I ran to the store to buy more feeders and several rolls of film. Over the next 2 weeks, I went through a 10-pound bag of sugar, and got some great photos (above). I think they must have been fueling up for their fall migration south.

At one time, I counted 32 hummingbirds in the same area. Now I can't wait until next year! —*Stacy Hays*
Kimberly, Alabama

Meet "Harriet Hummer"

While sitting on our patio one spring day, my husband, John, noticed a small bird buzzing around his head. He looked up and realized that a hummingbird was building a nest on the Christmas icicle lights hanging over the table. We were more than a little surprised to see the bird had chosen such an exposed site to raise its young.

My husband soon named her "Harriet Hummer," and we spent plenty of time watching her. When the wind blew, Harriet looked like she was the sailor of a very small boat on the high seas. She never seemed to mind that we often ate dinner just 2 feet below her nest, and she was perfectly happy to pose for the many pictures we took of her.

—*Karen Williams, Mesa, Arizona*

Pick Yourself Up

One summer day as I was sitting on our deck, a little hummer landed on our vinyl-covered clothesline. As soon as the bird landed, it started falling backward on the slippery surface. The hummingbird fluttered its wings until it was upright, then started falling back again. The bird picked itself up over and over again, but it didn't give up!

Finally, after falling backward at least 10 times, the hummingbird hung itself upside down for a few seconds and then flew off. I couldn't believe how determined that bird was. It was entertaining to watch. —*Denise Maxwell*
East Moline, Illinois

Fond Farewell

Last summer, I rescued a hummingbird from our garage. It had flown in there, and then it was trapped. After I brought it out, the bird was poised to fly away, but it didn't move. It remained perched on my hand long enough for my granddaughter Kali to touch it gently and bid it farewell. We'll always remember sharing this special moment.

—*JoNette Eason*
New Bern, North Carolina

A Very Eager Reader

My husband and I enjoy relaxing on our deck each morning while sipping our coffee and watching the many ruby-throated hummingbirds that frequent our yard.

We got a thrill one day when a juvenile hummingbird landed on my husband's arm while he was reading the newspaper (above photos). I guess the hummer wanted to know what was going on in the world! —*Mary Rayner, Deerbrook, Wisconsin*

A Nest in the Pines

My neighbor Ted Hofecker took this picture of a hummingbird nest, which was the first I'd ever seen. It was right outside his kitchen window, about 7 feet high in a long-needled pine. The female bird even incorporated pieces of the tree's bark into the tiny nest for her two babies.

—Helen King, Vermilion, Ohio

Ranger Rescue

I'm a ranger in Rocky Mountain National Park. Broad-tailed hummingbirds sometimes find their way into our visitor center and fly to the top of the high ceiling. It was frustrating to watch them trying to fly out of the closed windows. Enticing them down didn't work. Eventually, the birds would fall to the floor, unhurt but weak.

One day when this happened, I decided to try making sugar water from a soda in the break room refrigerator. We poured the cola into a tiny bottle cap and added a little water. I sat outside the building, holding the hummer and gently pushing its bill into the diluted soda. It drank reluctantly at first, but then with more excitement.

Visitors watched the progress of this experiment as they came and went. Finally, the bird tried its wings. It failed the first couple of times, but then flew off.

I've since saved two more hummingbirds with this method, but we don't think soda is good for hummers. Now we keep a hummingbird first-aid kit with sugar packets, a bottle cap and a recipe at all our visitor centers.

—Marilyn Irwin, Estes Park, Colorado

Where's the Nectar?

As we were enjoying our morning coffee while camping in Minnesota's Hennepin State Park, my husband and I observed a hummingbird looking for breakfast. The rising sun cast its rays across Mille Lacs Lake, causing the red taillights of our truck to glow. The hummingbird hovered around one of the taillights. Then, to our amazement, it began to probe its bill at the light.

Although the red glow looked like it would yield a tasty treat, the hummer soon realized it would have to look elsewhere for its next meal.
—Linda Mallin Sykes
Minnetonka, Minnesota

On Her Guard

I have a number of hummingbird feeders at my home, but one is dominated by a female (right) that thinks it's just for her. She guards it from a nearby tree and dive-bombs any intruder who comes near.

One day this summer, I was cleaning the feeder at the kitchen sink. She flew to the window and looked in as if to ask, "OK—are you about done?"
—Flora Marlatt
Galena, Ohio

Sweet Attraction

My husband works a lot and seldom has time to enjoy the natural beauty of our backyard. But one evening he got the chance as we sat outside on our swing, relaxing in the great outdoors.

Out of nowhere, a hummingbird flew up and hovered right in front of his face. I watched in awe, amazed at how close it was.

Then my husband turned to me and smiled. "See, I told you I was sweet."
—Amanda Robertson
Raymond, New Hampshire

Suspicious Activity

We had lots of hummer activity last summer. For several weeks toward the end of the season, I watched the ruby-throated hummingbirds feed throughout the day and into the early evening in preparation for their long flight south.

The feeder was on a porch post, where I took several photos through the open kitchen window. This cunning hummingbird really caught my attention. It acted so suspicious!

If the bird detected even the slightest movement, it would fly away. It always came back, though. Like clockwork, the hummer would return 15 minutes later to feed again.
—Jim Irwin
Kirkwood, Missouri

After admiring the stunning hummingbirds in *Birds & Blooms*, Dale Harmer of Sequim, Washington decided to write about his favorite "humdinger."

"I'd like to add the rufous hummingbird to your list of these amazing and beautiful creatures," Dale says.

"We look forward to the arrival of this little gem each spring and make sure to put up sugar-water feeders as soon as the first one appears."

You're right, Dale. Rufous hummingbirds are pretty remarkable.

The male rufous is the only North American hummingbird with reddish-brown feathers covering its entire back and much of its head and tail (thus the name "rufous," which means reddish).

It also sports green wings and an orange-red iridescent throat that sparkles like burnished gold in the right light. The female has little of the namesake rufous coloring, however. Instead, it has green feathers on its back, head and tail with a bright, orange-red spot on its throat.

The rufous inhabits a summer range that's farther north than any other hummingbird. It nests from Oregon and Idaho to southern areas of Alaska and the Yukon.

READER TIP

The rufous travels farther north during the summer than any other hummingbird, from Oregon and Idaho to southern areas of Alaska and the Yukon.

But you don't have to live in the Northwest to spot one of these brilliant birds. Rufous hummingbirds migrate through most western states. They follow a coastal route northward in spring, then fly over the Rocky Mountains in fall.

They're also one of the most common vagrants, sometimes drifting off course during southern migration. They've showed up in just about every state and province, even spending winter in some southern states.

Most hummingbirds are aggressive, but the rufous becomes especially territorial when defending temporary feeding areas during migration "pit stops" or when nesting. No creature is safe from attack, whether it's larger birds like blackbirds and thrushes, or critters like chipmunks.

THE RUFOUS HUMMINGBIRD boasts many distinctive characteristics, including reddish-brown feathers and a northern summer range. They will also nest in loose "colonies" of up to 20 pairs in a small area.

RUFOUS HUMMINGBIRD

HUMMINGBIRD
HOT SPOT

Sonny Manley

Create a flowering oasis with this easy garden plan.

Want to create a hummingbird hot spot in your backyard? It's easy. Just plant nectar-producing flowers like these and add water—no cooking necessary!

For those who are starting from scratch, we've included an entire hummingbird garden plan (at right) to help. If you don't have the room or time to create the full garden, just add some of the plants shown on the opposite page to your existing flower beds.

After your blooms are in place, don't forget to include a sugar-water feeder, a birdbath or a mister among the blooms. This will attract even more visitors. With these things in place, your backyard should be buzzing with activity in no time!

Chapter 6

1
Columbine
(*Aquilegia* species)
PERENNIAL
Hardiness: Zones 3 to 9.
Height: 1 to 3 feet.
Width: 6 to 24 inches.
Light Needs: Shade to full sun.
Bloom Time: Late spring to early summer.

Richard Shiell

2
Bee balm
(*Monarda didyma*)
PERENNIAL
Hardiness: Zones 4 to 9.
Height: 3 feet.
Width: 18 to 36 inches.
Light Needs: Full sun; tolerates afternoon shade.
Bloom Time: Summer.

R. Todd Davis

3

Mimosa
(*Albizia julibrissin*)
SMALL TREE
Hardiness: Zones 6 to 9.
Height: 20 to 35 feet.
Width: 20 to 35 feet.
Light Needs: Full sun.
Bloom Time: Summer.

Connie Toops

4

Lilac
(*Syringa* species)
SHRUB
Hardiness: Zones 3 to 7.
Height: 7 to 15 feet.
Width: 5 to 15 feet.
Light Needs: Full sun.
Bloom Time: Spring.

Dianne Dietrich Leis

5

Canna
(*Canna* species)
TENDER PERENNIAL
Hardiness: Zones 8 to 11.
Height: 1-1/2 to 6 feet.
Width: 20 inches.
Light Needs: Full sun.
Bloom Time: Summer.

Donna and Tom Krischan

6

Daylily
(*Hemerocallis* species)
PERENNIAL
Hardiness: Zones 3 to 10.
Height: 1 to 4 feet.
Width: 1-1/2 to 4 feet.
Light Needs: Full sun to partial shade.
Bloom Time: Early summer until first frost.

Daniel Leach

7

Scarlet runner bean
(*Phaseolus coccineus*)
ANNUAL
Height: 15 feet.
Width: 12 inches.
Light Needs: Full sun.
Bloom Time: Early summer.

Alan and Linda Detrick

8

Butterfly weed
(*Asclepias tuberosa*)
PERENNIAL
Hardiness: Zones 4 to 9.
Height: 1-1/2 to 3 feet.
Width: 12 inches.
Light needs: Full sun.
Bloom Time: Midsummer, early fall.

Donna and Tom Krischan

9

Zinnia
(*Zinnia* species)
ANNUAL
Height: 6 to 36 inches.
Width: 1-1/2 to 2 feet.
Light Needs: Full sun.
Bloom Time: Summer.

Richard Shiell

10

Hosta
(*Hosta* species)
PERENNIAL
Hardiness: Zones 3 to 8.
Height: 6 to 36 inches.
Width: 8 to 36 inches.
Light Needs: Full to partial shade.
Bloom Time: Summer.

Michael Gadomski

11

Gayfeather
(*Liatris* species)
PERENNIAL
Hardiness: Zones 3 to 9.
Height: 2 to 6 feet.
Width: 18 to 24 inches.
Light Needs: Full sun.
Bloom Time: Midsummer to early fall.

Michael Gadomski

12

Hollyhock
(*Alcea rosea*)
BIENNIAL
Hardiness: Zones 3 to 9.
Height: 2 to 9 feet.
Width: 1-1/2 to 2 feet.
Light Needs: Full sun.
Bloom Time: Summer.

Richard Shiell

Richard Day/Daybreak Imagery

FLOWER POWER FOR HUMMINGBIRDS

Ray Herrick/Racinphoto.com

Put out the welcome mat for these tiny miracles with a nectar-filled garden.

By Jeff Nowak, Executive Editor

Sid and Shirley Rucker

I'll never forget the look of amazement on our friends' faces when a hummingbird buzzed over the patio, past our picnic table right to the bright-red bee balm just a few feet away.

Their jaws dropped in amazement. They had never seen a hummingbird that close before. In fact, they'd never even seen a hummingbird!

That's when my chest swelled. "Oh, yeah," I said. "They come every day at this time."

"The hummingbirds zip from flower to flower," I boasted. "It's part of our dinner routine—to see who spots one from the kitchen window first."

Judging by the roll of my wife's eyes, I knew what she was thinking…if they only knew my "lazy-man's approach" to attracting these iridescent wonders.

My secret is simple—plant nectar-filled flowers hummingbirds can't resist, and kick back and enjoy the show.

Chapter 6

Sid and Shirley Rucker (vertical text, left margin of upper image)

Hummingbird Buffet

Hummingbird gardening is something anyone can try in most parts of the country and, yes, expect success.

You don't need a huge manicured garden to get started. A simple hanging basket, container or window box packed with mostly red nectar-producing flowers does the trick. And once you see an iridescent hummingbird flitting from flower to flower, I guarantee you'll want to expand your plantings next year to bring in more of these unbelievable birds.

What Is Nectar?

Nectar is nothing more than sugar water produced naturally by all kinds of flowers. Some, like Queen-Anne's lace and zinnias, produce nectar on their shallow clusters of flowers. These attract bees, butterflies and other insects, along with hummingbirds.

The real surefire plants designed to appeal to hummingbirds are deep, tube-shaped flowers. Hummingbirds probe these

DIGGING FOR NECTAR. There are many sweet flowers that will attract hummingbirds (like the ones at left) to your backyard. For the best results, plant bright-red varieties that have tube-shaped blooms.

blooms with their long bills and tongues to lap up the energy drink that keeps their high-revving motors humming.

What do the flowers get in return?

"Hummingbirds play a large role in pollination," explains backyard bird expert George Harrison of Hubertus, Wisconsin. "As hummingbirds dip their bills down into each flower, pollen clings to their bills and feathers (see photo at left), so they transfer it from plant to plant."

The pollen fertilizes the flowers, which produce seeds that ensure their survival.

Hummingbird Gardens

Reader Marie Harrison of Valparaiso, Florida started her hummingbird garden, admittedly, by accident.

"It was a little bit of luck," she says. "The first flowers that attracted hummers to my garden were planted simply because I love flowers. When I started noticing the hummingbirds coming to certain flowers, I wanted to attract more of them. So, I started planting the flowers they liked best."

Among her favorites are red pentas, Turk's cap lilies, butterfly weed and honeysuckle.

Over the years, Marie has learned what many hummingbird lovers have discovered—if you know exactly what flowers hummingbirds are looking for, you're almost guaranteed regular visits.

Ready to set out the welcome mat for hummingbirds in your backyard? Here are some tips to get started:

■ **Seeing red.** A patch of red flowers to hummingbirds is like a neon "EAT" sign along a lonely highway. These birds search out nectar from many different colored flowers, but it's the red ones that really have magnetic drawing power.

Scientists believe hummingbirds are attracted to red flowers because they've learned through experience that red tubular flowers contain the most nectar. So anything red—be it a flower, baseball hat or tricycle—triggers their instincts to investigate. That's why hummingbird feeders usually have red feeding ports.

■ **Tube-shaped blooms.** Many plants on hummingbirds' hit list are tube-shaped flowers that provide large amounts of nectar deep at the base of their blooms. Hummingbirds can easily reach this sugar water, while bees and most other nectar-loving insects are left out.

Trumpet vine is an excellent example of tube-shaped nectar producers. It offers hummingbirds 10 times more sugar water than other plants!

■ **Less fragrant, more filling.** Many flowers hummingbirds flock to surprisingly have little to no scent. And, as nature would have it, there's a good reason.

Sweet-smelling flowers attract bees and other insects. Hummingbirds, like most birds, have a poor sense of smell. They rely on sight to find food. So, by remaining odor-free, these flowers cater largely to hummingbirds.

■ **Cascading blooms.** Hummingbirds are in a flying class of their own, with the ability to fly forward, backward, hover and even upside down!

Some nectar flowers, like fuchsia, have adapted specifically to accommodate hummingbirds. Their blooms hang downward, so only agile hummingbirds can reach their sweet treat.

Planting Your Hummer Garden

Planting a hummingbird garden is no different than creating a perennial border, mixed container or any other garden. The basics are the same—soil rich in organic matter that drains well will keep the flowers healthy. And healthy nectar plants produce loads of the sweet stuff.

There are hundreds of sweet blooming plants—annuals, perennials, trees, vines and shrubs—that hummingbirds will feed from. Which ones should you choose? How should you plant them? It's easier than you think:

■ **Mix plenty of annuals.** Annuals ensure long-blooming flowers that immediately produce nectar, from the time the migratory hummingbirds return north from their tropical winter grounds, until they leave in fall.

■ **Aim for continuous blossoms.** Perennials, flowering trees and shrubs are excellent additions to a hummingbird garden, but plan carefully before you plant. Seek a mix of nectar producers that bloom in succession, from early spring to fall.

■ **Plant in clusters.** Again, red is a sure bet for attracting hummingbirds. To get their attention, cluster red blooms together so they shout out, "Dinnertime!"

But that doesn't mean your garden has to be monochromatic. These sweet-toothed birds will gladly feed from any color nectar flower, but use red to draw them in.

■ **Plant low to high.** Consider your hummingbird garden as a stadium, placing shorter plants in front of taller ones. This gives the birds a chance to easily get to all the blooms, without plant stems and leaves interfering with their whirring wings. As a bonus, you get to see them better from your patio or window.

■ **Add to existing gardens.** You don't have to start from scratch. Many hummingbird plants blend in beautifully with existing flower gardens.

■ **Deadhead for more blooms.** The longer your nectar-producing plants produce flowers, the more hummingbirds you'll attract.

Even though many hummingbird plants are low-maintenance annuals and perennials, take time to deadhead blooms before they go to seed.

This keeps the plants pouring energy into flower production…a sure way to convince hummingbirds to stay near your backyard, and come back year after year.

Sweet Results at Hummingbird Feeders!

"I believe the ultimate goal for a hummingbird garden is to attract hummingbirds to eat at sugar-water feeders," says George Harrison. "In spring, I place my feeders right among red flowers, then move them a few feet each day until they're

Mark Werner/The Image Finders

DUAL ACTION. Once hummingbirds are accustomed to visiting your garden's blooms, put out a sugar-water feeder to attract even more visitors (like the one above). You won't be disappointed!

close to the windows where we can see them."

Here are more feeder tips…

■ **Make your own nectar.** Mix 4 parts water to 1 part sugar, boil and cool before filling feeders. It's that easy!

Change the solution every 3 days or so, keeping leftovers in the fridge for up to a week.

■ **Red accents help.** While most feeders are red plastic, try this clever trick so your hummers see the feeder: Place a bright-red bow on it to draw attention.

■ **Hang feeders in shady areas.** This keeps the nectar solution from fermenting and algae from messing up your feeders.

■ **Protect from pests.** Sugar water is sure to attract the attention of ants and bees. A small ant guard above the feeder's hanger keeps ants from reaching your feeder. Buy one for a few bucks from a birder's store, or make one from an inverted spray paint can cap.

The most effective way to keep bees and yellow jackets from the feeders is by using a feeder with plastic "bee guards." These mesh covers allow only the hummingbirds to reach the nectar.

'GLAD YOU ASKED!'

Expert answers your hummingbird questions.

By George Harrison, Contributing Editor

What's on the Menu?

I'm wondering how hummingbirds feed their young. My neighbor thinks they hold nectar or sugar water in their mouths and feed it to their babies, but I think their bills are too narrow to do this. Can you solve the mystery?
—Millie Howard
Little Rock, Arkansas

George: I'd be happy to settle this discussion. Hummingbirds usually feed tiny insects and spiders to their young. They insert them right into the mouths of their babies.

They'll also feed nectar and pollen to the young birds. They do this by holding it in their throats and then squirting it into the mouths of the nestlings. Sometimes this will cause the youngster's throat to swell temporarily, resembling a goiter.

MOUTHS TO FEED. This female hummingbird tends to hungry nestlings.

This is true of hummingbirds because most of their food comes from flower blooms into which the birds thrust their long bills to draw out nectar.

Water Color

I've heard you're not supposed to add red food coloring to the sugar-water mixture for hummingbirds. Is this true?
—Florence Neilson
Duchesne, Utah

George: One of the older red food colorings was found to be toxic to birds, but with the new formulations, I don't believe that's still true.

However, it isn't necessary to dye sugar water for hummingbirds under most circumstances. The feeders usually have red or orange parts, which provide enough color to attract hummingbirds or orioles.

Clear sugar water (one part sugar to four parts water) will work just fine.

Have a Drink

I've heard pigeons and doves are the only birds that drink by suction. But what about hummingbirds? I've never seen a hummingbird tip its head back to swallow.
—Calvin Wheeler
Auburn, Washington

George: You're right, hummingbirds can be included in this select group. They are one of the few species of birds that swallow liquid without throwing their head back to allow gravity to help them swallow.

Aggressive Behavior

Why do the hummingbirds around our sugar-water feeders act so aggressive? There's plenty of room for several to feed at once, but one often chases the others away.
—Matthew Welch, Hyrum, Utah

George: There's usually a dominant male hummingbird that controls which birds feed from sugar-water feeders and flower beds in its territory. Females that are sociable with the dominant male usually are allowed to feed, while other males and females are sent packing.

338

347

357

369

CHAPTER 7

PLAN A GREAT GARDEN

Ken Thommes

366

360

Alan and Linda Detrick

Plan a Great Garden

ONE WITH NATURE

*Eco-minded planning led
to a lush oasis in the desert.*

By Shelley Grossman, Carlsbad, California

Today, we live in the midst of a big, vibrant garden that's filled with flowers, a mini orchard, vegetables, a pond and more. There isn't a blade of grass in sight. And that's quite a change from the way it was when we purchased the property almost 20 years ago.

Back then, it featured an expansive lawn lined with perfectly trimmed hedges and a few fruit trees. That kind of yard might be ideal to some—but all I could see was a place that lacked life. Birds flew through it, but didn't stay.

What's worse was the fact that the yard took gallons of water and lots of chemicals to keep everything green, and the constant mowing and pruning wasn't much fun either.

Becoming Water-Wise

Our area receives less than 11 inches of rain per year, making water a precious commodity that I didn't want to waste. And, as a master composter, I was more interested in recycling and enriching the soil than tossing anything out. In short, I was determined to do things differently, and my husband, Jay, was in complete agreement.

The first thing to go was the lawn, which I covered in grass clippings, mulch, newspaper, compost and black plastic. After about 3 weeks, the grass was gone and I was able to create a patchwork of flower beds lined with stone walls.

Once the walls were in place, I did some planting, but held off on completely filling the beds so I could continue adding compost and improving the soil. A year later, those beds were full of fertile dirt and ready to go.

It was hard to be patient, but the wait paid off when I added California poppies, geraniums, Joe Pye weed, nasturtiums, freesia and other beautiful blooms, and watched them flourish almost overnight.

There were a few plants that didn't take to one spot, so I'd move them to another. Over time, I learned to place new container-grown plants, still in their pots, out in the garden. Then I'd watch them for a week or two to see how they responded and looked amid the other blooms. This has saved me the extra work of transplanting many flowers, or worse, watching them die.

Composting and Conservation

At the same time I was working on the soil, I built compost bins so I could recycle any yard waste we created, along with herbicide-free clippings from our neighbors. I also introduced earthworms to my compost bins to speed up the process—and thanks to those creatures, I was able to churn out compost in about 10 days instead of 3 weeks.

To conserve water, we started to collect rain in barrels, and we actually found we could retain enough to fill a small swimming pool and pond 4 to 6 months out of the year.

Then we took it a step further. We checked with the regulations of our local municipality, and devised a way to divert water from the shower and washing machine into the garden. There, it irrigates plants, including a pair of 30-year-old orange trees, or is stored for later use.

As time passed, our yard began to take on a lush yet completely natural appearance. I replaced all of the stiff, manicured hedges with rambling bougainvillea, lantana, nandina, a luxurious bottlebrush tree and romantic wisteria vines.

We also put in a meandering, stone-lined waterfall and creek that feed into the small pond where I planted lotus and water iris. I've included other plants that require more water, too, like my cape tubular fuchsia. These beauties take advantage of the moisture in the fog that regularly rolls in from the ocean, about 1-1/2 miles away.

Vegetable gardening has long been a passion of mine,

SAVVY IRRIGATION. With water in short supply around her California area, Shelley Grossman (opposite page) had to get creative in her garden. She uses a water-recycling system and more than 60 rain barrels to create a yard filled with vegetables, fruit trees and flowers (like California poppies, above).

ever since I helped my dad grow tomatoes when I was young, so including one in my yard was always part of the plan. Compost and our warm weather help me grow a year-round bumper crops of eggplants, peppers, tomatoes, lettuce, cucumbers, melons and carrots.

Those same conditions ensure that my mini fruit orchard of apricot, pear, apple, plum and orange trees, as well as a variety of herbs, thrive, too.

I rarely have to shop for produce these days because we're pretty self-sufficient.

Our conservation efforts have come in handy as well, especially when it was dry enough in our area to require water rationing not long ago.

Unlike others around us who watched lawns turn brown, our yard continued to bloom, thanks to our water recycling system and the 68 rain barrels I now have installed throughout the property.

When I think back on what this place used to look like, I'm amazed and pleased. This once formal-but-bland property is now bursting with vitality. And, best of all, the birds are back!

GREEN THUMB TIP

You can practice good water conservation and have a thriving garden. I use rain barrels to collect water, and it really adds up fast! —*Shelley Grossman Carlsbad, California*

FRONT TO BACK. The front of Shelley Grossman's house is just as impressive as the back. With colorful flowers filling the entire area with blooms, you wouldn't guess that this California yard receives less than 11 inches of rain fall per year.

Planting List

1. Freesia
2. Joe Pye weed
3. Geranium
4. California poppy
5. Wisteria
6. Water iris
7. Lotus
8. Fuschia
9. Avocado tree
10. Nandina
11. Bougainvillea
12. Lantana
13. Japanese maple
14. Nasturtium
15. Fennel
16. Bottlebrush
17. Fruit orchard
18. Vegetable garden
19. Ivy geranium
20. Cape tubular fuchsia

House

DIGGING COLORADO

This couple battled rocks, deer and a fickle climate to create a mountain oasis.

By Ramona Boone, Colorado Springs, Colorado

Living in Colorado has its advantages. My husband, Steve, and I enjoy breathtaking views of 14,000-foot mountains and fields of wildflowers. But as someone who grew up in Illinois, I couldn't stop dreaming of a lush, colorful garden filled with sweetly scented flowers.

Unfortunately, the deer that live near our home seemed to share the same dream. They regularly came down from the mountains to forage. Apparently, our 1-acre property was a great place to nap and snack!

As a result, the landscaping around the house took on a very "native" look—just pine trees and rocks. For one small area of the yard, we brought in three truckloads of dirt, put mulch on top of that and laid flagstone paths. But I didn't plant anything there. I knew the deer and bears would munch it away.

A Blank Canvas

But there was hope. The previous owners had turned the large side yard into a dog run and surrounded it with a 6-foot-high fence. This space contained nothing but flat ugly dirt, plus a few trees. It was perfect for a deer-proof garden.

At least we *thought* it was perfect. Then we started trying to dig holes in the soil for planting.

Colorado clay doesn't even come close to the rich, black soil

WORTH THE WORK. Ramona and Steve Boone (above inset) had to clear out loads of rocky dirt and bring in new soil to create a fertile area for their thriving—and protected—garden (top).

of Illinois. There's a reason our neighborhood is called "Rockrimmon." With every shovelful, we unearthed nothing but rocks, from egg-sized lumps to small boulders. And what we dug up was unusable for planting, so we had to bring in new soil.

If we had it to do again, we would have skipped the digging and trucked in soil to make raised beds.

Still, we were fortunate. There were some natural assets within the enclosure, including a 40-foot pine tree, a shimmering aspen, a grove of small oak trees and a wonderful 4-foot by 2-foot boulder neatly located against the inside fence.

The first summer, we cleared weeds and laid out a design. Then Steve thought of a fish pond and decided to add a small water garden. Little did he know that after digging 6 inches down, he'd have to rent a jackhammer to punch through solid sandstone to finish the job.

Blossoming Landscape

We planted the basics that year—peonies, asters, rudbeckia and other hardy plants capable of withstanding the late snows and dry seasons of the High Plains. As a Midwestern native, I always thought abundant snow meant moisture. But in the Front Range of the Rocky Mountains, the snow often evaporates in the dry air instead of melting into the ground.

The next summer, I started trying the flowers I'd been dreaming about—roses, lilies and garden phlox. Although we're in Plant Hardiness Zone 5, there are pockets in the yard that are colder. And some years, it's like we're living in Zone 2! I spent a couple of years moving plants around and adding new ones to replace those flowers that froze in these cooler microclimates.

The existing oaks gave us an opportunity to try shade-loving plants like hostas that the deer would devour if planted outside the fence. Columbine loves the dappled shade, as do bleeding heart, rubrum lily, astilbe, hellebore and lamium.

Nature Takes Root

As the garden matured, we were thrilled to see volunteer plants emerge. Fragrant Hyperion daylilies appeared one summer, and a low-growing purple dome aster spread like crazy. One plant I mistook for a wayward oak—and almost yanked out—turned out to be a celandine poppy. It gives us lovely yellow flowers every spring.

Birds must have dropped some hollyhock seeds, because we never planted any, but have a nice array of them against the fence.

We turned an empty corner of the enclosure into a seating area by laying a flagstone patio. We loved it so much that the next year we tripled its size, adding an area for a hammock where we can relax while watching the hummingbirds and bees enjoy what the deer would love to eat.

Deer did manage to come in a few times when I forgot to close the gate, however. They sure enjoyed the tulips!

I put in a few annuals each year, like cosmos, but most of the plants in the garden are perennials.

To keep digging to a minimum, I use containers for anything that needs to be stored inside for winter, such as dahlias, an-

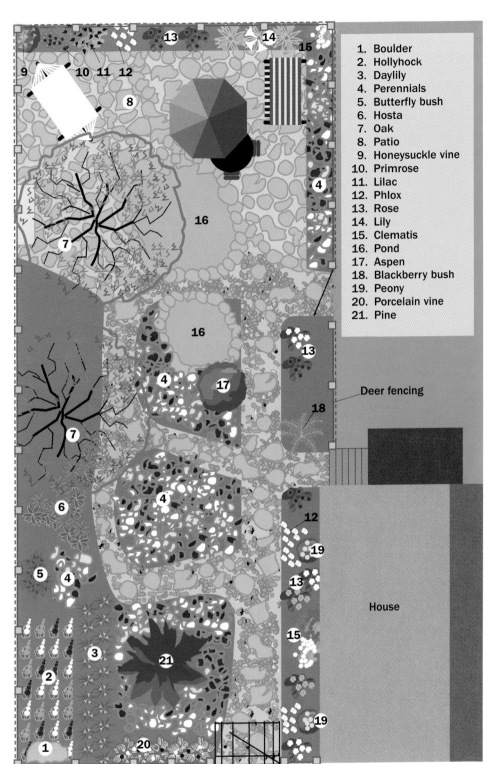

1. Boulder
2. Hollyhock
3. Daylily
4. Perennials
5. Butterfly bush
6. Hosta
7. Oak
8. Patio
9. Honeysuckle vine
10. Primrose
11. Lilac
12. Phlox
13. Rose
14. Lily
15. Clematis
16. Pond
17. Aspen
18. Blackberry bush
19. Peony
20. Porcelain vine
21. Pine

Deer fencing

House

FENCE THEM IN. Deer used to eat every single plant in sight. Then the Boones decided to transform an empty fenced-in spot into a sanctuary for their favorite flowers, including many *deer*-lectable varieties, such as (from top) lily, dahlia and rose.

gels' trumpets and gladiolas. That way, I just dump out the containers in fall, wrap up the tubers, and repot them the next year.

Lessons Learned

Now that I've figured out where everything should be, the perennials are doing well. The roses are thriving, thanks to the wood chips I place over them every fall for protection from the cold weather and the fish fertilizer I recycle from one of Steve's ponds.

To conserve moisture, we use lots of mulch, and we installed a drip irrigation system. This gives the roses a little extra moisture, and I water them by hand a couple times a month, too.

Now we have gravel paths dotted with flagstones that meander past two ponds. Our flower beds are bursting with scented charmers like phlox and sweet peas. And the entryway features a welcoming wrought-iron archway covered with Iceberg roses.

It's just like the garden in my dreams.

Large photo, R. Todd Davis; inset, Alan and Linda Detrick

GROWING A PATIO

Create a year-round retreat right outside your back door.

By Melinda Myers, Contributing Editor

When you look out your windows onto your patio, what do you see? Is it a beautiful, inviting space filled with vibrant blooms? Or is it a drab, cluttered area with withering plants that need your attention?

If you have been avoiding your patio, then it's time to do something about it. I'm going to show you some quick changes that will allow you to enjoy this space now and throughout the year.

A good time to give your patio a facelift is when summer is still lingering, so you can see what you'd like to keep and what you'd rather change for next season. And when fall arrives, that means bargain time for outdoor furniture, plants and gardening equipment. But before you go shopping, let's start with a few improvements you can make to your current space.

Devise a Plan

If your patio surface is a bit dull or out-of-date, you can liven it up without tearing it out. Concrete paints, modular decking, a layer of pea gravel and even a few ground covers squeezed into unsightly cracks can improve its appearance dramatically.

If you're looking to create a sense of privacy or screen bad views, then plants are a great way to do it. With just a little effort, you can train a few vines to grow up a trellis. It adds color and interest to the area.

You can also take things a step further by grouping ornamental grasses and tall shrubs nearby. Before you know it, the eyesore that was there before will be long gone, and you can relax in your own private space.

If the summer sun has been driving you off the patio, then create your own shade. Plant a tree or large shrubs nearby to help, but if you're looking for a faster fix, invest in an umbrella, arbor or awning.

Keep in mind that any shade you add will impact your plants below. This shouldn't deter you from adding shade or plants to your area. Just plan accordingly.

Plenty of Plants

Now it's time to put your green thumb to work. If it's not the traditional outdoor growing season, you can still plant in containers.

If you're trying to create year-round interest, there are plenty of perennials, dwarf trees and ornamental shrubs that will provide interest to your patio garden throughout the season. Select plants at least one zone hardier for better winter survival. Northern gardeners should also provide a bit more winter protection.

At the beginning of next growing season, start by adding some containers filled with annuals, perennials, bulbs and even edibles to your patio. Increase your planting space by changing annuals throughout the season.

Begin with frost-tolerant pansies in early spring. Then replace them with butterfly-attracting pentas when the weather warms, and finish with cold-tolerant ornamental kale. And don't forget a few evergreen boughs for a bit of winter color.

Never underestimate the power of color. Use a wide range of mixed plantings in the containers on and around your patio for added color and interest to the area.

Be sure to have variety, too. To do this, look beyond your traditional growing patterns. Try adding bulbs in your ground covers, a summer and a fall blooming vine together on one trellis, or herbs such as purple ruffle basil and tricolor sage with your flowers.

Get the greatest show from your patio garden by using plants with four-season interest. Look for those with flowers, fruits, colorful bark and other features that will allow you to enjoy them throughout the year. And don't forget to include a few to attract the birds and butterflies. You'll be glad you did when you spot these fliers enjoying your backyard.

So get started on creating your patio retreat. Whether you tackle the entire area or just add a few plants, you can make your patio a place you want to spend time. ◀

OUTDOOR ACCESSORIES. If you don't have the space for a large garden, or you already have your flower beds filled, then use your patio or deck space. Containers make great accessories outdoors, and there are lots of flowers to choose from.

Photos: above, R. Todd Davis; below, Darrell Gulin/Dembinsky Photo Assoc.

Plan a Great Garden

FROM WET TO WONDERFUL

Changing the drainage pattern brought out the best in their backyard.

By Bonnie Hare, Campbellsport, Wisconsin

The home I share with my husband, Pat, is my family's homestead. I grew up here and am familiar with every inch of the yard. Still, it has changed over the years. We lost a number of old, established trees to various natural causes, and eventually it became clear that we needed to do a little outdoor "remodeling."

In redesigning the yard, the mental picture we had of our dream gardens was breathtaking. A number of barriers stood in the way of making the vision a reality, however—including one really big, wet dilemma.

Starting from Scratch

We discovered we had a major drainage issue, one that become very obvious when we showed the property to a local landscaping professional and wound up standing in ankle-deep water in the backyard. Figuring out a way to get water away from our 1880s fieldstone house instead of toward it became a priority.

We also wanted to save an old smokehouse on the property, build a garage and, of course, shape our dream gardens. With our landscaper, we drew up plans and got to work.

The first chore involved clearing the yard, which quickly looked so barren that I took to calling our place "little house on the prairie." Soon, though, berms and swales, designed to disperse the water throughout the yard, began to pop up on the flat area. In turn, this created a "flower island" in the center of the yard.

Our efforts to save the smokehouse paid off. Today, it functions as my potting shed and is attached to our new garage. One side of the smokehouse shed's stone exterior also serves as the inside wall for the new three-season room we installed so we could further enjoy the gardens.

The only trouble we ran into with this phase of the proj-

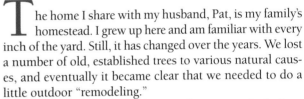

AWAY ON A ISLAND. Bonnie and Pat Hare (above left) use thousands of blooms to create a "flower island" (left) in their Wisconsin backyard. The lush area has red towering cannas, a small waterfall and plenty of blooms around a sitting area.

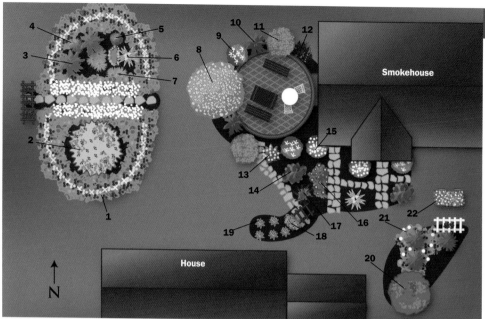

Planting List

1. Flower island
2. Mountain ash
3. Blue spruce
4. Arborvitae
5. Dwarf Austrian pine
6. Stella de Oro daylily
7. Canna
8. Honeylocust
9. Spirea
10. Juniper
11. Dogwood
12. Burning bush
13. Potentilla
14. Miss Kim lilac
15. Dwarf tree hydrangea
16. Purple coneflower
17. Lavender
18. Climbing rose
19. Hosta
20. Red maple
21. Shade garden
22. Flower cart

FLOWERING WALKWAY. The path leading to the arbor and seating area on the flower island (left) is filled with colorful blooms.

ect was that we were forced to take down a beautiful honeylocust tree to construct the garage.

My father and I had planted the tree when I was young, and I was heartbroken to lose it. At that point, I knew that the flower island would also hold a new honeylocust tree, one that we'd never have to cut down.

Once the honeylocust was in place near the island, we added old stone steps that invite visitors to walk into our new backyard focal point. We also installed a granite waterfall, then filled in around the tree and hardscaping with an abundance of blooms.

Flowers Galore

Perennials and more than 1,000 annuals call the island home each year. Wander along the stone path and you'll see Stella de Oro daylilies, foxgloves, cannas, impatiens, Wave petunias, marigolds and more.

I also added quaint stone paths near the smokehouse shed, three-season room and adjacent brick patio, then surrounded these structures with plantings that create a casual "cottage" look. Kaiser lilies, hollyhocks, mint, lavender, lilacs, spirea, dwarf tree hydrangea, dogwood, Miss Kim lilac, boxwood, burning bushes and irises all provide a warm welcome and a cozy feel.

We planted a large perennial bed at the back of the property, then turned our attention to the front yard, where we added a triangular white shade garden.

A red maple, Norway maple and China rose tree anchor the three corners of this garden. It also features a simple white arbor bearing a hanging basket of mixed pink impatiens. Boxwood, Shasta daisies and white impatiens fill in the ground below.

Pink Carefree Wonder roses grace the front of the house, and a beautiful handcrafted cart resembling an old-time English flower wagon stands near the driveway. I've loaded the cart with containers of flowers, including roses and lavender.

One thing I discovered while selecting and installing plants around our yard was to "go with the flow." I'm not referring to water, but the importance of choosing flowers that complement our old farmhouse.

I tend to stick with "old-fashioned" blooms like lilacs, pussy willows, roses, daisies and lilies. Sure, I'm tempted when I walk through the garden center and spot something really new or unusual, but if it won't enhance the historic nature of our home, I don't buy it. Bringing out the best in our property is my top priority.

Pat and I have found great satisfaction as we work in our gardens or enjoy the flowering vista from our patio. We consider it part of our contribution to nature—and we're always delighted to share it with others!

GREEN THUMB TIP

Plant blooms that complement your home. If you have an old house like me, then try using "old-fashioned" flowers like lilacs, pussy willows and roses.

—*Bonnie Hare, Campbellsport, Wisconsin*

SOMETHING FROM NOTHING

Starting from scratch, this gardener built a blooming paradise.

By Lena Jascur
Flora, Indiana

When we moved into our home 9 years ago, the yard was pretty much flower free, with the exception of a lone peony. But that plant didn't stay around for long—the former owner had a sentimental attachment to it and asked if she could take it with her!

After I dug up the plant, I surveyed the landscape, which consisted mostly of grass and weeds. Still, I could see plenty of potential.

What encouraged me most was a beau-

BIRDS &BLOONS

WELCOME

BATHS

341

IT'S HARD TO BELIEVE weeds once dominated the yard of Lena and Mike Jascur. Now, plants and decorative objects reign. Items like birdhouses, arbors, feeders, benches and birdbaths dot their yard, making it a cozy retreat for both people and birds. Above, son Cody stands with an arbor made from an old ladder (left), while daughter Hannah hangs wind chimes (right).

tiful willow shading the front of the house, and the stately pines that outlined the lot. I knew that hard work and perseverance would pay off in the end.

One Garden That Grew

I started with a simple bed of irises, positioned so I could see the blossoms from the kitchen window. That garden turned out so nice, I decided to make it bigger by adding more flowers—and I have yet to stop!

Putting in a new patch or two of flowers or enlarging an existing bed is my springtime ritual. I've also gotten into the habit of choosing plants for each new flower bed that will bloom at the same time. This way, different spots in our yard burst into color well into fall.

I've also developed a routine of planting bulbs each autumn after the current year's flowers have faded. Over the years, I figure I've planted more than 1,000 tulips, hyacinths and daffodils, and seeing them come up each spring is a real treat.

I haven't focused solely on flowers to brighten our yard, however. I've also included pear and crabapple trees, lilacs and a number of eye-catching shrubs, including barberry, weigela, viburnum and rhododendron.

Share and Share Alike

In the beginning, I used cuttings of various perennials to fill new flower beds. Annuals came in handy when I needed to cover up empty spots, and I quickly learned how to save the seeds to use the following year.

Now my gardens burst forth with everything from azaleas to hydrangeas, purple coneflowers, assorted lilies, zinnias and more. I always make sure to share the bounty by giving cuttings of my plants to family and friends, as well as seeds gathered from the annuals.

I have encountered challenges as I've expanded my gardening efforts. The biggest test has been finding out how to get around the many shady areas on our property. Packing the spots that receive the least amount of sun with different kinds of hostas and

ivy has proven to be the perfect solution.

Getting my husband, Mike, and our two children involved hasn't been any trouble, however. They're eager to dig in beside me.

In fact, I think I have two budding green thumbs in daughter Hannah and son Cody (photos above). They like to help me put in annuals, including marigolds and morning glories, and we all enjoy watching them bloom.

Mike likes to tackle heftier jobs, whether it involves hauling tons of fieldstones to the beds or building garden structures.

Accent on Handmade

We have a number of beautiful arbors and a stately pergola gracing our gardens, all built by Mike. He also put together one item I can't do without—my potting bench. That bench sees plenty of activity as soon as spring arrives!

His can-do attitude has rubbed off on me, and I'm happy to say I've constructed the many birdhouses, bird feeders and benches that garnish these gardens. The two outhouses are projects of mine, too. One is purely decorative, the other holds my shovels.

Everything we have made has cost us nothing but time. Rather than invest in building supplies, we're constantly on the lookout for old barns and sheds that are being torn down, in the hopes we can salvage some wood to create more clever fixtures to use in our yard.

Old items like balusters, sections of fence, chairs and railings that other folks toss out find new life at our place. We even found a novel way to use a wooden ladder from an old outdoor play set. It now tops one of the arbors and provides a solid climbing surface for the vines planted at the arbor's base like morning glo-

PERSONALITY APLENTY. A double-decker birdhouse became a mailbox (above), and a homemade potting bench is a useful accent in a shady nook (above).

ry and wisteria.

I've also planted rustic signs around our property and trimmed empty walls with simple grapevine wreaths. A wheelbarrow full of blossoms greets visitors near the path to the front door. Even our mailbox (above) is crafty—it was made from a two-story birdhouse.

Room for More

Gardening is definitely a passion of mine, and I'm constantly coming up with new ideas. That's a good thing, because I still have a lot of space to fill.

My goal is to eventually eliminate the grass (and the need to mow) and have a series of pretty pathways meandering among the many flower beds. Maybe someday I'll be done. But in the meantime, I'm happy to keep my garden growing.

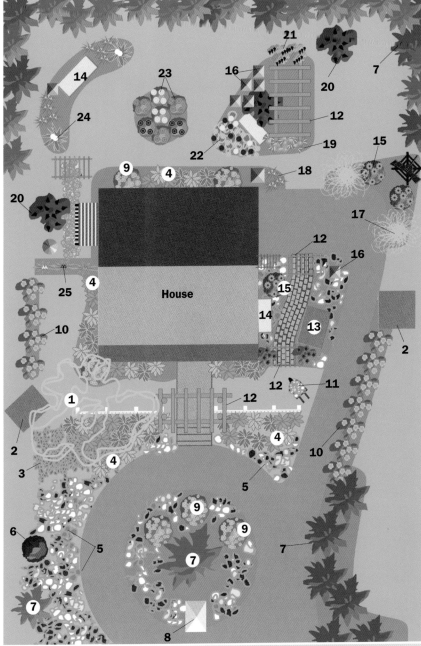

1. Willow
2. Outhouse
3. Ivy
4. Hosta
5. Annuals/perennials
6. Barberry
7. Pine
8. Birdhouse mailbox
9. Azalea
10. Rose of Sharon
11. Wheelbarrow
12. Arbor
13. Potting bench
14. Bench
15. Purple coneflower
16. Birdhouse
17. Zebra grass
18. Daylily
19. Morning glory
20. Lilac
21. Wisteria
22. Moss rose
23. Zinnia
24. Yucca
25. Iris

3 STEPS TO A BEAUTIFUL BACKYARD

FINISHING TOUCH. After planting, add a layer of mulch (like the gardeners at left and below) to keep weeds down and conserve moisture. Pull weeds (above) when they appear.

A former nursery owner shares her simple system for a thriving and healthy garden.

By Nancy Herman, Montague, New Jersey

W hen I owned a nursery and garden center, I heard a lot of questions from novice gardeners, but they all seemed to boil down to one thing: "Why did my plants die?"

I understood their frustration. It's discouraging to spend time and money on new plants, only to have them die over the winter—or survive, but fail to flower.

No wonder these gardeners thought they had "brown thumbs."

I knew from experience that skipping the basics could be a recipe for disaster, and I wanted to do whatever I could to help

Plan a Great Garden

345

ALL BUNDLED UP. Some shrubs benefit from the winter protection of burlap (above). Another important garden duty is regular watering at the plant's base (left) to avoid evaporation.

these newcomers flourish. So I developed this easy-to-understand three-step system for gardening success.

1. Prepare the Soil

This is the most important step. Skip this one, and I can almost guarantee that your garden won't live up to its full potential.

First, you need to determine what kind of soil you have. One test is to squeeze a handful of your garden soil and then rub it between your fingers.

If the soil feels gritty, you have sandy soil. If it sticks together or feels slippery, it's clay.

This will tell you something about how your garden uses water and nutrients. Sandy soil dries out quickly, so your plants' roots dry out faster, too. In hard clay, the soil stays wet, but it's difficult for the roots to absorb the water, as well as nutrients and oxygen.

For most plants, loam is ideal. It contains clay, sand and silt, plus organic material—decaying plant matter—which encourages the growth of microorganisms and bacteria, providing food for plants.

Adding compost is the single best thing you can do for your soil. It adds heft to sandy soil and helps it hold moisture, while making dense clay soil lighter and fluffier. And it provides nutrients in any type of soil.

You can buy a bag at the local garden center if you don't have your own compost pile.

To apply compost to an entire garden, spread about 2 inches over the soil, then till or turn it under to a depth of 6 inches or more, and plant as usual. Top-dress the garden every year with 1 inch of compost.

2. Proper Upkeep

Once your plants are in the ground, you need to pay attention to three duties during the growing season: watering, fertilizing and keeping your garden tidy.

I prefer to water my garden by hand—I think it's the only way to ensure all plants get the moisture they need. Lawn sprinklers

> **READER TIP**
>
> Adding compost is the single best thing you can do for your soil. It adds heft to sandy soil and makes dense clay soil lighter and fluffier.
>
> —**Nancy Herman**
> **Montague, New Jersey**

lose water through evaporation, and can overwater some plants while missing others.

Water only in the morning, and when the soil is dry down to a depth of 2 inches. Use a nozzle that produces a gentle flow, watering each plant at its base for about 30 seconds before moving to the next one. When you've watered all the plants, return to the first plant and water everything again.

Check the top 6 inches of soil. When that's moist, you've watered enough.

Fertilizer can be another necessary component—but don't overdo it. Nature has its own feeding process, and if you planted with good compost, you probably do not need extra fertilizer.

When in doubt, take a soil sample to your county Extension office. For a small fee, the soil lab will test it and tell you what type of nutrients your soil might need.

Keeping a clean garden also is important. Pull out weeds, prune dead and unwanted branches and remove spent flowers. One thing that helps reduce weeds is a 2-inch layer of bark mulch. This keeps the soil cool and retains moisture, which means less watering, too.

3. Get Ready for Winter

Your work doesn't end because it gets cold outside. Rake leaves and put them in your compost pile, and protect tender shrubs by surrounding them with burlap.

After the ground freezes, put mulch around your dormant plants. This keeps soil temperatures even, protecting roots from frequent freezing and thawing in colder climates. Later, as the mulch breaks down, it will add beneficial organic material to your soil.

And before you settle in for the winter, clean and oil your garden tools (WD-40 works well), and store them so they'll be ready to use in spring.

That's all there is to it. I have recommended this three-step method hundreds of times over the years…and it's a delight to see beginners turn into budding gardeners.

If you're new to gardening, try them yourself. Start enjoying your own beautiful, healthy garden—and stop wondering if you have a brown thumb!

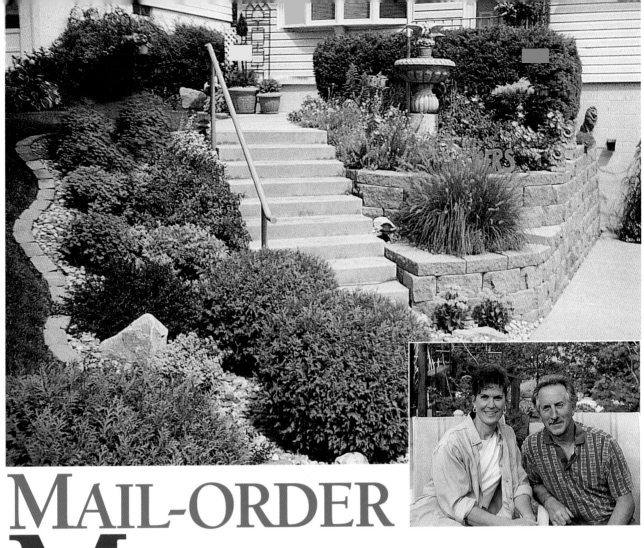

MAIL-ORDER MAKEOVER

This reader found an easy way to give her backyard a fresh look.

By Kathy Orean, Omaha, Nebraska

In the beginning, my plan was simple. We had just moved into our new home, and the landscape was fairly plain with just a few hedges, some hostas and an old apple tree.

My main goal was to gain a little privacy for the patio and some shade in the backyard. But it didn't stop there. Before I knew it, I was reading gardening books, and my mind was racing as I pictured all the things that could be done with my blank slate. I wanted the kind of yard that begged you to take a stroll.

Soon, I began looking through plant catalogs, eager to find the perfect shrubs and flowers for my area. It was wonderful. I loved the convenience, variety and price of ordering plants by mail.

Then one day, I realized it had happened. There was no denying it and no turning back—gardening had drawn me in for good. And my mail-ordering days had just begun.

That was 10 years ago. Since then, my husband, Ted, and I have come a long way.

In those first few months, we were mostly concerned with improving the front yard.

Ted does concrete work, and he got busy right away laying a new driveway, front sidewalk and steps (top photo). While he was doing that, I was relocating numerous hostas and yews from the front yard to other areas. It was then that I noticed my passion for "digging in" and giving plants new homes.

Front to Back

As we shifted our efforts to the backyard, Ted continued working on construction projects, and I kept on planting. Using concrete, he designed walkways and an octagon-

Plan a Great Garden

347

HAND-IN-HAND. Kathy and Ted Orean created a relaxing garden getaway in their backyard. Ted did most of the initial construction work while Kathy followed behind with planting. She made sure to use plenty of shrubs throughout the area so her feathered friends would have plenty of good shelter.

shaped pad for the gazebo he built from a kit.

The results were amazing. Ted had turned our ordinary space into a parklike setting, and it was up to me to add the finishing touches. He could barely get his projects complete before I was rushing in to soften the landscape with colorful plants like chrysanthemums, goatsbeard and burning bush.

I take pride in the fact that Ted and I have done all of the work on our own. He always seems to be crafting something impressive, and I have also taken on projects beyond planting. I installed all of the pavers in our yard myself, and I've created several garden structures—from a mosaic birdbath to several copper trellises and an arbor designed from PVC pipe (above left).

It's in the Mail

If you look around my yard, you'll quickly notice my love for shrubs and ornamental grasses. They hold up year-round, and more importantly, provide protection for wildlife.

I can't imagine an area without my backyard friends. It's such a treat to listen to all the different birdsongs while the squirrels are chattering away.

My love for these creatures started with a single birdbath and quickly expanded from there. I couldn't keep the one I had filled, so I added more. Now I have seven baths as well as four bird feeders, two squirrel feeders and several birdhouses, which are always filled with nestlings in spring.

Nearly all of the plants and shrubs for my feathered friends have come from mail-order catalogs. I was skeptical of this method at first. But I decided to give it a try after I couldn't find a specific variety of privet hedge at my local greenhouse. I ordered the shrubs, and they came right to my door, healthy and strong.

I've been using mail order ever since. It saves me in cost, especially with those end-of-season specials, and everything I've ever received has thrived in my garden. Plus, it gives me something to do in the winter.

I love poring through the catalogs, searching for more

Planting List

1. Arborvitae
2. Yew
3. Coreopsis
4. Ornamental grass
5. Coral bells
6. Blue Muffin viburnum
7. Buckthorn
8. Dwarf burning bush
9. Forsythia
10. Juniper
11. Green velvet boxwood
12. Spirea
13. Little Henry sweetspire
14. Minuet weigela
15. Butterfly bush
16. Chrysanthemum
17. Crabapple
18. Topiary spruce
19. Caryopteris Blue Mist
20. Hydrangea
21. Variegated dogwood
22. Goatsbeard
23. Privet hedge

plants and ideas. It's about this time—when I get a faraway look in my eyes—that Ted breaks into my daydream.

"You know, I'm not sure how much more we can add to the yard," he'll say with a knowing smile.

"There's always more room," I assure him.

Digging Up a Hobby

It's funny how you discover new hobbies and interests. I never would have imagined that gardening would be such a big part of my life, but I wouldn't have it any other way.

I love spending my free time outdoors. When anyone who knows me comes to visit, they always stop by my backyard first. In fact, the sign of my front porch reads, "If no answer, come to the garden."

I never get tired of the work involved. Anytime I try to sit down for a moment, the sights and sounds beckon me to become a part of them. I can't wait to indulge myself in the world of nature, from the birds and squirrels to the bees and plants.

Maybe someday I will actually kick back and relax, but for now, I'm enjoying myself too much.

GREEN THUMB TIP

If you want to find great deals on plants, try ordering through the mail at the end of each growing season. You can get beautiful flowers and shrubs for amazing prices.

—*Kathy Orean, Omaha, Nebraska*

Plan a Great Garden

A WOODLAND WONDER

This adventurous gardener turned mistakes into marvelous results.

By Sylvia Hoehns Wright
Glen Allen, Virginia

SHADY SANCTUARY. Colorful tulips and eye-popping azaleas light up Sylvia's lush wooded landscape with beautiful bursts of color (above). A pretty garden bench and path beckon visitors to pause and enjoy the natural scenery around them (near left).

Sometimes, a garden emerges through experimentation. The only drawback is that you never know what you'll get with trial and error as your guide. I learned that firsthand when I started landscaping the heavily wooded yard around my new home.

Somewhat overwhelmed by the space, I decided to begin my landscape overhaul by constructing a simple rectangular patio. Patio blocks, sand, a wheelbarrow and a carpenter's level provided me with the structure, while surplus azaleas from a nearby nursery offered instant hedging and privacy. A large shade arbor added later was the perfect finishing touch.

Right Plant, Right Place

With the patio complete, I moved on to developing the rest of the yard. It didn't take me long to realize, however, that the 100-year-old oak trees scattered throughout the property were going to be a formidable challenge.

Although the stately trees provided shelter from the glaring sun and occasional windstorm, the trees' dense canopies made it difficult for much of anything to grow beneath them.

In the beginning, I made the typical mistakes. I often considered my preference for showy flowers rather than soil requirements, plant endurance and prac-

> *I learned the hard way what would, and would not, thrive in my shady yard.*

ticality. I learned the hard way what would—and would not—thrive in my shady yard.

Eventually, I discovered it's as easy as choosing the right plant for the right place. That meant selecting shade-tolerant plants, like vinca, ivy and some evergreen shrubs.

Flowering bulbs, such as tulips and daffodils, provided a welcome punch of color in the wooded landscape. And in areas that couldn't support plants, I spread wood mulch to help

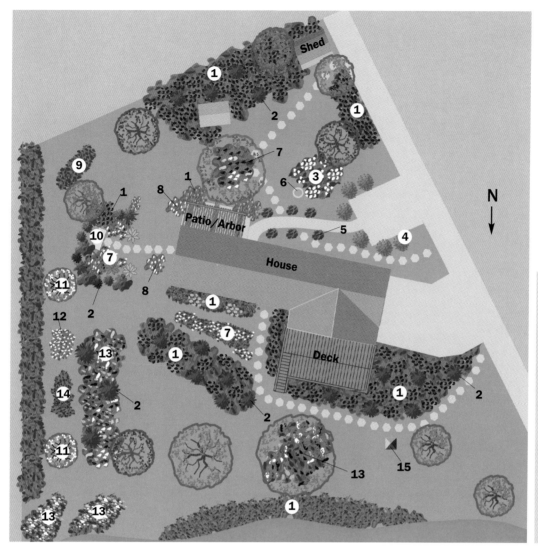

1. Azalea
2. Evergreen
3. Hydrangea
4. Boxwood
5. Holly
6. Birdbath
7. Bulbs
8. Flowering dogwood
9. Ivy
10. Bench
11. Weeping cherry
12. Mock orange
13. Perennial bed
14. Lilac
15. Bird feeder

N

naturalize the garden and protect the trees' vulnerable roots.

Clusters of trees provided the best planting sites. Tree drip lines became natural flower bed borders, and the sparse area beneath the trees' leaf canopies provided an empty palette on which to paint my woodland garden.

And because I began to work with the natural environment, something unexpected occurred. Volunteer seedlings of native plants, such as flowering dogwood, mountain laurel, lady's slipper and cardinal flower, began springing up.

After establishing the basic framework, I moved on to different challenges. The first was a relatively basic perennial and annual bed. Framing the area with colorful azaleas first, I planted the flower bed with a variety of hostas, ferns, lilies and iris. The addition of seasonal annuals kept the bed buzzing with continuous color all year.

READER TIP

In areas that won't support plants, spread wood mulch to help naturalize the garden and protect the trees' vulnerable roots.   **—Sylvia Hoehns Wright**
Glen Allen, Virginia

A Change of Plan

My next project, an herb garden, didn't quite turn out as I envisioned. The design included a bed of herbs around two large oak trees.

Yet, regardless of my dedication, the project remained plagued by problems as the fragile herbs competed for vital sunlight. I finally transferred the less shade-tolerant plants into some sunlit containers, where they thrived.

My birdhouse garden encountered a similar result. I designed the garden specifically for birds, including nest boxes and berry-producing shrubs, but it wooed no winged activity. Maybe the birds preferred the vast woodland sanctuary instead.

The project wasn't a total loss, however, as a flying squirrel finally moved into one of the birdhouses.

It was then that I made the choice to join the Virginia Master Gardener Program. After completing the course, my mistakes became less, and my successes grew.

Although it would be easy for me to second-guess my early gardening endeavors, I try not to be too hard on myself. After all, it was through those first efforts that I developed an awareness of nature's "big secret."

I learned I'm only a caretaker of the surrounding woodland environment—and working with it produces the best results.

THINK SPRING

With leaves to rake and mums to transplant in fall, spring flowers are probably the farthest thing from your mind. But by planting bulbs in autumn, you can set the stage for a showstopping, make-the-neighbors-green-with-envy color explosion next year.

Before you dig in, check out these common questions and answers to planting spring bulbs. If you're looking for more, simply log on to the Netherlands Flower Bulb Information Center's Web site at *www.bulb.com.*

Q: How soon after buying bulbs should I plant them?

A: Plant bulbs when you get them, but not before cooler fall temperatures arrive. Six weeks before the ground freezes is ideal.

If summer lingers, store your bulbs in the crisper of your refrigerator until cooler temperatures return. Just be sure to keep the bulbs away from fruits, which emit a gas as they ripen that's harmful to bulbs.

Q: How do I plant spring bulbs?

A: The easiest way is to dig a flat-bottomed hole about 12 to 18 inches wide and drop several bulbs into it. Plant large bulbs, such as tulips and daffodils, about 8 inches deep in well-draining soil, 6 inches in heavy. Smaller bulbs, like snowdrops, crocus and scilla, should sit about 5 inches deep.

Plant the bulb's pointy end up, and don't worry about fertilizing. Just give them a good soaking after planting. Mulching can be beneficial, but wait until the ground freezes lightly.

Q: How can I create the most impact with my bulbs?

A: Here are three simple planting rules you can use to get the most from your bulbs.

Plant in clusters. This concentrates the colors, making them look like bouquets.

Plant shorter bulbs in front. This is a good rule for bulbs that bloom at the same time, such as grape hyacinths and tulips. However, if the low-growing bulbs bloom early and the tall late, plant the taller-growing flowers in front. Their display will camouflage the dying foliage of the smaller bulbs.

Plant a double-decker. Plant small bulbs right on top of large bulbs. If they flower at the same time, it creates a colorful two-tone effect.

Q: What should I do after the flowers fade?

A: It's important to keep the leaves on the plants until they brown, or 6 weeks have passed since blooming. The leaves feed the bulb so it can flower next spring.

Clip tulip blooms after they fade so they don't go to seed, but leave daffodils alone.

READER TIP

Want to keep squirrels and other critters from digging up and raiding your newly planted bulbs?

■ Try planting daffodils and other Narcissi bulbs, because most animals don't like the way they taste.

■ Lay wire mesh, such as chicken wire, on top of bulb plantings. Squirrels can't dig through it, but flowers grow through the holes.

■ Use repellents or a variety of scare tactics—dog or cat hair spread around the flower bed, aluminum pie tins on twine or plastic scare owls and hawks—to fend off hungry critters. Be sure to vary your tactics, or the critters will catch on.

ABUNDANT BEAUTY. Well-manicured plants line the curving pathways (right) that Sumiko and Doyal Holmon (above) created in their yard.

This couple transformed an overgrown yard into a green-thumb showcase.

By Sumiko Holmon
Escondido, California

PARADISE FOUND

When I look at our yard today, with its lovely islands of flowers and trees amid winding stone paths, it's hard to believe it wasn't always this way. A mere 6 years ago, the property wasn't so picturesque.

We bought this 1/2-acre property because the spacious lot seemed perfect for gardening and provided room for a workshop for my handy husband, Doyal. We knew the lawn—consisting of scraggly patches of Bermuda grass interspersed with weeds—needed work, but we were unprepared for the huge number of gopher holes we discovered after moving in that summer. The size of the project mushroomed.

It wouldn't do any good to complain, however, so we both dug in and started cleaning things up. First, we had to cut down several overgrown berry and eu-

READY FOR A WALK? The Holmons' yard is a lush retreat packed with plants that thrive in southern California's heat. They edged pathways (above and below left) with trees, shrubs and flowers, and fashioned small sanctuaries (like the one far lower left) with evergreens, a homemade lantern and river rocks. At left, dusty miller and rosemary surround a lemon tree.

calyptus trees along the side of the house. Then we addressed the gopher problem by hiring a professional pest remover. It took the better part of a year, but it was worth it!

Digging up the front yard was next on our list. We eliminated the grass and weeds and decided to install rock gardens and plant trees to add shade. This plan seemed so perfect, we adapted it for rest of the property.

On the Rocks

Finding interesting shade trees became a regular activity on the weekends. We first chose peppermint willows (*Agonis flexuosa*) and carrot woods (*Cupaniopsis*)—and that's when we hit another snag.

Planting those pretty specimens turned out to be a much bigger task than either of us thought, thanks to bone-dry soil that was hard as a rock. We had to water the dirt just to soften it, then dig it up a bit and water some more. It was quite a process!

Finally, we were able to dig big enough holes and finish planting the trees. As a precaution, Doyal covered the softened soil with chicken wire to keep any nosy gophers from returning.

In addition to the willows and carrot woods in front, we added a variety of other trees along one side and in the back, including a Japanese black pine and juniper that we sur-

rounded with river rocks. A Japanese lantern Doyal crafted from concrete was the perfect Zen touch for that peaceful nook (see photo bottom far left).

The next challenge we faced was choosing flowers to plant around the trees. I wondered what varieties would thrive in the poor soil. Finally, I decided to try whatever caught my eye and settled on begonias, asters, salvia, vinca, anemones and dianthus, which all thrived.

Since we have no grass, our last task was to cover the bare areas of dirt by placing permeable weed barrier on the ground and covering it with granite chips. I could hardly believe we were finished! The 6 months of hard work truly paid off, though, when a neighbor stopped by and asked, "Do you do this for a living?" I couldn't stop smiling.

Separate Paths

Up until that point, Doyal and I had been working side by side, but we headed in different directions once the front was finished.

I tackled the side yard. Day after day, I hacked away thick, tough weeds and dried-up old bushes. After everything was cleared, I filled in the sloping area with durable geraniums, ornamental grasses, daisies and ice plants.

In the meantime, Doyal busied himself out back, building a shed, an arbor, a wooden arch, a covered bench, a gazebo and a deck, and putting in a vegetable patch and a koi pond.

READER TIP

To keep gophers from returning to our yard, we covered the soft soil around our newly planted trees with chicken wire.

—**Sumiko Holmon, Escondido, California**

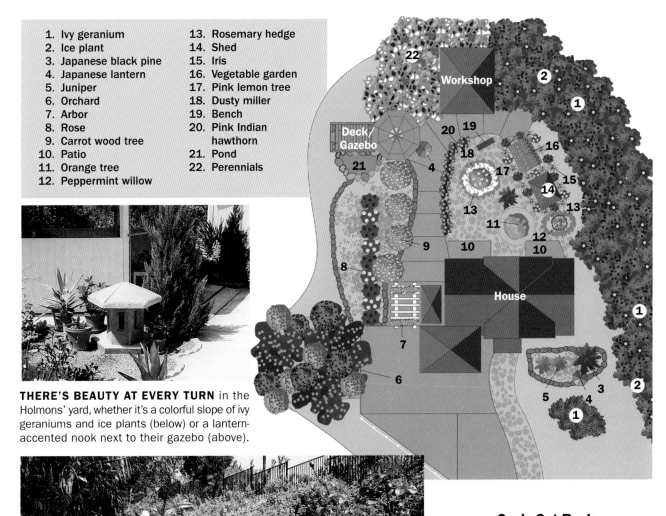

1. Ivy geranium
2. Ice plant
3. Japanese black pine
4. Japanese lantern
5. Juniper
6. Orchard
7. Arbor
8. Rose
9. Carrot wood tree
10. Patio
11. Orange tree
12. Peppermint willow
13. Rosemary hedge
14. Shed
15. Iris
16. Vegetable garden
17. Pink lemon tree
18. Dusty miller
19. Bench
20. Pink Indian hawthorn
21. Pond
22. Perennials

THERE'S BEAUTY AT EVERY TURN in the Holmons' yard, whether it's a colorful slope of ivy geraniums and ice plants (below) or a lantern-accented nook next to their gazebo (above).

His next job involved fashioning concrete rocks and using them to form meandering paths around the trees and rock gardens in the backyard, turning them into instant islands.

Just as we'd done in the front, we filled in any remaining bare areas with granite chips.

The whole process of shaping the yards took about 2 years. But that doesn't mean we've stopped working in the yard. We regularly try new shrubs, fruit trees and flowers, replacing varieties that haven't worked out, or planting new ones that appeal to us.

Oasis Out Back

While the front yard is lovely, everyone agrees that the backyard is the showstopper. As soon as visitors pass through the side gate and walk under the arbor, they're greeted by fragrant roses and a view of our small fruit orchard, filled with tangerine, kumquat, plum, nectarine, apple and avocado trees.

The path runs past the patio and a cluster of rock gardens that feature junipers, yuccas, a tangerine tree, a pink lemon tree and flowers galore. We've also tucked in silver garlic grass, rosemary and various ornamental specimens among the trees and blooms, along with several graceful pieces of driftwood.

Farther down the path sits the bench Doyal made, nestled among pink Indian hawthorns, roses and irises. The gazebo is stationed nearby, connected to the deck by a small Japanese bridge called a *taikobushi*. This is the best spot to enjoy the water garden with its colorful koi, cattails, waterfall and water lilies.

Whether we choose to walk along the path, rest in the gazebo or entertain on the patio, this plant-filled space offers so much. I love to relax and enjoy the flowers and the sight of butterflies and birds among the blooms, and appreciate all the wonderful things my husband and I created.

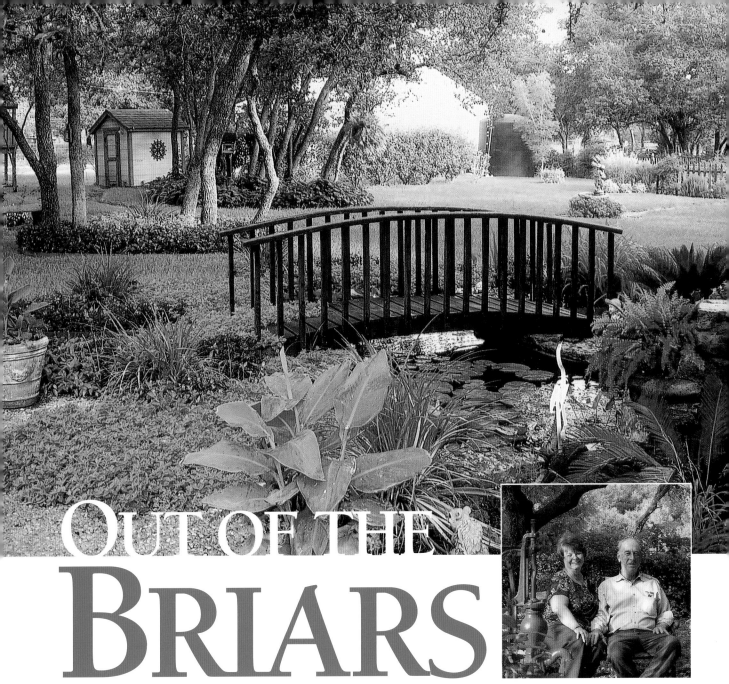

OUT OF THE
BRIARS

Over a decade, this couple transformed brambles into beauty.

By Connie Brewster, Bulverde, Texas

When we purchased our property back in 1993, I knew it had potential. After all, it consisted of 6-1/4 acres of prime farmland, giving us room to build our dream home and oceans of space for as many gardens as I could imagine.

The fact that unruly blackberry briars and thorn-covered bushes dominated the landscape didn't stop my dreaming, although it was hard to know exactly what we had because the pesky bushes had even outgrown the trees.

Clearing the land for the house was our first priority, and it took my husband, Wilson, and me the summer to finish.

The next problem we had to tackle was the herd of deer that called our place home. I knew I would never get my gardens going if I didn't figure out a way to handle them.

I considered fencing, but that wasn't practical. Then I hit on the idea of getting a dog to serve as a garden protector.

I had a feeling that a spirited pup—one spunky enough to chase anything that came into the yard—would solve the problem. Boy, did my hunch pay off!

We adopted "Yukon" from the animal shelter, and he's worked tirelessly ever since to keep our gardens clear of critters. Not even squirrels are safe. What's more, Yukon rarely digs or destroys my plants. He's worked out so well, I brought home another young dog, "Misty."

Once the pest problem was under control, I turned my

thoughts to gardening and let my imagination run wild. I was brimming with ideas to create a lush backyard filled with greenery and blooms.

One Step at a Time

After devising a master plan and sharing it with Wilson, we were ready to go. We agreed, however, that we couldn't accomplish everything overnight and decided to tackle one project per year. With Wilson's background in construction, I knew we would be able to handle much of the work ourselves.

We did get some help building the big features from time to time. For instance, a contractor poured our large cement pond, then Wilson and son Kevin built a rock waterfall to flow into it. I contributed by planting daylilies, begonias and Red Apple ice plants around the edges of the pond.

We also called in extra hands to help create our "park," a corner of the yard filled with oak trees. Wilson and I had already put in winding paths and were ready to develop the area further, when Wilson had a heart attack. While he recuperated, a landscaper placed shrubs among the oaks, in-

PULL UP A CHAIR. Connie Brewster invites visitors into her garden with plenty of colorful flowers and a calming water feature. Above, a waterfall pours out into a pond from a mound of rocks. At right, red begonias encircle a group of oak trees near the house.

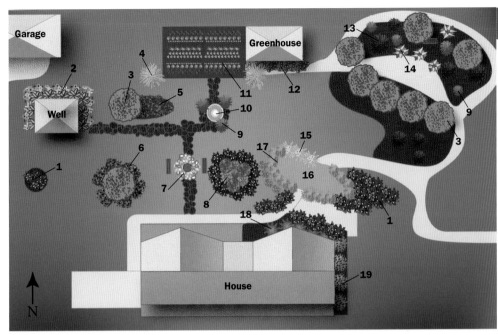

Planting List

1. Begonia
2. Hosta
3. Live oak
4. Ornamental grass
5. Ivy
6. Purple heart
7. Impatiens
8. Liriope
9. Dwarf nandina
10. Fountain
11. Vegetable garden
12. Lantana
13. Barberry
14. Esperanza
15. Daylily
16. Pond
17. Red Apple ice plant
18. River fern
19. Crape myrtle

MADE FOR THE SHADE. There are plenty of vibrant shade plants in this garden, since trees completely fill the backyard. Above, hostas and pink and white impatiens surround the shed.

cluding barberries, esperanza and dwarf nandina.

As soon as he regained his health, Wilson jumped back into gardening, tackling projects with me, and our sons Kevin and Wayne.

The process was slow, but over the course of 10 years, we transformed the yard from a dry and barren expanse to the flower-filled place that it is today.

Along the way, Wilson supported every one of my ideas and proved to be the real backbone of our operation. He built our garden fence, a greenhouse and a swing set for the grandchildren. I simply couldn't have done any of this without him.

It was and still is my job to fill and tend the flower beds—and I'm so pleased with the results. The gardens now overflow with color and consist mostly of perennials, although annuals are part of the mix, too.

I've discovered that choosing bright blossoms and planting a lot of them makes a greater impact on the landscape. That's why you'll find an abundance of my two favorite annuals, red begonias and red impatiens, near the patio and pond and around the well. They also pop up in various planters I've positioned in different spots.

Other flowers in my yard include mums, bougainvilleas, roses and crape myrtles. The lantanas that line the greenhouse thrive in our hot Texas weather and put forth colorful flowers that attract butterflies.

Simple Upkeep

Wilson and I mulch the gardens each year, which helps conserve moisture and results in rich, loose soil. I also add a slow-release fertilizer any time I put in a new plant to help it thrive. Water is key in our dry area, so we've installed a sprinkler system. Personally, though, I love to take the hose out and give the plants a drink myself, checking on each one as I douse its roots.

I recently told Wilson that I didn't think there were any more garden projects left to do. He laughed and said, "Yeah, right!" He knows me too well to think our yard will ever be "finished."

Honestly, I guess I have to agree with him. I feel best when I'm elbow deep in plants. Gardening is pure daily therapy for me.

GREEN THUMB TIP

Red is a great color in the garden. Try planning red begonias or impatiens for a powerful impact in your yard.

—*Connie Brewster, Bulverde, Texas*

SHADY CHARACTERS

Low-light ground covers add beauty anywhere the sun doesn't shine.

Shade—you either love it or hate it.

Gardeners often fall into the latter category because low-light conditions prevent the development of lush lawns, leaving shady areas looking bare, or worse yet, weedy.

That doesn't mean you should write off shady sections of your yard as no-grow zones, however. There are plenty of perennial ground covers that can be used in place of standard grass. These ground covers will naturally spread over time to create a lush carpet under trees, between buildings or in other places that don't see much sunlight.

Before you grab any garden tools, it's important to consider exactly what kind of shade you have.

Study the Shadows

Survey the area at various times of day to gauge how much light it receives…and keep in mind that the amount of shade can vary from one season to the next due to the changing position of the sun and the density of the tree canopy.

So, what did you see? If sunlight is only partially blocked

by open structures or trees with small leaves, like birch or honeylocust, chances are good the shade is dappled or filtered. This means that plants will receive a mixture of bright light and shade throughout the day, a situation that is suitable for many flowers and ground covers.

Or perhaps the area gets 4 to 6 hours of light per day, and the rest of the time it's in shade. This is considered partial shade and often occurs on the east or west sides of a house, or on the edge of a stand of trees. A wide variety of plants will grow in these conditions.

Spots that receive no direct sunlight, such as ground directly underneath Norway maples, oaks, spruces, pines and other trees with dense canopies, are in full shade, and only plants that tolerate low-light conditions will thrive there.

Once you've determined what kind of light conditions you have, you're ready for the next step—preparing the site prior to planting.

"Even at this point, I caution gardeners to go slow, especially if they're trying to fill in bare spots under trees where grass won't thrive," says *Birds & Blooms* garden expert and contributing editor Melinda Myers.

"The feeder roots for most trees are in the top 12 inches of soil directly under the tree, and if you dig too deeply when removing grass or installing ground covers, you can damage these roots. The goal here is to create an attractive cover for a barren area, but not at the expense of the trees."

Easy Does It

Melinda suggests removing the grass beneath trees in one of two ways. Cover the shady area with several layers of newspaper, grass clippings, wood chips or other organic mulch to eliminate what is growing there, or use an all-vegetation-killing chemical.

The second method produces immediate results, but be sure to read and follow all label directions carefully to avoid damaging nearby plants. It will also tell you how long to wait before planting again, which is generally 4 to 14 days.

The first method of grass removal is preferable because it is chemical free, though it does require patience. It typically takes about a year to complete, but it enriches the soil and won't harm future plantings.

After the grass is gone, it's time to consider what ground cover is most suitable for your climate and soil. If you live in the Southwest, where the weather is hot and dry for long periods, bearberry and lady's mantle are good choices because they don't require much water, and they thrive in heat.

Pachysandra and lamium can handle colder Midwestern and New England winters and are easy to control. Traditional lily-of-the-valley and periwinkle also thrive well in these regions,

Canadian ginger   Bugleweed

Deadnettle   Variegated pachysandra

GET IT COVERED. Ground covers don't have to be ordinary. There are plenty of unique varieties to choose from. Below, the bright green leaves of sweet woodruff share a flower bed with daffodils, alliums, white bleeding heart and various ferns.

10 Plants That Make the Most of Shade

Here's a quick list of ground covers that will add pizzazz to shady spots. To make sure these plants aren't considered invasive in your area, check with your local county Extension service. And while you're at it, ask what they recommend for shade ground covers that perform well in your area.

1. Bugleweed (*Ajuga*)—This beauty features masses of green, bronze or variegated foliage. Spires of blue flowers appear in late spring to early summer. Bugleweed may invade lawns, making it more suitable for areas surrounded by stones or other barriers. Zones 3 to 9.

2. Bearberry (*Arctostaphylos*)—Rocky and sandy soils are perfect for this hardy, low-growing evergreen, making it good for drought-tolerant gardens. The plant also produces white or pink flowers in spring and red berries in fall. Zones 2 to 8.

3. Ginger (*Asarum*)—Both evergreen and deciduous varieties are available. It will tolerate extremely low-light conditions and do well in the dense shade at the base of an evergreen. Zones 4 to 9.

4. Japanese painted fern (*Athyrium niponicum*)—This low-maintenance plant was named Perennial Plant of the Year in 2004. It flourishes in moist, humid areas, and the texture and color of its fronds make it a great ground cover for any shade garden. Zones 3 to 8.

5. Lady's mantle (*Alchemilla*)—Soft-green leaves form a nice mat and spread steadily. Chartreuse flowers appear in late summer or fall. Zones 3 to 8.

6. Lamium (*Lamium maculatum*)—Good in dry shade, the variegated leaves add a bright note from spring to fall. Pretty white or mauve flowers show up in May or June. Zones 4 to 8.

7. Pachysandra (*Pachysandra terminalis*)—This well-known shade lover offers glossy evergreen foliage with white flowers in spring. Zones 4 to 8.

8. Partridgeberry (*Mitchella repens*)—This evergreen features fragrant white flowers and red berries, prefers acidic soil and can handle moist to dry conditions. Zones 4 to 8.

9. Sweet woodruff (*Galium odoratum*)—Despite its delicate appearance, this plant is tough and well suited to wooded areas. Its white spring blooms last for several weeks, and even its leaves have a pleasant scent. Zones 4 to 8.

10. Winter creeper (*Euonymus fortunei*)—Trailing types of this mounding evergreen make great ground covers for shade. Winter creeper spreads easily, forming roots where its stems touch the ground. Zones 4 to 9.

BRIGHT SOLUTIONS. You don't need sun-loving plants to have color in your yard. Above, yellow corydalis blooms and Herman's Pride yellow archangel grow beneath a flowering azalea plant.

but they need to be contained or they can quickly spread and become invasive.

Florida violets and Japanese painted fern prefer lots of shade, moisture and heat, making them ideal for humid climates…and that's just the tip of the iceberg. There are plenty more to choose from.

Many of these ground covers do more than green things up in the shade—they also produce flowers that will add delightful dashes of color where you least expect them.

Time to Sow

Planting is pretty simple. The only thing to keep in mind is to avoid disturbing tree roots, which you can do by digging slightly wider and shallow holes rather than tilling up the entire planting area.

After gently tamping the plants in place, apply a generous layer of mulch and water thoroughly—then keep an eye on things.

"Although much of the work is now done, the first few years are critical," Melinda says. "Your ground cover will thrive if you put in a little extra effort in the beginning.

"People often don't realize that areas under trees, particularly those with heavy canopies, are actually dry and require regular watering. Those thick layers of leaves shed rain pretty well. Even a lengthy downpour might not penetrate the soil enough to make a difference."

And just like any newly planted garden, it's important to stay on top of weeding. Removing unwelcome plants reduces competition for water and nutrients and gives the ground covers the opportunity to become established.

But it won't be long before that once-barren area under the maple or next to the house is lush and green. And that's when you know you've got it made in the shade! ◄

FROM WILDERNESS TO WONDERFUL

Couple carves out a delightful hillside garden retreat.

By Fran Parr, Field Editor, Eldon, Missouri

The house sat in a wasteland of weeds and unkempt trees. Just 2 years old, the building had not been cared for or even inhabited. Still, when Wayne and Eva Studley saw the place, they fell in love with it.

From its spacious interior to the deck that overlooked a wooded lot, this home on the outskirts of Jefferson City, Missouri was the private haven the couple had been looking for. The only drawback—and it was a big one—was the sloping lot.

Not only was it overgrown, but from the street to the rear property line it pitched downward at a steep 25% grade, ending in a deep ravine. It was so extreme that erosion threat-

ened the rear deck, as well as the foundation of the house.

But after 27 years of farming, Wayne was accustomed to terracing and longed to work the soil again, enriching it and bringing beauty and utility to neglected land. Eva, a retired teacher, loved working in the yard and tending flowers. So, despite the visible shortcomings, these two experienced gardeners bought the home.

The first order of business after the Studleys moved in was

SHADY RETREAT. Wayne and Eva Studley (above inset) transformed the overgrown ravine in their backyard by planting hostas and ferns to create a secluded low-light landscape (top).

DARKNESS AND LIGHT. Shade garden favorites like goatsbeard (above left) and spiderwort (above right) thrive in the backyard. In front, sun-lovers brighten the landscape, including dwarf zinnias lining the flower beds (below) and a stunning rose of Sharon (bottom) towering over artemisia, perennial salvia and iris.

to landscape the backyard and stabilize the exposed foundation.

Sudden downpours and flash floods are common springtime occurrences in their area, so Wayne installed drainage pipes from the upper to the lower levels to prevent further erosion. He also added terraces and berms and cleared the underbrush in the ravine, leaving many large native trees for shade, including several kinds of oak, hickory, cedar, sassafras and dogwood.

Hauling in loads of mulch was the next step—and an important one, Wayne says.

"I prefer to use shredded mulch instead of the chipped kind," he says. "It decomposes faster, strengthening the soil and feeding the roots of the plants."

Although he lost track of how many pickup-truck loads he brought in, when the project was done, they'd applied a 6-inch layer of mulch over much of the area.

Then the couple designed various flower beds, walkways and peaceful retreats. The plans included a stepping-stone path encircling a sunken garden. Wayne made the "stones" himself, using forms and concrete.

Picking the Right Plants

Finally, it was time to plant...but what would work best? To find out, Wayne and Eva turned to experts at a local nursery for advice on plants, particularly those that tolerate shade and others that could handle the steep situation of their backyard.

Today, many plants known for foliage rather than flowers flourish in the Studleys' yard, including eight varieties of hostas and five different kinds of ferns that fill the sunken garden.

"A plant doesn't need to bloom for me to think it's beautiful," Eva explains.

That's not to say their place isn't blooming. The gardens burst with color, thanks to the bleeding hearts, quince, hydrangea, lilies, astilbe, columbine and moneywort.

"I really enjoy the pink and white bleeding heart blossoms that are the first to bloom each spring," says Eva.

"The moneywort is nice, too," adds Wayne, "but it tends to 'crawl' down the hill. I think I'll replace it with something else once it travels on."

Fun in the Sun

The backyard might be shady, but that's not the case out front. Eva took full advantage of the rays that area receives by filling curving beds with sun-loving plants.

"While we planned on having 95% perennials in front, we simply cannot resist adding a selection of annuals each year," she says.

Both Wayne and Eva are particularly fond of dwarf zinnias, which they use to line the beds. Pink Wave petunias are another favorite and look especially pretty spilling out of a sunken old oak bucket near the front door.

"Honestly, my favorite is whatever's blooming at the moment," Wayne says.

Looking to the future, this green-thumb twosome want to improve a wildflower garden they created. They originally bought a large can of mixed wildflower seeds, scattered them on a hillside and then watched as Queen Anne's lace took over.

"We don't mind that plant at all, but we'd like more variety and color in the bed," Wayne says.

Also waiting in the wings is a playground for their grandchildren. They'll construct it on the two vacant—and flat—lots next door.

Sage Advice

"The most important thing I'd share with others is to learn as much as you can about what you want to plant," Wayne says.

They've learned the hard way that some varieties can be too aggressive, like Missouri primrose. The couple loved the pink flowers it produced...but weren't pleased when the plant sent runners underground that popped up in their lawn. They've learned that such plants should be confined to pots buried in the soil...or avoided.

And others, like wisteria, wouldn't produce flowers in shade, no matter how much they pampered the plant.

"We fed that baby, urging it to grow up a 20-foot pole Wayne had secured in cement so it would stay on that hillside," Eva says. "It thrived and threw out 10- to 15-foot suckers, latching onto neighboring trees and shrubs, without one hint of a flower."

Aside from those few experiences, the Studleys believe in blooming where you're planted.

"We feel very lucky to have happened upon the house nobody wanted," they say. "It was a wilderness, but now it's a wonderful place to call home."

READER TIP

I prefer to use shredded mulch instead of the chipped kind. It decomposes faster, strengthening the soil and feeding the roots of the plants.

—Wayne Studley, Jefferson City, Missouri

1. Artemisia
2. Rose of Sharon
3. Zinnia
4. Salvia
5. Iris
6. Holly
7. Barberry
8. Rose
9. Cherry
10. Cedar
11. Birdbath
12. Ajuga
13. Periwinkle
14. Bleeding heart
15. Honeylocust
16. Hosta
17. Redbud
18. Fern
19. Moneywort
20. Astilbe
21. Bench
22. Hydrangea
23. Sassafras

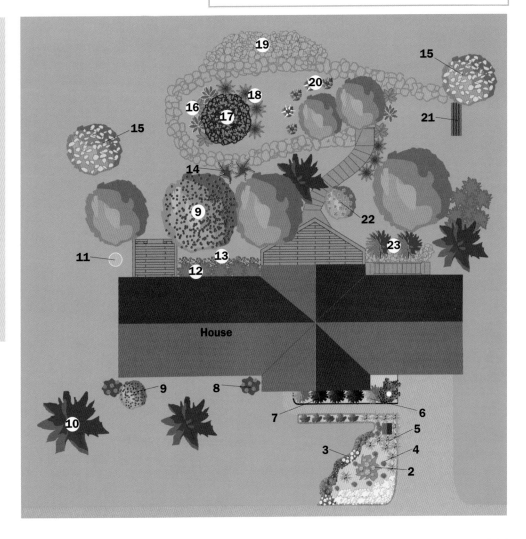

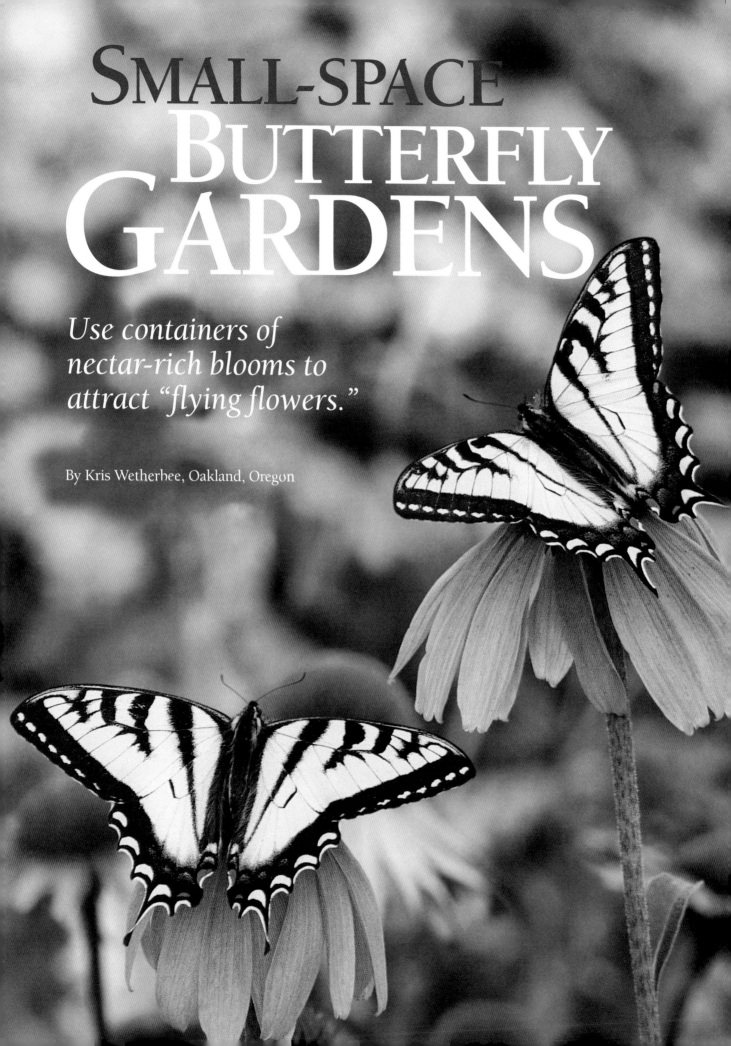

SMALL-SPACE
BUTTERFLY
GARDENS

*Use containers of
nectar-rich blooms to
attract "flying flowers."*

By Kris Wetherbee, Oakland, Oregon

There's no doubt that a container garden can add an instant punch of color to balconies, patios, porches and small yards. But did you know that planting the right selection of flowers can transform these small spaces into culinary havens for butterflies, too?

Imagine the excitement of watching as a myriad of beautiful butterflies—from small skippers to sizeable swallowtails—drift from one pot of flowers to another. They'll uncoil their tongues and sip nectar from each bloom…right before your eyes!

Just about any nectar-rich flowering plant, shrub, vine or small tree will grow in a container. Garden centers and nurseries offer a variety of pots and planters in various styles, colors, materials and sizes.

Container Chic

Options include plastic, wood, metal, stone, glazed pottery or clay, as well as lightweight planters made of polyethylene, fiberglass resin or other materials.

And, if you think beyond the confines of a standard pot, you'll uncover a wealth of items to recycle into creative containers. For example, a rustic wash basin, worn wheelbarrow or leaky birdbath can make stylish containers for butterfly plants.

Pots as small as 10 inches in diameter are fine for single plant displays, but 18 inches or larger is best when growing shrubs, trees or multiple plants. Larger containers are also less subject to temperature changes, and because they hold more soil, plant roots stay moist longer.

Whatever container you use, be sure it drains well. If a pot lacks adequate drainage, add holes to the bottom. Elevating containers on pottery feet, bricks, stones or even an upside-down pot also helps improve drainage.

Design Strategies

Want to know how to create a stunning plant display? The same design elements that make winning plant combinations for people to enjoy are also essential for attracting butterflies.

The key is to balance unity with variety—having some of the same colors and plant types in a container while still varying the heights, hues and bloom times. This will create multilayered and multi-season container gardens that appeal to many types of butterflies.

Plants arranged at varying heights also draw a diverse crowd of butterflies because they offer nectar flowers at different levels. Achieve this by mixing plants with trailing, bushy and upright growth habits.

For instance, grow a butterfly buffet featuring a chaste tree (*Vitex agnus-castus*) with catmint and trailing scaevola underneath. Or grow butterfly bush in a container with coral bells and garden verbena or sweet peas spilling over the edge. Garden phlox with candytuft and trailing geraniums (*Pelargonium*) also make an attractive combination.

If you find that a single tree or shrub looks lonely in its pot, fill it out by adding low-growing or trailing flowers, such as sedums, trailing lantana or verbena.

You can also feature a single species in a container and create the multilayered appeal by grouping several containers at varying heights. Use items like bricks, cement blocks,

SWEET TREATS. Butterflies love nectar-rich blooms, and it's easy to offer some in your garden. Left, tiger swallowtails feast on purple coneflowers. Above, a painted lady feeds on butterfly bush.

plant stands, pedestals, wooden stools or upside-down pots to raise the containers.

Blooms for Butterflies

While a flower's color, shape or scent will attract butterflies to some degree, the biggest draw by far is the bloom's nectar.

Adult butterflies typically have very cosmopolitan tastes, best served with a smorgasbord of nectar-rich flowers, especially those with flower clusters or daisy-like blooms, such as purple coneflower, mums, yarrow and butterfly weed, as well as tubular or bell-shaped flowers.

Not every nectar flower is suitable as food for butterflies. The amount of nectar a flower produces can vary within the species. Sometimes more fanciful double-flowered varieties are bred to impress the eye and not the appetite. So it's best to go with species plants whenever possible, rather than cultivars.

Don't Forget the Caterpillars

In addition to attracting adult butterflies, you can transform any small area into a butterfly nursery. Just grow a few containers of host plants, such as milkweed, mallow or asters. Adult female butterflies lay their eggs on these plants, and young caterpillars feed on them after hatching. Growing caterpillar foods also will bring in more butterflies for longer periods of time. You might even catch sight of species you've never seen before.

Unlike adult butterflies, caterpillars are very picky eaters. As a result, each species seeks out a specific plant or plants for its eggs.

Monarch caterpillars (left) feed exclusively on milkweed, while skippers mostly feed on grasses, sedges and legumes like wisteria and peas. Host plant preferences can vary within a species. Tiger swallowtails seek out trees like poplars, cherries and tulips, while black and anise swallowtail caterpillars dine on dill, fennel and parsley.

Some winning container combinations to attract several species are milkweed, fennel and grasses; and dogwood and violets with mallow.

With a little planning, you can also make your container garden do double duty. Some nectar sources, like penstemon and nasturtium, also are tasty meals for caterpillars.

Remember that a butterfly container garden isn't limited to patios, decks and entrance areas. Use potted plants to fill in bare spaces in a newly planted perennial bed or garden border. Stagger them on steps, encircle a tree or use them to line a walkway or path. Northern gardeners will need to provide protection for their overwintering plants and shrubs.

One thing is certain: A group of containers in a bright, sunny area can go a long way to providing habitat for butterflies...and a beautiful oasis for you.

Top Butterfly Picks for Containers

Annuals

Floss flower	Lantana	Sweet alyssum
Globe amaranth	Moss rose	Sweet william
Heliotrope	Salvia	Zinnia

Perennials

Agastache	Gaillardia	Salvia
Aster	Goldenrod	Scabiosa
Butterfly bush	Liatris	Sea pink
Butterfly weed	Oregano	Sedum
Candytuft	Penstemon	Verbena
Chrysanthemum	Phlox	Veronica
Coreopsis	Purple cone-	Yarrow
Delphinium	flower	Wallflower
Dianthus	Rudbeckia	

PLENTY TO CHOOSE FROM. Try any of the sweet blooms listed above to attract butterflies to your garden, whether it's big or small. Photos above: A monarch feeds on a type of butterfly bush, and woodland skippers find nectar from a pink zinnia bloom.

GARDENING ON MAIN STREET

Couple makes the most of their prominent location.

By George Traeger, Melrose, Minnesota

Spring might not arrive until Mother's Day in our part of the country, but the wait is well worth it. As soon as the snow retreats, over 1,000 tulip bulbs burst into bloom in our yard, while numerous shrubs change from drab to dramatic almost overnight.

And that's just the start of the show. As the tulips start to fade, snapdragons, poppies and roses begin to flourish, followed by daylilies, coneflowers, marigolds and more.

My wife, Ruth, and I live on Main Street, right next to

the local hospital, and we've made it our mission to keep our flower beds always in bloom. With people constantly passing by our home, it's almost as if our gardening efforts are on display...and we aim to please!

Of course, our yard wasn't always such a centerpiece. It was quite basic when we first bought the property, but Ruth and I could see potential in the swathe of green grass surrounding our house.

At first, we gardened within the confines of our yard. It

FOR ALL TO ADMIRE. George and Ruth Traeger created a gorgeous garden on Main Street. They filled sweeping flower beds (like the ones above and at left) with colorful flowers like dahlias, petunias and daylilies.

wasn't long before we ran out of room, however. My solution? I purchased the empty lot next door so we could spread out.

Greenhouse Gives a Head Start

Now, over 15 years later, we focus more on maintenance than expansion—and for good reason. We have a dozen planting beds, several ponds and a stream to take care of during the growing season, as well as a 12- by 24-foot greenhouse.

That structure began as a way to compensate for our short growing season. We used it as a place to prepare plants for the garden. Over the course of about 10 years, however, I reconfigured it several times until it reached its present size.

Today, it offers all the space I need to give the seedlings we purchase at the local garden center a head start each spring.

Some of those annuals are destined to go directly into our flower beds, while others are earmarked for the large pots I fill with flowers and set out in the yard. And, because it isn't unusual for temperatures to dip below freezing as late as Memorial Day, I rely on the greenhouse to provide shelter for those containers if frost is in the forecast.

No one else in our small town had a pond when we first decided to install one many years ago, and you can

imagine the interest this project generated. The locals regularly asked if they could stop by to see what we'd done.

Those requests keep coming each summer, thanks to the 4,000-gallon pond we put in a few years back. This water feature is stocked with 30 fish, including goldfish and koi, and sports a waterfall, a stream with a bridge and cattails. Geranium-filled planters brighten the banks, while a stately tree surrounded by hostas adds a touch of shade.

The Finishing Touches

Most of our flower beds hold the annuals we cultivate in the greenhouse. Although using annuals means we have to replant each year, the pansies, marigolds, petunias, alyssum and begonias keep our yard brimming with color well into fall.

Perennials have a place in our landscape, too. We've planted many varieties of tulips, which do exceptionally well in this part of the country. By selecting both early- and late-blooming types, we always have something flowering in spring.

A decorative steel fence marks the property line between our original yard and the lot we purchased next door, and we use this to support climbing roses, honeysuckle vines and clematis. Yellow, orange and red lilies encircle this spot as well.

Nearby is a garden devoted to roses, and just a few feet

away is one my favorite flower beds. This 40-foot-long patch is home to 50 or so dahlias (left) that bloom from mid- to late summer. These showy flowers are so amazing—I can't get enough of them!

Ensuring that our yard is constantly full of blossoms is a bit of a trick. The key, though, is planning ahead. Ruth and I spend all fall and winter plotting out what to grow and where to grow it.

Then we can act on those plans when warm weather returns...and before you know it, we're smack dab in the middle of summer, busy deadheading and removing weeds.

Our efforts pay off any time our seven children and 17 grandchildren visit and enjoy the gardens. We also participate in a garden tour and welcome local garden clubs to come see our yard. We've even had tour buses full of vacationers stop by our house.

See what I mean about our backyard always being on display? It's a good thing Ruth and I love planting and pruning, because when you garden on Main Street, everyone pays attention!

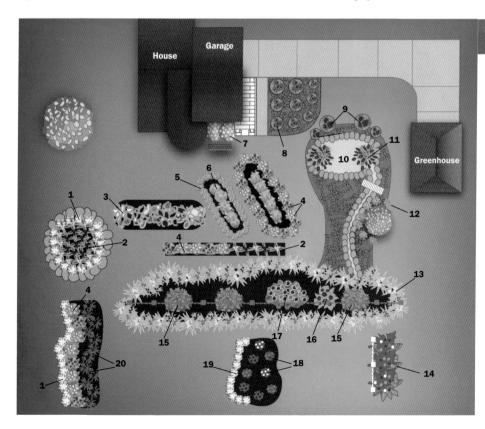

Planting List

1. Alyssum
2. Tulip
3. Annuals
4. Pansy
5. Begonia
6. Marigold
7. Hydrangea
8. Potted garden
9. Geranium
10. Pond
11. Cattail
12. Hosta
13. Lily
14. Dahlia
15. Honeysuckle vine
16. Clematis
17. Climbing rose
18. Rose
19. Dusty miller
20. Daylily

Plan a Great Garden

FULL OF APPEAL

Once an empty field, this colorful yard is now the apple of their eyes.

By Doris Witzgall, Bay City, Michigan

A jumble of dirt and weeds—that's what our yard looked like back in 1964. We'd just built our home on an acre of farmland, and things couldn't have been more barren. Little did I know that some 40 years later, we'd be surrounded by a garden paradise, complete with an apple orchard!

My husband, Wayne, and I weren't experts, but we were eager to brighten the scenery, so we dug right in and encountered our first major gardening challenge—clay soil. We decided then and there to create raised beds to deal with this problem. We also added a lot of organic matter to help break up the hard clay.

Vegetables and evergreens were the first items we cultivated. Next we fashioned a few flower beds and started adding annuals and perennials, from alyssum and columbine to lilies, petunias, hostas, roses, chrysanthemums, salvia, hollyhocks, phlox and more. Things just kept growing from there!

Weather Woes

It didn't take long to run into another stumbling block. The weather in our area is unpredictable, thanks to nearby Lake Huron, which can trigger unexpected changes in temperature and erratic conditions in general.

Some years we've had a severe frost as late as June and lost all our blooms. Since fall temperatures often start in September, we can wind up with a very short growing season. Other times, we've been lucky and had delightful weather from April to October.

Wayne and I quickly learned to roll with the punches. We know if one season is too short, too wet or too cool, the next one likely will be just perfect. We've also been careful to stay away from exotic plants and to pick hardy flowers, trees and shrubs.

Experimenting with different varieties in our garden beds is the secret to our success. After all, you never know what will work in your yard until you try it!

There certainly have been surprises over the years. In some instances, we've found flowers that were supposed to do well in sunny spots that performed better for us in shady areas, and other shade lovers that preferred brighter locations. And from time to time, we've tried species that just haven't worked in our yard at all.

Seed of an Idea

One addition that took off in a big way is Wayne's apple trees. He started with a few and kept adding more until we had 6 acres of orchard to the south of our yard and across the road.

I often describe our apple grove as a hobby that got out of hand. Honestly, though, the orchard is a real delight. We open it to the public each fall and sell apples and cider, along with the birdhouses and feeders Wayne crafts during winter. Anyone who stops in is welcome to wander through our gardens.

Friends and visitors alike often comment on all the work we've done…and all the rocks we've used to build our raised beds. By our calculations, we've hauled *150 tons* of stones over the years.

We also learned some important lessons about how to use the rocks. Proper placement is critical!

Position the stones from largest at the bottom to smallest along the top and offset each row so it interlocks with the one below it. Then the formations will last for years. It's also a good idea to stack the stones at a slight angle so they settle into

NO STONE UNTURNED. Rocks encircle almost every flower bed in the Witzgalls' yard. They estimate they've used 150 tons of them in areas like this shady retreat (right). Their butterfly garden (above left) is packed with nectar-rich perennials, and even a decorative butterfly house (top).

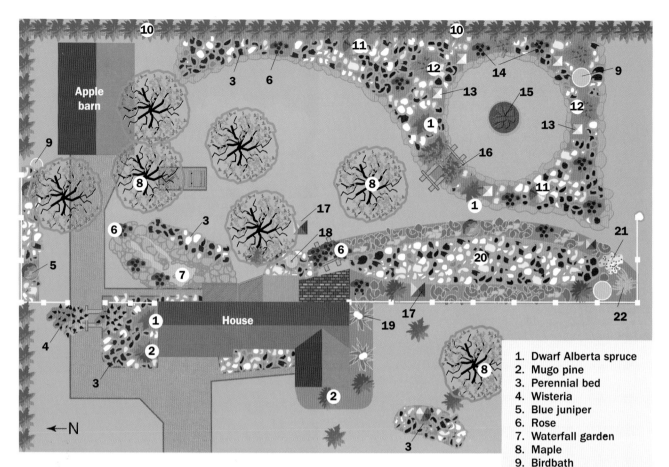

Apple barn

House

← N

1. Dwarf Alberta spruce
2. Mugo pine
3. Perennial bed
4. Wisteria
5. Blue juniper
6. Rose
7. Waterfall garden
8. Maple
9. Birdbath
10. White cedar
11. Birdhouse
12. Butterfly bush
13. Butterfly house
14. Rose of Sharon
15. Raised fire pit
16. Honeysuckle
17. Bird feeder
18. Fountain
19. Yucca
20. Angel garden
21. Spirea
22. Weigela

ROSE TO THE CHALLENGE. A variety of roses keep the Witzgalls' yard looking, and smelling, sweet. One of the most striking is a William Baffin climbing rose (above) next to the angel garden.

the dirt.

Three Seasons

We've never really had an overall design in mind for the yard. We just wanted to make sure it was blossoming from spring to fall.

Wayne is very creative and likes to try new things, like the waterfall garden he completed last spring near our hosta-filled shade garden. I pitch in by "decorating" with flowers, birdhouses, lanterns and more.

In addition to the waterfall and pond, we've created a butterfly garden filled with bee balm and other nectar-rich perennials they love, plus butterfly houses and stone benches. Not far away is an angel garden with a rose arbor and a collection of angel accents. Shrubs like spirea, arborvitae and weigela outline many of the beds. Maples, spruce and other trees add interest all through the year.

We no longer grow vegetables, since our daughter, who lives nearby with her family, put in a patch for us at her house. Our son and his family live across the road from us (many of our apple trees are behind his house). We love being so close to the kids and grandkids—and they're happy, too, especially when Wayne works in their gardens.

There's still plenty of work to be done at our place. The backyard is full, but we have a whole front yard for more gardens. I doubt we'll ever finish—and that's just fine with us! ◂

SECRETS TO GROW ON

The "best of the best" home-tested gardening secrets.

Watering Hole

A little leak doesn't stop me. When my three-tiered birdbath developed leaks in the top two tiers, I wanted to find a way to still use it.

I lined the top two bowls with pantyhose to prevent soil from spilling through the holes. Then I filled the bowls with potting soil and planted impatiens in them. I added water to the bottom bowl, which was still sound, for the birds to enjoy. It looks so pretty in our garden (above).

Last summer, a few petunias made their way into the planter portion of the birdbath and cascaded over the side, complementing the impatiens I put in there again. They looked so nice that I left them right where they were.
—*Bessie Rhiner, De Soto, Missouri*

Go for The Garlic

For years, I had trouble with Japanese beetles ruining my roses. Then I tried planting garlic. Just break open a head of garlic and scatter the bulbs around your bushes. I now have garlic growing in my rose beds...but no more Japanese beetles.
—*Elnora Hooper Leoma, Tennessee*

Sticking Together

Instead of buying plant stakes, I collect small, straight limbs and branches that fall into my yard from the trees. They blend in nicely with my gardens...and it is a lot cheaper than purchasing stakes.
—*Lindy Richee, Burbank, Illinois*

Compost Convert

I can't say enough about the benefits of amending your garden with compost.

In fall, I worked it into one of my beds, and the cannas I planted the next spring were taller than ever. The largest measured 10 feet, 2 inches (see photo at right). I planted bulbs from the same batch of cannas in a different bed, with no compost, and they grew to the usual 5 or 6 feet.

Now when I give plants or bulbs to friends, they want a bucket of compost to go with it!
—*Sherrie Schafbuch Belle Plaine, Iowa*

Bargain Trellises

Instead of investing in expensive trellises for climbing plants, I bought an old folding wicker screen for $10 and removed the hinges. Now I have three trellises that are quite attractive.
—*Janice Meisner, Cottage Grove, Oregon*

SEED STARTING

Jump-start your garden weeks ahead this year. It's easier than you think!

By Stephanie Jones, Syracuse, New York

There comes a day in every gardener's life when the notion of starting plants from seeds takes root. Usually, it's a restless winter day…a day on which you've paged through the colorful pages of a seed catalog and marveled at the offerings. And yet, if you've never done it before, you may hesitate, wondering if the project is too complicated or difficult. Good news! Seed starting is amazingly easy,

consumes little time, energy and money, and brings you a whole new level of gardening satisfaction. It's an adventure that, once begun, leads you to a brand-new sense of pride and joy in the plants you grow.

A Whole New World

If you have been buying mainstream seedlings down at your garden center each spring, mail-order seed offerings are a real eye-opener. There are dozens, indeed, hundreds of varieties to explore. The only difference is you'll be raising them!

Fans of seed starting often tout how much money they save. True, seed packets tend to be fairly inexpensive compared to bedding plants, which have time, effort and storage factored into their pricing. And seeds can lead to a lot of small plants (you might even make a little money on the side if you decided to sell the surplus).

The actual truth: In the end, you might not save a significant amount of money starting your own plants from seeds, simply because this hobby is addictive. As your confidence and expertise grow, you may end up plowing any saved money back into buying more seed packets. There are so many interesting varieties to try!

Still looking for an excellent reason to raise your own plants? By giving them a little TLC from seed to planting, you know the seedlings are well rooted because you've seen them grow day to day and tended to their needs. The seedlings will be naturally husky if you raise them in good soil at the proper distance from a light source, and you don't hurry them along with chemicals.

You'll also know they're healthy because the soil-borne diseases that sometimes plague big operations are easily prevented at home.

Making Wise Choices

As with any other garden purchase, you need to shop wisely so you'll enjoy success down the line. Make a wish list by flagging catalog pages with sticky notes or scraps of paper. Then return to the beginning and consider each choice one by one, paying particular attention to two important dates: when to start the seeds indoors based on your last spring frost; and how long it takes from seed planting until the time it produces flowers or fruit.

This helps you decide if the plant is suited for your climate and if it must be started indoors for longest bloom and greatest productivity once moved outdoors. This information also appears on the back of seed packets, too.

Starting seeds too early will force you to keep husky or unwieldy seedlings happy indoors too long. On the other hand, if you start something too late, you will be able to plant it, but it's likely to produce flowers or fruit later than usual, making the plant more vulnerable to summer's heat or an early frost.

Getting Started

Having done the necessary counting-backward math to determine when you want to start your seeds, you may discover you need to place your order right away! Seed companies get very busy in winter and early spring and fill orders on a first-come first-served basis. I recommend ordering spring seeds as early as you can for the most selection. While you're waiting for your packets to arrive, here are a few tips...

Prepare a spot to grow them. In milder climates, gardeners are able to sow seeds in a cold frame or greenhouse, if they have one. The rest of us have to make do indoors. The best spot to grow seeds is in an area out of the path of household traffic. You won't want people bumping into your tender sprouts, or curious pets coming around. It should also be a spot that is warm and out of drafts. A basement, sunporch or spare room are all good options. Some people even raise seeds on the tops of dressers, cabinets or refrigerators!

Think I'm kidding? The top of the refrigerator is an excellent place to grow seedlings because it generates a little warmth. Many seeds germinate better with some heat. You could even place your seed containers on top of a ra-

Seed Starting Steps

Basic Supplies
- Containers (see below)
- Soilless seed-starting mix. (It should be lightweight and labeled "sterile" so there's no risk of soil-borne diseases.)
- Labels (wooden Popsicle sticks are fine)
- Spray bottle or watering can

Recycled Seed Starters
You can recycle many containers for seedlings. Be sure they have drainage holes, as "wet feet" is a leading cause of seedling death. Remember...wash them in a 10:1 bleach solution before planting. Some perfect picks are:
- Shallow aluminum-foil trays
- Cups, including yogurt cups and margarine tubs
- Milk cartons, cut down
- Peat pots or peat pellets
- Plastic pots or plastic flats
- "Seed-starter" kits (consist of bottomless Styrofoam cells underlaid with water-wicking "fabric" and covered over with a plastic lid).

Freshness Test
Often, a seed packet contains more seeds than you'll ever need. Most of us simply fold down the edge and set the packet aside.

It's better to seal surplus seeds in small airtight jars (like baby food or spice jars) or plastic resealable bags and keep them in a refrigerator or a cool dark place, out of the light. Be sure they're labeled!

If stored properly, most seeds will germinate easily next season or even the one beyond. Some may last even longer!

TIP! Bulkier seeds, such as beans and peas, survive long-term storage best. Tiny ones, like those of lettuce or primrose, eventually dry out and won't grow—they may not even be worth storing.

diator, so long as the heat source is not too hot and is consistent.

Provide sufficient light. Some seeds germinate under a thin layer of soil mix, some are pressed lightly right on top, but in all cases the seedlings that sprout will require between 12 and 16 hours of light per day.

Sunlight from a window is not at all ideal. It's pale and limited in late winter and early spring. To make it work, you'll need artificial light. Fluorescent is best, and a timer at the outlet will help you regulate the hours it is shining on your baby plants.

Given these two critical requirements—location and light—some gardeners purchase a seed-starting setup for their house, while others make their own.

Time to Start Planting

Planting seeds indoors is not as hard as you think if you keep these simple tips in mind…

Get the mix. Begin with damp (but not drenched) sterile seed-starting mix, filling containers about three-fourths full. Tamp the surface flat and level with the flat of your hand or a small piece of wood before sowing.

Read the backs of seed packets. This gives information you need about sowing depth (or whether the seeds need light to germinate). The backs of seed packets have a wealth of important information, such as how far apart to sow the seeds, how many days they usually take to germi-

nate and when to plant. Sow carefully by hand. A pencil tip can be a very helpful tool when placing small seeds.

Don't sow too many seeds. This can lead to a forest of seedlings growing too thickly for you to thin without damaging them. Make little furrows if you're using flats,

Vegetable Seeds FOR SUCCESS

Eggplant
(Solanum melongena)

Planting depth: 1/4 inch
Best soil temperature for starting: 70°
Days to germination: 10 to 15
Special notes: A good plant to start indoors, as it is sensitive to cold. Move plants outdoors only after weather and soil have warmed up.

Pepper
(Capsicum species)

Planting depth: 1/4 inch
Best soil temperature for starting: 75° to 85°
Days to germination: 10 to 15
Special notes: Because some peppers, especially hot peppers, need a long growing season to ripen, they're an excellent choice for starting indoors.

Tomato
(Lycopersicon lycopersicum)

Planting depth: 1/4 to 1/2 inch
Best soil temperature for starting: 70° to 75°
Days to germination: 8 to 10
Special notes: Tomato seedlings can be moved easily from flats to larger pots, but when you do, set their stems a little deeper into the soil mix to anchor them better.

spacing seeds up to an inch apart (closer if seeds are tiny).

Cover seeds with plastic. Do this the very day you plant. This holds in warmth and humidity, giving the seeds the best chance of absorbing moisture and getting going. Don't seal tightly, though. That causes condensed water to drip back down onto the mix, making things too soggy.

Check on the seeds daily. The planting mix must not dry out, or seeds' growth will immediately halt. The best way to keep seedlings evenly, consistently moist is with bottom watering. Just set the container into a few inches of water (in the sink or in a tray) and let it wick up what water it needs before returning the container to its designated spot.

Seed leaves appear first

True leaf

RP Photo

Seedling Care

It usually takes a week or two for the first little leaves to poke up their heads. But what a thrill it is to see them! Once they begin to sprout:

Snip away extras. When the first true leaves appear, use sharp scissors to snip some of the weaker seedlings right at soil level. The properly spared survivors gain better air circulation, important for their health, and their roots won't have to compete for precious nutritional resources.

Water from above. Use a fine spray as the seedlings grow bigger. The plastic covering can be shifted on and off as your developing plants need ventilation. After a while, they'll be too tall, and you'll have to remove it completely.

Fertilize. After seedlings germinate, use a diluted flowering houseplant fertilizer (about 50% of the recommended dilution). Do this about every 2 weeks or less until you begin "hardening off" outdoors.

When seedlings are husky, well-rooted (tug gently on the leaves, never the stem, to check) and several inches high, it's time to get them ready for outdoor life.

In their original containers or transplanted into new individual pots, they may be moved outside in late spring to a sheltered spot out of the sun. Bring them indoors or cover them on chilly nights or if a frost threatens. A few days or a week of gradually introducing them to the sun and outdoors makes them much better in your garden.

GREEN THUMB TIP

"Pricking off" refers to the careful removal of seedlings from the soil as they begin to outgrow their original container.

Flower Seeds FOR SUCCESS

Photos (lower half of both pages) · RDA, Inc.

Nasturtium
(Tropaeolum majus)

Planting depth: 1/4 inch
Best soil temperature for starting: 65° to 70°
Days to germination: 7 to 14
Special notes: Can be difficult to transplant, to start seeds in peat pots. These seeds germinate in darkness, but the seedlings, of course, will need light.

Pansy
(Viola species)

Planting depth: 1/4 inch
Best soil temperature for starting: 65° to 70°
Days to germination: 7 to 21
Special notes: Cover the flats to exclude light until the tiny seeds germinate. They prefer cooler soil below 75°). If they fail to sprout, refrigerate for a few days to hasten germination.

Sweet Peas
(Lathyrus odoratus)

Planting depth: 1/2 to 1 inch
Best soil temperature for starting: 55° to 65°
Days to germination: 10 to 15
Special notes: These have hard seed coats; soak the seeds overnight in warm water before sowing.

386

396

394

BACKYARD SHOWPIECE

388

391

Photos, clockwise from top left: R. Todd Davis; Richard Day/Daybreak Imagery; Mark E. Gibson/Unicorn Stock Photos; Michael Wendt; Derek Fell

Steve Terrill; inset: Skip Moody/Dembinsky Photo Assoc.

FLOWERING DOGWOOD

When it comes to four-season appeal, this showy tree is "top dog."

By Rachael Liska, Associate Editor

As the days grow longer and warmer, the flowering dogwood readies itself for an unrivaled spring show. That's when its elegant flowers burst forth, lighting up forests, orchards and country roads with a lovely wash of white or pink.

So reliable is this harbinger of warmer weather that some gardeners decide when it's safe to plant by watching for the flowering dogwood's emerging blooms.

"The wooded area on my grandparents' Ohio farm was home to many dogwoods, so this tree holds special memories for me," shares *Birds & Blooms* Contributing Editor Melinda Myers. "Their early blooms brightened the landscape and signaled the start of spring. When I see them now, it reminds me of good times on the family farm."

It's easy to understand why this ornamental tree has also captured the fancy of home owners everywhere. But as striking as it is in spring, the flowering dogwood wins praise all year with its four-season appeal.

Legendary Pedigree

The flowering dogwood has a long and colorful history.

According to legend, it once equaled the mighty oak in size…until its wood was used for Jesus' cross. This saddened the dogwood, and it never grew so large again. As a reminder, its four petals form the shape of a cross and each is marked with a nail print. In the center is a crown of thorns.

History also tells of American Indians using the aromatic bark and roots as a remedy for malaria.

Today, the tight grains of dogwood make it ideal for golf club heads, knitting needles and tool handles.

Found in natural woodlands from New England south to Florida and west to Texas, flowering dogwoods evolved as so-called "understory trees."

Understory trees fill a unique niche since they grow in the shade of taller mature trees. In this microclimate, dogwoods receive filtered sunlight, high humidity and protection from drying winds—three conditions to keep in mind when adding a dogwood to the home landscape.

Best in Show

When properly cared for, flowering dogwoods will reward their owners with year-round pageantry in almost any landscape setting.

In spring, the blossoms appear before the leaves. But while this showy display is unmistakable, these "flowers" are actually modified leaves known as bracts, just like a poinsettia.

The true flower is insignificant and yellowish green, located in the center of the four "petals." White is the common color found in the wild, but some cultivars boast pink bracts.

Once the blossoms fade, green leaves unfurl. Their smooth, bright-green surface contrasts with the muted, silver-green underside. The small flowers then transform into dense clumps of green berries by early summer.

Autumn paints the leaves and twigs rich scarlet, while the fruits ripen to a glossy red. Various birds and other wildlife soon arrive to pick off the nutritious berries before the chill of winter sets in.

Sometimes said to resemble alligator skin, the flowering dogwood's rough, gray-brown bark makes it a standout in winter, too. This, combined with tiered branches and button-shaped buds at the tips of the twigs, makes for an attractive silhouette against a snow-covered yard.

Unleash the Beauty

The flowering dogwood's versatility has made it a popular choice for home landscapes. Slow growing, it does extremely well as a specimen plant or accenting a patio. And because it's a woodland native, flowering dogwoods are ideal for planting at the edge of a woods or in naturalized areas. Try pairing it with rhododendrons and azaleas for an informal yet pretty landscape feature with a lot of spring interest.

Flowering dogwood is a beautiful landscape plant, but is susceptible to many insects and disease if not kept healthy. Minimize the risk by purchasing healthy, pest-free plants from a reliable nursery.

Container-grown dogwoods may be transplanted any time of the year. Northern gardeners, however, might want to consider planting from late winter to early spring, so the tree has time to establish itself before the next winter. Southern gardeners should plant in fall to late winter, well before the heat

---

GARDENER'S BEST FRIEND. With its white (right) or showy pink (opposite page) blooms and attractive shape, flowering dogwood complements any backyard landscape. The eye-catching bracts (above left inset) are modified leaves, but are often mistaken for petals. The true flowers are at the center.

Backyard Showpiece

of summer arrives.

Grow in a partially shaded location with moist, well-draining soil. Add a 3-inch layer of mulch around the tree, being careful not to pile it against the trunk. Water thoroughly during dry, stressful periods and as needed the first few years after transplanting.

Follow these few simple steps, and you're on your way to enjoying the grace of this sensational showstopper. ◄

Plant Profile

Common Name: Flowering dogwood.
Botanical Name: *Cornus florida*.
Height: 20 to 30 feet.
Spread: 20 to 30 feet.
Leaves: Oval-shaped with prominent veins. Ranging from 3 to 6 inches long, they are medium green in summer and crimson in fall.
Flowers: Small, yellow-green flowers surrounded by four, 2-inch-long white or pink bracts.
Hardiness: Zones 5 to 9.
Light Needs: Full sun to full shade. Best in partial shade.
Soil Type: Prefers moist, well-draining, humus-rich and acidic soil.
Planting: Northern gardeners should plant from late winter to early spring. Southern gardeners should plant in fall to late winter. Avoid planting in compacted or shallow soils.
Prize Picks: Cherokee Chief is a popular pink flowering dogwood, though it doesn't tolerate extreme cold.

A heavy white bloomer, Cloud Nine is slow growing and more compact than most other varieties, making it ideal for smaller gardens.

With pink and yellow variegated foliage, Cherokee Sunset boasts red flowers and is disease-resistant.

Alan and Linda Detrick

These majestic trees gallop into spring with a winning flower display.

HORSECHESTNUT

For sheer showstopping spring beauty, few ornamental trees can compete with the horsechestnut. This magnificent shade tree is one of the first to leaf out, setting the stage for sensational flower plumes in May.

Except for a handful of shrubby or smaller species, such as the bottlebrush buckeye, horsechestnuts grow to impressive heights, making their springtime performance even more magnificent. The most familiar tree, the common horsechestnut, tops out at 75 feet, with a spread of up to 70 feet.

White flowers appear in early to mid-May, forming upright clusters 2 to 5 inches wide and 5 inches to 1 foot or more in length. The blossoms are white with yellow markings and have a pink blotch at the throat of each flower.

Known botanically as *Aesculus hippocastanum*, this plant is native to the mountains of Greece and Albania. The palmlike leaves have pointed lobes, giving the foliage a graceful look. The color of its bark ranges from dark gray to brown, with attractive, platelike scales similar to that of apple trees.

With its imposing size and pretty spring show, the horsechestnut is a popular landscape choice for parks, college campuses, golf courses and other expansive settings with room to showcase its charms. It's particularly popular in the eastern U.S., where, as one tree expert notes, "Virtually every campus has a horsechestnut."

While prevalent in North America, the horsechestnut is truly prized in Europe. France's Palace of Versailles boasts extensive horsechestnut plantings, and the trees line many Paris boulevards, including the famed Champs-Elysees.

Going Nuts

Horsechestnuts are landscape mainstays in the United Kingdom, where their smooth shiny nuts are used for a popular game called "conkers."

These nuts are known as "buckeyes" in parts of North America because they resemble that of the Ohio buckeye tree, a cousin of the horsechestnut. The tennis ball-sized spiny fruits contain one or two nuts, and attract deer and squirrels when they begin to fall in September.

Where wildlife visits or fruit clean-up causes problems, Baumannii horsechestnut (*Aesculus hippocastanum* 'Baumannii') is a good alternative. This cultivar produces no fruit and has an especially long blooming period with double flowers.

The Right Fit

Because of its size, common horsechestnut is a good fit for only the largest home landscapes. However, the red horsechestnut (top right), *Aesculus x carnea*, is sized right for suburban lawns. At maturity, it's 30 to 40 feet tall, about half the height of a common horsechestnut, and has rose-red flowers.

This smaller variety also is more resistant to leaf blotch and powdery mildew. Both diseases can make horsechestnut leaves discolor and drop, but cause no permanent damage in otherwise healthy plants. Prompt raking and disposal of diseased leaves helps reduce the risk of future outbreaks.

Horsechestnuts don't grow true from seed, so it's best to purchase a tree from a nursery and plant it in spring. Choose a site with full sun to partial shade, moist soil and good drainage. Keep soil moist throughout the growing season, and give the tree room to spread. In time, you'll have a horsechestnut worthy of the backyard triple crown. ◀

UNBRIDLED BEAUTY. The horsechestnut puts on a showy spring floral display, whether it's the statuesque common horsechestnut (opposite page) or the smaller red horsechestnut (above). Although known for its unique flowers (opposite page inset), you can't miss its spiny hulls as they mature (left).

Plant Profile

Common Name: Horsechestnut.
Botanical Name: *Aesculus hippocastanum*.
Height: 50 to 75 feet.
Spread: 40 to 70 feet.
Leaves: Large five- to seven-pointed leaflets that are greenish-yellow in spring, dark-green at maturity and yellow or brown in autumn.
Flowers: White panicles up to 5 inches wide and 1 foot long.
Hardiness: Zones 3 to 7.
Light Needs: Full sun to light shade.
Soil Type: Moist and well draining.
Planting: Plant balled-and-burlapped trees in spring; container-grown plants anytime during the growing season. Dig a hole as deep as the root system and 2 to 4 times the width of the root ball. Root flare should be at or slightly above soil. Do not amend soil in planting hole.
Fruit: Shiny, light-brown nuts inside spiny hulls.
Prize Picks: *Aesculus hippocastanum* 'Baumannii' produces long-lasting double white flowers and no fruits. Red horsechestnut (*Aesculus x carnea*) grows 30 to 40 feet tall and boasts rose-red flowers.
Backyard Benefits: Its flowers attract butterflies.
Caution: Plant parts are poisonous if ingested.

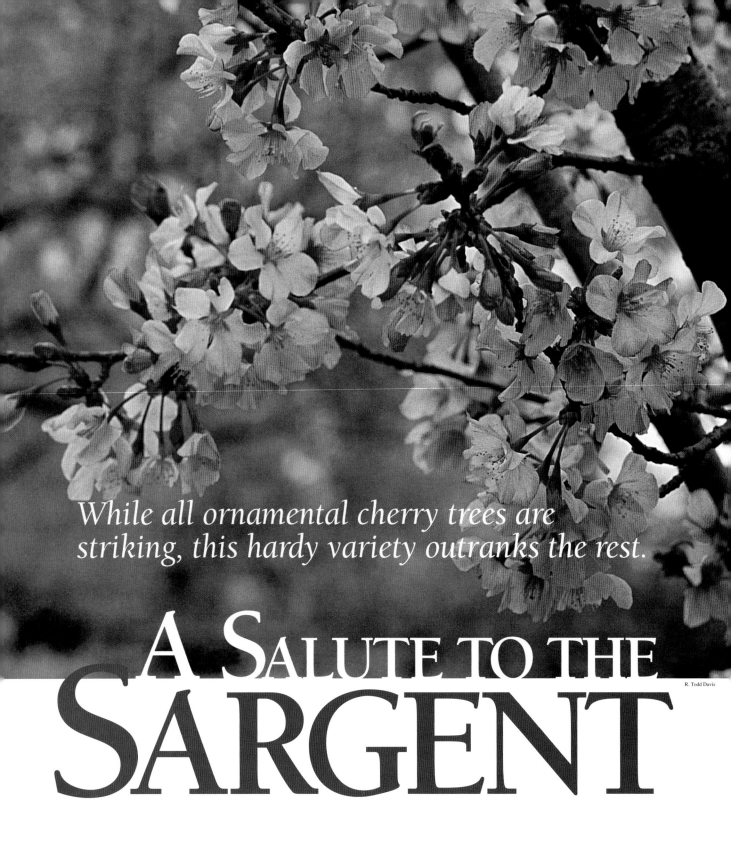

While all ornamental cherry trees are striking, this hardy variety outranks the rest.

A SALUTE TO THE SARGENT

There's no question that ornamental cherry trees are nature's showstoppers. These beauties produce a truly breathtaking cloud of blossoms to greet each spring.

In fact, the fragrant display is so amazing that many communities across the country host celebrations to honor them, including the National Cherry Blossom Festival, held each spring in Washington, D.C.

But ornamental cherries aren't reserved for arboretums and parks, the flowering specimens make appealing additions to home gardens as well. The problem is that many types are susceptible to disease or pests like borers. Luckily, the Sargent cherry is the exception to that rule.

BLOSSOMS AND MORE. When it comes to ornamental trees, it's hard to top the beauty of Sargent cherry. This colorful tree is a good choice for home landscapes—it's relatively carefree and offers year-round interest, producing pink flowers in spring as well as brightly colored leaves in fall. Even its marked mahogany bark (right inset) is attractive.

<small>Mark Turner; inset: R. Todd Davis</small>

Tough Enough

First brought to the U.S. from Japan in the 1890s by its namesake, noted arborist Charles Sprague Sargent, this variety has long demonstrated its hardiness, as well as its ability to withstand insects and disease.

What's more, the tree thrives in Zones 4 to 9, making it an ideal addition to gardens in most parts of North America. Plus, the Sargent cherry will live for 30 to 50 years.

Best of all, this ornamental beauty puts on a show all year long. In spring, it produces clusters of graceful, pink blossoms that cover every branch. But the show doesn't stop there.

Shortly after the flowers appear, new red-tinged leaves emerge. When fully unfurled, the tree's oval leaves deepen to an attractive, dark-green hue and measure about 3 to 5 inches long.

By summer, pea-sized cherries appear, starting out reddish and ripening to a purplish black. Because of their diminutive nature, the fruits are rather inconspicuous, but they attract plenty of birds that will devour most of the cherries before they can hit the ground, keeping mess to a minimum.

Come fall, the Sargent is ready to shine again. As the days shorten and nights cool off, the leaves turn a brilliant, flaming orange-red before dropping in late September.

Then, during winter, the bare branches and multiple upright trunks are visible—and even that's a treat. Satiny bark the color of rich mahogany covers the tree and features extended horizontal markings called lenticels (right inset), which add interest to the otherwise dull landscape.

Most Sargent cherries grow 20 to 40 feet tall and wide with a rounded shape that works in varied settings.

A Place in the Sun

As with most ornamental fruit trees, spring is the preferred time to transplant a Sargent cherry. And the best place to put one is in a very sunny spot, although the tree will tolerate a little shade. Avoid low spots or areas subject to late-spring frost, however.

It isn't terribly fussy about soil and will do well in almost any conditions as long as the drainage is good. You'll need to dig a hole that's the same depth as the roots but wider to give the roots room to spread out. Then gently position the tree in the hole, fill it with soil, water thoroughly and apply mulch.

The tree grows fairly quickly, though it may take 5 to 6 years to flower.

You don't need to worry about pruning the tree until it's well established—and even then you don't need to do much more than create a basic framework and remove broken, misshapen or very low branches each fall.

Other than that, all you have to do is sit back and watch this tree parade its beauty in your yard throughout the year. And that's something worth celebrating!

READER TIP

If space is an issue, the columnar Sargent cherry (*Prunus sargentii* 'Columnare') is a good option. It attains the same height as its cousin, but only spreads 10 to 15 feet.

Plant Profile

Common Name: Sargent cherry.
Botanical Name: *Prunus sargentii.*
Hardiness: Zones 4 to 9.
Height: 20 to 40 feet (can grow up to 70 feet in the wild).
Spread: 20 to 40 feet; 10 to 15 feet for the Columnare variety.
Flowers: Bowl-shaped, 1- to 1-1/2-inch pink flowers in clusters in spring.
Leaves: Oval or rounded leaves 3 to 5 inches long with serrated edges. Leaves are reddish tinged in spring, deepening to dark green in summer. By fall, they turn bright orange-red.
Fruit: In summer, inconspicuous, glossy 1/2-inch round cherries that start out reddish and ripen to purplish black; are readily consumed by birds.
Light Needs: Full sun.
Soil Type: Moist, well-draining and moderately fertile.
Planting: Plant trees in spring. Add mulch and water well to encourage strong root development.

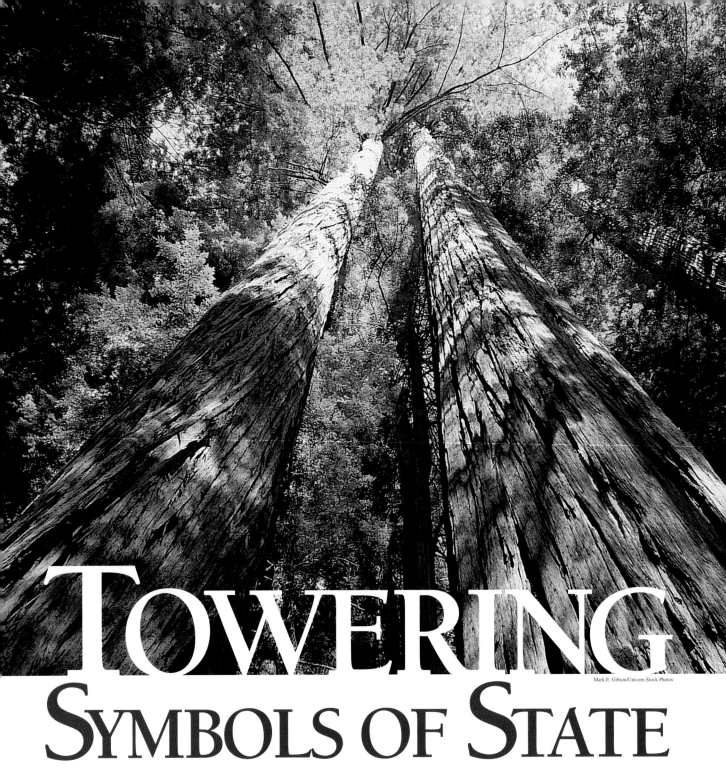

Mark E. Gibson/Unicorn Stock Photos

TOWERING
SYMBOLS OF STATE

Official trees have roots in each region's history and character.

By Karen Sutherland, Downers Grove, Illinois

For centuries, trees have been an important natural resource to Native Americans, pioneers, farmers and city dwellers alike.

They've offered shelter, fuel and building materials for everything from transportation to toys. And wood continues to be invaluable today.

All 50 U.S. states have recognized the role of these woodland beauties by selecting official state trees.

Varieties selected for this honor include the tallest (California redwood, at top), the largest (giant sequoia), the oldest (bristle-

HISTORIC ROOTS. All 50 states have acknowledged the importance of trees by selecting one as an official state symbol. At left, California redwoods are just one of the lofty emblems of The Golden State. They also recognize the giant sequoia as one of their state trees. New Hampshire claims the distinctive peeling bark of the white birch (above). Also known as a paper and canoe birch, this tree produces decorative, dangling catkins in spring. These long clusters of seeds resemble a cat's bushy tail.

Find Your State Tree

State	Tree
Alabama	Longleaf pine
Alaska	Sitka spruce
Arizona	Palo verde
Arkansas	Loblolly pine
California	California redwood / Giant sequoia
Colorado	Colorado blue spruce
Connecticut	White oak
Delaware	American holly
Florida	Cabbage palmetto
Georgia	Live oak
Hawaii	Kukui/candlenut
Idaho	Western white pine
Illinois	White oak
Indiana	Tulip tree
Iowa	Oak
Kansas	Cottonwood
Kentucky	Tulip poplar
Louisiana	Bald cypress
Maine	Eastern white pine
Maryland	White oak
Massachusetts	American elm
Michigan	Eastern white pine
Minnesota	Red pine
Mississippi	Magnolia
Missouri	Flowering dogwood
Montana	Ponderosa pine
Nebraska	Cottonwood
Nevada	Single-leaf pinyon / Bristlecone pine
New Hampshire	White birch
New Jersey	Northern red oak
New Mexico	Pinyon
New York	Sugar maple
North Carolina	Pine
North Dakota	American elm
Ohio	Buckeye
Oklahoma	Redbud
Oregon	Douglas fir
Pennsylvania	Eastern hemlock
Rhode Island	Red maple
South Carolina	Palmetto
South Dakota	Black Hills spruce
Tennessee	Tulip poplar
Texas	Pecan
Utah	Blue spruce
Vermont	Sugar maple
Virginia	Flowering dogwood
Washington	Western hemlock
West Virginia	Sugar maple
Wisconsin	Sugar maple
Wyoming	Plains cottonwood

Canada's Provincial Trees

Province	Tree
Alberta	Lodgepole pine
British Columbia	Western red cedar
Manitoba	White spruce
New Brunswick	Balsam fir
Newfoundland	Black spruce
Northwest Territories	Jack pine
Nova Scotia	Red spruce
Ontario	Eastern white pine
Prince Edward Island	Northern red oak
Quebec	Yellow birch
Saskatchewan	Paper birch
Yukon Territory	Quaking aspen

cone pine) and some of the showiest (the redbud and the flowering dogwood).

All told, 38 different tree varieties are state symbols, with a number of states picking the same tree.

For example, the flowering dogwood is the state tree of both Missouri and Virginia; the white oak represents Connecticut, Illinois and Maryland; and the sugar maple is the tree that has been selected by four states—New York, Vermont, West Virginia and Wisconsin.

A pair of states even adopted more than one tree to share the top honor. California recognizes the prominence of the redwood *and* the giant sequoia, while Nevada designated the single-leaf pinyon and the bristlecone pine, both common in its desert countryside.

Began with Arbor Day

The state tree movement dates back to the inauguration of Arbor Day in 1872.

Settlers in Nebraska were encouraged to plant trees to help

Backyard Showpiece

Redbud, flowering dogwoods

Joseph Kayne/Dembinsky Photo Assoc.

Sugar maple

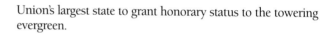

Ann Trulove/Unicorn Stock Photos; top photo: Adam Jones/Dembinsky Photo Assoc.

Bristlecone pine

celebrate the new holiday. One of the most popular varieties used to seed the vast prairies was the cottonwood, which later became Nebraska's woody mascot.

The first state to choose a tree officially, however, was Texas. In 1919, the Lone Star State picked the pecan in memory of a much-loved former governor who passed away in 1906.

His last request was that a pecan be planted on his grave, and the nuts from that tree shared so people could plant more.

Other states followed suit for a variety of reasons. Minnesota, Montana, Oregon and Maine all recognized coniferous trees that were important to their lumber or shipbuilding industries.

History Lessons

History played a role in the selection of Massachusetts' state tree. The legislature selected the American elm, in honor of the "Liberty Elm," under whose branches the colonists made plans for gaining America's independence from Britain.

Connecticut singled out the white oak to commemorate the important role of its famous "Charter Oak." In 1687, England's King James II sent representatives to retrieve a charter he'd granted the colony, so colonists hid it in a hollow section of the white oak's trunk.

More modern events have had an impact on state tree selection, too. Charles Lindbergh's famous airplane, the *Spirit of St. Louis*, had wings made of Alaska's Sitka spruce, prompting the

Union's largest state to grant honorary status to the towering evergreen.

Child's Play

Children played a role choosing trees in three states, where they voted for their favorite species. Mississippi youngsters elected the magnolia, and kids in West Virginia and Wisconsin gave the nod to the sugar maple.

All but one state—Hawaii—picked trees native to their particular regions. People there decided to acknowledge the kukui or candlenut, a variety imported from Malaysia. This tree's small, white blossoms often appear in leis, the floral necklaces associated with the Aloha State.

Only a handful of the hundreds of tree species growing in this country are honored as official emblems. But that doesn't mean they're hard to find. Take a good look at the trees near your home, and you're sure to spot a few with stately roots.

READER TIP

Hawaii is the only state that didn't pick a tree native to their region. The people there chose the kukui or candlenut, imported from Malaysia, because the tree's white blossoms often appear in the state's signature leis.

—Karen Sutherland, Downers Grove, Illinois

ENJOY THE SHOW

Richard Day/Daybreak Imagery

Our resident plant expert explains the "mystery" of fall color.

By Melinda Myers, Contributing Editor

As summer turns to fall, the leaves on many trees start changing from shades of green into yellow, red and orange hues. The transformation is spectacular, so it's not surprising that I hear two common questions each autumn:

First, how does the magnificent process work? And second, why do some leaves change color while others that should don't?

Back to Basics

Let's start with a little basic biology. Plant leaves actually contain a variety of colors, but the green pigment in the chlorophyll found in leaves is the most dominant. Because of this, it masks the other colors, and we see brilliant greens throughout most of the season.

The green chlorophyll is critical to the life of the plant. It captures energy from the sun, and then through the process of photosynthesis, combines it with carbon dioxide and water to produce the plant's nourishment in the form of sugars.

During the process, the chlorophyll slowly breaks down, but the cycle doesn't stop. The plant continues to produce new chlorophyll to maintain the vivid-green leaves we know and love in summer.

Transformation Explanation

But as fall takes over with its shorter days, the cycle changes. Plants must begin to get ready for winter.

To do this, the leaves develop a layer of corky cells between the leaf stem and branch to prepare for fall leaf drop. This layer slows the production of chlorophyll, and the green leaf color begins to fade. As it does, it exposes other color pigments (called carotenoid pigments), unveiling the pleasant hues of yellow, brown and orange.

These pigments are responsible for the gorgeous yellow leaves of ginkgo, redbud, witchhazel, larch and birch trees. The warm browns and tans often found on oaks are due to the accumulation of tannins in the leaves as the green chlorophyll disappears.

Now add in the effects of cool fall nights. If temperatures drop below 45° while the days are still sunny and warm, the plant is unable to use all the sugars produced in the leaves during the day. To avoid a toxic buildup of these sugars, the plants use the excess to produce a chemical called anthocyanin. These pigments are what give us the red and purple leaves of red maple, burning bush, black gum, flowering dogwood and sweet gum.

Delayed Display

Magnificent yellows, oranges and reds help give autumn its vibrant identity, but not every season sparkles like we want it to. A poor fall color display, like so many gardening woes, can be blamed on the weather.

Gray days and warm nights will dim the display, and early frost may damage leaf tissue, causing it to turn black before it has a chance to show off its rich colors. Cool, wet springs or warm, humid summers also can cause leaf spot and early leaf drop, eliminating the canvas on which nature paints its colorful season finale.

Gardeners can influence the intensity of the fall show as well. Too much nitrogen fertilizer may dim the color, preventing the beautiful red hue from developing on red maples, burning bush and others. Sun-loving plants placed in shade also can lose their fall luster.

Although you can do your part to ensure a great fall show by monitoring the environment of your plants, the rest is up to nature. So as the crisp autumn weather takes over, just sit back and enjoy the transformation. ◄

READER TIP

Be careful using nitrogen fertilizer. Too much may prevent the beautiful autumn hue from developing on red maples, burning bush and others.

SENSATIONAL SHRUBS

Make an impact in your backyard with these flowering stars.

Scott E. Zir>ck

Camellia

Botanical Name: *Camellia*.
Bloom Time: Late winter to early spring.
Hardiness: Zones 6 to 11.
Flower Color: Red, pink and white.
Height: 3 to 20 feet.
Width: 3 to 20 feet.
Light Needs: Partial shade.
Planting: Plant root ball even with surrounding soil. To keep roots moist, cover base with 2 inches of mulch.

Robert Domm

Forsythia

Botanical Name: *Forsythia*.
Bloom Time: Early to mid-spring.
Hardiness: Zones 3 to 8.
Flower Color: Yellow.
Height: 1 to 10 feet.
Width: 3 to 10 feet.
Light Needs: Full sun.
Planting: Plant in hole as deep as, but wider than, the root ball. Space plants 2-1/2 to 6 feet apart.

Dereck Fell

Heavenly Bamboo

Botanical Name: *Nandina domestica*.
Bloom Time: Midsummer.
Hardiness: Zones 6 to 9.
Flower Color: White.
Height: 6 to 8 feet.
Width: 4 to 6 feet.
Light Needs: Full sun to partial shade.
Planting: Check with your county Extension service to make sure it isn't invasive in your area. For more impact, plant several in a grouping.

Hydrangea

Botanical Name: *Hydrangea.*
Bloom Time: Summer.
Hardiness: Zones 4 to 9.
Flower Color: Pink, white and blue.
Height: 6 to 22 feet.
Width: Up to 8 feet.
Light Needs: Partial shade.
Planting: Place in hole the same depth as the root ball, but wider. Water thoroughly, keeping the soil moist but not soggy.

Mary Jane Hayes

Jasmine

Botanical Name: *Jasminum.*
Bloom Time: Spring.
Hardiness: Zones 6 to 10, depending on variety.
Flower Color: Yellow, white or pink.
Height: Shrubs generally are 3 to 10 feet. Jasmine can also be used as a climber, which will reach 12 to 40 feet.
Width: Up to 10 feet.
Light Needs: Full sun to partial shade.
Planting: Plant container-grown shrubs whenever they're available.

Richard Shiell

Mountain Laurel

Botanical Name: *Kalmia latitolia.*
Bloom Time: Late spring to midsummer.
Hardiness: Zones 4 to 9.
Flower Color: Pink, white and red.
Height: 7 to 15 feet.
Width: 7 to 15 feet.
Light Needs: Full sun to deep shade (produces fewer flowers).
Planting: Sow seeds immediately after harvesting.

Dick Keen / Unicorn Stock Photos

Rose of Sharon

Botanical Name: *Hibiscus syriacus.*
Bloom Time: Late summer to mid-autumn.
Hardiness: Zones 5 to 9.
Flower Color: Pink, red, purple, blue and white.
Height: 10 to 12 feet.
Width: 6 to 8 feet.
Light Needs: Full sun to partial shade.
Planting: In northern areas, plant in spring. Thrives in moist soil that drains well.

Dereck Fell

Michael Wendt

WHITE ASH

These trees provide a dazzling autumn show.

By Kathleen Zimmer-Anderson, Waukesha, Wisconsin

Each fall, I pat myself on the back when I look at our yard. Why? Because I had the bright idea to add a white ash to the garden several years ago, and now we're blessed with a glowing autumn display when shorter days and cooler temperatures prompt the tree's leaves to change color.

The only downside is that the leaves turn in September, and the ash is bare well before winter—but that smoldering purple hue is worth it in my book. And besides, those ash-gray branches add texture and interest to our yard until spring coaxes pretty new leaves to emerge.

There's much more to like about the white ash besides autumn color, however. For one thing, they can grow as much as 2 feet a year, so gardeners don't have to wait long for their trees to be tall enough to provide shade.

White ash is the largest of the ash trees, rising anywhere from 50 to more than 100 feet when mature. Branches can spread about 50 feet wide, making this deciduous specimen ideal for larger yards, where a lush crop of leaves will cool down sunny decks and patios or provide an oasis in the middle of an open space.

Well-Rounded Selection

Another key quality is the tree's ability to tolerate a wide range of soil conditions. Moist, well-draining loam is preferred, but the white ash can handle clay and sand, too.

It thrives in a variety of climates as well. This North American native can be found throughout eastern Canada and the eastern half of the U.S., from Nova Scotia to Minnesota and as far south as Florida and Texas. It is a common sight in forests and parks from north to south.

Although flowers do bloom in spring, the red or purple clusters lack petals and don't attract much attention. Winged

seeds develop later in summer and can be a bit of a nuisance. Seedless varieties such as Autumn Purple are a clean alternative. Other seedless options to try include Autumn Applause and Rosehill, both of which turn a rich, bronze red in fall.

What a Sport

The wood of the white ash is light yet strong and nicely pliable, allowing it to endure storms and high winds better than many other types of trees. These characteristics also make it a top pick for crafting sports equipment like tennis rackets and oars, although it's probably best known as the preferred lumber used to make baseball bats.

Well before becoming an important resource for our national pastime, the white ash was regularly used by Native Americans to shape bows and arrows for hunting. And woodworkers have long relied on the timber to make furniture and cabinets.

Of course, gardeners prefer to enjoy living trees, not lumber. And from its handsome bark to its pleasingly symmetrical crown, the white ash is an asset in any setting.

There aren't any special planting requirements for the white ash, which handles transplanting quite well. Simply select a sunny spot with room for the tree to grow. Once it's in the ground, cover the roots with moistened soil and then top with mulch to help retain moisture.

Continue to water regularly, and don't fertilize until the ash has been in the ground for a year. Once it's fully grown, the tree shouldn't require any fertilizer.

Unfortunately, the white ash is susceptible to several pests and diseases, including various borers, ash plant bug, cankers, leaf rust and anthracnose. One pest of recent concern is the emerald ash borer, which was first discovered in Michigan and has been found in nearby states. Gardeners in these areas should monitor their ash trees, and contact their county Extension service for more information if a problem arises.

It's important to remember that most vigorous specimens don't succumb to these culprits, but it still pays to keep an eye out for any trouble.

Chances are good, though, that your experience with the white ash will be nothing but positive, just like mine has been. And your reward will be year after year of beauty, with a brilliant "fashion show" each fall!

READER TIP

Monitor your white ash, keeping an eye out for pests and diseases. If you suspect a problem, contact your county Extension service for additional information.

Plant Profile

Common Name: White ash.
Botanical Name: *Fraxinus americana.*
Height: 50 or more feet.
Spread: Up to 50 feet.
Leaves: Usually 8 to 12 inches long and composed of five to nine leaflets that are 2 to 6 inches long. Leaflets are oval or spear shaped and finely toothed along the edges. They are dark green on top and lighter underneath, turning purple or yellow in autumn.
Bark: Ashy brown or gray, divided by narrow, interlaced ridges when mature.
Flowers: Inconspicuous, dark-red or purple clusters that appear before leaves in the spring.
Seeds: 1- to 2-inch-long, winged, light-brown seeds that hang in clusters.
Hardiness: Zones 3 to 9.
Light Needs: Full sun.
Soil Type: Prefers moist, well-draining soil, but will tolerate less hospitable conditions as long as water is plentiful.
Planting: Plant balled-and- burlapped trees as soon as possible; container-grown trees can be transplanted throughout the growing season. Dig a hole that is as deep as the tree's roots but three to five times wider. Remove container, burlap, wire or twine and place tree in hole. Fill with existing soil, water and add mulch.

PURPLE REIGNS. The white ash has many admirable characteristics, but its typically reddish-purple autumn leaves attract the most attention. Varieties like Autumn Purple (above and opposite page, left) are especially eye-catching. These trees are handsome in other seasons as well with their attractive leaflets (above left) and graceful branching habit (opposite page, right).

Derek Fell; inset: Bill Marchel

ELDERBERRY

Put out the welcome mat for birds with this fruity favorite.

By Deb Mulvey, Associate Editor

Want to turn your backyard into a bird buffet? Planting an elderberry is an easy way to do it. These native plants produce a bounty of berries that birds absolutely love.

Elderberries, or elder, grow wild in woodland borders and thickets in much of North America, providing birds with food, habitat and cover. And they can perform the same function in your home landscape.

There are about 25 species of elderberry, but the type known as American elder (*Sambucus canadensis*) is the best for attracting birds. This species blooms profusely in June and July, producing flat-topped white flower clusters that resemble Queen-Anne's lace.

Beauty, Then Buffet

These clusters, known as cymes, attract butterflies—another backyard bonus. The cymes are so dense that they sometimes cover the plant completely, obscuring the bright-green foliage. As the blossoms fade, they begin forming glossy purplish-black fruits, which ripen in August and September.

Once the fruits appear, keep your binoculars and bird guide handy, because they attract a multitude of species (see the list in "Plant Profile" at right).

Don't worry about running out of berries, though—a single plant is enough to feed a hungry crowd. An American elder produces so much fruit that branches may bend to the ground under the weight of the berries.

BEAUTIFUL BENEFITS. What elderberry lacks in looks, it makes up for with an ability to attract a bounty of interesting birds (like the cedar waxwing left inset). Photos, from left: white flower clusters emerge in spring…berry bunches droop from the branches…unique cultivars like Aurea offer bright-golden foliage.

READER TIP

Try growing this free-growing plant along naturalized gardens, property lines and fencerows.

Growth Spurt

As you might expect with a native plant, the elderberry is fairly easy to grow. Started from seed or suckers (these are shoots that grow from the roots), it can quickly reach 12 feet in height and width.

For home landscapes, the big issue is the American elder's unkempt appearance. The branches arch and sprawl, and suckers pop up constantly. If your goal is to keep this plant looking tidy, you're in for a never-ending task.

While aggressive pruning will keep it in bounds, a more suitable solution is to use it in spots where its "untamed" look won't be an issue.

Naturalized gardens, property lines and fencerows are good choices. A woodland border is even better. This creates a "transitional zone" for birds, luring more of them to nest and feed close to your yard.

Many Choices

If a manicured landscape is your first priority, however, you might be happier with another type of elderberry that offers a more shrublike appearance.

Some varieties of *Sambucus nigra*—also known as black elder or European elder—have a neater, more upright growth habit. The cultivar Gerda, also sold as Black Beauty, produces pink, lemon-scented flowers and purplish-black leaves, and reaches heights of 10 to 12 feet. A type called Black Lace has similar features, but is even more compact at 6 feet.

Another species, *Sambucus racemosa*, known as European red elder, has cone-shaped yellow flower clusters and shiny red fruit. One of the best cultivars, Sutherland Gold, has leaves that are copper colored in spring but turn gold in summer.

These plants won't produce the same bumper crop of berries as American elders, and may need to be cut back in winter or early spring. But they'll still attract birds and butterflies to your yard—and look good doing it.

Plant Profile

Common Names: Elderberry, elder.
Botanical Name: *Sambucus* species.
Height: 5 to 12 feet.
Spread: Up to 12 feet.
Leaves: Bright-green and toothed; some varieties have yellow or purple leaves.
Flowers: Clusters of small white, pink or yellow blooms.
Fruit: Shiny, purplish-black fruits 1/4 inch in diameter appear in August and September. Some cultivars produce red fruit.
Hardiness: Zones 3 to 9.
Light Needs: Full to partial sun. Colored-leaf varieties produce the best color in dappled shade.
Soil Type: Prefers fertile, moist and well draining.
Planting: Plant in spring or fall, or propagate by seeds or suckers.
Prize Picks: American elder Aurea is one of the most attractive cultivars, with golden foliage and cherry-red fruit.
Backyard Benefits: Attracts birds and butterflies. The bird species that eat its berries include: American robin, Baltimore oriole, blue jay, brown thrasher, Carolina wren, cedar waxwing, common grackle, eastern bluebird, eastern towhee, gray catbird, hermit thrush, indigo bunting, mourning dove, northern cardinal, northern flicker, northern mockingbird, red-bellied woodpecker, ring-necked pheasant, rose-breasted grosbeak, ruffed grouse, scarlet tanager, song sparrow, summer tanager, Swainson's thrush, tufted titmouse, wild turkey, wood thrush and yellow-bellied sapsucker.
Warning: All plant parts can cause digestive discomfort if ingested raw, but the fruits are safe to eat if cooked. Contact with leaves can cause skin irritation.

SHRUBS ADD WINTER 'WOW'

Try these plantings for color that doesn't cool off with the weather.

By Melinda Myers, Contributing Editor

When winter arrives, the beauty of your garden doesn't have to be locked away in cold storage. You can keep your yard bright and interesting by adding a few shrubs with eye-catching seasonal appeal.

The first step is to tour your winter landscape. There's no need to throw on a coat yet—we're starting indoors.

Examine your yard through the windows you use the most during winter. For instance, I always start my day with a cup of coffee in the kitchen. So the view outside that window is important to me.

Now grab your coat and go for a walk through the yard. Look for spots with room to plant shrubs or for flower beds that can be expanded. Note the light and soil conditions of each area so you can match new plants to the growing condi-

tions.

With the chosen spaces in mind, you're now ready to make a list of specific shrubs for your backyard.

Color is a good place to start. The holiday lights and decorations that adorn many homes this time of year are clues that we all crave a little more brilliance in winter. Planting a few shrubs can fill that need.

Bark Is a Pretty Sight

Red twig dogwood, also known as redosier dogwood, is a long-time favorite. It has unique red stems that make a nice backdrop to overwintering perennials or an accent plant for evergreens.

Regular pruning keeps the color vibrant year-round (though

Mark Turner

Kim Hawks

Kim Hawks

Steve Terrill

Kim Hawks

A FLURRY OF CHOICES. From berries to evergreen leaves, winter shrubs offer plenty of variety. Clockwise from top left: winterberry features vibrant fruit…evergreen holly paints a pretty holiday picture…witch hazel unfurls cold-weather flowers…clusters of purplish berries make beautyberry a unique sight…the crooked branches of Harry Lauder's walking stick stand out once the leaves fall.

in spring and summer, the leaves disguise it). Simply remove older brown stems at ground level in late winter. This encourages new growth, which is the most vivid.

The yellow twig variety, Flaviramea, adds a different look to the garden. Just a few of these yellow-stemmed beauties pack a punch in the landscape.

Another shrub with colorful stems is Japanese kerria. Its glossy, bright-green stems are sure to catch a second look. The slender stems stand upright and provide welcome contrast.

But it's not just about color. The texture of the bark can add interest, too. Burning bush, also known as winged euonymus, has stems with corky ridges that look especially pretty after a snowfall. However, gardeners in parts of the Northeast and Midwest, where this plant is invading native woodlands, should

avoid using it. Instead, consider its native counterpart, eastern wahoo. Although it lacks the corky bark, it produces small pink and orange fruit.

The oakleaf hydrangea has several attractive features for winter. The coarse textured older stems are covered with peeling, cinnamon-brown bark. This, combined with the dried flowers, creates cold-weather charm.

Another way to increase appeal is with uniquely shaped shrubs. Harry Lauder's walking stick is the first to come to mind. Its curled and twisted stems, which become more apparent after the leaves have fallen, make this a nice focal point in a patio garden, mixed border or foundation planting. Remove any straight stems that sprout from the roots beneath the graft.

Serving Up Fruit

One of the most common ways to create a bright spot amid the snow is with fruit-bearing shrubs. You'll appreciate the color—birds will appreciate the food.

Holly is the traditional berry for the holidays, and these shrubs (and trees) come in many evergreen varieties that also produce colorful fruit.

Southern gardeners have a wider selection of evergreen types that work in warmer climates. Northern gardeners need to look for hardier cultivars of the Meserve hollies, such as China Boy, China Girl, Blue Boy, Blue Girl, Blue Prince and Blue Princess. As the names imply, there are both male and female plants. I suggest at least one male for every five females to help guarantee fruit.

A hardier alternative is the deciduous holly, known as winterberry. The lack of leaves in winter is not a problem, since red fruit covers the upright stems.

And take a second look at the off-season potential of a long-time garden staple—the rose. Not only are the rose hips colorful, but you can also gather some of the hip-covered stems for unique

These 19 Shrubs Shine in Winter

Name	Hardiness/Zone	Size	Light Needs
Beautyberry (*Callicarpa*)	5 to 8	4 to 10 ft. tall; 4 to 6 feet wide	Full sun to partial shade
Burning bush (*Euonymous alatus*)	4 to 8	Up to 15 to 20 ft. tall and wide	Full sun to partial shade
Chokeberry (*Aronia*)	3 to 9	6 to 10 ft. tall; 3 to 5 ft. wide	Full sun to partial shade
Eastern wahoo (*Euonymus atropurpureus*)	4 to 9	12 to 24 ft. tall; half as wide	Full sun to partial shade
Harry Lauder's walking stick (*Corylus avellana* 'Contorta')	4 to 8	8 to 10 ft. tall and wide	Full sun to light shade
Meserve hollies (*Ilex x meserve*)	5 to 9	Up to 12 ft. tall and wide	Full sun to partial shade
Hydrangea, oakleaf (*Hydrangea quercifolia*)	5 to 9	4 to 6 ft. tall and wide	Full sun to partial shade
Hydrangea, panicle (*Hydrangea paniculata*)	3 to 8	Up to 15 to 20 ft. tall; 10 to 20 ft. wide	Full sun to partial shade
Hydrangea, snowball (*Hydrangea arborescens*)	3 to 9	3 to 5 ft. tall and wide	Partial shade to full sun
Kerria (*Kerria japonica*)	4 to 9	3 to 6 ft. tall; 6 to 9 ft. wide	Full sun to full shade
Northern bayberry (*Myrica pennsylvanica*)	3 to 6	5 to 12 ft. tall and wide	Full sun to half shade
Red twig dogwood (*Cornus sericea*)	4 to 8	Up to 10 to 15 ft. tall and wide	Full shade or sun
Running serviceberry (*Amelanchier stolonifera*)	4 to 8	4 to 6 ft. tall and wide	Full sun to partial shade
Shrub roses (*Rosa* species)	2 to 9*	Up to 10 ft. tall	Full sun
Southern wax myrtle (*Myrica cerifera*)	8 to 9	10 to 15 ft. tall and wide	Full sun to partial shade
Viburnums (*Viburnum* species)	3 to 9*	Up to 15 ft. tall and 12 ft. wide	Full sun to partial shade
Winterberry (*Ilex verticillata*)	3 to 9	6 to 10 ft. tall and wide	Full sun to partial shade
Witch hazel, common (*Hamamelis virginiana*)	3 to 8	15 to 20 ft. tall and wide	Full sun or shade
Witch hazel, vernal (*Hamamelis vernalis*)	4 to 8	6 to 10 ft. tall and wide	Full sun or shade

*size and hardiness varies with species

indoor arrangements.

The colorful fruit of beautyberry adds a seldom-seen pinkish-purple hue to the winterscape. For the best fruit display, prune regularly and avoid excess fertilizing.

When selecting this plant, look for the American beautyberry, which puts on a good show of berries. But if you like a challenge, search for the purple beautybush (*Callicarpa dichotoma*). It's more difficult to find, but its graceful appearance and impressive fruit display will make the effort worthwhile.

Cool Flowers

Hydrangeas, a shade-garden favorite, take on new character in winter. Both the snowball and panicle types produce flowers that dry on the plant. These brown blooms and tiny, capsule-like fruit provide a nice contrast to the fine texture of nearby overwintering ornamental grasses or perennials.

And let's not forget about flowers. No, I'm not just speaking for southern landscapes. Most gardeners can enjoy the fall and winter blooms of witch hazel. Common witch hazel unfurls fragrant, strap-like flowers for about a month between October and December.

For those who like an early start to the growing season, plant vernal witch hazel. These long bloomers start flowering as early as January in the South, to late February or March in the North. The blooms last for 3 to 4 weeks, providing a much-needed winter flower fix.

Ever-Popular Evergreens

We can't discuss winter shrubs without at least mentioning evergreen conifers. They've long been the backbone of a winter garden, providing a green ray of hope in otherwise barren landscapes.

Although thousands of varieties provide virtually endless possibilities, there are a few basic pointers for selecting the right conifers for your yard.

Look for dwarf pines, spruces or junipers for hot sunny locations. Arborvitae and false cypress add texture with their somewhat lacy appearances. And hemlocks and boxwood provide a bit of year-round greenery in sunny or shady locations.

These shrubs also form great backdrops to the other colorful and interesting shrubs we've discussed. For a winter yard that really stands out, consider planting mixed borders of evergreens, deciduous shrubs and perennials.

Each will lend its own form of beauty to awaken your slumbering yard.

READER TIP

Create a bright spot in your yard during the winter with fruit-bearing shrubs. You'll love the color, and the birds will appreciate the food.

TREE TRIMMING KNOW-HOW

With the right tools and techniques, a professional-quality tree trimming job is a snap.

By Jean Bartholome, Durango, Colorado

Trees are an important part of any yard. And as any tree owner knows, they need occasional trimming. Properly done, trimming controls the shape of the tree, keeps the tree healthy, and eliminates branches that endanger property or could potentially interfere with overhead wires or nearby structures.

Rather than using the haphazard hacking approach, with the right equipment and a little patience, you can trim your own trees and save a bundle over hiring a professional tree trimmer.

A word of advice: The most common mistake is to over-trim a long-neglected tree. If you haven't had the pruning saw out for a long time, take it easy! Your tree will thank you.

The Anatomy of a Tree

In trimming, the most important parts of the tree are the buds (Fig. A and inset). The direction the tree will grow is determined by the buds. When trimming, spare the buds that are pointed in the direction you want the tree to grow.

The terminal (end) buds continue the outward or upward growth. The removal of a terminal bud causes the growth of side branches, making the tree bushier.

Buds that lie dormant for many years are called latent buds. They may only start to grow after the tree has sustained damage to other branches.

Proper Trimming Technique

The photo on page 231 (far right)) shows the best way to trim a branch larger than 2 inches. The initial undercut is important, as it prevents the weight of a branch from pulling a strip of bark off the tree. Your goal is a cut that's close to the trunk, angled up and flush with the branch collar (Fig. B).

When to Cut

The best time to trim living branches (dead branches can be trimmed any time) is late winter, when the tree is dormant, or very early in the spring prior to new growth. Technically, most trees can be trimmed any time, but some trees are more susceptible to disease and infestation if trimmed in the summer. Elms and oaks should be trimmed in dormant season to reduce the chance of developing Dutch elm disease or oak wilt.

What to Cut

When you're ready to trim, you'll have to decide what to cut and what to leave alone. You should look for:

■ **Dead or dying branches.** Cut them back to another healthy branch or back to the main trunk. If trimming a diseased tree, be sure to disinfect tools between each cut.

■ **Branch stubs.** Remove all too-long stubs back to the nearest healthy branch or trunk.

■ **Chances to correct the tree's shape.** Familiarize yourself with how the tree should look naturally. An ideal tree has a strong central trunk and scaffold limbs that are spaced along the trunk with no two of them directly above and shading the other branches.

■ **Branches growing too close together.** The process of removing excess branches is called thinning. It opens up the tree to let in air and light for the leaves on the inside and lower portions of the tree, improving fruit and flower production.

■ **Rubbing branches.** Remove any branches that rub against each other or might in the future. These branches often develop open wounds where insects can enter and disease can start.

■ **Suckers and water sprouts** (see Fig. A). Remove any suckers growing at the base and trunk of the tree, as well as water sprouts that grow on branches vertical to the trunk.

■ **Weak crotches.** Remove branches that have weak or narrow-angle (less than 30 degrees) crotches. These branches are the most likely to tear away in storms, damaging the bark and nearby branches.

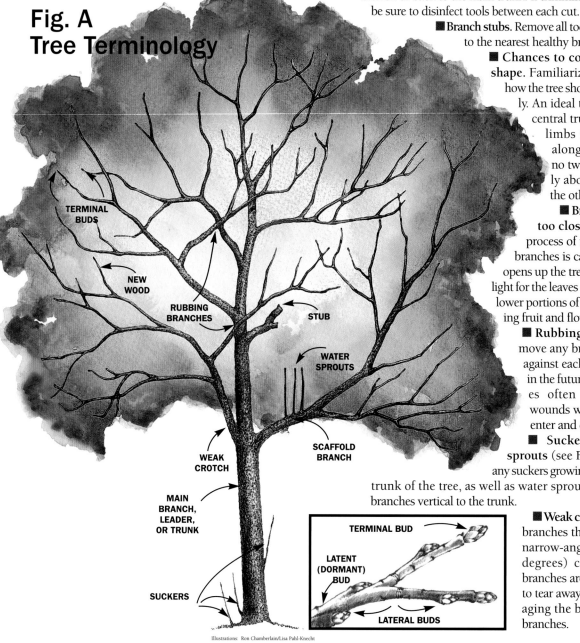

Fig. A
Tree Terminology

TERMINAL BUDS

NEW WOOD

RUBBING BRANCHES

STUB

WATER SPROUTS

WEAK CROTCH

SCAFFOLD BRANCH

MAIN BRANCH, LEADER, OR TRUNK

SUCKERS

TERMINAL BUD

LATENT (DORMANT) BUD

LATERAL BUDS

Illustrations: Ron Chamberlain/Lisa Pahl-Knecht

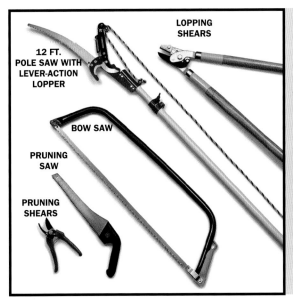

12 FT. POLE SAW WITH LEVER-ACTION LOPPER

LOPPING SHEARS

BOW SAW

PRUNING SAW

PRUNING SHEARS

The Right Tools Make All the Difference

If you buy a few moderately priced tools and rent others as needed, you'll be able to properly maintain your trees for years. With good pruning shears (around $20), you'll be able to cut flush with the branch collar. Position the thin blade on the trunk side to keep the resulting stub as short as you want it to be. Use the shears for branches up to a 1/2 inch thick.

If you have to struggle with the shears, you should move up to the lopping shears (around $45). You'll be able to cut branches around 1-inch thick with loppers. For larger branches, use a pruning saw or a bow saw. Never use a regular shop saw because it will require much more effort and it won't do a good job.

For really high branches, you can rent ($25 per day) or buy (around $48) a pole saw. Some have a small curved saw on the end and others have a cord- or rod-operated lever-action pruning shear.

What About Safety?

First off, always wear eye protection and gloves when trimming trees. Second, stay away from all utility wires.

If you must remove a large limb over a patio or close to your house or garage, take steps to reduce the risk of damage as it drops. One good way to control the drop is to tie a rope around the limb to be cut and throw the other end of the rope over a higher limb. Have a helper keep just enough tension on the rope to control the limb without binding the saw blade. Caution: Watch for the thick end of the limb as it falls. If the job just seems too dangerous to tackle yourself, don't hesitate to call a certified arborist.

Fig. B Cutting Technique

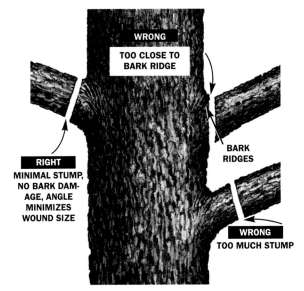

WRONG
TOO CLOSE TO BARK RIDGE

BARK RIDGES

RIGHT
MINIMAL STUMP, NO BARK DAMAGE, ANGLE MINIMIZES WOUND SIZE

WRONG
TOO MUCH STUMP

RIGHT AND WRONG. Correct cutting technique prevents damage to the bark and bark ridges, leaving a clean, slightly angled cut that produces the smallest wound, and avoids long stumps, which are avenues for insect infestation and rot. For the best results, always use sharp tools for the cleanest cuts.

SECOND CUT

FIRST CUT

THIRD CUT

BRANCH COLLAR

EASY AS 1-2-3. Remove a limb using the three-cut method. Make the first cut (an undercut) from below, about 12 inches from the trunk and approximately one-third of the limb's thickness. Make the second cut from above, about 1 inch out from the undercut, going completely through the limb. Then the third cut removes the small remaining piece of limb.

READER TIP

If you are trimming a diseased tree, be sure to disinfect your tools between each cut.

—Jean Bartholome, Durango, Colorado

426

408

432

418

Chapter 9

GLAD YOU ASKED!

416

428

Photos: Viceroy butterfly, Skip Moody/Dembinsky Photo Assoc.; potted plants, Alan and Linda Detrick; yellowthroat, Maslowski Productions.

MAKE IT BLOOM

Discover why your plants are not flowering.

By Melinda Myers, Contributing Editor

"My lilacs didn't bloom this year. I pruned them, fertilized and did everything right. Can you help?"

This is just one of the many blooming mysteries I am asked to solve each year. Unfortunately, there is no single, easy solution. The cause for non-blooming plants can be anything from improper care and unsuitable growing conditions to the weather.

So before you give up on your garden, let's unravel the mystery behind why some of our favorite plants fail to bloom. It might be an easier fix than you think.

Timing Is Everything

I'll start with lilacs (above), since they are one of the most common non-bloomers. Like forsythia, bridal wreath, spirea and other spring flowering shrubs, lilacs set their flower buds in late summer. So if you prune these plants af-

ter the buds are set—from summer through the next bloom time—it will eliminate the spring flowers. If you do need to prune, then you should do so right after the plant has flowered.

If pruning is not the problem for your shrubs, then take a look at the winter weather conditions. Many plants like forsythia or oriental wisterias fail to bloom after a cold winter. While we can't control the weather, we can select plants with flower buds that are more likely to survive winter. There are several to choose from.

The University of Minnesota Landscape Arboretum has introduced many cold-hardy plants, including Meadowlark forsythia and Minnesota snowflake mock orange. If you live in Zones 4 to 5 and are looking for wisteria, try the Kentucky cultivar (*Wisteria macrostachya*). Unlike its oriental cousins, this wisteria has shorter, 12-inch

blooms that appear with the leaves. It's not as impressive as a Japanese wisteria in bloom, but it's certainly better than no blooms at all.

Southern gardeners have the opposite problem with weather. Plants in warmer zones may not have blooms due to a lack of cold. Certain plants like lilacs and spring-flowering bulbs need a cold period to set their flowers. If this affects you, look for varieties that set blooms in your region, or buy precooled bulbs and flowering plants suited to your mild climate.

Late-spring cold snaps can interfere with some flowering plants. Though they are cold hardy when dormant, the flower buds are subject to frost damage as the protective bud scales separate, exposing the tender petals. Some early-spring blossoms are damaged by the cold, while others never expand beyond the swollen bud stage.

Older and Wiser

Another reason a plant might lack blossoms is from a lack of maturity. Flowering is part of the reproductive process in plants, and they need to reach a certain level of maturity to reproduce.

For annuals, this happens in the first year. For biennials and most perennials, flowers emerge in the second year. And for trees and shrubs, it could be years.

Most nut trees don't blossom and produce fruit until they are 15 years old or more. Standard apple trees are usually 6 or 7 years old before they begin to flower. Landscape plants like wisteria (right) and trumpet vine may take as many as 7 years to reach a flowering stage. In these cases, all you can do is be patient.

Excess fertilization can also interfere with flowering. For example, trumpet vines love nitrogen and will steal it from any source that their roots can reach. This overindulgence leads to large plants that are covered with leaves but lack overall blooms.

Avoid high-nitrogen fertilizer near these plants. And if that doesn't work, try giving your trumpet vine a little root pruning. Don't overdo it—that can cause your plant to

SPRING FLOWERS. The cause of non-blooming plants could be as simple as timing. Forsythia (top) and lilac (opposite page) both set their flower buds in late summer. If you prune after the buds are set, you will not have flowers come spring. Other plants like wisteria (above) may take years before flowering.

die—but a little can help encourage flowering.

A lack of other nutrients, such as phosphorous, can also result in a lack of blooms. This nutrient encourages root growth, flowering and fruiting. But don't reach for the fertilizer. Many soils are already high in phosphorous, and adding more can be harmful to the plant and the environment as well. This is a case where you should take some extra time to test your soil.

Sunlight can also interfere with flowering, so make sure your plants have proper growing conditions. Check the label or ask your local Extension service to match the right plant to your growing conditions.

Next time you need to solve a blooming mystery, take a few clues from your growing environment and gardening practices. You might be surprised to find that the answer is likely within your reach!

'GLAD YOU ASKED!'

Expert answers your garden questions.

By Melinda Myers, Contributing Editor

A Clue About Blue

Do blue spruces bloom? This one (below) is about 40 years old, and I'd never seen anything but plain pinecones grow on it until these bright-pink blooms emerged. —Donald Schweyer, Hudson, Indiana

Melinda: Although your tree's bright-pink display is impossible to miss, the blooms of spruce trees are often much more subtle.

Spruce trees produce separate male and female flowers on the same tree. The pollen-bearing male flowers can be quite colorful, like the ones on your tree. These will release pollen to the female flowers, resulting in the development of seed-filled cones. The cones are actually the fruit that forms once fertilization occurs.

After they've done their job, the male flowers dry up and drop off the tree. Though it happens every year, it often goes unnoticed.

Pretty Surprise

Last spring, this lovely flower (left) appeared in my mother's garden. Do you know what it is? Will we see it again this spring?

—Pat Pietras
Weeki Wachee, Florida

Melinda: This beautiful bloom is commonly known as rose turmeric (botanically it's *Curcuma elata*). It is one of a group of 40 plants that are native to the rain forests of Asia and Australia.

Since it's hardy in Zones 7 to 11, you should see it next season. This adaptable plant grows best in partial shade, but will tolerate full shade through full sun as long as the soil is moist.

Ready for the Holidays

I'd like to bring my potted red and green caladiums inside as holiday decorations. However, I've heard they must rest in winter to return in spring. Is this true?
—Amanda Henry, Wimberly, Texas

Melinda: The shorter, cooler days of autumn usually send this plant into its resting stage. But all you need to extend its show of colorful leaves is a little extra warmth and some added light.

Caladiums are tropical plants that can be grown as perennials outdoors in Zones 10 and 11 or as annuals in colder climates. To maintain them indoors, grow the plants in a warm area with 16 hours of light. Use artificial lights to extend the natural daylight.

For added humidity, place the plants on a saucer of pebbles that's filled with water. The pot should sit on the pebbles, not directly in the water.

Then allow them to rest for several months after the holidays by placing them in a cooler and darker location.

When the weather warms in the spring, set your plants outdoors and get ready for another spectacular display of striking foliage.

Weeds Gone Wild

How can I get rid of the wild strawberries (like the ones below) that are invading my backyard? They are growing into my lawn.
— Jean Kline
Reading, Pennsylvania

Melinda: Pulling is the only nonchemical solution. Or you can spot treat these unwanted plants with Roundup or Finale. These total vegetation killers will destroy the tops, roots and runners of these weeds. Just be careful not to get any of these chemicals on nearby grass or flowers—it will kill them, too.

Try painting the weed killer directly on the strawberry plant to avoid damaging the surrounding plants. Or create a makeshift shield to contain the herbicide.

To do this, remove the bottom of a plastic milk jug or carton. Place it over the weed, keeping grass and other desirable plants outside the container. Spray the weed through the top and wait for the dripping to stop. Carefully move the jug to the next weed.

As always, read and follow the manufacturer's label directions and wear the recommended protective gear when applying any herbicide.

Going Nuts

About 6 years ago, I planted two self-pollinating pecan trees. Though the trees are growing well, they have yet to bloom or produce any pecans. What's wrong? — Chuck Himebauch, Port Byron, Illinois

Melinda: Patience is the answer to your problem. All plants must reach a mature state before they produce flowers and fruit. For nut trees, that waiting period can be as long as 10 to 20 years.

Mulch the soil around the trees and water thoroughly when needed. By taking proper care of your trees over the next few years, you'll ensure a future full of bountiful and tasty pecan harvests.

Unknown Beauty

This beautiful wildflower (at left) shows up in the woods behind my house every June. Can you tell me what it is?
— Karen Britton Tamaroa, Illinois

Melinda: Known as Indian pink or Maryland pinkroot (its botanical name is *Spigelia marilandica*), this beauty is native to moist woodlands. You can find Indian pink from Maryland south to Florida and west to Texas, Missouri and Oklahoma. Watch closely, and you'll notice the colorful flowers open from the bottom up during spring and summer.

If you'd like to extend its display, remove the spent flowers. They thrive in fertile well-draining soil and partial shade.

Mysterious Beauty

I planted this perennial (below) 20 years ago, but I don't know what it is. It's hardy, drought tolerant and blooms in May. Can you solve this mystery?
— June Lake, Cayce, South Carolina

Melinda: A quick look may remind you of a cornflower. But the bloom time, foliage and growth habit reveal it's a Stokes' aster (*Stokesia laevis*). This native of the southern United States is hardy in Zones 5 to 9, and blooms from late spring through most of summer. Northern gardeners, however, have to wait for summer to enjoy its show.

This lavender beauty grows 12 to 24 inches tall with a mounded growth habit. Plant it in full sun with well-draining soil for best results. Add mulch in winter to increase its hardiness in northern gardens.

Dogwood Is a Dud

I have a dogwood tree that never blooms. How can I coax spring flowers out of my reluctant tree?
— Hattie Wiant, Weston, West Virginia

Melinda: Age, fertilization, pruning and sunlight all affect flowering.

Young trees will often bloom in the containers when you buy them, but expend their energy developing a root system when transplanted into a landscape. Once established, however, the blooms should return.

The second most common problem is overfertilization. Too much nitrogen can produce large plants with few or no flowers. Make sure your dogwood isn't getting extra fertilizer from a nearby garden or lawn area.

Though shade tolerant, dogwoods need sufficient light to flower. Those growing in excess shade have sparse growth and very few blossoms.

Lastly, save all pruning chores until after the tree blooms or should have bloomed. Flowering dogwoods set their flower buds the previous season, so winter pruning might eliminate the spring show.

Family Flower

My grandmother gave me the seeds to this pretty plant (at left). What is it?

—Shari Lemke
Waterloo, Wisconsin

Melinda: Known as Texas plume or scarlet gilia (*Ipomopsis rubra*), this biennial makes a nice addition to a naturalized planting area or perennial garden.

During its first year, the plant grows only 3 inches tall and produces no flowers. The next year, however, it stretches toward the sky and can reach heights of 6 feet. The long, orange-red flower spikes provide color throughout summer.

Grow it in full sun and well-drained soil for the best results. Because it's a biennial—flowering only in its second year—sow seeds several years in a row to ensure colorful blooming plants each summer.

Mosquito Control

I'd like to discourage mosquitoes from breeding in my backyard pond. Is there anything I can add to the water? —Gwyn Pollard, Ontario, Canada

Melinda: Water gardens that contain fish or have moving water usually are not the cause of overabundant backyard mosquitoes. Standing water in trash cans, discarded tires and birdbaths is more often the culprit.

Still, you can use a larvacide to kill any mosquito larvae that might be in your pond.

Use ones that contain Bacillus thuringiensis israelensis (also known as Bti), a bacterium that kills the larvae without harming fish, people or wildlife. It's available in dough-nut-shaped blocks, called dunks, which you can place into the water to control these pests.

A Vine to Share

I'd like to share my honeysuckle vine with friends. Can I start it from a cutting? If so, how?

—Sue Shepherd, Greenfield, Indiana

Melinda: Woody plants, such as shrubs and perennial vines, are tricky to start from cuttings.

To do this, take several 4- to 6-inch cuttings from the tips of the new growth in spring or early summer, and dip them in a rooting hormone. Place the treated cuttings in moist sand, vermiculite or perlite, and set them in a shaded location.

Once rooted, plant the cuttings in a container filled with a well-draining potting mix. Move the established plants to the garden in fall, or keep them in a protected location and bury the pot over winter, then plant them the following spring.

Layering is another way to propagate vines. To use this method, bend a stem to the ground or to a container of potting mix, and nick it 9 inches below the tip. Bury this portion of the stem, leaving the tip above the ground and the stem attached to the parent plant. Roots will form on the buried portion. Once rooted, disconnect the stem from the parent plant and move to a permanent location.

Strange Sight

Several years after we planted this evergreen, it grew a section at the top that looks like a ball (below). We've never seen anything like it. Can you explain how this happened?

—Lucille Adams
Reynolds, North Dakota

Melinda: The tree's bizarre growth is called a broom. Brooms can be caused by insects, disease, environmental stresses or plant mutation.

A single broom on a healthy tree is usually a harmless mutation. In fact, cuttings and seeds from cones produced on these growths are sometimes used to propagate many of the uniquely shaped or dwarf evergreens that are available in the market today.

Bird's Nest spruce is one popular plant that had its start from a broom that grew on a Norway spruce.

You may want to contact a local nursery to see if their propagator is interested in trying to develop a new variety using cones from the broom on your tree. Otherwise, just continue enjoying this unique feature and the attention it brings from passersby.

Not What You Think

I watched this lovely cactus bloom (below) over the course of a month, but haven't had any luck identifying it. Can you help?

—Dieter Hain
Walla Walla, Washington

Melinda: This plant has the look of a cactus, but it's really a bromeliad. This particular bromeliad is known as urn or vase plant (the botanical name is *Aechema fasciata*) and is one of over 200 bromeliad species.

Most are native to rain forests and are a type of epiphyte, meaning they anchor onto trees or shrubs with their roots, and use their leaves to gather water and nutrients from the environment. Once the flower fades, the plant will start to decline.

But don't worry. New plants called offsets or pups will soon appear. These can be divided and planted in individual containers.

Mystery Growths

These weird growths (below) showed up in my front lawn last summer. They lasted 1 day, and then withered away and disappeared. They came up about 2 feet from where I had cut down a plum tree. Do you know what they are?

—Ken Buchholz,
New Hope, Pennsylvania

Melinda: These strange growths are mushrooms, the fruiting bodies of fungus that usually grow underground.

A type of fungus that feeds on rotting wood in the soil is like-

ly feeding on the decaying roots of your plum tree, helping speed up decomposition. When it's wet, the fungus sprouts mushrooms. These are not harmful to your lawn, they just look bad. When dry weather returns, the mushrooms shrivel and disappear, while the fungus continues its work underground.

As soon as the plum roots have fully decomposed and there is no food for the fungus, it—along with the mushrooms—will disappear. In the meantime, you may want to rake and destroy any mushrooms that pop up to prevent kids and pets from eating them.

A Pox on Phlox

How can I eliminate white mold from my garden phlox? The plants continue to bloom, but they don't look very nice.

—Mary Boocher, Tipp City, Ohio

Melinda: It sounds like powdery mildew has infected your plants. Gardeners growing other flowers, including bee balm, lilacs and zinnia, may know this disease as well.

Avoid the problem by using resistant cultivars of garden phlox, such as David, Kathryn and the Flame Series, or try its look-alike cousin, *Phlox maculata*.

You can reduce the problem on susceptible plants with proper management of the growing conditions. Garden phlox should be in full sun with good air circulation. Accomplish this by allowing plenty of room between plants, or by thinning individual plants in spring—removing about one-quarter of the stems as they emerge.

Fungicides can also reduce the symptoms. You'll need to treat the plants weekly once the disease appears. Remember to always follow the manufacturer's directions when selecting or using fungicides and other chemicals.

A Name for Lily

I love these beautiful blooms (below), but I have no idea what they are. Can you identify them and let me know if it's okay to leave them outside over winter?

—Marge Moffitt, Armstrong, Iowa

Melinda: A relative of the amaryllis, this plant is commonly called zephyr lily, rain lily or rocket lily (botanically known as *Zephyranthes grandiflora*). It is hardy only in a few southern areas—Zones 10 and 11—so all other gardeners must winter it indoors.

This is a fairly easy plant to grow. Those who'd like to try can purchase and pot rain lily bulbs in spring. Then water the plant often enough to keep the soil moist, and use a dilute flowering houseplant fertilizer once the flowers appear.

In late August, begin to nudge the plant into dormancy, so it will stop actively growing. Cut back on watering so leaves begin to wither. Once the leaves are dried, store the plant in a cool, dark location.

Bring your rain lily out of hiding in February to start the growing season again. Place it in a sunny window in your home, and keep the soil slightly moist—leaves and blossoms will soon follow.

Toppling Flowers

My recent crop of zinnias and gladiolas were quite spindly. The zinnias grew 5 feet tall and the glads reached 6 feet. The stems were so weak they could barely support the blooms, even with the help of stakes. What happened?
—Jo Smith, Summerville, South Carolina

Melinda: Lack of light or excess nitrogen can cause the growth you describe, so take a look at the conditions in this garden area.

Have your trees matured and started shading these plants? Perhaps a new fence, shed or other addition is blocking some much-needed sunlight.

Next, take a soil test to find out what, if any, fertilizer is needed. Avoid high-nitrogen fertilizer that can promote excess growth.

And finally, monitor the soil's moisture. Excess rain or watering can lead to the spindly growth you've noticed as well as certain disease problems.

Stars in the House

This houseplant has unique, star-shaped blooms. Do you know what it is, and can you tell me more about it?
—Suzanne O'Bryan
Sheffield, Texas

Melinda: A favorite of mine, the wax plant, known botanically as *Hoya,* has attractive foliage and, when the conditions are right, will produce these beautiful, fragrant blooms.

Grow this houseplant in a container filled with a well-drained potting mix in bright light. Water thoroughly whenever the top few inches of soil start to dry. Keep the soil more moist during the summer when the plant is actively growing. Allow the soil to dry slightly when the plant is resting over winter.

High humidity in spring and summer followed by cooler temperatures and drier soil in winter will encourage flowering. Limit pruning. Many wax plants develop long, leafless flowering stems. Leave these and the shorter flower stems intact for next year's blooms.

Coneflower Seeds

I often admire the purple coneflowers (like the ones at right) growing in my neighbor's yard. Can you plant them using seeds from the cone tops?
—Patty Duffield
Strange Creek, West Virginia

Susan M. Perren

Melinda: Yes, and anyone growing purple coneflowers probably would be happy to share the offspring of these prolific seeders.

Collect seeds in fall, and sow outside or store in the refrigerator over winter. Stored seed can be started indoors or planted directly outdoors in spring.

You won't see flowers until the second season. Also, the offspring of hybrids may look different than the parents.

Vine Won't Climb

I planted hummingbird vine 2 years ago, but it will not grow. The vine won't even try to climb the fence that's next to it. Can you give me some advice? *—Thomas Lowe*
Constantine, Michigan

Melinda: Several plants go by the name hummingbird vine. The large orange and yellow flowered trumpet vine (*Campsis radicans,* like the one at right) attaches to structures with aerial roots.

The bright-orange, coral-red or scarlet blooming honeysuckle vine (*Lonicera*) also attracts hummingbirds. It attaches to structures by twining around the support.

Once you know which variety you have, make sure you give it the right support. A brick wall is good for trumpet vine, while a trellis or arbor is more suitable for the honeysuckle. Secure the branches to the structure with twine or staking tape. Once the vine makes contact, it should continue to grow and cling to the structure.

Proper growing conditions and care should get your vine off and growing. Trumpet vine prefers full sun and well-drained soil. Honeysuckle vines like full sun to part shade.

Afraid of Heights

My friends have a ranch in the mountains of Montana. Due to the high altitude, flower buds don't open well. Any suggestions? *—Barbara Wingel, Frenchtown, New Jersey*

Melinda: Your friends and other high-altitude gardeners face some of the most challenging growing conditions. The cold nights, scorching sun, thin and rocky soil, short growing season and the hungry wildlife make it difficult.

The best place to start is with plant selection. Encourage your friends to include native plants that are adapted to these harsh conditions. They can contact local nature centers for sources and care of native plants. Local garden clubs and Extension services will have other helpful tips.

In addition, they may want to try arctic poppy, alpine aster, bellflower, blanket flower, columbine, gilia (*Ipomoea rubra*), lupine, penstemon, peony, dianthus and soapwort.

Trees from Seeds

I would like to start a new tree from the seeds that come off of red maples. How should I do this?　　　—*Ruth Edwards*
Poland, Maine

Melinda: I always look to nature for clues about starting trees and shrubs from seeds. The true red maple (*Acer rubrum*) produces seeds in early summer. These don't need a special treatment to germinate. Store them in a cool (41°) location for 60 to 75 days to increase sprouting success.

The other "red" maple is truly a red-leafed variety of Norway maple, botanically known as *Acer platanoides*. Its seeds ripen in the fall. They drop to the ground, get chilled through winter and sprout the following spring. To start these seeds, mimic nature by storing them in moist peat moss in a cool location for 90 to 120 days.

After storing the seeds, plant them in a well-drained potting or seed-starting mix. Place in a warm location and keep the soil moist. As soon as the seeds sprout, move to a sunny location or under artificial lights. Water thoroughly and often enough to keep the soil moist.

Many gardeners grow their seedlings in containers for a season or two before moving them into the ground. If you do this, be sure to sink the potted seedlings into the ground for winter to help insulate the roots against the cold.

Change It Up

How often should you replace the soil with potted plants (like the ones below)? Can you walk me through the process?
—*Jo Lough, Bloomington, Indiana*

Melinda: Outdoors, I try to replace the soil in my annual containers with each season. I would rather invest in new potting mix than to risk the buildup of disease that could wipe out a planting. I do recycle the soil, though. I combine old potting mix with my

Alan and Linda Detrick

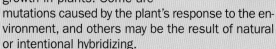
compost to use in my outdoor garden area.

Indoors, I let the plants and my growing goals dictate how to proceed. Stunted houseplants with undersized new growth and those where the water quickly passes through the pot are good candidates for a change. A few days after watering is a good time to relocate the plants. The soil is moist enough to hold together but not too wet to handle. Slide the plant out of the pot. Loosen or cut any roots that are growing around in a circle. Then move it to a pot one size larger.

Avoid the temptation to move plants into a much larger container. If you do this, the plant will spend its energy sending out roots instead of top growth. Plus, the extra soil will hold moisture, increasing the risk of root rot.

If you're trying to slow the growth of larger plants, allow them to stay in the same container a bit longer. Flowering houseplants and cacti prefer to be in pots. You even may consider pruning the roots of larger plants that have reached the maximum pot size available.

Berry Compatible

The first year I planted blackberry bushes, they produced lots of fruit. Then I planted raspberries right next to them, and the berries dried up. Is it true that you should not plant these two berries together?　　　—*Ben Friesen*
Hutchinson, Kansas

Melinda: There's no problem growing blackberries and raspberries in the same garden. Just give them plenty of growing room and properly prune them. Overcrowded plantings can result in anthracnose. This fungal disease causes purplish lesions on the stems and crumbly, dry fruit. Reduce the problem with proper pruning and regular thinning. Better circulation helps leaves dry quickly, lessening the risk of disease.

Remove canes that bear fruit to ground level right after harvest. Fall raspberries can be pruned to the ground each autumn if you do not want a summer crop.

In late winter, thin the remaining raspberry canes to three or four per square foot, removing no more than a quarter of the growth of each stem. At the same time, tend to your blackberries by removing any dead canes. Then cut back the remaining stems to about 15 inches. This will reduce disease problems and increase the harvest.

Hibernating for Winter

I have a beautiful bougainvillea plant. How should I care for it over the winter? —*Mrs. Alex Sesko*
Winsted, Connecticut

Melinda: Keeping bougainvillea and other tropical plants alive over winter can often be challenging. With small plants, place them in a sunny window or under artificial light. Then just water and manage like your other houseplants.

Large plants that won't comfortably fit in your home may need cool storage so they go dormant for the winter. To

Stumped by the Stem

Every year, this flower comes up—no leaves, just a stem—then it produces flowers in July. What is it?
—Bob and Linda Knuteson
Arlington, Wisconsin

Melinda: This bloom is sure to surprise and please. Its long, strappy leaves emerge in spring. The quiet plant is often overlooked or forgotten after it dries up and disappears... then surprise! Beautiful flowers, without a leaf in site, appear in summer or early fall.

This growth pattern is the source of its common names—surprise lily, resurrection lily or autumn amaryllis.

Though it goes by many common names, it is known botanically as *Lycoris squamigera*.

The plant prefers full to partial sun and well-drained soil. Most books rate it only hardy to Zones 5 or 6, but many gardeners like you have had luck growing it in Zone 4.

store, find a cool place that doesn't freeze. Water thoroughly whenever the soil is crumbly and only slightly moist to prevent the roots from drying.

I know several gardeners that have successfully kept their bougainvilleas alive for more than 5 years. Then there are the rest who allow the plants to die quickly from a hard fall frost. You can compost the remains, and start with fresh plants each spring.

Flustered Forester

I spotted this tree (above) growing on a sand hill in southeastern Texas and can't determine its identity—and I'm a retired forester! Can you help? —*Jack Dillon*
Cleveland, Texas

Melinda: Your mystery tree is a callery pear. It is often used as a street tree or landscape plant because of its ornamental value. It also has a tough drought- and pollution-tolerant nature, which landscapers love.

The small tree is covered with white blossoms in spring followed by the small, brown "pears." The glossy-green leaves are beautiful all summer, turning a brilliant red in late fall.

This tree was introduced from China to the United States in an attempt to breed disease (fireblight) resistance into our edible pears. Instead, it moved into the landscape as a tree.

The proliferation of fruit has made it an invasive plant in some regions. As birds eat the fruit, they distribute them throughout natural areas. This is probably how your mystery tree found its way to the sand hill.

Root of the Problem

Is it okay to plant poplar trees near a water line? I've heard the trees send out roots to nearby water sources and disrupt the lines. —*Mary Ann Gove*
Cottonwood, Arizona

Melinda: You're right to avoid poplars near a water line, but tree roots in general like the damp, oxygen-rich soil above sewer and water lines. When a crack develops in a sewer

Cacti Conundrum

My sister-in-law has a collection of cacti in her home, and during a recent visit, I took a photo of this lovely bloom. Can you help me identify it?

—Hazel Graham, Portland, Oregon

Melinda: Take a close look at the flower, and you can see why it is commonly called orchid cactus. This large group of cactus, known as *Epiphyllum*, contains many members that produce red, purple, white or yellow flowers that are often fragrant in spring or summer.

It's best to grow these in a bright location, allowing the soil to dry slightly between waterings. Keep the plant a little drier during its rest period (when it's not actively growing) and slightly moister when in bloom. In winter, give the plant a break from flowering by moving it to a cooler (50°) location.

Cool temperatures and drier soil during the rest period will encourage blooms. Move it to a warmer location when the plant is flowering or actively growing.

---

line, moist vapor is released and the tree roots follow this to the pipe. The roots infiltrate the crack and eventually cause a blockage.

Clay tile and even concrete can be vulnerable to tree-root invasion. PVC pipe, with fewer and tighter-fitting joints, is less susceptible.

Moisture-loving trees like poplar, willow, elm, ash, silver maple and birch are common culprits when it comes to blocked sewer lines. Avoid planting these near water and sewer lines to reduce the risk of clogged pipes.

All Mixed Up

I planted a wildflower mix several years ago, and now I can't get rid of the yarrow. It is beginning to take over! How can I control it? —Marion Critz, Bay Shore, New York

Melinda: Thanks for sharing your story as a warning to others. Many wildflower mixes contain plants that may not be native to your region, and others contain seeds like yarrow that can become weeds.

You can reduce the yarrow population with some effort and persistence. The only nonchemical method is to weed them out by hand.

You can also try a total vegetation killer like Roundup or Finale. If you do this, be sure to protect nearby plants. A Master Gardener I know has a good method for this. Cut out the bottom of a plastic milk jug and place it over the weed. Then spray the herbicide through the opening. Once the product drips off the leaves, move the container to the next plant. This is time-consuming, but it keeps nearby plants safe.

New vinegar and clove oil-based herbicides are now on the market. These should be more environmentally friendly, but may require repeat applications.

If more than 50% of your garden is yarrow, you may just want to start over. Kill off all the plants in the area and start with a weed-free site. Then use a wildflower mix from a local and reliable source.

Jack's Beanstalk?

We don't know if this strange plant (below) in our yard is a weed or a tree. I cut it down, but it always comes back. This picture shows just 1 year of growth. The plant was nearly 22 feet tall! Can you tell us what this is? Should we be concerned because it is growing near our foundation?

—Leroy Parsons Rogersville, Tennessee

Melinda: Your mystery plant is a princess tree (*Paulownia tomentosa*). But whether it's a weed or not depends on where you live.

Its invasive nature has lead some states, including yours, to add it to their list of invasive exotic plants. In this case, it should be avoided in the garden.

This tree was brought to the United States from Japan over 150 years ago. Gardeners liked its fast growth, impressive foliage and fragrant, lavender flowers, and they thought it would be a great addition to the backyard. However, that same fast growth, as well as its plentiful seeds, made it a problem plant in some areas.

This tree can reach 30 to 40 feet in height and width, much too big for its current location. Save yourself some money and help the environment by digging it up.

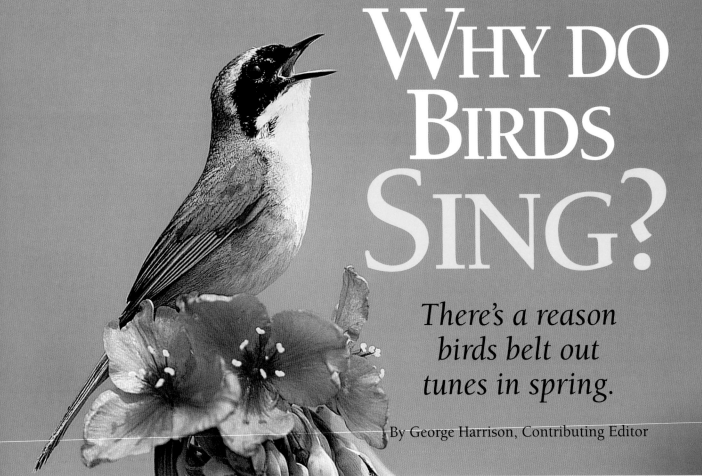

WHY DO BIRDS SING?

There's a reason birds belt out tunes in spring.

By George Harrison, Contributing Editor

"In the spring, a young man's fancy lightly turns to thoughts of love," the saying goes.

The same may be said of birds. That's because spring is when most birds turn to family obligations—they mate, build nests, lay eggs and raise young.

Singing is an important part of the breeding cycle, which begins when migratory male birds reach their nesting grounds. They usually arrive before the female birds, giving each male time to establish a nesting territory and defend it against other males of the same species.

Singing is a form of communication that reinforces this ownership—announcing through song that "this is my territory."

Female songbirds usually arrive on the nesting grounds a week or two after the males. As they pass through, they hear the males singing. If a song attracts them, a female will stop to look over the male, check his plumage to determine if he has desirable genes, and then explore his territory. It is the female that selects a mate.

Music to Their Ears

Birdsongs aren't always sweet music. Male ring-necked pheasants crow like chickens, mourning doves coo somberly, kingfishers rattle and owls hoot.

Woodpeckers peck on a sounding board, such as the siding of a house. This springtime hammering is not an effort to find food. It's a communication with other woodpeckers.

Male ruffed grouse attract mates and defend territories by "drumming," a booming noise they make by beating the air with their primary wing feathers, usually while perched on a fallen tree or log. Other grouse, like prairie chickens and sage grouse, make a booming sound by filling the air sacs on the sides of their necks with air and exhaling.

Singing usually is a male trait, but some female songbirds croon, too. Female northern cardinals create a softer version of the male's song, sometimes in unison with their mates. This likely is a courtship ritual to strengthen the bond between a pair.

Surprisingly, a bird's mouth or bill sometimes plays little or no part in singing. In fact, birds like warblers and vireos can sing with their bills closed, or with their bills full of food. That's because birds create the sound deep in their throats by exhaling air from their lungs.

However, many birds do belt out tunes in a loud, showy fashion, like the common yellowthroat or the eastern meadowlark.

Although we're not entirely sure how birds learn to sing, we do know it's a combination of heredity and mimicking. Juvenile songbirds will begin to rehearse their songs during their first autumn and winter. They graduate to mature singing during their first spring. These younger birds will hear other males of their species and imitate them, often adding a slight touch of their own.

There is a big difference between a bird's song and its

call. Singing usually is a more melodious sound, while calling often is sharper and more direct.

Calls are used either as a loud alarm note to communicate danger, or as quiet chatter to locate mates and other birds of their species. For example, a northern cardinal's loud "chip" call is very different from its musical "what-cheer, what-cheer, birdie, birdie, birdie" song.

Northern cardinals (like the one at right) are one of the few songbirds that sing almost all year long. At my southeastern Wisconsin home, I hear them at least 10 months a year. It is a welcome sound when the woods are snow-covered.

Early Bird Gets the Worm

The best time to hear birds sing is at dawn on a spring morning. Often called the "dawn chorus," birdsongs reach a fever pitch at daybreak in late May and early June, the peak of breeding season in most parts of the United States and Canada. It is well worth getting up early to hear nature's finest musical show. Sometimes it is so loud that the birds drown out each other's finest efforts.

Though most songbirds sing short songs, averaging only 2 to 6 seconds each, a few are known for continuously repeating their song.

Birders have made a sport of counting some amazingly high numbers of repetitive, nonstop songs. One was a male song sparrow in Ohio that performed 2,305 songs nonstop. In Virginia, I heard a whip-poor-will repeat its nighttime chorus at least 800 times before I fell asleep. The world record could be a red-eyed vireo that sang 22,197 times in a single day.

The songs of birds are one of nature's great gifts. Not only are they a treat to the ear, but bird-watchers who recognize the sounds can easily identify the singer without seeing it.

CARRY A TUNE. Spring is a great time to hear the feathered friends singing in your backyard. Below, a northern cardinal and an eastern meadowlark belt out tunes. Opposite page, a common yellowthroat puts on quite a show during his song.

Photos this page: Marie Read

BIRD-WATCHER'S SECRET
Try imitating a bird's song to draw them into your backyard. Or if that doesn't work, try "squeaking," which is essentially a kissing sound.

'GLAD YOU ASKED!'

Birding expert answers your questions.

By George Harrison, Contributing Editor

Grosbeak Guest

I live in the Rocky Mountains and saw this colorful visitor (below) at my bird feeder one day. What is it?
—*Richard Loos, Granby, Colorado*

George: Your mystery bird is a male pine grosbeak, an inconspicuous bird that lives in the spruce and fir forests of the northern United States and Canada.

Often seen in small groups, its main diet in winter is berries. Though it's not rare to see pine grosbeaks in the forest, they only occasionally visit backyard bird feeders.

1-Year Lease

Last summer, a pair of bushtits raised a brood of four young in an elaborate, 9-inch-long pouch in my climbing rose. Will they use the nest again this year?
—*Bernice Lebeau, Whittier, California*

George: Most birds, including bushtits, do not use a nest for more than one brood. The exceptions are those birds that use birdhouses for nesting, such as bluebirds and chickadees.

There is a very good reason why birds that build nests in trees, shrubs or on the ground need a new nest for each brood. By the time the youngsters are ready to leave the nests, they've grown so much that the nest has expanded to accommodate their size. In doing so, the nest is unfit for another brood.

Cardinal Divide

Although we are longtime birders, we can't figure why there are no northern cardinals west of the continental divide. They seem to be so widespread in the East. Any ideas? —*Nancy Howard, Puyallup, Washington*

George: There are records of northern cardinals sighted in California and Nevada, and breeding records in western and southern Arizona and throughout Texas

However, you are correct that cardinals generally are not found west of the Rockies, probably because the habitat and food available are not suitable to this species.

With the popularity of backyard bird feeding, northern cardinals have already extended their historically southern range well into the North and West, and perhaps someday they will appear at a feeder in your yard in Washington.

Keeping a Neat Nest

I watched as this house wren (below) came and went from its nest all day. What is that object it's carrying away from the birdhouse?
—*Donna Neal Odenton, Maryland*

George: That white object is called a fecal sac. Nature has devised an extraordinary way to keep birds' nests clean by having nestlings pass their waste in a little white sac.

This makes it easy for the parent birds to carry it away from the nest in order to avoid attracting predators.

Pretty Mystery

I spotted this unusual little visitor (below) in my birdbath. What kind of bird is it? —*Frances Collier*
Ogdensburg, New York

George: Your mystery bird is an ovenbird, a member of the wood warbler family. Easy to identify by their markings, this bird's orange crown patch and a heavily streaked white breast make it a real standout.

Like other members of the warbler family, the ovenbird migrates in the fall to spend winter in the warmth of southern Mexico and Central America.

The stout ovenbird gets its name from the shape of its domed nest, which resembles an oven. Usually found on the leaf-covered forest floor, the neatly formed nest is typically made with grass, leaves and twigs.

Keeping It Clean

How can I protect the inside of my wooden bird feeder from water damage and mold, and what's the best method for cleaning out old birdseed?

—*Beatrice Bailey, Newcomb, New York*

George: Start by trying to prevent water from getting into your feeder. You can mount a dome above it to keep out the rain, snow and, perhaps, even squirrels. If wind continues to blow rain and snow into the feeder, try applying caulk to the corners and cracks where the moisture is entering.

To clean it, a good shot from a garden or pressure hose will wash away the old clumps of seed.

Buzz Off

Do you have advice to keep flies away from oriole feeders? I bought a feeder that holds grape jelly and fruit, but, unfortunately, the bugs seem more interested in it than the birds are. —*Karina Alpers*
La Porte City, Iowa

George: Switch to sugar water to attract and keep orioles throughout the summer and into September.

Sugar water (one part sugar to four parts water, boil then cool mixture before serving) in an orange, plastic oriole feeder is easy to maintain and will attract a minimum number of bees and flies.

Don't Go, Goldfinch

American goldfinches appear at my feeders near the end of April, then disappear about 2 weeks later. How can I convince these birds to stick around?

—*Doug Goodgion, Falls Church, Virginia*

George: In May, American goldfinches may move from your backyard to habitat that's more suitable to their nesting needs. They seek out fields with plenty of thistle plants, which they use to build nests and feed young.

All you can do to keep them around is offer the foods they prefer, such as nyjer (thistle) or sunflower seeds in the shell or medium cracked.

Also, it's possible that these finches have been in your backyard before April as well. Their olive-brown winter plumage is so dramatically different from the yellow summer plumage they begin to sport in spring, that it's possible they have been visiting your feeders incognito.

Strange-Looking Sack

I found this strange object (below) near our farm. It was originally hanging from one of our cottonwood trees. Can you tell me what it is?

—*Karen Provost, Navarre, Ohio*

George: It appears to be the nest of a Baltimore oriole.

An oriole nest is made in the shape of a pouch with the entrance at the top. But the female oriole weaves the nest in such a way that it can close up like a purse, sometimes concealing its identity as a nest.

Often suspended from a branch near the top of a tree, the female incorporates various plant fibers and hair into the nest. This woven sack can be as deep as 8 inches.

Frequently, Baltimore orioles will return to the same territory in subsequent years, though they seldom reuse old nests.

Mealtime for Mockers

I always see northern mockingbirds at my birdbath, but never at my feeder. What types of food should I set out for them? —*Wilma Mitchell, Fayetteville, Tennessee*

George: Northern mockingbirds are omnivorous, with about half of their diet consisting of various insects, such as beetles, ants, bees, butterflies, wasps and grasshoppers.

But mockingbirds are also quite fond of both wild and cultivated fruit. If you want to attract them to your bird feeder, simply place small pieces of fruit on a tray feeder or inside an empty grapefruit half. Pieces of apples or citrus, or grapes and berries are an open invitation for mockers to dine.

Mystery Visitor

I spotted this unusual bird (below) at my backyard finch feeder. I was able to get several good pictures, but still can't identify it. Can you? —Mikelyn Burnell
Kimball, Michigan

George: This unusual species is a European goldfinch, a common bird in Britain and Europe. Like American goldfinches, it will eat sunflower seeds and nyjer at bird feeders.

Unlike the American goldfinch, the European species does not change plumages in winter, so the red on its face gives it a spectacular appearance year-round. Also, the sexes look alike, so we can't speculate if your visitor was a male or female.

Many attempts have been made to introduce this species into North America, but none have been successful. The bird that appeared at your feeder was probably an escaped pet.

Where Do Swallows Go?

I've always wondered where barn swallows migrate. Do they ever return to their original place of birth?

—Lola Carlson, Bowdoin, Maine

George: All swallows, including barn swallows, are long-distance migrators. Barn swallows abandon their breeding range in the fall to wing their way through the Caribbean to spend winter in Central and South America. A few may irregularly winter as far north as southern Florida and the southwestern United States.

They usually return to the same general area where they were raised. Most nest within 20 miles of their birthplace, while some even nest much closer.

Out of the Ashes

Several hummingbirds visit my yard to feed from the flowers and feeders. However, they also seem to relish the ash piles from my paper burner. Why is the ash so popular with these hummingbirds?

—Ruby Barth, Reedsport, Oregon

George: Although I have never seen hummingbirds feed from an ash pile, I suspect the ashes offer a mineral they need for laying eggs. A bird's reproduction cycle often requires special nutrients it must acquire prior to laying eggs.

Changing Tastes?

I've noticed the woodpeckers in my backyard eating sunflower seeds, while the black-capped chickadees have developed a taste for nyjer. Can birds learn to eat new kinds of food? —Lillian Marcotte
Hartland, Vermont

George: Yes, many species of birds are eating new foods as they adapt to what's available at bird feeders.

Some other changes I've heard include finches and doves eating safflower seeds, and American robins feasting on cracked sunflower. Dark-eyed juncos, which typically feed on the ground, are flying up to eat sunflower seeds off tray feeders.

And while it's a fairly common sight today, orioles, house finches and tanagers didn't used to sip sugar water from backyard hummingbird feeders.

These adaptations not only help increase the populations of these birds, but also allow them to pioneer into new regions.

Ants in Your Feathers?

I witnessed blue jays taking large red ants in their bills and rubbing them under their wings and on other parts of their bodies. Why would they do this?

—Thomas Kintz, Homosassa Springs, Florida

George: Blue jays and many other species will use crushed ants to rid their bodies of parasites. The ants contain formic acid that will kill parasites or cause them to abandon birds. Some birds will also roll on anthills to obtain the same relief from parasites.

Table for One

Many birds visit my feeders, often in pairs. However, the males of some species, such as indigo buntings and rose-breasted grosbeaks, always arrive solo. Why don't I see them with a mate? —Debby Videto
Bowden, West Virginia

George: There's more than one answer to your question. First, if it's nesting season, the females may be incubating eggs or feeding young.

The other possibility is that, in some cases, the males and females look so different from one another that they may not appear to be a pair. For example, the rose-breasted grosbeak female looks like a brown-striped sparrow, and the female indigo bunting is light brown with little or no blue in her feathers.

Finally, it's common behavior among many species for males and females to feed and bathe separately during the breeding season. This may help defend the pair from being preyed upon at the same time.

Long Live the Birds?

What is the life expectancy of common backyard birds, such as northern cardinals, bluebirds, mourning doves, chickadees and towhees?

—Yvonne Dragonette, Beverly Hills, Florida

George: If a backyard bird survives its first year, and 80 percent do not, the bird may live an average of 5 or 6 years.

The first year is the most hazardous for birds. From nestlings to fledglings to inexperienced juveniles, these young birds face a wild world fraught with danger.

Averages aside, some backyard species have lived much longer. For example, records show that a northern cardinal lived in the wild 13-1/2 years; a mourning dove lived 10 years; and a black-capped chickadee reached 12 years, 5 months.

Soak Up the Sun

I spotted this greater roadrunner at the Red Rock Visitor Center in Nevada. I followed it around for a bit, then it sprawled itself on the patio in this strange position (below). What is it doing? —*Peggy Hamlen Las Vegas, Nevada*

George: This is a very interesting and colorful photograph

of a greater roadrunner sunning itself. Birds will do this in very hot conditions to help rid their feathers and bodies of parasites. The insects cannot stand the heat, and leave the bird.

When they are sunning, the birds are also absorbing vitamin D, which is essential to their health.

Whip-poor-will Watch

Is it my imagination, or is the whip-poor-will population diminishing? Is there anything we can do to protect these birds? —*Keith Etzel Shippenville, Pennsylvania*

George: You are not imagining it. Whip-poor-will numbers have declined dramatically in recent decades due to loss of their wooded habitat in both summer and winter ranges, pesticides that kill the insects they eat, and nocturnal predators, such as great horned owls, that hunt them.

They are on the watch list, but not yet endangered. One of the only things people can do to help is to save the mature woodland habitat where whip-poor-wills live.

Editor's Note: Learn more about whip-poor-wills in "Top Billing" on pages 40-41.

Why the Cold Shoulder?

Every winter, I put out plenty of suet and birdseed. A few birds visit my backyard, but not like they do in summer. What's the problem? —*Margo Magwood Kitchener, Ontario*

George: Most people who feed backyard birds find that winter is the busiest time of the year. The fact that you don't have more activity in winter may have something to with the amount of evergreen habitat in your yard.

When the leaves of deciduous trees disappear in the fall, a yard without evergreens provides no adequate cover for birds to use when they are threatened by predators or inclement weather.

You can correct this by planting some pines, spruces and firs near the feeders to reestablish a comfort level for the birds that visit in winter. A quick fix would be to stand an old Christmas tree near your feeder. This will provide some temporary cover for the birds.

"Hairy" Hawk

My husband and I believe this backyard visitor (below) was a young red-tailed hawk. However, a friend of ours said it can't be because they won't stay close to humans, and their feathers don't go as far down on their legs. Can you clear up this mystery?

—Jill Johns, Perrysville, Ohio

George: You and your husband were right in your identification. This bird is a juvenile red-tailed hawk, which is apparent because of its lack of red tail, and the abundance of white on its breast and upper legs.

All red-tails have feathers on their upper legs, but your photograph makes it look like they extend down farther than they really do. These birds actually have yellow featherless legs from the knee joint down to the toes.

Red-tailed hawks commonly nest in mature forests in rural subdivisions, and are used to humans in their habitat. Because this bird is a juvenile, perhaps just out of the nest, it may not yet have acquired a strong fear of people.

Shared Parenting

Before we could take down our Christmas wreath one spring, two bird pairs built nests in it. House finches claimed the center hole and American robins took the top. It made for some wonderful bird-watching.

Then one day we spotted something remarkable—an adult robin feeding the finch babies (see the photo at right). Can you explain this unusual behavior?

—Margaret and Allen Denney, Huntington, Indiana

George: This behavior is not as unusual as you might believe. The urge to feed young is so strong in parent birds that they will even feed the young of other birds.

The American robin nest was located so close to the house finch nest, that when the parent robin saw the open and begging mouths of the finch babies, it instinctively fed them.

This kind of behavior will sometimes even occur after young birds have left the nest.

Ruffled Feathers

I spotted this tousled looking American robin last spring. What's wrong with its feathers? —Angela Saylor Paxtonville, Pennsylvania

George: The unkempt feathers on the robin you noticed were probably the result of the bird's brooding activity. The strange markings are located where a female typically has a brood spot. This is a warm area of skin under the feathers that female birds use to incubate eggs and brood young.

This bird must have been recently brooding on a nest, and you saw it with its breast feathers still out of place.

Colorful Diet

I was thrilled when American goldfinches began visiting my backyard last January. After about a week of feasting at my thistle feeder, they began to get their gold color back. Was this change due to their diet? —Marjorie Coulter Owens Cross Roads, Alabama

George: The seasonal color changes for American goldfinches, and most other birds, have nothing to do with diet. But they have everything to do with the amount of daylight each season brings.

A gland in the bird's brain signals the plumage to change as the amount of daylight increases or decreases. The American goldfinch's brilliant yellow summer plumage is its breeding garb; the olive-green winter plumage is designed as protective coloration. The change you noticed was simply the start of this seasonal molt.

In Full Color

Last spring, my husband put out short lengths of red and green yarn for nesting birds. Within 45 minutes, they'd taken all the red yarn, but left the green. We put out more batches of red, which the birds grabbed, but they still didn't touch the green.

Can you tell us if birds are able to distinguish colors and why they might have left the green yarn?

—Bev LeCount, Elkhart, Indiana

George: Birds can see the same colors we can. That's why male birds usually are more colorful than females. Males are trying to attract mates, while females need to blend in with the habitat when incubating eggs and feeding young.

However, it's difficult to answer why your birds preferred the red yarn to the green yarn for nesting material. Perhaps the red blended better with their selected nesting habitat or the bird sitting on the nest. Or, maybe the red color was meant to warn predators to stay away.

Although we can't be sure of the exact reason, it definitely has something to do with survival.

A Clean Bill

I often see birds stroking their bills over tree branches. It doesn't seem connected with gathering food or nesting material. Do you know what they're doing? —Kim Spain Spangle, Washington

George: When a bird is stroking its bill over a tree branch, it usually is cleaning its bill after having eaten something messy or sticky, such as suet, peanut butter or a juicy insect.

Birds are fastidious about cleanliness, and spend a great deal of time preening their feathers, bills and feet.

California Bird

While in California, I saw this pretty bird sitting in an orange tree. Can you tell me what kind of bird it is and some information about it?

—Carol Kalscheur
Madison, Wisconsin

George: The bird is the Eurasian collared-dove, a nonnative species that has spread across North America rapidly during the last decade. It was first introduced from Europe and is now found in most parts of the United States.

The Eurasian collared-dove is a member of the dove and pigeon family. It has a call, a hooting coo, like the mourning dove, but is slightly larger in size and heavier. Its diet is similar to the mourning dove's, so you will often see it at backyard feeders, looking for seed.

Food and Water

We have a small birding business, and many customers ask us whether it's more important to provide water or food for birds in winter. What is your advice? —Linda Libby
Windham, Maine

George: Food will attract more birds to the backyard in winter than water, though a heated birdbath may be a popular site. Your region has an abundance of snow, so birds can find sufficient moisture without looking far. That's why food will be a greater attraction.

Attract birds with variety. Offer a selection in various feeders around your yard to get the greatest number of birds.

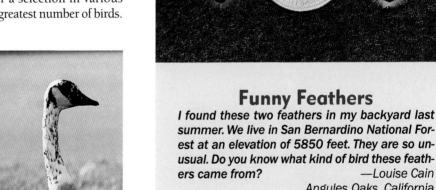

Stumped by Spots

This unusual goose has me stumped with its black and white spotted neck. Do you know why it looks like this?

—Harry Johnson
Prospect Heights, Illinois

George: The strange-looking bird is either a partial albino or a crossbreed. Partial albinism is not that rare among many species of birds.

If is it a crossbreed, it looks like a mix between a Canada goose and a domestic white goose. This happens occasionally, and this is what you probably witnessed here.

Two of a Kind

I found these birds (above) on my patio one afternoon. Can you help me identify this amiable pair? —Joanne Fabian
Souderton, Pennsylvania

George: These birds are juvenile northern mockingbirds, evident because of the spots on their breasts. Males and females of this species look alike, so I'm not able to identify the gender.

This species has moved farther and farther north in recent decades, and are now found in New England and the Midwest. They are feisty birds with a song repertoire that imitates dozens of man-made sounds and many other birds' songs, too.

Funny Feathers

I found these two feathers in my backyard last summer. We live in San Bernardino National Forest at an elevation of 5850 feet. They are so unusual. Do you know what kind of bird these feathers came from?

—Louise Cain
Angules Oaks, California

George: I can only take a guess as to what bird these feathers came from. Because each one shows a black spot, we have to consider all birds with black spots that live at low elevations in southern California.

My guess is that these came from a northern flicker. This flier has black spots on its breast, so it looks like it would be a match. They certainly are interesting feathers.

Daytime Owl Sighting

While on a walk, I spotted this cute owl on the lower branch of a tree. What can you tell me about it, and why was it out during the day?
—Linda McGrath, Appleton, Wisconsin

George: You saw a northern saw-whet owl, a nocturnal species that was probably roosting. This northern forest owl hunts almost entirely at night, mostly for mice. It finds its prey by sight and sound, and swoops down on it from a tree branch.

Saw-whets prefer to live in coniferous trees, though the one in your photograph is roosting in a deciduous tree. The bird's name comes from its song. It reminded settlers of the sound a whetstone makes when sharpening a saw.

Change of Plans

We regularly have purple martins in our yard during nesting season, but one year they were acting strange. A pair began building its nest, and then a few days later, disappeared. Do you know why they had a change of plans?
—La Vonne Propst, Brownsville, Oregon

George: Because purple martins nest in colonies, and there was only one pair in your house, they may have left to move into a colony nearby.

Another possibility is that they may have been chased away by European starlings or house sparrows, both non-native pests that compete with native species. Or perhaps a cold snap, even a short one, limited the number of insects they could find around the birdhouse to keep them alive.

It sounds like you have the right setup to attract purple martins. I hope the success you've had from previous years returns next spring!

When to Call It Quits

Someone once told me that you should not keep sugar-water feeders out after Labor Day because it will keep hummingbirds from flying to their wintering grounds until it is too late. Is this true?
—Emma Miller
Middlefield, Ohio

George: It is not true that sugar-water feeders control bird migrations, so you don't have to worry about taking yours down any time soon. The length of daylight actually controls when birds migrate.

In fact, you should keep your feeders up as long as possible. This helps fuel the birds that are passing through the area on their migration routes. You never know when you might see a straggler passing through and searching for a sweet treat.

The End of a Song

Someone once told me that mockingbirds don't sing in August. I began to notice this the past 3 years, and sure enough, they stop singing at the end of July. Why is this?
—Lois Gibbs, Athens, Georgia

George: Like most birds, northern mockingbirds only sing during certain times of the year. You will hear their song during courtship and when they are defending their breeding territories.

After breeding season ends, there is no reason for them to sing, so they stop. In winter, the birds establish feeding territories that are completely different from nesting territories. You may occasionally hear northern mockingbirds sing to defend those areas, but for the most part, these birds do stop singing by August.

Bullfrog Bully

The bullfrog in my neighbor's backyard fish pond stalks and eats small birds. Is this normal behavior?
—Sharon Bannister, Perrysburg, Ohio

George: It is not unusual for a large bullfrog to capture and consume small birds, given the chance. Unfortunately, there's not much you can do.

If you want to protect the area birds, you'll have to capture the bullfrog and release it in a lake or other wetland at least a mile away.

Seeds for Bluebirds?

I read in a past issue that bluebirds don't visit seed feeders, but my son, who lives in Virginia, disagrees. He took this picture of eastern bluebirds feeding on sunflower hearts in his yard. What's your take on this unique situation? —Betty Lambert
Gainesville, Florida

George: While it's not typical bluebird behavior, your son is right. Both bluebirds and American robins have adapted to eating cracked (hulled) sunflower seeds.

I, too, was amazed when I saw a parent robin on my tray feeder one day. It was gathering cracked sunflower seeds in its bill. Then it fed them to its four fledglings nearby. This is an example of how birds have changed or adapted their feeding habits to the foods available at feeders.

Under Attack

I was walking by the yew in my front yard when a mockingbird attacked me. This continued for about 2 weeks, until I realized there was a nest with young birds nearby. Is this a common form of behavior for this species?
—Phillip Mauro, Fort Lee, New Jersey

George: It is typical of northern mockingbirds to attack people and pets during nesting season. They do it to protect their eggs and young.

I knew a house cat that ruled a yard until a pair of northern mockingbirds built a nest in one of the hedges. From that point on, the cat was afraid to go outside because of the aggressive birds.

Red-winged blackbirds and tree swallows will also attack to protect their nests, so try to steer clear until nesting season is over.

Hanging Out

I think I may be on to something. After several years of testing bluebird houses, I believe these interesting birds prefer a hanging birdhouse (right). Do you think this makes sense?
—Robert Walshaw
Coweta, Oklahoma

George: You may, indeed, be on to something with a hanging bluebird house—if, for no other reason, than it may keep predators from destroying the nest.

Bluebirds prefer to nest near open areas, such as grassy fields where they can catch insects for themselves and their young. Fence posts often face grassy fields, and that is why nearly all bluebird houses are on posts.

Historically, bluebirds nested in natural cavities in tree limbs or stumps, often made by woodpeckers. Prior to your letter, I had not heard of a successful hanging bluebird house, but it should work if it is near an open field.

Is More Better?

Let's say I have a bird feeder that gets 100 birds. If I add a second feeder with the same amount of seed, do you think I will attract even more birds? In other words, does the quantity of feeders increase the number of birds coming to feed
—Duane Bellingham, East Sandwich, Massachusetts

George: The short answer is yes. Generally, if you have more feeders, more birds will be attracted to your yard. So if you have three different feeders, you can accommodate three times the number of birds.

It might not be easy to notice, though. In winter, feeder birds move around a great deal, so the ones that are there in the morning are not the same ones there in the afternoon. They may look the same, but you're likely attracting a lot more birds than you realize.

Late-Night Surprise

My husband works third shift and I drive him to work around midnight. One night, when I came home, I saw a beautiful green hummingbird hovering in the car lights above my morning glories. Do you know why it would have been out at that late hour? —Sharon Johnson, Alvarado, Texas

George: My guess is that the car lights frightened the hummingbird that was roosting in the morning glories. In general, it is not common for these magnificent birds to fly in the middle of the night. However, they will fly in the dark during migration when they have to make the long trip across the Gulf of Mexico to the tropics.

THAT'S AN IMPOSTER

These butterflies will make you do a double take.

By Tom Allen, Contributing Editor

Imitation is the sincerest form of flattery. If that phrase is true, then the monarch and pipevine swallowtail have it made. Both of these popular flying flowers are toxic species other butterflies imitate.

This behavior, known as Batesian mimicry, has developed over time. It is an evolutionary process whereby a species changes its color or pattern through genetic mutation to closely resemble a toxic species. Butterflies are just one of the insects that use this behavior.

They do this for protection. Other than their look-alike technique, these butterflies have no defense against predators. If they resemble a toxic butterfly, then they have a bet-

ter chance of surviving and passing their traits to off-spring

Model Behavior

When it comes to understanding mimic butterflies, you must first look to their source. For instance, the toxic butterfly that another butterfly copies is the source model.

Predators recognize toxic butterflies because of their warning colors, which often consist of black, yellow, white and red combinations. These colors provide maximum visibility against the greens and browns of natural habitats. It's like sending a big warning sign to predators.

One of the most common examples of mimicry behavior is that of the viceroy butterfly (below left). It looks and behaves like the monarch (above left), which feeds on the toxic milkweed plant. It wants to fool predators into thinking it is also toxic,

Above, below: Tom Allen

Above, Richard Day/Daybreak Imagery

so the viceroy appears at the same time of year as the monarch and uses similar habitats.

The queen and soldier butterflies also resemble the monarch, but they are not mimics. They feed on milkweed and are toxic, so they are yet another model for the viceroy.

Since viceroys are found throughout most of North America, the butterflies have different options. In the northern part of the United States, the orange and black fliers mimic the monarch. Farther south, they tailor their look after the queen and soldier butterflies, which have slightly different coloring in certain regions.

For example, I live in Florida, and queen and soldier butterflies are much darker brown than monarchs. Because of this, the viceroys here have evolved to a darker coloration pattern to give them even better protection against predators in their natural habitat.

Pipevine Impersonator

The Diana fritillary, the red-spotted purple, the spicebush swallowtail and female tiger swallowtail all mimic the chemically toxic pipevine swallowtail (see photos above). Since the pipevine is found from the central U.S. southward, these mimics—at least the black forms—are in the same region.

In northern states, female tiger swallowtails remain yellow, since pipevines don't exist in that region. But the

CON ARTISTS. Pipevine swallowtails (above) are toxic, therefore many other butterflies try to mimic their coloring. Top, the red-spotted purple (right) and the female tiger swallowtail (left) both resemble the pipevine's coloring as a form of protection.

true mimics of pipevines use similar woodland habitats within their range and fly during similar periods of the year.

The female Diana fritillary is a rare and beautiful woodland butterfly that is truly dimorphic, meaning the males and females look very different. For years, it fooled scientists into thinking that the males and females of the Appalachian species were two different butterflies.

These unique butterflies live in moist and shaded woodland habitats in the Appalachian and Ozark Mountains. Their only form of protection is to mimic the pipevine.

So the next time you think you see a pipevine swallowtail or monarch, be sure to take a closer look at their markings and coloring. You could be looking at a different species altogether!

> ### BUTTERFLY BIT
> The viceroy, queen and soldier are all butterflies that resemble the monarch. However, the viceroy is the only one that is a true mimic.

'GLAD YOU ASKED!'

Our butterfly expert answers your questions.

Winged Wonder

I spotted this striped butterfly (above) perched on a pine tree in my yard. It looks like a tiger swallowtail, but I didn't think these butterflies were in this part of the country. Can you tell me what kind it is?

—Jeanne Hardy, Paulden, Arizona

Tom: The butterfly is a female two-tailed swallowtail. This butterfly, which occurs throughout the western United States, is very similar to the common tiger swallowtail, but can be easily distinguished by the double tails on its hind wings.

You can tell this one is a female because it has a large amount of blue on the hind wing. This is also a good way to identify a female tiger swallowtail.

Make Your Own Nectar

I purchased a butterfly feeder to help attract more butterflies to my garden. I already make my own hummingbird nectar. Can I use this recipe to feed butterflies?—

Niceta Field, Ray, Michigan

Tom: While hummingbird nectar typically is a 4-to-1 ratio of water to sugar, butterfly nectar is a bit weaker. Try a 10 percent sugar-water solution (about 1 part sugar to 10 parts water), and add a pinch of multivitamins, if you'd like, from a children's vitamin capsule. Or, use Gatorade with a little sugar added—about 1/2 teaspoon of sugar per cup.

One word of advice, though. You'll want to have some sort of trap to keep ants from taking over the sweet liquid.

Another thing to keep in mind is that butterflies are attracted to flowers by the amount of ultraviolet reflection they emit. Since some colors emit better than others, certain feeders may not emit the correct wavelengths to attract butterflies. Purple, lavender, orange and red usually work well, but you'll just have to try them.

In addition to feeders, there are a few other simple ways to attract butterflies. You can put bananas or fermented fruit in your feeder to attract butterflies like mourning cloaks, anglewings or tortoiseshells.

Also, don't forget the flowers. Because of the differences in UV reflections, some flowers are better than others. One to try is lavender or purple butterfly bush (*Buddleia*), which should attract fritillaries and swallowtails.

Group Shot

I snapped this picture (below) at a resting area in a nearby national forest. I believe there are three different species of butterflies here. Why are they grouped together like this? There did not appear to be any water on the ground.

—Bill Campbell
Kingsport, Tennessee

Tom: This activity is called "puddling" and it's a common sight, especially during early spring in wooded areas of the Appalachian Mountains and elsewhere. Newly emerged male butterflies of several species will gather at moist spots to sip minerals and salts from the wet soil.

Although you mentioned that there didn't appear to be water on the surface, all the butterflies need is a slightly damp area from which to extract the collected minerals.

In your photo, the two dominant species are tiger swallowtails and pipevine swallowtails. They have also been joined by one or two spicebush swallowtails and a few duskywing skippers.

A Blooming Mystery

This royal walnut moth was in my garden early one morning (below). I've never seen this kind of flying flower on my blooms before. Was this a rare sighting?
— *Paul Wolf, Hanover, Pennsylvania*

Tom: The royal walnut is also known as the hickory horned devil because of the long horns on the caterpillar. This flier belongs to the same family as other large moths such as the luna and cecropia.

This moth is fairly common in your area, especially where hickory and black walnut trees are found. However, it's not a flier that visits flowers. These moths do not have mouths for feeding, so you're not likely to see it on a bloom.

Home Sweet Home?

I have two butterfly houses, but I'm not sure where to hang them. Do these houses really attract butterflies? — *Donna Hoppes, Pendleton, Indiana*

Tom: Butterfly houses are more of a garden decoration than a way to attract butterflies to your yard.

Although a few butterfly species seek shelter for winter hibernation or a shady roost during the hot summer, most butterflies usually rest on vegetation or in trees.

However, if you put your houses in a protected area near woodlands, you could attract a mourning cloak or question mark to them. And in areas where Milbert's tortoiseshells are found, a butterfly house might be effective, since these butterflies hibernate in large groups.

Be aware that butterfly houses also make good homes for wasps and hornets.

Butterfly Assistance

Four monarch caterpillars recently hatched on my milkweed, and I've noticed some ants and aphids on the plant, too. Do monarchs need these insects, or should I get rid of them?
— *Mrs. John Mecozzi Camarillo, California*

Tom: Many butterflies in the hairstreak and blue families have a cooperative relationship with ants. The ants protect the caterpillars from predators, and in return, the ants feed on a sugary solution the caterpillars secrete.

However, monarch caterpillars don't secrete a sugary solution, and they don't need protection, either, because the milkweed they eat produces toxins that ward off predators.

So while the ants and aphids don't pose a threat to the caterpillars, they could be a problem for your milkweed. You can deal with the pests by applying a little soapy water to the plant when the caterpillars aren't present.

Glad You Asked!

ATTRACTING BUTTERFLIES

By Tom Allen, Contributing Editor

It seems everyone wants to know how to attract butterflies to their gardens. It's one of the most common questions I hear. But before you can create a successful habitat for butterflies, you need to consider your own "habitat."

Are there features like open fields, wooded areas or wetlands? What region is it? What's the climate like? All of these factors determine what butterfly species inhabit the area around your home, as well as the types of plants you can grow to attract them.

Time to Play Host

A good place to start is with the foods—or host plants—that butterflies require during the caterpillar stage. Most butterflies, especially females, do not stray far from host plants.

The most well-known example of this is milkweed, the host plant for monarchs and a great nectar source, too. Some other examples are everlastings for American ladies, clovers for sulphur butterflies, and tulip trees, ash or choke cherry for tiger swallowtails.

In addition, you also need to be aware of some of the characteristics of the butterflies you'd like to attract.

Monarchs migrate in fall, therefore it helps to plant late bloomers for them, such as asters or chrysanthemums.

Another important trait to consider is the length of a butterfly's proboscis—what they use to sip nectar.

Some butterflies, including swallowtails and skippers, have a long proboscis and can reach into deep-throated flowers, such as cardinal flower, honeysuckle, bee balm and azalea.

Other species, especially small ones (like the acadian hairstreak above), can only reach into flowers with short corollas. So planting milkweed (including butterfly weed), purple coneflower, blazing star, phlox, buckwheat, butterfly bush and lilac will attract them.

Butterfly Buffet

In addition, there are a number of butterfly species that don't like flower nectar as a food source. These are the anglewings, the admirals and the tortoiseshells, to name a few.

They are mainly sap feeders and get their nutrients from tree wounds, rotting fruit and even animal dung. To attract them, you can set out various crushed ripe fruits and allow them to ferment.

While no one can attract all the butterflies that are common to their region, planting a few of the flowers mentioned here should increase the fluttering activity in any backyard.

Cause and Effect

I found a monarch chrysalis hanging from a black-eyed Susan plant with moisture on it. I thought it was from the dew, but no other plants around were wet. When the monarch emerged from the chrysalis (at right), it had a large hole in one of its wings. Why is this, and does it have anything to do with the moisture on the chrysalis?
—Debbie Welch, Sioux Falls, South Dakota

Tom: There a couple of possible explanations for what you saw. First, the moisture on the chrysalis could simply be moisture that hadn't evaporated. Another reason for the moisture is that a parasitic wasp could have penetrated the chrysalis, causing fluid to exude from the puncture wound.

The tear in the butterfly's wing is a separate issue altogether. It probably happened when the butterfly emerged from the chrysalis.

When a butterfly first emerges, its wings are fragile and soft. Since the wing is complete and simply has a tear, I believe this is what happened in this case. So the moisture on the chrysalis and the torn wing are probably not related at all.

Unknown Beauty

While visiting a friend in Pennsylvania, I noticed this beauty on a butterfly bush. Can you tell me what it is and give me more information about it?
—Shirley Mathews, Wilmington, Delaware

Tom: The butterfly is a female tiger swallowtail. Females have a lot more blue on their hind wings than males, so they are easy to distinguish.

These butterflies should be common in your area. They feed on cherry and tulip poplar trees as caterpillars, and the adults often visit flower gardens to obtain nectar.

If you want to attract them, try planting butterfly bush (as your friend did). It's one of the best nectar-producing plants in summer gardens.

Blooming Attractions

Two of my favorite butterflies are the eastern tiger swallowtail and zebra longwing, but I can't seem to attract them to my yard.

I keep thinking, if I plant it, they will come. But I have tulip trees, willow trees and passionvines, and still no butterflies. Can you offer more tips?
—Austin Miller Sugar Land, Texas

Tom: Tiger swallowtails will only visit your yard if they are common in the area. You are near the edge of their range, but if you see them in your area, you should be able to attract them.

By planting plenty of nectar plants, you will catch the eye of strays. In particular, try cottonwood, sweet bay and cherry.

For zebra longwings, keep using native passionvines, as they will work the best. These butterflies prefer shaded habitat, so try growing this vine up a tree.

Good luck. I hope your persistence pays off!

Long Live Monarchs

Can you tell me how long monarch butterflies typically live?
—Jean Caldwell, Saint Helen, Michigan

Tom: Monarchs are considered a long-lived butterfly compared to other species. The monarchs we see from spring through summer generally live 3 to 4 weeks—which is similar to the lifespan of many other butterflies. But those that belong to the migrating fall generation live from October to February or March, a period of 5 to 6 months.

The longest-lived butterfly is the mourning cloak, at up to 10 months.

Adult mourning cloaks emerge from their chrysalises around June. They become dormant during the hot summer months and hibernate for winter before emerging in spring to breed and lay their eggs. Adults generally die in late April or May.

In contrast, many small, fragile hairstreaks or blues are lucky to survive 4 to 6 days as butterflies.

A Moth Face-Off

I was walking to the mailbox one morning when I found these two moths staring each other down. Can you tell me what they were doing? The bigger moth looks like an Imperial to me, but do you know what the smaller one is?
—Brett Dawson, Aylett, Virginia

Tom: The two moths appear to be an Imperial moth, on the left, as you thought, and a male Royal walnut moth. They were probably both attracted to a light overhead or nearby, and coincidentally happened to land at the pole facing each other.

While it appears that the moths might be attracted to one another, that's probably not the case. They most likely just settled down next to each other. It's a very interesting photo, though.

Bountiful Butterflies

I took this photo (above) last year in my neighbor's yard. I have never seen so many butterflies together. Can you tell me what these are and explain more about them?
—Nora Glick, Waterloo, Iowa

Tom: These are painted ladies, a species most common west of the Mississippi. These fliers build up huge populations that migrate in large numbers, usually from the south to north.

You probably witnessed one of these migrations. This species feeds on a number of plants as caterpillars, but are particularly fond of thistles.

Down and Out

I just found a queen chrysalis on the floor of my patio. I think it fell off a flowerpot. What should I do with it?
—Nancy Boatwright, Zephyrhills, Florida

Tom: Look at the tail end of the chrysalis. You should see a tiny black hook called a cremaster. Caterpillars use this to attach themselves to stems. Take a piece of thread and tie it around this tiny hook. Then tie it to a twig to help give the chrysalis support.

This will help the butterfly emerge in spring, but even if you don't do this, there's still a good chance it will pull itself out of the chrysalis.

Looking for a Name

I see lots of bright-yellow butterflies in my backyard. Do you know what these common fliers are?
—Evelyn Willis Goodrich, Texas

Tom: If they are small to medium-sized butterflies, they are most likely sulphurs. Sulphurs are quite common around yards. Many of them feed on legumes as caterpillars and especially like clover.

Next time you see the sunny fliers, look closely at the markings on the wings. Then use a field guide to compare. It will probably list the host plant they are attracted to. Then you can see if you have it growing in your backyard.

Autumn Blues

Every fall these pretty blue beauties show up in our yard. They flutter away as quickly as they land, but one day I was able to snap this photo. Can you tell me what they are?
—Teresa Kollmar Grandview, Washington

Tom: You've discovered the common checkered skipper, a butterfly that has two broods—one in spring and another in late summer and early fall. The butterfly's blue appearance comes from long, bluish hairs on the inner part of the wings. The species prefers fields and pastures with low-growing mallows, where it feeds.

The caterpillars of this butterfly make leaf nests by rolling or attaching a group of leaves together with silk near the top of mallow plants. If you carefully look inside, you will see the greenish caterpillar, with a dark head and covered with short, whitish hairs. The caterpillars will winter fully grown in these leaf shelters.

Glad You Asked!

MEET OUR EXPERTS

We have some of the friendliest and most knowledgable pros in the whole industry.

MELINDA MYERS
Plant Doctor

There's no such thing as a typical day for Melinda. Awake some days as early as 4 a.m., Melinda says it seems like she's always writing something for somebody. Her work has even taken here across the globe, to places like the Netherlands and Zimbabwe.

So how did this plant doctor get her start?

Melinda's experience with horticulture goes way back to the days growing up in the suburbs of Columbus, Ohio, while spending many weekends at her grandparents' farm. Her father had an extravagant vegetable garden, but Melinda was relegated to deadheading petunias.

By the second grade, Melinda could already name the parts of a plant. By high school, she knew she was on the right path.

"In 10th grade, most people dissect frogs in science class," she says. "I dissected plants."

Her interest in plants continued to grow, leading her to a master's degree in horticulture. She's also a certified arborist and started the Master Gardener program in Milwaukee.

Melinda has shared her expertise through a variety of media. In addition to answering your questions in *Birds & Blooms* and *Birds & Blooms EXTRA*, Melinda has written several books, hosts *Great Lakes Gardener* on PBS, writes a column for the *Milwaukee Journal Sentinel* and *Backyard Living* magazine, holds planting clinics and lectures, and has taught horticulture classes at Milwaukee Area Technical College.

When Melinda's not writing or answering questions, she's in her own backyard, weeding and watering. Transforming her entire small-space yard into a garden, Melinda often enlists the help of her daughter, Nevada.

"She's a great weeder," Melinda says.

Irene Jeruss

Melinda admits her garden isn't perfect. She's even grown a few weeds in her day, battling persistent backyard ribbon grass for 15 years. She says gardening is still a learning experience for her. Even after 27 years of writing and teaching, there's always a gardener with a new question.

"Some women get flowers," Melinda says. "People bring me dead plants and insects."

GEORGE HARRISON
Backyard Bird-Watcher

Nancy Rotenberg

"It's in my genes." That's how George describes his lifelong fascination with birds and nature. His father, Hal, was a nature writer and photographer, and George used to accompany him to locations, where he would take still photographs while his father shot movies.

Since George always knew he wanted to follow in his father's footsteps, he decided to get a degree in journalism from Penn State University.

"I knew the subject of nature from living it," George says. "I just needed the formal training in writing."

Since then, George has written 13 books, produced six specials about backyard birds for PBS television and has written for six different nature magazines. He even helped start *Birds & Blooms*!

George enjoys life more by doing less—even though he's still pretty busy. Most of his time is taken up by writing, and his backyard wildlife habitat provides plenty of inspiration.

"Something's going on outside my window all the time," George says.

Helping people discover the enjoyment of bird-watching is what George loves most about his job. He encourages newly interested bird-watchers to provide food, cover and water as a sure-fire way to attract birds to any backyard.

When he's not answering questions, George takes advantage of living on a lake by fishing. Not even a frozen lake will stop him—he likes ice fishing, too. Practice must make perfect, since George says he never has any trouble catching fish!

TOM ALLEN
Butterfly Guide

Mark Werner/The Image Finders

From the moment Tom learned to walk, he was out chasing butterflies. He says his passion for the outdoors was something he was born with.

When he was young, Tom collected and studied butterflies in Massachusetts, where he was born. After obtaining undergraduate and master's degrees from the University of Maine in entomology and wildlife, Tom accepted a position as a research biologist for the West Virginia Division of Natural Resources until his recent retirement. He studied big game animals, especially black bears, and also butterflies. He's written two books—one about butterflies and caterpillars in West Virginia; another about caterpillars across North America.

Now living in Florida, Tom continues researching and studying nature with the Florida Fish and Wildlife Conservation Commission. Tom also teaches an environmental course at Edison College in Fort Myers. He joined the staff of *Birds & Blooms EXTRA* as a contributing editor for its launch in March 2005.

In his free time, Tom enjoys working in his backyard butterfly garden. "There's always a lot of work to be done in my yard," Tom says.

An active participant in the Florida Yards and Neighborhoods program, Tom's yard serves as a model backyard butterfly habitat.

Tom says the trick to attracting butterflies is to think in terms of their life cycle.

"You have to provide nectar for the butterflies and a host for the caterpillar," Tom says. "That's the key to continuous populations of butterflies."

BEST OF 'GLAD YOU ASKED!'

Here's a compilation of the most common questions.

By George Harrison and Melinda Myers,
Contributing Editors

Bald Bird

This strange looking cardinal (below) has visited my yard for the past two summers. Why does it look this way? —T. Markman, Chagrin Falls, Ohio

George: This male northern cardinal has a parasite problem that causes it to lose the feathers on its head, exposing the dark skin underneath. This is a very common condition that's most seen among cardinals, blue jays and other songbirds.

The feathers will eventually grow back, and the cardinal will survive. But during the several weeks that it takes for the new feathers to appear, the bird looks ill. I often remark that we have a "Frankenstein cardinal" when we see a bird with this condition in our yard.

Multitasking Tree

I'd like to plant a tall-growing deciduous tree near my deck. Can you recommend one that will flower and produce the kind of berries birds enjoy? —Lottie Edwine, Rapid City, South Dakota

Melinda: Look for a tree that's suitable to your growing conditions, hardy to your area and doesn't create a mess with its fruit.

Serviceberry (botanically known as *Amelanchier*) is tolerant of partial shade and hardy in Zones 2 to 9. It produces blueberry-like fruit that the birds will pick clean off the tree. The size varies with the cultivar selected.

European mountain ash (*Sorbus aucuparia*) grows 20 to 40 feet tall, prefers cool, moist soils in the summer and is hardy in Zones 3 to 7. Many birds, but especially cedar waxwings, enjoy its fruit.

A close relative that's more tolerant of hot, dry summers is the Korean mountain ash (*Sorbus alnifolia*). Hardy in Zones 4 to 7, it can reach heights of 40 feet. It has bright, pinkish-red fruit and beautiful fall color.

And don't forget about crabapples. Select cultivars bred for their disease resistance and persistent fruit. Some, like Birdland, are especially attractive to birds. Visit a reliable nursery to find the cultivar that best suits your needs.

Show Your True Colors

I know American goldfinches lose their bright-yellow feathers in winter. So why do some birds, like northern cardinals and blue jays, keep their bright plumage all year? —Ethel Richards, Poland, Ohio

George: American goldfinches turn olive-brown in winter for protective coloration against predators. They're bright in the summer, when bolder colors abound, to attract mates and defend territories. Once breeding season is over, they don drabber feathers to match their surroundings.

Although appearing bright to our eyes, the feathers of northern cardinals and blue jays must provide whatever protection these birds need. Keep in mind that animals see color differently than humans.

Woodland Wonder

I found this wildflower (below) growing under a canopy of cedar trees. What is this beautiful plant? —Marilyn Bilsbarro, Dryden, Ontario

Melinda: What a lucky find! This native fairy slipper orchid is primarily found in Canada and Alaska, with a few localized populations elsewhere in the United States. Its numbers are dwindling, especially in the southern parts of its range.

Watch for these natives to appear in cedar (*Thuja*) swamps or dry pine, fir and cedar woods. The fairy slipper (*Calypso bulbosa*) prefers cool soils and doesn't tolerate close contact with human activities. For more information about this and other native Canadian orchids, visit *www.osrbg.ca/orchid_native.html*.

Just Stopping By

Will you help us identify the hawk (above right) we spotted in our backyard? We were thrilled to see it until we realized it was hunting the birds at our feeder, so we took down the feeder until the hawk left. Is there anything else we should have done? —Robert Keller, Scottsbluff, Nebraska

George: I believe that your large visitor was a juvenile northern goshawk, a bird that spends most of its life in the Rocky Mountains and northern regions into Canada and Alaska.

Occasionally, these raptors will move south in search of food, which includes songbirds, squirrels and rabbits.

Because the bird was just passing through, the most damage it could have done was to take a couple of mourning doves or juncos.

Witnessing a hawk hunt your favorite songbirds can be upsetting, but it's important to remember that they have to eat, too, and it is all part of the balance of nature.

If you'd like to help protect your songbirds against future hawk visitors, provide dense shrubs for cover near the feeders. Small birds can retreat into the branches for protection.

Backward Blooming

Every summer, I set my pots of bougainvillea outside, but never get more than a couple of the colorful bracts. In winter, however, they spring to life. How can I coax the plants to produce beautiful fuchsia-colored bracts outdoors? —Kathy Phipps, Tulsa, Oklahoma

Melinda: Bougainvillea's beautiful bracts, what most gardeners call flowers, are a colorful addition to northern and southern gardens. These plants grow well in containers, but need to be moved indoors before the temperatures drop below 40°.

The plants require sun, warmth and regular fertilization to bloom. There are a few things you can try to encourage bracts to form in summer, rather than during winter.

Switch to a balanced or flowering plant fertilizer. This will avoid adding excess nitrogen, which can delay blooming.

Another suggestion is to keep the soil slightly dry. This will often encourage blooming.

Also, try pruning the plant in spring. The pruning promotes new growth where the flowers will develop.

As evening temperatures increase to about 70°, the warmth initiates flowering, and blossoms (like the ones at left) appear in a couple of months.

Make the needed adjustments, and you might be able to coax your plant to bloom earlier in the season.

Clean House

A family of wrens nested in my birdhouse several years ago, but I haven't seen any since. Do wren houses need to be cleaned out after nesting season? If so, how do I go about cleaning them?

—Nancy Fields, Isanti, Minnesota

George: You can clean out a wren house like any other birdhouse. Remove a panel, take out all the contents, wash out dirt or parasites and reassemble the house. Doing this after the nesting season gets rid of insects or other debris that might discourage birds from nesting in it next spring.

In the case of wrens, however, researchers have found that leaving a couple of sticks in the house improves the chances of a wren using it again for future nesting. Apparently, the wren believes that if the house was used in the past, it must be a good place to nest.

Reblooming Poinsettia

My poinsettia plant lost all its bright-red foliage. Should I trim it back so it will bloom for me again next Christmas?

—Isaac Zook
Gordonville, Pennsylvania

Melinda: Continue to grow your poinsettia in a sunny window, watering it thoroughly and often, enough to keep the soil slightly moist. Encourage fuller growth by cutting it back to 4 to 6 inches in mid-March.

Once the danger of frost has passed, you may move your plant outdoors. Just bring it inside before the first fall frost.

Then fertilize occasionally in spring and early summer with a flowering plant fertilizer.

Starting October 1, cover the plant or move it to a dark lo-cation where it can receive 14 hours of complete darkness each night. During the day, uncover and place the plant in a sunny window or under artificial lights.

Continue this process until the top bracts (the petal-like leaves) are fully colored. Keep the soil slightly dry and temperatures a bit cooler during the dark treatments for even greater success.

Every missed dark treatment delays the bloom by 1 day. But don't give up if you miss a couple of days. You can always go for a Valentine's Day poinsettia and start a new trend!

Two-Time Nesting

Last year, we had an eastern phoebe build two nests in the rafters over our deck. In one nest, we saw her caring for three fledglings. In the other nest, she incubated three eggs, sitting on them at night. Is it common for phoebes to make two nests?

—Sharon Dennison, La Plata, Maryland

George: Phoebes normally raise two broods each summer, but not at the same time. One possibility is that the pair you witnessed started on the second nest when the fledglings in the first nest were ready to fly.

In that case, the male would feed the youngsters, while the female incubated eggs in the new nest. Male and female phoebes look alike, so it would be impossible to tell the parents apart.

It is common, however, for phoebes to construct multiple nests. They are known for their lack of orientation, and often build several nests on one rafter before deciding which one to use.

In addition, sometimes the female will lay three eggs in one nest and one egg in another, but both nests will not be successful.

Out of the Zone

I harvested a few seed pods from a Japanese iris while visiting New York. So far, the resulting plants are doing well at my Florida home, but will they continue to grow in this climate?

—Vito Derasmo
Sebastian, Florida

Melinda: Japanese iris can grow as far south as Zones 9 and possibly 10. Many gardeners in mild climates will grow the iris in pots so they can keep them out of the wet, boggy soils in winter.

However, since your plant came from a northern garden, it may be a cultivar more suited for the north, or it could have difficulty adjusting to your warmer climate. This is just another gardening situation where you will have to wait and see what happens.

And be patient. It can take 4 to 5 years for iris to flower when grown from a seed pod. To increase your chance of success, keep the plants somewhat dry during the dormant period when they aren't actively growing.

Change of Appetite?

My mother always told me that bluebirds won't visit feeders because they don't eat seeds. So I was really surprised to see several eastern bluebirds lined up on my feeder one fall day (above). Do you have any idea what would draw them there?

—Debbie Nagle, Dimock, Pennsylvania

George: Your mother was right—it is rare to see these birds at seed feeders. Bluebirds mostly eat insects and fruits. The visitors at your feeder that day were probably searching for worms, grubs or larvae in the seed.

I suspect the seed got wet and attracted insects that laid eggs and hatched larvae. I'm sure it was a treat for those bluebirds, and you can be confident your mother was true to her word.

Look What Sprouted

To spice up our yard, we planted a wildflower seed mix. These purple flowers (below) came up, but we don't know what they are. Can you tell us?

—Dave Clevenger, Laguna Beach, California

Melinda: Your mystery plant is globe gilia, also known as blue or Queen Anne's thimbles (its botanical name is *Gilia capitata*).

This beauty tolerates hot and dry conditions, and is a native of western North America. A relative of phlox, it blooms from June through October and works well in native flower gardens, informal plantings and water-wise landscapes.

This annual will reseed itself in gardens where the soil is not disturbed. This allows the seedlings to sprout and develop into mature, flowering plants.

Glad You Asked!

Unwanted Alarm

My friend has a problem with a woodpecker that wakes her each morning by knocking its bill on her metal chimney. Do you have any suggestions to stop it?

—Rosemary Brown, Dickson, Tennessee

George: Although it may not seem like it at 5:30 a.m., think of the noise the woodpecker makes on the chimney as its song. It uses the sound to attract and court females and establish a breeding territory.

The noise will end when the breeding season ends, in mid- to late summer. In the meantime, try covering the chimney with a wire mesh that has small holes the woodpecker can't penetrate (like hardware cloth). This should stop the noise.

In fact, any kind of temporary enclosure around the chimney should keep the woodpecker—and your friend's mornings—quiet.

Orange Surprise

This bright-orange plant (below) appears in my garden every year. Can you tell me what it is?

—Joan Langille, Truro, Nova Scotia

Melinda: Your mystery plant is commonly called Maltese cross and goes by the scientific name *Lychnis chalcedonica*.

This perennial is relatively easy to grow in full sun and most soils. Avoid wet or poorly drained areas, since these conditions tend to shorten its lifespan.

Over the years, you should see more and more of this perennial. It readily self seeds, resulting in plenty of seedlings to grow and share. Avoid cultivating the soil early in the season, which tends to "weed out" such seedlings.

Letting nature do the work is the easiest way to propagate this plant. You also can dig and divide your existing plant in early spring or late summer to expand your planting.

Spring Pruning

What's the correct way to trim my forsythia?

—Wendy Cloutier, Dover, New Hampshire

Melinda: Forsythias are very tolerant of pruning. You can prune these and other spring-flowering shrubs right after they bloom. That way, you get to enjoy the flowers and still control the plant's size.

For the best results, remove one-third of your forsythia's older stems (they're the thickest) to ground level every year. If you'd like, reduce the height of the remaining stems by one-third as well.

Do this for 3 years, and you'll have a smaller and better-looking plant. Then remove a few older canes each year. This will keep new growth coming from the base and maintain the size you want.

440

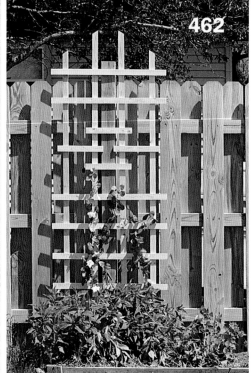

462

460

463

452

466

HERE'S THE PLAN

444

Here's the Plan

Birdhouse Has CLASS

Inspired by a reader's photo, we developed a simple plan that you can customize.

By Cliff Muehlenberg
Editorial Assistant

R eaders send lots of photos of backyard birdhouses, and as a weekend woodworker, I love to study them all. Once in a while one catches my eye, and I just have to build it for myself.

That was the case with this schoolhouse birdhouse sent by Patty and Bill Martin of Bonita Springs, Florida. The one-room birdhouse ranked high on my wife's cuteness meter, and I could tell it was easy to assemble, even for the first-time birdhouse builder. Best of all, I knew this basic design could be easily customized. I can see it now... the perfect birdhouse fishing shanty ...general store...church...or firehouse. You decide.

Start Building!

1. Enlarge the front/back wall pattern at right by 200% on a copy machine, then enlarge it about another 154% to a final height of 10-1/4 inches (copiers may differ, so final enlargement could vary).

Cut two pieces of board 11 inches long. Tack the two boards together using four 1-1/4-inch brads. Tape the pattern to the boards. Cut out the pattern with your saber saw.

2. Cut the pieces for side walls.

3. Create the windows with a chisel. Start by tapping an outline,

RP Photo

Here's What You'll Need...

- ❏ One 6-foot 5/8-inch x 6-inch cedar fence picket
- ❏ 1-1/2-inch finishing nails
- ❏ 1-1/4-inch brads
- ❏ One #6 1-1/4-inch galvanized wood screw
- ❏ Wooden match sticks
- ❏ Acrylic paints
- ❏ Decorative items (available at most craft and hobby stores)

Recommended Tools...

- ❏ Saber saw or hand saw
- ❏ Chisel
- ❏ Hammer
- ❏ Drill
- ❏ Hand plane
- ❏ Combination square
- ❏ Nail set
- ❏ Hot-melt glue gun

then chisel a smooth even surface about 1/16 inch deep. Paint chiseled-out surfaces black.

4. Nail the sides to the front and back. Set the nails just below the surface.

5. Cut the four roof pieces to size. Cut one edge of the lower roof pieces at a 45° angle.

6. Cut and plane to a thickness 1/4 x 1/4 inch trim for the door frame. The window trim is made from wooden matchsticks. Paint the trim on all sides.

7. Cut wood 1/8 inch thick for the door and shutters (you'll also want to cut the chalkboard at this time if you're making the schoolhouse birdhouse). It can be planed to 1/8 inch or sawn to this thickness on a band saw. Exact thickness is not important.

Make one piece that is large enough for all the pieces to be cut from it. Cut the door and shutters to size and paint.

8. Glue on shutters, door and all trim pieces. Nail on front porch and add a small step below the door made from a scrap piece of door trim.

9. Cut the birdhouse floor to fit. Drill four 1/4-inch holes near the corners for drainage.

Recess the floor 1/4 inch. Predrill a hole on the back wall of the house for a 1-1/4-inch screw, which holds the floor in place. Add additional support to the floorboard by drilling pilot holes about 1-1/8 inches deep on each side for a finishing nail. The nail heads will stick out so you can remove them when cleaning.

10. Glue on roof pieces. (Note the vent space above the lower roof. This keeps the house cool in summer.) When glue is set, nail in place. Also glue awnings over windows.

11. Drill an entry hole approximately 6 inches above the floor. Use 1-1/8 inches for wrens and 1-1/4 inch for chickadees. Decorate as desired and let dry before hanging it in your backyard.

If a bird takes up residence, you've passed the test!

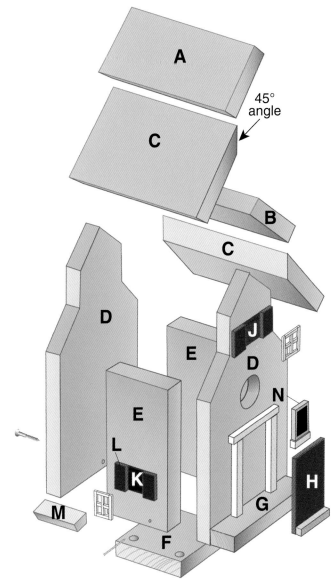

45° angle

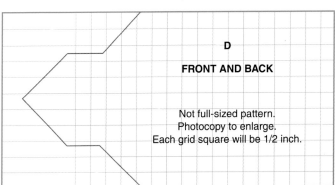

D

FRONT AND BACK

Not full-sized pattern.
Photocopy to enlarge.
Each grid square will be 1/2 inch.

CUTTING LIST

Part	Name	Qty.	Dimension
A	upper roof	1	3-5/8" x 6-3/4"
B	upper roof	1	2-3/4" x 6-3/4"
C	lower roof	2	3-1/8" x 6-3/4"
D	front/back	2	5-1/2" x 10-1/4"
E	side walls	2	4" x 6-3/8"
F	floor	1	cut to fit

OPTIONAL DETAILS:

Part	Name	Qty.	Dimension
G	porch	1	1-1/4" x 5-1/2"
H	door	1	1/8" x 1-3/4" x 4"
J	front window	1	chisel 1-1/4" square
K	side windows	2	chisel 1-1/4" x 1-1/2"
L	shutters	6	1/8" x 3/4" x window height
M	awnings	2	3/4" x 3-1/4" with a 15° bevel on one side
N	chalkboard	1	1/8" x 1-1/4" wide x 1-3/4" high

Coffee Can
Birdhouse

Simple plan starts with an empty coffee can.

Here's a terrific birdhouse that's as enjoyable as the aroma of the morning's first pot of coffee.

And it has a lot more going for it, too. The house is simple to build, costs pennies to make and is a great way to recycle coffee cans and scrap wood. As a bonus, it's a breeze to clean out after nesting season—just slip out the dowel and empty the can.

You don't have to paint it, but if you're like reader Jean Walters of Fort Worth, Texas who shared this plan, you might want to dress it up.

"These are great projects for children's groups, and they cost about $2 to make," Jean says. "Have your friends and neighbors save their coffee cans and precut the wood yourself. Then let the kids paint and assemble them. (If you plan to decorate your birdhouse, Jean suggests sanding and painting the pieces before assembly.) They're easy as store-bought pie to make, and sell faster than a cup of coffee in a doughnut shop.

Here's What You'll Need...

- ❑ Two scraps of 3/4-inch-thick pine board, measuring at least 4-1/2 inches square
- ❑ Two 1/4-inch-thick plywood or paneling scraps, measuring at least 6 inches x 9 inches each
- ❑ 1/4-inch dowel, 8-1/2 inches long
- ❑ 1-1/4-inch finishing nails
- ❑ One 11-ounce coffee can
- ❑ Hooks, wire or a chain for hanging the birdhouse

Recommended Tools...

- ❑ Table saw
- ❑ Power drill

Start Building...We'll Keep the Coffee Warm!

1. Cut the ends of the birdhouse 4-1/2 inches square from scrap pine boards.

2. Locate the entrance hole in one board by measuring 3-7/16 inches from one corner. (When measuring, place your ruler diagonally from corner to corner and draw a light pencil line.) Be sure to mark the corner from which you're measuring—you'll need to measure from it again in step 4.

3. Drill a 1-inch entrance hole for wrens or the appropriate-size hole for other small birds you'd like to attract. (See the birdhouse-building guidelines on page 39.)

4. Hold the front and back pieces together in a vise or clamp them together. Locate the perch by measuring 1-1/4 inches from the same corner used in step 2 and mark this spot on the pencil line. Then drill a 1/4-inch hole through the front piece (with the entrance hole) and most of the way through the back. (See "Workshop Wisdom" at right for a helpful hint.)

5. Cut the roof pieces from 1/4-inch plywood or paneling scraps. Cut one piece to measure 5-3/4 inches x 9 inches, and the other 6 inches x 9 inches.

6. Nail the roof pieces to the front and back boards with 1-1/4-inch finishing nails. The large roof piece should overlap the smaller at the peak. (If you're using paneling, the back side should face out.) Leave enough room between the front and back pieces so you can easily insert the coffee can.

7. Clean and dry the coffee can (watch out for sharp edges). Drill two 1/4-inch holes in one side of the can for drainage. Drill two more 1/4-inch holes on the opposite side of the can for ventilation.

8. Place the coffee can between the front and back boards. Cut a 1/4-inch dowel to 8-1/2 inches long and insert it through the perch holes. If the fit is too snug, lightly sand the dowel, which holds the can in place.

9. Attach a chain, hooks or wire for hanging the birdhouse. With any luck, you won't have to wait long for your feathered friends to discover the new home you've provided. Just sit back, have another cup of coffee and enjoy the show.

Workshop Wisdom
Drilling Holes Partially Through a Board

If you need to drill a hole only partway through a board, here's an easy method to make sure you don't drill too deep.

1. Lay the drill bit against the outside edge of the board to determine the proper depth you need to drill.

2. Mark the depth on the bit with a piece of masking tape, making sure the bottom edge lines up at the depth you should stop drilling. Wrap the piece of tape around the drill bit.

3. Drill the hole into the board, stopping when you reach the bottom edge of the tape.

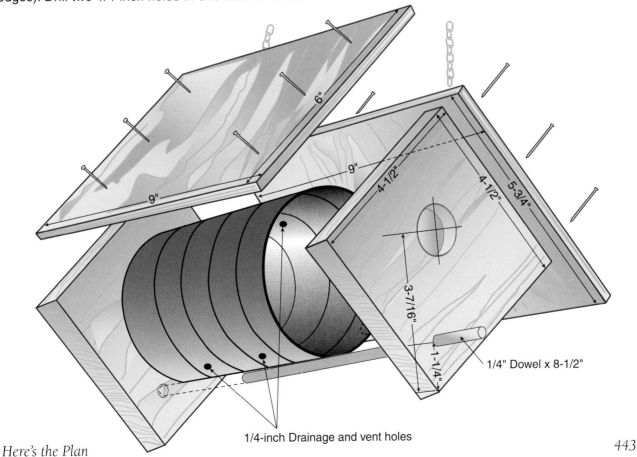

1/4" Dowel x 8-1/2"

1/4-inch Drainage and vent holes

Here's the Plan

443

GOURD
Birdhouse

James R. Hill, III

If properly preserved, a homegrown gourd birdhouse will last for decades.

Gourds make great birdhouses, and the time spent creating one is a worthwhile investment. Cured hard-shell gourds are almost as tough as plywood. And they will last up to 30 years if properly coated with a preservative and handled with a little care.

Gourds have been used to make purple martin houses for centuries. Native Americans used to hang them to attract martins to their settlements. Today, martins depend on people to supply them with houses and gourds. If you live east of the Rocky Mountains, you may want to give the martins a hand.

These basic gourd birdhouses are popular with the birds and purple martin "landlords". The best part is, there's no limit to the number you can produce and hang right in your yard. We've heard of one martin enthusiast who puts up and maintains more than 600 gourd houses every year!

Other birds will nest in a gourd, too. Just customize it with the proper-size entrance hole for the species you're trying to attract and place it in the right habitat. (See "Gourds Will Attract Other Birds, Too" on page 446.)

Because many *Birds & Blooms* readers have expressed an interest in learning how to make gourd houses specifically for purple martins, we've included this project.

Here's What You'll Need...

- ❑ One hard-shell gourd, also known as a bottle gourd or birdhouse gourd
- ❑ Bleach (for disinfectant)
- ❑ Fine steel wool
- ❑ Wood preservative or copper sulfate
- ❑ Oil-based primer
- ❑ Oil-based white enamel paint
- ❑ Plastic-coated copper wire, 24 inches long
- ❑ Face mask (see "Safety First!" tip at far right)

Recommended Tools...

- ❑ Power drill
- ❑ 2-1/8-inch hole saw or a keyhole saw

444

Chapter 10

Step 2

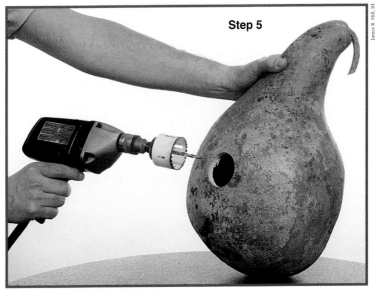

Step 5

HOMEGROWN BIRDHOUSE. Gourd houses are easy to make—but they take a bit of time and patience. It may take 3 to 6 months before a gourd completely dries and you can begin working on it. Mold will form on the gourd as it dries (at left). Don't throw it away like many first-time gourd crafters do. This is just part of the natural drying process. Eventually you'll wash the mold off and drill a 2-1/8-inch entrance hole (above) when it's completely dry. See the illustration below to help locate the entrance.

Let's Get Gourding

1. Harvest a hard-shell gourd when the vine has withered. Be careful to leave the stem attached. It's best to cut the stem with a pruning shears so you don't bruise it.

A good purple martin gourd has a diameter of about 8 to 13 inches. Wash it thoroughly in water, rinse in a solution of 1 part disinfectant (bleach works fine) and 10 parts water, and dry it with a towel.

2. Hang the gourd in a sunny spot or place it on newspaper in a warm dry spot (such as an attic or basement) for 3 to 6 months. If the gourd is lying on a flat surface, be sure to frequently turn it.

The gourd will begin to mold as it dries (see photo above left)—*don't throw it out!* This is a natural part of the curing process. Gourds dried indoors will grow the most mold and should be wiped clean frequently with the same concentration (1 to 10) of disinfectant you used for cleaning. However, discard any gourds that become soft or wrinkled.

3. Check if the gourd is dry by giving it a good shake—if the seeds rattle, you can begin making a birdhouse.

4. Soak the gourd for 15 minutes in hot soapy water, then scrape it with a dull knife to remove the outer skin and mold. Scrub the gourd in the water with fine steel wool. Rinse it well and allow it to thoroughly dry.

5. To locate the entrance hole, hold the gourd by its stem between your index finger and thumb and let it hang. Mark a center point along the outer-

most part of the curve so the hole faces straight out— not towards the sky or the ground (see illustration below).

The hole should measure 2-1/8 inches and can be easily and quickly drilled with the proper-size hole saw as pictured above. (Be sure to wear a face mask.)

You can also use a keyhole saw to cut the entrance by hand. If you do, it's best to cut the hole immediately after washing the gourd, while it's still wet.

6. Make seven drainage holes in the bottom of the gourd about 2 inches apart using a 5/16-inch drill bit.

7. With the same bit, drill two sets of holes about 2 inches from the top of the gourd's neck for hanging and ventilation. One set should be drilled perpendicular to the entrance hole and the other in line with it. (You'll only use one set of holes for hanging. Choose the pair that will allow the entrance hole to face the most open direction.)

(Continued on next page)

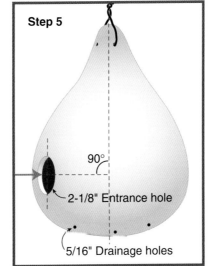

Step 5

90°

2-1/8" Entrance hole

5/16" Drainage holes

Safety First!

Protect Yourself from Harmful Gourd Dust

Gourd dust is a caustic substance. Always wear a tight-fitting dust mask when drilling gourds or scraping out seeds. You should also wear a mask when removing bird nests from the gourds in fall.

Here's the Plan

445

8. Remove seeds and membrane through the entrance hole with a long-handled metal spoon, screwdriver or a wire coat hanger (wear a face mask). If this is difficult, soak the gourd in water for several hours. The inside does not have to be completely clean.

9. Dip the gourd in a wood preservative for 15 minutes, weighting it down with a brick. Then remove the gourd and hang it up to dry for several days.

For a cheaper alternative, dissolve 1 pound of copper sulfate (available at garden centers and farm-supply stores) in 5 gallons of warm water and dip the gourd as instructed above. Wear rubber gloves while handling it.

HOUSE PAINTING (WITHOUT A LADDER). Purple martins prefer white houses, so painting the gourds (below) is an important part of the process. Use an oil-based primer and top coat with white exterior enamel paint. Paint only the outside, and be careful not to clog the drainage holes. Gourd houses need to be repainted every few years, but if properly maintained, they'll last for decades to come.

Step 10

Gourds need to be retreated and repainted every few years. So whatever preservative you use, store the solution in a covered plastic bucket for reuse, but keep it away from children and pets.

10. Sand the gourd smooth and paint with an oil-based primer. Allow it to dry.

11. Paint the gourd house with white exterior enamel paint with a nylon brush. (Do not use water-based latex paint because it will peel.) Apply two coats. Be careful not to clog drainage holes.

12. When dry, you can hang your gourd (you'll need at least 4 to 6 gourds to attract martins) from a 24-inch plastic-coated copper wire. Thread the wire through two of the holes directly across from each other and hang it from a support line (see page 12), below a martin house (like the one on page 34) or on a specially made gourd rack. The gourd will swing, making it less attractive to nest competitors, such as starlings.

Hang the gourd 10 to 15 feet high, with the entrance hole facing an open area.

13. In late August or early September, after the martins depart for their winter homes in the tropics, take the gourd house down for cleaning. Break up nests with the handle of a wooden spoon and shake out the contents. Then store until early spring (the martins return as early as February in the deep South) in a spot inaccessible to rodents.

Your gourd house will be ready to use again, but you might want to prepare a few more over winter, because the martins will probably bring along a few more friends!

Editor's Note: *Want to know more about gourd houses for purple martins? A 12-page booklet, "Growing & Preparing Gourd Homes for Martins," is available from the Purple Martin Conservation Association, 301 Peninsula Dr., Suite 6, Erie PA 16505. Or see the association's Web site at purplemartin.org.*

Gourds Will Attract Other Birds, Too

If you live in an area that's not the most suitable for attracting purple martins, don't despair. Gourds make fine homes for several varieties of cavity nesters, including bluebirds, swallows, chickadees, wrens, woodpeckers, great crested flycatchers, titmice, screech owls, kestrels and nuthatches.

Each bird has its own requirements for habitat, entrance-hole size and cavity dimensions. For instance, house wrens need a 1-inch entrance hole in a gourd 5 to 6 inches in diameter and prefer gourds hung in a shady area close to brush.

Chickadees need a 1-1/4-inch hole and like to nest in wooded areas. Bluebirds and tree swallows require a 1-1/2-inch hole and prefer to nest in open areas. For flycatchers, make the hole 1-3/4 to 2 inches in diameter and hang the gourd in a tree close to a brushy area.

Birdhouse For Beginners

One-board project fits in anywhere.

While this birdhouse is as simple as it gets, it has a lot going for it. It can be made very quickly…uses minimal materials and tools…and boasts a sleek look that will make any budding woodworker proud to say, "I built it myself!".

"We've had a simple one-board birdhouse like this in our yard for the past 3 years, and have had occupants each spring," says Loron Holden of Lillian, Alabama.

We simplified Loron's design a bit so even kids can take on this project with a little help from an adult. So clear off your workbench, grab your hammer and tape measure and start showing that young woodworker-in-training how it's done.

Here's What You'll Need...

❑ One 5-foot 1-inch x 6-inch No. 2 pine board
❑ 1-5/8-inch galvanized deck screws
❑ 2-inch galvanized finishing nails

Recommended Tools...

❑ Power drill   ❑ Appropriate-size spade bit
❑ Hand saw

Let's Saw That Board!

1. Using the full width of the 1-inch x 6-inch board, cut out the pieces as shown in the board layout below.

2. Drill a centered entrance hole about 2-1/2 inches from the top of the front piece. See the "Build a Better Birdhouse" chart on page 39 for recommended hole sizes and placement.

3. Attach the front to the sides with 1-5/8-inch deck screws. Predrill the holes in the front piece to prevent the wood from splitting.

After nesting season when it's time to clean out the birdhouse, remove these screws for easy access.

4. Attach the back to the sides with 2-inch finishing nails. Be sure each nail goes in straight. We recommend predrilling holes using the method described in "Workshop Wisdom" on page 63.

5. Cut about 1/2 inch off each corner of the floor for drainage.

6. Recess the floor 1/4 inch up from the bottom of the house, then attach it with 2-inch finishing nails from the sides and back. *Do not nail the floor from the front or you won't be able to open it for cleaning.*

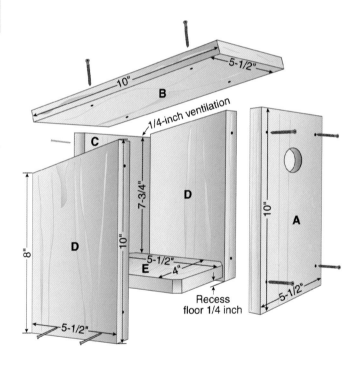

7. Attach the roof to the sides with 1-5/8-inch deck screws.

You're finished—your board is now a birdhouse. Nice job!

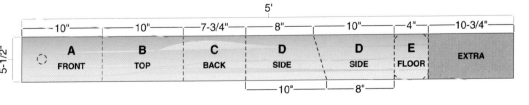

FLOWERPOT
Birdhouse

This clay pot will "grow" generations of wrens.

Here's a rather interesting twist—a flowerpot project that has nothing to do with plants and everything to do with birds.

With a little bit of remodeling, you can put out the welcome mat for wrens with this easy-to-build birdhouse, which requires a minimum of tools and effort.

Susan Vater created this birdhouse for her garden in Middleton, Wisconsin. Because the house is small, she says it's perfect for hanging in the thick vegetation that wrens prefer.

The only difficult part of this project is making the entrance hole in the flowerpot. The hole should be 1 inch in diameter, or as veteran wren house builders say, "large enough for a quarter to pass through".

Glass drill bits work best for drilling into the clay, but masonry bits work almost as well. If you don't have either, don't worry—regular drill bits will do the job, too. They'll just need sharpening after you're finished. But if you think you can take a shortcut by using a spade bit, don't try it. You'll end up with a broken pot.

A Little at a Time

1. Locate the entrance hole and use a small drill bit (1/8 inch or less) to start a hole at its center. Then work your way up to larger bits, gradually enlarging the hole. Here are some suggestions that may help:
- Use a slow speed while drilling.
- Wipe the bit often with a damp rag to clean it. (Keep electric drills away from water!)
- Do not use force as you drill.

2. Once you've used your largest drill bit, it's time to test your patience—the rest of the hole will be enlarged by hand with a rat-tail file and finished with a half-round file. This may take up to 30 minutes.

There's a secret to making steady progress—keep your file clean. Tapping or brushing out the dust won't be enough; you'll need to rinse the file in a bucket of water before continuing.

Once the entrance is just large enough to pass a quarter through, the most difficult work is finished. But be careful...this is no time to accidentally drop the flowerpot!

3. Trace the open end of the pot on a piece of 1/4-inch or thicker plywood to make the floor to the house. (Be sure to use plywood and not particle board, which soaks up water like a sponge.) Cut the circular base with a saber saw about 1/4 inch wider than the guideline.

4. In the center of the plywood base, drill a hole large enough for the eyebolt to pass through. Then set the flowerpot upside down on top of the plywood base.

5. Slip a fender washer onto the eyebolt and pass it through the pot's drainage hole and through the plywood base. Slip another washer over the end of the eyebolt and secure it with a nut. (Be careful not to over-tighten the nut—you might break the pot.)

Now your wren house is ready to hang. Using a hook or chain, suspend the house from a sturdy support 5 to 10 feet above the ground, preferably in an area with plenty of low growth. Then wait for the your tenants to arrive.

There'll be no doubt when the wrens do move in—they're especially robust singers, with a distinctive trill at the end of each song.

Because the wrens' diet consists primarily of insects, you'll not only be grateful for their beautiful serenade. They'll police your garden, eating many uninvited pests.

Trace the mouth of the flowerpot onto plywood and cut 1/4 inch wider than the guideline.

Here's the Plan

Build a Better Birdhouse!

Here are some basic guidelines you'll find helpful when building birdhouses for specific species.

Species	Dimensions	Hole	Placement	Color	Notes
Eastern bluebird	5" x 5" x 8"h.	1-1/2" centered 6" above floor	5-10' high in the open; sunny area	light earth tones	likes open areas, especially facing a field
Tree swallow	5" x 5" x 6"h.	1-1/2" centered 4" above floor	5-8' high in the open; 50-100% sun	light earth tones or gray	within 2 miles of pond or lake
Purple martin	multiple apts. 6" x 6" x 6" ea. (minimum)	2-1/8" hole 2-1/4" above floor	15-20' high in the open	white	open yard without tall trees; near water
Tufted titmouse	4" x 4" x 8"h.	1-1/4"	4-10' high	light earth tones	prefers to live in or near woods
Chickadee	4" x 4" x 8"h. or 5" x 5" base	1-1/8" centered 6" above floor	4-8' high	light earth tones	small tree thicket
Nuthatch	4" x 4" x 10"h.	1-1/4" centered 7-1/2" above floor	12-25' high on tree trunk	bark-covered or natural	prefers to live in or near woods
House wren	4" x 4" x 8"h. or 4" x 6" base	1" centered 6" above floor	5-10' high on post or hung in tree	light earth tones or white	prefers lower branches of backyard trees
Northern flicker	7" x 7" x 18"h.	2-1/2" centered 14" above floor	8-20' high	light earth tones	put 4" sawdust inside for nesting
Downy woodpecker	4" x 4" x 10"h.	1-1/4" centered 7-1/2" above floor	12-25' high on tree trunk	simulate natural cavity	prefers own excavation; provide sawdust
Red-headed woodpecker	6" x 6" x 15"h.	2" centered 6-8" above floor	8-20' high on post or tree trunk	simulate natural cavity	needs sawdust for nesting
Wood duck	10" x 10" x 24"h.	4" x 3" elliptical 20" above floor	2-5' high on post over water, or 12-40' high on tree facing water	light earth tones or natural	needs 3-4" of sawdust or shavings for nesting
American kestrel	10" x 10" x 24"h.	4" x 3" elliptical 20" above floor	12-40' high on post or tree trunk	light earth tones or natural	needs open approach on edge of woodlot or in isolated tree
Screech owl	10" x 10" x 24"h.	4" x 3" elliptical 20" above floor	12-40' high on tree	light earth tones or natural	prefers open woods or edge of woodlot

Nesting Shelves

Species	Dimensions	Hole	Placement	Color	Notes
American robin	6" x 6" x 8"h.	none—needs roof for rain protection	on side of building or arbor or in tree	light earth tones or wood	use is irregular
Barn swallow	6" x 6" x 8"h.	none—does not need roof	under eaves of building	light earth tones or wood	prefers barns or outbuildings
Phoebe	6" x 6" x 8"h.	none—does not need roof	under eaves of building	light earth tones or wood	prefers water nearby

Note: With the exception of wrens and purple martins, birds do not tolerate swaying birdhouses. Birdhouses should be firmly anchored to a post, a tree or the side of a

Source: *Garden Birds of America* by George H. Harrison. Willow Creek Press, 1996.

Simple Tray Feeder

Sturdy feeder serves all sorts of wildlife.

If you enjoy seeing a variety of animals feeding in your backyard, this easy-to-build triangular feeder is all you'll need to attract a crowd.

Cardinals and other "tray feeders" will love it…and the low platform will attract birds that feed close to the ground like dark-eyed juncos and mourning doves.

You'll also see plenty of squirrels and chipmunks, so keep the tray well stocked with cracked corn. (If these furry critters can count on a reliable food supply here, they'll be less likely to disturb other feeders set up only for birds.)

One of our *Birds & Blooms* editors came up with the idea for this unique triangular feeder. The three legs prevent wobbling no matter where you put it in your yard. Plus, it's lightweight enough to move with ease.

Here's What You'll Need...

- ❏ One 8-foot 2 x 2
- ❏ One 3-foot 1-inch x 8-inch board (or 4-foot 2 x 4)
- ❏ One 2-foot-square piece of metal window screen
- ❏ 2-1/2-inch and 2-inch galvanized deck screws
- ❏ Waterproof carpenter's glue
- ❏ Masking tape

Recommended Tools...

- ❏ Table or miter saw
- ❏ Heavy-duty stapler

Start with the Tray

1. To make the seed tray, cut three 24-inch lengths from an 8-foot 2 x 2 with 60° opposing angles on each end (remove 30° on each cut).

2. On a flat surface, fit the pieces together with the edges overlapping and temporarily fasten them with carpenter's glue. Hold the joints tight with masking tape. When the glue is dry, drill a pilot hole in each corner and secure with 2-1/2-inch deck screws.

3. From a 2-foot-square piece of screen, cut out a triangle that fits the frame, extending about halfway between the inner and outer edge of the frame. Staple the screen to the wood securely, leaving about 1 inch between staples.

4. For the legs, rip three 2-1/2-inch widths from a 3-foot 1-inch x 8-inch board. Cut each piece to 16 inches. If you want a more finished appearance, bevel the tops of the legs 15°. The legs can also be made from 2 x 4's to reduce warping.

5. Position a leg so it bridges the joint of the frame (see plan and photo at right). Then predrill two holes for the screws, being careful not to hit the screws holding the seed tray together.

6. Use 2-inch deck screws to attach each leg to the frame. (To make the tray a little sturdier for chunky wildlife, you can glue the leg joints with carpenter's glue before driving the screws.)

Now fill the tray with seed and cracked corn—it shouldn't take long for the neighborhood critters to discover the banquet you've set out for them!

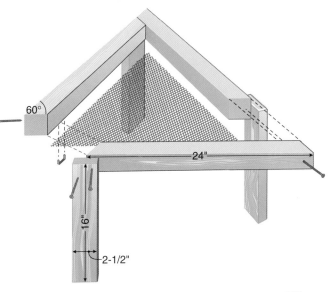

Here's the Plan

Suet Feeder

They'll Love

Spilled birdseed leaving a mess on your patio or deck? This feeder offers a tidy alternative.

The spirit of holiday gift-giving inspired Robyn MacDuff of Sandy, Utah to develop this easy-to-use suet feeder.

"I wanted to make Christmas gifts for friends and family to share my enjoyment of feeding birds," Robyn recalls. "Some people on my gift list didn't like spilled birdseed on their patios, so I decided on suet feeders—they're perfect for attracting winter birds and don't spill seeds on the ground."

Searching for an attractive design, Robyn perused back issues of *Birds & Blooms* and found some great ideas. "Then I set up my drafting table and got to work," she says.

Robyn's feeder is designed to hold the premade suet cakes that can be purchased at bird-supply stores, hardware stores and garden centers. Before making this feeder to the dimensions shown, we recommend finding out the standard size of the suet cakes available in your area and adjust the measurements if needed.

Time for Tools

1. Begin with a 3-foot 1-inch x 6-inch pine board. Rip the board on a table saw so one piece measures 1-1/4 inches wide. From that board, cut:
- Two side pieces 6 inches long
- One bottom piece 6-1/4 inches long
- One top piece 4-3/4 inches long

2. Adjust the blade in your table saw so it is low enough to make a groove, called a "dado", 1/4 inch deep. (Check the depth of the dado on a scrap board. For safety, be sure to use push sticks when cutting—see photo next page.)

Here's What You'll Need...

- ❏ One 3-foot 1-inch x 6-inch No. 2 pine board
- ❏ One scrap piece of 1/4-inch plywood (4 x 4 inches minimum)
- ❏ One piece of hardware cloth with 1/2-inch or 1/4-inch squares
- ❏ 1-1/4-inch and 3/4-inch wire brads
- ❏ Netting staples
- ❏ Three double-headed (duplex) nails
- ❏ Waterproof carpenter's glue
- ❏ Two screw eyes
- ❏ Chain for hanging the feeder

Recommended Tools...

- ❏ Table saw   ❏ Tin snips   ❏ Pliers

Cut the dado lengthwise in the center of the 6-1/4 inch long piece. This will accommodate the tail support, which will help keep unwanted birds like European starlings off your feeder. You'll need to make a few passes over the saw blade until the dado is 1/4 inch wide.

Cutting the dado will require you to adjust your saw's fence—the guide used for ripping a board—a few times. It may be tempting to leave the saw running during these adjustments, but don't! *Always* shut off the saw when ad-

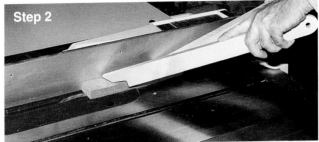

SAFETY FIRST! When cutting small wood pieces and making "dado" cuts on a table saw, use push sticks to guide the wood (as pictured above). This keeps your hands and fingers a safe distance away from the dangerous saw blade.

justing the fence.

3. For the tail support, you'll need a scrap piece of 1/4-inch plywood at least 4 inches square. Cut this piece 3-1/2 inches wide at the top and taper it to a width of 2-3/4 inches at the bottom. The angle is 5°...or you can just measure in 3/8 inch from each bottom corner, draw a pencil line to the top corner and then cut off the waste.

4. Rip the remaining 3-foot-long pine board 2-1/4 inches wide (remember to use a push stick!). Then cut a 7-3/4-inch-long piece from it for the top of the feeder.

5. Using 1-1/4-inch wire brads, nail the framework together following the plan at right. The 4-3/4-inch piece should be centered under the top piece and fastened with 1-1/4-inch brads from below. *Make sure the groove in the bottom piece is facing down.*

6. To hold the suet cake in the feeder, you'll need enough 1/2-inch-square or 1/4-inch-square screening to cut two pieces measuring about 5-1/2 inches x 6 inches. Trim the wire nubs with a tin snips as closely to a full square as possible. This will give the feeder a finished look and keep you and the birds from being poked by sharp ends.

7. Attach one piece of screening on one side of the feeder with netting staples on all four sides.

8. On the front side, staple the screening *only at the bottom edge*, fastening with three or four staples. These staples act as a hinge, allowing you to swing open the screen to fill the feeder. If the screen doesn't swing open easily, loosen the staples a bit.

9. To hold the "screen door" closed, drill three holes 3/8 inches from the edge of the top board for double-headed (duplex) nails. These will protrude through the top and extend past the screening to keep the door tightly shut (see photo at top left).

(*Hint:* We suggest drilling the center hole first and testing the fit with one of the nails. Then adjust the end holes

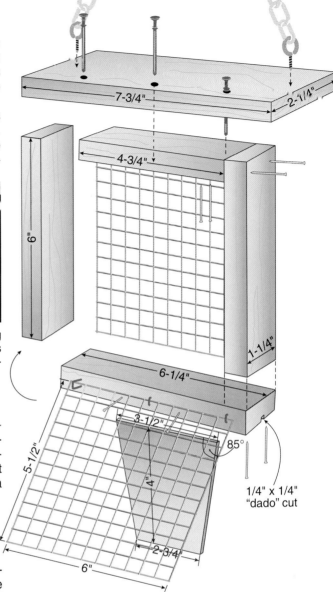

if needed so the screen is held tightly in place.)

Choose a drill bit slightly larger than the nails, since they will be removed each time you fill the feeder. Don't make them too loose, or this feeder will be an easy target for a crafty squirrel.

For a finished look, cut the nails with a hacksaw so they're about 1-3/4 inches long.

10. Center the tail support into the dado and fasten with waterproof glue and 3/4-inch wire brads from both sides.

11. Before adding the chain, open and screw the eyes into the top board. Then insert the ends of the chain into the screw eyes and squeeze them shut with a pliers.

Fill the feeder with a fresh suet cake and hang from a tree or feeding station, or attach to a tree trunk. Soon the birds in your neighborhood will be in "fat city".

Step 7: Staple back hardware cloth on all four sides.

RECYCLED
Bird feeder

Old juice bottle and wood scraps become a feeder.

Homemade bird feeders don't have to be homely. This one is made mostly from recycled materials, yet looks as attractive as an expensive store-bought product.

Kenneth Higgins designed this feeder for his yard, which overlooks Lake Buchanan in Burnet, Texas. Filled with sunflower seed, it is a favorite of the tufted titmice in his area.

It's a great project for builders on a budget or those who would like to try something new. Kenneth points out that he made three feeders like this one from a leftover piece of cedar fencing.

"That's pretty cheap," he observes. "One board is all it takes, and you feel good about it because you're recycling, too."

Since wide boards tends to warp, we recommend making the roof and feeding tray from plywood, which stands up to weather well (it won't warp). Although plywood isn't as attractive, we've disguised it a bit by edging the tray with cedar.

Here's What You'll Need...

❑ One 1-gallon plastic juice bottle with cap
❑ Plywood scraps, at least 1/2 inch thick
❑ Cedar or pine scraps
❑ 1-1/4-inch galvanized deck screws
❑ 1-1/2-inch wire brads
❑ Small sheet-metal screws
❑ 18-inch-long light-duty rustproof chain
❑ Two S hooks

Recommended Tools...

❑ Table saw   ❑ Saber saw
❑ Utility knife   ❑ Compass
❑ Power drill

Finish Your Juice, It's Time to Start Building!

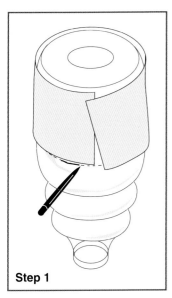

Step 1

1. Wash and dry a 1-gallon plastic juice bottle (we used an Ocean Spray juice bottle). Mark at least 3/4 inches below the point where the bottle straightens out.

Wrap a piece of paper around the bottom of the bottle, lining up the edge of the paper with the point you've marked. Make sure the paper is straight as it wraps around the bottle. Then trace around the edge of the paper with a permanent marker to make a cutting line (at left).

Carefully cut (away from yourself) along the line with a utility knife or scissors. Take your time with this step because the plastic will become flimsy as you cut.

2. Cut or drill three 1/2-inch holes in the narrowest part of the bottle's neck. Don't worry too much about the size of the holes—you can always enlarge them later if necessary. Start by using a smaller bit.

3. Cut a scrap of plywood 6-1/2 inches square for the seed tray.

4. Rip trim pieces that will make a tray 1 inch deep (thickness of plywood plus 1 inch).

They'll overlap at the corners, so the four bottom trim pieces should measure 6-1/2 inches *plus* the thickness of the wood you're using. Attach them to the tray with 1-1/2-inch wire brads. Drill a 1/4-inch drainage hole in each corner of the seed tray.

5. Cut a scrap of plywood 10-inches square for the roof. The larger roof will protect seed in the feeding tray from rain and snow. Trim the roof edging in the same manner as the seed tray in step 4.

6. From another scrap of plywood, cut a disk to fit the diameter of the wide part of the bottle. Measure the diameter of the wide opening and use a compass to draw the circle, or trace around the bottle. Cut the piece with a saber saw right on the cutting line. This will allow the piece to slip in and out of the bottle easily when you fill the feeder.

Center and attach the disk to the underside of the roof with four 1-1/4-inch deck screws.

7. Drill a hole through the center of the roof pieces. Connect opposite corners with straight pencil lines. They'll meet in the center of the board. (It's important that this hole be centered or the feeder will not hang straight.) Make the hole just large enough to accommodate the chain you'll use to hang the feeder.

8. Remove the cap from the bottle and carefully drill two holes near its outside edge. Start with a small drill bit and gradually increase the size until the small sheet-metal screws fit through it easily. *Do not apply pressure while drilling.* Going slow and sure like this will help prevent the plastic cap from cracking.

Attach the cap centered in the feeding tray with the small screws, but don't tighten them too much or the cap may crack.

9. Drill a hole through the center of the bottle cap and tray. Again, increase the drill bit size gradually. Be very careful when starting the hole—drill slowly so the cap doesn't break.

10. String the chain through the roof, bottle and tray. Loop the top of the chain or use an S hook for hanging. Attach another S hook at the bottom to keep the chain from slipping up through the feeder. Close the hook with pliers.

Hang it, fill it and let the wild birds come and get it!

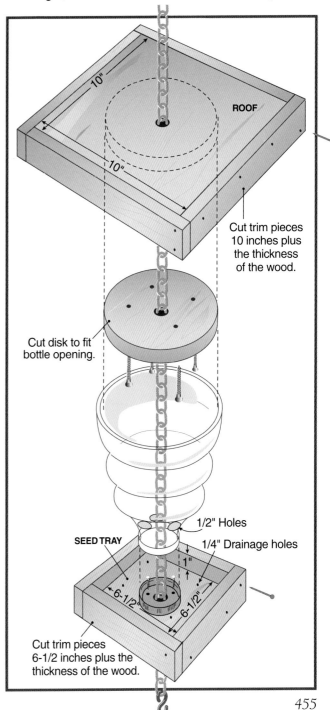

10"
10"
ROOF
Cut trim pieces 10 inches plus the thickness of the wood.

Cut disk to fit bottle opening.

1/2" Holes
1/4" Drainage holes
SEED TRAY
1"
6-1/2"
6-1/2"
Cut trim pieces 6-1/2 inches plus the thickness of the wood.

Easy Orange Feeder

Simple project will attract colorful diners.

No need to break the budget when it comes to feeding orioles. With this simple orange feeder, you're sure to bring these beautiful birds to your backyard—after all, they can't resist citrus in the spring.

The best part is this project may not even cost a dime, because there's a good chance you probably already have enough scrap lumber and hardware around the house to build several of these surefire feeders.

This feeder was inspired by one designed by Daniel Medbury of Plymouth, Michigan. We've simplified it a bit so anyone can build it—even a child with a little adult supervision. In less than an hour, you'll be hanging your own exclusive oriole feeding station.

Here's What You'll Need...

❑ One scrap 2 x 4, at least 13 inches long
❑ One 1-inch x 8-inch board, about 12 inches long
❑ One 1/4-inch dowel, at least 18 inches long
❑ Four 2-1/2-inch galvanized finishing nails
❑ Four common nails
❑ Waterproof carpenter's glue
❑ One screw eye for hanging the feeder

Recommended Tools...

❑ Table saw
❑ Power drill
❑ Combination square

BALTIMORE ORIOLES can't resist citrus in the spring.

Easy as Orange Pie

1. Cut a scrap 2 x 4 at least 13 inches long.

2. Cut two 45° angles to form a centered peak on one end (this will become the top). Use a combination square or tri-square to help draw the cutting angles.

3. "Dog-ear" the corners at the bottom end of the 2 x 4 by sawing about 3/4 inch off each corner at a 45° angle.

4. Drill two 1/4-inch holes through the 2 x 4. Center one hole 1-1/4 inches from bottom of the board and the other 6-1/2 inches from bottom. Make sure you drill the holes perpendicular to the 2 x 4. This will ensure that your perches will be straight. (See "Workshop Wisdom" at bottom right for a helpful hint.)

5. Cut two roof pieces from the 1-inch x 8-inch board. One section should measure approximately 6 inches x 7-1/4 inches and the other 5-1/4 inches x 7-1/4 inches. If you'd like, dog-ear the outside corners of the roof pieces by cutting off about 1 inch from each corner at a 45° angle.

6. Nail the roof pieces to the 2 x 4 peak with two common nails. The longer piece overlaps the shorter.

7. The oranges are held onto the feeder by spearing them onto 2-1/2-inch finishing nails. Center these nails on each side of the 2 x 4 about 3 inches above each perch hole. Drive the nails about 1 inch into the 2 x 4 at a downward angle so they hold the oranges better.

8. Cut the 18-inch dowel in half for perches. Insert the dowels into the holes and center them. A little waterproof carpenter's glue in the holes will hold the perches firmly in place.

9. File or cut a flat spot in the center of the roof peak for a screw eye, which is used to hang the feeder. Drill a pilot hole first—this will prevent the wood from splitting.

A coat of deck stain is optional, but it'll help protect the wood from weather. Be sure the stain is dry before using the feeder.

Then cut two oranges in half, spear them onto the nails and wait for the orioles to show up while you enjoy a glass of iced tea.

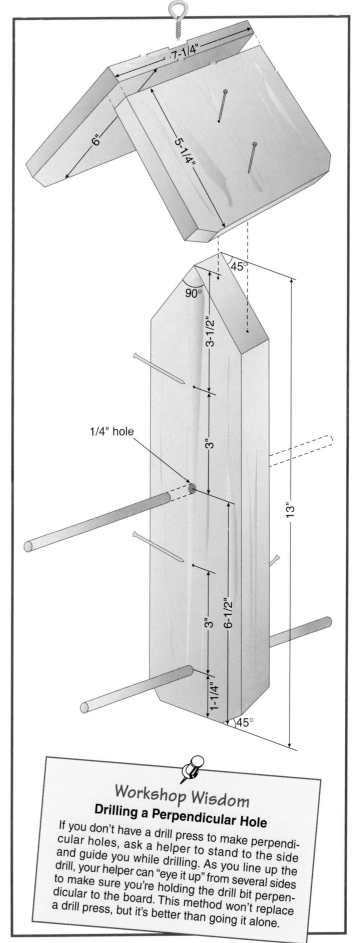

Workshop Wisdom
Drilling a Perpendicular Hole

If you don't have a drill press to make perpendicular holes, ask a helper to stand to the side and guide you while drilling. As you line up the drill, your helper can "eye it up" from several sides to make sure you're holding the drill bit perpendicular to the board. This method won't replace a drill press, but it's better than going it alone.

Birds will go NUTS

Simple feeder keeps out squirrels.

If you want a parade of new birds coming to your backyard, try offering them something new... peanuts!

One of our editors added a simple peanut feeder like the one pictured at left to his backyard. Birds he's never seen near his place—woodpeckers (both hairy and downy), nuthatches and blue jays—came out of their shell to sample the peanuts.

We've received a lot of interest in this type of peanut feeder ever since we pictured one like it on the cover of *Birds & Blooms* (October/November '98 issue). The wire feeder caught the eye of Alice Schultz of Gasport, New York.

"I'd sure like to make one for myself," Alice writes. "I figure it must be made for squirrels since it's filled with peanuts."

Actually, the wire hardware cloth keeps those furry critters from getting to the goobers. Squirrels can be persistent and destructive though (some even chewed through the wire when we filled it with peanuts out of the shell), so we recommend filling the feeder with peanuts *in the shell*.

This makes it even more difficult for squirrels to get to the feed, while woodpeckers, nuthatches and other birds have little trouble breaking the shells and finding the hidden treasures inside.

Here's What You'll Need...

- ❑ One 2-foot 1-inch x 6-inch board
- ❑ Approximately 12 inches x 18 inches of hardware cloth with 1/4-inch squares
- ❑ 36-inch-long light-duty chain
- ❑ One screw eye
- ❑ Netting staples
- ❑ Waterproof carpenter's glue (or 1-5/8-inch deck screws)

Recommended Tools...

- ❑ Band, saber or scroll saw
- ❑ Wire cutter
- ❑ Needle-nose pliers
- ❑ Soldering iron (optional)

Let's Start Building

1. Cut out four disks—two should measure about 4-3/4 inches across and two should measure about 3 inches across—with a band, saber or scroll saw. Make the circles with a compass, or simply trace the rims of quart and 1/2-pint paint cans (or other cans similar to the dimensions above).

Cut the smaller disks carefully—they should be as close to identical as possible.

2. Center and glue (or predrill and fasten with three 1-5/8-inch deck screws) each of the small disks to the larger disks. Clamp these pieces together until the glue dries. This will form the top and base of the feeder.

3. Fasten one end of the chain to a screw eye. Open the eye with two small pliers. (With the pliers parallel to the screw, twist in opposite directions until the eye opens just enough for the chain to be inserted.) Close the eye with a pliers.

Drill a pilot hole in the center of one of the small disks and turn in the screw eye. This will become the feeder's base.

4. Wrap hardware cloth around the completed base. (If using a 1/2-pint paint can to determine the size of the smaller disks, wrap the hardware cloth around the base and the can, which should be positioned about 10 inches higher than the base. Wrap heavy-duty rubber bands around the base and can to form a cylinder.)

Cut the hardware cloth about 1/4 inch beyond the last complete square where it comes together. This will leave small wire tabs on one end (see illustration at lower left). Remove the rubber bands and paint can.

5. Bend hardware cloth into a cylinder and attach to the feeder's base with netting staples (with the chain inside).

6. Join the two ends of hardware cloth to form a cylinder. Secure by wrapping the tabs around the other end using needle-nose pliers. Make sure the cylinder isn't too tight at the feeder's top, otherwise it will be difficult to lift up and close when filling with peanuts.

We recommend spot soldering the wire at the seam about every 2 inches for a better hold. If there is excess wire at the tabs, trim with a wire cutter.

7. Drill a hole in the center of the feeder's top large enough for the chain to easily slide through. Thread the chain through it and place the top of the feeder onto the cylinder.

The chain can be looped for hanging or attached to a S hook.

8. Slide the top up along the chain and fill the cylinder with peanuts. We think you'll enjoy watching the parade of feathered friends from the "peanut gallery".

18"

3"

4-3/4"

Dimensions can vary as indicated in step 1.

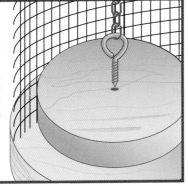

Step 4: When cutting hardware cloth, leave wire tabs on one 18-inch side. Roll the cloth into a cylinder and bend the wire tabs around the other end to hold them together.

Here's the Plan

Butterfly House

Whimsical project is a conversation piece.

Over the years, our magazines have received a lot of mail about butterfly houses. Do they really work? How do you attract butterflies to them? What should be placed inside?

So we set out to do our own research on these "flying flower" abodes to find some answers. As of yet, we have not been able to confirm that garden-variety butterflies will actually take up residence in these popular butterfly houses.

But don't let that discourage you from making this project. We're fairly certain placing a butterfly house in your garden will attract quite a few comments and generate lots of interest, even if it doesn't really attract butterflies.

Spread Your Wings With This Project!

1. From the 8-foot 1-inch x 8-inch board, cut the pieces as shown in the board layout at far right. If you do not plan on painting your butterfly house, we recommend using cedar, which will weather well.

2. Cut 60° angles on a table saw to form a peak on the front and back pieces.

3. Locate and cut 5-inch slits as shown in diagram at far right. Use a 3/8-inch bit to drill holes 5 inches apart at the top and bottom of each slit. Then cut between the holes with your saber saw. The slits can also be made with a router mounted to a router table, using a 3/8-inch straight bit.

4. Since wasps like to use these butterfly houses, we recommend stapling a piece of roofing paper or other dark material on the inside over the entrance slits. This will keep unwelcome insects out.

5. Attach sides to back with 1-1/2-inch finishing nails, setting the heads just below the surface.

6. Glue a 3-inch-long 2 x 2 to the inside of the back piece, making sure the bottom of it is recessed 1 inch. Clamp and allow to dry.

7. Nail the floor in place through the sides. The floor should sit up against the block attached in the previous step. (The floor will be recessed 1/4 inch.)

8. Drill a 7/8-inch hole in the rear corner of the floor and into the block approximately 2-1/2 inches deep.

9. Nail the front to the sides with 1-1/2-inch finishing nails, setting the heads just below the surface.

10. Make a 30° bevel cut on the top edge of each roof piece to form the peak. To make this cut on a table saw, tilt the blade 30°. Hold the board upright on end against the fence and push the piece through the saw blade. To do this safely and accurately, make an auxiliary fence like the one pictured at right.

11. Attach the roof pieces to the top of the butterfly house with 1-1/2-inch finishing nails, setting the heads just below the surface.

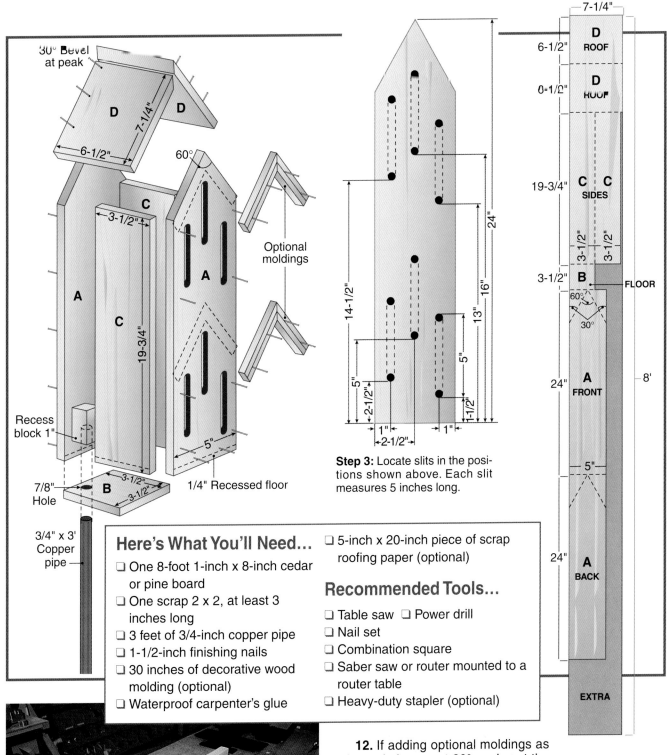

30° Bevel at peak

D D

7-1/4"

6-1/2"

60°

30° Bevel at peak

C

3-1/2"

A

A

C

19-3/4"

Optional moldings

Recess block 1"

7/8" Hole

B

3-1/2"

3-1/2"

5"

1/4" Recessed floor

3/4" x 3' Copper pipe

24"

14-1/2"

16"

13"

5"

5"

2-1/2"

1-1/2"

1" 1"

2-1/2"

Step 3: Locate slits in the positions shown above. Each slit measures 5 inches long.

7-1/4"

6-1/2"

D ROOF

6-1/2"

D ROOF

19-3/4"

C C SIDES

3-1/2" 3-1/2"

3-1/2"

B FLOOR

60°

30°

24"

A FRONT

5"

24"

A BACK

EXTRA

8'

Here's What You'll Need...

- ❑ One 8-foot 1-inch x 8-inch cedar or pine board
- ❑ One scrap 2 x 2, at least 3 inches long
- ❑ 3 feet of 3/4-inch copper pipe
- ❑ 1-1/2-inch finishing nails
- ❑ 30 inches of decorative wood molding (optional)
- ❑ Waterproof carpenter's glue
- ❑ 5-inch x 20-inch piece of scrap roofing paper (optional)

Recommended Tools...

- ❑ Table saw ❑ Power drill
- ❑ Nail set
- ❑ Combination square
- ❑ Saber saw or router mounted to a router table
- ❑ Heavy-duty stapler (optional)

12. If adding optional moldings as pictured above, cut 30° angles at the peaks and attach with 1-1/2-inch finishing nails.

13. Hammer the 3/4-inch copper pipe about 12 to 18 inches into the ground. Use a scrap block of wood on top of the pipe while hammering to prevent damaging the top of the pipe.

Make sure the pipe is straight and slide the house onto it. Then show your friends and family you've put out the welcome mat for butterflies!

MOVABLE AUXILIARY FENCE

PUSH PIECE

ROOF

Step 10: Use a 2 x 4 as a movable auxiliary fence to help cut the beveled peak. Fasten a push piece to the 2 x 4 and perpendicular to the table saw. Then clamp the roof to the movable fence. Push the fence, roof and push piece through the blade. (Note: Make sure your clamp is tight and positioned as shown.)

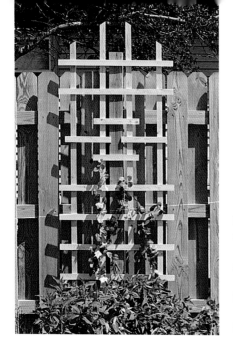

Simple Trellis

Easy project...big payoff.

How can something so simple be so useful? Just ask Pamela Hill of Gilbertsville, Kentucky.

"My trellis was just the thing needed to hide an old tree stump," Pam explains. "I anchored it in front of the stump, then planted clematis and daylilies around its base.

"The clematis climbed the trellis. It's truly a beautiful sight when the flowers are in bloom. The rest of the season, greenery hides the stump."

We thought you'd have use for this project as well. After all, when it comes to growing upwards, nothing could be "viner" than a well-built trellis.

Wrap Your Tendrils Around This Project

1. Rip just enough material off of the 2 x 4's to eliminate the rounded edges. For your safety, use push sticks when cutting the materials needed for this project.

2. From a 2 x 4, rip two outside vertical pieces 3/4 inch x 79 inches. Cut a 30° angle on one end of each piece as shown in plan at right. These pieces are a bit thicker than the rest because they're the main supports. Make sure these supports do not have any large knots or they will be weak.

3. Rip the rest of the 2 x 4's into strips 3/8 inch thick.

4. Cut two of these strips 74-1/4 inches long (pick the ones with the fewest knots). These will be the trellis' center vertical slats. Cut a 30° angle at the top of each piece as shown.

5. From the rest of the material, cut seven 30-inch pieces and four 12-inch pieces for the horizontal slats, eliminating knots whenever possible.

6. Lay out the slats according to the plan at right. Assemble using waterproof construction adhesive and two 3/4-inch brads at each joint. (The joint's strength comes from the adhesive—the brads only hold them in position while the glue dries.) We suggest using a piece of 3/8-inch scrap board for support when nailing.

Be sure to square each piece and double check the measurements before gluing and nailing. And here's a helpful hint...mark the position of each horizontal strip with a pencil line below it so you know where to put the construction adhesive.

Allow the adhesive to dry for 24 hours. When completely dry, flip the trellis over and blunt the points of the brads that protrude.

7. To protect your trellis from weather, give it a coat of deck stain.

8. If free standing, drive the metal pipes 18 to 24 inches into the ground, spacing them 24 inches apart at the outside edge. Place a scrap block on top of the pipe when you hammer. Attach the outer legs of the trellis to the pipes with several 7-inch plastic cable ties, plant a vine and let it climb!

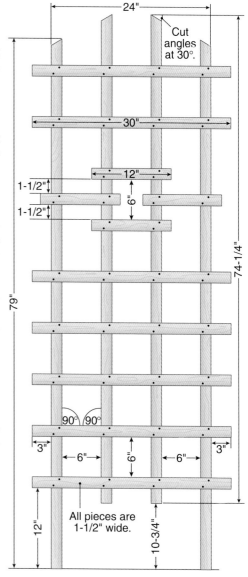

Here's What You'll Need...

❑ Two 7-foot 2 x 4's (with as few knots as possible)
❑ 3/4-inch wire brads
❑ Waterproof construction adhesive
❑ Six 7-inch cable ties (optional)
❑ Two 3-foot pieces of 1-inch pipe (optional)
❑ Wood preservative or deck stain (optional)

Recommended Tools...

❑ Table saw   ❑ Clamps
❑ Combination square

Chapter 10

Clay Pot Display

Add plants along a wall or corner.

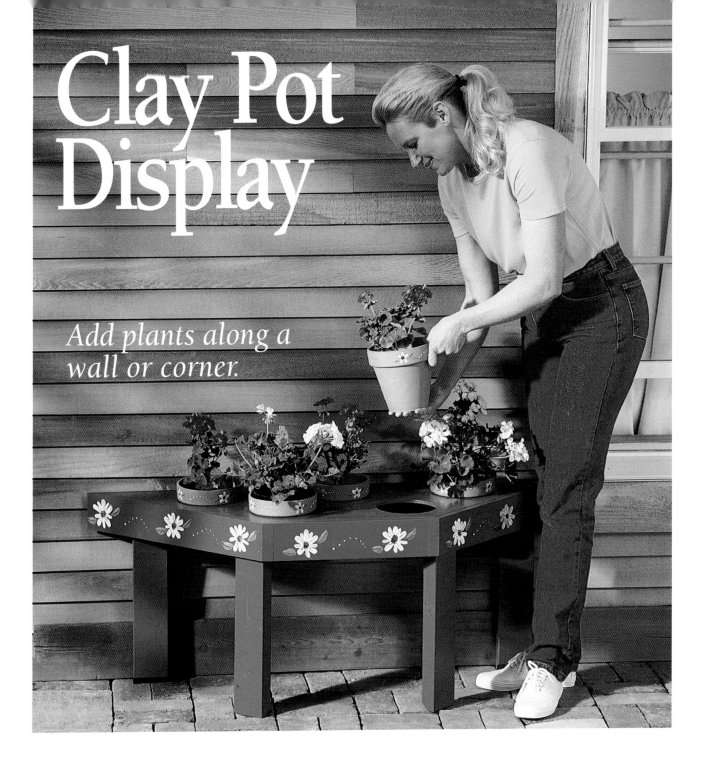

This handy little clay-pot stand is a painless way to brighten your yard—especially if you have a bad back.

The knee-high stand will save you from the deep bending associated with a ground-level garden. You can even tend your plants from the comfort of a lawn chair or a small stool.

Here are many more great features worth pointing out:
- The stand fits neatly against a straight wall (above), or can be turned around and tucked snugly into a corner (at top right).
- There's little to no weeding necessary.
- When the pots are removed, the stand becomes portable. It's light enough to easily move from one place to another.

- The sturdy stand holds its ground on windy days. You won't have to pick up tipped flowerpots.
- It's also ideal when placed near the back door closest to the kitchen—just grow a different herb in each pot for an instant herb garden.
- If you have a taste for fresh vegetables but don't have space for a garden, don't worry. Just find a sunny spot large enough to accommodate this clay-pot stand and fill it with some of the new container vegetables specifically bred for flowerpot gardening.

If that's not enough from one project, here's one more thing to add to the list. When someone asks, "How's your garden growing?" you can actually say, "It's gone to pot"…and smile about it!

Here's the Plan

Build Your Pots a Home

1. Find five 6-inch clay pots. You may want to buy new ones from a single source to ensure the pots have the same diameter.

2. Cut the piece of 16-inch x 48-inch plywood to a width of 14-1/2 inches. Then cut the plywood with 45° angles on each end (see illustration below).

Be careful with this board so the pointed corners do not chip when moving it in your work area.

3. With a compass, draw a circle 5-7/8 inches in diameter (2-15/16-inch radius) onto a piece of heavy cardboard or scrap wood. Cut out the circle and check your clay pots for fit. Adjust the diameter if necessary until the lip of the pots sit on the surface of the test piece. Then set your compass for the radius of that hole.

Use the compass to lay out the remaining holes on the plywood as shown in the illustration below, then cut out

each one with a saber saw (see "Workshop Wisdom" on page 55 for a helpful hint).

4. Rip two lengths of 3-inch-wide board from the 8-foot 1-inch x 8-inch board. (Be sure to use a push stick when ripping boards. This will keep your hands a safe distance from the blade.) These become the trim boards around the plywood top.

5. Cut the trim boards to size. You will need to make 45° bevel cuts on each board. See diagram below for the approximate length of each trim board and to determine the direction the angles should be cut. Notice the side trim boards have parallel angles and the front and back boards have opposing angles. (See step-by-step method on following page.)

6. On a flat surface, lay the trim pieces around the *(Continued on next page)*

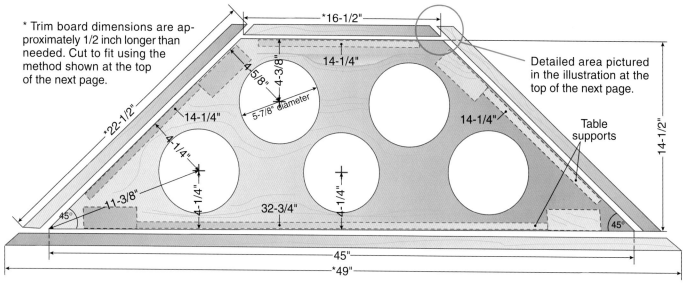

* Trim board dimensions are approximately 1/2 inch longer than needed. Cut to fit using the method shown at the top of the next page.

Detailed area pictured in the illustration at the top of the next page.

Table supports

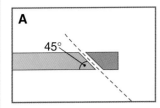

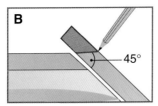

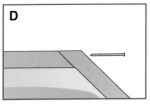

A 45°

B 45°

C

D

Step 5: To help determine where to cut 45° angles on the trim boards (shown above): **A.** Start by cutting a 45° angle on one piece. **B.** Place it in position, lay the next piece in place and mark where to cut it. **C.** Trim the board. Repeat these steps for the rest of the trim pieces. **D.** To attach the trim, clamp (as shown below), drill pilot holes (make sure they go partially into the next piece) and nail at the corners and into the plywood top with 2-inch finishing nails.

plywood top to make sure they fit together snugly, but don't attach them to the top just yet. Simply mark the depth of the plywood onto each trim board with a pencil. (Do this rather than measure since not all 1/2-inch plywood is exactly 1/2 inch thick.) Later, you will mount support boards along these lines to hold the plywood top flush with the trim boards (see step 8).

7. From the remaining 1-inch x 8-inch board, rip a strip 3/4-inch square (use a push stick) and cut the following table supports:
- One piece 32-3/4 inches long
- Three pieces 14-1/4 inches long (for the other sides)

8. Center the longest and shortest supports on the front and back trim boards and attach them below the pencil line (the line you made in step 6) with 1-1/4-inch finishing nails.

Mount the side supports as indicated in the illustration on page 73 so they do not interfere with the legs.

9. Attach the side trim boards to the plywood top with 2-inch finishing nails. Predrill the holes almost the full length of the nail into the plywood. (See "Workshop Wisdom" on page 63 for a helpful tip.)

Fastening angled pieces can be tricky, but clamping them to your workbench or table will make it much easier (see illustration at right).

10. To make the legs, cut four 17-1/2-inch pieces (they can be longer if desired) from a 8-foot 2 x 4. Add an optional 45° bevel cut to face inward at the bottom of each leg to give them a more finished look.

11. Attach the legs to trim boards (from the inside as shown in the plan at right) with construction adhesive and three 2-inch deck screws.

For each leg, drive in one screw, then square the leg before driving in the others. The screws holding the legs to the longest side will need to be driven in on a slight upward angle because of the tight corners, or you can secure them through the front trim board.

12. To prevent water damage, finish the stand with a coat of deck stain or exterior paint.

Now all you need is potting soil that drains well and a few of your favorite plants to fill those empty pots. Dig in!

Step 9: Fastening angled pieces can be tricky, but clamping them to a workbench or table will make it much easier.

CLAMP

PLYWOOD TOP

TRIM BOARD

WORKBENCH TOP

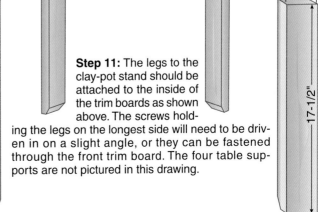

3"

17-1/2"

Step 11: The legs to the clay-pot stand should be attached to the inside of the trim boards as shown above. The screws holding the legs on the longest side will need to be driven in on a slight angle, or they can be fastened through the front trim board. The four table supports are not pictured in this drawing.

Here's the Plan

UNIQUE Window Box

Flowers look great in picket fence planter.

"Don't fence me in" was a sentiment sung by Bing Crosby and the Andrews Sisters. But *you* won't be singing that tune when you add this attractive picket fence planter to your home.

This nifty fenced planter is sure to spruce up any plain old windowsill. Better yet, its simple plans are easily expanded to fit any length of window, and you can choose the style picket that best suits your place!

Your favorite flowers will look lovely from either side of the window when you "fence them in" with your new planter.

Build This Planter…You'll Be Glad You Picked It

1. Measure your windowsill to determine the appropriate length for your window box. Once you decide on the length, cut the back piece of the box from a 1-inch x 8-inch board. Then rip the piece to a width of 6-3/4 inches.

2. Cut the floor of the box from 1-inch x 8-inch board, making it the same length as the back piece. Rip this piece to a width of 6 inches.

3. Cut the front of the box from 1-inch x 8-inch board to a length 3 inches longer than the back and bottom. Rip it to a width of 6-3/4 inches.

4. Cut the ends of the box. Rip a 2-inch x 8-inch board that is 13 inches long to 6 inches wide. Then cut two pieces 6 inches long, using the table saw's miter gauge.

5. Assemble the box. Start by attaching the back to the end pieces, using 2-inch deck screws (make

sure the grain runs horizontally on the end pieces and that the tops are flush). It's important to predrill and countersink the holes.

Next, fasten the floor to the end pieces with 2-inch deck screws. Then screw the back piece to the floor with the deck screws. Again, predrill and countersink the holes.

6. Center and fasten the front of the window box to the floor and ends the same way as in the previous step. The piece will extend 1-1/2 inches beyond both ends.

7. Determine the number of pickets needed based on the length of your box. (Select a style that works well with your house. We've provided a few examples at right, or you can design your own.)

The pickets measure 3-1/2 inches wide x 11-3/4 inches tall. They'll be spaced evenly along the face of the box and overhang the bottom by 1-1/4 inches.

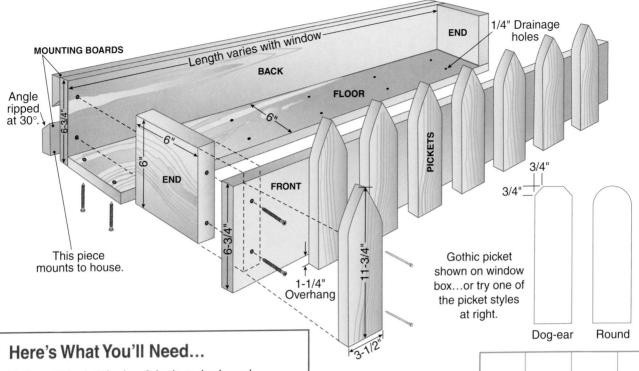

MOUNTING BOARDS

Length varies with window

BACK

END

1/4" Drainage holes

Angle ripped at 30°.

6-3/4"

FLOOR

6"

6"

END

6"

PICKETS

3/4"

3/4"

This piece mounts to house.

FRONT

6-3/4"

11-3/4"

Gothic picket shown on window box...or try one of the picket styles at right.

1-1/4" Overhang

3-1/2"

Dog-ear

Round

Here's What You'll Need...

❏ One 13-inch 2-inch x 8-inch cedar board
❏ 1-inch x 8-inch cedar boards (length determined by window width and number of pickets needed)
❏ 2-1/2-inch, 2-inch and 1-1/4-inch galvanized deck screws
❏ 1-1/4-inch galvanized finishing nails
❏ Waterproof construction adhesive

Recommended Tools...

❏ Table saw
❏ Saber saw
❏ Power drill
❏ Combination square
❏ Countersink
❏ Level

8. Cut the pickets from a 1-inch x 8-inch board. Use a saber saw to cut the tops (or a table saw for the dog-ear style).

If you want to paint the pickets a different color from the box (like in the photo at left), now is the best time to do it.

9. With the window box resting on its back, lay out the pickets across the front. Space them evenly and square to the box. (The end pickets on the box pictured above align with the end pieces of the box.) When set, mark their positions with a pencil line on the same side of each picket.

10. Set a combination square for 1-1/4 inch and position the pickets so they hang below the bottom of the box. Attach the pickets with construction adhesive and 1-1/4-inch finishing nails.

11. Flip the box over and drill 1/4-inch drainage holes in the floor.

12. Rip the window box mounting board 4-1/2 inches wide from a 1-inch x 8-inch board. It should be the same length as the back of the box. Rip the board in half with a 30° cut down the middle making two pieces.

Fasten one piece with the angle pointing down, flush with the top of the back piece. Use construction adhesive and 1-1/4-inch deck screws. Don't forget to predrill holes in the mounting board so it doesn't split.

13. The other half of the mounting board will be attached to the house or window frame with the appropriate-size screws. Predrill the holes and hang the board using a level to make sure the box sits straight.

Now all you have to do is fill your window box with potting soil that drains well and plant some attractive flowers. (If your spouse has been "impatiently" waiting, you might want to plant some impatiens!)

Before long, your windowsill will be blooming behind the nice, cozy "picket fence" that you put up yourself.

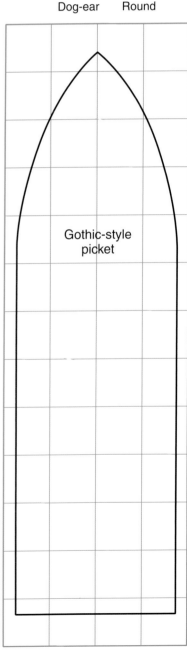

Gothic-style picket

Here's the Plan

Homemade COLD Frame

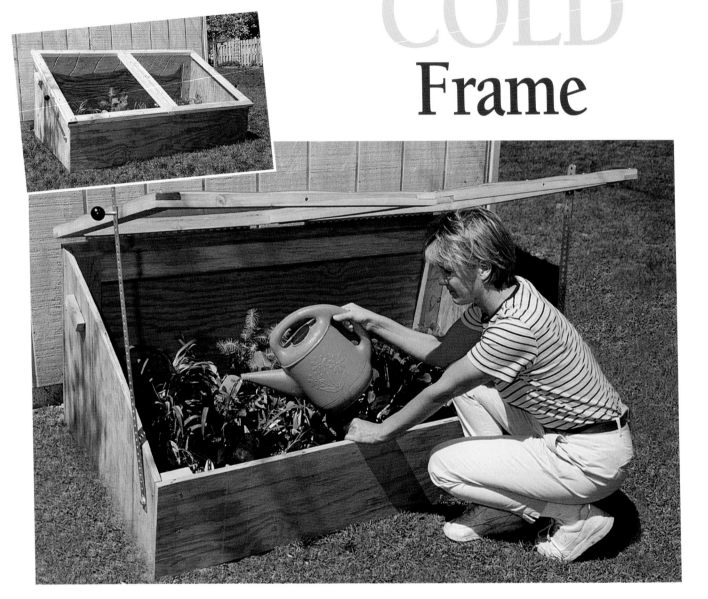

Jump-start garden plantings with this project.

To get a jump on the gardening season, there's nothing more practical than a simple cold frame.

Just a few winter hours spent in the workshop will produce this easy-to-make windowed frame that lets the warm sunshine in and helps keep the frigid air out—especially on chilly evenings.

We've seen several cold frames, and this one is inspired by many of the best ideas our readers sent in.

The frame is built on an angle to capture the most light,

especially when it's placed facing South. And the metal straps are a sturdy and secure way to make sure the open lids will stay that way. That's a comforting thought when you're working below the open panels.

On warm sunny days, the straps allow you to open the lids to several positions, letting hot air escape so your plants won't wilt from excess heat.

We used pressure-treated wood for this project, which will keep the frame in business for many gardening seasons to come. Just give the wood a week or so to dry out before actually building with it.

One word of warning—we were tempted to build our cold frame with old storm windows stored away in an editor's garage. For safety reasons, we opted to use Plexiglas instead. It may cost a bit more, but when it comes to safety, particularly when young ones are around, it's money well spent.

Heat Up the Workshop With This Cold Frame!

1. Rip just enough stock off two 5/4-inch x 6-inch deck boards to eliminate the rounded edge from both sides. Then rip both boards to widths of 2-1/2 inches. You'll end up with four pieces measuring 2-1/2 inches x 72 inches.

2. From each of these four pieces, cut a section 30-1/4 inches long and another section 36-1/4 inches long. These will be used to make the window frames.

3. Cut 2-1/2-inch half-lap joints (see plans on next page) on both ends of the frame boards. These joints, which are half the stock's thickness deep (approximately 1/2 inch), can be made on the table saw quicker with a dado blade, but you can also use a regular saw blade by making more passes.

4. Assemble the window frame on a flat surface using a rafter square to make sure each corner is 90°. Apply adhesive to each corner and interlock the half-lap joints. Fasten with two 1-inch deck screws on each corner. Predrill the holes first so you don't split the frame.

Here's a tip: Start by squaring and putting one screw in each corner. Check the frame with the rafter square. Then add a second screw to each corner. Make a second frame the same way.

5. Drilling holes in the Plexiglas must be done very carefully so it does not crack. Drill larger holes than the 1/2-inch sheet-metal screws so they easily fit through the holes. A sharp twist drill will work fine but *do not apply pressure* as you drill. If you have a variable speed drill, use a medium speed. Drill holes about 5 to 6 inches apart, starting about 1-1/2 inch from the corners of the Plexiglas.

6. Cut the plywood and 2 x 4's as shown in the plywood board layout at right and in the plan on page 86. From the 2 x 4's, cut two pieces 23 inches long for the back of the box, two more pieces 11-3/4 inches long for the front of the box and one piece 50-3/8 inches for across the back of the box.

7. Attach the 23-inch-long 2 x 4's to the back plywood piece, indenting 3/4 inch from the edges. Position the 2 x 4's so the wider (3-1/2-inch) side is against the plywood and fasten them with 2-inch deck screws. Here's another

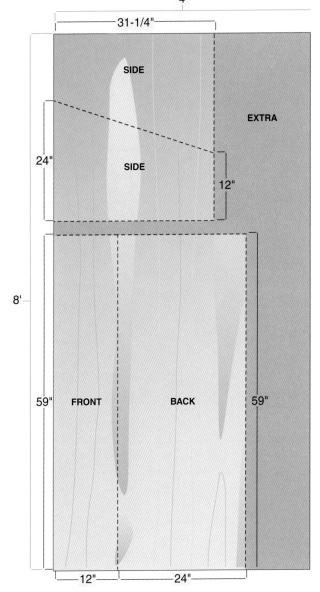

tip: Use a piece of 3/4-inch-thick scrap plywood to help set the indent needed to properly position the 2 x 4's.

Attach the 11-3/4-inch 2 x 4's to the front plywood piece, again indenting 3/4 inch from the edges.

8. Attach the plywood sides to the back and front 2 x 4's with 2-inch deck screws. Be sure to square all the cor-

(Continued on next page)

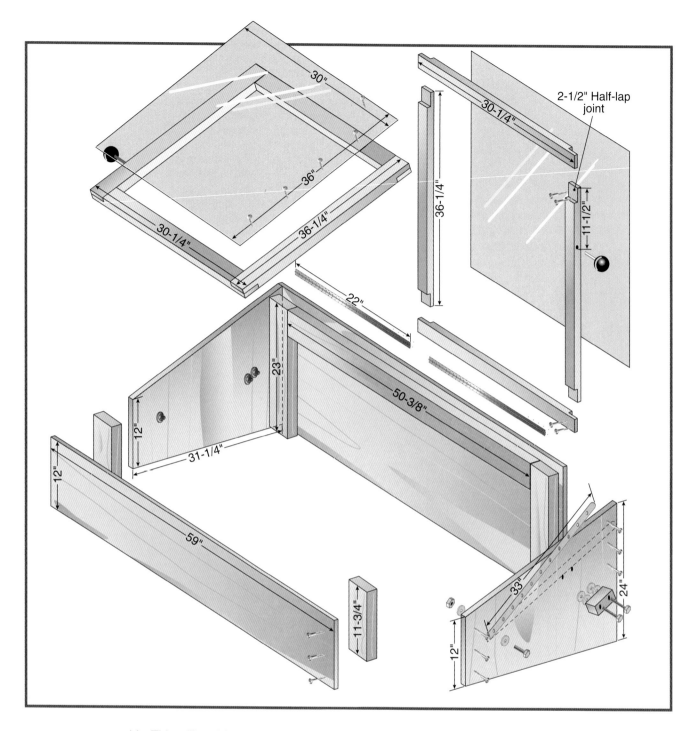

ners as you assemble. This will avoid problems later.

9. Attach the 50-3/8-inch 2 x 4 across the back wall. Position it flush with the tops and between the back vertical 2 x 4's. Attach through the back wall with 1-5/8-inch deck screws. This piece keeps the frame square.

10. Cut the piano hinge into two pieces 22 inches long with a hacksaw. Attach one hinge to the back of each window frame (one of the 30-1/4-inch sides) along the edge.

Lay windows in position on top of the cold frame—you may need an extra set of hands here. Allow about 1/2 inch between the two windows in the center.

11. Cut the metal straps 33 inches long and round the ends with a file or grinder. Attach each strap to a side with 3/8-inch x 1-1/2-inch bolts, washers and nuts as shown.

12. On the outside edge of each window frame, drill a 3/8-inch hole 1-1/2 inches deep and 11-1/2 inches from the front corner for locking pins. The pins will hold the metal straps in place when the windows are propped open.

To make the pins, cut the heads off each 3/8-inch x 4-inch bolt with a hacksaw and file the ends smooth. Then screw a plastic knob onto the threads of each bolt.

13. To make a rest for the metal straps, which are used when the windows are closed, cut two 3-inch-long pieces from a 2 x 2. Predrill two holes through each and attach to the sides of the box with 1/4-inch x 2-1/2-inch bolts. Place two washers stacked between the 2 x 2 and the side boards on each bolt.

Go ahead—it's time to start planting, even if there is a threat of frost!

Concrete Memories

Stepping-stones last a lifetime.

Here's a great project to personalize your garden as well as give your kids or grandkids something fun to do on a warm summer day.

"A friend suggested putting my children's handprints and footprints in concrete stepping-stones," writes Charlene Schneckenberger of East Aurora, New York. "It was such a great idea, I ended up making a stone for each member of our family, including our dog, 'Molson'.

"We used wood stencils to add our names," she says. "Then we personalized each stone by making an impression with objects—such as a dog biscuit for Molson."

Beads, buttons and other small objects can also add color to your stepping-stones. Just press them into the concrete while it's still wet.

"We placed our garden stones by a swing I love to sit in. They're now the focal point of our backyard—and we'll always treasure this keepsake."

These stepping-stones make perfect gifts for Mother's Day, Father's Day, or just to celebrate those lazy days of summer when there's "nothin' to do".

Create a Great Impression

1. Cut four 14-1/2-inch-long pieces from a 2 x 4 to make a 13-inch-square concrete form. (You can adjust the size of these pieces to make larger or smaller forms.)

2. Lay out the boards on edge to form a square (each board should overlap the end of the next piece). Drill pilot holes and fasten them together with 2-1/2-inch deck screws. Set the form on level ground or place it on a piece of cardboard or scrap plywood.

3. Mix concrete in a large bucket according to the manufacturer's directions. If using quick-drying concrete, work fast—it begins to set in minutes.

4. Pour the concrete into the form so it's at least 2 inches thick. Smooth the surface with a spatula or wide putty knife.

5. Press hands or feet into wet concrete. Rinse hands immediately with a garden hose because materials in concrete mix are dangerous to the eyes. (Read the package label for other warnings.) Decorate as desired.

Here's What You'll Need...

- ❏ One 6-foot 2 x 4
- ❏ 2-1/2-inch galvanized deck screws
- ❏ One 40-pound bag of concrete mix (approximately half a bag for each 13-inch-square stone)

Recommended Tools...

- ❏ Power drill
- ❏ Hand saw
- ❏ Large bucket
- ❏ Garden hose
- ❏ Spatula or wide putty knife (to smooth concrete)

STUNNING STEPPING-STONES can be made in your own backyard. Just pour concrete into a premade form, add handprints or footprints and decorate with buttons, beads or other personalized items.

6. Let the concrete dry completely and remove the stepping-stone from the form. Be careful not to crack the stones...loosen the form screws first and carefully pull the boards apart.

7. Bury the stepping-stone in a visible place so it sits flush with the ground.

Tighten the form screws and you're *set* to make another priceless stepping-stone, as well as a priceless memory.

Here's the Plan

Windowsill HERBS

Plant a garden... right out the window.

Here's a project that is doubly satisfying. That's because this window-box herb garden will not only perk up your sill, it will also add some zest to your cooking.

It can be sized to fit any window, but it makes the most sense to hang it near the kitchen, where you can snip whatever herb best complements the meal of the day.

Growing herbs in pots is a great way to keep them under control and have a variety right at your fingertips. It also eliminates many chores of large-scale gardening.

If herbs aren't your thing, that doesn't mean you have to write off this project. The clever design is perfect for holding pots of colorful annuals, too.

In fact, you can easily extend the growing season by planting early spring bloomers, such as violas, then as they begin to fade, swap the pots with new ones filled with summer annuals. Late in the season, change the pots again, adding ones filled with chrysanthemums, which will brighten your windowsill until the first frost.

Here's What You'll Need...

- ❏ 1-inch x 8-inch rough cedar board (the length will be determined by the width of your window)
- ❏ One 2-inch x 8-inch rough cedar board, 15 inches long
- ❏ 2-1/2-inch and 2-inch galvanized deck screws
- ❏ 2-inch galvanized finishing nails
- ❏ Waterproof construction adhesive
- ❏ 6-inch clay flowerpots   ❏ Glue stick

Recommended Tools...

- ❏ Table saw   ❏ Power drill
- ❏ Saber or band saw   ❏ Level
- ❏ Combination square

Let's Build a Window Garden

1. Measure your window to determine the overall length of your window box.

2. Make two photocopies of the end-support pattern at right (outlined in red). With a scissors, cut out the paper patterns 1/2 inch beyond the guidelines. Tack each pattern to the 2-inch x 8-inch board with a glue stick. Place the straight sides flush with the corners of the 2-inch x 8-inch board. (Notice that the grain runs horizontally.) If necessary, square the corners of the board first.

Cut out each end support with a saber saw or band saw and sand the edges smooth.

3. Cut the top to length from a 1-inch x 8-inch board.

4. Cut the back to length from a 1-inch x 8-inch board, making it 7 inches shorter than the top. Rip it 5-1/4 inches wide.

5. Locate the center points for the pot holes in the top board. To do this, draw a line the length of the board 1/8 inch off center (*closer* to the front). Then mark the

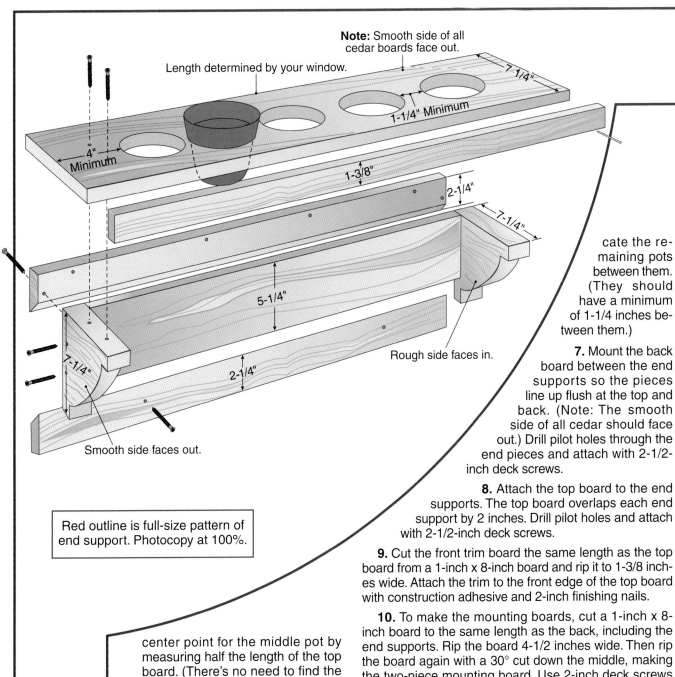

Note: Smooth side of all cedar boards face out.

Length determined by your window.

7-1/4"

1-1/4" Minimum

4" Minimum

1-3/8"

2-1/4"

7-1/4"

5-1/4"

Rough side faces in.

2-1/4"

7-1/4"

Smooth side faces out.

Red outline is full-size pattern of end support. Photocopy at 100%.

cate the remaining pots between them. (They should have a minimum of 1-1/4 inches between them.)

7. Mount the back board between the end supports so the pieces line up flush at the top and back. (Note: The smooth side of all cedar should face out.) Drill pilot holes through the end pieces and attach with 2-1/2-inch deck screws.

8. Attach the top board to the end supports. The top board overlaps each end support by 2 inches. Drill pilot holes and attach with 2-1/2-inch deck screws.

9. Cut the front trim board the same length as the top board from a 1-inch x 8-inch board and rip it to 1-3/8 inches wide. Attach the trim to the front edge of the top board with construction adhesive and 2-inch finishing nails.

10. To make the mounting boards, cut a 1-inch x 8-inch board to the same length as the back, including the end supports. Rip the board 4-1/2 inches wide. Then rip the board again with a 30° cut down the middle, making the two-piece mounting board. Use 2-inch deck screws to attach one mounting board flush with the top and end supports, making sure the angle points down. Attach the other mounting board to your house (above or below the windowsill), making sure it's level and the angle points up (see illustration at right).

Hang the window box, fill your pots with a potting mix that drains well and plant your own "window-grown" herbs or flowers!

center point for the middle pot by measuring half the length of the top board. (There's no need to find the center point of the board if you're using an even number of pots.)

Locate the center points for the end pots by measuring 7 inches from the ends of the top board. (The far edge of the outermost pots will need to be at least 4 inches from the ends of the box so they will clear the end supports.)

6. Determine the hole diameter for your pots. (If you made the clay-pot stand on page 72, you can try to use the same template if it fits the pots used in this project.)

To make a template, use a compass to draw a circle 5-7/8 inches in diameter (2-15/16-inch radius) onto a piece of heavy cardboard or scrap wood. Cut out the circle and check your clay pots for fit. Adjust the diameter if necessary until you find the proper fit.

Draw the center (if using an odd number of pots) and end circles using the center points already marked. Lo-

494

483

486

500

488

BONUS

476

496

Photos this page: dandelions, Alan and Linda Detrick; hummingbird, Francois Gohier; opposite page: pond, Nick Johnson/Positive Images; fence garden, Terry Wild Stock Inc.

WAR
OF THE
WEEDS

Battle plans begin with knowing thy enemy.

By Teri Dunn, Gloucester, Massachusetts

A few years ago, when my husband and I were house hunting, I nixed a perfectly nice place because of the weed I spotted growing in the yard. He and the real estate agent were making their way through the front door when I gasped in horror, trotted after them and declared, "No way!"

I led them back outside and pointed to an extensive patch of Japanese knotweed encroaching on the lawn. We were back on the road in minutes, the real estate agent looking annoyed.

Several weeks later, I noticed our agent had sold the house to someone else—someone who didn't know about nasty weeds, evidently.

Japanese knotweed, also known as Mexican bamboo (its tall, hollow stems resemble bamboo), is perhaps one of the most aggressive weeds ever. Like many problem plants, it's not native to the United States—giving a weed a leg up because it lacks native predators.

This one grows in dense patches, so you know it has spreading underground roots. If you chop or mow Japanese knotweed down, like the heads of the scary Hydra creature in ancient Greek legend, several more will soon grow back in its place.

The grim truth is that this plant, like a number of other tenacious weeds, resists even an application of strong garden poison. What to do, then?

Controlled Fury

Once you are convinced you have a problem plant on your hands, perhaps the worst thing you can do is lash out in ignorance. A vigorous attack that involves ripping out, cutting back or chopping down may be your first inclination, but it may not be a long-term solution. On top of

Chapter 11

Jeff Greenburg/Unicorn Stock Photos

this, the effort can be exhausting!

You may be tempted to resort to garden chemicals. However, be aware that using the wrong herbicide, or too much, can kill more than your targeted foe. You might inadvertently damage nearby garden shrubs and flowers, or the poison could seep into your soil, entering tree roots, tainting groundwater and even killing off earthworms and other wildlife. This is not a tactic to employ lightly.

Before you begin your battle, take a deep breath and take the time to understand the weed. It will help!

What Is a Weed?

The renowned writer and orator Ralph Waldo Emerson famously said, "What is a weed? A plant whose virtues have never been discovered."

To him, I say: "Oh, really? Ever garden, Ralph? Ever try to have a nice lawn, buster?"

Virtues? Bah! This is war, and I don't have time to admire my opponent's virtues!

That said, it is important and worthwhile to find out what the weed's name is and a little bit about it. Its so-called virtues turn out to be virtues only from its point of view—like any other living thing, it wants to keep on living.

Because you're a gardener to begin with, your powers of plant observation should be pretty good.

If not, look up the weed in a reference book or on the Internet. Alternatively, show a typical piece (a stem with leaves on it, plus a flower or seed head) to a staffer at your local garden center or a landscape contractor.

You might also try calling or visiting a lawn-service company; keeping weeds out of their clients' lawns and adjacent flower beds is their business, and they are often quick and accurate in their diagnosis.

Finally, determine how your weed reproduces, for this is the key to fighting its spread and hopefully eliminating it from your yard altogether. Many weeds—such as the common dandelion—reproduce with windblown seeds.

They may release thousands, in the hopes that most will find hospitable ground to grow in. Others will reproduce using their underground runners, poking up new stems here and there, like the aforementioned Japanese knotweed. Then there are even other tougher weeds, sorry to say, that employ both methods.

So to Emerson I say, a weed is "a plant that is very successful at increasing its own numbers."

Prevention

Weeds, like all other plants, require hospitable growing conditions to get a foothold, and then they really start to thrive. The most pernicious ones are widely adaptable—they don't seem to mind poor soil, periods of drought or soggy soil, and competition from other plants, including your beloved garden plants.

Indeed, as you know, many weeds can overrun the less-tough but desirable plants. How can you control these backyard bullies?

Keep disturbance to a minimum. Dug-up, raked, rototilled or otherwise disturbed soil brings up weed seeds that may be lingering in the ground, waiting for some light to germinate.

Eliminate "free and clear" conditions. Bare ground is an open invitation to weeds. The elbow room you wisely allow your flowers and shrubs is an opening for weeds, at least until the garden plants mature and cover it over or shade it.

So always lay down several inches of mulch, or cover the open areas with several layers of newspaper. Then add 2 to 4 inches of wood chips on top of that.

This method effectively smothers developing weeds, depriving them of the sunlight and the water that they need to survive. (Mulch is also nice for your desirable plants, reserving the resources in the soil for them and conserving moisture.)

Don't give 'em a foothold. Weeds rush in to recently cleared land. So… before creating a new flower bed, or even before clearing brush from the edges of your yard, look carefully.

If weeds are already growing there, deal with them first

Proper Disposal

Do not underestimate your enemy! Never toss weeds or weed fragments onto your compost pile, or even back into the woods or brush surrounding your property. Surviving bits may simply grab on, start growing anew and march back into your yard. (True, some compost piles get quite hot, especially in the interior, but this may still not be sufficient to kill surviving weeds or weed seeds.)

Your best bet is to bag all weed parts and send them away with your household garbage if allowed. Alternatively, if you have a big pile, and if it is allowed in your municipality, you could burn the weeds.

before starting the project. Otherwise, you're just inviting them into your yard.

Battle Tactics

Here are effective weed-controlling methods, starting with the easiest and least intensive. Pick one you think will work and see the battle through to victory, or work your way down the list, employing the tactics until you win.

Dig or pull weeds out, early and often—get every last bit, because some weeds can regrow from root fragments. If a weeding fork or trowel isn't up to the job, resort to a sharp garden spade. Hack off top growth and trace it back to its point of origin.

Cut off flower heads before they go to seed.

Mow down the area repeatedly, starting early in the year, when the weed starts to poke up and before they go to seed. Repeat again and again if it regrows—eventually, this assault will deprive the roots of food (because you chopped off leaves and stems that energize them), and they will die.

Smother the area. Use clear plastic for 6 to 8 weeks during the hottest part of the year. Or try a combination of newspaper and wood chips. It will smother the weeds and improve the soil as it eventually breaks down.

Use a herbicide specifically labeled for control of your weed, then read the label carefully before using. The label will give you the application instructions, including the best timing (time of year as well as time of day), waiting time before you can replant the treated area and dosage amounts —follow these exactly.

Weed killers may be applied in various ways (sprayed on leaves, painted onto leaves and stems or sprayed over an entire patch).

Again, the label will provide the information you need. Protect nearby garden plants with a tarp, work on a dry, windless day, and wear protective gear if necessary. Good luck with those weeds. I hope you win the battle! ◀

GREEN THUMB TIP

If weeds have infested your lawn grass, try letting the grass grow a bit higher in the hopes of shading out lower-growing weeds.

NINE NASTY WEEDS...
and how to rid your yard of them.

Thistle

Botanical Name: *Cirsium.*
Description: Annual, biennial and perennial species that is found throughout the U.S. and southern Canada. Though it can have pretty flowers, it's still a pest.
Control: In the garden, pull weeds, mulch and use a pre-emergent herbicide. Spot treat with total vegetation killer. For the lawn, use broadleaf herbicides labeled for controlling thistles. Paint total vegetation killer on unresponsive weeds.

Ground Ivy, Creeping Charlie

Botanical Name: *Pilea nummularifolia.*
Description: Perennial that hugs the ground. It has round scalloped leaves with a distinct aroma when crushed. It has purple flowers in spring.
Control: Hand-pull from the garden, taking care to remove all roots and stems. If this does not work, spot treat with a total vegetation killer. Treat lawns with traditional broadleaf weed killers in fall after a hard frost or in spring when plants are in full bloom.

Crabgrass

Botanical name: *Digitaria ischaemum.*
Description: Summer annual. Seeds sprout when soil temperatures reach 50°. Found throughout the U.S. and tolerates a wide range of conditions, especially heat and drought.
Control: A dense, healthy lawn can crowd out crabgrass and other annual weed grasses. Taller grass, mowed at the proper height, will shade the ground, preventing seed germination. Treat infested areas with a crabgrass pre-emergent.

Bindweed

Botanical Name: *Convolvulus arvensis.*
Description: Twining, creeping stems branched at the base; deep-rooted. Resembles its relative, the morning glory, but with much smaller, pinkish white flowers. An annual, it reproduces via seeds and loves open, bare dirt.
Control: Pull out or cut down as early in the growing season as possible, but certainly as flowers appear—it must not be allowed to go to seed.

Chickweed

Botanical Name: *Stellaria media.*
Description: Very low-growing, many-branched, with tiny leaves and dainty white flowers. An annual, it reproduces via seeds, as well as stems rooting at the nodes. Loves fertile garden soil.
Control: Hand pulling is easy—do it while they're young! Smothering and mowing are also options if the plants haven't seeded themselves between all your desirable plants.

Dandelion

Botanical name: *Taraxacum officinale.*
Description: Ground-hugging rosette; golden-yellow flower heads emerge from center on a smooth, hollow stem and segue to a fluffy white puffball of seeds. Deep taproot!
Control: Pick off or mow down the flowers in spring before they go to seed. Pull plants out by their long roots (easier after a rain or watering). If in your lawn, remember that they adore poor soil, so maybe some soil enrichment is in order.

Japanese Honeysuckle

Botanical Name: *Lonicera japonica.*
Description: Twining or trailing vine; reproduces by seeds and by creeping stems rooting at the nodes. Small yellow or white fragrant flowers are followed by purplish black berry.
Control: Cut back or mow, relentlessly. It might take some time, but they should eventually start to die back. Then be sure to pull or dig out the root systems, so they don't come back.

Japanese Knotweed, Mexican Bamboo

Botanical Name: *Polygonum cuspidatum* or *Fallopia japonica*
Description: Tall, straight, bamboo-like stems, heart-shaped leaves; small white flowers appear in sprays in the summer.
Control: Depends on the size of the patch. Digging out and/or smothering may work for smaller ones. You can also spray a total herbicide (such as Roundup or Finale) in late summer or early fall, when the plant flowers.

Quackgrass

Botanical Name: *Elytrigia repens, Agropyron repens.*
Description: Creeping rootstocks produce wiry grass blades; flowers are spikelets.
Control: If there isn't a lot (yet), try hand digging or smothering. Black plastic and/or a total herbicide should work. Farmers have had luck with tilling an infested area in midsummer so the exposed roots dry out in the hot sun, then raking them off and disposing of them. It's worth a try.

Secrets to
Colorful
Containers

The splash of a container garden adds brilliance where you least expect it. Here's how to help yours steal the show.

By Melinda Myers, Contributing Editor

I've been growing plants in containers for as long as I've been gardening. My first container garden started on the balcony of my apartment.

Now that I have my own backyard, modest as it may be, I still rely on containers.

To me, they're the perfect way to brighten up your front entrance, expand a vegetable garden or soften your deck, porch or patio. Often, I'll use containers to add color and interest to areas that need instant color. One of my favorite tricks is placing pots of annuals among ground cover or in flower beds to add additional color and a new dimension.

If you haven't tried container gardening, you're missing out on the fun. And I'll let you in on a secret…it's easy!

Location, Location, Location

Before starting, I recommend taking a simple walk around your house. Are there entrances you want to highlight? Views you want to block or spots that need a bit more color? If the answer is yes to any of these, then containers are the perfect answer.

But remember, just like selling a home or planting a garden, there's no doubt location is the most important factor to success.

Container gardens can be grown in sun or shade. Just match the plants to the light, and you already have put yourself in position for quick success.

And, I'll save you some frustration—avoid windy locations that can break tall plants, increase water needs and even knock over and crack the pots. I know because I learned the hard way.

Everything…Plus the Kitchen Sink

Once you've determined where you're going to use containers, it's time to think about what kinds of pots will work the best.

Plain pots, even black nursery pots, make the plants the star. Decorative pots complement your decor, so look for plants that mix with their style, too. And don't forget to check out neighborhood yard sales. Old boots, coffeepots, weathered barrels, an old kitchen sink and other recycled items can have new life as garden containers.

Here are a few tips for selecting the right container for your plants:

Always provide drainage holes. This prevents water from collecting in the bottom, which could lead to root rot and the early death of your plant. If your pot doesn't have drainage holes, drill a couple in the bottom yourself using a cordless drill.

Complement your garden. Select pots that blend well with your gardens. Unglazed clay pots are heavy and dry out faster than other materials. Plastic, fiberglass, metal and other materials reduce watering chores because they cut down on evaporation and help hold the moisture in the soil longer.

Select lightweight pots. This way, you can move them around in your backyard. This is also important if you're going to display them on a balcony, where you'll want to keep weight to a minimum.

Bigger is better. Select a container large enough to fill the space and hold the plants you select. Small containers require frequent watering and often get lost or look out of place in the landscape.

Fill It Up

Even more important than selecting the right container, is what

RP Photo

WELCOMING ENTRYWAY. Numerous pots of brilliant annuals can liven up even a modest front entrance. The containers are easy to maintain and the payoff is instant curb appeal.

WHAT IS INSIDE COUNTS. Potting mix that drains well, not garden or topsoil, is the most important ingredient to healthy container plantings.

TAME THE BULLIES. Aggressive plants can take over a container. Trimming back the overgrown coleus (above) created a more balanced container in about 2 weeks.

goes inside. Don't take a shovel of garden soil and toss it in a pot. The drainage, water-holding ability and growing conditions in a pot are drastically different from your regular garden. Containers require a special mix. You can make your own potting mix or purchase a container mix at the garden center. Most ready-to-use potting mixes contain basically the same ingredients: perlite and/or vermiculite mixed with peat moss. Some have fertilizer added and many have water-holding polymers, a great addition that helps reduce watering needs.

Planting mix with good drainage and water-holding ability will minimize your work. Unfortunately, all the bags look basically the same, so experience, yours or others', may be your best guide.

If you prefer to blend your own potting mix, follow this basic step-by-step recipe:

1. Combine 1/3 peat moss, 1/3 perlite or vermiculite and 1/3 garden soil. If you have some already, you may substitute compost for peat moss.
2. Mix it well in a wheel barrow, on a potting table or in another large container.
3. Add more peat moss or vermiculite, if needed, to help increase drainage.
4. Mix in water-holding crystals to keep soil from drying out quickly.

Time for Design

To me, this is when the real fun begins. Just about any plant will do well in a container if it receives the light it needs and the proper amount of water. With a little planning, container gardens will look their best and require less work.

Here are the basics you should think about before you start planting:

Look for perfect matches. Combine plants that have the same light and water needs, making sure they are the right choice for the light, wind and temperatures of the location you've selected.

Save water…and chores. Drought-tolerant plants are perfect for beginning container gardeners. Moss roses, zinnias and gazania are more tolerant if you need a forgiving watering schedule.

No bullies. Use plants that are equally assertive. Otherwise, fast-growing plants take over and hide their more timid neighbors.

Maintaining Good Looks

Because they dry out fast, containers should be checked daily to see if they need watering. Use your fingers as a moisture meter. If the top few inches of soil feel crumbly yet slightly damp, it is time to water.

Water thoroughly until excess water runs out the bottom drain holes. Here are some more tips for outstanding container gardens with less work:

Group near water. Be sure containers are close to a water source. Try my favorite shortcut—empty your dehumidifier water into a watering can and use that to water containers. Two chores, one step!

Give them a boost. Poor growth, lack of flowers and pale leaves may indicate your plants need a nutrient boost.

To save time, guesswork and the mess of mixing and applying fertilizer, mix slow-release fertilizer into the soil at planting time.

If you missed this opportunity, just sprinkle some on the soil surface even after it's planted.

If you like to mix and apply the fertilizer yourself, check out one of many fertilizers at your garden center. You can either apply a small amount often, or use a stronger concentration less frequently. Let your plants and the fertilizer label be your guide.

Routine chores. Deadhead, trim back and control weeds in your containers just like other gardens. Because container gardens can be moved, soilless mixes are weed free and the smaller size makes the chores manageable, they work for even for the busiest schedules.

Now you're armed with all you need to know to get a container garden off to a great start. Look through the garage, check out a few yard sales or pick up a few pots at your area garden center. Then fill 'em up and watch a beautiful container garden bloom.

Secret Ingredients for Container Combos

Container gardening may not be a perfect science, but there are three basic ingredients—vertical, filler and trailing plants. Mix those together in one container and you're virtually guaranteed a perfect combination.

Vertical accents. Look for tall, narrow plants, or consider growing a vine on a small trellis for your vertical accent.

Keep in mind that tall plants may need support. To keep them from tipping, try adding some extra weight, such as a rock, for ballast.

Trailing plants. These plants anchor a container and soften the look. Like your vertical accent, it's important to remember to pick something that doesn't take over the container.

Filler plants. The remaining space between vertical and trailing plants should be packed with fillers. These are medium-sized plants that round out the container.

Fillers give containers personality. Color echoing, repeating the color or foliage of the vertical or cascading plant, is a great way to tie it all together. You can also select contrasting colors for a visual punch or mellow it out with plants in complementary colors. The options are endless.

Here are my favorite surefire container picks that can be mixed and matched. It's that easy!

Vertical Plants	Trailing Plants	Filler Plants
Bronze fennel	Dichondra	Coleus
Dwarf papyrus	Lamium	Geranium
Ornamental grasses	Licorice vine	Impatiens
Purple Majesty millet	Petunia	Penta
Spike (Dracaena)	Sweet potato vine	Verbena

BEAT THE HEAT

Blazing sun and drought wilting your garden? Don't worry...here are answers for an always refreshing summer garden.

By Julie Drysdale, Aptos, California

It's hot out there! Whether you garden in a naturally arid climate, or a dry spell moves in and overstays its welcome, heat is supremely stressful on backyard plants across the country.

Surely, you feel the effects of heat, too. When outdoors without the protection of shade and sufficient water, our bodies begin to feel weak and woozy. We begin to wilt.

The same fate befalls our garden plants. And if there is no relief, once-vibrant flowers drop, leaves droop, and the plants eventually collapse and perish.

If this discouraging scenario takes a toll on your garden in summer, you might be tempted to do the obvious—pour on the moisture with frequent waterings. That is, if your area doesn't have water-use restrictions, or if your water bill isn't already sky-high.

There's good news...plan ahead, and you won't have to douse your thirsty plants. A much better solution is to grow flowers that stand up to the heat. With the right selections, you'll have plants that put on a terrific show even through the blazing, dog days of summer.

That leaves you with only one worry—keeping *yourself* well-hydrated. And don't forget the hat and sunscreen when you go outdoors to enjoy your vibrant heat-resistant garden.

Pick the Right Plants

Contrary to what most people think, you don't need cactus and a desert landscape to have a heat-tolerant garden. Though cacti and succulents are well suited for these conditions, and even occasionally produce bright flowers, they may not be your first choice. Or, your area's climate may be too humid or cold for them to survive. Luckily, there are plenty of other flowering plants that can beautify your yard in a hot summer season. (See our top 12 picks on page 239.)

If heat is a yearly problem in your garden, begin by choosing plants that are known to stand up to hot and dry conditions. There are many, and they share certain key qualities:

Smaller flowers and leaves. Smaller flowers mean smaller petals, and narrow leaves mean less surface area for evaporation. Ideally, look for plants that produce lots of small flowers, so the show is bountiful and their color makes an impressive impression, even from across the yard.

Strong root systems. Another quality that helps plants tol-

erate heat is below the soil line. It's in the roots of the plant.

Root systems of drought- and heat-tolerant plants tend to be stockier and to grow deeper and wider. This makes sense when you imagine the stress that dried-out soil can cause. Thin and wispy roots, or shallow ones, simply won't survive these tough conditions.

So seek out plants that are clearly labeled as adapted to dry

---

A LITTLE BREAK. Even the hardiest plants that survive hot dry conditions need a little relief from the blazing sun. A fence (below), lattice or a trellis offer a bit of welcome shade in sunny areas.

Terry Wild Stock, Inc.

Starve 'Em When It's Hot!

Hot, dry weather is the worst possible time to fertilize your flower garden. This is because plant roots respond to the difficult conditions by slowing or shutting down, and the nitrates in plant foods will only injure them in this state.

You could try fertilizing earlier in the year, before the blazing weather arrives, but that may only produce a flush of tender growth that is much more easily scorched or killed than hardened older plant tissues. It is better not to feed at all...or, if you feel you must, use a slow-release fertilizer early in the season.

---

climates, including desert natives, dry-meadow natives, prairie natives and plants that survive at high altitudes.

Incidentally, if you purchase seeds or plants of wildlings from the local native-plant nursery, don't worry about them looking as weedy as they might in nature. Garden conditions are always less stressful, and you will be pleasantly surprised at how beautiful they turn out to be when treated to a better life. This is especially true of garden-grown penstemons and coreopsis.

Also, it pays to seek out cultivars (cultivated varieties) of suitable native plants. These have been selected or bred to be better looking, with more compact growth habits, showier flowers, longer bloom periods—or all of the above. A perfect candidate is the prairie coneflower, which has seen a flurry of pretty new introductions in nurseries and mail-order catalogs in recent years.

A Fighting Chance

The best part of heat-resistant gardens is that extra effort on your part is not a requirement. Here's all you need to do:

Choose the right site. Even plants billed as sun-lovers need a little relief, especially at midday. So the number one rule is to avoid growing them in a full sun, especially on south-facing exposures. Part-day shade minimizes stress and also preserves flower color longer. So choose a spot where your house, garden shed, or even a tree or shrub, casts some shade at some point during the day. You may want to build a fence, lattice or trellis to help.

Improve the soil. Few plants actually enjoy dry, dusty nutrient-poor soil and hot conditions.

While you can't change the heat, you can change the growing medium. Work in plenty of organic matter prior to planting. This not only improves the soil texture, fertility and its ability to retain any moisture, it also helps the soil stay cooler. This should be an annual task.

Protect the vulnerable. Just-planted flowers are very susceptible to damage from a heat wave. It's important to give them a little extra shelter for their first few weeks. Temporary shelter works just fine, such as lawn chairs or boxes that create a bit of shade and shield them from drying winds.

Mulch! You may think of mulch for mainly fall or winter plant protection, but it's just as important to plant survival in very hot summer weather. Mulch keeps resource-stealing weeds at bay and retains whatever moisture there may be for your plants.

An inch or two can make a world of difference. If you can't cover the entire garden bed, at least sprinkle mulch over the root area of each plant. Use natural mulch, from bark chips to herbicide-free

Ben Phillips/Positive Images

grass clippings, but avoid pebbles and stone because they tend to soak up and reflect heat.

Water Works

Scientists studying the effects of heat and drought on plants have made an interesting discovery. Only about 10 percent of water supplied is actually retained by a plant in the best of circumstances. The remaining 90 percent is lost through evaporation and transpiration. This is not wasted water, however—it is used to cool the plant.

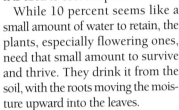

While 10 percent seems like a small amount of water to retain, the plants, especially flowering ones, need that small amount to survive and thrive. They drink it from the soil, with the roots moving the moisture upward into the leaves.

A plant naturally gives priority to feeding its leaves before developing buds or open flowers. This is why you see heat-stressed plants jettisoning buds and flower petals first.

If heat stress is bad enough, the next thing you'll see is damage to the leaves. Their edges and tips will appear scorched and brown, or entire leaves will wilt. In the final stage, the leaves will simply fall off the plant, dry and dead.

You don't want things to come to this point, of course. Proper, not indiscriminate, watering will help a lot. Instead of frequent, shallow watering sessions, soak your plants slowly over a few hours, with a trickle from the hose, soaker hose or a sprinkler set on low.

If your flower garden is large, consider investing in an in-ground irrigation system. These are regulated with a timer. (For containers, consider a drip-water system.)

In any event, always water at ground level so as much water as possible will soak into the root area. The watering area should be extended at least as far out as the plant's spread above the ground, and sometimes even a little farther so all the roots are moistened.

For the best floral display, remember to supply as much water as you are able to when you spot buds on your plants—this will allow them to plump up, develop properly, produce more color and finally, unfurl their very welcome beauty in your garden.

12 Tough-as-Nails, Drought-Tolerant Flowers

Annuals

1. California poppy. Though the deep-orange petals of this beautiful wildflower are silky and large compared to some heat-tolerant plants, they hold up very well. The ferny, somewhat succulent foliage is light blue to green.

2. Fan flower. These plants have a nice trailing habit, dense foliage of small, narrow leaves, and loads of small, fanlike flowers that are usually purple or blue. Some varieties have an accenting white dot. The plant is very durable.

3. Mexican sunflower. Forms a clump 3 or more feet wide and high, with somewhat coarse leaves. It's studded with bright-orange or red 4-inch daisies starting in late summer. Hummingbirds and butterflies flock to them!

4. Moss rose. Though the flowers are not large (no more than an inch across) and are carried on spreading, low stems of fleshy leaves, these plants are very charming. Flowers come in many bright hues, including yellow, orange, red, hot pink, purple and white.

5. Strawflower. Papery flower heads look great in the garden and in a vase, fresh or dried. They come in red, pink, white and yellow. Small, lance-shaped grayish leaves accompany them.

6. Zinnia. Bushy plants with tough, durable leaves and reliably perky flowers. The colors are always bright. Butterflies love them!

Perennials

7. Artemisia. Valued for their beautiful silver leaves on tall arching stems or low "cushion" mounds. These plants are reliably tough and trouble-free. Hardiness Zones 4-8.

8. Blanket flower. Perky daisies in yellow, red and orange. The stems are stiff, the leaves coarse and the plants bushy. Hardiness Zones 3-9.

9. Coreopsis. Scads of pretty little yellow daisies cover an airy mound of thin-needled foliage. Hardiness Zones 3-9.

10. Lavender. Stiff, gray-green leaves on mounding plants that are often taller than they are wide. The hauntingly fragrant flower spikes come in various shades of purple as well as plain white. Hardiness Zones 5-9.

11. Penstemon. Arching stems laden with showy, tubular flowers that attract hummingbirds. The plants can get tall (up to 4 feet) and rather shrubby in habit. Hardiness Zones 4-8.

12. Yarrow. Lacy, flat-topped flower clusters and thin, feathery sage-green foliage. Usually white or yellow,

SMALL-SPACE GARDENING

Get the most out of your yard with these easy tips.

It's only natural to have huge aspirations for your garden. But what if your space is tiny rather than sprawling? How do you achieve a high-impact garden in tight confines?

Don't worry. With the right plants and structures, even small spaces can have great gardens. Here's how:

Make every inch count. If you're working with a small space, layering helps make the most of it. Work from ground level upward, filling each layer with plants. Start with ground covers, annuals and perennials, then work up to shrubs and trees.

Go vertical. Plant flowering vines along fences, arbors and trellises for maximum visual impact without eating up lots of precious garden space. Brighten privacy fences with trellises and flat-backed planters.

Double your pleasure. Mix bulbs with perennials. This provides spring color as the bulbs emerge, and summer color when the perennials bloom. And as a bonus, perennials also mask the withering bulb foliage as it dies back. (Don't cut these leaves; they're the energy source for the bulbs to flower next year.)

Try a tabletop garden. This is ideal for gardeners with limited space—or aching knees! Select a sturdy table that can hold about 50 pounds, and fill it with pots of flowers, vegetables and herbs. Upkeep is minimal—you won't need to hoe, weed or rake. This garden is easy on your back and knees, too, since you don't have to squat or kneel to tend it.

Plan for season-long color. Select plants with staggered bloom times. This guarantees you'll have something flowering throughout the season.

Pot 'em up. Containers are a quick and easy way to add flowers anywhere, especially soil-free areas like patios, porches and decks. To minimize watering, choose drought-resistant plants and use larger pots, which won't dry out as quickly. Use potting soil with moisture-retaining crystals, or add your own.

Find space for veggies. Tuck tomatoes and peppers among sun-loving flowers, and train sprawling veggies, like cucumbers and pole beans, to climb up a trellis. Use lettuce as a border plant, or combine several varieties to make a low-growing bed. Think small—compact squares work just as well as long rows.

Most veggies also grow well in containers. And when they're portable, it's easier to find the perfect spot for them—like a sunny spot for tomatoes, or partial shade for lettuce. Start plants in pots indoors to get a jump on the season. You'll save even more time—there's no transplanting!

Don't forget the trees. Even the smallest yard needs trees or evergreens for a sense of structure. Many varieties of dwarf trees are ideal for small landscapes. Check out your local nursery and garden center…and make sure a plant marked "dwarf" is truly small enough for your landscape.

Make room to relax. No matter how small your garden is, create an area for a bench or a chair or two. After all, gardening isn't just about planning, planting and maintaining. It's also about enjoying!

Photo opposite page: RP Photo

POND MYTHS REVEALED

Nancy Rotenberg.; opposite page, Meredith Hebden/Positive Images

Forget what you've heard about water gardens… it's time to set the record straight once and for all.

By Rachael Liska, Waukesha, Wisconsin

There's no arguing that the soothing sound of gurgling water washing over stones…tumbling over a waterfall…or lapping at water lilies…can wash away the stress of the most chaotic day. But can all the maintenance, money and muck some people associate with a backyard water garden bring that tension back twofold?

For years, backyard ponds and water gardens had a bad reputation—and rightfully so. The methods of yesterday's ponds yielded high-maintenance monsters (*Creature from the Black Lagoon* come to mind?) that sucked time and money quicker than a high-output pump sucks water.

Today, that's all changed. Thanks to new, back-to-nature techniques and technologies, a water garden can be a low-maintenance—and a relatively affordable—personal paradise.

Still, common myths persist that may discourage those longing for lush lilies and colorful fish in their backyards. So, before you pull the plug on the idea of building your own backyard water garden, check out the facts.

Myth: Small water features are less work.
Fact: Larger and mature water gardens are easier to maintain. Aquarium hobbyists know it's easier to achieve a healthy, stable tank with more water, not less. Smaller water features rarely have the flow or capacity necessary for long-term stability, leading to more maintenance than larger ponds.

Properly designed ponds are able to achieve ecological balance. As a water garden matures, it becomes more stable with each passing year as plants, bacteria colonies and other vital life become established.

Myth: You should never have algae in your pond.
Fact: Some types of algae, in proper proportion, are a natural and beneficial part of a water garden's ecosystem. They lend a pleasing patina to rocks and a natural color to the water, and they provide food and oxygen for fish and other aquatic life. Chemically treated water is dead by comparison.

What turns people off is too much algae. Usually, this has a simple cause—an overabundance of sunlight. That's why a well-designed natural pond includes aquatic plants that shade 50% of the pond's surface.

Myth: Maintaining a water garden is a constant headache.
Fact: Ecologically balanced water gardens let Mother Nature do the work. So look for systems and kits that work with her, not against. These include ones with mechanical and biological filtration, lots of aquatic plants, fish, active bacteria and plenty of rocks. Find the right balance, and you don't have to worry about water testing, chemicals, clogged filter screens or a mucky bottom that needs constant cleaning.

In fact, a well-designed, eco-friendly pond needs only a few things:

First, remove large debris (leaves and twigs) from the

pond's surface and your skimmer basket as needed—approximately every 2 weeks in summer and weekly in spring and fall. Second, plan an annual draining or clean out of your pond in cold climates.

In gardening terms, a well-thought-out pond is about as much work as maintaining an established perennial border, minus the time-consuming weeding and watering.

Myth: Water gardens are not practical in colder climates.

Fact: In colder climates, water gardens can run through the winter or be shut down. Shutting down a pond minimizes energy costs. But even if a pond is put to bed for the winter, a certain level of activity must be maintained, especially if you choose to overwinter plants and fish. A floating heater will ensure a breathing hole in the ice for fish. And running a small pump will keep the water properly oxygenated.

Letting a pond run through the winter offers stunning aquatic landscapes of frozen waterfalls and crisp, shimmering water. It also requires occasional attention.

It's important that the water keeps moving in winter. Slow or still water can be caused by debris buildup or ice dams. This can cause water to overflow the liner. Also, evaporation continues through the winter months, so it's important to maintain an appropriate water level in the pond.

Myth: To keep fish, water gardens need to be deep.

Fact: Two feet deep is as good as a mile. Fish, including koi, hibernate in ponds just 2 feet deep through winters as cold as Minnesota's chillers. A small circulating agitator pump and heater are all you need to keep a breathing hole in the ice and oxygenate the water for your finned friends.

As a general rule, avoid over-populating a pond with fish. An overcrowded pond can suffer from poor water quality, which leads to excessive algae growth and sick fish.

Never exceed 1 inch of fish for every square foot of pond surface area (be sure to calculate the number of fish based on their mature size).

For example, a 10- by 15-foot pond (150 square feet) would be able to handle a total of about 150 inches of fish—meaning a pond this size could include 15 10-inch fish, 10 15-inch fish or 30 5-inch fish.

Myth: Water gardens provide breeding grounds for mosquitoes.

Fact: A well-designed backyard water garden has lots of water flow, which inhibits mosquito breeding. That's because

AQUATIC PARADISE. Don't be afraid to try a water garden or pond in your backyard. Believe it or not, you don't have to spend a lot of time or money to get beautiful results. Water is a great way to attract birds to your backyard (like the great blue heron, above right). If you are worried about these birds eating your pond's fish, read the fact at right to learn more.

mosquitoes breed in still, standing water.

Ponds and water gardens also support fish, frogs, toads and other wildlife that find mosquito larvae a tasty treat.

Small water features and birdbaths should have their water changed regularly, however. And be sure to keep the rest of the yard clear of containers where water can collect and stagnate.

Myth: Water gardens take up too much space.

Fact: Water gardens come in all shapes and sizes, with container and tub gardens being popular choices. A small container water feature can add life to even the darkest corner of your deck or yard.

Any nonporous container can be used…decorative ceramic pots, stone troughs and antique stone sinks all have what it takes to be an enchanting pint-sized paradise. Even a whiskey barrel lined with heavy-duty plastic makes a wonderful water garden. Whether you opt for a formal or casual look, just be sure to add a small fountain, oxygenating plants or fresh water to keep the system in balance.

There are several aquatic plants available today that are in scale with container or tub gardens. Miniature water lilies, floating fairy moss, dwarf cattail and baby doll water lotus will add all the charm of plants twice their size.

Myth: Water gardens cost a fortune.

Fact: A water garden is certainly an investment, but it doesn't have to be a money pit. At the most affordable end of the spectrum, DIY kits with everything you need retails for $700 to $900, plus another $600 for the other stuff that doesn't come in the box (rocks, pebbles, fish, plants and so on). Plus, you'll want to add in a healthy amount of sweat equity for that 8- by 11-foot pond and waterfall you'll be installing yourself if you want to keep costs down. Professional installations start at around $4,000 and average $6,000 to $8,000.

Running a high-efficiency pump 24/7, 365 days a year, will tack $20 to $40 onto your monthly electric bill. Winter pumps and heaters are less expensive.

Something to keep in mind…water gardens are considered landscaping investments. They pay for themselves in increased home equity. So what may seem like a lot up front, chances are, will be money well spent down the road.

Myth: Predators will eat your fish.

Fact: Predators are out there, but there are things you can do. Koi lovers beware—in shallow water, your prize specimens are at risk, mainly from great blue herons or raccoons. But you can fight back! An inexpensive, motion-activated scarecrow system will deter these anglers with a timely spray of water.

Smart and kind pond owners also install underwater tunnels, rock ledges or other hiding spots, such as submerged drain tiles, for their fish. These act as aquatic "panic rooms," plus fish find them interesting places to explore.

Raccoons don't care to swim for their supper, but will dip into the buffet from the banks. A pond that's at least 8 feet wide will deprive these varmints of dry access to the deepest part of the water garden.

Myth: Any landscaper can build a water garden.

Fact: Building a pond and building it right are two different things. Building ecosystem ponds is a relatively new specialty. A good landscaper isn't necessarily knowledgeable about the concept, design or construction that makes an organic water garden system work.

If you do hire someone to install your water garden, make sure that he or she is certified as professionally trained in the installation of ecosystem ponds.

If you decide to do it yourself, take time to read as much information as you can on the subject before sticking a spade into your soil. The Internet has a tremendous amount of information on pond building.

GREEN THUMB TIP

Save money on your backyard pond by installing it yourself. There are plenty of good do-it-yourself kits that will walk you through the steps.

GETTING INTO THE ZONES

By Melinda Myers
Contributing Editor

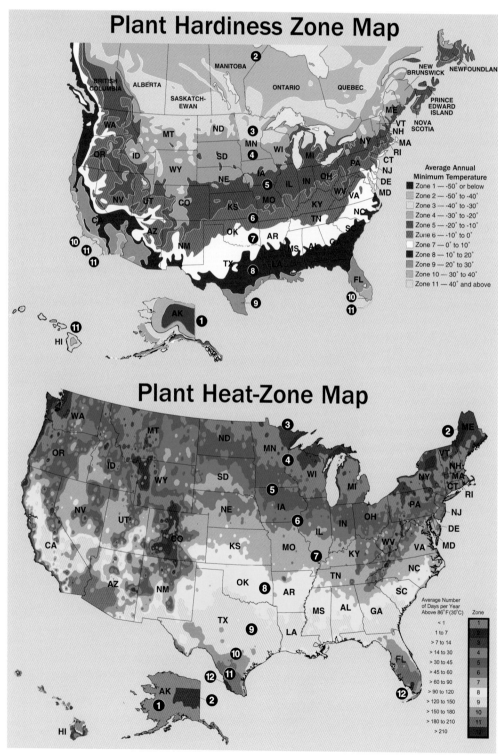

Plant Hardiness Zone Map

Average Annual Minimum Temperature

Zone 1 — -50° or below
Zone 2 — -50° to -40°
Zone 3 — -40° to -30°
Zone 4 — -30° to -20°
Zone 5 — -20° to -10°
Zone 6 — -10° to 0°
Zone 7 — 0° to 10°
Zone 8 — 10° to 20°
Zone 9 — 20° to 30°
Zone 10 — 30° to 40°
Zone 11 — 40° and above

Plant Heat-Zone Map

Average Number of Days per Year Above 86°F (30°C)

	Zone
< 1	1
1 to 7	2
> 7 to 14	3
> 14 to 30	4
> 30 to 45	5
> 45 to 60	6
> 60 to 90	7
> 90 to 120	8
> 120 to 150	9
> 150 to 180	10
> 180 to 210	11
> 210	12

Since my garden is in Wisconsin, I always look at a plant's hardiness to cold first. Likewise, my Southern gardening friends are particularly concerned with heat hardiness. Fortunately, there's help for all of us—heat and cold hardiness maps to help with making plant selections.

Cold hardiness ratings are based on the average minimum winter temperature in an area. The USDA Cold Hardiness Map is the most commonly accepted.

The American Horticultural Society more recently developed the Plant Heat-Zone Map. This rating reflects the duration and extremes of heat in each region. It's based on the average number of 86° or hotter days per year from 1974 to 1995. The 86° mark is where heat starts damaging plants.

On both maps, you'll notice small islands of warmer or colder areas surrounded by other zones. This is typically where elevation differences, bodies of water or urban areas create different growing conditions in a particular zone.

Your own landscape may have such islands, too. Fencing, stonework, construction materials and existing plants may block cold winds, reflect heat, cast cooling shade or create sheltered beds. These areas can be one whole growing zone warmer than the rest of your yard! Luckily for you, these microclimates can stretch your planting palette beyond what's recommended for your area.

To get a better idea of the microclimates in your backyard, conduct a hardiness rating of your own. Just monitor temperatures in different areas and record your planting successes and failures. Soon you'll have a personalized hardiness map customized to your yard.

BIRD GARDEN BASICS

Want to know a secret? It's not hard to bring birds and butterflies to your backyard blooms. Really. You just have to know what to grow.

We've chosen a mix of flowers, trees and shrubs that will work for different climates, color schemes and garden layouts. Pick your favorites, pick a spot—and get planting!

BIRDS:

Seed
Attract seed-eating birds like chickadees, northern cardinals and American goldfinches by planting seed-bearing perennials and annuals. Some top choices:
Purple coneflower (Zones 3 to 9)
Liatris (Zones 3 to 9)
Black-eyed Susan (Zones 4 to 9)
Sunflower (Annual)

Berries
For our feathered friends who prefer to dine on berries (American robins, cedar waxwings, catbirds and more), try planting trees and shrubs like:
Juneberry (Zones 3 to 9)
Sea Green juniper (Zones 3 to 9)
Gray dogwood (Zones 4 to 8)
Mulberry (Zones 4 to 9)

Shelter
All birds seek spots to nest and hide from predators. Ornamental grasses—which come in all sizes, shapes and colors—serve as great shelter. Also try trees and shrubs like:
Spruce (Zones 2 to 9)
Pine (Zones 2 to 11)
Fir (Zones 3 to 9)
Hemlock (Zones 3 to 9)

BUTTERFLIES and HUMMINGBIRDS:

Color
Hummingbirds are drawn to brightly colored, trumpet-shaped flowers, such as:
Serbian bellflower (Zones 3 to 8)
Trumpet vine (Zones 4 to 9)
Fuchsia (Zones 9 to 11)

Host plants
Try this trick: offer host plants to feed the caterpillars that will eventually become the butterflies you desire. Here are a few:
Willow (Zones 2 to 9)
Elm (Zones 2 to 9)
Dill (Annual)
Parsley (Annual)

Nectar
The best bet to bring in all types of butterflies and hummingbirds is to fill your backyard with nectar-packed plants. Try shrubs, perennials and annuals, such as:
Delphinium (Zones 3 to 7)
Aster (Zones 3 to 9)
Bee balm (Zones 3 to 10)
Weigela (Zones 4 to 9)
Butterfly bush (Zones 5 to 9)
Salvia (Annual)
Snapdragon (Annual)

BEST ALL-AROUND BLOOM:

Honeysuckle vine (Zones 4 to 9). The nectar of this pretty plant attracts hummingbirds and butterflies, birds relish its summer fruits, and its leaves grow into a tangle of foliage that's suitable for nesting.

GARDENING FOR BIRDS

These plants are sure to attract birds to your backyard.

Flowering Dogwood

Botanical Name: *Cornus florida*.
Hardiness: Zones 5 to 8.
Birds Love: Its crotches provide a place for birds to build their nests, while bright-red berries provide nourishment in fall.
Height: 20 to 30 feet.
Width: 20 to 30 feet.
Light Needs: Full sun to partial shade.
Planting: In the North, plant in late winter to early spring; in the South, fall to late winter.

Skip Moody/Dembinsky Photo Assoc.

John Lewandoski

Honeysuckle

Botanical Name: *Lonicera*.
Hardiness: Zones 3 to 9.
Birds Love: Hummingbirds prefer its funnel-shaped blossoms.
Height: Vines, 8 to 30 feet; shrubs, 2 to 15 feet.
Width: Shrubs, 3 to 15 feet.
Light Needs: Full sun to partial shade.
Planting: Space plants 3 to 4 feet apart in holes the same depth as the root balls.

RP Photo

Blue Spruce

Botanical Name: *Picea pungens*.
Hardiness: Zones 3 to 8.
Birds Love: Its thick branches of prickly needles provide shelter, while cones produce seed for food.
Height: 30 to 60 feet.
Width: 10 to 20 feet.
Light Needs: Full sun.
Planting: Plant bareroot seedlings in early spring, balled-and-burlapped trees soon after purchase and container-grown trees anytime during growing season.

Sunflower

Botanical Name: *Helianthus annuus*.
Hardiness: Annual.
Birds Love: In early autumn, the seeds of this blooming beauty attract a variety of birds.
Height: 2 to 15 feet.
Width: 18 to 24 feet.
Light Needs: Full sun.
Planting: Sow seeds 6 inches apart in spring. Thin to the strongest growers so the plants are 18 to 24 inches apart.

Firethorn

Botanical Name: *Picea pungens*.
Hardiness: Zones 3 to 8.
Birds Love: Its thick branches of prickly needles provide shelter, while cones produce seed for food.
Height: 30 to 60 feet.
Width: 10 to 20 feet.
Light Needs: Full sun.
Planting: Plant bare-root seedlings in early spring, balled-and-burlapped trees soon after purchase and container-grown trees anytime during the growing season.

Alan and Linda Detrick

Guy Bumgarner

Hollyhock

Botanical Name: *Alcea rosea*.
Hardiness: Zones 3 to 9.
Birds Love: Hummingbirds relish its red, pink, yellow, white or purple blossoms in early summer.
Height: 3 to 8 feet.
Width: 1 to 3 feet.
Light Needs: Full sun.
Planting: To force blooms during the first summer, sow indoors in winter and transplant in early spring.

Richard Shiell

Crabapple

Botanical Name: *Malus*.
Hardiness: Zones 2 to 8.
Birds Love: The 1/4- to 2-inch red, yellow or orange apples this tree boasts are irresistible to birds.
Height: 8 to 25 feet.
Width: Up to 25 feet.
Light Needs: Full sun but will tolerate light shade.
Planting: Dig the planting hole the same depth as the root system, and three to five times wider.

HUMMINGBIRD
BASICS

Lure hummingbirds to your yard with these seven simple tips.

If you don't have hummingbirds buzzing around regularly in your yard, then you don't know what you're missing. These tiny fliers are some of the most entertaining and beautiful birds around.

Bird lovers have long been fascinated with the hummingbird, and it's not hard to see why. Their tiny bills and amazing flights make them one of the most sought-after birds to attract in the backyard, and they are easy to lure with sugar-water feeders.

You can have "flying jewels" right outside your back door, too. These seven tips will tell you everything you need to know to start offering sugar water to hummingbirds. Before you know it, they'll be frequent visitors to your yard.

1. First Things First

Mix a sweet treat. Hummingbirds have a mighty big appetite. If humans ate like hummingbirds, they'd each have to consume more than 300 pounds of food a day! Satisfy a hummingbird's hunger with sugar water.

Here's the recipe: Mix 4 parts water to 1 part sugar, boil and cool before filling hummingbird feeders. Change the solution every 3 days or so. You can keep leftovers in the refrigerator for up to a week.

RP Photo

Reader Tips: To save on fridge space, try this sugar water shortcut recommended by *Birds & Blooms* reader Carole Miller of Meeker, Colorado. Make a concentrated one-to-one ratio of water to sugar. When you fill the feeders, mix a cup of the concentrate with 3 cups water.

Freezing is a great way to store sugar water, says Walter Norvell of Fort Worth, Texas. Measure out the amount of liquid needed to fill your feeders and pour them into freezer bags. As you need refills, remove the mixture from the freezer, thaw and pour into your feeder.

2. Hummingbirds Love Red

Use this power color to your advantage. Hummingbirds can zip along at speeds approaching 60 mph, and nothing grabs their attention like the color red. Put a bright-red bow on top of your sugar water feeder, or hang a feeder among a patch of red flowers to lure hummingbirds to your backyard.

Reader Tips: No detail is spared when Anne Speers of Conroe, Texas welcomes spring's first hummingbirds. She sets out a bright-red tablecloth in her yard to catch the attention of migrating hummingbirds, hungry after their long journey. You can find a red plastic tablecloth at party supply stores, but a red oilcloth or bedsheet works just as well.

With dozens of backyard feeders to choose from, there are two main things to keep in mind: The feeder should have plenty of red on it, and be easy to clean and refill.

3. Aggressive "Bully Birds"

Don't let their size fool you! It's common for a dominant male hummingbird to chase other hummingbirds away from a feeder to protect his feeding territory. In fact, these fearless fliers will attack creatures of any size and will even hover near humans in an attempt to scare them.

One way to solve the problem of bully hummingbirds is to hang another feeder around the other side of your house, out of sight of the first feeder. If the male can't see both feeders, he can only protect one.

Reader Tips: Multiple feeders work well for Pamela Lockard of Bayfield, Colorado, but she also has another secret. Start the season with several feeders spaced around the yard. As more hummers return to the area, move them closer together. This gives juveniles and females a chance to feed while the aggressive males are busy chasing each other. Best of all, you get to watch the hummingbirds all in one spot.

Susan Manchulenko, above left; Harry McClelland, above right; Sid and Shirley Rucker; opposite, Francois Gohier

4. Up Close and Personal

Get a front row seat. Hummingbirds are the only birds that can fly upside down and in reverse. You don't want to miss that!

With a little planning, you can have hummers as close as your favorite window. But it takes time to get them used to feeders that close to your house.

Start by placing a sugar-water feeder among red blooms in the garden. As soon as they get comfortable eating there, move the feeder a few feet every day until it's close to your

RP Photo

favorite viewing spot. But watch closely—hummers have been clocked as fast as 55 to 60 mph!

Reader Tips: Since hummingbirds need to eat almost constantly to replenish energy, Kimberly Bestys of Hamondsport, New York is always sure to offer a wide array of food to her feathered friends. Besides keeping sugar water feeders full, Kimberly puts out apples, oranges, grapefruit and kiwifruit. Not only are the hummers happy, but a variety of other birds are also attracted to the fruit buffet.

Be sure to hang feeders in shady areas. This keeps the nectar solution from fermenting and algae from messing up your feeders.

5. Stay Out

Keep thieves at bay. Say good-bye to ants, bees and wasps—the most common feeder invaders.

The best way to keep sweet-toothed ants away is by hanging a small ant guard above your feeder. This cuplike device is filled with water, creating a moat ants won't cross. The most effective way to keep bees and wasps from feeders is to install bee guards. These plastic mesh covers allow only hummingbirds to reach the nectar.

Nectar thieves aren't limited to just insects. Orioles are often attracted to the bright red of hummingbird feeders and will gladly feast upon the sugary treat inside. Even squirrels, woodpeckers and deer will snack on sugar water. Hang feeders high off the ground and away from branches to keep these intruders away.

Reader Tips: Hang a bee trap (a bottle filled with sugar water) near your feeder to eliminate many of the invading flying insects.

Francis & Janice Bergquist, top; Carolyn Kirchner

Kathy Dewine

Hummingbirds can even help manage other garden pests. Joanne Sumter of South Carolina suggests hanging sugar-water feeders above rosebushes—the birds will help keep pesky aphids away.

6. Take It to the Cleaners

Eliminate the dirty work. Keep your feeders clean. When sugar water ferments, algae grows and clogs feeder ports and reservoirs. In hot weather, feeders should be cleaned at least once a week. The easiest way is to wash with a solution of hot water and vinegar, using a pipe cleaner to wash the ports.

Reader Tips: To clean those hard-to-reach spots, try this technique from Margarita Delbrook Villa of Santa Barbara, California. Pour 1 tablespoon of uncooked rice into the feeder, fill halfway with water and shake. Discard the rice when you're finished. Unpopped popcorn kernels and sand works, too (top right).

RP Photo

Denture-cleaning tablets work wonders for hummingbird feeders, says Rachel LeBlanc of Shrewsbury, Massachusetts. Fill the feeder with water, drop in a tablet and let it soak. Rinse the feeder well when finished and refill with fresh sugar water.

7. Do-It-Yourself Feeders

Get creative, be resourceful. Believe it or not, a few recycled items are all that's needed to make your own hummingbird feeder. And since hummingbirds often return to the same locations year after year, you'll want a feeder that works.

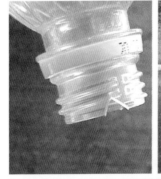

Reader Tips: A jar makes a quick feeder that is easy to clean, says Linda Bussell of Imperial, Nebraska. Drill holes in the top of the lid, fill with sugar water and hang from a string in the top (right). Keep the jars filled so the hummers can reach the solution easily.

An empty 2-liter plastic bottle is what Cindy Sexton of Monroe City, Missouri uses (center right photos). Cut four V-shaped notches in the rim of a bottle. Drill four small holes through the bottle's cap and line up with the notches.

Attach the cap to the center of a larger lid using hot glue or silicone. Fill the bottle with sugar water, screwing the cap on so the liquid slowly dribbles out into the larger lid when held upside down. Hang with a wire and wait for your feathered friends to feast.

BIRD-WATCHER'S SECRET

Leave hummingbird feeders up into fall to attract migrants. It won't interfere with the hummingbirds' migration, and they will appreciate the energy boost.

BIRD TALES HALL OF FAME

Amazing bird encounters from the past year.

Stick Your Neck Out

I consider myself one of the lucky ones to have seen a pileated woodpecker up close, and I have my mom to thank for it. She is an avid birdwatcher, and has only seen these large woodpeckers once. She was visiting my aunt, who lives nearby, when she saw a pileated near a tree cavity at the edge of the yard. It had been gathering food for its nestlings.

My mom told me about the sighting, and I decided it would be the perfect opportunity to photograph the birds. I knew I had to act quickly before the babies flew the nest, so I put on my camouflage and went to my aunt's house to wait.

I sat there for several hours on 2 different days, but finally got a great shot of the pileated family (left). I love how the nestlings' heads are sticking out of the hole.

—*Donald Mayville, Blossvale, New York*

Try, Try Again

I was sitting under my carport one spring morning when a black-capped chickadee came looking for nesting material. The determined bird landed nearby on a small piece of carpet. It tried to pull the threads out of it, but had no success.

Then the chickadee flew to my hand, trying to pull the hair out of my arm. When that didn't work, it moved on to my heavy eyebrows and then went back down to the hair on my arm. But still, the hair wouldn't budge. Finally, the little bird gave up and flew away. I sure hope it found something to make its nest.

—*Robert Albright
North Canton, Ohio*

Springtime Welcome

We look forward to the American goldfinches that come to our yard in spring. The birds are always well fed. We start early in the season by providing plenty of food in multiple feeders and place them in our garden among blooms like these red-hot pokers.

We have between 50 and 70 goldfinches visit each day, and it's such a delight to see them hanging upside down or sitting upright as they feed. The colorful sight is a wonderful welcome to spring!

—*Norma and Mike Origer
Cloverdale, Oregon*

Rare Encounter

Several years ago, my husband, Harry, and I were in Big Basin Redwood Park in California. This park was the first state park established in California and is home to magnificent groves of ancient redwoods.

I was there to attend a business meeting, so Harry decided to pass some time by taking a walk along the park's creek. While he was out, Harry spotted a black-and-white bird with webbed feet, sitting in the middle of the path. Harry wondered why a web-footed bird was in a redwood forest.

He squatted down, put his hand out, and the bird hopped onto his palm. They studied one another, and then Harry took the bird down to the creek where he gently set it down on the bank.

After a while, Harry returned to park headquarters and told us about his encounter. The staff showed him a picture, and Harry positively identified the bird as a marbled murrelet. Everyone erupted in excitement. Marbled murrelets are a very rare species. They do nest in old-growth redwood forests, but no one had ever seen one of the birds in Big Basin.

Since then, there have been other murrelet sightings in the park. But, as far as I know, no one else has ever had such a personal experience with this elusive bird.

—Ellen Weaver, Deseronto, Ontario

Winter Fountain

We don't usually have to worry about our birdbath freezing here in the Southwest. But one night, a cold spell, combined with a power outage, gave our feathered friends an icy surprise.

The next morning, I poured warm water in the bath to thaw the ice so the birds could drink. Afterward, this American robin and house sparrow stopped by to enjoy a sip from the open water.

I call this photograph "Winter Fountain." I snapped it before all the ice melted away. *—Celestyn Brozek*
Albuquerque, New Mexico

"Oh Say Can You See..."

My mother-in-law loved her feathered friends and belonged to the VFW Ladies Auxiliary. She combined the two interests by hanging patriotic birdhouses around her porch. But the birds never nested in them.

When Mom passed away, we hung her birdhouses around our deck. One day, I heard the chirps of baby birds, but it didn't occur to me that the sounds could be coming from a birdhouse. They were, though. After all those years, a family of eastern bluebirds decided to make one of Mom's birdhouses their home.

It was fun to watch the babies and share the experience with our granddaughter Paige. Mom would have loved this photo (above). We like to imagine the baby bird is singing the national anthem. "Oh say can you see, by the dawn's early light..." *—Rose Feorene, Pittsburgh, Pennsylvania*

Bad "Hair" Day

We spend winters in Florida, and every day while we're there, a beautiful great egret comes to visit.

Early in the morning, it sits on top of our car, looking in the kitchen window. When we're outside, it follows us around the yard. Even our yellow lab seems to have made friends with the gregarious bird.

Then one day we had a bad windstorm, and we didn't see the bird the next morning. Later in the day, we finally spotted it. The weather must have ruffled the egret's feathers (right). We think this is a bad feather day at its best!

—Jackie Walters
Rodney, Michigan

Use Your Head

Pine siskins, redpolls and several finches inundated our yard last spring. These birds were so hungry that it was easy getting them to eat from our hands.

Once the excitement of hand-feeding wore off, my daughter Sage figured out a way to spice things up. She placed the seed on her head. It didn't take long for the birds, like this common redpoll, to find the food. It was a season of feeding the birds we'll remember.

—*Vicky Gehring*
Caribou, Maine

Out with the Trash

I was taking the trash out one summer day, when three warblers came out of nowhere and dive-bombed me. I had no idea why.

As I got closer to the garbage can, I heard a chirping sound. I looked inside and found a baby bird peering up at me. I think it must have been learning to fly when it fell into the can.

I turned the garbage can on its side, and the fledgling quickly came out and ran away. After that, the parents stopped bothering me, and I never again forgot to put the cover on my garbage can. It was a good lesson for me— and the bird! —*Gloria Loa, El Paso, Texas*

Canine Solution

During spring nesting last year, a pair of Carolina wrens by-passed the nine wren boxes I have. Instead, they built their nest in a hanging pot of ivy. The only problem—the pot was in my greenhouse, which I keep open during the day and then close at night.

Knowing that the birds are up at the crack of dawn, much earlier than me, I had to figure out a way for them to get in and out.

I found an old door with a cutout section where a doggie door had been. Then I took down one of the doors to the greenhouse and replaced it with the other door. I turned it upside down so the opening would be near the top.

In less than 2 hours, the wrens were going in and out of the greenhouse, using their new door. Now I can continue sleeping in! —*Lafon Moughon, Flatonia, Texas*

A Vine Surprise

When John Fesperman went out to gather tomatoes in his Salisbury, North Carolina garden, he almost picked a bird's nest instead! A chipping sparrow had built a nest atop two tomatoes that had grown together, as if it knew the fruit would provide a solid foundation during the summer.

The next day, John found two speckled, pale blue eggs in the nest, and two more followed. The four babies hatched a few weeks later.

Each time John and his daughter went to the garden to pick okra or tomatoes, the mother bird would start hollering and carrying on about the intrusion. She never left the edge of the nest, no matter how close they got.

—*Carolyn Bost, Field Editor*
Rockwell, North Carolina

Office Mascot

When I was a child, I dreamed of talking with animals like Dr. Doolittle. I even smeared peanut butter on trees in attempts to draw birds to my yard.

I've now been birding for several years, and there's always a new surprise around the corner. Last year, I was astonished when a pair of sandhill cranes showed up where I worked.

When I first saw them, I couldn't believe it. There they were—two gigantic birds, each standing 4 feet tall. I went outside to get a closer look, and we stood there studying each other for about 10 minutes. I talked to them softly, and they buried their enormous bills into the ground, as if they were searching for food.

After some research, I learned that these birds like to eat grains. I began feeding them, and they came to visit me often at work. Occasionally, they would even come to greet me at my car when I pulled into the parking lot. It sure made my workdays more enjoyable.

—*Candace Rouse, Sandford, Florida*

Hitching a Ride

Our vacation home on Hilton Head Island is next to a lagoon, and we often see wildlife and birds there.

One morning, my wife called me over to take a look at the water. Floating down the lagoon was a canoe that had broken loose from a nearby rental dock.

The surprising thing about it was the regal blue heron standing on the prow, almost as though it was guiding the craft. I raced for our camera and was able to snap a long-distance shot. My wife and I wondered how long the heron's ride lasted.

—*Jack and Lois Christ, Saginaw, Michigan*

Be Our Guest

At least once every 2 weeks one year, we welcomed a special visitor to our garden. A juvenile Cooper's hawk would fly in to check things out, usually perching in the pine trees on our property. It also seemed to enjoy spending time near our well and fish fountain (above), where it would sit for a few minutes and occasionally take a quick sip of water.

We knew when the raptor was around because our yard became incredibly quiet. The birds and squirrels knew better than to romp around when this bird of prey made an appearance!

—*Harriet Bricker, Camp Hill, Pennsylvania*

Dazzling Duet

My parents and I were attending a concert in the Hollywood Bowl, the legendary amphitheatre in southern California. The guest artist was the soprano singer Elizabeth Schwarzkopf.

Shortly after the program began, we heard a second voice singing with her. After looking around, we noticed a northern mockingbird in a nearby tree, singing the impressive notes. Apparently, it decided to rise to the challenge!

For the rest of the evening, we listened to duets sung by two very beautiful voices. It was a concert experience we'll never forget!   —*Julian Schofield, Sonora, California*

Keep It Together

When I bought a plain birdhouse from a craft store, I hung it outside with the intention of painting it before nesting season. Before I could, a pair of house wrens had already moved in to raise a family.

One day, I noticed that the simple birdhouse was looking a little soggy— probably from the wet spring weather. I touched the house, and the bottom of it came apart, right there in my hand. The roof was still hanging in the tree, and three baby wrens were in the nest.

I went to the garage and grabbed a small bungee cord to reconnect the house back to the roof. Then I added some ever-useful duct tape and wire for extra support (above). The nestlings didn't seem to be phased by the commotion.

The wren parents returned and finished raising the babies, and I've since replaced the house with something more sturdy.   —*Linda Townsend, Stoughton, Wisconsin*

Determined Doves

Mourning doves are one of the most persistent and faithful birds I know. I learned this a few years ago when a couple of doves came to our backyard deck, looking for a place to nest.

The doves first chose the air conditioner—not a convenient spot for them or us. After the first set of babies left, I knew I had to do something, since mourning doves often have several broods in one season.

To discourage the birds from nesting there again, I placed a large planter on the air conditioner. Turns out, the birds thought the planter would be the perfect spot for their second nest.

After those babies left, I decided enough was enough. We didn't want the doves to take over our deck area all summer, so I covered anything that could make a nesting spot. That didn't stop the doves, though. They still managed to find a pot of sticks for their third brood; a planter stand for their fourth; and a decorative wrought iron bowl on my patio table for their fifth and final nest (above).

We didn't get to use our deck as we'd hoped that season, but it was an entertaining summer. Even when we were outside, those dedicated doves were always just a few feet away, incubating their eggs.
—*Shirley Thiessen*
Gladstone, Missouri

Beware of Mockingbird

It all started early one morning at a vacant lot across the street from my house. I was sitting on my porch when a flash of movement caught my eye.

Soon, I saw a squirrel running across the street, with a northern mockingbird following close behind. As the duo made its way to the roof of my neighbor's house, I saw the bird pecking away at the squirrel's head.

I had seen this bird at my suet feeder before, but never like this! I think it must have had a nest nearby that it was protecting.

Some time later, the same mockingbird was seen chasing a red fox through my yard.

I guess this is one bird you don't want to mess with. I'm sure glad it was them and not me!
—*Barb Mikesell*
Greenwood, Indiana

Reindeer Games

My son was working on the mechanical reindeer for our Christmas display when a hawk suddenly flew at him. It dove toward him, but it soon became clear that the hawk was not interested in my son.

Instead, it grabbed the deer display with its claws and began hissing and flapping its wings. The show didn't stop there, though.

The reindeer continued its automated movements, knocking the hawk off its perch and into the snow. The bird rolled over, stared up at the deer, spread its wings and then disappeared in a flash. I guess the hawk was no match for a reindeer!
—*Barbara Folger*
East LeRoy, Michigan

Some Like It Hot

It's common to see American robins in our backyard during winter, but I don't usually see them up close and personal.

One morning last January, I stood at our sliding glass doors and watched the flurries of our first major snowstorm. I had my camera ready, hoping the weather would draw the birds to our feeders and heated birdbath. I hoped to take a few good pictures, but I never could have imagined the results.

Our tiny yard was a hub of activity. At least a dozen robins descended on our yard at once to use the steaming birdbath. They landed on it, under it, and some even hovered overhead, looking for an opening. Those amazing birds were only a few feet away and oblivious to my camera and me!

I snapped pictures as fast as I could, until the birds left as suddenly as they had arrived. It was a morning I will always remember.

I hope the robins will make us a regular rest stop for many winters to come.
—*Joyce Fleming*
Reston, Virginia

David and Goliath

I was on my way to work when I saw two great egrets peacefully eating in a pasture. I had my camera with me, so I stopped the car to take a few pictures.

As I crouched behind a sign for cover, a red-winged blackbird flew in and began attacking the egrets—probably because they were near its nest. I tried to photograph them without bursting into laughter at their antics.

The blackbird would dive at the egrets, and they would squawk and run. This scenario continued for about half an hour, until a large logging truck passed through and scared all the birds away. I did manage to get this humorous picture (above), though. You can see the egret running away as the blackbird flies in for another attack.

—Arenett Grant, Emmett, Idaho

Following Directions

When I moved to central Pennsylvania, my mom gave me a wreath to hang on the front door of our new house. The wreath features mini birdhouses and a sign that reads "Home Is Where You Build Your Nest."

Apparently, a pair of house finches took the sign literally and made themselves comfortable on the wreath. You can see the babies peeking out from behind the birdhouses in the photo I took (above). Fortunately, we don't use our front door very much!

—Jennifer Portwood
Lewisberry, Pennsylvania

Bluebird Buddy

I've been nurturing mountain bluebirds for the past couple of years, and they are used to me being around. This photo shows me feeding mealworms to a female out of my hand.

The parent birds seem to appreciate my assistance. The mama bluebird always looks up at me while perched on my fingertips, with her head cocked to the side as if she's thanking me.

—Skip Hengel, Gallatin Gateway, Montana

INDEX

Index